7th International Metrology Conference (CAFMET 2018)

Marrakech, Morocco
9 - 12 April 2018

ISBN: 978-1-5108-7471-8

Printed from e-media with permission by:

Curran Associates, Inc.
57 Morehouse Lane
Red Hook, NY 12571

Some format issues inherent in the e-media version may also appear in this print version.

Printed by Curran Associates, Inc. (2018)

For permission requests, please contact Comite Africain de Metrologie (CAFMET)
at the address below.

Comite African de Metrologie (CAFMET)
62 av. Notre Dame du Lac
49000 Angers
France

Phone: 33 (0) 6 73 62 32 62
Fax: 33 (0) 2 41 88 84 21

contact@cafmet.com

Additional copies of this publication are available from:

Curran Associates, Inc.
57 Morehouse Lane
Red Hook, NY 12571 USA
Phone: 845-758-0400
Fax: 845-758-2633
Email: curran@proceedings.com
Web: www.proceedings.com

Table of contents

S1 – Health

S2 – Environment

S3 – Agri-food

S4 - Measurement, calibration and uncertainty

S5 – Energy

S6 - Measurement and Metrology

S7 - Uncertainty and validation

S8 - Measurement and competency

Table des matières

S1 – Santé

S4 – Mesure, étalonnage et incertitude

S5 – Energie

S6 – Mesure et métrologie

S8 – Mesure et compétences

Traceability of measurements in stereotactic radiosurgery in Romania

E. Iliescu[1], S. Bercea[1], C. Tuta[1], A. Celarel[1], S. Patrascu[1], C. Cenusa[1], F. Stoica[2], R. Stempurski[2]

[1] "Horia Hulubei" National Institute for R&D in Physics and Nuclear Engineering (IFIN-HH), Magurele, Romania, [2] "Bagdasar-Arseni" Emergency Hospital, Bucharest, Romania

Received:

Abstract. Conventionally, dosimetry reference in stereotactic radiosurgery (SRS) for treatment with ionizing radiation using linear accelerator (LINAC) is done by measuring the absorbed dose in water (D_W) in a field of radiation reference (10x10 cm^2). Unlike the situation encountered in the use LINAC for other specific equipment, such as the Leksell Gamma Knife units of (LGK), large field of 10x10 cm^2 reference required by existing protocols, there are no exist. Dosimeters ideal for use in these application areas ionizing radiation should be equivalent water and also should have small size and provide a millimeter resolution [1]. Various types of passive dosimeters (radiochrome films, TLD, alanine) were used for measurements in radiation fields with diameters between 4 mm and 35 mm in a LGK equipment. Dosimeters are being calibrated in terms of absorbed dose in water (D_W) using an ionization chamber calibrated in a calibration laboratory. A first finding is reported concerns that water absorbed dose rate calculated from measurements made with radiochrom films (MH -V2 - 55) was higher than values obtained with other substances. Another conclusion drawn from various researches is that the alanine dosimeter can provide a high precision, but not for fields with a diameter less than 20 mm, while TLD are not suitable for fields with a diameter less than 10 mm; a suitable method in these cases remains dosimetry film radiochrom (Gafchromic). Alanine-RES dosimetry system is able to measure the cumulative total dose received by the patient. Ionisation chambers, which are commonly used in clinical dosimetry are not suitable for small and non-standard radiation field, because, at on one hand, the lack of spatial resolution, and, on the other hand, the lack of precision of the measurement of absorbed dose and the disturbance caused to the photon fluency. This paper deals with the research dedicated to the implementation of the alanine/RES system in the dosimetry for stereotactic radiosurgery in Romania.

Keywords: stereotactic radiosurgery (SRS); ionizing radiation; alanine.

1 Introduction

Protocols published until now, such as IAEA-TRS-398 and AAPM-TG-51 [1,2], describe the method of measuring the absolute dose in water in a reference field of 10x10 cm^2 using a ionization chamber, while output factors are measured and / or calculated by the user [3-7].
For Leksell Gamma Knife (LGK), the determination of the absolute dose in water for SRS treatment is often done by calculating the product between the water absorbed dose (Dw), measured in the largest available radiation field (16 mm or 18 mm in diameter), using a small volume ionization chamber according to conventional protocols, and the output parameter provided by the manufacturer (or user) for each treatment range [8].
After many years of research, major concerns for reference dosimetry in the radiation fields used in SRS remain. This is due to the difficulty of making accurate dose measurements, difficulties caused by various factors such as: the partial closure of the photon beam in the measuring point [6]; the absence of the charged particle balance; the steep gradient of the absorbed dose rate; the effect of the average volume on the detector response; fluctuation of photon fluctuations in the lateral direction of the beam [6,9,10].

2 Theoretical background

Data from literature [8,9] presents the analysis of the use of passive dosimeters for reference dosimetry in small fields (subject to acceptable measurement accuracy). Various types of passive dosimeters (radiochrome films, TLD, alanine) have been used for measurements in radiation fields with a diameter of between 4 mm and 35 mm in a LGK equipment. Dosimeters were calibrated in terms of the absolute dose in water (Dw), using a calibrated ionization chamber calibrated in a calibration laboratory.
A first reported finding relates to the fact that the water absorbed dose rate calculated from the radiochrome (MH-V2-55) measurements was higher than the values obtained with other types of dosimeters. A possible explanation for this is the lower mediating effect on the dosimeter volume. The ratio of the water absorbed dose (w) obtained with each dosimeter and those obtained with the film was evaluated. For LGK, the ratio decreases as the dosimeter increases and remains constant for collimator diameters larger than 8 mm. The same behavior was also observed when LINAC was used, and the ratio increased with field size, independent of the dosimeter used. This behavior could be explained as a volume mediation effect, effect due to dose gradient and loss of electronic balance.
The estimation of the output factors for the LGK collimators indicated that, and if there was a concordance between the Monte Carlo simulations and the measurements made with various dosimeters, there is no certainty that the Dw in the radiation field was known with the correct precision, research in reference dosimetry is still an important aspect. The output factor is the ratio between the absorbed dose rate for a field size and the absorbed dose rate obtained for the field size under reference conditions. This size allows for the evaluation of scattering changes when changing the collimator setting and linking the absorbed dose rate for a given collimator to the dose rate absorbed for the field reference size.
Another conclusion drawn from these research is that the alanine dosimeter can provide high accuracy but not for fields with a diameter of less than 20 mm, whereas TLDs are not suitable for fields smaller than 10 mm in diameter; a suitable method in these cases remains radiochrome film dosimetry (Gafchromic).

3 Experimental setup

The Leksell Gamma Knife C stereotactic radiosurgery equipment, which is equipped with the Bagdasar-Arseni University Clinical Hospital (SCUBA), shown in Figure1, is a complex installation whose main component of interest in the research that is carried out in this project is the Irradiation Unit (Figure 2, Figure 3). With a total mass of 18,300 kg (including shielding

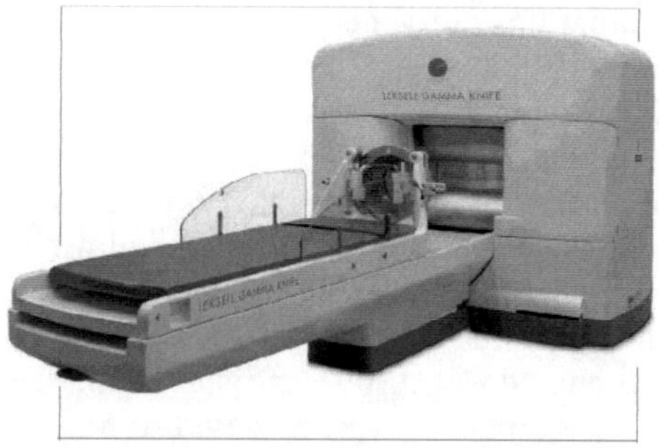

Fig.1. Leksell Gamma Knife C

systems), the irradiation unit contains 201 Co-60 radioactive sources (Figure 3); the total activity of these sources (at the time of their introduction into the installation) is 6000 Ci, which ensures a flow value the absorbed dose of min. 3 Gy / min (the values commonly used are in the range of 3 Gy / min - 5 Gy / min) [28].

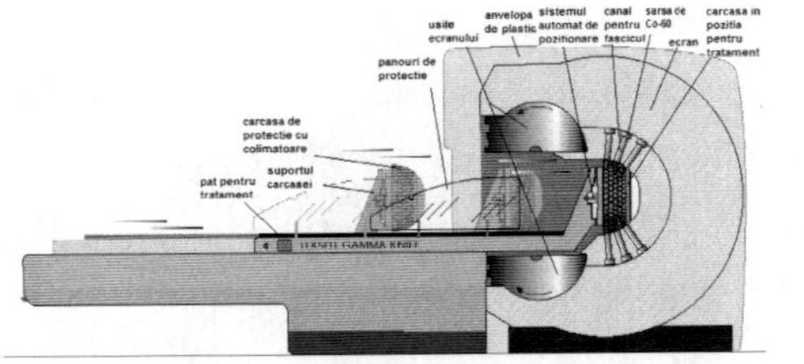

Fig. 2 . Irradiation Unit

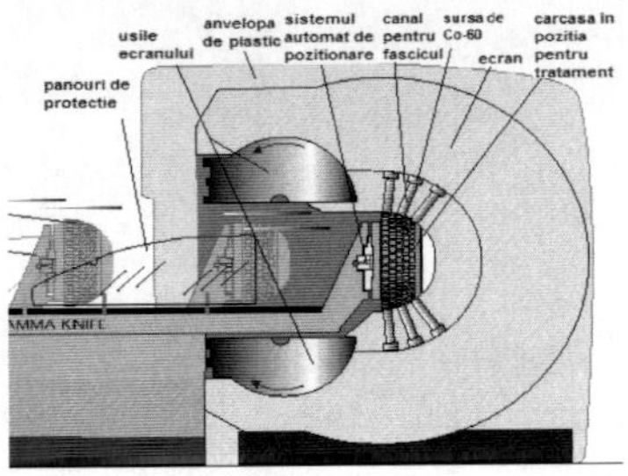

Fig. 3. Irradiation Unit

• Mass 18 300 kg; door weight 800 kg; 201 sources of Cobalt-60; Co-60 Source Activity: 6000 Ci ; Dose rate: min 3 Gy / min; Radiation screen: 40 cm cast iron.

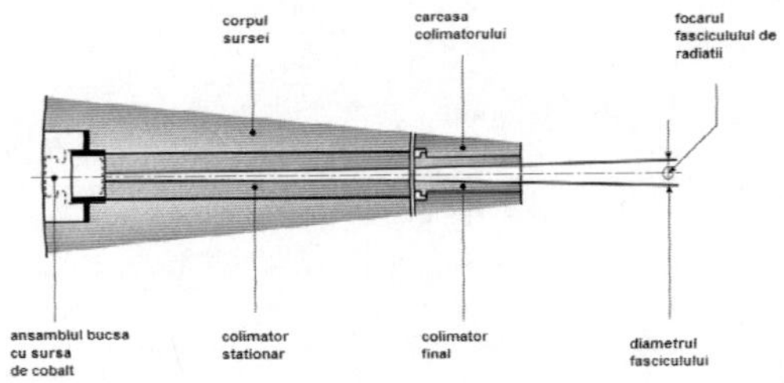

Fig. 4. Gamma radiation beam geometry

Each of the 201 radioactive sources is provided with a fixed collimator and a final collimator, whose role is to define the gamma ray beam geometry emitted by the sources (Figure 4).

Each radioactive source is triple encapsulated in welded stainless steel cylinders (Figure 5).

Fig. 5. Stainless steel cylinders

The shape of the irradiation enclosure as well as its positioning within the LGK / C equipment are presented in Figure 6.

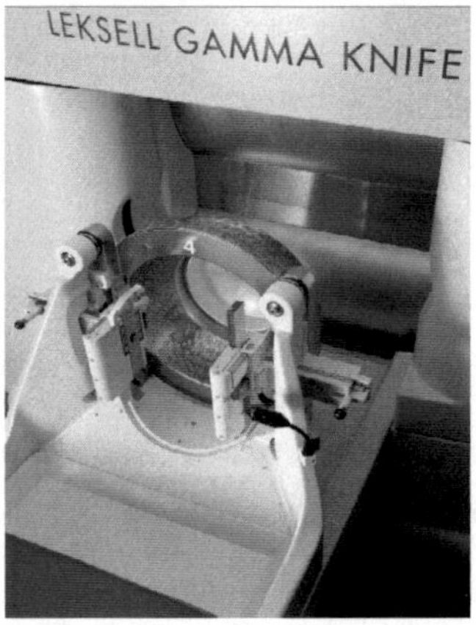

Fig. 6. Automatic positioning system

To perform the various experiments necessary to achieve the objective of this project, the spherical phantom(Figure 7), made of an equivalent tissue material, will be used for irradiation. The use of this phantom is imposed by the need to measure the absorbed dose in the tissue

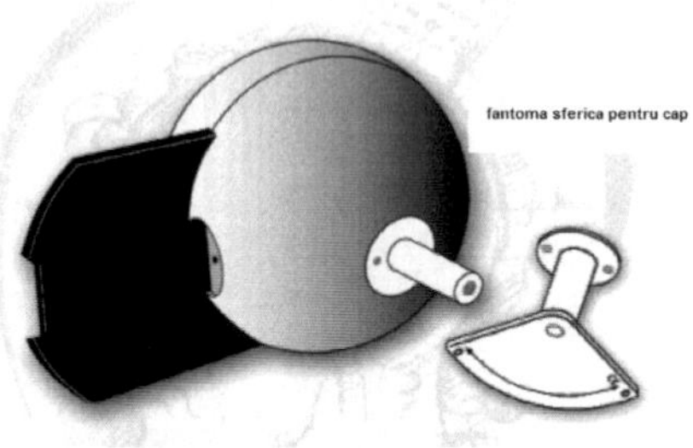

Fig. 7. The phantom

The phantom is thus designed to allow the insertion into its equatorial area of a plate also made of a tissue equivalent material (PMMA). In this plate, the dosimeters (radiochrome film, alanine, etc.) will be inserted into a geometry to be set. This will take into account the radiation geometry but also the shape and dimensions of the detectors used. In this way, the necessary irradiation conditions will be ensured to measure the dose absorbed in Dw tissue) at various points in the area of interest for stereotactic surgery.

4 Results and discussions

Based on the studies conducted and taking into account the data reported in the literature, we can conclude the following: For the first time, to check the calibration conditions of the LGK, two alanine pills with the following dimensions: diameter 4.8 mm; a thickness of 3 mm and a mass of 67.5 ± 0.1 will be placed in the special box (Figure 7). Another approach will be to use radiochrome films placed in the same box type. After testing the functionality of this dosimeter irradiation configuration, attempts will be made to calibrate them. For

this purpose, the same type of cassette, which is inserted into the ghost-head (from ABS - acetylbutadienstirene), will be used. In this case, however, the box will be designed to allow simultaneous insertion of the alanine / film pills and the PTW 31010 ionization chamber used for reference measurements together with the UNIDOS electrometer.

5 Conclusion

Considering that the objective of this phase of the project is to establish the characteristics of the alanine dosimeters required for use in stereotactic dosimetry, we consider that the amount of information accumulated during the studies conducted and presented in this report allows the programming of the research to be carried out in the next stage, in order to achieve the overall objective of the project

References

1. IAEA (2005) Absorbed Dose Determination in Photon and Electron Beams, An International Code of Practice, Technical Report Series, vol. 277, Viena-Austria

2. Almond PR, Biggs PJ, Coursey BM, Hanson WF, Saiful Huq M, et al. (1999) AAPM's TG-51 protocol for clinical reference dosimetry of high-energy photon and electron beams, *Med. Phys.,* 26: 1847-1870.doi:10.1118/1.598691

3. Heydarian M, Hobany PW, Beddoe AH (1995), A comparison of dosimetry techniques in stereotactic surgery , *Phys. Med. Biol.* 41:93-110.doi:10.1088/0031-9155/41/1/008

4. Sánchez-Doblado F, Hartmann GH, Pena J, Rosello JV, Russiello G, et al. (2007), A new method for output factor determination in MLC shaped narrow beams, *Physica Medica,* 23: 58-66, doi:10.1016/j.ejmp.2007.03.002

5. Sauer OA, Wilbert J (2007), Measurement of output factors for small photon beams, *Med. Phys.* 34:1983-1988.doi:10.1118/1.2734383

6. Das IJ, Ding GX, Ahnesjö A (2008), Small fields: Nonequilibrum radiation dosimetry , *Med. Phys.* 35:206-215.doi:10.1118/1.2815356

7. Fan J, Paskalev K, Wang L, Jin L, Li J, et al. (2009), Determination of output factors for stereotactic radiosurgery beams, *Med.Phys.* 36:5292-5300. doi:10.1118/1.3232217

8. Massillon G, Cueva-Procel D, Dosimetry for small fields in stereotactic radiosurgery using gafchromic MD-V2-55 film, TLD and alanina dosimeters, published may 9, 2013, http://dx.doi.org/10.1371/journal.pone.0063418

9. Massillon-JL G (2010), Dosimetry in steep dose-rate gradient radiation fields: A challenge in clinical applications. *Eleventh Mexican Symposium on Medical Physics AIP Conference Proceeding* 1310:23-28.doi:10.1063/1.3531600

10. Alfonso R, Andreo P, Capote R, Saiful Huq M, Kilby W, et al. (2008), A new formalism for reference dosimetry of small and nonstandard fields, *Med. Phys.,*

35:5179-5186.doi:10.1118/1.3005481

Improving better measurements on metrology for health

E. Batista, M. Ferreira*, and I. Godinho
Portuguese Institute for Quality, Metrology Department, Caparica, Portugal
* Correspondence: mcferreira@ipq.pt

Abstract. Based on the work developed by the multidisciplinary Health Metrology Task Group (HMTG), this paper depicts novel approaches for best practices in health metrology. Aiming to enhance its metrological traceability, the case study is applied to an infusion technology where translational research is emphasizing. The specific role of metrology education is highlighted, focusing on the framework of hospitals' policy and the related background of health professionals. The discussion is structured around the ongoing project EMPIR 15SIP03- Infusion Uptake.

Keywords: Errors, Health, Metrology, Measuring Instruments, Traceability.

1 Introduction

Although metrological tools are well established for measurements in the technical fields of economic transactions, environment, road safety and food, they remain comparatively insufficient for measurements in the medical field.

Interest and debates on metrology [1] for health have grown over the last years and led to discussion about the key role of metrological and statistical principles applied in health care and health monitoring systems. One of the major challenges is the enormous diversity of measurements and the strong interdisciplinary nature of the topic.
Evaluating technological progress in the field of measurements and measuring instruments, it is straightforwardly understandable that a lot of work is yet to be done with respect to metrology applied in health services facilities.

Considering a backwards and forwards approach, on the one hand for the medical device industry and applications in medicine including medical equipment manufacturers, all of them must have performed periodic testing and calibration of equipment as parts of a quality control regime that guarantees the reliability of medical instruments. On the other hand, the health care professionals assume that results obtained by the instruments are accurate, reliable and comparable over time. This assumption implies that measurement results are metrologically traceable. Nevertheless, there should be awareness that errors and uncertainties of measuring instruments and incorrect handling procedures could lead to unsuitably wrong diagnoses and inadequate treatments.

Although the measuring errors are present and quantified in a wide range of medical measurements, the majority of health care professionals believe that the most serious errors in medical measurements is motivated by any other purposes than the lack of metrological traceability.

Notwithstanding the health professionals lack of awareness about metrology issues, when this topic is applied to the framework of health care, it is acknowledged that there are no broad consensus.

Therefore, the growing awareness about the key role of metrology in health care creates new areas of metrological opportunities to the sphere of health quality assurance. In this context and under the real framework of metrology in Portuguese health care organizations, a study was performed in 2014 among Portuguese hospitals to identify and analyze issues concerning the concept of metrological traceability [2]. One key output pointed the lack of awareness of health professionals regarding metrology as a topic requiring further evaluation. Moreover, it was also considered that the interoperability between metrology, quality assurance and health care was not contextualized within the current European legal framework [3]. Therefore, under the framework of the Sectoral Commission for Health-CS/09 at the Portuguese Quality System, a multidisciplinary Health Metrology Task Group (HMTG) was created by the Portuguese Institute for Quality (IPQ).

2 Method

Metrology in health is a rather new subject and many potential topics exist. Based on this approach, it has been observed that the meaning of calibration and metrology are not known by many medical instruments users. In addition, tests, measurements and calibration of bio-medical instruments are becoming increasingly significant, when accuracy in diagnosis and effectiveness in treatment is required. Nowadays, the traceability of medical metrology instruments is not addressed at the health organizations in a systematic manner. Therefore, the metrology community needs a strong collaboration with clinical experts and health-related industry.

Considering the key role of metrology best practices in health care facilities, the ad-hoc Working Group HMTG consists of engineers, chemists, nurses, physicists, pharmaceutics and other technical experts from several official organizations.
Public hospitals, institutions from the Portuguese ministry of health and other top-level stakeholders are currently members of the HMTG, who are also active on other technical committees ensuring a greater flow of information.

Facing the needs to achieve best practices in health care facilities and taking into account clinical practices, the main goal of this multidisciplinary Task Group (TG) is to improve the metrological knowledge of non-metrology professionals. For that, HMTG developed a set of Metrology guidelines for several different measuring instruments aiming to the metrological best practices of health professionals from Portuguese hospitals [4], [5], [6], [7].
The first published guide [4] is a transversal document applied to all fields of metrology, and focusing on the specific filed of health metrology. The guides followed are technical documents that cover key tools of metrological and technical requirements of blood pressure devices [5], clinical thermometers [6], and infusion pumps [7]. Those items are available from IPQ website (free download[1]).
As the medical community and government authorities are considered the target of this reference documents dissemination, the task group organizes discussions, workshops and conferences with stakeholders such as clinical experts and health professionals. All activities developed after publishing the guides were the response to a strong demand from health professionals and from whom is engaged in the usage of medical instruments and measurements. Training to the medical devices users must be one of the adopted means to make them aware of the role of metrology and also the methodologies of measurements and calibration described on the aforementioned guides.

From a metrological point of view, the national task force has been the key to establish and supporting confidence in medical instruments and clinical measurements.

3. Infusion technology

The complexity of some medication and the multiple steps involved in their preparation, administration, and monitoring create a scenario that demands close attention to detail and heavily relies on human intervention to detect and mitigate errors. In order to support this clinical procedure, medical infusion instruments are widely used and are fundamental for primary health care, namely for providing drugs, nutrition and hydration to patients such as syringe pumps and peristaltic pump. Hence, it is crucial that the volume and flow generated by these instruments are as accurate and precise as possible. To ensure this, it is necessary to have appropriate calibration methods and standards. These instruments present different measuring features and capacities according to their use and therapeutic application [8].
Two different calibration methods can be used to determine the flow error of infusion pumps [9]. One is the gravimetric method, considered as a primary method and commonly used by the National Metrology Institutes. The other is a comparison method where an Infusion Device Analyser (IDA) is used as a flow generator, which is typically used in the hospitals' maintenance offices.

3.1 Translational research

Regarding the potential topics applied on health Metrology, priorities have been identified and a strategic research agenda for research projects within the European Association of National Metrology Institutes (EURAMET), such as the European Metrology Programme for Innovation and Research (EMPIR), have been developed.
In this framework, the EMPIR Metrology for Drug Delivery Project (MeDD - HLT07) [8] had as main concern the improvement of such calibration methods.
Aiming to disseminate the knowledge obtained from MeDD Project, a new EMPIR project standards and e-learning course to maximize the uptake of infusion and calibration best practices (Infusion Uptake - 15SIP03) started in May of 2016.

The 15SIP03 EMPIR Project has two main goals:

- To develop an -learning module made available on the E-learning platform of the European Society for Intensive Care Medicine (ESICM), with aim at creating awareness and understanding of multi infusion risks, and thereby reducing dosing errors, thus decreasing adverse patient incidents and increasing the quality of medical treatment;
- To incorporate the best metrology practices concerning calibration of infusion devices according to ISO standards, namely ISO 7886-2 and IEC 60601-2-24.

Furthermore, according to the terms of reference of the HMTG and considering that IPQ is a partner on EURAMET within the research project from Infusion Uptake - 15SIP03, a new guide of infusion technology was design and developed for the health professionals. This guide [7], as a delivery of the EMPIR project 15SIP03, will provide helpful information to support accurate measurements where the success of a treatment relies on accurate doses of the prescribed drug delivered at the specified time. In addition, as a great percentage of the errors can be avoided if the users of infusion technology have a better understanding of the instruments, it was also created a networking forum by the main Portuguese public hospitals.

The reference guide information [7] will be included on the e-

[1] Permanent accessed by URL http://www1.ipq.pt/PT/SPQ/ComissoesSectoriais/CS09/Pages/CS09.aspx

learning modules of the EMPIR project 15SIP03, which also emphasizes the real impact of testing, maintenance, calibration and legal metrological control procedures applied.

Under the scope of this work, the cooperation in the field of health Metrology has been established at IPQ applied to a translational research methodology.
On the one hand, the work developed by HMTG and EMPIR 15SIP03 project consortium have provided new knowledge and useful technical experience exchanges among practitioners, improving the metrological traceability of infusion instruments rather than maintenance operations [7]. One the other hand, the engagement on new practices for health professionals also brought new inputs for the current available standards dealing with metrological traceability of infusion technologies and accessories, e.g. ISO 7886-2 [10], IEC 60601-2-24 [11] and further insights to recommendations from the International Organization of Legal Metrology (OIML).

4 Conclusions

The joint work of HMTG reaches a strong collaboration with clinical experts and health-related professionals. In this way, the impact of metrology in health has been demonstrated by not only improving accuracy and comparability of measurements but also in assessing the benefits of clinical decisions. Also represents a bridge for realization and further development of scientific and technical cooperation among universities, metrology institutions, health organizations, hospitals and manufactures.
Considering that the main participants are from the Portuguese Ministry of Health, the authors believe that, in the near future, a vast experience on how to assure the metrological traceability of infusion technologies with the best possible practice could be generated. Therefore, the authors emphasize the possibility of using this approach on other different types of measuring instrument and strongly believe on further efforts to improve new scientific and technical joint working groups in the framework of EMPIR or other research projects.

References

1. JCGM 200. (2012). International Vocabulary of Metrology. Basic and General Concepts and Associated Terms.

2. Ferreira, M.; Matos, A.; Leal, P. (2015). Evaluation of the role of metrological traceability in health care: a comparison study by statistical approach. Accreditation and Quality Assurance. Volume 20, Issue 6 (2015), Page 457-464.

3. Ferreira, M. (2011). The role of metrology in the field of medical devices. International Journal of Metrology and Quality Engineering. 2: 135-140. DOI:10.1051/ijmqe/2011101.

4. Comissão Sectorial da Saúde. (2015). Metrologia na Saúde – Guia de Boas Práticas. 1.ª Edição. Instituto Português da Qualidade. ISBN 978-972-763-158-2.

5. Comissão Sectorial da Saúde. (2016). Metrologia na Saúde – Guia de Boas Práticas: Instrumentos de Medição da Pressão Arterial. 1ª Edição. Instituto Português da Qualidade. ISBN 978-972-763-160-5.

6. Comissão Sectorial da Saúde. (2016). Metrologia na Saúde – Guia de Boas Práticas: Termómetros Clínicos. 1ª Edição. Instituto Português da Qualidade. ISBN 978-972-763-161-2.

7. Comissão Sectorial da Saúde. (2017). Metrologia na Saúde – Guia de Boas Práticas: Bombas de Perfusão. 1ª Edição. Instituto Português da Qualidade. ISBN 978-972-763-161-2.

8. Batista, E., H Bissig, H., Petter, et al. (2015). Assessment of drug delivery devices. Biomedical Engineering, 2015, 60(4).

9. Batista, E., Ferreira, M., Godinho, I., et al. (2017). Comparison of infusion pumps calibration methods. Measurement Science and Technology. 28(2017)124003(5pp). DOI.org/10.1088/1361-6501/aa8474.

10. ISO 7886-2:1996, Sterile hypodermic syringes for single use, Part 2: Syringes for use with power-driven syringe pumps.

11. IEC 60601-2-24:2012, Medical electrical equipment - Part 2-24: Particular requirements for the safety of infusion pumps and controllers.

Factors influencing the perpetuation of the quality approach in health care centers of the Medical Prefecture of the city of Fes, Morocco

M. Hmidani[1], S. Maniar[2], B. Zaadoud[3], A. Charki[4], A. El Ouali Lalami[1*]

1- Institute of Nursing Professions and Health Techniques of Fez, Regional Health Directorate, El Ghassani Hospital, Fes 30000, Morocco.
2- Service of the Public Health, Regional Health Directorate Fès-Meknès, Hospital El Ghassani, Fes 30000, Morocco.
3- Epidemiology Unit, Medical Delegation of My Yacoub, Hospital Ibn EL Khatib Regional Health Directorate Fes-Meknes, , Fès 30000, Morocco.
4- ISTIA (Institut des Sciences et Techniques de l'Ingénieur d'Angers) – University of Angers, French.

Received:

Abstract. The quality approach, which has been implemented since the year 2000 at the pilot sites of the Medical Prefecture of Fes, was aimed to be generalized to all primary health care centers (PHCCs) in the outpatient network. This result is far from being reached at the present time. The objective of this study, performed for the first time in the center of Morocco, was to describe the factors that influenced the implementation and the perpetuation of the quality approach in the PHCCs of the Medical Prefecture of the city of Fes in the center of Morocco. For that, we carried out a survey of the managers of the PHCCs of the Medical Prefecture of Fes. We also had an interview with the quality facilitators and the managers of the Service of the Network of the Health care institutions. We have acquired a percentage of answer to the questionnaire equal to 99%. On the 36 PHCCs touched by the formation, the quality cycle could be initiated only in 17 PHCCs and only in 10 PHCCs could be completed. Currently this approch was given up by all PHCCs. The analysis of the results revealed that there are several factors which impeded the implementation and the perpetuation of the quality approch, in the ambulatory network of the prefecture of Fes. Concerning the factors related to the internal environment, we noted the insufficient commitment of the managers of the central service, the insufficiency in the accompaniment, the follow-up and the communication of the hierarchical managers of all the PHCCs involved in our study. Similarly, the insufficiency of human resources and the overload of work discourage PHCCs managers, to initiate, to complete and to ensure the continuity of the quality improvement cycle.Regarding the functions of support, we found that the supervision, the facilitation, the motivation and the reward are determining factors that have been lacking in the context of this study. As for the organization for quality, this study also revealed an insufficiency of the coordination of the improvements actions of quality between the operational actors and piloting.

Keywords: Quality approch, Factors of Perpetuation, Cycle Improvement of Quality, Primary health care center, Medical Prefecture of Fes, Morocco.

1 Introduction

Historically, the quality approach (QA) developed with the beginning in the industrial companies. Thereafter, they conquered the nonindustrial organizations in particular the sector of health [1].

In Morocco, it is only with the advent of the political reforms, institutional, economic and social committed since the Nineties that the context became more favorable for the introduction of an approach quality structured into the units of care [2]. These include the clinical audits, the team approach to problem solving, development of standards and norms in the context of different national public health programs… Thus, in 1999 the Ministry of Health (MH) has developed a National Quality Assurance Program (NQAP), which provided and constituted the reference framework for institutionalizing quality assurance at all levels of the health system [2].

* Correspondence: eloualilalami@yahoo.fr
Institute of Nursing Professions and Health Techniques of Fez, Regional Health Directorate, El Ghassani Hospital, Fes 30000, Morocco.

The Fes-Meknes region is among the pioneering regions in the field of quality. Indeed, since the end of the 1990s, a large number of people have been trained in Quality Approaches, Principles and Tools and the Quality Circles (QC) have been established and made up in practically in all primary health care centers (PHCCs). However, seven years later, this approach has only been implemented and established only in a small number of PHCCs.

These difficulties have even been encountered in developed countries. Indeed, the majority of QCs implanted at healthcare institutions in Canada have encountered difficulties [3] and some have ceased operations before reaping benefits. The insufficient degree of implication of leaders, the ambiguity surrounding their motivations and the organizational context inside of which they exert their functions are factors that may be incriminated [4].

The implementation of QC in health facilities requires the respect of several phases: a preliminary study, the implementation of a QC action plan with the instruments for monitoring and evaluation [5]. They also ask the installation of a sequence, primarily coherent, stages characterized by: the

convergence of the efforts towards a common goal, activities which take as a starting point a decision-making process, the implication of all the hierarchical levels in the maintenance of the points of excellence and in the correction of the gaps as well as the identification of the responsibilities for the speakers [6].
Several factors of order organizational, cultural, economic and environmental determine the success or failure of QC [7]. The dysfunctions and obstacles that influence QCs do not appear in the majority of cases during the implantation phase, but they occur during the phase of perpetuation [6]. These obstacles can be classified into two categories: "visible and invisible barrier", the first of a technical and operational nature. Second is of a strategic and relational nature [8].
The essential factors that determine and condition the success and the perpetuationof QCs can also be grouped into four categories: strategic, technical, structural and cultural [9]. Another category called "regulatory or lawful", was added by Tabuteau [10] because the health facility is managed differently than a company. Similarly, they can be classified in three dimensions: 1) that related to the enabling internal environment, 2) that related to the organization for quality, and 3) that related to support functions [11].

It is in this context that it seemed to us interesting and necessary to consider the possible factors that have influenced the sustainability and the perpetuation of the (QA) in the PHCCs at the level of the city of Fes. This study was performed for the first time in the center of Morocco.

2 Material and Methods

Type of study
This is a retrospective descriptive study.
Study area
This study proceeded in the city of Fez in central Morocco, who counts to 1079,000 inhabitants. The city had 36 ESSPs during the study period. Each ESSP is managed by a Chief Medical Officer and a Head Nurse. All PHCCs are managed and supervised by the service of the networks of health institutions.
Population
It includes in this study a population of two groups of actors, namely: all the managers (doctor and head nurses) of the PHCCs who are 72 in number and the responsible for the service of the networks of health institutions.
Methods and instruments of collection and data analyzes
For doctors and nurses managers of PHCCs, we conducted a survey using a self administered questionnaire that included questions "closed" and "open" questions. All questions flow from the terms of reference of the study.
We conducted with the officials of the service of the networks of health institutions, a semi-directive interview through a interview grid including the major axes to discuss in relation to the research question.

The collected data was processed and analyzed using the software Epi info (version 3.3.2 2005) and Microsoft office Excel 2007.

3 Results and discussion

All 36 PHCCs were included in our study. Of the 72 questionnaires distributed, we recovered 71, about 99% of respondents. 65% of respondents have a seniority at the position than 3 years.

At the level of the networks of health institutions we included 5 people directly involved in the establishment and perpetuation of the quality cycles (QC) namely the chief doctor, the major nurse and 3 quality facilitators.
Implementation of the QC
On the 36 PHCC formed in QA, 53% of PHCC could not initiate the QC. Moreover, 20% of PHCC began a cycle but could not finish. For the remainder, 6 PHCC have buckled only one QC is 16%, 2 PHCC have buckled two QC (6%), only one PHCC could complete 3 QC (3%) and onther PHCC could buckle 4 QC (3%) (Figure 1). Currently, all PHCC gave up this approach.
Several factors could explain the difficulty of initiation and perpetuation of this step on the level of the health care institutions. According to a study initiated in the Hospital of the Specialities of Rabat in Morocco, the causes of non the perpetuation of the QA which was raised by the participants are: lack of the shared vision of quality, the insufficiency of implication of the persons in charge, the failure of coordination between the structures and not-control of the method of the project of quality [12].

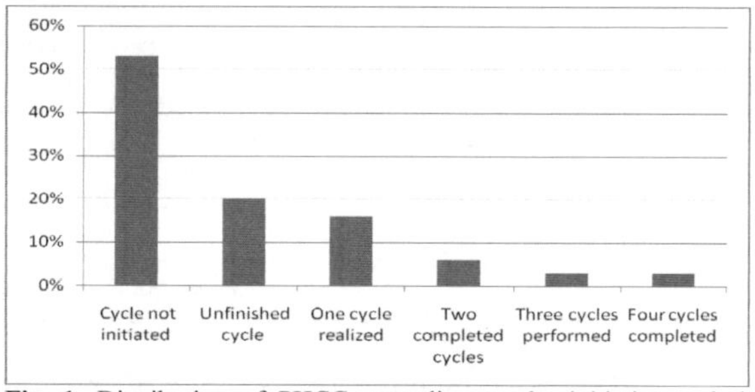

Fig. 1. Distribution of PHCC according to the initiation and the completion of the Quality Cycle.

Training of the managers of PHCC in step quality
As shown in the figure 2, 65% of the participants in the study profited from a formation on quality. On the other hand the persons in charge of the service of the networks of health institutions affirmed that the training has been assured for all the personnel of PHCCs concerned at the level of prefecture of Fes. The 35% of the health workforce not formed are probably lately assigned to the level of the town of Fes.
The formation in QA, constitutes a determining factor in the establishment and in perpetuation of the quality step. However, in the context of our study, the formation is not seemed to be lacking, since an significant effort in terms of formation was made as our results prove it. Thus, we can wonder about the quality of this formation. Indeed, implementation the perennial of the QA, requires three types of formation namely: competences of base in QA, the framing of the personnel at the time of the realization of the activities, and monitoring and the supervision of the efforts of the personnel as regards QA [11].

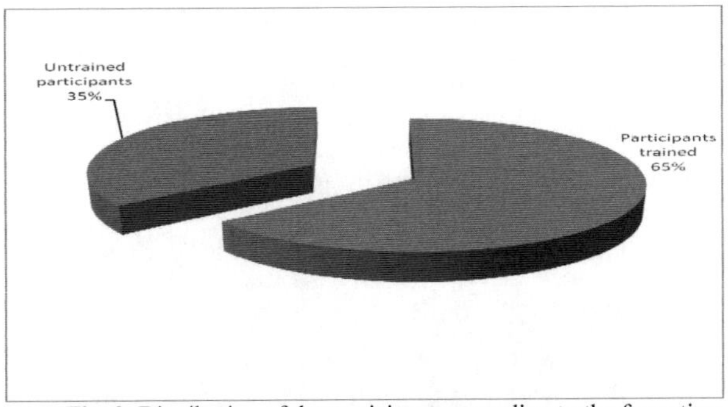

Fig. 2. Distribution of the participants according to the formation in QA.

Supervision, follow-up and evaluation of the quality team.

As shown in the figure 3, 67% of PHCCs which initiated the QC declared that they were not the subject of a supervision, and that they were not convened by their superiors, for meetings of exchange, follow-up and of evaluation. This could be a source of demotivation for the teams and thus constitute factors, in the context of this study, having could block the perpetuation of the QC.

This is compatible with what was brought back by certain authors [11,13] who affirmed that the continuous improvement of quality requires the monitoring, the supervision, the follow-up of the respect of the standards and the measurement of the achievements as regards quality on all the levels. In the same way an investigation [14] realized by the national center of the French scientific research in twelve establishments of care carrying into perception of quality at the professionals of the health care institutions concluded in the need for supporting a culture of the quality evaluation as well at on the level of the indicators installed as on the level of the quality step itself. This in order to maintain the dynamic of the actions undertaken in the name of quality.

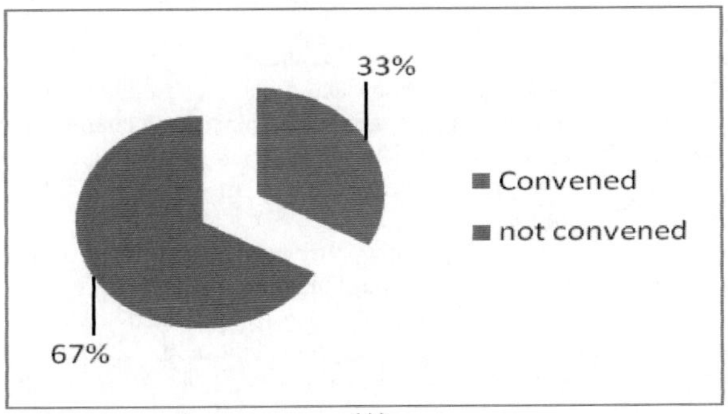

(A)

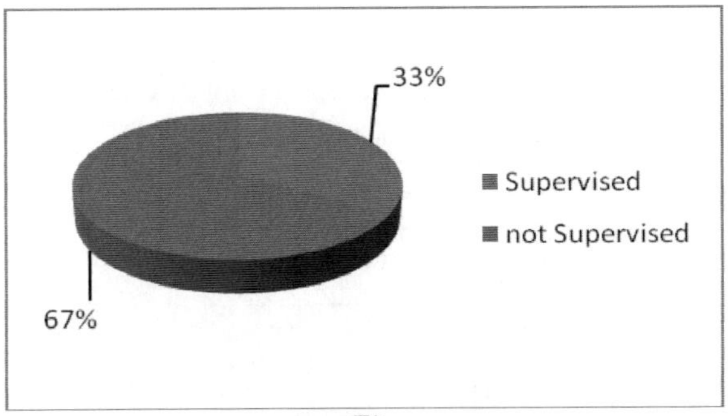

(B)

Fig. 3. The distribution of PHCCs according to the supervision (A), the follow-up and the evaluation (B).

Accompaniment (support and facilitation) by the persons in charge of the networks of health institutions

56% of the respondents declared that they were not accompanied by their hierarchical person in charge during control of the QC (Figure 4).

This result agrees only partially with all what was advanced by the people interviewed. Indeed, the two persons in charge of the service of the networks of health institutions affirmed the support, the facilitation and the systematic accompaniment of the teams of the QC and coordination with the referents quality to frame them and support them. However, two referents quality out of three announced that their support and facilitation are not systematic, but it is started under the request of the team of QC.

Knowing that the perpetuation of QA is difficult to obtain, if the managers do not provide an accompaniment and a solid framing to all the levels. This could be done by showing their attachment and their support for a culture of quality and to the people which take part in the activities of improvement of quality [15,12]. We can consider that the insufficiency in the accompaniment is a factor which have influenced the perpetuation of the QA negatively.

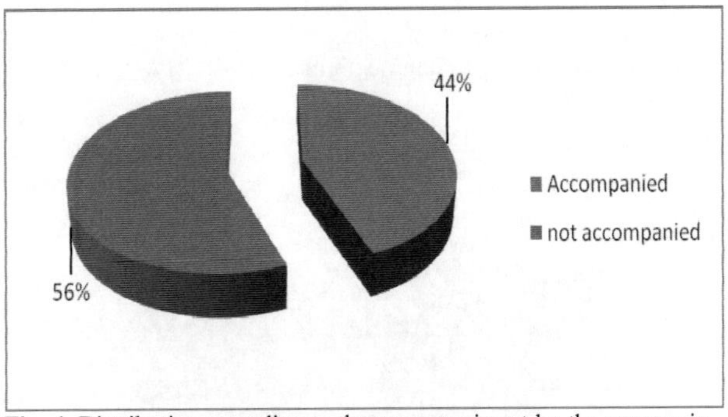

Fig. 4. Distribution according to the accompaniment by the persons in charge of the networks of health institutions.

Availability of human resources

77% of the persons in charge affirm not to have the essential resources to carry out the activities of the QA (Figure 5). This finding has been confirmed by the networks of health institutions officials.

The insufficiency of human resources and the overload of work are two factors which can slow down the perpetuation and the continuous development of QC. Indeed, the insufficiency of the resources, especially human, resounds on the motivation of the professional to carry out the activities of the QA [11,6]. This known as, the human insufficiency of resources is a national problem which is sometimes easily advanced to justify certain resistances to change.

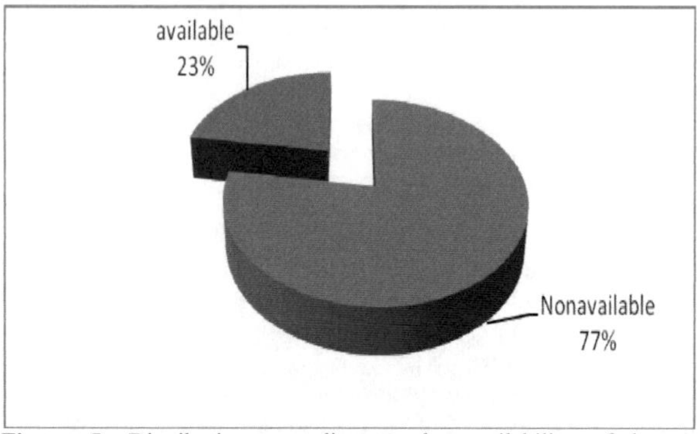

Figure 5: Distribution according to the availability of human resources.

Reward of the efforts quality

81% of the respondents belonging to PHCCs where the QA was initiated, declare that they were not rewarded for their efforts as regards improvement for quality (Figure 6). In the same way, the persons in charge of the service of the networks of health institutions were all agreements which the lack of reward is one of the key factors, which blocked the perpetuation of the QA, in the primary health care centers of Fes.

The lack of reward demotives the personnel who sees the quality approach, an overload of work [16]. Thus, the reward symbolic system of the teams, who reserve part of their times and their effort to the QA, could play a determining role for its perpetuation on the level of the establishments medical [11]. In the context of this study, this shows that the non-rewarding quality efforts have a non-negligible impact on the non-perpetuation of QC.

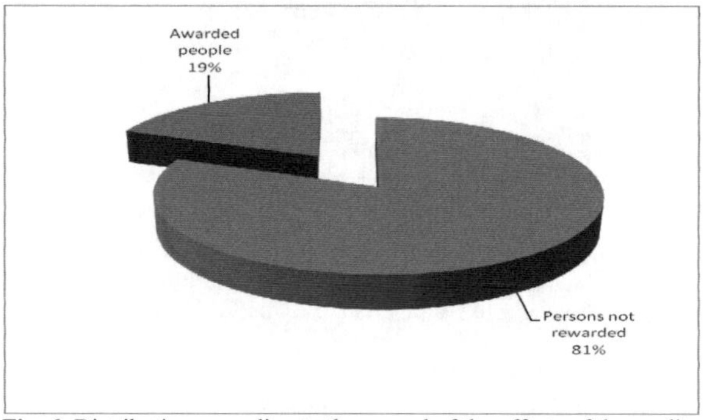

Fig. 6. Distribution according to the reward of the efforts of the quality teams.

Causes of non completion and perpetuation of QA

As shown in the figure 7, the causes of non completion and non perpetuation of the quality steps most frequently quoted by the participants are: the overload of work (82%) and the insufficiency of human resources (73%). The demotivation, lack of spirit of voluntariate and the support of seniors in rank, and their accompaniment are quoted by approximately the one third of the participants.

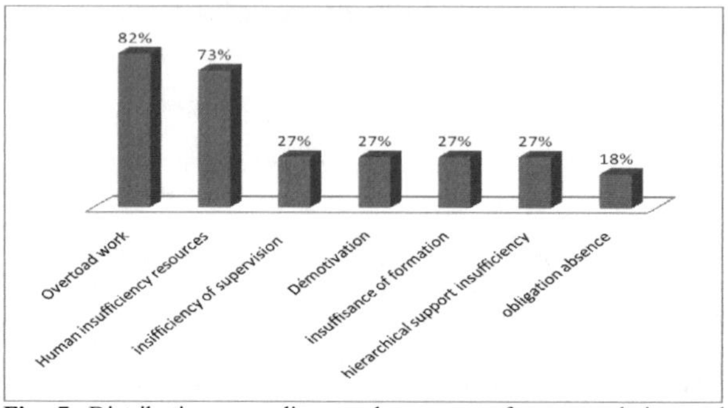

Fig. 7. Distribution according to the causes of noncompletion and perpetuation of QA.

The results of the semi semi-structured interview with the persons in charge of the service of the networks of health institutions confirm this observation, because they specified that the causes influencing the perpetuation of the QC negatively at the ambulatory level are presented thus: the insufficiency of human resources and the overload of work as well as lack of the motivation through the material reward or symbolic system. Recognition through motivation could to pay homage to the quality teams and to recognize their efforts as regards improvement of quality.

The persons in charge the service of the networks of health institutions also noted, that the partiality and the subjectivity of the listeners in the first price of national competition quality demotivated completely the teams which took part in this national competition.

Moreover, all interview them stressed that the insufficiency of coordination between the various actors of this step, the not implication and the non engagement of the persons in charge on the level of the central service, at regional level played a determining role in non the perpetuation of the QA in the medium of this study.

This result is in agreement with a study carried out in Morocco on the level of the Hospital of the Specialities of Rabat city. In the same way, several authors [17,11,5,18] affirmed that the success of a policy of continuous improvement of quality within the health care institutions requires the explicit engagement of the persons in charge institutional and the implication of all the hierarchical levels.

The orientation of the persons in charge for quality is decisive to exceed two types of obstacles: that of individual and structural resistances to the change, and that of possible professional defense reactions sometimes met in the health care institutions [19,20].

As for their recommendations, the persons in charge of the service of the networks of health institutions suggested all the structuring of national plan of quality assurance, by allocating

its own human and financial resources to him, like the other programs of health.
Various studies have emphasized and recommended the necessity of a framework to institutionalizing quality approach [21,22,23].

4 Conclusion

This study, could highlight certain factors affecting the capacity of the CS of the prefecture of Fes to establish and perennialize the QA, in particular: lack of engagement of the persons in charge of central service, the insufficiency in the accompaniment and the support of the hierarchy, the overload of work, lack of reward and the insufficiency in coordination between the operational actors and of piloting of the QA.
The catch in consideration of the recommendations of this study will be of a great contribution to support the initiation and the durability of cycle of improvement of quality. This study was interested in the local managers, it would be interesting to generalize it near the whole the personnel implied in the quality sites.

References

1. ANAES, Principles of implementation of a step quality in health care institution. National agency of accreditation and evaluation in health, Paris, (2002)
2. Ministry for health, Main road plan of quality assurance, Morocco, (2000)
3. D. Loseau, When the management of quality becomes a ritual. Inspiration and news bulletin for public managers. **15** (2000)
4. D. Lozeau, Tortuous ways of the management of quality in the public hospitals in Quebec". Management. **27**, 113-122 (2002)
5. B. Monteil, M. Périgord, and G. Raveleau, Tools of the circles and improvement of quality. Paris. Editions of Organization, (1985)
6. R. Grenier, The process of management of the quality of the care - services; Care Frameworks. **43**, 29-34 (2002)
7. F. Bruno, University of Quebec with Three-Rivers, Correspondence to Université of Quebec with Three-Rivers, CP 500, Three-Rivers (Quebec) G9A. **5**, (2008)
8. A. Jacqueyrie, Obstacles with quality: visible and invisible barriers; topicality and file in public health. **35**, 42-43 (2001)
9. S.M. Shortell, CL. Bennett, GR. Byck, Assessing the impact off continuous quality improvement one clinical practice: what it will take to accelerate progress; The Milbank Quarterly. **76**, 593-624 (1998)
10. B. Tabuteau, management by quality in the health care institutions. Stakes, brakes and levers of action professional Thesis for obtaining specialized Mastr in Management by Quality. (2008)
11. L.M. Frnco et al., Franco LM, Silimperi DR, Veldhuyzen van Zanten T *et al.,* Sustaining quality of health care: institutionalization of quality assurance. *QA Monograph Series*. Bethesda, MD: published for USAID by the Quality Assurance Project, 2002.
12. N.R. Salhi, The factors which block the perpetuation of the step quality on the level of the hospital of the specialities of Reduction. Memory of the ENSP (2014): http://ensp.sante.gov.ma/CDS/Documents/Memoires/mem_2014/SALHI.pdf
13. D. Nicholas, Organization of quality: option of the national plans. (1999)
14. J-P. Claveranne et al., Perceptions of quality at the professionals of the health care institutions; DHOS; Ministry for health, the family and the handicapped people; http://www.sante.gouv.fr/htm/dossiers/quali_profsante/qual_profes.pdf
15. F. Douguet, J. Muñoz, Effects of the accreditation and measurements of improvement on the quality of the care and the activity of medical staffs. Paris: Direction of the research of the studies, the evaluation and the statistics. **172**, (2005)
16. D. Boudin, Accreditation and quality of the hospital care. Key to success factors of a step quality. Actual Back Public health. **35**, 25-61 (2001)
17. K.S. Gautam, Cal for board leadership there is quality in hospitals", Quality Management in Health Care. **14**, 18-30 (2005)
18. B.J. Weiner, S.M. Shortell, J. Alexander, Promoting clinical involvement in hospital quality improvement efforts: the effects off signal management, board, and physician leadership"; Health Services Research. **32**, 491-510 (1997)
19. B. Lucet, The place of the formation in the establishment of the culture quality"; Topicality and file in public health. **35**, 38-40 (2001)
20. E. Hassani, Etude des facteurs influençant la reconduction du concours qualité: cas de la région du grand Casablanca. Mémoire INAS, (2010): http://www.sante.gov.ma/inas/mem/mem-2010/HASSANI%20MEHDI.pdf
21. D.R. Silimperi, L.M. Franco, T.V.V. Zanten and C. Macaulay, A framework for institutionalizing qualityAssurance. International Journal for Quality in Health Care. 14, 67–73 (2002)
22. J. Hermida, The road to institutionalizing quality assurance in Ecuador in an environment of health sector reform. Int J Qual Health Care; **11:** 447–450 (1999).
23. Project Report. Institutionalization of Quality Assurance. Bethesda, MD: published for USAID by the Quality Assurance Project, 2000.

Infectious risk management in hemodialysis through the implementation of a quality approach case of a hospital in Fez' city.

S. Berrada* [1, 2, 3], T. G. Benjelloun [2, 4], L. Bennani [1, 4], B. Oumokhtar [4], L. A. El Ouali [1], H. F.Z. Squali [3], H.T. Sqalli[5]

(1): Specialized Institute of nursing professions and health techniques of Fez. (2): LRDEHM-Fez.
(3): Laboratory of Neuroendocrinology and Nutritional and Climatic Environment, Faculty of Sciences Dhar El Mahraz, Fez.
(4): Laboratory of Human Pathology, Biomedicine and Environment, Faculty of Medicine, Fez
(5): Department of Nephrology, CHU Hassan II, Fez.

Summary: Nosocomial infections are a global public health problem, with significant consequences and repercussions, both at the individual and at the economic level. In order to reduce the risk of infection in a hospital hemodialysis center, we have implemented a quality approach that aims to the assess and control of elements that may cause direct or indirect contamination of patients, such as compliance with standards and specific practices, also monitoring the treatment room environment's quality. The objectives were to evaluate standards and specific practices, and to perform microbiological monitoring of this center's environment.
The first component, that was reealized in order to evaluate compliance with the standard and specific precautions at the center, was based on two descriptive and observational surveys conducted one year apart, before and after renovation of the center. The overall analysis has shown that compliance with these practices is variant according to the type of measures considered, but remains globally insufficient. As for the second part, we carried out the control of the hemodialysis rooms' air' s quality and the surfaces of the objects most commonly handled by the patients. This control showed high contamination rates, which maximum was in the case of air and that was very high in the case of surfaces (86.9%).
The most contaminated surface points were mattresses, remote controls, tensiometers, trolleys and scales. The tables and generators also revealed high contamination rates. The identification of isolated germs showed the presence of bacteria and molds, with a predominance of bacteria. The examination of the molds found revealed neither the presence of *Aspergillus* nor *Candida albicans*. The distribution of the bacteria found showed a high proportion of Gram-positive bacteria (85.81%) compared to Gram-negative bacteria (14.19%). This high rate could result from the lack of hygienic measures and the respect of standard precautions we raised in a previous study by patients and staff.
This work showed a lack of standard and specific precautions, a high microbial colonization and a high presence of opportunistic and pathogenic bacterial flora. To improve the quality of care and control the infectious risk in hemodialysis, it would be essential to reinforce the training of staff in hospital hygiene, evaluate and optimize the disinfection protocol applied to surfaces.

Key words: Quality approach, Nosocomial infections, Environment, Fez Hemodialysis, Standard and specific precautions, Quality of care.

* Correspondence: berrsanae@yahoo.fr

1 Introduction

Nosocomial infections are a worrying situation worldwide because of their high morbidity and mortality, but also because of their considerable human and economic impact [1–4]. Due to the frequent and prolonged exposure to various contaminants in the hemodialysis environment, the multitude of skin entry gates and the circumstances of exposure, the immunodeficiency of patients, nosocomial infections represent in hemodialysis the second leading cause of death after cardiovascular disease, a quarter of hospitalizations related to vascular access infections and three-quarters of bacteremic infection-related deaths [5,6]. If the eradication of these infections is impossible because the risk of contracting them can never be zero, prevention as for it, remains the mean to slow down their progression. It is based on the mastery and control of the hospital environment, and the respect of standard and specific precautions [5–8].

As part of improving the quality of care and preventing infectious risk in hemodialysis, we implemented a quality approach to control the elements that can cause direct or indirect contamination of patients. Carried out at the hemodialysis center of the Al Ghassani hospital in Fes, our study included two components and aimed to the assess of compliance with standard and specific practices, also monitoring the microbiological quality of the environment of the halls of the hospital, treatment and evaluation of the corrective actions put in place.

2. Materials and methods

Framework and type of study

The study included four cross-sectional descriptive surveys carried out at the hemodialysis center of the Al Ghassani hospital in the city of Fes (Morocco), before and after renovation of the center. The first part was spread out over a period of 4 months (February-March 2012, March-April 2013), while the second part, was fanned out over a period of six months (April, June, September to November) of the year 2012.

Study population and data collection procedure

For the first component, the survey population included all paramedical staff at the center as well as common patients treated during both periods of the study. Patients excluded from the study are new recruits at the center after renovation and those who left the center or died after the first survey. The information was collected by observation and monitoring of the target population, on anonymous grids developed from the recommendations guide of the French Society of Hospital Hygiene [7]. The grids included 58 questions, including hand hygiene for patients and staff, wearing the recommended dress code, adherence to standard and specific precautions, and cleaning and disinfecting generator surfaces.

For the second component, the population concerned was the environment of the patient treatment rooms. Surface swabs were taken between hemodialysis sessions using the swab technique, which involves rubbing a sterile and moistened swab over a defined area of 25cm^2 [9]. The points chosen were those closest to patients such as generators, tables and mattresses, as well as objects most commonly handled by patients such as remote controls. The analysis of the samples was carried out according to the method described by Meunier [10]. Each swab was immersed in a liquid nutrient broth (Brain Heart Infusion [BHI]) and was incubated at 37 ± 1∘C for 18 to 24 hours. By exhaustion, this broth was then used to inoculate two culture media: blood agar and chloramphenicol Sabouraud, respectively incubated at 37 ± 1∘C for 48 hours, and at 20 ± 2∘C for 5 days. As for the air samples, and because of the absence of biocollectors, the sampling technique used consisted in exposing open petri dishes containing PCA medium for 16 minutes and incubating them at 37 ± 1. ° C for 48 hours. The identification of bacteria was based on classical cultural, morphological and biochemical traits and the one of mold is based on appearance, size and shape. The culture's environments used were prepared according to standard [11] and checked before use (pH, sterility). In addition, an internal quality control (distilled water, consumable, oven, autoclave, environmental conditions of the analysis environment,..), was carried out daily according to the Canadian guidelines [12].

Ethics and confidentiality

The study protocol was submitted to the regional ethics committee, which authorized us to start the study. The confidentiality of the information obtained on the subjects of the study was respected, because neither the names of the patients nor those of the paramedical personnel appeared on the documents of the study.

Statistical analysis

All variables are summarized by the use of descriptive statistics. The qualitative variables are described in terms of proportions, and the quantitative variables were described in terms of mean standard deviation. The statistical analysis of the data was carried out with the software Epi Info 3.4 (version 2007). A value of $p < 0.05$ was considered significant. Data entry was done using the Excel software.

3. Résults and discussion

The hemodialysis center of Al Ghassani hospital in Fes, underwent a restructuring in 2012 according to national and international standards. The renovated center provides treatment for more than 132 patients with chronic end stage renal failure. Due to many factors such as frequent antibiotic therapy and the multitude of invasive vascular acts, patients treated with hemodialysis have a high risk of infection [13]. The evolution of the transmission potential of these infections prompted national and international organizations to make recommendations for their prevention. They concern the design of premises, the rules for the maintenance of equipment and surfaces, also standard and specific precautions designed to minimize the risk of cross-transmission of micro-organisms between caregivers and patients [7, 8]. In order to improve the quality of care in this service and to reduce the infectious risk in hemodialysis patients, we conducted this study, and which is about the respect of standard and specific practices and the monitoring of the environment of treatment rooms hemodialysis.

Based on observation, we conducted two descriptive surveys and completed 344 grids, ie 177 in 2012 and 177 in 2013, which allowed us to evaluate the compliance with standard and specific precautions at the pre- and post-development center, and follow their evolution following the corrective actions that we carried out. These actions included the transmission to the center leader of a report of the strengths and weaknesses raised in 2012, and an awareness of the entire healthcare team by

exposing the findings found, while showing on their role in improving and emphasizing the objectives to be achieved [6].
Standard precautions are measures that rely especially on hand hygiene and the application of barrier measures when applying care such as gloves and gowns [14-17]. Respect for hygiene for patients has varied from one type to another, but remains globally insufficient. Thus, during the connection, the hygiene of the patients' arms was not carried out, but it was noted after the disconnection and improved significantly in 2013. The percentages of the hand hygiene practice before the connection and after the disconnection have also changed. However, the significant improvement of this practice is noticed only before the connection. These results could be linked to a lack of knowledge of these measures, and should be improved by an awareness campaign concerning the good level of daily hygiene, the wearing of a clean and appropriate dress allowing to clear the fistula, and the systematic washing using a foaming antiseptic solution of the hands and the arm where the fistula is located [5, 7, 8].
In the health care staff, compliance with hand hygiene varied from one type to another. Thus, the hygienic washing was not practiced, the simple washing of the hands decreased significantly (41.86% in 2012, 2.32% in 2013), whereas the application of the hydro-alcoholic friction knew a significant improvement between the two surveys (6.98% in 2012 against 23.25% in 2013). Although the National Technical Committee on Nosocomial Infections [CTIN] has recommended, since 2001, hand rubbing by hydro-alcoholic solutions by replacing handwashing, its compliance isn't sufficent despite the availability of hydro-alcoholic solutions in the refurbished center [18]. The lack of hand hygiene observed shows that efforts should be made to remind and encourage the health care staff to respect hand hygiene since it is the first step to prevent the cross-transmission of germs between patients and that it must be performed between each patient and for all care [7, 19]. It would also be interesting to highlight the multiple advantages of hydro-alcoholic solutions, namely their effectiveness, availability, tolerance and especially when they contain emollients, and their speed of action [20, 21]. All these advantages have made hydro-alcoholic friction the reference technique for hand disinfection and an alternative for countries with limited resources where the water supply and the equipment available to it are a real obstacle to the practice of washing water hands [20] (Table 1).

Table 1 : Respect of hygiene practice by patients and paramedical staff

Hygiene practice	**2012**	**2013**	**P**
Patients			
Hygiene of the arms before connection	0%	0%	-
Hygiene of the arms after disconnection	2.90%	25%	<0,05
Hygiene of the hands before connection	1.16%	10.46%	<0,05
Hand hygiene after disconnection	16,25%	25%	>0,05
Staff			
Simple wash	41.86%	2.32%	<0,05
Hydro-alcoholic friction	6.98%	23.25	-
Hygienic wash	0%	0%	

Gloves are an effective barrier against cross-transmission of germs as they reduce the level of contamination of the hands by the flora acquired during care [21]. They must be worn systematically when there is a risk of contact with blood, or any other product of human origin, during various manipulations of biological sample tubes, or soiled equipment, during care [7,8, 22]. The results related to compliance with these measures are shown in Table 2. Indeed, we found that this barrier was used systematically during the two surveys, this was objectified by the absence of notifications of cases of viral hepatitis. The wearing of sterile gloves was predominant both during the connection and during disconnection. Although the recommendations advocate the use of clean gloves, and their change between two patients and between two activities [5, 7, 14], we noticed the systematic use of sterile gloves and their change between activities and patients. The use of sterile gloves instead of clean gloves may be an unnecessary expense since the cost of sterile gloves is higher than that of clean gloves. As for the assessment of the wearing of clothing precautions by the staff, we found that they were rarely respected during the 1st survey, with frequencies of 4.07%, 10.46% and 5.23% respectively. On the other hand, a significant improvement in mask wear and eye protection was noted in 2013. However, the frequency of use of the mask remains relatively lower compared to those mentioned in previous work [23-25]. According to Girou and al (2002), the wearing of protective clothing should not be systematically performed, the over-coat should be worn during any act of care exposing to a contamination of the workwear by biological fluids, the mask and protective goggles must be worn when exposing gestures to splashes or aerosolizations of body fluids [14].

Table 2: Respect for the wearing of gloves and the recommended clothing.

Pratics	2012	2013	P
Wearing sterile gloves:			
Before connection	93.02%	97.67%	>0,05
After disconnection	95.35%	98.83%	
Port de gants non stériles:			
Before connection	6.98%	2.33%	>0,05
After disconnection	4.65%	1.17%	
Dress code:			
Mask port	5.23%	20.34%	<0,05
Wearing eye protection	4.07%	18.60%	>0,05
Wearing the over-blouse	10.46%	8.72%	

The compression of the puncture points, shown in Table 3, proved that it was performed by the patients in almost all the cases observed (98.28% in 2012 and 99.42% in 2013). As for the placement of the dressing on the puncture points (Table 3), it was carried out frequently by the nursing staff (67.44% in 2012 and 61.62% in 2013). Its execution by the patients themselves, the other patients and the caregivers, was also observed. The compression and placement of dressings, performed by the hands of unwashed patients and colonized by commensal cutaneous flora, could generate nosocomial infections, resulting from endogenous contamination [26].

Table 3 : Compression of puncture points and placement of dressings.

Gesture performed	2012	2013	P
Compression of the puncture points performed by:			
The nurse	1.72%	0.58%	>0,05
Patient himself	98.28%	99.42%	
Placement of dressings made by :			
The nurse	67,44%	61,62%	>0,05
Other patient	28,50%	33,14%	
Patient himself	2,32%	4,66%	
Caregiver	1,74%	0,58%	

The practice of internal and external disinfection of generators is presented in Table 4. We noted that the internal disinfection of generators between the hemodialysis sessions was systematic, while the cleaning of their surfaces was not. However, we found that it increased significantly from 18.60% in 2012 to 40.12% in 2013, but overall remains insufficient. In order to prevent the spread of environmental transmissible pathogens, Karkar *and al* (2014) routinely recommend cleaning and disinfecting external surfaces of generators between hemodialysis sessions [5].

Table 4 : Cleaning and disinfection of the generators.

Desinfection	2012	2013	P
From the surface	18.60%	40.12%	<0,05
Internal	100%	100%	>0,05

Although the share of nosocomial infections related to environmental contamination is difficult to assess, and the importance of microbiological control is controversial [27-29], international recommendations currently indicate the multiple interests of microbiological monitoring of the environment in the prevention of nosocomial infections, namely the consideration of surface contamination and the search for microbial tanks at the origin of grouped cases of infections or epidemics [18, 30]. In this context and as part of the implementation of a quality approach in this center, and before any corrective intervention, we conducted a monitoring of the air quality and surfaces of patient treatment rooms. The results are presented in Table 5.

Table 5 : Percentage of surface contamination and air.

Type of sampling Point removed	Type of sampling Point removed	Number of Analyzed point	Percentage of contamination	P
Surface Total number:184	Generator	84	79.8%	>0,05
	Table	63	88.9%	
	Mattress	21	100%	
	Trolley	4		
	Remote control	4		
	Blood Pressure	4		
	Balance	4		
Air Total number :12	Room 1	4	100%	>0,05
	Room 2	4		
	Room 3	4		

Indoor air quality in health facilities has become a growing concern, resulting from changing care practices and the presence of frail people [31]. Its microbiological control showed a maximum positivity rate, caused in all the samples analyzed by a bacterial contamination. The high level of contamination has been reported by other authors [32, 33]. However, this contamination would not be a problem itself if the contaminants would remain permanently in the air, and would be a real risk if the contaminants would settle on the surfaces [34]. This risk would be worse in at-risk patients such as immunodepressed patients and hemodialysis patients [35].

As for the microbiological monitoring of surfaces, it showed a contamination rate of about 86.9%. This rate is comparable to that found by other authors. Meunier and al (2005) reported in Strasbourg a positivity rate of 87% [10]. Saouide El Ayne *and al* (2014) reported to Kenitra a positivity rate of around 92.85% [36]. Touijer (2014), revealed a percentage of contamination of 97.92% in a study conducted in four hospital departments of the city of Fez [33]. However, Méité *and al* (2010), had noted Abidjan a lower positivity rate than we found, or 46.7% [39]. Barbut and al. (2006) note that the level of contamination varies qualitatively and quantitatively over time and according to services and patients [37]. The most contaminated surface points were mattresses, remote controls, tensiometers, trolleys and scales. The tables and generators also showed very high contamination rates. This could be due to the fact that these objects are commonly handled by the nursing staff and patients, and secondly to a lack of sanitary practices, which could potentially promote the transmission of microorganisms [38]. These results recall those of Méité and al (2010), who found that the most contaminated sites were those used by staff or visitors [39]. These frequent contact surfaces located in the immediate vicinity of the patient can serve as microbial reservoirs and come into contact with patients either directly or indirectly through medical devices or the hands of patients and staff [10,38 40]. The frequency of germs isolated from air samples and surfaces is shown in Figure 1. The distribution of germs found in air samples, showed the absence of mold, and a predominance of gram-positive bacteria with a percentage of 83.67%. We noted a predominance of Staphylococcus and in particular those with coagulase negative compared to other bacteria isolated (Bacillus sp, gram negative oxidase positive non-fermentative bacilli (BGN Ox P NF). This result recalls that of other studies [32, 33], but does not agree with that found by Thilbaut (2011), who noted the prevalence of Staphylococcus aureus over other isolated bacteria [41].

The isolated saprophytic and pathogenic microorganisms can agglomerate and settle in dry media such as dust and inert carriers, and are also very resistant in the external environment. In addition, a multiplication of these germs could occur if the necessary conditions are favored, especially if careful maintenance is not ensured, which could lead to a high or critical concentration of these microorganisms. On the other hand, continuous or discontinuous mechanical disruption of microbial tanks releases microorganisms from their sources and causes biocontamination, which could lead to exogenous contamination of patients [42].

The identification of germs isolated from surfaces showed the presence of bacteria and molds, with a predominance of bacteria. The examination of the molds found revealed neither the presence of Aspergillus nor Candida albicans. This result does not agree with other authors who isolated Cladosporium sp, Aspergillus sp, Penicillium sp and Microsporum canis within controlled surfaces [43-45]. However, surveillance studies conducted by both Saouide El Ayne and al (2014) and Méité and al (2010) reported only bacterial contamination [36, 39]. The distribution of bacteria found, showed a high proportion of Gram-positive bacteria (85.81%) compared to Gram-negative bacteria (14.19%), which is in agreement with previous studies [10,36] but differs from the bacteriological profile reported by other authors [39,45, 46,47].

Schmitt and al (2009) noted that the environment is a tank for Gram positive bacteria, widely dispersed by human activity. These bacteria are more resistant to desiccation than gram-negative bacteria and especially if the surfaces are only biionettaged daily without disinfecting effect of the product [48]. The bacterial flora is mainly represented by Staphylococcus coagulase negative (61.70%), Bacillus sp (12.78%), Streptococcus (11.34%), non-fermenting Gram-negative bacilli (10.64%). %), and fermentative Gram-negative bacilli (3.54%). The predominance of Staphylococci, especially those with coagulase negative, has been noted in previous studies [36, 49]. The frequency of the genus Staphylococcus compared to other genera of bacteria does not agree with the results found by other authors. Touijer (2014) reported the predominance of Bacillus sp over coagulase-negative and positive coagulase Staphylococci [33].

While coagulase-negative Staphylococci and Bacillus were ubiquitous in all contaminated surfaces, Staphylococcus aureus was only found in generators and mattresses. Streptococci have been isolated from generators, mattresses, tables, remote controls and scales. Non-fermentative gram-negative bacilli (BGN) were present on all types of dots except scales, whereas those with fermentative negative oxidase were found only at mattresses, generators and tables. The flora found on the surfaces depends in fact on several factors such as the human activity which brings a contribution of micro-organisms by the patients themselves and by the nursing staff, the inefficiency of the biocleaning, the quality of the air [37], as well as microorganism-related factors such as lifespan on inert carriers, surface adhesion, ability to produce a biofilm, and ability to withstand adverse conditions [36].

4. Conclusion

This work is part of the improvement of the quality of care and the reduction of nosocomial infections in the hemodialysis department of Al Ghassani hospital. He showed that the observance of standard precautions and hygienic practices was not perceived as obligatory by the nursing staff as well as by the patients. The corrective action taken was not effective since the application of these measures remains globally unsatisfying. This could be mainly related to staff reluctance to change, lack of motivation, old age, and lack of information, training and awareness.

The environmental control of the treatment rooms of hemodialysis testifies to a strong microbial colonization of both the surfaces and the air of the center. The surface contamination rate is 86.9%, that of air is 100%. The most contaminated surface points were mattresses, remote controls, tensiometers, trolleys and scales. The isolated bacterial flora was largely represented by Gram-positive bacteria with a clear predominance for Staphylococcus coagulase-negative. To control the infectious risk in hemodialysis, it would be essential to reinforce the training of staff in hospital hygiene, to invest in effective and innovative training programs both practical and theoretical based on educational technologies and responding to the staff's needs and evaluate the disinfection protocol applied to the center environment.

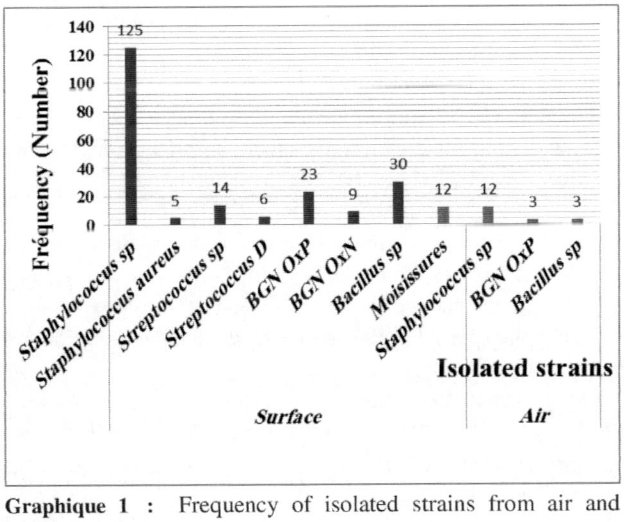

Graphique 1 : Frequency of isolated strains from air and surface samples.

References

1. R.W. Haley, D.H. Culver, J.W. White, W.M. Morgan, T.G. Emori, V.P. Munn, and al. The efficacy of infection surveillance and control programs in preventing nosocomial infections in US hospitals. Am J Epidemiol. **121**, 182-205(1985).

2. D. Pittet, S. Harbarth, C. Ruef, P. Francioli, P. Sudre, S. Pétignat. Prevalence and risk factors for nosocomial infections in four University hospitals in Switzerland. Infect Control Hosp Epidemiol.**20**,37-42 (1999).

3. K. El Rhazi, S. Elfakir, M. Berraho, N. Tachfouti, Z. Serhier, C. KAnjaa, and al. Prévalence et facteurs de risque des infections nosocomiales au CHU Hassan II de Fès (Maroc). Rev Sante Mediterr Orient.**13**, 56-63 (2007).

4. S. Berrada, T. G. Benjelloun, L. Bennani, A. S Diarra, B. Oumokhtar, L. A. El Ouali, H. F. Z Squali., H. T. Sqalli. Exploration microbiologique des surfaces d'un centre d'hémodialyse de la ville de Fès : étude descriptive transversale. Revue francophone internationale de recherche infirmière. **3**, 120-128 (2017).

5. A. Karkar, M.B. Bouhaha, M.L. Dammang. Infection control in hemodialysis units: a quick access to essential elements. Saudi J Kidney Dis Transplant. **25**, 496-519 (2014).

6. S. Berrada, H. T. Sqalli., B. Oumokhtar, L. Bennani, L.A. El Ouali, H. Hanin, S. El Fakirl, N. Benaich, H. F. Z. Squali. Évaluation de la conception et des pratiques standards d'un centre d'hémodialyse au Maroc. Revue francophone internationale de recherche infirmière. **1**,225-232(2015).

7. Jacques *and al.* Bonnes pratiques d'hygiène en hémodialyse. Recommandations de la SFHH. Hygiènes. **XIII** (2005).

8. Recommandations de bonnes pratiques médicales, affection longue durée, insuffisance rénale chronique terminale CIM 10 : N 18 Code ANAM: L008. Maroc: Ministère de la Santé (2013).

9. Norme ISO 14698-1. Salles propres et environnement maîtrisés apparentés. Maîtrise de la biocontamination. AFNOR; (2003).

10. O. Meunier, C. Hernandez, M. Piroird, R. Heilig, D. Steinbach, A. Freyd. Prélèvements bactériologiques des surfaces : importance de l'étape d'enrichissement et du choix des milieux de culture. Ann Biol Clin. **63**(5), 481-6 (2005).

11. Norme NM 08.0.155. Guide pour la préparation et la production des milieux de culture en laboratoire. 1-16 (2006)

12. Lignes directrices concernant l'application des contrôles de qualité en microbiologie. DR-12-SCA-02. Québec: Centre d'expertise en analyse environnementale du Québec. 1-36(2011).

13. B. Oumokhtar , M. El Azhari, M.Timinouni, K. Bendahhou, B. Bennani, M. Mahmoud, L.A. El Ouali, S. Berrada, M. Arrayhani, H.T. Squalli. *Staphylococcus aureus* nasal carriage in a Moroccan dialysis center and isolates characterization. Hemodialysis International. **17**, 542-547(2013).

14. E. Girou, R. Girard, C. Chémorin, A. Simon. Précautions standards. Reanimation. **11**, 257-9 (2002).

15. OMS. Manuel d'hygiène hospitalière et de prévention des infections nosocomiales. Royaume du Maroc: Ministère de la Santé(2009).

16. Centre de coordination de la lutte contre les infections nosocomiales inter-région sud-est. CCLIN. Rapport final du groupe d'experts concernant l'hémodialyse(2010).

17. M.L. Atif, A. Brenet, S. Hageaux, M.H. Fave, C. Cochet, E. Baticle, C. Pourrier, D. Wolny, P. Astagneau, Z. Kadi. Connaissances des précautions standards chez 4439

professionnels de santé dans 34 établissements de France. Médecine et maladies infectieuses. **43**,10-16(2013).

18. Comité technique national des infections nosocomiales (CTIN). Avis du CTIN du 5 décembre 2001 sur la place de la friction hydro-alcoolique dans l'hygiène des mains lors des soins. Bulletin officiel n° 2001-52.

19. Guide des bonnes pratiques pour la prévention des infections liées aux soins réalisés en dehors des établissements de santé Ministère de la Santé, de la Famille Et Des Personnes Handicapées (2002).

20. F. Dicko-Traore, C. Gire, V. Brevaut Malaty, M. Busutil,l A.S. Monnier, V. Brunel. Évaluation des connaissances et des pratiques d'hygiène des mains au niveau de l'unité de néonatologie et soins intensifs au service de médecine infantile et néonatologie de l'hôpital Nord, Marseille. J Pediatr Puericult **24**,172-7(2011).

21. E. Girou, R. Girard, C. Chemorin, A. Simon. Précautions standards. Réanimation. **11**, 257- 259(, 2002).

22. D. Thiveaud, A.M. Grimoud, N. Marty, C.Roques, J.P. Lodter, G.Chabanon. Hygiène : structures, matériels, méthodes. EMC- Ondontologie.**1**, 307-339(2005).

23. N. El Mikatti, P. Dillon, T.E. Healy. Hygienic practices of consultant anaesthetists: a survey in the north-west region of the UK. Anaesthesia. **54**, 13-18 (1999).

24. A. Carbonne, B. Veber, J. Hajjar , D. Zaro-Goni, S. Maugata, J.C. Seguier, A. Chalfine, K. Blanckaert, M. Aggoune, C. Auboyer. Évaluation des pratiques en anesthésie exposant au risque infectieux par transmission croisée. Annales Françaises d'Anesthésie et de Réanimation. **25**, 1158-1164 (2006).

25. A.J. Ryan, C.S. Webster, A.F. Merry, D.J. Grieve. A national survey of infection control practice by New Zealand anaesthetists. Anaesth Intensive Care. **34**, 68–74 (2006).

26. S. Anselme, S. Boileau, M. Vedel, C. Muller, M.F. Blech, H. Bouaziz . Evaluation des pratiques d'hygiène en anesthésie entre 1998 et 2007 en Lorraine. Annales Françaises d'Anesthésie et de Réanimation. **28**, 28-34 (2009).

27. T. Bauer, E. Ofner, H. Just, F.D. Daschner. An epidemiological study assigning the relative importance of airborne and direct contact transmission of microorganisms in a medical intensive care unit. J Hosp Infect. **15**, 301-309 (1990).

28. W.R. Jarwis, J.R. Edward, D.H. Culver. Nosocomial infection rated in adult and pediatric Intensive care units in the United States. AM J Med. **91**, 185-191(1991).

29. G.A. Ayliffe. Environmental Sampling in hospitals. Host, **6**, 3-5 (1992).

30. L. Sehulster, Y.W. Raymond, A. Matthew, Carpenter, P.E. Rodney-Donlan. Infection Control Practices Advisory Comitee. Recommandations of CDC and healthcare. Guidelines for environmental infection control in health care facilities. MMWR. **52**, RR10 (2003).

31. Guide. La qualité l'air intérieur dans les établissements du réseau de la santé et des services sociaux. Québec (2005).

32. M. El khadir. Surveillance microbiologique des surfaces de l'hôpital Ibn El Khateb de Fès. Mémoire de Master en Biologie, Université Sidi Mohamed Ben Abdellah, Faculté Des Sciences Et Techniques Fès, Maroc (2011).

33. H. Touijer. Prévention des infections nosocomiales : Ecologie bactérienne en milieu hospitalier et sensibilité aux antibiotiques et aux désinfectants. Mémoire de Master en Biologie. Université Sidi Mohamed Ben Abdellah, Faculté des Sciences Dhar Mehraz-Fès, Maroc (2014).

34. M. Combet. Salles propres à l'hôpital : un historique. Salles propres et maîtrise de la contamination. 05, 15-19 (2009).

35. F. Jacques *and al.* Surveiller et prévenir les infections associées aux soins. Hygiène. XVIII , **4**, (2010).

36. N. Saouide El Ayne, A. Echchelh, A. Chaouch., N. Auajjar, S. Hamama, A. Soulaymani. Rôle de l'environnement hospitalier dans la prévention des infections nosocomiales : Surveillance de la flore des surfaces à l'hôpital EL Idrissi de Kénitra- Maroc. European Scientific Journal. **10**, 238-247(2014).

37. F. Barbut, D. Neyme. Les difficultés d'interprétation des contrôles microbiologiques environnementaux. Revue Francophone des laboratoires. **382**, 27-32 (2006).

38. L.S. Munoz–Price, D.J. Birnbach, D.A. Lubarsky. Decreasing operating room environmental pathogen contamination through him proved cleaning practice. Infect Control Hosp Epidemiol. **33**, 897-904 (2012).

39. S., Méité, C. Boni-cissé, P. Monemo, A.P. Mlantanoa, H. Faye-ketté, H. Dosso. Surveillance microbiologique des surfaces au niveau d'un établissement hospitalier de niveau tertiaire : Exemple du CHU de Yopougon, abidjan, Cote d'ivoire. J sci pharm. biol. **11**, 73-81(2010).

40. Comité consultatif provincial des maladies infectieuses (CCPMI). Pratiques exemplaires en matière de nettoyage de l'environnement en vue de la prévention et du contrôle des infections dans tous les établissements de soins de santé. 2ème Edition (2012).

41. M. Thilbaut. Les infections nosocomiales : l'importance d'un suivi épidémiologique et de l'identification rapide des bactéries en cause (2011).

42. F. Squinazi. Analyses en microbiologie Environnement microbien (air, surfaces, eau). Techniques de l'ingénieur. **3**, 3551-3555 (2006).

43. J.T. Li, Y. Li. J. Wang. Surveillance on gram-positive bacteria isolated from patients with hospital acquired infections or community acquired infections. Zhonghua Yi Xue Za Zhi. **83**, 365-374 (2003).

44. P.E. Santos, S. Cordoba, A. Carrillo-Munoz, L. Rodero, E. Rubeglio, M. Soria. Epidemiology of fungaemia in a paediatric hospital of high complexity. Rev Iberoam Micol. **27**, 200-202 (2010).

45. C.P. Garcia-Cruz, M.J. Najera-Aguilar, O.E. Arroyo-Helguera. Fungal and Bacterial Contamination on Indoor Surfaces of a Hospital in Mexico. Jundishapur J Microbiol. **5**, 460-464 (2012).
46. R. Djerfaour, D.J. Benhaddouche, M. Bensenane, U. Bouk, C. Hacene, k Meguenni. Infections nosocomiales à bactéries multirésistantes en reanimation polyvalente 12 mois de surveillance sur 250 patients. J Magh' Réa Urg. **17**, 205-208 (2010).
47. C. Njall, D. Adiogo, A. Bita, N. Ateba, G. Sume, B. Kollo, F. Binam, R. Tchoua. Ecologie bactérienne de l'infection nosocomiale au service de réanimation de l'hôpital Laquintinie de Douala, Cameroun. Pan African Medical Journal. **14**, 140-148 (2013).
48. A. Schmitt, N.Glasser, D. Stainbach, O. Meunier. Études expérimentales de l'effet rémanent d'un détergent désinfectant pour surfaces sur une souche d'*Escherichia coli*. Pathologie Biologie. **57**, 463–469 (2009).
49. J. Nelson, A. Bivens, A. Shinn, L. Wanzer, C. Kasper. Microbial flora on operating room telephones. AORN J. **83**, 607-626 (2006).

Management tools help prevent scientific misconduct: a field study in Lyon

M Estienne, S. Chesnais, C Chevalier, S Rémy, Béatrice Baudoin-Massot, Valérie Gall and E. Giesen*

Institut National de la Santé et de la Recherche Médicale (Inserm), Paris, France

Received:

Abstract. We have developed the concept of Ethical and Efficient Research Management and believe that managerial tools sustain high quality research and are useful in the prevention of scientific misconduct. The way a team, a project, or a study is managed will determine the degree of confidence among the people involved. Management also sets the standard of conduct. Honesty, accountability, professional courtesy, fairness and good stewardship (Singapore Statement on Research Integrity, 2010) can be practiced without special tools, but management tools and a coherent management system make special attention easier, give more visibility and the engagement for the principles and responsibilities associated with Research integrity and are more efficient. As a part of a management system, Research integrity turns from an implicit understanding into an explicit rule in the lab.

Keywords: Research integrity, tools for responsible and good quality research; documentation architecture

1 Introduction

Although some cases of fraud and plagiarism have been reported from the early days of science on, the awareness of the necessity of scientific integrity has increased over the last 10 to 15 years and cases of professional misconduct in research are regularly commented by scientific journals. A definition of scientific integrity was provided by the American Office of Research Integrity and the scientific community organized several conferences on scientific integrity in order to develop the subject. Reasons and causes of undue behavior have been analyzed and actions have been taken at the level of the scientific community. Standards and declarations of good conduct are available, scientific journals have set rules for reviewing and editing (white paper and retraction policies) and in many institutions values are communicated and serve for guidance ; also, protection of whistle-blowers has been enforced by law in certain countries (Loi Sapin II, in France).

Now, most institutions worldwide have set up "Offices of Research Integrity" where allegations of fraud and misconduct can be reported. Scientific misconduct leads to retraction of scientific articles, exclusion from grant funding and, in severe cases, loss of an academic position.

Preventive actions at the level of a research team or the individual researcher, however, are rarely presented in the literature. At this level, the general conclusion often is that scientists are human beings after all, that the pressure to produce and to publish is constantly increasing and that scientific misconduct is just part of the "system". Some preventive actions, among which figure better information and training of young researchers on scientific practice and methodology have lately been proposed at the Conference on Research integrity in Rio di Janeiro (2015).

In order to fill in this gap, we have developed the concept of Ethical and Efficient Research Management (EERM)[1]. EERM also contains managerial tools which sustain high quality research and are useful in the prevention of scientific misconduct. Honesty, accountability, professional courtesy and fairness and good stewardship (Singapore Statement on Research Integrity, 2010, [2]) can be practiced without special tools, but management tools and a coherent management system make special attention to scientific integrity easier, give more visibility to the engagement for the principles and responsibilities associated with Research integrity and is more efficient. As a part of a management system, Research integrity turns from an implicit understanding into an explicit rule in the lab.

The advantage of considering research integrity (and also project management, metrology, maintenance of equipment and so forth) as part of the management system, is that it will benefit from the attention, professionalism and management tools available in the lab. As being part of a coherent system, actions and checks are planned, run, improved and documented according to the PDCA (plan do check act) principle. When identified as a process of management (process oriented approach), Research integrity is declined into attainable objectives, which are followed by specific actions, checks and improvements. It can also be included into other processes. For example "Information on Good scientific Practice, What to do in case of suspicion of deviant behavior, Lab books, property of data, and authorship" can be part of the process "Integration of a new co-worker" [3]. The process "Departure" includes checks of the lab-books, check-list and time-table for transmission of information, biological samples and other tools. Record

* Correspondence: eva.giesen@inserm.fr

keeping, safety and completeness of raw data, results and additional scientific information can be part of a process "Documentation".

2 Theoretical background

Today, in many fields of research, the scientific community is concerned with scientific misconduct (SM) and Questionable research practice (QRP), and their potential deleterious effects on both science as such and its intrinsic organization and on society and the trust that is put into the word of a scholar. In general terms, as pointed out by the US Office of Research Integrity [4], "responsible conduct in research is simply good citizenship applied to professional life". It concerns very different issues that range from data collection and handling to documentation and record keeping, publication and reviewing of articles, teaching and working with students or with co-workers in a team, or with national and international collaborators. Put more succinctly, responsible conduct concerns the entire spectrum of the work of an investigator.

Scientific integrity (which is the opposite of SM), can therefore be as clearly defined through "FFP" (fabrication, falsification, plagiarism): either data have been fabricated or falsified or they are real; either a text was copied (without citation of the authors) or is genuine. Misconduct relates to a deliberate action; not an honest error or scholarly differences in interpretations or judgments, unless they are considered grossly deviant.

Questionable research practice is related to scientific practice, poor quality of data and research, inappropriate methodology and so forth. Science can be of good, mediocre or poor quality, excellently and sloppily performed, at a different extent. Questionable research practice is therefore sometimes referred to as a "grey zone". "Questionable research practice" (QRP) is defined as:

. Inappropriate or poor methodology, incorrect data mining, interpretation and storage

. "Cherry picking" (reporting only data that support the hypothesis or leads to a positive result), or "massaging" or "cooking" data (deleting undesired data points or observations, taking only the desired data or information into account). These serve to maintain the viewpoint of a given researcher or support a biased theory, sometimes based on strong political, social or religious beliefs and in clear conflict with the assumption of "openness" of science.

. Photo manipulation for "improving" images and photo records by using computer software without giving precise information on the software used and what was modified on the image

. Inadequate record keeping

. Guest (gift, ghost) authorship

. Deletion from the list of authors of a person who contributed significantly to the article

. Not giving credit or recognition to persons who helped or supported the research or provided technical assistance, without qualifying for the author-status.

. "Salami-slicing" of a publication (cutting down coherent data and findings into "smallest publishable unit")

. Failure to disclose conflicts of interest

. Failure to share information, methods, tools etc. with the scientific community

Today, different codes and standards exist and define "good research practice": In 2010, the 2nd World Conference on Research Integrity released the "Singapore Statement on research integrity" [2]. It is based on fundamental principles of honesty, accountability, professional courtesy and fairness, and good stewardship of research. The European charter for researchers focused on recruitment and mobility of researchers in Europe [5]. The European Code of Conduct for Research Integrity explained the principles of research integrity and gave some advice on prevention of MR and QRP [6].

The NFX 50-553 standard was published by the French Standardization body in 2014. It is part of the ISO 9001 family of standards for sound and efficient organization and conduct of activities and specialized on the "Management of research activities" [7].

3 Experimental setup

We developed the concept and tools of EERM (Ethical and efficient research management) that contains management tools for different challenges in scientific integrity, good research practices and ethical management issues, which can easily be used by any scientific community and by different stakeholders in the community. EERM is a concept of good research management and at the same time a toolbox, containing managerial tools that are currently used in project management, quality management, knowledge management and risk assessment. These tools are commonly used in industry and increasingly in the service sector. We have selected those items which seem the most useful and adapted them to the culture and the needs of scientific research. Project management, quality management as such are well documented and international standards exist. Particular aspects of Quality management in research and EERM have been published previously by our team [8].

In this study we decided to test three particular tools of the EERM tool box with the help of three Inserm Research Units based in Lyon who previously agreed to participate. In the case that the laboratory had already set up a Quality management system, the quality manager was asked to pilot the field study and in case it had not, the quality manager of another lab helped out.

The first tool is related to communication of the importance of scientific integrity (in analogy to §5.11f to h (leadership) and §

7.2 (competences) of the ISO 9001: 2015 standard). A 60min conference on scientific integrity was given to each of the three labs by one of us (EG). Before and after the conference, participants were asked to answer 10 questions about the topic (written, anonymous questionnaire). The questions were chosen so that interest in scientific integrity and individual practice could be measured.

The second tool is related to the step-wise elimination of dysfunctions. Usually, allegations of misconduct are reported by coworkers and other members of the institution. Whistle blowers often hesitate to report an allegation, because relationships (also dependencies) are strong in science. Students and young researchers sometimes do not dare report what seems to them to be SM or QPR because they depend on the head of a team or institution for their research and their career. Senior researchers and reviewers may not report items of concern because they realize that they may be in a situation in the future where they depend themselves on a favorable outcome of an evaluation. For these reasons and in order to keep to a positive and preventive approach, we decided to inquire in an anonymous way about research practice. The participating labs were given access to a specific inquiry web-site which does not record incoming e-mail addresses and invited to record to this “RIQ-box” (RIQ: Recherche Intègre et de Qualité) observations of concern and questions which they may have. The RIQ-box is opened every month and observations and questions are discussed during the lab meeting with the head of the lab and the quality manager in order to alert the members of the lab and to make them gradually more aware of scientific integrity.

Responsible research conduct refers also to the ability to justify scientific conclusions based on the data acquired (data management), the ability to account for the data (organization, protection and storage), its verification by the scientific community (availability of data and tools, reproducibility, debate) and sharing of information and tools with other researchers. Science is based on the sharing of knowledge, however, in practice the handling of the requests by colleagues and competitors differs substantially from individuals and from disciplines. Wicherts et al reported that of the 141 articles examined, 73% of the authors did not share their data despite considerable insistence and effort to request those data. Wicherts et al admit that in their field, psychology, most people “fail to document their data in a way that allows others to quickly and easily check their work” [9].
For this reason, our third tool is concerned with data storage and the capacity to quickly and totally be able to find raw data upon request. An architecture of data is proposed leading from a given table or figure to synthetized, then treated data, to raw data. This architecture is written down in parallel to the elaboration of a scientific article.

For the time being, only data for tool 1 are available and reported in this article.

4 Results and discussions

This study is based on the participation of 86 persons, of which 38% were research staff, 28% technical staff and 22% PhD students. About half of them had some knowledge of research integrity ("Recherche intègre et de qualité" (RIQ)). Before (and after) the conference 87% (89%) declared that their "research is always or mainly RIQ". However, only 5% declared that "everybody in the lab does RIQ" (before and after the conference. Moreover, 82% wish to "reinforce integrity and quality of their research" (asked after the conference) and 54% would like to have specific training in research integrity (asked before the conference).
Asked after the conference, 91% of participants stated that the conference had clarified their thoughts about scientific integrity. For 78% this conference was sufficient, but 19% wished additional training.

We conclude that the topic is considered important by nearly all participants and that they wish to further develop it.

To the question whether scientific misconduct is rare or not so rare, 17% of participants answered "rare" and 76% "not so rare" (before and after the conference).

When asked before the conference to give three key words for scientific integrity, the associated terms appear to be very scattered. They range from "honesty, sincerity, confidence, transparence" (14%) to "traceability" (13%) and "rigor, preciseness, treatment of results" (11%) before the conference and "honesty, sincerity, confidence, transparence" (14%) to "traceability" (15%) and "reliability" (8%) (Table 1). Note that participants had a free choice to write down the key words; for this reason, a large variety of words have been used. A total of 258 key words were given. The authors gathered expressions which seemed similar or have a similar meaning in order to reduce scatter.

Table 1. Give three key words for integer and good quality research (RIQ)

Key words	T0(%)	T1(%)
honesty, sincerity, confidence, transparence	14	14
reliability	6	8
traceability	13	15
methodology, validated protocoles	10	9
rigor, preciseness, treatment of results	5	11
reproducibility	5	4
respect, loyality, curtesy	2	5
competence, knowledge	2	1
responsibility	2	3
training, awareness	4	6
Integer interpretation of data	4	3
Objectiveness	3	4
Ethicis, absence of conflict of interest	8	4
Documentation	3	2

Fig. 1. Have you already whitnessed cases of scientific misconduct?

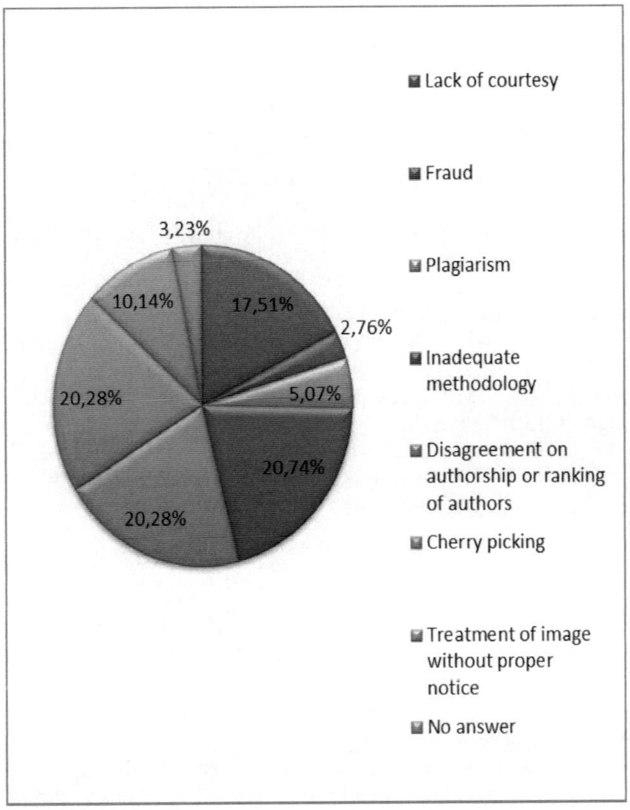

Fig. 2 Have you discovered during this conference items considered as misconduct, which you had not been aware of priviously?

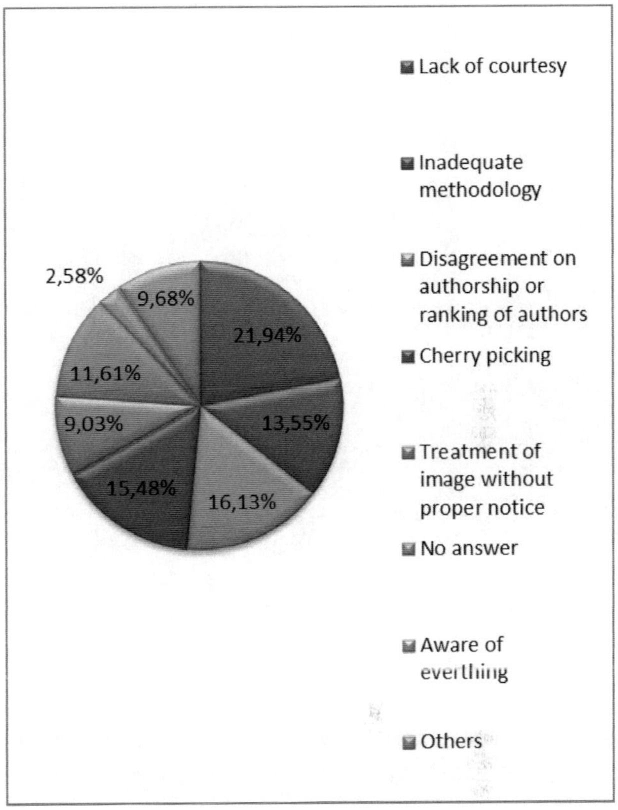

Figure 1 shows that 18% of participants had whitnessed a lack of courtesy (manque de courtoisie). Although this is also noted in every day life, at the workplace courtesy is part of quality of life and deserves special attention. Inadequate methodology, disagreement on authorship and "cherry-picking" collect each 20% of responses. "Treatment of image without mention" (another form of cherry-picking) gathered 10%.

Figure 2 shows that most of the presented items had not previously been identified by participants as scientific misconduct.

Fig. 3 Which items of scientific integrity would you like to reinforce in the future?

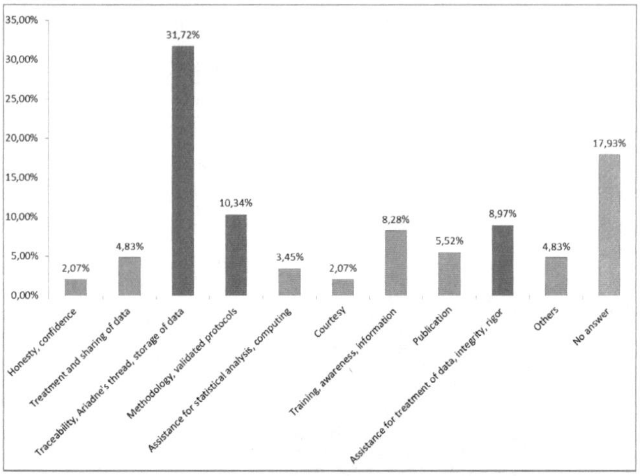

Although 18% of the participants did not anwer the question, a large majority (32%) wants to improve the tracability of data.

5 Conclusion

An ethical mind-set has to be "internalized" individually, by each researcher and kept alive during his/her career through input from the scientific community, debate, and collective problem-solving, particularly when there are occurrences of poor research practice. Through our initial Quality Management approach, we developed Ethical and Efficient Research Management and proposed to use specific management tools to address the principles and recommendations made in the Singapore statement [1] in favor of scientific integrity.

The presented data, collected in a field study which is ongoing, show that scientists care about responsible conduct of research, however it is not always easy to identify what "best practices" are and, especially, how to translate them into daily life. Researchers share a common set of values but these have to be translated into applicable and practical objectives and actions. Currently, codes of conduct exist for scientific integrity in general and different codes of conduct have also been established for various areas of science. However, the sole fact of their existence does not change the practice of research or research management. Some mechanisms for detection and handling of bad research practice are used by institutions and scientific journals. Preventive actions however, aside from teaching and building awareness are scarce. For this reason, we suggest to make use of the tools that EERM offers to those individuals and teams who wish to improve their practice and prevent SM and QRP as much as possible.

The present study is in the process of extension to a larger number of participants and to different cities in France. Moreover, awareness is being fostered by an additional tool, the RIQ-box, which will reveal topics of concern and opportunities to inform and train participants through short workshops addressing scientific integrity under different angles. The "Ariadne's thread" tool will be tested as to being efficient for simple and rapid retrieval of treated and raw data when requested by a reviewer or after publication.

6 Adresses of authors (alphabetical order)

Béatrice Baudouin-Massot, UMRS 1155, Hôpital Tenon, 4, rue de la Chine, 75970 Paris Cedex 20
Sabrina Chesnais, U1032 (LabTAU) Inserm, 151, cours Albert Thomas69424 Lyon CEDEX 03
Catherine Chevalier, UMS 016, Inserm, Université de Nantes, IRS-UN, 8, quai Moncousu, 44007 Nantes
Monique Estienne, UMR Inserm 1060 - Inra 1397 - Insa Lyon, 15 Avenue Jean Capelle, Bâtiment IMBL, 69621 Villeurbanne
Valérie Gall, UMR S 910, Faculté de la Timone, 27 Bvd Jean Moulin, 13005 Marseille
Séverine Rémy, Centre de Recherche en Transplantation et Immunologie UMR1064, INSERM, Université de Nantes, 30 Bd Jean Monnet, 44093 Nantes

7 References

1. Giesen E., « Efficient and ethical research management: A new challenge for an old problem » Int. J. Metrol.Qual.Eng. 6, 406 DOI: 10.1051/ijmqe/2015028 (2015)

2. Singapore Statement on Research Integrity, www.singaporestatement.org (2010)

3. Bareille R, Baudouin-Massot B, Careno M, Fournier S, Lebret N, Remy-Jouet I, Giesen E « Preventive actions to avoid questionable research practices. Use of Ethical and Efficient Research Management during arrival and departure of a co-worker» Int. J. Metrol.Qual.Eng. 8, 10 DOI: 10.1051/ijmqe/2016029 (2017)

4. N. H. Steneck Introduction to the. Responsible Conduct of Research. (2007) https://ori.hhs.gov/sites/default/files/rcrintro.pdf

5. The European charter for researchers (2005) (www.europa.eu.int/eracareers/europeancharter)

6. The European Code of Conduct for Research Integrity (2017) (www.esf.org/fileadmin/Public_documents/Publications/Code_Conduct_ResearchIntegrity).

7. NF X50-553 Management des activités de recherche (2014) ; https://www.boutique.afnor.org

8. Alvarez M, Chevalier C, Gall V, Moreau E, Pégorier-Lelièvre M, Remy-Jouet I, , Rémy S, Schiltz C, Giesen E, « Quality management for robust and reliable research », Int. J. Metrol. Qual. Eng. 6, 407 (2015), DOI: 10.1051/ijmqe/2015029

9. Wicherts JM, Bakker M, Molenaar D, Willingness to Share Research Data Is Related to the Strength of the Evidence and the Quality of Reporting of Statistical Results. (2011) PLoS ONE 6(11): e26828. https://doi.org/10.1371/journal.pone.0026828.

Performance of laboratories participating in Waters (Chemical) Proficiency Testing Program in 2016

D. Mihaila, P. Briggs and M. Bunt

Proficiency Testing Australia (PTA), Sydney, Australia

Abstract. Proficiency Testing Australia (PTA) conducts a comprehensive proficiency testing scheme for water testing. The Waters (Chemical) Proficiency Testing (PT) Program has a tradition of more than 25 years and regularly offers laboratories the opportunity to assess their analytical capabilities for a large variety of chemical parameters monitored for water quality. The performance of laboratories participating in the program in 2016 was evaluated for 17 rounds of the program finalised in this year, comprising 78 different parameters in matrices simulating potable and effluent water. The study applies to 3,854 results from 117 laboratories, mainly from Australia and other Asia-Pacific countries. A robust statistical analysis was used for evaluation of laboratories' performance based on the z-score criteria, according to ISO/IEC 17043:2010 [1]. The study indicates that, on average, 85.8% of the submitted results were satisfactory, 5.7 % questionable and 8.5% were outlier results.

Keywords: water, proficiency

1 Introduction

Proficiency testing results from the Waters (Chemical) PT Program published during 2016 were used for this paper. The program is conducted by PTA, a proficiency testing provider operating from Australia, which offers programs in various scientific fields of Chemical Testing, Biological Testing, Construction Materials, Mechanical Testing, Non-Destructive Testing and Calibration.

For more than 25 years, Waters (Chemical) PT Program has provided proficiency testing programs on a large range of parameters, routinely tested by laboratories involved in water quality. Participation in the program is voluntary and it is open to all laboratories, regardless of their accreditation status or country of residence.

Waters (Chemical) PT Program is organised in rounds of interlaboratory testing programs, designed for a set of parameters. The rounds are conducted periodically, with different frequencies, depending on the set of parameters selected. For each round, subsamples of the same water sample are simultaneously distributed for testing to participating laboratories. Many rounds of the program involve a "split-level" design, when two separate samples, with different levels of the parameters to be tested, are included.

The results are returned to PTA and compared with the consensus values, in order to evaluate the performance of individual laboratories. A robust statistical approach, using z-scores, is used to assess laboratories' testing performance.

In year 2016, 17 rounds of the Waters (Chemical) PT Program were completed, including determinations for metal ions, halogen ions, residues, organic concentration, volatile organics, and others. The goal of this study was to investigate the performance of participants in the program in 2016, to identify possible patterns in outlier reporting and opportunities for quality improvement.

2 Methods

2.1 Waters (Chemical) PT Program

For each round of the Waters (Chemical) PT Program, participating laboratories usually receive one or two water samples and are asked to measure a set of parameters. On few occasions, rounds are designed with three or five samples. Samples are artificial water solutions, simulating potable, effluent water or, on very few occasions, standard solutions. Some rounds of the program, where two or more samples are offered, include samples with matrices of different complexities, challenging the ability of laboratories to measure the parameters requested.

Laboratories were instructed to test the samples according to their usual procedures and methodology. The results were reported to PTA within two weeks from the samples dispatch. Results are requested to be reported together with an estimate of the measurement uncertainty (MU), however, results without MU are not excluded from analyses and reports

2.2 Performance of participants

With few exceptions, the results of the program are numerical values and are evaluated based on the z-score criteria, according to ISO/IEC 17043:2010 [1] and ISO 13528:2015 [2]. The z-score gives a measure of the departure of the result from the assigned value for the parameter tested and is calculated as:

$$z = \frac{x - X}{s_{PT}}$$

where X is the assigned value and S_{PT} is the standard deviation for proficiency assessment. The assigned value for each parameter tested is the median of all results. The normalised

interquartile range (NIQR) is used to estimate the standard deviation S_{PT}.
Results are evaluated as satisfactory, questionable or outliers based on the absolute value of the z-score associated:

- | z | ≤ 2.0 indicates a "satisfactory" result
- 2.0 < | z | < 3.0 indicates a "questionable" result
- | z | ≥ 3.0 indicates an "outlier" result

Occasionally, there are laboratories reporting results as "less than values" when the majority of participants return numerical results. When these "less than values" lie more than 3 x NIQRs below the median they are deemed to be outliers.
For a limited number of parameters, the consensus of laboratories results is a "not detected" or "less than" response. In these cases, a result reported as a numerical value will be evaluated as outlier if it exceeds a determined critical level.

2.3 Proficiency Testing (PT) participation

The number of submitted PT results in year 2016 was used as measure of PT participation. The level of PT participation was coded as "low" for laboratories with less than 15 submitted results, "moderate" for those with 15-49 submitted results and "high" for those with 50 or more submitted results.

2.4 Sample matrix

In this study, 2,157 results were for potable water samples, 1,541 for effluent water samples and 156 for standard solutions. For the 156 results obtained in standard solutions, for statistical analysis, these were included in the same category with the potable matrix results.

2.5 Participants' country of residence

Similar to data observed in a previous study [3], 67% of laboratories participating in Waters (Chemical) PT Program in 2016 were from Australia. The international participants (33%) were mainly from the Asia-Pacific region, with the largest representation from Malaysia (8.5%). For the statistical analysis, laboratories were grouped in two categories, Australian and international residents.

2.6 Statistical analysis

Binomial regression with a logit link function was used to assess the proportion of outlier results, based on a model:

$$logit(\pi_i) = log\left(\frac{\pi_i}{1-\pi_i}\right) = \beta_0 + BX$$

where π_i is the proportion of outliers in group category i and BX represents the change in logit of proportion of outliers for one unit change in the vector of independent variables (sample matrix, country of residence and PT participation).
Statistical significance was ascertained at 95% level. For interpretation, results are presented as odds ratios with 95% confidence intervals (CIs) and exemplified as proportion of outliers. Statistical analyses were performed using STATA 13.0 (STATACorp LLC, Texas, USA).

3 Results and discussions

Waters (Chemical) PT Program included 17 rounds finalised in 2016 and offered 78 different parameters for testing. A total of 117 laboratories participated in the program and 3,854 results were submitted.
The large majority of results (3,749) were numerical results and were evaluated based on the z-score criteria. There was a small number of qualitative results (105) which were evaluated according to pre-established criteria. These results were not excluded from statistical analyses.
The median number of results per testing parameter was 32. Parameters with high levels of participation were offered in more than one sample and, some of them, in more than one round. The highest number of results were reported for pH (224 results) and Conductivity (192 results), while the lowest participations were observed for various volatile halocarbons, with 10 or less reported results.
The proportion of outliers showed considerable variation between parameters and ranged from 0% to 20.6%. High percentages of outliers (more than 15%) were obtained for Bismuth (15.7%), Total Recoverable Oil and Grease (16.7%), Silver (16.8%), Sulphate (17.4%), Total Alkalinity (17.4%) and Total Kjeldhal Nitrogen (20.6%).
Parameters with no outlier results were either qualitative tests or parameters with a low number of results (15 or less). It is worth mentioning the good performance of participants for Total Suspended Solids, with only 0.9% outliers in 110 results. Other parameters with less than 3% proportion of outliers were Calcium, Copper, Lead and Nickel (each with more than 30 results).
Laboratories from Australia accounted for 67% of the total participants and contributed with 2,851 results (74%). International participants with the largest representations were from Malaysia (8.5%), New Zealand (3.4%), Singapore (3.4%) and Indonesia (2.6%).
The number of submitted PT results in year 2016 by a single laboratory ranged from 1-137, with a median of 18 results submitted. Australian laboratories had an average results submission of 36.6 submitted results per laboratory, higher then the average of 25.7 results submission for international participants, however, the difference was not statistically significant (p = 0.12).
For the entire study, participants reported the measurement uncertainty (MU) for 76.8% of the results. Australian participants had a higher level of MU reporting, with 83.8% of their results being supported by an estimate of MU, compared with only 56.8% of results submitted by international participants. MU reporting also varied considerably between parameters tested. The extremes were observed for different volatile halocarbons, where MU reporting was around 40% for

the qualitative parameters and 100% for quantitative parameters.
Overall, out of the total of 3,854 results submitted, 85.8% were deemed satisfactory, 5.7 % questionable and 8.5% were deemed to be outlier results.
At laboratory level, there was no correlation between the number of submitted results and the proportion of outliers (r= -0.08, p= 0.37). However, after grouping laboratories on three levels of PT participation, a regression model adjusted for sample matrix and country of residence indicated that on average laboratories with high and moderate levels of participation had a lower proportion of outlier results. Compared to the group of high PT participation, laboratories with low PT participation were 1.6 times more likely to report outlier results (OR: 1.66; 95% CI: 1.18-2.35). A similar result was obtained in comparison to the moderate PT participation group (OR: 1.63; 95% CI: 1.10-2.41).
Thus, for results obtained by Australian laboratories in effluent water samples, the model estimates 13.1% outliers in the low PT participation group and 8.3% outliers in the high PT participation group (95%CI: 6.0%-11.3%). A similar trend was observed for potable water, the model predicting 10% outliers in the low PT participation group and 6.2% outliers in the high PT participation group (95%CI: 4.5%-8.6%) for Australian laboratories.
These findings are in agreement with observations from our previous study on a single parameter [3] and suggest that a quality program including consistent participation in proficiency testing could have a notable impact on improving laboratory performance.

4 Conclusion

In studying the performance of laboratories participating in the Waters (Chemical) PT Program in year 2016 it was found that overall 8.5% of the results submitted were scored as outliers and required to be investigated by the reporting laboratories.
The rate of outliers varied considerably between analytes (0-20.6%) and it was affected by samples matrix, as suggested by other papers assessing performance of participants in PT programs [4, 5].
The study found that there was an inverse correlation between the level of PT participation and the proportion of outlier results. After adjusting for sample matrix and country of residence, it was shown that laboratories with low levels of PT participation (less than 15 results) were more likely to report outliers than laboratories with moderate (15-49 results) or high (50 or more results) levels of PT participation.
While these data indicate an association between the level of participation and proportion of outlier results, this association is not to be interpreted as a cause-effect relationship. Moreover, the variation in proportion of outlier results is likely to be influenced by many other factors than those considered in this study.
In spite of these limitations, our findings add to evidence from several other studies, in fields of food or water testing, indicating that regular PT participation could improve the quality of laboratory results [3, 5, 6, 7].

This was the first time PTA conducted an evaluation of the performance of participants in the Waters (Chemical) PT Program within a one year interval. Future studies should investigate whether the trends and associations observed continue, as more data become available.

References

1. ISO/IEC Conformity assessment — General requirements for proficiency testing, ISO/IEC Standard 17043, 2010
2. ISO Statistical Methods for use in proficiency testing by interlaboratory comparison, ISO Standard 13528, 2015
3. P. Briggs, D. Mihaila, Overview of a long-lasting proficiency program for water testing, Proc. of the 5th International Proficiency Testing Conference, 1–7 (2015)
4. H.Z. Senyuva, J. Gilbert, Assessment of the performance of pesticide-testing laboratories world-wide through proficiency testing, Trends in Analytical Chemistry **25**, No. 6 , 554–562 (2006)
5. C. Ferreri, S. Caimi, C. Paneghetti, P. Campostrini, S. Caroli, The proficiency testing programme for trace elements of the CORILA project, Microchemical Journal **79**, 159–163 (2005)
6. M. Abdelmassih, V. Planchon, M. Polet, K. Dierick, J. Mahillon, Analytical performances of food microbiology laboratories - Critical analysis of seven years of proficiency testing results, Journal of Applied Microbiology **120**, Issue 2, 346–354 (2016)
7. L. Noel, C. Vastel, R. Chekri, C. Chafey, C. Testu, T. Guerin, Evaluation of 10-years French NRL proficiency tests for lead, cadmium and mercury analysis in foodstuff of animal origin, Microchemical Journal **92**, 73–79 (2009)

Evaluation of Measurement Uncertainties by the GUM Method in an Analytical Process of Certain Base Metals

A.EL BAHRAOUI*, M.BAKASS and M.HAMCHI

Faculty of Sciences Semlalia, Prince Moulay Abdellah Boulevard, Marrakech 40000

Abstract

Our work objective is to apply the GUM method to evaluate the analytical process uncertainty of the base metals in order to comply with NF EN ISO / IEC 17025 requirements and to make our contribution to the accreditation of the laboratory. First, a study was conducted on the analytical process of base metals and its different steps; ranging from the chemical sample preparation. to flame atomic absorption spectrometric analysis. The quantities that influence the analysis results have been deduced. After setting up a work plan for the entire analytical process, we followed the methodology for estimating measurement uncertainties, namely the measurand specification - the identification of the different sources of uncertainty - the the uncertainties quantification in each step and compound and expanded uncertainties calculation. The case of the iron element has been studied as an example of a test. this study allowed us to deduce the steps that can generate the most uncertainties based on the relative weight of measurement uncertainties. This is actually, in descending order, the analysis and pipetting step as well as the skill of the operator that has a noticeable effect on the analysis results.

Key words: Uncertainties assessment; GUM; NF EN ISO / IEC 17025; Analytical process Basic metals; Atomic absorption spectrometry.

Introduction

To characterize the quality of the result of a "measurement" is to evaluate and express its uncertainty. This term has connotation rather negative shows our degree of ignorance and doubt about the result, but it's in fact a valuable tool for characterizing the measurement results quality and, more generally, the information provided by these results. In fact; many error causes affect the gross result of a "measurement"(1).

For this reason, the laboratory must take into account the error causes by referring to standard NF EN ISO / IEC 17025, which is a document intended mainly for laboratories, stating the "General requirements concerning the competence of calibration and testing laboratories ". The laboratory must consider the NF EN ISO / IEC 17025 standard as an operating model that allows it to logically achieve the level of quality necessary to satisfy its customers, rather than as a list of rules on the respect of which it must justify itself to its customers. an evaluator. This approach will allow the laboratory not to over-quality or the standard misinterpretation, but also to be able to establish the provisions to meet the requirements of the standard NF EN ISO / IEC 17025, in relation to the need induced by the demand of its customers or its market(2).

For this, a sufficient and meaningful approach has been used to evaluate and express the analytical process uncertainty. This is indeed based on the procedure described by the standard "Guide to the Expression of Uncertainty in Measurement "(abbreviated GUM). The proposed methodology has the advantage of being applicable to most chemical measurements as well as in the context of routine analyzes.

* Correspondence: ayoubelbahraoui95@gmail.com

Theoretical part

According to the GUM method, the estimation of a measurement uncertainty comprises a certain number of steps, successively following each other(2):

- Measurement specification:

Definition of what you want to measure "the quantity to be measured"

- Identification of sources of uncertainty:

After performing the measurand specification operation, it is necessary to identify each source of elementary uncertainty in order to assign a value that will be taken into account when calculating the uncertainty associated with the final result. Analysis of the analytical process can be performed using an Ishikawa diagram (or fishbone diagram).

- Quantification of standard uncertainties:

The quantitative evaluation of the different components of uncertainty consists of estimating the standard uncertainties of each of the components involved in the measurement.

Two types of methods can be used:

-Evaluation of Type A: Uncertainty assessment method by statistical analysis of series of repeated measures observations. It is then a simple statistical treatment of errors:

The empirical standard deviation of the series is calculated as follows:

$$\sigma=\sqrt{\frac{\Sigma(Xmoy-Xi)^2}{N-1}}$$

And uncertainty type A is then estimated as (3):

$$u_\sigma=\frac{\sigma}{\sqrt{N}}$$

Type B evaluation: method of assessing uncertainty by means other than statistical analysis of observation series. It can be characterized by standard deviations, evaluated from probability density functions based on experience or other information.

To arrive at expressing the Type B uncertainty in the form of a standard deviation, it's necessary to resort to probability laws, the most used of which are summarized in the following table:

Table 1. Typical Uncertainties of Probability Distributions.

Law	uncertainty	Curves
Normal	$u = \frac{a}{k}$	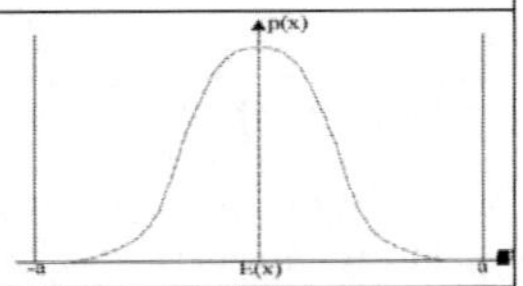
Uniform	$u = \frac{a}{\sqrt{3}}$	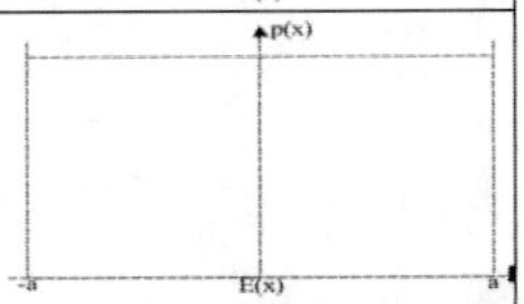
U-shaped	$u = \frac{a}{\sqrt{2}}$	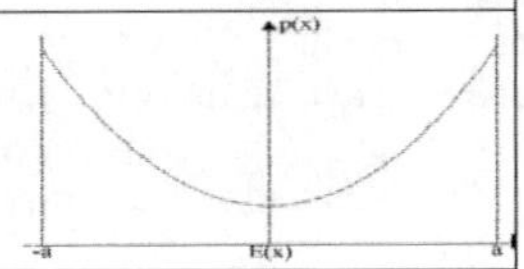
Triangle	$u = \frac{a}{\sqrt{6}}$	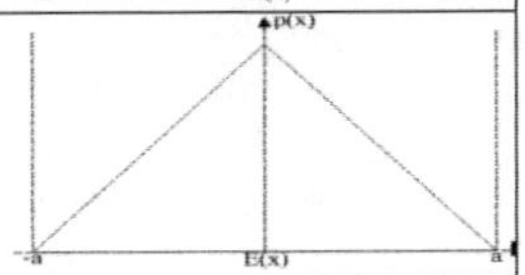

Calculation of combined standard uncertainty and expanded uncertainty.
combined standard measurement uncertainty:
There are two methods for calculating compound uncertainty:

- Direct measurement:

In the case where the measurand is written as follows: y – (p + q + r + ...) and taking into account all the sources of error, we can then express the composite uncertainty in the form:

$$uc(y(p,q,...)) = \sqrt{u(p)^2 + u(q)^2 + \cdots}$$

- Indirect measurement:

In this case, a calculation is necessary in order to access the desired quantity. These are often calculations of the type: y = (p × q × r × ...) or y = p / (q × r × ...). Composite uncertainty can be expressed as:

$$uc(y) = y \times \sqrt{\left(\frac{up}{p}\right)^2 + \left(\frac{uq}{q}\right)^2 + \cdots}$$

- Expanded measurement uncertainty

The final step is to obtain an extended uncertainty by assigning a coefficient k that depends on the confidence interval. it's expressed as:

$$U = k \times uc$$

Final expression of the measurement result:
The writing measurement results must incorporate the measurement uncertainty, the level of confidence and the appropriate units:

Y= y±U, unité, niveau de confiance

3 Expirational part

3.1 Description of the analytical process

The analytical process of the base metals consists of several steps as shown in Figure 1. The first step is to start with the chemical preparation and that consists in dissolving the sample. This first step is based on the weighing operation for which the balance control has great importance. For this, the balance is controlled by the use of a standard charge, the same mass as the sample of measurement (0.5g), at the beginning of the weighing of the sample. The preparation of the mother solution is thus obtained by attacking the mass of the weighed sample with a known volume of aqua regia and in order to obtain a total dissolution of the metals. Dissolving is then done in a 200 mL flask compolling by adding the demineralised water up to the flask mark. After the mother solution is obtained, the pipetting step is started, in which the pipette is checked first and then 1 ml is taken from the stock solution. The daughter solution is then prepared in a 100 ml flask after completion with demineralised water. Both solutions are sent to the flame atomic absorption spectrometric analysis step. The washing of the nebulization chamber and the burner is so necessary to avoid contamination of the sample. The use of a range of standards for each element to be analyzed makes it possible to draw the calibration line corresponding to each analysis element. The content of each element is then measured as a percentage.

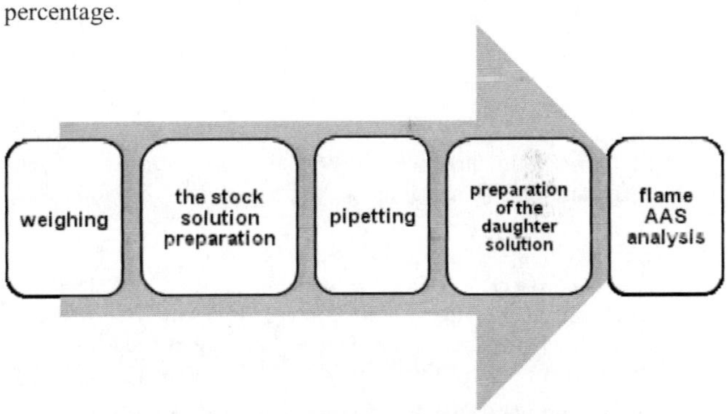

Figure 1. Analytical process of base metals.

3.2 Application of the GUM method on the analytical process

For the application of the GUM method on the analytical process to be organized, we followed the methodology of the estimation of the uncertainty indicated in the theoretical part.

- Measurand specification:

The quantity to be determined in this process is the content of a base metal in a sample, which is calculated by the following relation:

$$T(\%) = \frac{C \times SSV \times Df}{10000 \times m}$$

T = The base metal content of in%;
C = Base metal concentration in milligram / liter;
SSV = The stock solution volume in milligram;
Df = Dilution factor;

m = Mass weighed in grams.

Then the important steps for the evaluation of the uncertainty in the analytical process will be: weighing, preparation of the stock solution, dilution containing pipetting and preparation of the daughter solution and analysis by AAS.

- Identification of uncertainty sources:

After determining the important steps in the analytic process, we have been able to identify the uncertainty sources influencing the result in each step of the analytical process. After several tests and observations, using the cause-and-effect diagram (Figure 2) that encompasses all this process steps.

Figure 2. The analytic process Cause-effect diagram.

- Standard uncertainties quantification:

The 5M (Method, Means, Medium, Labor, Material) are replaced by the analytical process steps in the cause and effect diagram Figure 2 to facilitate the quantification of standard measurement uncertainties in each step:

For the weighing step, type B evaluation is used, starting with the standard measurement uncertainty of measurement standard calculated from the uncertainty announced in the calibration certificate, this uncertainty is expressed by the following formula (2): $u_{et} = \frac{Uet}{2}$

Then we proceed to the reading which is affected by a standard measurement uncertainty u_r function of the resolution "the real step" (d) which corresponds to the difference between two successive indications. It's equal to(2): $u_r = \frac{d}{2\sqrt{3}}$

The uncertainty associated with the balance linearity, which characterizes the ability of the balance to follow the linear ratio between the input value and the output value, is expressed by maximum permissible measurement error (MPME) of the balance. divided by the root of three.

As for standard measurement uncertainty due to the effect of temperature on the balance, it's estimated based on the sensitivity coefficient C which is variable from one instrument to another (4) and this by applying the following formula :

$$u_T = \frac{C \times \Delta T \times m}{\sqrt{3}}$$

Because of weighing can be affected by the sample position to be weighed on the scale plate, the standard measurement uncertainty of the eccentricity is evaluated by a triangular distribution (5): $u_{exc} = \frac{|Ii - IC|max}{\sqrt{6}}$

$|I_i - I_C|_{max}$ being the maximum difference between the center weighing position and the other positions.

The glassware tolerance (flask, pipette) given by the manufacturer and the temperature effect, are two sources of uncertainties that are estimated in the same way in the preparation steps of the stock solution, dilution and the preparation of the daughter solution.

Then we estimate the tolerance by the following formula (6): $u_t = \frac{tol}{\sqrt{6}}$

The temperature can be quantified as follows (6): $u_t = \frac{2,1 \times 10-4 \times V \times \Delta\theta}{\sqrt{3}}$

V being the glassware volume and Δθ the difference between the temperature measured during the experiment and that mentioned on the glassware.

Concerning to the analysis, which is indeed the last step in the analytical process of the base metals, the readings uncertainties of the atomic absorption spectroscope display and the balance are estimated in the same way as previously in the step of weighing.

Before reading the results we go through the calibration curve step, which is a diagram generated by a range of standards prepared experimentally, representing the concentration on the abscissa axis and the absorbance of the solution carried on the ordinate axis. However, the calibration measurements uncertainty train on these concentrations a systematic error, whose the standard deviation is estimated by

(2) : $u_{cet} = \frac{Sy}{a} \times \sqrt{\frac{1}{N} + \frac{1}{p} + \frac{(X - Xmoy)^2}{\Sigma(Xi - Xmoy)^2}}$

N: measurement standards number

p: repetition

a: the origin to the ordinate

x: the sample concentration

xi: measurement standard concentration i

s_y: residues standard deviation estimated by : $s_y = \frac{\Sigma(yi - ycalculé)^2}{N - 2}$

$y_i - y_{calculé}$ is the difference between the absorbance calculated from the line **y= ax+ b** and the experimental absorbance called residue.

With $a = \frac{\Sigma(xi - xmoy)(yi - ymoy)}{\Sigma(xi - xmoy)^2}$ et $b = \frac{\Sigma yi - a\Sigma xi}{N}$

Seen that the calculations complexity, we have programmed an Excel spreadsheet to ensure the ease of carrying out the various calculations.The last uncertainty source is the operator effect, which is very important. This operator effect is estimated by type A evaluation of measurement uncertainty at the end of the analytical process to avoid the calculation repetition of this effect in each step. This so-called repeatability uncertainty is in fact the standard deviation of a measurements series that encompasses the operator effect during the analytical process and the device effect. (5): $u_s = \frac{1}{\sqrt{N}} \times \sqrt{\frac{\Sigma(x - xmoy)^2}{N - 1}}$

- Combined standard measurement uncertainty and expanded measurement uncertainty calculation

In each step combined standard measurement uncertainty is calculated by the direct measurement method announced at the beginning.

And from the relation: $T(\%) = \frac{C \times Vsm \times Fd}{10000 \times m}$, we can deduce that the combined standard measurement uncertainty of the analytical process is calculated by the indirect measurement method.

For expanded measurement uncertainty and at a 95% confidence interval, it is equal to: $\mathbf{U = 2 \times u_c}$

u_c being the analytic process standard measurement uncertainty.

The standard uncertainties and compound types contained in the analytical process of base metals are estimated in each step and grouped together in Table 2.

Table 2.standard measurement uncertainties of the distribution laws

Step	Uncertainty Source	Standard measurement uncertainty calculation	Type
Weighing	Standard	$uet = \frac{Uet}{2}$	B
	Resolution	$ur = \frac{d}{2\sqrt{3}}$	B
	Linearity	$ulin = \frac{EMT}{\sqrt{3}}$	B
	Temperature	$uT = \frac{C \times \Delta T \times m}{\sqrt{3}}$	B
	Eccentricity	$uexc = \frac{\lvert Ii - IC\rvert max}{\sqrt{6}}$	B
Weighing combined standard measurement uncertainty		$ucp = \sqrt{uet^2 + 2 \times ur^2 + ulin^2 + uT^2 + u}$	
The stock solution preparation	Flask tolerance	$ut = \frac{tol}{\sqrt{6}}$	B
	Temperature	$uT = \frac{2,1 \times 10-4 \times V \times \Delta\theta}{\sqrt{3}}$	B
The stock solution combined standard measurement uncertainty		$ucsm = \sqrt{ut^2 + uT^2}$	
Pipetting	The pipette Tolerance	$ut = \frac{tol}{\sqrt{6}}$	B
	Temperature	$uT = \frac{2,1 \times 10-4 \times V \times \Delta\theta}{\sqrt{3}}$	B
Pipetting combined standard measurement uncertainty		$ucpi = \sqrt{ut^2 + uT^2}$	
The daughter solution preparation	Flask tolerance	$ut = \frac{tol}{\sqrt{6}}$	B
	Temperature	$uT = \frac{2,1 \times 10-4 \times V \times \Delta\theta}{\sqrt{3}}$	B
The daughter solution combined standard measurement uncertainty		$ucsf = \sqrt{ut^2 + uT^2}$	
Analysis	Reading	$ul = \frac{h}{2\sqrt{3}}$	B
	Calibration curve	$ucet = \frac{Sy}{a} \times \sqrt{\frac{1}{N} + \frac{1}{p} + \frac{(X - Xmoy}{\Sigma(Xi - Xmo}}$	A
	Operator	$us = \frac{1}{\sqrt{N}} \times \sqrt{\frac{\Sigma(x - xmoy)^2}{N-1}}$	A
Analysis combined standard measurement uncertainty		$uca = \sqrt{2 \times ul^2 + ucet^2 + s^2}$	
Analytical process combined standard measurement uncertainty		$u_c = t_{el} \times \sqrt{\left(\frac{ucp}{m}\right)^2 + \left(\frac{ucsm}{V200}\right)^2 + \left(\frac{ucpt}{V1}\right)^2 + \left(\frac{uca}{Cel}\right)^2}$	

➢ The measurement result Final expression

After calculating the analytical process combined standard measurement uncertainty and the expanded measurement uncertainty. The measurement result can be expressed in this form:

$T_{el} = (t_{el} \pm 2 \times u_c)$ at a 95% confidence interval.

4 Results and discussions

In our case we studied the iron which is part of the base metals and we followed the steps of quantifying the uncertainties mentioned before.

During the weighing step, and to estimate the different standard uncertainties, it's necessary to have:

- The certified standard uncertainty charge of 0.5g and which is given by the research center: 0.08mg.
- The resolution of the balance that is mentioned on the technical poster of the scale which is 0.0001g.
- The scale maximum permissible measurement error which is: MPME = 0.5mg.
- The temperature effect. Indeed, the variation observed during the weighing operation of a mass of 0.5g is $\Delta T = 0.3$ ° C and with a sensitivity coefficient [3] equal to 15×10^{-6} which is deduced from the maximum number verification steps of the weighing instrument. This coefficient is only the ratio between the maximum range of the scale and the verification scale ($e=10 \times d$).
- For eccentricity it has no effect on our weighing measures. Indeed the positioning of a mass of 0.5g in five different positions of the plate has allowed to obtain the same value in all these positions, which gives a standard uncertainty of zero eccentricity.

The standard measurement uncertainty estimation are calculated in the same way during the preparing the stock solution steps, pipetting and preparing the daughter solution. It's useful to know that the tolerance of the 200 mL flask, the 1 mL pipette, the 100 mL flask are respectively; 0.15 mL, 0.004 mL, 0.1 mL. The temperature measured during these steps is 20.2 ° C.

Finally, concerning the analysis step, we start with the reading standard measurement uncertainty, deduced from the resolution of the device which is equal to 0.01 mg / L.

The linear least-squares adjustment procedure used, suppose that the x-axis (the abscissa) uncertainties values are significantly smaller than the uncertainty on the y-axis (7). Therefore, the uncertainty calculation estimate for the concentration reflects the uncertainty in the absorbance and not the uncertainty of the standards designated for calibration. The four standards for calibration were measured three times each (7), giving the results shown in Table 3.

The concentration of iron in the once-prepared solution was measured at 44.38 mg / L. The standard measurement uncertainty of the calibration line calculated using the Excel spreadsheet is:

$$u_{cet} = \frac{Sy}{a} \times \sqrt{\frac{1}{1} + \frac{1}{12} + \frac{(X - Xmoy)^2}{\Sigma(Xi - Xmoy)^2}} = 0.4222 \text{ mg/l}$$

Table3.Calibration results.

Standards concentration in mg / L	Absorbance measurements 1	Absorbance measurements 2	Absorbance measurements 3
0	0.0033	0.0014	0.0051
10	0.1526	0.1177	0.1282
20	0.2846	0.2303	0.2442
60	0.6928	0.5886	0.5757

Finally, in order to estimate the operator effect, ten measurements were taken during the entire analytical process and afterwards the values dispersion around the average was estimated (C_{moy}=44.45mg/L et σ=0.3058). to deduce the standard measurement uncertainty that is equal to:

$$u_s = \frac{0.3085}{\sqrt{10}} = 0.09756 \text{mg/L}$$

After the uncertainties quantification, combined standard measurement uncertainty of each step and which are grouped together in Table 4 are calculated. Since in the case of iron, the content in % is equal to the concentration in mg/L, we calculated the combined standard measurement uncertainty of analytic process that equals: **u_c=0.4407%**

And at a 95% confidence interval the expanded measurement uncertainty is equal to: **U=0.8814%**

Finally according to GUM the final result can be written as follows:

T_{fer}=(44.4± 0.9)% à 95%

Table 4.the analytic process combined standard measurement uncertainties

Step	Standard measurement uncertainty	Relative standard measurement uncertainty	Relative weight
Weighing	**u_{cp}=0.000293 g**	$\frac{ucp}{m} = \frac{0.000293}{0.5}$ = **0.00059**	**4.63%**
The stock solution preparation	**u_{csm}=0.0614ml**	$\frac{ucsm}{V200} = \frac{0.0614}{200}$ **=0.00031**	**2.42%**
Pipetting	**u_{cpi}=0.00163ml**	$\frac{ucpt}{V1} = \frac{0.00163}{1}$ = **0.00163**	**12.8 %**
The daughter solution preparation	**u_{csf}=0.0409ml**	$\frac{ucsf}{V100} = \frac{0.0409}{100}$ **=0.00041**	**3.22%**
Analysis	**u_{ca}=0.4333mg/L**	$\frac{uca}{Cfer} = \frac{0.4333}{44.45}$ **=0.00975**	**76.88 %**

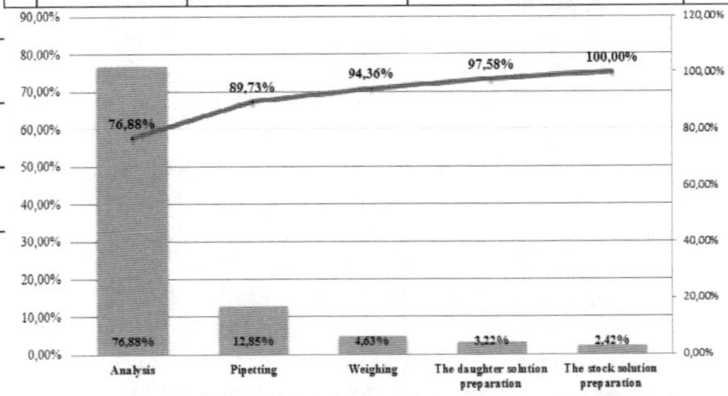

Figure 3. Pareto diagram of relative weights

From the relative weights of the analytical process steps, obtained from the ratio and all relative combined standard measurement uncertainty and all of relative combined standard measurement uncertainties, and from a Pareto diagram shown in Figure 3; it was possible to deduce the steps which prevail in the measurement uncertainties calculation. Indeed the contribution of each step to the uncertainty on the analytical process differs from one stage to another. The ranking of the main sources of error in descending order is: the analysis step with a relative weight of 76.88% followed by the pipetting step with a relative weight of 12.85%. This is why we must be attentive during these two steps, and more specifically regarding the preparation of the calibration line. This calibration line should be done carefully and with greater certainty. On the one hand, a good preparation of the standards ranges has great importance in the analysis of this material type and on the other hand it must be ensured that there is no contamination. during the line using AAS drawing . The concentrations situation in the curve middle leads us to minimize the calibration line uncertainty without forgetting the the operator contribution in the whole analytical process and which plays a very important and crucial role to achieve results reliable. Generally, the way to realize the calibration line assumes, of course, that there is a linear relation between signal and concentration. However, the linearity domain of the measurement method can be very limited. It's therefore in the first place to have perfectly determined the method linear range for the analyte considered. Regarding the measuring medium, which may contain not only the analyte whose concentration is to be determined but also many other physico-chemical species from the matrix. We must then try to control in which measure these species can disrupt the analytical signal, to take into account, these matrix effects. Therefore, it's necessary to be able to refer to a calibration line constructed for the analyte considered in its measurement medium.

5 Conclusion

Uncertainty in measurement is essential in any discipline,

especially in laboratories where decisions need to be made. The objective of our laboratory is to be accredited NF EN ISO / CEI 17025. To reach this goal we made an uncertainties estimation during all the steps of the analytical process while starting with the measurand specification until the expression final measurement result. Through this uncertainty measurement estimation of the different steps, it has been possible to know the measurement step referring to the relative weight of the uncertainties. Our work has been closed with recommendations to help in minimizing these uncertainties as much as possible. Reliable results will only be achieved once the calibration is rigorously performed in an exact and logical manner. The analysis method is actually corrected only if, in the absence of the analyte under consideration, the analytical signal of the measuring medium is zero. In other words, the measurement medium without the analyte must not give an answer that corresponds to an "additive" matrix effect, because we are in the presence of non-specific interference. For this, must be used a simple calibration model that takes into account all interactions. But the mere fact of changing the matrix can affect the results trueness and we can't escape the validation step of the method.

References

1. B.Gaumont, J.Laurent. **De l'incertitude à la précaution : le rôle de la métrologie.** ***Annales des Mines - Responsabilité et environnement.*** **2010, pp. 82 - 91.**
2. **D.Maton.** *Guide pour l'évaluation des incertitudes de mesures analytiques* . s.l. : BRGM, 2000.

3. **Ministère de l'éducation nationale, de la jeunesse et de la vie associative.** Ressources pour le cycle terminal. *Mesure et incertitudes.* France : s.n., 2012. Vol. 37.

4. **Métrologie, Collège Français de.** *Guide de métrologie à l'usage des laboratoires d'analyses de biologie médicale.* France : Lexitis Editions, 2013.

5. **Commission SFSTP, D. Louvel,C. Barbier, M.-D. Blanchin, M.-C. Bonenfant, X. Chavatte, C. Chmieliewski, X. Dua, R. Dybiak,C. Imbernon, C. Lebranchu, L. Louvet, M. Vandenhende.** Balances. *Partie III. Incertitude de mesure d'une balance.* s.l. : STP PHARMA PRATIQUES , 2009. Vol. 19, 4.

6. **C.DUCAMP.** Concentration de la solution d'EDTA. *Estimation de l'incertitude de la mesure :Application à l'incertitude sur le calcul de la concentration d'EDTA lors de la détermination de la dureté d'une eau naturelle.* s.l. : ENFA, 2011. Vol. 11.

7. **members, EURACHEM.** *Quantifying Uncertainty in Analytical Measurement.* s.l. : S L R Ellison(LGC-UK),M Rosslein(EMPA-Suisse),A Williams(UK), 2000.

Machining Granite Materials: Effects of Polishing Conditions on Part Quality, Fine and Ultrafine Particles Emission

V. Songmene*, A. Miazza, J. Kouam and O.A. Olufayo

École de Technologie Supérieure (ÉTS), 1100 Notre-Dame Street West, Montréal (QC) H3C 1K3, Canada

Received:

Machining is necessary to shape parts but it is also an important source of pollution (for example contaminated cutting fluid, non-recyclable chips, dust and aerosols) and constitutes hazards to machine-tools operators. The shop floor air quality is of great concern when shaping dusty materials such as granite, marble and engineering stones. It is therefore important to deal not only with productivity, but also with air quality as occupational health and safety regulations are becoming more and more severe. On the 24th of March 2016, the US department of Labor's Occupational Safety and Health Administration (OSHA) announced the reduction of the exposure limit for inhalable crystalline silica dust by half and has given industries up to five years according to their sector to comply. This policy affects industries involved in transforming and manufacturing of granite and marble products. To quickly comply with these new regulations, engineers and researchers must help industries in developing strategies which limit workers risk of exposure to silica. This paper investigates the part surface finish as well as the emission of fine and ultrafine particles during granite polishing. The main goal is to determine machining conditions leading to less dust emission while maintaining acceptable part quality and productivity.

Keywords: Granite, polishing, machining conditions, surface finish, dust, Occupational Health and safety

1 Introduction

Natural and engineering stones are usually shaped and finished using a wide a variety of machining processes which include sawing, milling, profiling, drilling and polishing. Hard stones products are found in variety of applications such as in houses (kitchen counters tops, bathrooms ties) and exterior buildings (landscaping, walls) and monuments. Some of these monuments in North America are the Martin Luther King memorial (Washington, DC); National 911 memorial (New York, NY) and the World War II memorial (Washington, DC).

The main purpose of hard stones polishing is to improve the part surface quality, accuracy and the glossiness. Fig. 1 for example shows the evolution of the surface quality and the roughness profile as a function of the polishing stage or the abrasive grit size used. In industries, different combinations of abrasives grit sizes ranging from rough to fine are used for polishing. The machining of natural and engineered hard stones, and especially the crystalline silica (SiO_2) it generates, is being pointed out as a source of occupational diseases: silicosis, lung cancer and other respiratory diseases, [1, 2-6]. In March 2016, the United States of America reduced the maximum exposure limits for respirable silica dust by more than half of it current values [2]. It is now 50 μg/m^3 for an eight hours working shift. This revision was also the result of the following [7]: (i) more evidence that old exposure limits did not adequately protect workers; and ii) evidence that exposures to crystalline silica below 100μg/m^3 caused silicosis and cancer.

* Correspondence: victor.songmene@etsmtl.ca

According to NIOSH [1], the most common forms of crystalline silica in the workplace are quartz, cristobalite and tridymite. Silicosis is caused by inhalation and deposition of respirable silica (quartz and cristobalite) particles less than 10 μm in diameter (PM_{10}). The size of the particles has an influence on its place of deposition in human body, [8], and on its harmfulness.

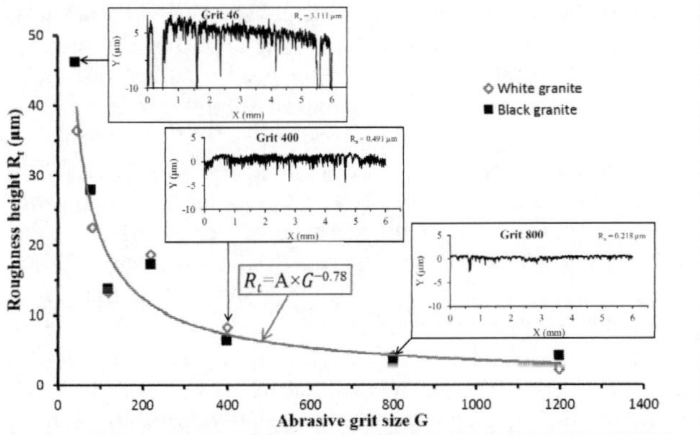

Fig. 1. Effects of polishing stages on granite surface roughness: Spindle speed: 1000 rpm, feed 8.3 mm/s, pressure 0.23 bar. *Adapted from Saidi et al. (2015)*

The inflammatory effect of granite nanoparticles on lung tissue is greater than that of micro particles, [9]. Let us also note that

silicosis is latent and incurable. OSHA [10] distinguishes three classes of silicosis: 1-Chronic silicosis is the most common form of silicosis that occurs after 15 to 20 years of moderate to low exposure to respirable crystalline silica. 2- Accelerated silicosis can occur after 5 to 10 years of high exposure; 3- Acute silicosis, fatal, occurs a few months to two years after exposure to extremely high concentrations of respirable crystalline silica. Workers who inhale very small particles of crystalline silica are at risk for silicosis, an incurable, progressively debilitating or even fatal disease, [11].
This problem is very serious and critical: OSHA estimates that: i)-in the United States of America, about 2.3 million workers are exposed to respirable silica in their work; ii)- The net monetary benefits of the new standards, in USA, are expected to be $ 7.6 billion annually due to reduced mortality and morbidity from exposure to crystalline silica, [12].
Therefore, it is critical to found solutions for limiting workers exposure to these harmful particles. To do so, industries need engineers and researchers to help them find new and safe ways to shape these materials containing crystalline silica. Kitchen countertops and other granite and marble products (ornamental, building) manufacturers will have to meet the new exposure limits (50μg/m^3). The machining of natural stones and artificial stones generates dust containing crystalline silica [1-9]. The emission rates and particle size distribution of this dust depends on operations, processes, materials and tools used to shape or polish these hard materials [13]. Scientists are still lacking data (number, area and mass concentrations) of particles generated to test correlations [14] and build a database for model calibration [15], useful for studying and characterizing the emission of nanoparticles and ultrafine particles.

Some research works have been made on part surface quality when machining granite and others hard stones products, but only limited work focuses on the surface quality, productivity and dust emission. While investigating belt polishing of granite, it was found that more fine particle are produced while operating at high speed during belt polishing [16]. Saidi et al. [13] have shown during polishing of granite that fine particle dispersion depends more on spindle speed used rather than on the sizes of the particles. High concentrations of fine particles with diameters size lower than 2.5 microns (PM2.5) were found away of the polishing zone (source of emission). This suggested that any worker close to the machining area but away from the particle emission source could be exposed to these particles known to be dangerous as they contain silica, [13].
A study by Songmene et al. [17] has shown that the use of water in MQL mode is effective in reducing fine particles in the air during semi-wet polishing of granite, but not ultrafine particles. Yilma [18] has shown that the analysis of the chips generated during granite polishing can provide information on the use but not of optimal cutting conditions in terms of productivity and efficiency of the process. Therefore, an economic method based on the minimization of friction forces for machining granites was proposed [18], but the authors did not pay attention to the generation of dust.

As Songmene et al. noticed [19], air quality control or characterization of airborne suspended particles often uses the mass concentration as the principal parameter. For many instruments, this parameter is evaluated by counting the number of particles identified by the detector of the measuring instrument and by calculating the mass concentration. This is based on the density of the particles, according to the assumption that the particles are spherical. These parameters (mass and number concentrations) are adequate for large or fine particles, but not necessarily for nanoparticles and ultrafine particles [20]. The specific surface area was suggested as an essential parameter for nanoparticle studies [20], as there would be a better correlation between this metric quantity and the nanoparticles' toxicity.

The purpose of the current article is to study the part quality, fine particle (FP) emission and ultrafine particle (UFP) emission during polishing of granite materials, in relation to the machining conditions and abrasive tools used. The work is intended to provide manufacturing information and understanding that could be used to limit the dust emission at the source while improving the part quality and the productivity. The metrics used for dust characterization include the particle's shape, number concentration, specific surface concentration and mass concentration.

2. Experimental setup

The polishing was conducted in a closed Computer Numerical Control (CNC) milling machine (10,000 rpm), allowing the dust sampling to be carried out in a closed environment. This increases the measurement efficiency, as fewer particles are capable of escaping into the environment. Polluted air in the machine was aspirated into the particle measurement equipment through a 10 mm diameter polyester tube (back tube in Fig. 2b). The tube is about 304.8 mm, and kept up straight in order to minimize particle loss inside. The polishing tool (Fig. 2b) was a 50.8 mm diameter diamond abrasives tool mounted in a rigid tool holder. The abrasives grit size and the polishing conditions are listed in Table 1.
Fine particle (FP) emissions were measured using an APS (Aerosol Particle Sizer, Fig. 2c) capable of sampling particle size ranging from 0.5 to 20 μm. Ultrafine particle (UFP) emissions were measured using an SMPS (Scanning Mobility Particle Sizer), equipped with a nano DMA (Differential Mobility Analyzer), Fig. 2d. This system can measure particle size ranging from 7 to 300 nm. These two instruments (APS and SMPS) measure particle number concentration, specific area concentration and mass concentration as a function of particle aerodynamic diameters.
The workpiece materials used were two granites (black and white). Fig. 3 presents scanning electronic images and compositions of the granites tested. The white granite (Fig. 3a) was found to be of medium to large grains sizes granite with granular and porphyric automorphic texture. It contains 41% of quartz, 33% of plagioclase and 23% K-feldspar.

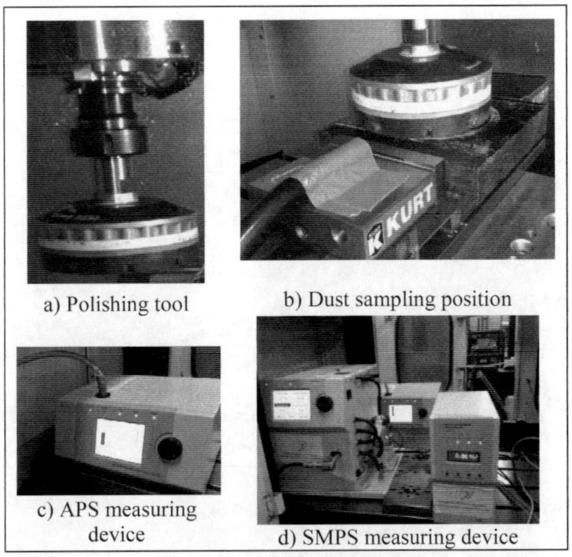

Fig. 2. Experimental setup & equipment.

The black granite (Fig. 3b) is an anorthosite with coarse grains, consisting mainly of plagioclase (about 83%). It does not contain quartz. The compositions of the white and black granites were also confirmed with MEB analysis and petrographic examinations on thin blade samples. Mineralogical analysis has shown that the grain size of the black granite (0.2 to 17 mm) is greater than that of white granite (0.5 to 7 mm). Although the black granite contained no quartz (SiO_2) and no feldspar, it does however contain silicon as plagioclase ($CaAl_2Si_2O_8$-$NaAlSi_3O_8$) does. The tested white granite contains about 52% of silicon while the back granite contains only 12% Si [16]. This silicon (Si) is sometimes the cause of respiratory diseases of workers during polishing of the granite, especially when it is in the form of quartz [11].

Table 1: Polishing conditions

Abrasives grit sizes	60, 120, 220, 400, 800, 1200, 1800
Feed rates: V_t	
mm/min	254-2032
(ipm)	(10-80)
Spindle speed: Vs (rpm)	250, 500, 750, 1000, 1250, 1750, 2000, 2250, 2500
Polishing tool diameter	50.8 mm (2.0 in)
Type of polishing	Rotation + translation
Depth of polishing	0.0508 mm (0.002 in)
dust sampling distance	1.9 mm (0.75 in)

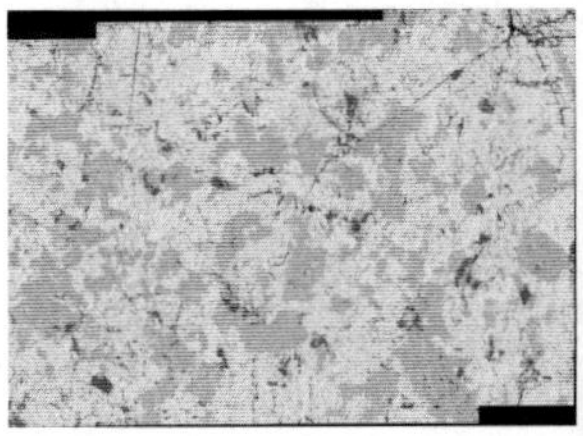

	Minerals	Proportions (%)
	Quartz	41.38
	Plagioclase	32.39
	K-feldspar	23.14
	Biotite	1.14
	Oxydes/ biotite	1.95

a) White granite

	Minerals	Proportions (%)
	Plagioclase	83.61
	Olivine	1.51
	Biotite	2.83
	Oxydes/ sulfures	5.20
	Orthopy-roxene	6.85

b) Black granite

Fig. 3. Granite workpiece materials tested.
(IOS Services Géoscientifiques, Chicoutimie, Canada)

4 Results and discussions

4.1 Chips and particle morphology and Si content

A preliminary analysis of the percentage of silicon in black and white granite during dry polishing revealed that the dust collected during the polishing of white granite contained more silicon than the one collected when polishing the black granite (Fig. 4). This result can be explained by the fact that the white granite contains 40% more silicon than the black granite [16]. This high amount of silicon in white granite dust can be further explained by the presence of quartz within the white granite (quartz 41%) compared to the black granite which is mostly composed of plagioclase (83%), Fig. 3.

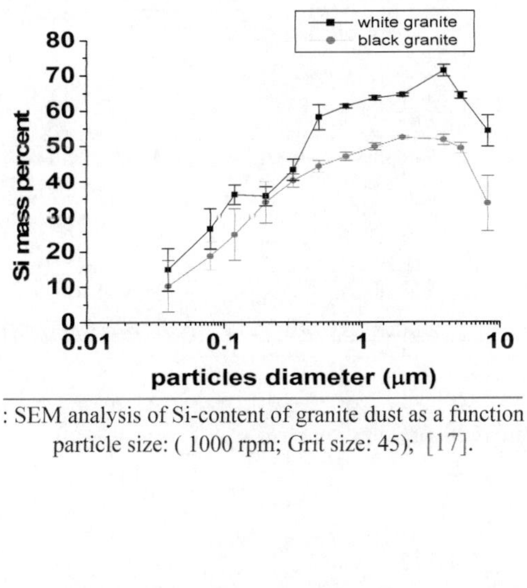

Fig. 4 : SEM analysis of Si-content of granite dust as a function of the particle size: (1000 rpm; Grit size: 45); [17].

a) b)

Fig. 5. SEM images of collected granite dust: a) rotational and translation-free polishing, b) conventional polishing

Fig. 5 displays the SEM images of dust collected during the polishing process. It appears that during polishing without travel motion (translation-free), the dust generated is spherical (Fig. 5a). This can be explained by the rubbing action between the chip and the abrasives. In the case of conventional polishing combining the rotation and the translation of the tool, the machined surface is constantly renovated, creating quite a different shape of chip and dust (Fig. 5b). The difference in the dust shape can impact the accuracy of the measurement as it was demonstrated that conventional dust sampling methods, assuming spherical particles underestimates the results [21].

Fig. 6 presents SEM morphology images of particles obtained when polishing black and white granites at different speeds. The effect of the polishing speeds tested on particles shapes was not significant; however, particles are more agglomerated with an increase in the polishing speed for black granite as compared to white granite. This observation could be due to their mechanical property difference, as well as to the fact that white granite contains more abrasive Si particles than black granite.

Polishing speeds	White granite	Black granite
500 rpm		
1000 rpm		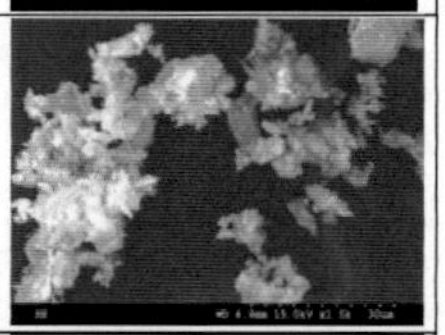
1500 rpm		

Fig. 6. SEM images of particles obtained during polishing (Feed rate: 508 mm/min; tool grit size: 60; pressure:0.2 bar)

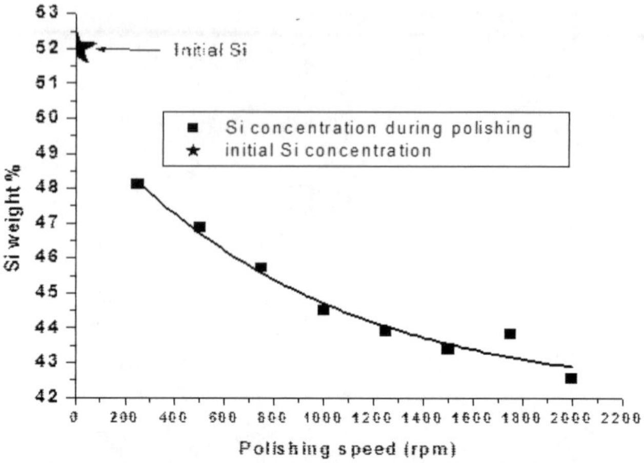

Fig. 7: Variation of Si-content of emitted particle obtained at different polishing speeds for white granite (Vt:8.4 mm/s; Abrasive grid size: 60; pressure :0.2 bar)

For a given polishing process (rotation + translation), the particle morphology did not vary with the polishing speed (Fig. 6) nor with the feed rate. However, the composition of the emitted dust and especially its Si-content varied with the cutting speed and the feed rates used (Figs. 7 and 8). The tested white granite contains initially more silicon (about 52%) and the back granite contains only 12% Si [16]. The variation of the initial Si-content within the particle as a function of the machining speeds and feed rates can be due to the change in chip sizes as already noticed by Yilma [18].

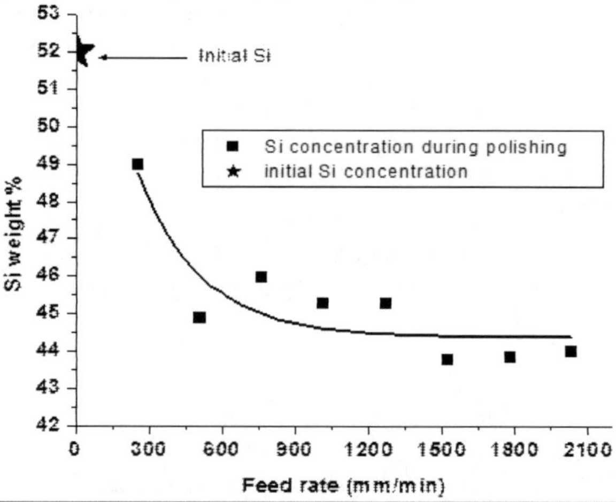

Fig. 8: Variation of Si-content of emitted particle obtained at different polishing feed rates for white granite (Vs: 1000 rpm; Abrasive grit size: 60; pressure: 0.2 bar)

Figs 9-11 display the evolution of the normal forces during polishing as a function of the abrasive grit sizes (Fig. 9), polishing speeds (Fig. 10) and feed rates (Fig. 11). For a given feed rate, the normal polishing force did not vary with the tool grit sizes nor with the polishing speeds. However, as expected, an increase in the feed rate led to an increase of the normal force. By increasing the feed rate, the chip load and the chip sizes are increased and this leads to higher normal force as each abrasive removed therefore a large amount of materials.

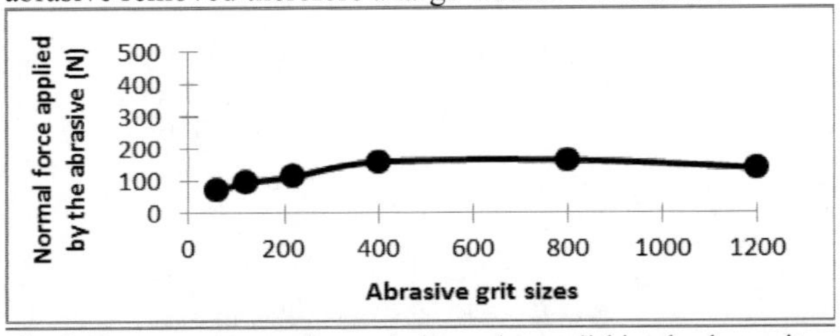

Fig. 9: Forces acting on the workpiece when polishing back granite as a function of the abrasive grit sizes (Vs: 1000 rpm; Vt: 508 mm/min)

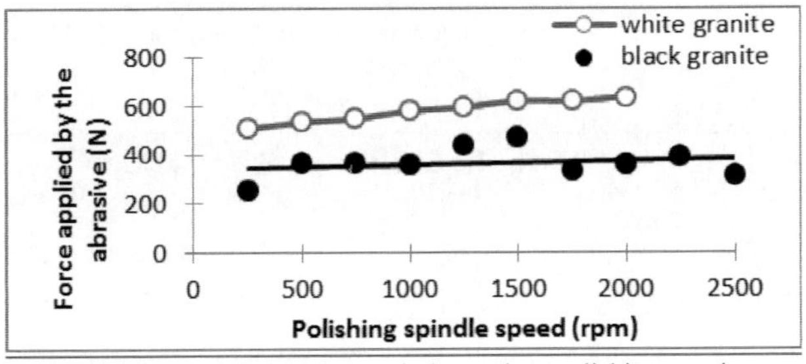

Fig. 10: Forces applied to the workpiece when polishing granites as a function of polishing speed (Vt: 508 mm/min; Abrasive grid size: 60)

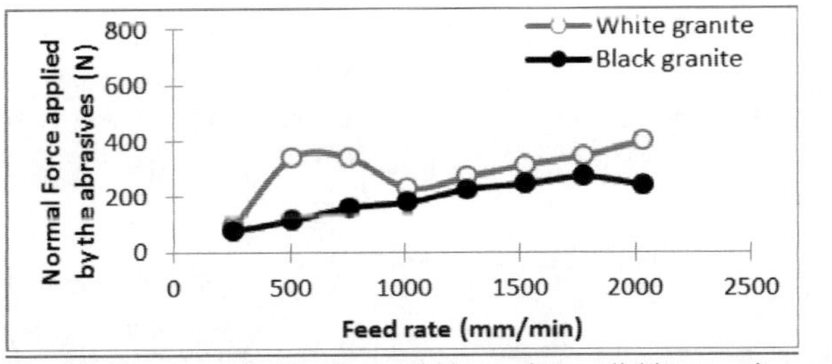

Fig. 11: Forces applied to the workpiece when polishing granites as a function of the feed rate (Vs: 1000 rpm; Abrasive grid size: 60)

4.2 Part surface finish

The part surface finish was evaluated using the following metrics:

- The arithmetical mean roughness value: Ra
- The total height of the roughness profile or maximum peak-to-valley roughness height: Rt
- The core roughness depth average: Rpk
- The reduced peak height average Rvk

Figs 12-14 display the evolution of the Ra-values and Rt-values as a function of polishing speed (Fig. 12), feed rate (Fig. 13) and abrasive grit sizes (Fig. 14). Higher speeds, higher feed rates and higher abrasive grit sizes all led to better surface finishes. The use of the high speeds and feed rates also means that higher productivity is achieved.

Fig. 15 and Fig. 16 display the evolution of the surface roughness parameters as a function of the polishing parameters (spindle speed and feed rate). Better surface finish is obtained for spindle speeds higher than 1000 rpm and for feed rates higher than 508 mm/min. If the spindle speed is too high, the high temperature generated might lead to surface burning.

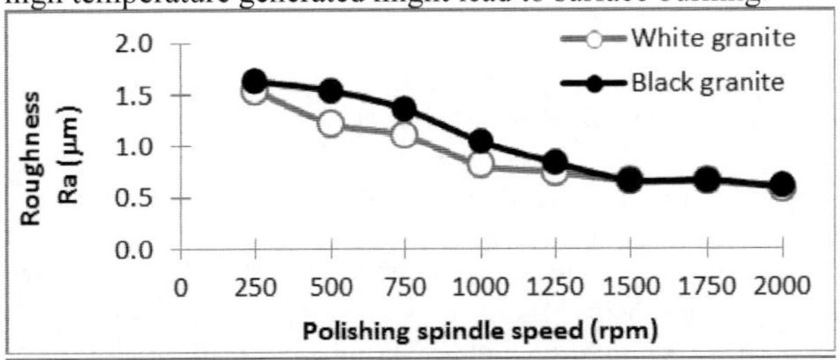

Fig. 12: Ra-values as a function of polishing speed (Vt: 508 mm/min; Abrasive grid size: 60)

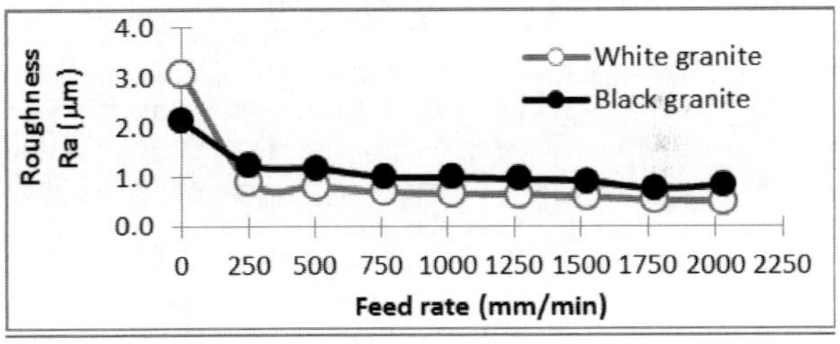

Fig. 13: Ra-values as a function of the feed rate (Vs: 1000 rpm; Abrasive grid size: 60)

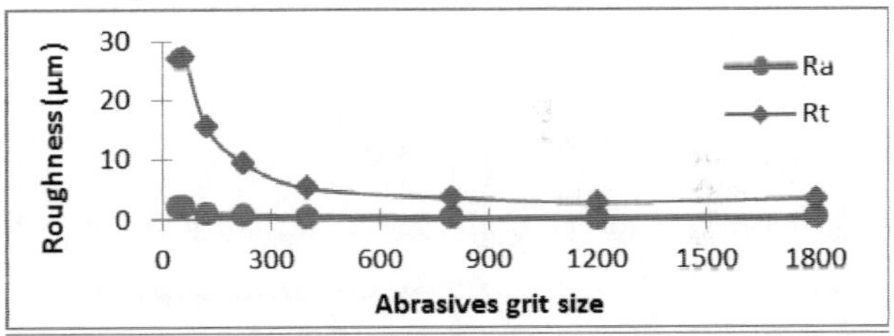

Fig. 14: Evolution of Ra and Rt as a function of the abrasive grit size (Vs: 1000 rpm; Vt: 508 mm/min; **black granite**)

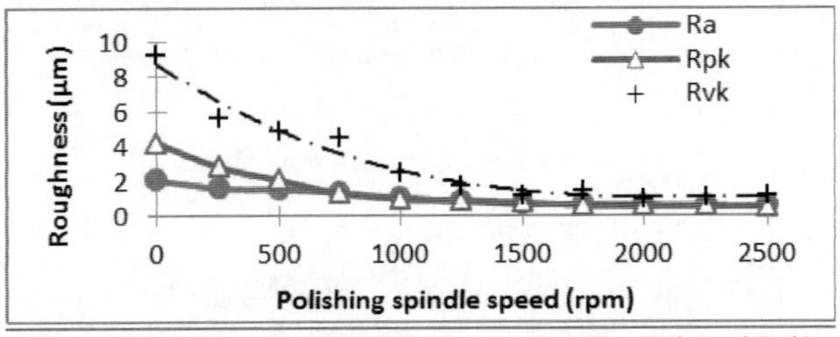

Fig. 15: Evolution of surface finish parameters (Ra, Rpk, and Rvk) when polishing **black granite** as a function of polishing speed (Vt: 508 mm/min; Abrasive grid size: 60)

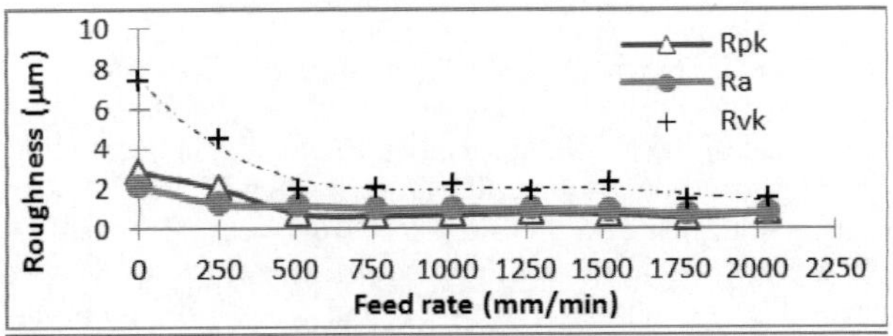

Fig. 16: Evolution of surface finish parameters (Ra, Rpk, and Rvk) when polishing **black granite** as a function of the feed rate(Vs: 1000 rpm; Abrasive grid size: 60).

4.3 Fine particles (FP) emission

Fine particles were sampled using an Aerosol Particle Sizer spectrometer capable of measuring particles with aerodynamic diameters ranging from 0.5 to 20 µm. The number concentration of the particle emitted increased with the abrasive grit sizes during roughing operations and was quite constant in finishing operations using large grit sizes (Fig. 17). This is in good agreement with observations made by [13] who observed that during roughing operations, the chip formation by brittle fracture leads to high amount of fine particle.

During the finishing process, the chip formation is by ductile flow [13] and this limit the quantity of fine particle emitted (Fig. 17). Fig. 18 shows that for a given grit size, in roughing conditions, the fine particle emission decreases with the feed rate. This behavior is understandable as the increase in feed rate leads to the generation of larger chips and particles, thus reducing the number of the later. As a consequence, their specific surface and mass are also reduced (Figs. 20 and 21). The percentage reduction of the particle number concentration reached about 22% when the feed rate was changed from the low to high value. There is however an interaction between these emissions and the workpiece materials that is still to be investigated (Figs. 19-21).

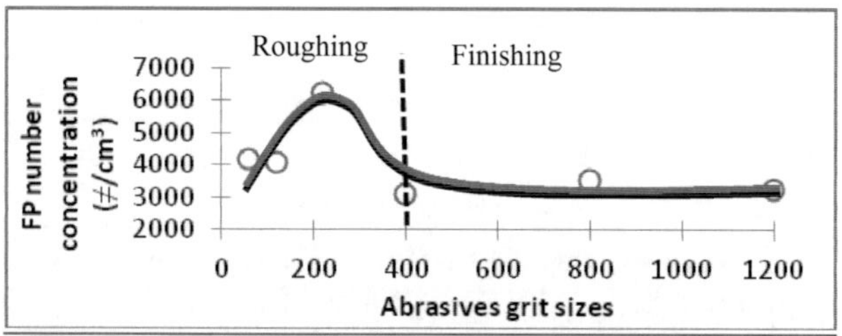

Fig. 17. Fine particle emission when polishing **black granite** as a function of the feed rate (Vs: 1000 rpm; Abrasive grid size: 60)

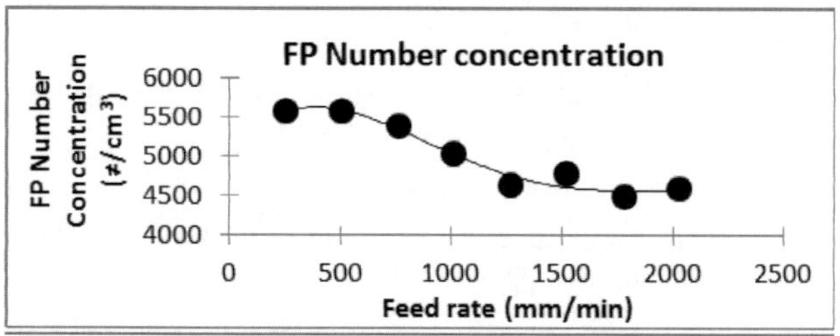

Fig. 18: Particle emission when polishing **black granite** as a function of the feed rate (Vs: 1000 rpm; Abrasive grid size: 60)

The effects of the polishing speed on FP number concentration and mass concentration are displayed in Figs 22 and 23. For black granite, there is a critical speed of about 1500 rpm at which the emission of the fine particle is high, while at lower speeds, the emission increases only slightly with the polishing speed. This evidence of this critical speed was already noticed during machining of metals by Songmene *et al.* [22]. Switching the speed from 1500 rpm to about 750 rpm led to a reduction of particle number concentration by about 71% (Fig. 22).

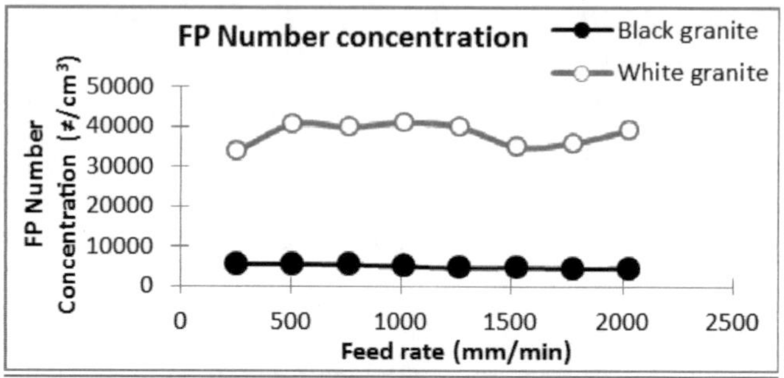

Fig. 19: Evolution of Fine particle number concentration as a function of the feed rate (Vs: 1000 rpm; Abrasive grid size: 60)

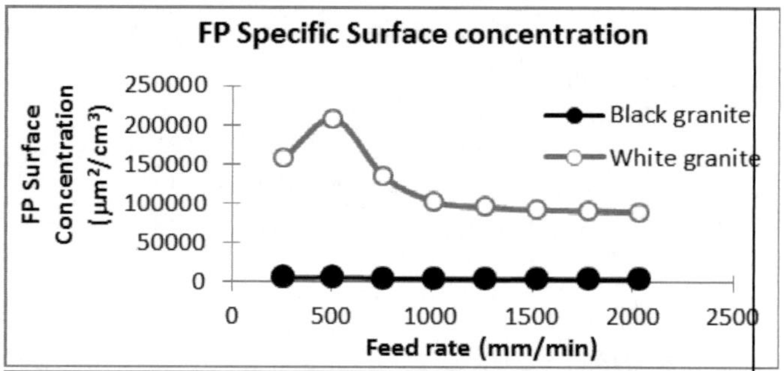

Fig. 20: Evolution of Fine particle specific surface concentration as a function of the feed rate (Vs: 1000 rpm; Abrasive grid size: 60)

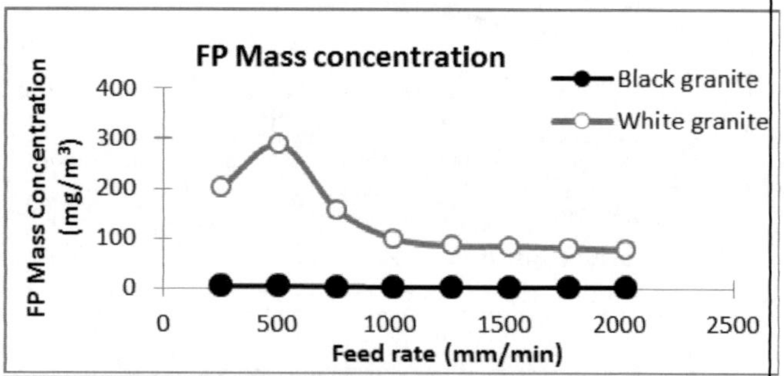

Fig. 21 Evolution of fine particle Mass concentration as a function of the feed rate or travel speed (Vs: 1000 rpm; Abrasive grid size: 60)

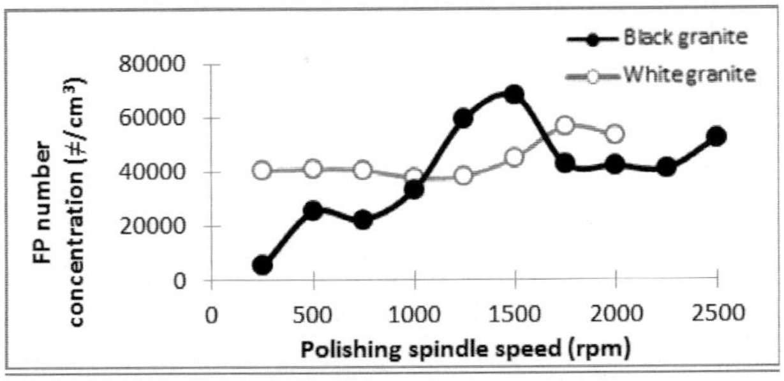

Fig. 22 Effects of polishing speed on fine particle number concentration (Vt: 508 mm/min; Abrasive grid size: 60)

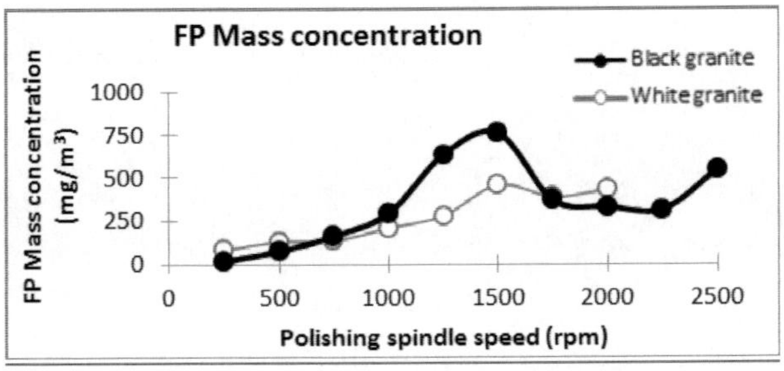

Fig. 23 Effects of polishing speed on FP **mass concentration** during granite polishing (Vt: 508 mm/min; Abrasive grid size: 60)

4.4 Ultrafine particles (UFP) emission

Ultrafine particle (UFP) emission was sampled using Scanning Mobility Particle Sizer (SMPS) capable of sampling particles of mobility diameters ranging from 7 to 300 nm. The effects of the feed rates on ultrafine particle emission are displayed in Figs. 24-27. It appears that the use of high feed rates is beneficial from the UFP reduction point of view, in addition to improving the productivity. The UFP number concentration reduction was about 84% when using a high feed rate as compared to the worst case (feed rate of 508 mm/min), Fig. 24.

The effects of the polishing spindle speed on UFP emission are displayed in Figs. 27-29. From these graphs, it comes that the use of low spindle speed is beneficial in reducing the UFP emission. As for UF particle, the speed of about 1500 rpm is still critical as the UFP concentrations are high at this speed. When a low speed of about 1000 rpm was used, the UFP number reduction reached 90% as compared to result obtained at the critical speed (1500 rpm).

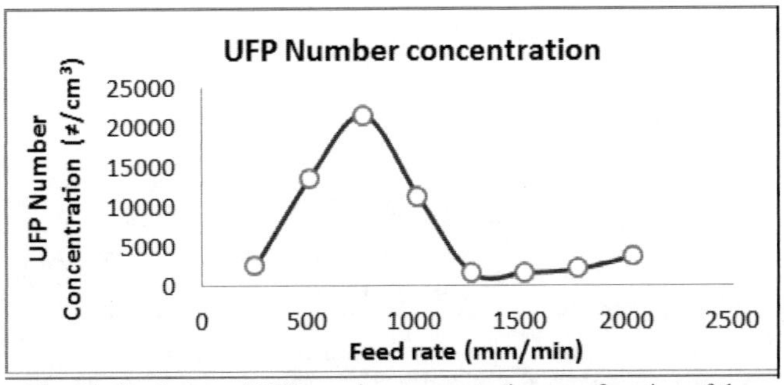

Fig. 24: Evolution of UFP number concentration as a function of the feed rate (Vs: 1000 rpm; Abrasive grid size: 60; white granite)

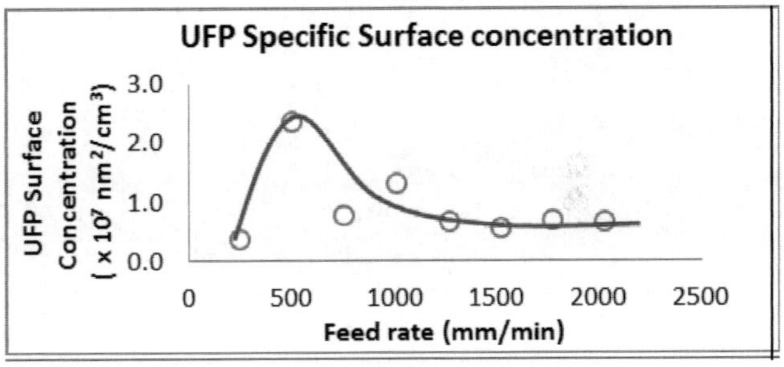

Fig. 25 UFP Surface concentration as a function of the feed rate (Vs: 1000 rpm; Abrasive grid size: 60; white granite)

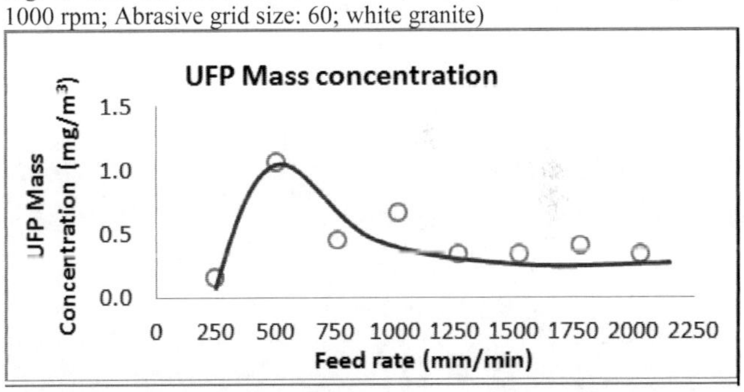

Fig. 26: Evolution of UFP Mass concentration as a function of the feed rate (Vs: 1000 rpm; Abrasive grid size: 60; white granite)

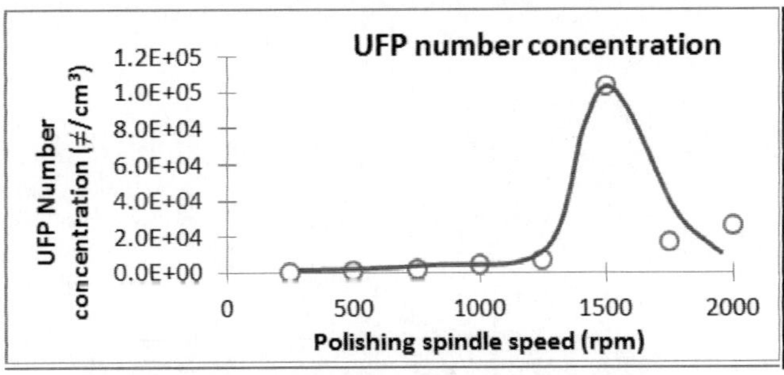

Fig. 27: UFP Number concentration as a function of polishing speed (Vt: 508 mm/min; Abrasive grid size: 60; white granite)

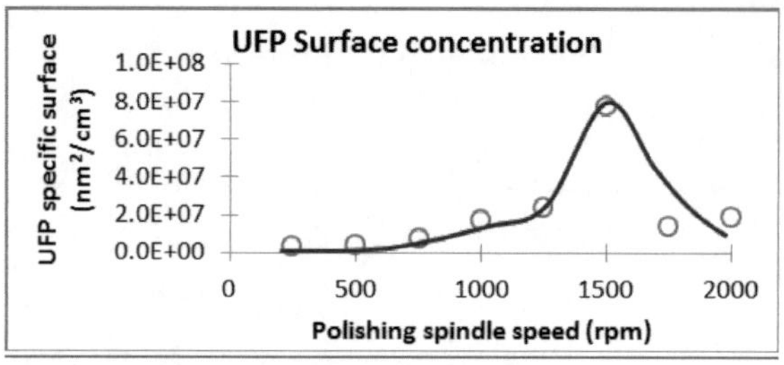

Fig. 28: UFP Surface concentration as a function of polishing speed (Vt: 508 mm/min; Abrasive grid size: 60; white granite,)

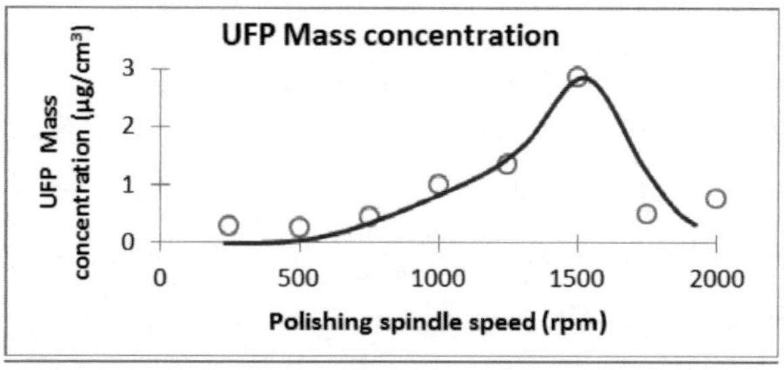

Fig. 29: UFP Mass concentration as a function of polishing speed (Vt: 508 mm/min; Abrasive grid size: 60 ; White granite,)

5 Conclusions

The polishing of granite was investigated in this article. It was found that:

- Rough polishing emitted more particles (fine and ultrafine) than finishing operations.
- Fine particle emission is controlled by the feed rate and the polishing speed while for ultrafine particles the feed rate appeared to be the parameter controlling the most the ultrafine particle emission.
- The polishing process can be engineered by selecting appropriate feed rates and polishing speeds so as to reduce the particle emission (PUF and UFP) and improve the part surface finish. The use of high feed rates led to limited emission of both FP and UFP. As far as the polishing speed is concerned, it was found that to limit the emission of FP and UFP a speed about 1000 rpm or lower should be used.
- In general, the reduction of particle number concentrations when varying the feed rate or the polishing speed was very effective for ultrafine particle. This particle number concentration was about 84% to 90% for ultrafine particles and 22% to 74% for fine particles, depending whether the feed rate or the polishing speed was varied.

5. Acknowledgment

This research work is part of a global Project on polishing granite (REF 2010-0047) funded by IRSST, Montreal, Canada. The authors also acknowledge A. Lacroix granit (Saint-Boniface, Qc, Canada) for donating granite samples and IOS Services Géoscientifiques (Chicoutimie, Canada) for performing SEM and petrographic analysis on granites samples used in this work.

References

1. NIOSH [2016]. Health hazard evaluation report: evaluation of crystalline silica exposure during fabrication of natural & engineered stone countertops. By Zwack LM, Victory KR, Brueck SE, Qi C. Cincinnati, OH: US Dept. of Health and Human Services, Centers for Disease Control and Prevention, National Institute for Occupational Safety & Health, NIOSH HHNE Report No. 2014-0215-3250.
2. OSHA (Occupational Safety & Health Administration), 2016, OSHA's Final Rule to Protect Workers from Exposure to Respirable Cystalline Silica- http:\\www.osha.gov/silica: Consulted oct. 5, 2016.
3. Kramer, M., Blanc, P., Fireman, E., Amital, A., Guber, A., Rhahman., N., 2012, Artificial Stone Silicosis. Disease Resurgence Among Artificial Stone Workers. Chest, 142(2), pages 419-424.
4. Margaret L. Phillips, David L. Johnson & Andrew C. Johnson (2013), Determinants of Respirable Silica Exposure in Stone Countertop Fabrication: A Preliminary Study; J. Occup. Environ. Hyg. 10, Iss. 7, 2013: 368-373.
5. Phillips, M.L. & Johnson, A.C. 2012, Prevalence of Dry Methods in Granite Countertop Fabrication in Oklahoma. J Occup Environ Hyg, 9, pages 437-442.
6. Marble Institute of America, 2008, Silicosis: An Industry Guide to Awareness and Prevention. Cleveland, OH: Marble Institute of America.
7. Trahan, C.; O'Connor, D. et Betit, E.; (2017) Understanding & Implementing the New Construction Silica Standard 20160519 1800 1 3; web seminar, The Center for construction research and training, https://www.youtube.com/watch?v=RgCO9SLhOjM&t=1s; consulted: 22 oct. 2017.
8. Ricaud, M., O. Witschger. 2012. Les nanomatériaux. Définitions, risques toxicologiques, caractérisation de l'exposition professionnelle et mesures de prévention. ED 6050: INRS, 48 p.
9. Ahmad, I., Khan, M.I. and Patil, G. (2011) Nanotoxicity of occupational dust generated in granite stone saw mill. Int. Conf. Nanoscience, Tech. & Soc. Impl., Bhubaneswar, 8-10 Dec. 2011.
10. OSHA (2002), Crystalline Silica exposure health hazard information for general industry employees. https://www.osha.gov/Publications/osha3176.html, vu: oct. 2017.
11. OSHA/ NIOSH, Occupational Safety and Health Administration/National Institute for Occupational Safety and Health, Hazard alert, 2015, Worker exposure to silica during countertop manufacturing, finishing, and installation, [online] https://www.cdc.gov/niosh/docs/2015-106/pdfs/2015-106.pdf.
12. AIHA (2016), Respirable Crystalline Silica in the Workplace: New Occupational Safety and Health Administration (OSHA) Standards; by Scott D. Szymendera, Congressional Research Service report R4447; https://www.aiha.org/government-affairs/Documents/CRS%20Silica%20Report-04-16.pdf; consulted 27 oct. 2017
13. Saidi M. N., Songmene V., Kouam J. and Bahloul A (2015), Experimental investigation on fine particle emission during granite polishing process, Adv. Manuf. Tech. v81(is9-12): 2109-2121
14. Brouwer, D. (2010), Exposure to manufactured nanoparticles in different workplaces, Toxicology, 269 (2-3), 120-127.
15. T. Schneider, D. H. Brouwer, et al. (2011), Conceptual model for assessment of inhalation exposure to manufactured nanoparticles, J. Exposure Sc. & Env. Epidemiology 21, 450–463.
16. Kouam J.; Songmene, V.; Balhoul, A. (2013) Experimental investigation on PM2.5 particle emission during polishing of granite, Health, 5, 29-35.
17. V. Songmene, J. Kouam, A. Balhoul, (2018) Effect of minimum quantity lubrication (MQL) on fine and ultrafine particle emission and distribution during polishing of granite, Measurement, doi:https://doi.org/10.1016/j.measurement.2017.10.012
18. Yilmaz, N.G. (2016) Size analysis of the chips generated during abrasive machining of granite in relation to productivity and efficiency parameters, Particulate Sc. & Tech., 34:5, 593-601.
19. Songmene, V.; Khettabi, R.; Viens et al. (2015). Nanoparticle measurement, control and characterization Procedure applied to machining and mechanical friction, Rapport R-864.100. IRSST
20. Witschger O, Fabriès F (2005). Particules ultrafines et santé au travail. 1 - Caractéristiques et effets potentiels sur la santé. INRS 199: 21-35.
21. Djebara A., (2011), Métrologie des particules ultrafines d'usinage : Optimisation de la caractérisation et de la mesure, PhD thesis, ÉTS, Montréal, Qc, Canada, Oct. 2011.
22. Songmene, V., Balout, B. and Masounave, J. (2008) Clean machining: Experimental investigation on dust formation: Part I

and part II. Int. J. Environmental Conscious Machining (ECDM), 14, 1-33.

Traceable Mass Determination and Uncertainty Calculation

T. Fehling, F. Hilbrunner*, S. Mühlich, M. Schreiber

Sartorius Lab Instruments GmbH & Co. KG, Otto-Brenner-Straße 20, 37079 Goettingen, Germany

Received:

Abstract. Numerous basic conditions are specified for weights and their mass comparisons in the OIML R 111-1 International Recommendation for Weights and Precision Mass Standards.
Based on the maximum permissible errors for the nominal values of weights of different classes, this guideline also specifies the geometric shapes and material characteristics for these weights besides the requirements for performing and evaluating mass comparisons. For instance, these requirements include limits for magnetic properties, surface quality and density of the material used for weights.
As the majority of mass comparisons are performed under atmospheric conditions, weights experience buoyant force, depending on their volume and the air density, where such buoyancy is directed opposite to the downward force exerted by these weights. This systematic effect can be eliminated if the air density and the densities of the materials of the test and reference weights are known. In mass metrology, two methods are commonly used for highly accurate determination of air density. In the first method, the air density is determined by measuring weights of a known mass and calculating the significant density difference. The second method analytically defines air density as a function of various influence quantities based on an updated formula. Air density can be calculated if the temperature, barometric pressure and humidity as the key influence quantities are known. The uncertainties in measuring these climate data result in an air density specification that has a component of uncertainty. In order to determine the uncertainty of an air buoyancy correction, the densities of the test and reference weight materials and the uncertainties of these weights must also be known besides the air density and its uncertainty. Under these aspects, requirements can be placed on the uncertainty of climate data measurements and on the uncertainty of the densities of materials.

Keywords: combined uncertainty; maximum permissible error; air bouyancy correction

1 Introduction

All models of the Cubis series of mass comparators are standard-equipped with a module for measuring the ambient conditions of air temperature, barometric pressure and relative humidity in order to determine the air density. This module is located within the weighing chamber of mass comparators with a draft shield to determine the environmental conditions actually prevailing at the time of measurement. On Cubis mass comparators without a draft shield, the climate data module is attached on an external stand and/or holder so that the relevant ambient conditions are measured in this case as well.

Fig. 1. Cubis MCM2004 / Climate Data Module

The plug-in connector of this module permits easy removal for calibration at regular intervals. The calibration data and associated characteristic curves for correction are stored in the internal memory of the climate data module. As a result, synchronous and metrologically traceable climate data and their measurement uncertainties are available for mass comparisons.

* Correspondence: falko.hilbrunner@sartorius.com

The following standard uncertainties are specified for a calibrated climate module:

Temperature: $u_t = 0.15$ K, in measuring range $t = (18 \ldots 24)$°C

Pressure: $u_p = 1$ hPa, in measuring range p (800..1100) hPa

Humidity: $u_{hr} = 1$ %, in measuring range $hr = (30 \ldots 70)$ %

Therefore, this module enables exact determination of the air density synchronous to measurement of mass in order correct for errors resulting from air buoyancy in a mostly automatic way.

In addition, Cubis mass comparators have built-in application software for mass determination. This software guides the user in a clearly structured and exactly timed way throughout the individual steps of mass comparison. A record is automatically generated that shows all relevant information on mass comparison in addition to the result of this comparison. The mass comparator provides a complete uncertainty budget of each mass comparison performed, along with the associated climate data, besides showing the conventional mass of the test weight used.

The following describes the essential fundamentals for determining an uncertainty budget during calibration of weights, as well as the permissible uncertainty contributions of the climate data quantities to an air buoyancy correction. In this description, it is assumed that the conventional mass of the test weight and the uncertainty of the conventional mass are to be determined by calibration of a test weight to a reference weight of higher accuracy.

2 Determining the Uncertainty in Compliance with OIML R111-1

The expanded uncertainty of the conventional mass of a test weight $U(m_{ct})$ is yielded by the expansion factor, or coverage factor, k and the combined standard uncertainty $u_c(m_{ct})$ according to [1, Equation (abbreviated as "Eq.") C.6.5-3] as follows:

$$U(m_{ct}) = k \times u_c(m_{ct}) \tag{1}$$

In this equation, the coverage factor determines the confidence internal. As a rule, a confidence interval of 95% is used, which corresponds to a coverage factor of $k = 2$. The expanded uncertainty of each weight must satisfy the condition below (cf. [1, Eq. 5.2-1]):

$$U(m_{ct}) \leq \frac{1}{3} MPE \tag{2}$$

The maximum permissible errors, MPE, dependent on mass and weight class are indicated in [1, Table 1]. Based on the values of this table, the maximum permissible relative errors plotted in Fig. **1** were calculated for the different weight classes. The highest requirements are placed on weight class E1 for weights with a nominal mass m_0 greater than 100 g. The maximum permissible relative error for this class is as follows:

$$\frac{\text{MPE}}{m_0} = 0.5 \cdot 10^{-6} \tag{3}$$

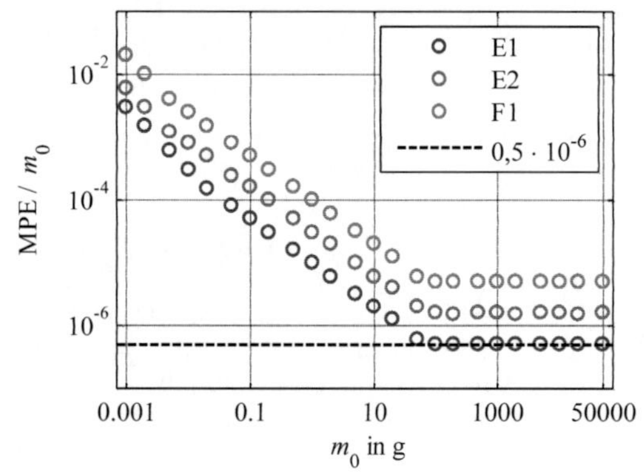

Fig. 1. MPE of OIML-compliant Weights from 1 mg to 50 kg

The combined standard uncertainty of the test weight is comprised of the standard uncertainty of the weighing process $u_w(\overline{\Delta m_c})$, the standard uncertainty of the reference weight $u(m_{cr})$, the standard uncertainty of air buoyancy correction u_b and the combined standard uncertainty of the weighing instrument u_{ba}. According to [1, Eq. C.6.5-1], the combined standard uncertainty is calculated using the following formula:

$$u_c(m_{ct}) = \sqrt{u_w^2(\overline{\Delta m_c}) + u^2(m_{cr}) + u_b^2 + u_{ba}^2} \tag{4}$$

The uncertainty of a weighing process is determined using the standard deviation of the individual mass comparisons $s(\Delta m_c)$ and the number of weighing cycles n [1, Eq. C.6.1-1]:

$$u_w(\overline{\Delta m_c}) = s(\Delta m_{ci})/\sqrt{n} \tag{5}$$

The standard uncertainty of a reference weight is yielded by the following [1, Eq. C.6.2-1]:

$$u(m_{cr}) = \sqrt{(U/k)^2 + u_{inst}^2(m_{cr})}, \tag{6}$$

where U represents the expanded uncertainty of the reference weight given on the calibration certificate and $u_{inst}(m_{cr})$ is the standard uncertainty due to instability of the reference weight. This can be determined based on the calibration history of the particular weight.

According to OIML R111-1, the standard uncertainty of air buoyancy correction is calculated as follows [1, Eq. C.6.3-1]:

$$u_b^2 = \left[m_{cr} \frac{\rho_r - \rho_t}{\rho_r \rho_t} u(\rho_a)\right]^2 + [m_{cr}(\rho_a - \rho_0)]^2 \frac{u^2(\rho_t)}{\rho_t^4} + m_{cr}^2(\rho_a - \rho_0)[(\rho_a - \rho_0) - 2(\rho_{al} - \rho_0)] \frac{u^2(\rho_r)}{\rho_r^4} \tag{7}$$

Assuming that $\rho_{al} = \rho_0$, [cf 2, Eq. 34.67], this equation is simplified to the following:

$$u_b = m_{cr}\sqrt{[(\rho_r - \rho_t)/(\rho_r \cdot \rho_t)\, u(\rho_a)]^2 + (\rho_a - \rho_0)^2(u(\rho_t)^2/\rho_t^4 + u(\rho_r)^2/\rho_r^4)} \tag{8}$$

Here, ρ_r and ρ_t are the densities of the materials of the reference weight and the test weight, respectively; ρ_a is the current air density, and ρ_0 is the reference value of the air density, where $\rho_0 = 1.2$ kg m^{-3}. Were the reference weight to be calibrated using the same weighing instrument to a reference weight of higher accuracy, there would be a correlation. In this case, the air density of the last calibration of the reference weight ρ_{al} would have to be considered in calculating the air buoyancy correction. As this is generally not the case, it is assumed that $\rho_{al} = \rho_0$ based on [2, Eq. 34.67].

The combined standard uncertainty of a balance is obtained according to [1, Eq. C.6.4-5]:

$$u_{\mathrm{ba}} = \sqrt{u_{\mathrm{s}}^2 + u_{\mathrm{d}}^2 + u_{\mathrm{E}}^2 + u_{\mathrm{ma}}^2} \tag{9}$$

This result is comprised of the standard uncertainty of the sensitivity of the mass comparator u_{s}, the standard uncertainty of the display resolution u_{d}, the standard uncertainty due to eccentricity (off-center loading error) u_{E} and the standard uncertainty due to magnetism (magnetic properties and influences) u_{ma}. The standard uncertainty of the sensitivity is obtained according to [1, Eq. C.6.4-1]:

$$u_{\mathrm{s}} = |\overline{\Delta m_{\mathrm{c}}}|\sqrt{u^2(m_{\mathrm{s}})/m_{\mathrm{s}}^2 + u^2(\Delta I_{\mathrm{s}})/\Delta I_{\mathrm{s}}^2} \tag{10}$$

A possible, universally valid simplification is given in [2, Sections 3.4.6.2–3.4.6.3], where

$$u_{\mathrm{s}} \approx |\overline{\Delta m_{\mathrm{c}}}|\, u(m_{\mathrm{s}})/m_{\mathrm{s}} \approx 5 \cdot 10^{-4} |\overline{\Delta m_{\mathrm{c}}}| \tag{11}$$

We have found that indicating the relative uncertainty as $5 \cdot 10^{-4}$ is a value that works in practice as it can be reliably obtained during regular calibration of the balance or mass comparator.

The standard uncertainty of the display resolution is obtained according to [1, Eq. C.6.4-2]:

$$u_{\mathrm{d}} = d\sqrt{2}/(2\sqrt{3}) \tag{12}$$

In conventional measurements, the standard uncertainty due to eccentricity is already included in the standard uncertainty of the weighing process $u_{\mathrm{w}}(\overline{\Delta m_{\mathrm{c}}})$. As a result, the following is yielded with reference to [1, Section C.6.4.4.1]:

$$u_{\mathrm{E}} = 0 \tag{13}$$

The uncertainty component due to magnetism can likewise be neglected to the extent that weights compliant to standards, such as OIML R111-1, are used (cf. [1, Section C.6.4.5]).

$$u_{\mathrm{ma}} = 0 \tag{14}$$

3 Determining the Air Density

The air density is an essential influence quantity in highly accurate mass comparisons. The reason is that systematic buoyancy effects can be corrected if the air density is known. To correct for the effect of air density, OIML R111-1 specifies the following equation [1, Eq. 10.2-1]:

$$m_{\mathrm{ct}} = m_{\mathrm{cr}}\,(1 + C) + \overline{\Delta m_{\mathrm{c}}} \tag{15}$$

with [1, Eq. 10.2-2]:

$$C = (\rho_{\mathrm{a}} - \rho_0)\frac{\rho_{\mathrm{t}} - \rho_{\mathrm{r}}}{\rho_{\mathrm{r}}\,\rho_{\mathrm{t}}} \tag{16}$$

However, the uncertainty of air density results in an uncertainty component in the difference in mass determined. The air density can be calculated according to the CIPM-2007 equation [3] from the climate quantities of temperature, pressure, humidity and from the molecular constituents of air, with the latter usually the average mole fraction of carbon dioxide in air. Assuming that the exact mole fraction of carbon dioxide is known and equal to $0.4 \cdot 10^{-3}$, we indicate a combined relative uncertainty (excluding the contributions of the climate quantities of temperature, barometric pressure and humidity) of $u_{\mathrm{F}}(\rho_{\mathrm{a}})/\rho_{\mathrm{a}} = 22 \cdot 10^{-6}$ for the CIPM-2007 equation. As an alternative to this CIPM-2007-formula, the air density can be calculated using a simplified equation [1, Eq. E.3-1].

$$\rho_{\mathrm{a}} = \frac{0.34848\,p - 0.009\,hr \cdot \exp(0.061\,t)}{273.15 + t}, \tag{17}$$

where hr is in % and t in °C

The relative standard uncertainty of this simplified formula is as follows (cf. [1, Section E.3]):

$$u_{\mathrm{F}}(\rho_{\mathrm{a}})/\rho_{\mathrm{a}} = 2 \cdot 10^{-4} \tag{18}$$

If we calculate the air density from the quantities of temperature, barometric pressure and humidity, the standard uncertainty of air density is obtained as follows: [1, Eq. C.6.3-3]:

$$u(\rho_{\mathrm{a}}) = \sqrt{u_{\mathrm{F}}^2 + (\partial\rho_{\mathrm{a}}/\partial p\ u_p)^2 + (\partial\rho_{\mathrm{a}}/\partial t\ u_t)^2 + (\partial\rho_{\mathrm{a}}/\partial hr\ u_{hr})^2} \tag{19}$$

The following values are given for the sensitivity coefficients under normal conditions (cf. [3, Section 2.2]):

$$\begin{gathered} \partial\rho_{\mathrm{a}}/\partial p \approx +1 \cdot 10^{-5}\ \mathrm{Pa}^{-1} \\ \partial\rho_{\mathrm{a}}/\partial t \approx -4 \cdot 10^{-3}\ \mathrm{K}^{-1} \\ \partial\rho_{\mathrm{a}}/\partial hr \approx -9 \cdot 10^{-3}, \text{ where } 0 \le hr \le 1 \end{gathered} \tag{20}$$

4 Budgeting the Uncertainty Components

It is necessary to budget the uncertainty components in order to generally verify whether a mass comparator is suitable for various accuracy classes. The following requirements have proven to be useful in practice:

$$u_{\mathrm{w}}(\overline{\Delta m_{\mathrm{c}}}) \le 4/5\, u_{\mathrm{c}}(m_{\mathrm{ct}}) \quad \text{and} \tag{21}$$

$$u(m_{\mathrm{cr}}) = u_{\mathrm{b}} = u_{\mathrm{ba}} \le 1/3\, u_{\mathrm{c}}(m_{\mathrm{ct}}) \tag{22}$$

If these individual requirements are met, the combined uncertainty of a mass comparator will always be lower than the uncertainty limit prescribed.

The required repeatability $s(\Delta m_c)$ of a mass comparator can likewise be derived from the required standard uncertainty of the weighing process $u_w(\overline{\Delta m_c})$.

$$u_w(\overline{\Delta m_c}) = s(\Delta m_c)/\sqrt{n} \leq 4/5\, u_c(m_{ct}) = 2/5\, U(m_{ct}) = 2/15\,\text{MPE; i.e.,} \quad s(\Delta m_c) \leq 2/15\,\text{MPE}\sqrt{n} \tag{23}$$

The required number of weighing cycles n is specified by OIML for the respective accuracy class of weights. Table 1 shows the minimum number of weighing cycles as a function of accuracy class along with the required repeatability for ABA cycles.

Table 1: Number of ABA weighing cycles for E and F class weights

OIML Class	E1	E2	F1	F2
n Cycles	5	3	2	1
$s_{max}(\Delta m_c) = 2/15\,\text{MPE}\sqrt{n}$	0.30MPE	0.23MPE	0.19MPE	0.13MPE

5 Uncertainty of Air Buoyancy Correction

In order to ensure that the total uncertainty budget for a mass comparison does not exceed the maximum permissible errors, a requirement has to be placed on the uncertainty of air buoyancy correction. With reference to the budget selected according to Equation (22), the uncertainty of an air buoyancy correction may be no more than 1/3 maximum of the permissible combined standard uncertainty of the conventional mass.

$$u_b \leq \frac{1}{3} u_c(m_{ct}) \tag{24}$$

Based on the equation above, it follows that the required uncertainty of air buoyancy correction in relation to the maximum permissible error (k = 2) is obtained by:

$$u_b \leq \frac{\text{MPE}}{3 \cdot 2 \cdot 3} = \frac{\text{MPE}}{18} \tag{25}$$

Therefore, the maximum permissible uncertainty of air buoyancy correction for class E1 weights with a nominal value greater than 100 g is yielded by:

$$u_b \leq \frac{0.5 \cdot 10^{-6}}{18} m_0 = 2.7\overline{7} \cdot 10^{-8}\, m_0 \tag{26}$$

The standard uncertainty of the air buoyancy correction is given in Equation (8), which can be broken down into three individual formulas.

$$u_b^2/{m_{cr}}^2 = u_{b1}^2 + u_{b2}^2 + u_{b3}^2 \quad \text{, where} \tag{27}$$

$$u_{b1} = \frac{\rho_r - \rho_t}{\rho_r\, \rho_t} u(\rho_a)$$

$$u_{b2} = (\rho_a - \rho_0) \frac{u(\rho_t)}{\rho_t^2}$$

$$u_{b3} = (\rho_a - \rho_0) \frac{u(\rho_r)}{\rho_r^2}$$

The term u_{b1} depends on the density difference between the reference weight and the test weight and on the uncertainty of the air density measured. Both terms u_{b2} and u_{b3} are each yielded by the product of the deviation of air density from the reference value $\rho_0 = 1.2\ \text{kg/m}^3$ and the uncertainty of the density of the test weight and of the reference weight.

Taking the problematic nature of this calculation into general consideration, we assumed that all three terms would yield the same uncertainty contribution to the air buoyancy correction; i.e.

$$u_{b1} = u_{b2} = u_{b3} = u_b/\sqrt{3} \leq 2.7\overline{7} \cdot 10^{-8}/\sqrt{3} = 1.6 \cdot 10^{-8} \tag{28}$$

This assumption enables us to derive the requirements on the uncertainty of the air density measured and, therefore, on the uncertainty of measurement of the climate quantities of temperature, barometric pressure and humidity.

6 Requirements on Climate Data Measurement

The starting point for considering these conditions is the requirement on term u_{b1}:

$$u_{b1} = (\rho_r - \rho_t)/(\rho_r\, \rho_t)\ u(\rho_a) \leq 1.6 \cdot 10^{-8} \tag{29}$$

Hence, the following is obtained as the required uncertainty of measurement for air density:

$$u(\rho_a) \leq 1.6 \cdot 10^{-8} \rho_r\, \rho_t/(\rho_r - \rho_t) \tag{30}$$

The permissible ranges for the density of the materials of weights are provided in [1, p. 17, Table 5]. For weights of accuracy class E1 with a nominal mass of at least 100 g, the density must be within the range of $7934\ \text{kg/m}^3 \leq \rho \leq 8067\ \text{kg/m}^3$. If we plug in such maximum permissible errors for measurement of the density into Equation (30), the following requirements will be yielded for the uncertainty of air density:

$$u(\rho_a) \leq 7.7 \cdot 10^{-3}\ \text{kg/m}^3 \tag{31}$$

and for the relative uncertainty:

$$u(\rho_a)/\rho_a \leq 7.7 \cdot 10^{-3}/\rho_a \leq 6.4 \cdot 10^{-3}, \text{ where } \rho_a = \rho_0 \tag{32}$$

The maximum permissible errors on measurement of the density are higher for weights smaller than 100 g. However, this error on measurement of the density is established as such: "... that a deviation of 10% from the specified air density (1.2 kg m^{-3}) does

not produce an error exceeding one-quarter of the absolute value of the maximum permissible error given in Table 1." [1, p. 17]. The ratio of the maximum permissible relative error of the weights to their maximum permissible errors on measurement of their density is therefore approximately constant.
The relative uncertainty of $2 \cdot 10^{-4}$ in simplified Equation (17) for calculating the air density is lower by a factor of 32 than the required uncertainty for air buoyancy correction. Hence, the uncertainty contribution of this equation is negligible. The relative uncertainty of air density, along with the corresponding sensitivities, is obtained using the three essential influence quantities for determining the air density, temperature, barometric pressure and relative humidity:

$$\frac{u^2(\rho_a)}{\rho_a^2} = (-4 \cdot 10^{-3}\,\mathrm{K}^{-1} \cdot u(t))^2 + (1 \cdot 10^{-5}\,\mathrm{Pa}^{-1} \cdot u(p))^2 + (-9 \cdot 10^{-3} \cdot u(h))^2 \leq (6.4 \cdot 10^{-3})^2 \tag{33}$$

Assuming that all three climate quantities have the same uncertainty contribution, the following is yielded:

$$u(\rho_a)/(\sqrt{3} \cdot \rho_a) = 4 \cdot 10^{-3}\,\mathrm{K}^{-1} \cdot u(t) \leq 6.4 \cdot 10^{-3}/\sqrt{3} = 3.7 \cdot 10^{-3}\text{, or} \tag{34}$$

$$\boldsymbol{u(t) \leq 0.92\ \mathrm{K}}$$

$$u(\rho_a)/(\sqrt{3} \cdot \rho_a) = 1 \cdot 10^{-5}\,\mathrm{Pa}^{-1} \cdot u(p) \leq 6.4 \cdot 10^{-3}/\sqrt{3} = 3.7 \cdot 10^{-3}\text{, or}$$

$$\boldsymbol{u(p) \leq 3.7\ \mathrm{hPa}}$$

$$u(\rho_a)/(\sqrt{3} \cdot \rho_a) = 9 \cdot 10^{-3} \cdot u(h) \leq 6.4 \cdot 10^{-3}/\sqrt{3} = 3.7 \cdot 10^{-3}\text{, or}$$

$$\boldsymbol{u(h) \leq 0.41}$$

The requirements calculated for the uncertainty of climate data measurement can be met using conventional climate data sensors. The uncertainty of the relative humidity of 0.41 means that the relative humidity may be measured using a standard uncertainty of 41%. Under this aspect, it would not be mandatory to measure the humidity.

7 Influence of Height above Sea Level

E1 laboratories place high requirements on air conditioning. Such requirements usually cover devices for controlling the temperature and relative humidity. However, the barometric pressure is not controlled. The average barometric pressure essentially depends on the height of a laboratory above sea level. Therefore, temperature and humidity play a subordinate role for determining the mean value of air density. Fig. indicates the correlation between air density and height above sea level [1, Eq. E.3-2].

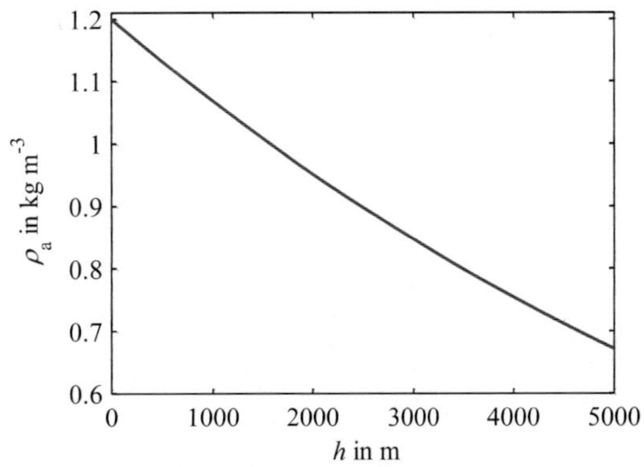

Fig. 3. Air Density as a Function of the Height above Sea Level

The deviation of the air density from the reference value of 1.2 kg/m³, in conjunction with the uncertainty of the density for the test weight and the reference weight, yields an uncertainty component for air buoyancy correction (Eq. 8). This correlation is clearly indicated by the two terms u_{b2} and u_{b3} in Equation (27). A maximum permissible error of $1.6 \cdot 10^{-8}$ is required for the relative uncertainty of air buoyancy correction according to Equation (28) for the three uncertainty components u_{b1}, u_{b2} and u_{b3}. For instance, if we plug in a value for the density uncertainty of $u(\rho_r) = u(\rho_t) = 5\ \mathrm{kg/m^3}$, (see also OIML R 111-1, Table B5 Estimated typical uncertainties on page 43), the curve depicted in Fig. **2** is yielded for the terms u_{b2} and u_{b3} as a function of the height above sea level. The dotted line represents the required maximum permissible error for the uncertainty of the air buoyancy correction.

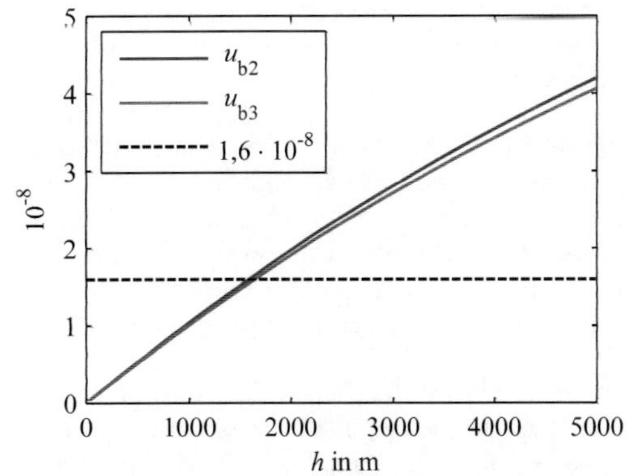

Fig. 2. Uncertainty Contribution u_{b2} and u_{b3} as a Function of the Height above Sea Level

It can be seen that independently of the uncertainty of climate data measurements, the required maximum permissible error for the uncertainty of air buoyancy correction is exceeded at an elevation of approximately 1,600 m (5,259 ft.). On the other hand, an unambiguous requirement can be derived for the uncertainty of test weight and reference weight density measurements as a function of height above sea level.

This correlation is shown in Fig. **3**. The calculation of this density is based on a density of 8,000 kg/m^3 for the material of a weight.

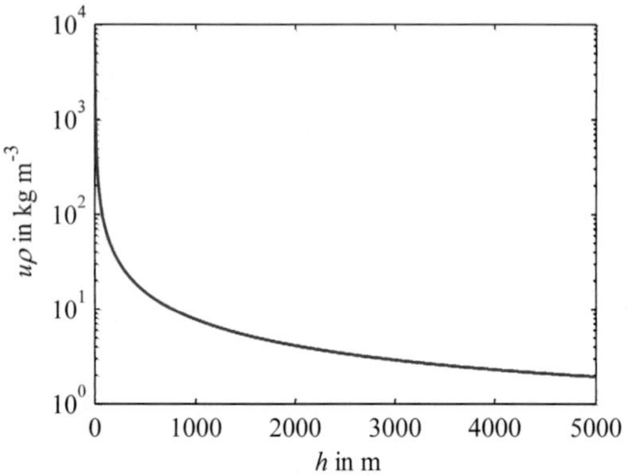

Fig. 3. Required Uncertainty of the Density of the Weights as a Function of the Height above Sea Level

To meet the requirement placed on the uncertainty of air buoyancy correction at higher elevations, the uncertainty of the density measurement for the test weight and the reference weight has to be reduced. For example, to fulfill the requirement on this uncertainty at elevations of up to 5,000 m (~16,404 ft.), the standard uncertainty of the density measurement for both the test weight and the reference weight must be less than 2 kg/m^3.

8 Conclusion

This article examines the essential aspects of calculating the uncertainty budget in compliance with international standards for the measurement of the conventional mass of weights. Special focus was given to the role of air density and its associated uncertainty. If air density is calculated from the climate quantities of air temperature, barometric pressure and relative humidity, uncertainty components will result from climate data measurements and from the equation for calculating the air density. By weighting the uncertainty components as prescribed, it is possible to specify the maximum permissible errors for the uncertainty of measurement of climate data. To determine the uncertainty of air buoyancy correction, the uncertainties of the density of the test weight and of the reference weight as well as the deviation of the air density from the reference value of 1.2 kg/m^{-3} must be considered besides the uncertainty of the air density itself. An uncertainty component of an air buoyancy correction will result from the height of a mass standards laboratory above sea level, regardless of the uncertainty of climate data measurements as the average air density essentially depends on elevation. On the other hand, the required uncertainties of the density measurements of test and reference weights can be derived as a function of elevation.
Cubis MC mass comparators permit exact determination of the conventional mass of a test weight, providing a detailed record of the associated uncertainty budget, which includes the air buoyancy correction and its uncertainty calculation under the limiting conditions described.

References

1 OIML R111-1, Weights of classes E1, E2, F1, F2, M1, M1–2, M2, M2–3 and M3, Part 1: Metrological and technical requirements, Edition 2004 (E)
2 Kochsiek, M., Gläser, M., "Comprehensive Mass Metrology", Wiley-VCH Verlag Berlin (2000), Sec.3.4, "Mass determination with balances" (Roman Schwartz)
3 Picard, A., Davis, R.S., Gläser, M., Fujii, K., "Revised formula for the density of moist air (CIPM-2007)", Metrologia 45 (2008) 149–155
4 GUM 1995, Guide to the expression of uncertainty in measurement, JCGM 100:2008, 2008

MCM2MCMC: Software for Bayesian uncertainty evaluation

Kavya Jagan and Alistair Forbes

Data Science Group, National Physical Laboratory

Abstract

The Guide to the Expression of Uncertainty in Measurement (GUM) and its Supplement 1 (GUMS1) use an input-output model based on the measurement equation. Both can be regarded as defining approximate, computational approaches to providing summary information about the same output distribution, one in terms estimates of the mean and standard deviation of the output distribution, the other in terms of a sample from the output distribution. The Monte Carlo method (MCM) described in GUMS1 can be regarded as a Bayesian posterior distribution corresponding to a particular type of prior distribution. Bayesian uncertainty evaluation works in terms of the observation equation and the posterior distribution is evaluated for a particular choice of the prior distribution. For systems with a nonlinear response, the posterior distribution describing the uncertainty associated with the measurand derived using a Bayesian approach will not be the same as the distribution specified by the GUM approach. However, the two distributions are linked in a straightforward manner and this enables a very simple Metropolis-Hastings independence Markov chain Monte Carlo algorithm to be implemented that uses the MCM sample generated by the GUMS1 approach as its basis.

In this paper, we describe a MATLAB function, MCM2MCMC, that implements the MCM-MCMC approach. We illustrate application of the software on a practical uncertainty evaluation problem. The software will be free to download from the NPL website.

1 Introduction

Uncertainty quantification using methods described in the GUM [1] or Supplement 1 to the GUM, GUMS1 [2], involve an input-output model, a measurement equation, that links the quantity of interest α to other variables about which we have information. For the case of an instrument response, we assume that an instrument response η can be written as

$$\eta = \phi(\alpha, \boldsymbol{\beta}), \tag{1}$$

where α is the quantity of interest, the measurand, and $\boldsymbol{\beta}$ are other influence factors for which a distribution $p(\boldsymbol{\beta})$ can be assigned. A response

$$\zeta = \eta + \epsilon$$

is observed where ϵ represents random effects associated with the measurement of η. The GUM approach converts the instrument response equation above to a measurement equation

$$\alpha = \psi(\eta, \boldsymbol{\beta}) \tag{2}$$

and uses the observed measurement ζ to assign a distribution $p(\eta)$ to η. Along with the distribution $p(\boldsymbol{\beta})$ for $\boldsymbol{\beta}$ and the measurement equation (2), the distribution for α is defined. Information about this distribution can be found by propagating the information about η and $\boldsymbol{\beta}$ through the measurement equation. The GUM uses the law of propagation of uncertainty (LPU) to propagate the means and standard deviations associated with the input distributions to estimate the mean and standard deviation of the output distribution for α. The GUMS1 procedure uses the Monte Carlo method for uncertainty propagation which involves sampling y_q and b_q, $q = 1, \ldots, M$, at random from $p(\eta)$ and $p(\boldsymbol{\beta})$. Then $a_q = \psi(y_q, \mathbf{b}_q)$ are draws from the distribution associated with α.

In a Bayesian context, the observation equation (1) is used directly and a distributional assumption is usually made on the realisations ζ of η, for instance

$$\zeta | \alpha, \boldsymbol{\beta} \sim \mathrm{N}(\eta, \sigma^2),$$

where $\eta = \phi(\alpha, \boldsymbol{\beta})$. This statement says that if we knew η, then we would expect observations ζ of η to be drawn from a Gaussian distribution centred on η with standard deviation σ.

The distribution $p(\zeta|\alpha, \boldsymbol{\beta})$ defines the likelihood of observing ζ given parameters α and $\boldsymbol{\beta}$. Bayes theorem is used to define the joint posterior distribution $p(\alpha, \boldsymbol{\beta}|\zeta)$ for α and $\boldsymbol{\beta}$ according to [9, 11]

$$p(\alpha, \boldsymbol{\beta}|\zeta) \propto p(\zeta|\alpha, \boldsymbol{\beta}) p(\alpha, \boldsymbol{\beta}), \tag{3}$$

where $p(\alpha, \boldsymbol{\beta})$ is a joint prior distribution assigned to α

and $\boldsymbol{\beta}$. Inferences about the parameter of interest, α are made from the marginal distribution

$$p(\alpha|\zeta) \propto \int p(\alpha, \boldsymbol{\beta}|\zeta) \mathrm{d}\boldsymbol{\beta}.$$

This distribution summarises the knowledge about α given that we have observed the measured response ζ.

Several papers, e.g., [3, 4, 5, 6, 7, 10], consider the relationship between the Monte Carlo method and Bayesian inference in the context of uncertainty evaluation. The analysis shows that from the point of view of Bayesian inference, the GUMS1 approach for propagating distributions through a measurement model imposes a particular type of prior distribution for the measurand and other influence quantities. For some models, the assigned prior distribution might not be plausible but if an alternative prior distribution is adopted then other, potentially more elaborate approaches, have to be employed.

Markov chain Monte Carlo [9] (MCMC) methods are widely-used algorithms for providing a sample a_q from a target distribution $p(a)$. However, their implementation is sometimes not straightforward as the user has to design the chain in such a way that it (a) converges quickly to the target distribution and (b) provides a sample that can be used efficiently to determine estimates of the distribution parameters such as its mean and standard deviation: if the sample has a high auto-correlation, then a large sample is required in order to determine useful estimates of the distribution parameters. As a result, for the sake of computational convenience, a GUMS1 approach is often adopted, sometimes in situations for which the underlying assumptions implicit in the GUMS1 approach are difficult to justify.

In this paper, we show that for many practical problems a sample produced using a GUMS1 approach can be used to define candidate steps in a particular type of MCMC algorithm, a Metropolis-Hastings independence chain. The algorithm gives users freedom to choose their preferred prior distribution for the measurand, rather than that implicitly assigned in the GUMS1 approach, thereby avoiding some of the problems that can arise when applying GUMS1 to certain types of measurement models. Many of the practical difficulties in implementing a Bayesian approach to uncertainty evaluation are largely eliminated by using this approach.

Section 2 describes the relationship between the posterior distributions for α obtained using the MCM method and Bayesian inference. Section 3 describes the Metropolis-Hastings algorithm used to convert MCM samples to MCMC samples from the Bayesian posterior distribution. A simple illustration based on single parameter model is provided in Section 4 and concluding remarks are presented in Section 5.

2 Relationship between measurement and observation equation approaches

The inferences about the system under study can be developed in terms of the parameters α and $\boldsymbol{\beta}$ or in terms of η and $\boldsymbol{\beta}$. The observation and measurements equations, (1) and (2), respectively, can be used to convert distributions $p(\alpha, \boldsymbol{\beta})$ to distributions $p(\eta, \boldsymbol{\beta})$ and vice versa using the change of variables formula in Appendix A.

From a Bayesian point of view, the essence of the GUM approach, in terms of the parameters η and $\boldsymbol{\beta}$, is the assignment of the distribution $p(\eta|\zeta)$. For example, if the likelihood $\zeta|\eta$ is modelled as $\zeta|\eta \sim N(\eta, \sigma^2)$ then $\eta|\zeta$ is assigned to be $\mathrm{N}(\zeta, \sigma^2)$. This accords with a Bayesian approach

$$p(\eta|\zeta) \propto p(\zeta|\eta)p(\eta).$$

if the prior for η is the improper prior $p(\eta) \propto 1$. A consequence of this prior is that the joint posterior distribution $p(\eta, \boldsymbol{\beta}|\zeta)$ is such that

$$p(\eta, \boldsymbol{\beta}|\zeta) = p(\eta|\zeta)p(\boldsymbol{\beta}).$$

In terms of the parameters α and $\boldsymbol{\beta}$, the GUM approach implicitly assigns the prior distribution

$$p_{\mathrm{MCM}}(\alpha, \boldsymbol{\beta}) \propto \left|\frac{\partial \phi}{\partial \alpha}(\alpha, \boldsymbol{\beta})\right| p(\boldsymbol{\beta}). \tag{4}$$

(The label MCM refers to the Monte Carlo method.) With this prior, the joint posterior distribution of α and $\boldsymbol{\beta}$ is given by

$$p_{\mathrm{MCM}}(\alpha, \boldsymbol{\beta}|\zeta) \propto p(\zeta|\alpha, \boldsymbol{\beta}) \left|\frac{\partial \phi}{\partial \alpha}(\alpha, \boldsymbol{\beta})\right| p(\boldsymbol{\beta}). \tag{5}$$

The main conceptual difficulty in the GUM approach interpreted as Bayesian inference is in the assignment of the prior in (4). The first issue is that the prior information for α depends on the prior information for $\boldsymbol{\beta}$,

$$p_{\mathrm{MCM}}(\alpha, \boldsymbol{\beta}) = p(\alpha|\boldsymbol{\beta})p(\boldsymbol{\beta}), \quad p(\alpha|\boldsymbol{\beta}) \propto \left|\frac{\partial \phi}{\partial \alpha}(\alpha, \boldsymbol{\beta})\right|.$$

The second issue is that the prior for α depends on the instrument response function ϕ, in other words, the prior information about a quantity depends on the type of instrument you plan to use to measure it. Both these features seem implausible. However, if ϕ is nearly linear in α, then we have $p_{\mathrm{MCM}}(\alpha, \boldsymbol{\beta}) \approx p(\boldsymbol{\beta})$ with a noninformative prior $p(\alpha) \propto 1$ for α.

Suppose we wish to perform Bayesian inference about α using the a prior distribution of the form $p(\alpha, \boldsymbol{\beta}) =$

$p(\alpha)p(\boldsymbol{\beta})$. Then the posterior distribution $p(\alpha, \boldsymbol{\beta}|\zeta)$ and from $p_{\rm MCM}(\alpha, \boldsymbol{\beta}|\zeta)$ are related through

$$\frac{p(\alpha, \boldsymbol{\beta}|\zeta)}{p_{\rm MCM}(\alpha, \boldsymbol{\beta}|\zeta)} \propto \frac{p(\alpha)}{\left|\frac{\partial \phi}{\partial \alpha}(\alpha, \boldsymbol{\beta})\right|}. \quad (6)$$

The relationship (6) leads to a particularly simple implementation of the Metropolis-Hastings independence chain algorithm [8, 9] in which draws from the approximating distribution $p_{\rm MCM}(\alpha, \boldsymbol{\beta}|\zeta)$ are converted to draws from $p(\alpha, \boldsymbol{\beta}|\zeta)$.

3 Metropolis-Hastings

Markov chain Monte Carlo methods (MCMC) [8, 9] are sequential, iterative schemes designed to produce samples from a probability distribution $p(\mathbf{a})$. They are constructed in such a way that sampled value at a particular iteration $\{\mathbf{a}_q\}$ only depends on the value $\mathbf{a}_{q-1}$ at the previous iteration. (They therefore satisfy the Markov property, hence their name.) The sampling scheme for generating the next element of the chain has to be designed in such a way that, eventually, the samples $\mathbf{a}_q$ represent samples from $p(\mathbf{a})$. One commonly used method to achieve this is the Metropolis-Hastings MCMC method.

Suppose we wish to sample $\{\mathbf{a}_q\}$ from a *target distribution* $p(\mathbf{a})$. Given a draw $\mathbf{a}_{q-1}$, a proposed draw $\mathbf{a}^*$ for the next member of the sequence is generated at random from a *jumping distribution* $p_0(\mathbf{a}^*|\mathbf{a}_{q-1})$. Then $\mathbf{a}_q$ is set to $\mathbf{a}^*$ with acceptance probability

$$P_q = \min\{1, r_q\}, \quad r_q = \frac{p(\mathbf{a}^*)p_0(\mathbf{a}_{q-1}|\mathbf{a}^*)}{p(\mathbf{a}_{q-1})p_0(\mathbf{a}^*|\mathbf{a}_{q-1})}. \quad (7)$$

Otherwise, $\mathbf{a}_q$ is set to $\mathbf{a}_{q-1}$. The simplest way to implement the acceptance step is to draw u_q from the uniform distribution $R(0, 1)$ and if $u_q < r_q$, set $\mathbf{a}_q = \mathbf{a}^*$, otherwise set $\mathbf{a}_q = \mathbf{a}_{q-1}$.

There are two common types of Metropolis-Hastings algorithms, random walk algorithms for which the $\mathbf{a}^* = \mathbf{a}_{q-1} + \mathbf{e}_q$ where $\mathbf{e}_q$ is a draw from a fixed distribution, e.g., a Gaussian

$$\mathbf{a}^*|\mathbf{a}_{q-1} \in {\rm N}(\mathbf{a}_{q-1}, V),$$

or an independence chain in which $\mathbf{a}^*$ itself is a draw from a fixed distribution $p_0(\mathbf{a})$ so that $p(\mathbf{a}^*|\mathbf{a}_{q-1}) = p_0(\mathbf{a}^*)$. For an independence chain, r_q in (7) is given by

$$r_q = \frac{p(\mathbf{a}^*)p_0(\mathbf{a}_{q-1})}{p(\mathbf{a}_{q-1})p_0(\mathbf{a}^*)} = \frac{p(\mathbf{a}^*)}{p_0(\mathbf{a}^*)}\frac{p_0(\mathbf{a}_{q-1})}{p(\mathbf{a}_{q-1})} \quad (8)$$

If p_0 is a good approximation to p, then this ratio is likely to be close to 1 so that the percentage of samples that are accepted is larger if the approximating distribution is closer to the target distribution. For a random walk chain, the sampling from the jumping distribution has to be done sequentially but for an independence chain it is possible to start with a sample $\{\mathbf{a}_q\}_{q=1}^M$ from the approximating distribution and then apply the accept-reject scheme sequentially. The scheme essentially samples from regions where p_0 has less probability mass than p at the expense of rejecting samples from regions where p_0 has more probability mass and in this way converts a sample from p_0 to a sample from p.

3.1 MCM-MCMC independence chain

It is seen that the calculation of r_q in (8) can expressed in terms of p/p_0. Equation (6) shows how the ratio of $p/p_{\rm MCM}$ can be evaluated in terms of the prior $p(\alpha)$ for α and the partial derivative of ϕ with respect to α. In particular, for a noninformative prior $p(\alpha) \propto 1$, the ratio only depends on the partial derivative. This observation is the key to converting a sample $\{(a_q, \mathbf{b}_q)\}_{q=1}^M$ generated using the Monte Carlo method of GUMS1 to a sample from the Bayesian posterior. All that is require to implement the scheme is to record

$$d_q = \frac{\partial \phi}{\partial \alpha}(a_q, \mathbf{b}_q),$$

as the MCM sample is being generated. NPL has developed software in MATLAB to perform these calculations and it will be made available to download for free from the NPL website. Sample code for the simplest case for $p(\alpha) \propto 1$ is presented in Appendix B.

4 Numerical example

This illustration involves the non-linear response model

$$\eta = \phi(\alpha, \boldsymbol{\beta}) = \beta_1 \exp(-\alpha) + \beta_2,$$

where $\zeta|\eta \sim {\rm N}(\eta, \sigma^2)$ and prior information about $\boldsymbol{\beta} = (\beta_1, \beta_2)^{\rm T}$ is of the form $\boldsymbol{\beta} \sim {\rm N}(\mathbf{b}, V_{\mathbf{b}})$. The corresponding measurement equation is

$$\alpha = -\log\left(\frac{\eta - \beta_2}{\beta_1}\right).$$

Also

$$\frac{\partial \phi}{\partial \alpha}(\alpha, \boldsymbol{\beta}) = -\beta_1 \exp(-\alpha).$$

and

$$p_{\rm MCM}(\alpha, \boldsymbol{\beta}) = |\beta_1 \exp(-\alpha)|p(\boldsymbol{\beta}). \quad (9)$$

Calculations were performed based on $\zeta = 0.92$, $b_1 = 5$, $b_2 = -5$, and

$$V_{\mathbf{b}} = \left[\begin{array}{cc} 0.5 & -0.1 \\ -0.1 & 0.2 \end{array}\right].$$

Given draws $y_q \in \mathrm{N}(\zeta, \sigma^2)$ and $\mathbf{b}_q \in \mathrm{N}(\mathbf{b}, V_\mathbf{b})$, $q = 1, \ldots, M$ we assign two arrays A_0 and D according to

$$\begin{aligned} A_0(q) &= a_q, \quad a_q = -\log((y_q - b_{2,q})/b_{1,q}), \\ D(q) &= |b_{1,q} \exp(-a_q)|\,. \end{aligned}$$

A_0 is the array of MCM samples from the distribution $p_{\mathrm{MCM}}(\alpha|\zeta)$ based on the GUMS1 approach propagating the distributions for η and $\boldsymbol{\beta}$ through the measurement equation. These samples were used in the Metropolis-Hastings independence chain algorithm to generate the array A of samples from the Bayesian posterior distribution using a non-informative prior for α as described in section 3. Figure 1 shows the distributions for $\alpha|\zeta$ obtained using both methods. The two distributions are similar but the distribution $p_{\mathrm{MCM}}(\alpha|\zeta)$ has more probability mass for smaller values of the α, reflecting the prior distribution in (9) implicitly assigned by the GUMS1 approach. Since the distribution $p_{\mathrm{MCM}}(\alpha, \boldsymbol{\beta}|\zeta)$ is reasonably close to the Bayesian distribution $p(\alpha, \boldsymbol{\beta}|\zeta)$, the acceptance percentage in the independence chain was reasonably high at 89%.

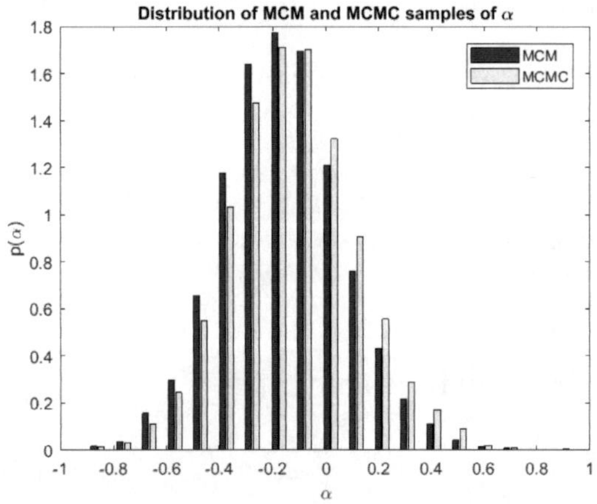

Figure 1: Normalised histograms of MCM (left) and MCMC (right) samples for α

5 Conclusion

This paper has been concerned with the relationship between the Monte Carlo method (MCM) of GUM Supplement 1 for evaluating measurement uncertainty and Bayesian approaches to uncertainty evaluation for an instrument response model. For nonlinear responses both approaches lead to nonstandard distributions associated with the measurand. Sampling methods can be used to determine samples from these distributions from which summary information such as means, standard deviations and coverage intervals can be estimated. A sampling scheme for the Monte Carlo method is generally straightforward to implement while for the Bayesian approach more sophisticated Markov chain methods are usually required. However, the relationship between MCM and Bayesian inference for the instrument response model allows for a particularly simple implementation of a Markov chain Monte Carlo implementation. We have described this implementation an illustrated its behaviour on a nonlinear model. MATLAB software that performs these calculations is presented in Appendix B. Software that performs more general MCM-MCMC calculations has been developed at NPL and will be available to download for free from the NPL website.

Acknowledgement

This work was supported by the UK's National Measurement System programme for Data Science.

A Change of variables formula

Suppose $\mathbf{x} = g(\mathbf{y})$ represents a change of variables with inverse $\mathbf{y} = f(\mathbf{x})$. If $\mathbf{y}$ has PDF $p_Y(\mathbf{y})$ then the PDF $p_X(\mathbf{x})$ associated with $\mathbf{x}$ is given by

$$p_X(\mathbf{x}) = |J_f(\mathbf{x})| p_Y(f(\mathbf{x})), \quad J_f(i,j) = \frac{\partial f_i}{\partial x_j},$$

if $\mathbf{x}$ is in the range of g and is zero otherwise.

B Software

MATLAB software that performs MCM-MCMC calculations as described in section 3 is provided below. It is assumed that MCM sampling scheme has been implement that determines $\{(a_q, \mathbf{b}_q)\}$ and

$$d_q = \frac{\partial \phi}{\partial \alpha}(a_q, \mathbf{b}_q).$$

The input arrays `A0` and `D` store a_q and $|d_q|$, respectively. The output array `A` is the MCMC sample and `aP` is the acceptance percentage for the independence chain.

```
function [A,aP] = mcm2mcmc1(A0,D)
% A0(M,1)            A0(q) = aq
%  D(M,1)             D(q) = abs(dq)
%
% A(M,1)             Samples from the
%                    posterior distribution for alpha

% Chain length
  M = length(A0);
% Initialise arrays
```

```
  A = zeros(M,1);
  I = zeros(M,1);
% The first MCM sample is accepted
  A(1) = A0(1);
  I(1) = 1;
  dq = D(1);
% Determine whether each element of A0 is
% accepted or rejected
  for q = 2:M
    % Acceptance ratio
      ds = D(q);
      rq = dq/ds;
      uq = rand(1,1);
    % Acceptance index
      I(q) = uq < rq;
    % Accept or replicate
      if I(q) == 1
          A(q) = A0(q);
          dq = ds;
      elseif I(q) == 0
          A(q) = A(q-1);
      end
  end % for loop
% Acceptance percentage
  aP = 100*sum(I)/M;
end % function
```

References

[1] BIPM, IEC, IFCC, ILAC, ISO, IUPAC, IUPAP, and OIML. Evaluation of measurement data — Guide to the expression of uncertainty in measurement. Joint Committee for Guides in Metrology, JCGM 100:2008.

[2] BIPM, IEC, IFCC, ILAC, ISO, IUPAC, IUPAP, and OIML. Evaluation of measurement data — Supplement 1 to the "Guide to the expression of uncertainty in measurement" — Propagation of distributions using a Monte Carlo method. Joint Committee for Guides in Metrology, JCGM 101:2008.

[3] M. G. Cox, G. B. Rossi, P. M. Harris, and A. Forbes. Reply to a comment on 'a probabilistic approach to the analysis of measurement processes'. *Metrologia*, 46:L9–L10, 2009.

[4] C. Elster, W. Wöger, and M. G. Cox. Draft GUM supplement 1 and Bayesian analysis. *Metrologia*, 44:L31–L32, 2007.

[5] A. B. Forbes. Approaches to evaluating measurement uncertainty. *International Journal of Metrology and Quality Engineering*, 3:71–77, 2012. DOI: 10.1051/ijmqe/2012017.

[6] A. B. Forbes. An MCMC algorithm based on GUM supplement 1 for uncertainty evaluation. *Measurement*, 45:1188–1199, 2012.

[7] A. B. Forbes and J. A. Sousa. The GUM, Bayesian inference and the observation and measurement equations. *Measurement*, 44:1422–1435, 2011.

[8] D. Gamerman. *Markov chain Monte Carlo: Stochastic Simulation for Bayesian inference*. Taylor & Francis, New York, 1997.

[9] A. Gelman, J. B. Carlin, H. S. Stern, D. B. Dunson, A. Vehtari, and D. B. Rubin. *Bayesian Data Analysis*. Chapman & Hall/CRC, Boca Raton, Fl., third edition, 2014.

[10] I. Lira and D. Grientschnig. Equivalence of alternative Bayesian procedures for evaluating measurement uncertainty. *Metrologia*, 47:334–336, 2010.

[11] D. S. Sivia. *Data Analysis: a Bayesian Tutorial*. Clarendon Press, Oxford, 1996.

Experimental study of the pyroelectric response of flexible PVDF film as function of air flow velocity generated in wind tunnel

M.H. RAOUADI[1,2], W. TOUAYAR[1]

[1]*Materials, Measurements and Applications Research Laboratory, Dépt. de Génie Physique et Instrumentation, National Institute of Applied Sciences and Technology, INSAT, University of Carthage BP676, 1080 Tunis Cedex, Tunisia*
[2]*LMEEVED Laboratory. CRTEn, Technopole of Borj Cedria BP. 95 2050 Hammam'Lif Tunisia*

Received:

Abstract. This paper presents the results of an experimental investigation on the response of the flexible PVDF pyroelectric film to a generated air flow in wind tunnel with open test section. The used wind tunnel has a DAkkS calibrated flow calculation system for the air flow velocity measurements and a velocity interval from 1m/s to 25m/s. The characteristic of the air flow are well controlled and presents an uncertainty budget below 1.4% in the open test section of the wind tunnel. A study of the response of the sensor as a function of air flow velocity was carried out. The response of the sensor in the airflow is also presented in relation with Reynolds number Re and the Nusselt number Nu. The Reynolds numbers examined in this study range from 3300 to 83000 and the Nusselt number range from 25 to 173. The experimental results show that the flexible PVDF film gives a response proportional to the rate of Re and Nu which projects its possible exploitation in wind velocity measurement (anemometry).

Keywords: Wind tunnel, Pyroelectric PVDF film, wind velocity mesearement.

1 Introduction

The air flow velocity measurement is very important in many applications such as the meteorology and environment study, the control of wind velocity produced by the turbine and gas leak detection. The most used instrumentations applied to study and characterize the air flow velocity (Anemometry) in small devices, wind tunnel laboratory or industrial applications are the Laser Doppler Anemometry LDA, the Ultrasonic Anemometer, Hot-Wires Film, the Pitot static Tube and the cup anemometer. LDA and Ultra-sonic anemometer can provide a high spatial and time resolution and high accuracy measurements but are difficult to apply in many environments and it consumes a lot of resources. The problems of the Hot-Wires Films anemometers are the internal noise of the probe, the effect of fluid temperature change, and the frequent breakage of the fragile filament caused by shock or vibration of the probe. The Pitot Static Tube and the cup anemometer are widely used and regarded as ones of the most economic and robust flow instruments for air velocity measurements in the engineering applications. But the use of Pitot tube and the cup anemometer still have some problems like measuring in unsteady air flow or wind with particle containing [1-6].

Thus, the challenge of designing an accurate, robust and inexpensive anemometer is still relevant. Some previous work developed the pyroelectric anemometry (PA) as a new method to measure the gas flow velocity. In fact, the work of H. Rahmanami described the theory of the relation between the heat transfer of the convective flow and the pyroelectricity. The application presented of the PA was the Microchannel gas detection in low velocity (max 0.1 m/s) using the LiTaO3 as a pyroelectric material and a heated electrode. The experimentation used to characterize the response of the PA sensor was basic. They used a gas flow rate which was adjusted and measured by a commercial flow controller and a lock-in amplifier to measure the response of the sensor [7-10].

We are inspired by the work cited above to develop and to test a new design of the PA with new pyroelectric material based on flexible PVDF film , very used generally in dynamic infrared pyroelectric detectors for its flexibility, very low cost, non-toxicity for the environment and high sensitivity and responsivity [11-14]. Comparing with these previous works, the proposed experimental method offers much larger measuring range of the wind velocity. In fact the experiment was performed inside a calibrated wind tunnel, which was recently renewed and adapted for all kind of anemometry measurements in accordance with ISO 17025 standards. The air flow velocity is measured with a DAkkS calibrated Pitot static tube anemometer from 1 to 25m/s.

We first present, in section 2, the theoretical mechanism describing the convection heat exchange in the vicinity of the interface fluid flow/solid. The detailed of the new experimentation based on the study of the response of flexible PVDF pyroelectric film as function of air flow velocity in wind tunnel will be presented in section 3. Finely we discuss, in section 4, the results of the response of the sensor.

2 Theoretical background

The pyroelectric effect consists in a generation of the spontaneous polarization (Ps) when its temperature (T) changes, p is called the pyroelectric coefficient:

$$dP_s = p dT \qquad (1)$$

$$\text{with } p = \frac{dP_s}{dT} \qquad (2)$$

Considering a pyroelectric material including charge collection electrodes then the pyroelectric current can be written as:

$$I_p = ps\frac{dT}{dt} \qquad (3)$$

Whereby, Ip is the pyroelectric current, p the total pyroelectric coefficient of the material, S the active surface area and dT/dt the time derivative of the temperature.

In the other hand, heat exchange by convection can be used to create temperature fluctuation and to generate the pyroelectric current. In fact, when a fluid flows over a pyroelectric material, convective heat flow affect its thermal equilibrium and consequently induces a change in the charge state of the pyroelectric material.

Generally, the heat flow exchanges δQ/dt (in Watts) between a fluid and a solid, by convection mode, is described by the Newton equation given by:

$$\delta Q/dt = h.(Tp - T\infty).dS \qquad (4)$$

Where h is the coefficient of exchange in Watts/m2K, Tp- T∞ (in K) is the Temperature difference between solid and fluid and dS is the surface exchange (m^2).

The direct estimation of the heat exchange δQ from equation (4) is difficult because h is a function of several variables like the fluid characteristics, the nature of the flow, the temperature and the shape of the exchange surface. That is why, for the heat exchange study by convection, we use the Reynolds number (Re) and estimation of Nusselt number (Nu) [15]. The Reynolds number allows us to determine the fluid flow characteristics and the Nusselt number estimates the importance of convection phenomena at the solid fluid interface. We use the Hilpert correlation presented in equation (6) to evaluate the evolution of the Nu as function of Re and also the Prandlt number Pr.

$$Re = \frac{U_\infty . d}{\nu} \qquad (5)$$

$$N_u = C.Re^m.Pr^{0,35} \qquad (6)$$

Where φ the heat flux density (W.m−2), λ is the thermal conductivity of the solid (W.m−1.K−1), d is the dimension of the solid (m), U_∞ is the velocity of the fluid flow (m.s-1) α is the thermal diffusivity of the fluid (m2.s-1) and ν is the kinematic viscosity of the fluid (m2.s-1). C and m are two constant which vary according to the defined interval of Re [15].

From the characteristics of the fluid flow in forced convection in the vicinity of the solid fluid interface, it is well known that when Re>>1, the coefficient of the heat exchange Nu between surface and fluid flow increases significantly. Considering our practical case in which the air flow velocity varies from 1m/s to 25m/s, Re>>1 and consequently a significant heat exchange can occur in the interface of the wind flow/sensor, allowing an exploitable responses of the pyroelectric film.

3 Experimental setup

3.1- Wind Tunnel description

The air flow is generated in a closed circuit wind tunnel with open test section (figure 1) intended for the calibration of all kind of anemometers in the range from 1 to 25m/s. It is equipped with 22 KW 3 phases motor connected to the blower. The plan of the open test section is 1m2 and its length is 1.3m.

The wind velocity is controlled by a computer through an interface known as the flux calculation system named (WESTIBOX) connected to the frequency converter. A calibrated Pitot static tube is connected to the WESTIBOX to control and to measure the air flow velocity; also a calibrated hygrometer is placed inside the wind tunnel and before the open test section and connected to the WESTIBOX to measure the temperature and the humidity of the coming air flow (figure 2). This system is developed by the company Westenberg-Engineering (Cologne, Germany) and calibrated with the international DAkkS standard. A pressure balancer is located between the collector and the divergent to evacuate the overflows and maintaining a constant pressure in the measuring section. The open test section is located in a closed box with controlled temperature and humidity (figure 3).

Fig.1. Architecture of the wind tunnel

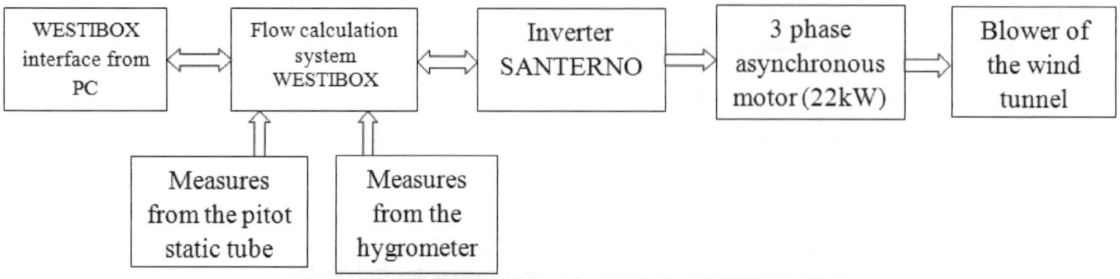

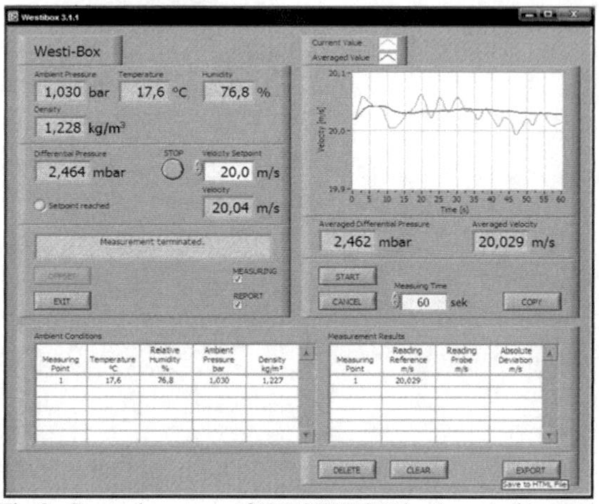

Fig.2. Control system of WESTIBOX in the wind tunnel

3.2 Measurements

We performed the measurements with a configuration of the flexible pyroelectric film as follows: the first electrode of the flexible PVDF film is in contact with the incident fluid flow and the second electrode is in contact with the substrate (figure 4). We use a substrate with a very high thermal conductivity to increase further the heat transfer by convection between the PVDF film and the wind flow and so amplify the pyroelectric current response. For the response characterization of the flexible PVDF pyroelectric film, we placed the sensor in the open test section of the wind tunnel.

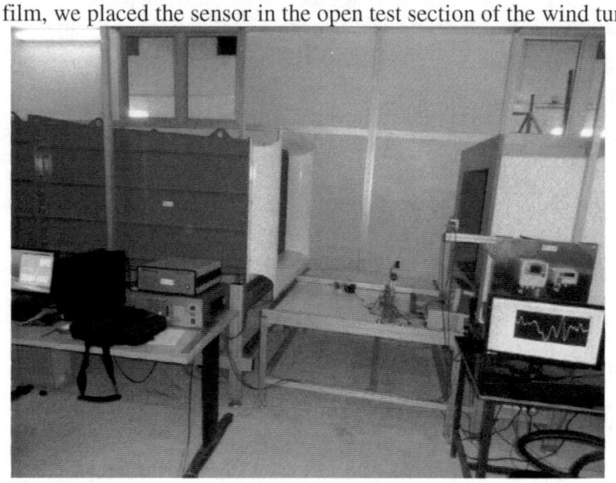

Fig.3. Open test section of the wind tunnel in controlled environment

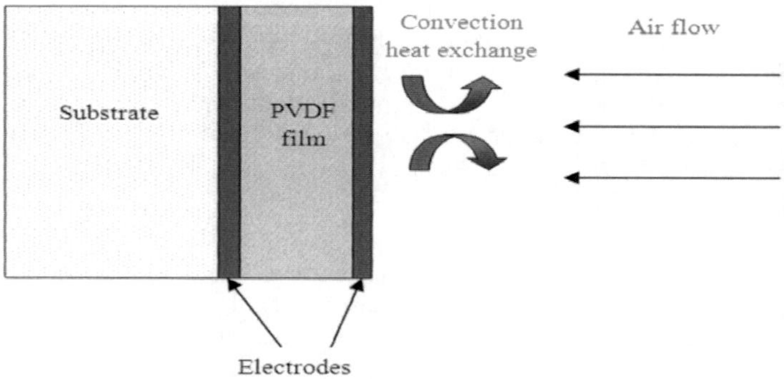

Fig.4. Proposed design of the PA in this work

To study the signal of our designed sensor, we used the oscilloscope MSO2024 and an amplification circuit. The PA signal is amplified and displayed in the oscilloscope and in the PC with the LABVIEW interface (figure 5). In the amplification system we have added to the current-voltage amplification a circuit Band pass filter in the input. This filter is placed in the amplifier circuit to eliminate the electromagnetic noise produced by the three-phase asynchronous motor of the blower and by the frequency inverter which controls the motor.

The response of the flexible PVDF pyroelectric film to a chopped Laser radiation has been previously studied (figure 6) [16].

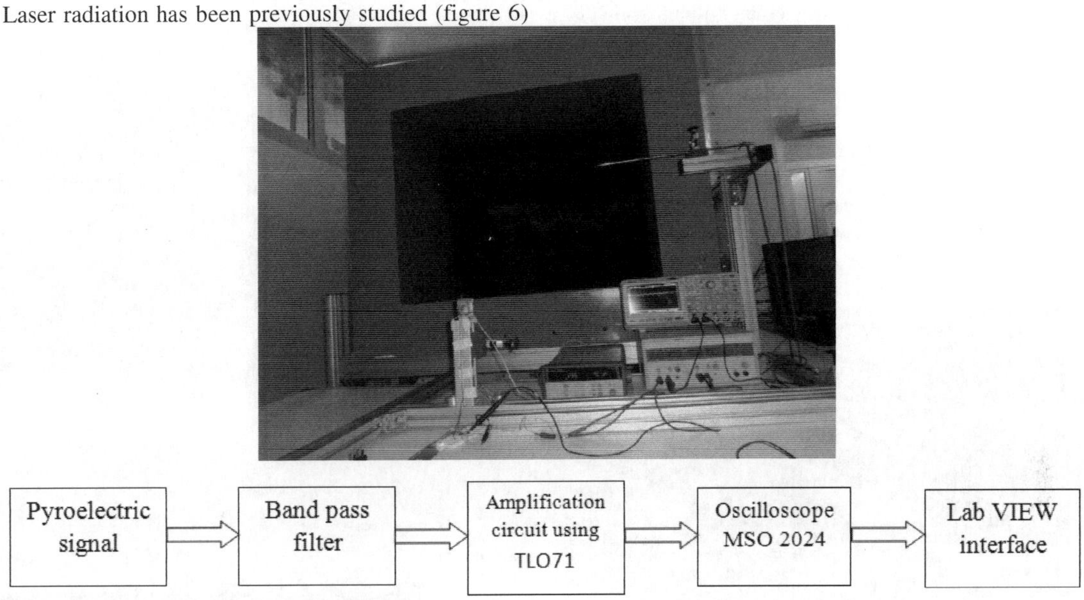

Fig.5. Used system to measure and visualize the pyroelectric signal

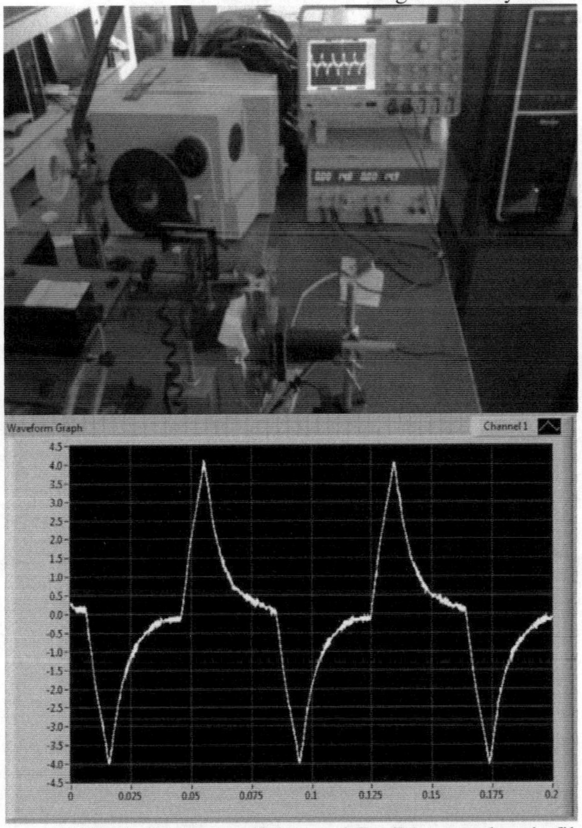

Fig.6. Response of the used flexible pyroelectric film studied using a conventional measuring system. It shows the regular signal of the response of the sensor [16].

4 Results and discussions

The system studied is constituted by an incident air flow with velocity varying in the interval [1-25] m/s and a pyroelectric PVDF film having the shape of a disc of diameter 3cm. Starting from these geometric considerations, we, firstly calculate the Reynolds number Re and secondly use equation (5), whose conditions of establishment are quite similar to our experience, to calculate the Nusselt number Nu. From calculated values of Re (3.103 <Re <8.104) and Nu (25<Nu<173), it appears that a significant heat exchange by convection can occurs with vortices and turbulent flow apparition near the interface sensor/air flow as signaled in B. S. Petukhov study [17]. In this case, velocity, temperature, and other physical properties of the fluid flow change continuously in time and at every point of a turbulent flow. These changes induce irregular fluctuations and are generally controlled by two mechanisms: molecular and convective. The first mechanism results in the appearance of viscous stresses proportional to the gradients of the averaged velocity and heat fluxes due to heat conduction which are proportional to the averaged temperature gradients. The second mechanism gives rise to turbulent stresses caused by momentum transfer due to velocity fluctuations and turbulent heat fluxes caused by heat transfer.

Our measurements, conducted according the measuring system described in figures 5 and 6, are in a good agreement with the above description. In fact, as it is shown in figure 7 (a, b, c, d, e and f), the pyroelectric responses of the flexible PVDF film are characterized by an irregular shape. The positive and negative values of the signal reflect the fluctuation of the convective heat exchange detected by the pyroelectric film .This deduction is confirmed by the increase in fluctuation (amplitude and frequency of the signal) observed when the velocity of the fluid increases (figure 7). So when the air velocity increases, the turbulences increase and the fluctuation of the pyroelectric film signal increases too. In fact, the number of positive and negative peaks (frequency of fluctuation) increases when the velocity increases as seen in figure 7 (2, 8, 12, 15, 18, 24, 30 peaks for respectively velocity 1m/s, 5m/s, 10m/s, 15m/s, 20m and 25m/s). Compared to the regular shape observed in figure 7, it appears clearly that the measured responses are closely related to the turbulent fluctuations of the heat exchange which explains their irregularity.

(7 a)

Pyroelectric signal in Volts

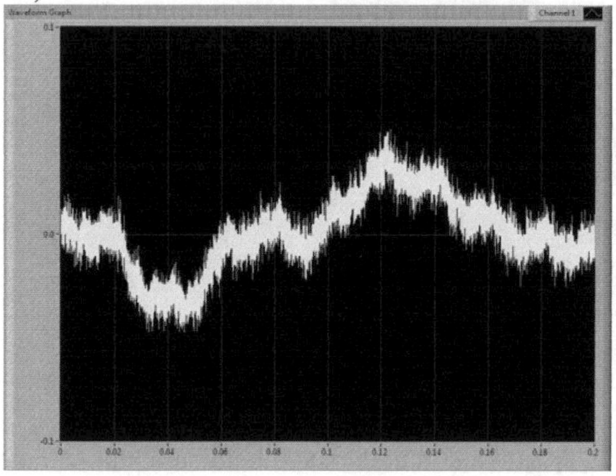

Time in 10^{-1}s

(7 b)

Pyroelectric signal in Volts

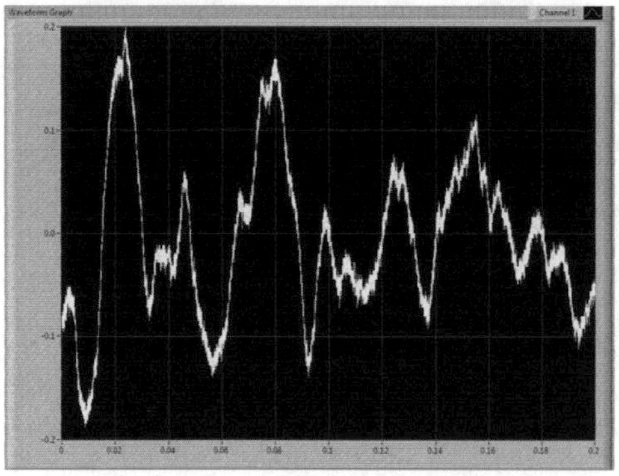

Time in 10^{-1}s

(7 c)

Pyroelectric signal in Volts

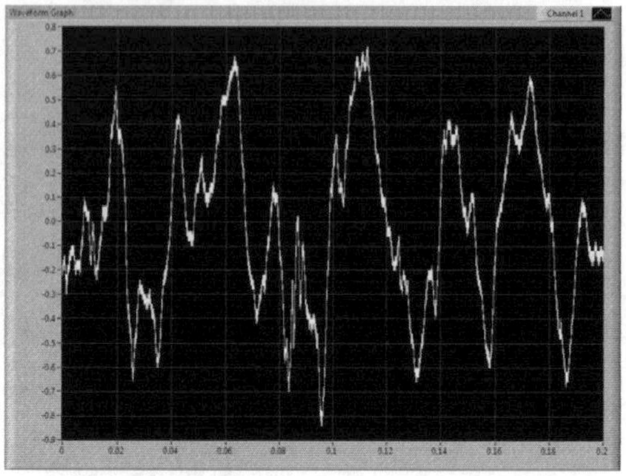

Time in 10^{-1}s

(7 d)

Pyroelectric signal in Volts

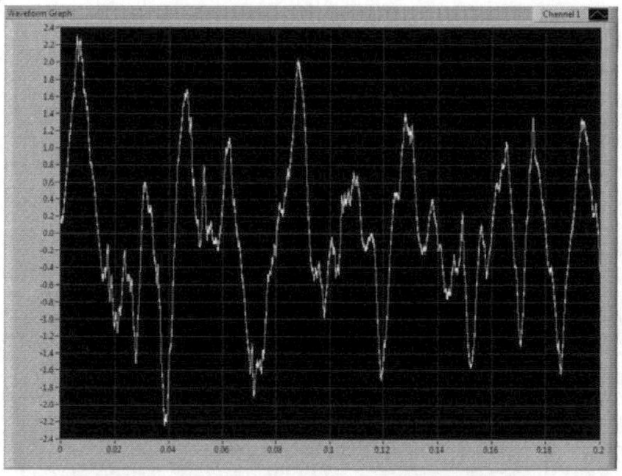

Time in 10^{-1}s

(7 e)

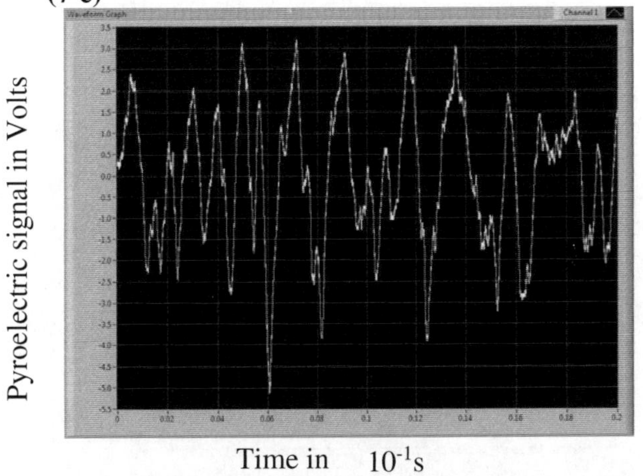

(7 f)

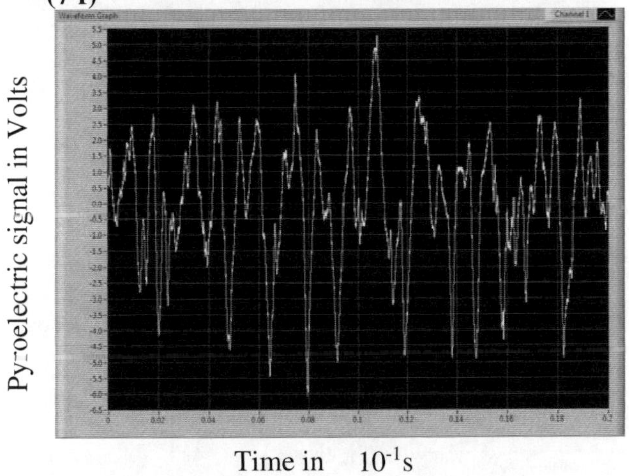

Fig.7. Response of the flexible PVDF film to different air flow velocity generated in the wind tunnel: a) 1m/s, b)5m/s, c)10m/s, d)15m/s, e)20m/s and f)25m/s

To give more quantitative aspect to our observations, we present, respectively in figure 8 and 9 the evolution of the amplitude maximum of the pyroelectric signal with Re number and the average of the absolute values of the peaks for different velocities in the period of 20ms. The two found curves are identical, which allows us to use, in our measurements one of these two characteristics of the signal.

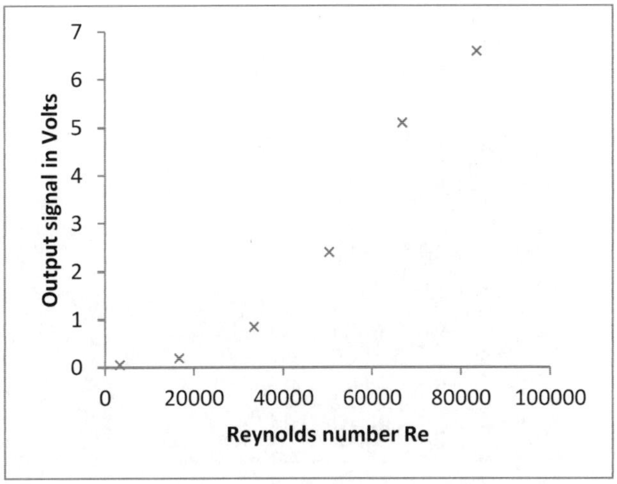

Fig.8. of the observed peaks in the period of 20ms for each velocity as function as the Re number

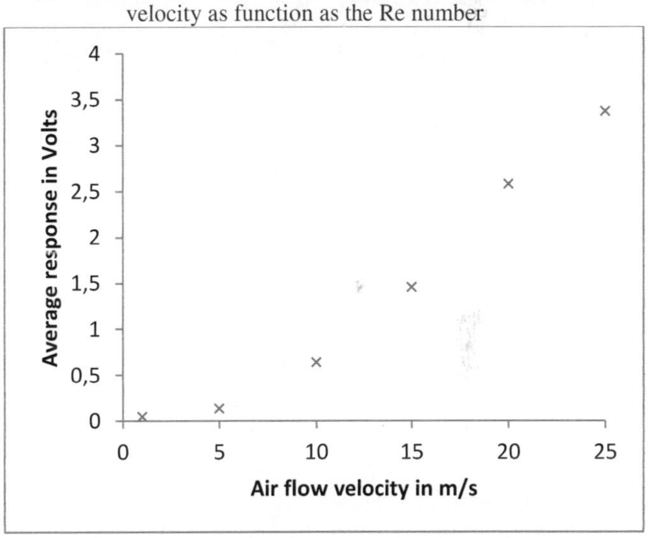

Fig.9. Average of the peaks measured as function of the velocity

In the other hand and to test our measurements, we have placed two identical PVDF flexible film cells with parallel thermal configuration in the open test section of the wind tunnel (figure 10) and we measure, using the bench described in figure 5, the sum of the output pyroelectric signals. The maximum of current generated by the parallel association for each velocity of the wind flow in the interval velocity [1-25] m/s is nearly equal to their algebraic sum of individual currents (figure 10). We also note that the frequency of the fluctuation of parallel cells response was the same for individual cell. These results are in concordance with the work of A. Cuadras et al [18]. However, for the velocity over 20m/s, the average of the values of the observed peaks for two cells is only multiplied by 1.4 of the average of the peaks of one cell. We attribute this observed non linearity to the increase of the turbulent fluctuation of the wind flow in the vicinity of the sensors. Indeed, strong fluctuation can induce a superposition of the two generated current or on the contrary an opposition of these currents (figure 11).

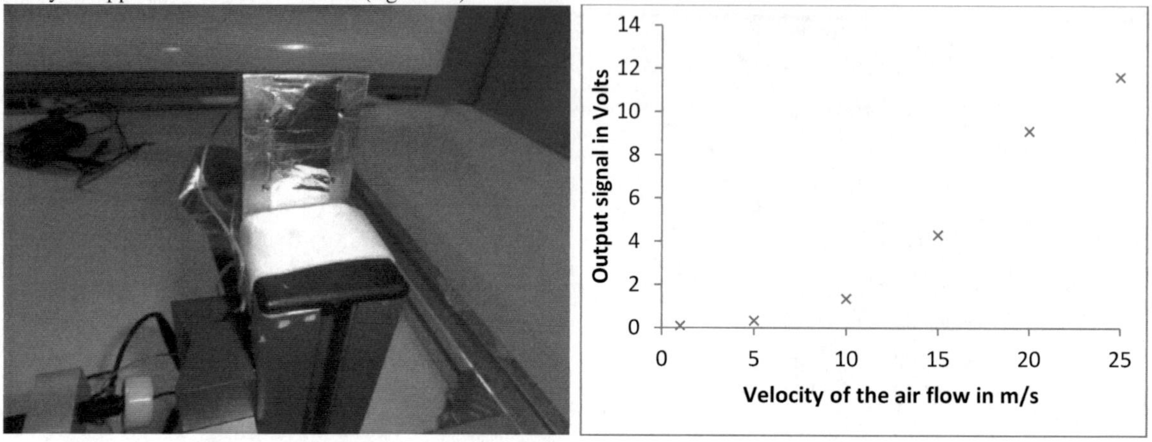

Fig.10. Matrix 2X1 cell of PVDF film placed in open test section of the wind tunnel and Maximum of the peaks measured for each velocity

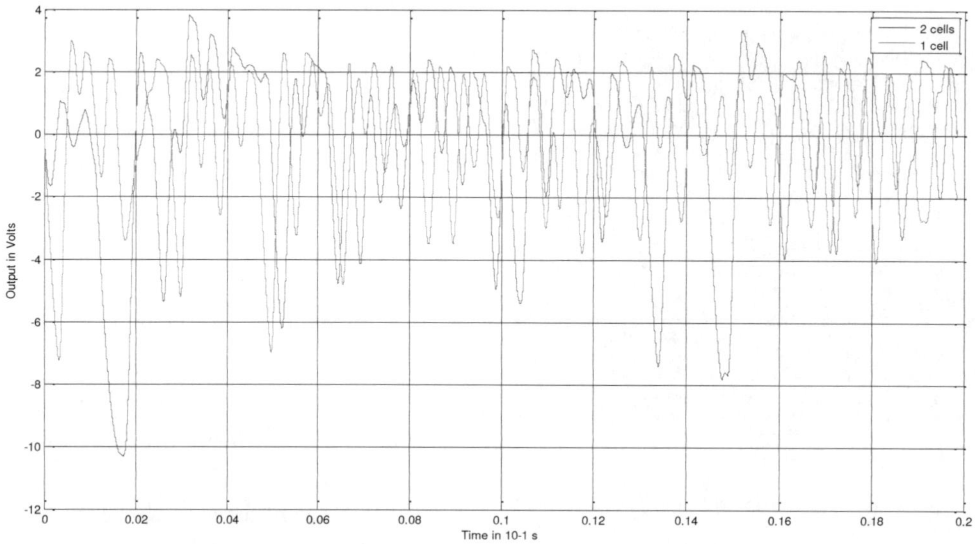

Fig.11. Signal of one cell in green and signal of matrix of two cells in blue for air flow velocity 25m/s.

5 Conclusion

In this paper, an experimental study had been done on the response of the flexible PVDF film placed in a wind tunnel with an open test section. The aim of this work is to characterize the response of the flexible PVDF film in the wind tunnel for possible application in anemometry (PA). We described the characteristics of the used wind tunnel and the appropriate measurement system. The experimental results and observations show that the pyroelectric signal of the flexible PVDF film is proportional to the rate of the heat exchange by convection induced by the air flow velocity around the sensor. These results are in concordance with theoretical concept of the heat exchange by forced convection. This concordance is seen in the irregularity of the pyroelectric signal which confirms the appearance of turbulence in the interface sensor/air flow. We think that these results can be exploited to develop anemometry application based on flexible PVDF film for very large scale of air flow velocity. However, further research would be required to control the effect of the sensor geometry and to stabilize the response of the film for eventual calibration.

Acknowledgements
The authors are grateful for the support provided by the German Institute of Metrology PTB and the Center for Research and Technology of Energy (CRTEn, Tunisia) for this work. The authors are also grateful to Dr. Harald Müller, Head of the Working Group on Fluid Measurement Techniques in PTB, for fruitful discussions on appropriate wind tunnel measurement methods.

References

[1] C.R. Wood, L. Pauscher , H.C. Ward, S. Kotthaus , J.F. Barlow, M. Gouvea, S.E. Lane, C.S.B. Grimmond, Wind observations above an urban river using a new lidar technique, scintillometry and anemometry, Science of the Total Environment 442 (2013) 527–533.

[2] Malick Ndoye, E. Dorignac, J. Delville, G. Arroyo, Physical analysis of velocity and temperature cross-correlations in a plane mixing layer using variable temperature hot wire anemometry, C. R. Mecanique 338 (2010) 688–697.

[3] Rolf-Erik Keck, A numerical investigation of nacelle anemometry for a HAWT using actuator disc and line models in CFX, Renewable Energy 48 (2012) 72e84.

[4] Evangelos Keramaris, Similarities and Differences Between Hot-Film Anemometry and Particle Image Velocimetry in Open Channels, Procedia Engineering 162 (2016) 388-395.

[5] Víctor Francia, Luis Martín, Andrew E. Bayly, Mark J.H. Simmons, Use of sonic anemometry for the study of confined swirling flows in large industrial units, Flow Measurement and Instrumentation 50 (2016) 216–228.

[6] B Maribo Pedersen, Troels Friis Pedersen, Helmut Klug, Nico van der Borg, Neil Kelley, Jan Åke Dahlberg, wind speed measurement and use of cup anemometry, Edition 1999 second print 2003, Edited by Raymond S Hunter Renewable Energy Systems Ltd Scottish Regional Office 11 Elmbank Street Glasgow G2 4PB United Kingdom.

[7] H Rahnamai and J N Zemel, Pyroelectric Anemometers preparation and flow velocity measurements, Sensors and Actuators, 2 (1981/82) 3 16.

[8] Hamid Rahnamai, Pyroelectric-Anemometer probe with improved sensitivity, Sensors and Actuators, 3 (1982/83) 17–22.

[9] Dun Yu, H. Y. Hsieh and J. N. Zemel, Microchannel pyroelectric anemometer, Sensors and Actuators A. 39 (1993) 29 35.

[10] H.Y. Hsieh a, Haim H. Bau b, Jay N. Zemel a, Pyroelectric anemometry: theory of operation, Sensors and Actuators A 49 (1995) 125-132.

[11] A. Pecora, L. Maiolo, F. Maita, A. Minotti, Flexible PVDF-TrFE pyroelectric sensor driven by polysilicon thin film transistor fabricated on ultra-thin polyimide substrate, Sensors and Actuators A 185 (2012) 39– 43.

[12] A. Aliane, M. Benwadih, B. Bouthinon, R. Coppard, F. Domingues-Dos Santos, A. Daami, Impact of crystallization on ferro-, piezo- and pyro-electric characteristics in thin film P(VDF–TrFE), Organic Electronics 25 (2015) 92–98.

[13] Wee Chen Gan, Wan Haliza Abd. Majid, Enhancing pyroelectric and ferroelectric properties of PVDF composite thin films by dispersing a non-ferroelectric inclusion La2O3 for application in sensors, Organic Electronics 26 (2015) 121–128.

[14] M.S. Jayalakshmy, J. Philip, Pyroelectric figures of merit and associated properties of LiTaO3/polyvinylidene difluoride nanocomposites for thermal/infrared sensing, Sensors and Actuators A 206 (2014) 121– 126.

[15] M. Favre-Marinet, S. Tardu, Convective Heat Transfer, First published in Great Britain and the United States in 2009 by ISTE Ltd and John Wiley & Sons, Inc.

[16] M.H. Raouadi, N. Sifi, and O. Touayar, Development of the PSO method for the determination of the dynamic response of a pyroelectric sensor, Int. J. Metrol. Qual. Eng. 7, 304 (2016).

[17] B . S . Petukhov, Heat Transfer and Friction in Turbulent Pipe Flow with Variable Physical Properties, High Temperature Institrite. Academy of Science of the USSR. Moscow.. USSR 1970.

[18] A. Cuadras, M. Gasulla, V. Ferrari, Thermal energy harvesting through pyroelectricity, Sensors and Actuators A 158 (2010) 132–139.

DEVELOPMENT OF A STANDARD FOR LNG FLOW METERING USING LASER DOPPLER ANEMOMETRY

R. Maury[1], A. Ouderdani[1], C. Auclercq[1], Y. Lehot[1]
S. Loubat[2], J. Chevalier[3], F. Ben Rayana[3]

[1]*CESAME-EXADEBIT/ LNE-LADG, 43 rue de l'aérodrome, 86000 POITIERS, France*
[2]*ELENGY, 11 avenue Michel Ricard, 92276 BOIS-COLOMBES, France*
[3]*Engie, 361, avenue du Président Wilson, 93211 SAINT-DENIS LA PLAINE, France*
r.maury@cesame-exadebit.fr

Abstract

A very promising alternative to the state-of-the-art static volume measurements for Liquefied Natural Gas (LNG) custody transfer processes is the dynamic principle of flow metering. As the Designated Institute (DI) of the LNE ("Laboratoire National de métrologie et d'Essais", being the French National Metrology Institute) for high pressure gas flow metering, Cesame-Exadebit is involved in various Research & Development programs. Within the framework of the first (2010-2013) and second (2014-2017) EURAMET Joint Research Project (JRP) named "Metrological support for LNG custody transfer and transport fuel applications", Cesame-Exadebit explored a novel cryogenic flow metering technology using Laser Doppler Velocimetry (LDV) as an alternative to ultrasonic and Coriolis flow metering.
Cesame-Exadebit is trying to develop this technique as a primary standard for cryogenic flow meters. Currently, cryogenic flow meters are calibrated at ambient temperatures with water. Results are then extrapolated to be in the Reynolds number range of real applications. The LDV standard offers a unique capability to perform online calibration of cryogenic flow meters in real conditions (temperature, pressure, piping and real flow disturbances). The primary reference has been tested on an industrial process in a LNG terminal during truck refuelling. The reference can calibrate Coriolis flow meters being used daily with all the real environmental constraints and its utilisation is transparent for LNG terminal operators.
The standard is traceable to Standard International units and the combined extended uncertainties have been determined and estimated to be lower than 0.6% (an on-going improvement to reducing the correlation function uncertainty which has a major impact in the uncertainty estimation).

This present paper is organized as follows. After a short introduction, the section 2 presents the technical solution to perform a cryogenic measurement with LDV system (optical windows, vacuum insulation, seeding...). Section 3 is focused on LDV measurement technique explanation. Section 4 presents experiments that have been realized in cryogenic conditions in the National Institute of Standard and Technology (NIST) in Boulder, Colorado using Liquid Nitrogen. Section 5 provides an uncertainty budget in cryogenic condition. Section 6 gives some information regarding on-site experiments in an LNG terminal during truck filling. Finally, section 7 gives some conclusions and perspectives for future work

1. Introduction

Liquefied Natural Gas is a strategic, and in the case of long distances, more economical alternative for pipeline gas. Indeed, there has been an increase in the global market for both pipeline and LNG transfer over the past decades. The application of LNG as a transport fuel is gaining wider attention and within Europe many LNG fuelling stations are already in operation with many more stations planned and to be built in the coming years. This is very much welcomed by the Europe Commission as the use of LNG as a fuel is one of the pillars of its Clean Fuel Strategy. LNG is particularly suited for long-distance road freight transport for which alternatives to diesel are limited. Furthermore, engines running on LNG produce much less noise than diesel-operated engines and therefore trucks on LNG are becoming the preferred choice for deliveries in urban areas. LNG is also an attractive fuel to meet the new limits for sulphur content in marine fuels and for NOx-emissions from marine engines.

Data from *Cheniere interpretation of Wood Mackenzie data (Q4 2016)*) shows that the amount of fuel traded as LNG is expected to nearly double from 2015 to 2030. Furthermore, 30 LNG trains are planned for construction to meet forecast demand through to 2030 and will lead to 150 mtpa of new liquefaction capacity. There is also new LNG cruise carrier available for tourism in the Mediterranean Sea.

Figure 1 presents the LNG demand in the North Africa and the middle East in 2016.

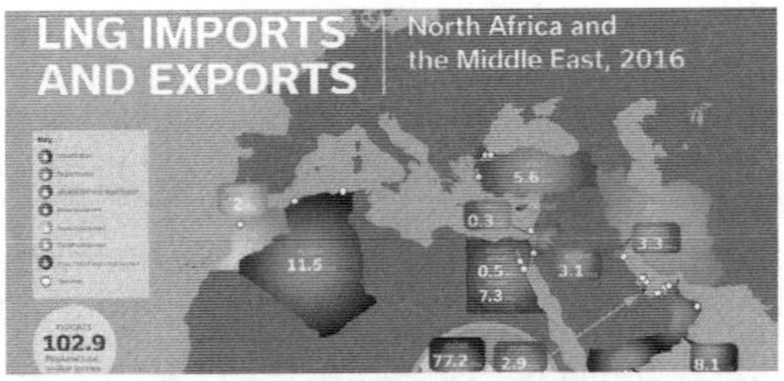

Figure 1 : MENA LNG imports and Exports in 2016.

Last year, regional gas producers Qatar, Algeria, Abu Dhabi, Oman and Egypt shipped out 102.9 mtpa. The region imported 22.5 mtpa. As our recent special report points out, both imports and exports are set to grow, making the MENA region one of the most exciting LNG markets to watch.

The measurement of this energy has to be efficient and accurate and the related uncertainties have to be extremely low with respect to the constant trading between suppliers. The objectives of LNG custody transfer operations are to measure the quantity of energy loaded from production facilities into an LNG carrier, or unloaded from an LNG carrier to a receiving terminal. To accomplish this, a number of elements must be measured and calculated: LNG volume (in m^3), LNG density (in kg/m^3), LNG gross calorific value (in *MMBTU/kg*), the energy of the gas displaced during the transfer of LNG in *MMBTU* and finally (if applicable) the energy of the gas consumed in the LNG carrier's engine room (see GIIGNL 2015 – [1]). The energy equation of unloaded LNG from a LNG carrier can be written as follow:

$$E = (V_{LNG} \times D_{LNG} \times GCV_{LNG} - E_{gasdisplaced} - E_{gastoER}) \quad (1)$$

LNG volume quantity is being measured on-ship using tank level measurement systems in combination with tank calibration tables. In comparison with other commodities like natural gas or gasoline, the total uncertainty of measured energy is high for LNG and has been estimated to be up to 1% (see Kerkhof [2]). When the ship suffers from wave motion (off shore), the measurement becomes even more difficult. The tank calibration creates an additional challenge.

The aim of the related JRP is to further develop the metrological framework for LNG, for both small and large-scale applications. This will lead to a significant reduction of uncertainties in the determination of transferred energy in LNG custody transfer processes. Cesame-Exadebit has been involved in the development and validation of novel and traceable calibration standards of LNG mass and volume flow for vehicle fuel dispensing and ship bunkering. To measure LNG volume, we studied the capability of a flow measurement system using Laser Doppler Velocimetry (see Strzelecki *et al.* [3]). The LDV system may provide an alternative traceability route for LNG volume flow meters. It can also be used as a non-intrusive instrument to perform flow profile measurements in a cryogenic medium.

LDV as a flow measurement technology has already been demonstrated under high pressure with natural gas (5.5 *MPa*) with an uncertainty of 0.22% (see Mickan *et al.* [4]) but its extension to cryogenic temperatures is especially challenging because:

1. The measurement of a velocity component in LNG by means of LDV requires the introduction into the fluid through one optical path of two laser beams which intersect to form the measurement volume. There are two features to be taken into account: the size of the volume measurement has to be calculated in order to capture the main aerodynamic features of the flow and most importantly, the fluid temperature is around -160°C whereas the flow measurement system is at ambient temperature. Icing on the optical path must be prevented in order to perform an accurate velocity measurement.
2. The LDV measurement requires the presence of micron-size tracers in the fluid. In the absence of natural micron-size tracers, it is essential to provide a clean seeding system that does not contaminate the fluid.
3. The objective is to measure instantaneous LNG flow rate with an uncertainty around 0.2% with traceability of the measurement.

The study focuses on the technological challenges and solutions for extending the LDV method to cryogenic temperatures by a two-step approach. First, the air-based experiments carried out at the Cesame-Exadebit facilities (in Poitiers, France) are presented, then the liquid nitrogen experiments on the traceable facility (at NIST, Colorado USA) are debated and an overview of on-site measurement in a LNG terminal is given.

2. Experimental setup

The LDV measurement package is composed of three main sections: the cryogenic seeding part, the conditioning part (containing the convergent) with the measuring cross-section and the divergent.

The seeding part is equipped with an access for the seeding probes in cryogenic conditions, and with two windows for particle visualization (see Figure 2). The conditioning part is provided with windows which allow passage of laser beams for measuring the velocity profile at the exit of the convergent. The downstream part of the Cryogenic LDV Measurement Package contains the divergent. These three parts are located inside a vacuum chamber to ensure thermal insulation.

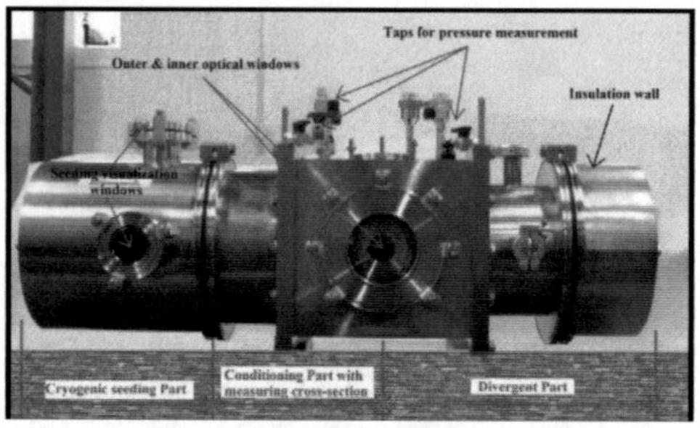

(a)

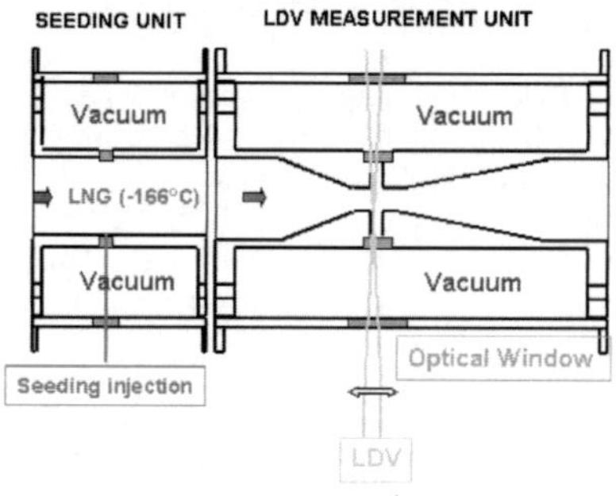

(b)

Figure 2 (a) Description of the simplified Cryogenic LDV Measurement Package and (b) 2D model horizontal cross-sectional view.

The main characteristics of the cryogenic LDV system are described in more details in Strzelecki *et al.* [5]. There are briefly restated below:

- •Internal diameter D=80 mm
- •Throat diameter d=40 mm
- •Beta ratio of the convergent d/D = 0.5
- •Length L=6D
- •Maximum operating pressure: 20 bar

The seeding unit is equipped with an access for external seeding forcing (probes under cryogenic conditions) and with two portholes for particle visualization. Indeed, LDV requires micron-size particle injection to achieve velocity measurements (if particles are not naturally in the tested fluid). Generally, there is enough material (micron-sized particles) to reach a statistical convergence of the mean and fluctuating velocities. Nevertheless, an external seeding might be needed to insure a higher and quicker statistical convergence.

The LDV measurement unit consists of an optimized convergent for conditioning the cryogenic flow before measuring the local velocity at the throat section by means of the LDV. Indeed, the shape of this convergent uniformizes the main stream and provides a thin axial velocity gradient at the nozzle exit.

Figure 3 shows the diagram of the optical configuration with the laser beams.

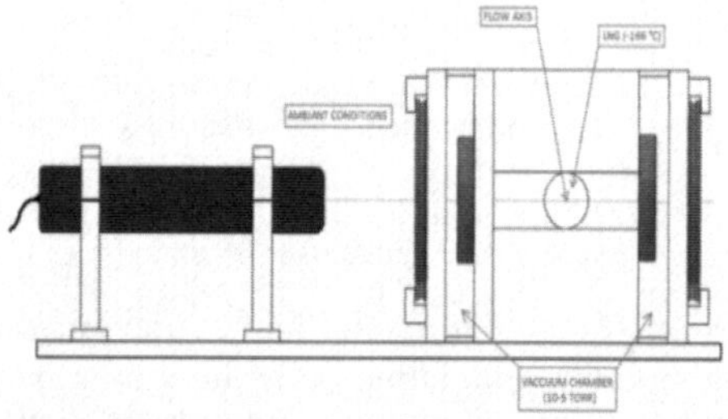

Figure 3 Optical configuration for the LDV package system (cross-sectional view of the nozzle).

The second porthole is an interface between the insulation vacuum chamber and the ambient atmospheric conditions. This assembly needs a very accurate spatial positioning to maintain the parallelism which provides beam intersection in the direction perpendicular to the flow. In addition, these portholes must withstand a large variation of temperature and pressure.

The velocity profiles are measured by means of a Laser Doppler Velocimetry from DANTEC in the backscattering mode with the following specifications. The laser wavelength is 532 nm (green beams) with a 160mm focal lens. The fringe spacing is 2.217 µm. The volume measurement is 0.41mm x 0.05mm. Further information regarding the LDV principle can be founded in Eder *et al.* [6].

The laser is traceable to SI units by the Doppler frequency and the fringe spacing. The velocity is calculated using the equation below:

$$v = \frac{I(f_D - f_S)}{cos(\gamma)} \quad (2)$$

where I is the fringe spacing, f_D is the Doppler frequency measured by the system as the particle flows through the measuring volume, f_S is a frequency shift deliberately added to one of the beams in order to retrieve directional information (see e.g. [6] for more details) and, γ is the offset from 90° at the measurement spot. The fringe spacing (I) of the LDV system has been calibrated by a notified body (CETIAT in France).

3. Axial velocity measurement by LDV: measurement principle

The method of determining the volume flow rate from a local velocity (measured downstream of a throat) is presented in this section. The basic idea is to design a flow conditioner (convergent) that provides a symmetrical and flat velocity profile in order to assure a very repeatable and fast profile measurement. Once the boundary layers are analytically determined or directly measured, the flow rate measurement can be reduced to a single point measurement (centreline axial velocity measurement).

To be a primary standard, a theoretical framework needs to be developed to accurately determine the shear layer influence on the mass flow rate assessment (with a single point measurement in the centreline axis). As an example, if the velocity profile is a piston profile, the shear layer influence is negligible, whereas in case of channel flow or free jet, the Reynolds stresses modify the velocity magnitude over the diameter significantly.

Cesame-Exadebit is currently working towards proposing this equipment as a primary standard for cryogenic flow meters. It is a challenging objective and Cesame needs to continue its journey to define the best theoretical approach to achieve this shear layer evaluation. In the meantime, the shear layer influence can also be determined experimentally by using a comparison with another standard. The Laser Doppler Velocimetry package then becomes a secondary standard.

The volume flow rate is obtained by measuring the mean velocity ($\bar{v}$) at the throat (if the velocity gradient has a small impact on the average flowrate). The governing equation can be written as equation 3:

$$Q_v = \pi \frac{d^2}{4} \bar{v} \tag{3}$$

Furthermore, the ratio between the velocity on the axis v_{axis} (measured by the LDV system) and the output of the mean velocity $\bar{v}$ is a constant value for each Reynolds number based on the throat diameter d. The function combining all the values is defined as A^* and the expression can be written as:

$$\frac{v_{axis}}{\bar{v}} = A^*(Re_d) \tag{4}$$

Where for a circular cross section duct of diameter d,

$$Re_d = \frac{\bar{v} d \rho}{\mu} = \frac{4 Q_m}{\pi \mu d}. \tag{5}$$

These relations allow the calculation of the volume flow rate from the axial velocity measured at one point downstream of the throat on the centreline axis. It can be written as follows:

$$Q_v = \pi \frac{d^2}{4} \bar{v} = \pi \frac{d^2}{4} \frac{v_{axis}}{A^*(Re_d)} \tag{6}$$

To implement this method, it is mandatory to establish a transposition function between the volume flow rate and the local velocity measurement (as a function of Reynolds number). Ideally, if the axial velocity profile was piston type or top-hat shape (at the nozzle lip), the transposition from local centerline velocity to volume flow rate will be straightforward. Indeed, the momentum thickness of the shear layer will have no influence ($\delta_\omega \rightarrow 0$). The mass flow rate will be the integration of the velocity on the centerline over the diameter.

From the boundary layer evolution theory, the growing of the vortices downstream the nozzle lead to an increase of the momentum thickness of the shear layer (δ_ω) and the transposition for single velocity point measurement to volume mass flow needs to be adjusted by a calibration factor (i.e. A^* function (depends to Re_d)) to takes this growing into account.

4. Experimental phase: Nitrogen-based experiments

a) *Objectives of the Nitrogen phase*

In a previous experimental campaign, Cesame Exadebit has carried out some tests in air in Poitiers (France) to determine a transposition function to assess the mass flow rate by having a one point measurement on the centreline at the nozzle throat vicinity ($A^*(R_e)$). This phase gave Cesame-Exadebit the opportunity to implement this function during the cryogenic tests and assess the accuracy of the model. The Objectives of the NIST campaign are reminded here. It will allow the validation of the technical choices and to test numerous hypotheses regarding the cryogenic conditions such as: mechanical behaviour in cryogenic conditions, the vacuum level required to perform velocity measurements without icing on portholes, the optical convergence of the beams with liquid nitrogen or the instrumentation permeability with cryogenic fluid.

b) *Experimental setup and test plan*

The LDV package test was run on the NIST cryogenic flow measurement facility in 2016. This facility has a combined uncertainty in the measurement of 0.18% for the totalized volume flow (k=2) (see Scott *et al.* [7]). This uncertainty statement applies to measurements made within a flow range of 75 to 750 *L/mn*. NIST have incorporated a newer equation of state for nitrogen (see Span *et al.* [8]), and the uncertainty in density for the new equation is 0.02% (k=2).

A rangeability test was run to determine flow meter performance over a range of flow rates and fixed temperature and pressure. The temperature was about 80*K*, the pressure range was about 5 bar. There were five separate flow rates selected which were repeated at least three times. During this experimental phase, Cesame-Exadebit only tried to calculate mass flow rate by using single point measurement in the jet centreline axis. The test plan is restated in Table 1 below.

Run	Qm (kg/s)	Throat velocity (m/s)	Mach Number	Re_d Col
1	2.00	2.0	0.005	$4.36E^{+05}$
2	2.46	2.5	0.007	$5.37E^{+05}$
3	3.55	3.5	0.010	$7.73E^{+05}$
4	4.91	4.9	0.014	$1.07E^{+06}$
5	7.11	7.1	0.020	$1.55E^{+06}$
6	9.17	9.2	0.027	$2.00E^{+06}$

Table 1 : Test plan during cryogenic experimental phase in NIST facility with the LDV package.

c) Single point measurement: results and discussion

The laser beam convergence was determined with accuracy by taking into account the length modification of the convergence beams due to nitrogen refraction indices. Convergence positioning (during experiments) was controlled using a remote camera mounted on one of the optical access points of the LDV package (on the top) since no one can be close to the laser during experiments (safety procedures for a class 4 laser). The laser system was not moved in order to ensure the convergence of the beams to the centreline axis close to the throat (x/D = 0.25 approximately). The experimental setup is visible in Figure 4:

Figure 4 Experimental setup for LDV measurement in the NIST facility.

The main goal of these tests was to determine the correlation function (A*(Re)) in cryogenic conditions (the same procedure carried out during air based experiments). During these experiments, the upstream pressure was fixed around 5 bar and the velocity was increased from 2 to 9 *m/s* resulting in a Reynolds number based on the throat diameter from $4.3E^5$ to $2.0E^6$. Each mass flow rate has been repeated at least three times to access standard deviation in the laser results. A trigger signal was sent from the NIST acquisition system to our laser/sensors acquisition system to provide a relevant set of data for performing the measurements and calculations.

Cesame-Exadebit applied the correlation function determined during the air-based experimental phase in Poitiers. The Reynolds number is the similitude criterion. Even if there is a fluid property modification (from air to cryogenic liquid), the correlation is not expected to be highly modified. Nevertheless, this NIST phase provided a new correlation function for cryogenic conditions that Cesame will test soon.

Cesame must take into account the low temperature constraints on the flow meter body. Indeed, the reduction of the throat diameter due to cryogenic temperature affects largely the assessment of the axial velocity. The paper of Thermeau [9] presents the length modification (Δl/l) as a function of temperature in Kelvin. In our case, the ΔT is 213K resulting in a length modification around 0.27% on the diameter.

Figure 5 presents the results of the bias in velocity between the standard facility and the LDV package. The extended uncertainty of the facility has been added to the results.

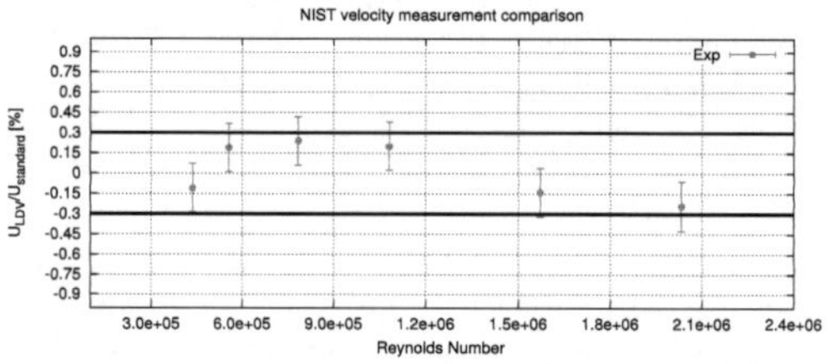

Figure 5 Velocity difference (with air based correlation function) between NIST standard facility and LDV package.

As a general comment, the trend observed during the air experiments is continued under cryogenic conditions since at low Reynolds numbers, the correlation function plays a higher role. The increasing Reynolds number leads to a reduction of the momentum thickness in the shear region. Figure 5 above shows that the comparison of the velocity between the standard facility and the LDV package is comprised between: -0.3% and 0.3% with 0.18%

of extended uncertainty. As a first attempt under cryogenic conditions, these results are really promising.

Cesame-Exadebit wants to investigate further by having another experimental phase during which the correlation function defined under cryogenic conditions will be used to reduce the bias observed in Figure 5.

d) Feedback on previous objectives:

During these tests, many topics required investigation. Cesame-Exadebit's knowledge of cryogenic conditions improved significantly during this experimental phase. The explanation for each topic is given below:

1. *Mechanical behaviour in cryogenic conditions*: the LDV package operated correctly throughout the experimental phase. No internal leakage was detected and the thermal constraints of the body part were correctly handled by all the seals / O rings used in the system.

2. *Vacuum level required to perform velocity measurement without icing on portholes*: the vacuum system operated effectively during the runs with a vacuum level around 1^{-4}mbar. This was enough to provide a sufficient vacuum level to avoid icing on the portholes.

3. *Optical convergence of the beams with liquid nitrogen*: the optical path had been calculated theoretically and it appears that it is relevant to what we saw during testing. The convergence of the beams allows us to perform LDV measurements with a high accuracy level.

4. *Instrumentation permeability with cryogenic fluid*: no leakage was detected during tests.

This method allows us to provide single point measurement velocity on the centreline axis of the jet over a large range of Reynolds numbers ($5E^4$ to $2E^6$). It can be used to calibrate on-site flow meters (Coriolis, ultrasonic flow meters...) which operate under cryogenic conditions. This technique has several advantages since it is much quicker and optical adjustments are much easier to make. The flow meters will be calibrated under real experimental conditions (temperature, pressure, fluid properties and large range of mass flow rates and Reynolds numbers).

5. Uncertainty budget evaluation:

The value of the measurand (the measurement) is obtained from a measurement of the time-averaged velocity on the centreline axis of the LDV instrument. The axial velocity is converted to a cross-sectional average by applying a scaling factor obtained from a calibration curve (model function A^*). The cross-sectional averaged velocity is then multiplied by the cross-sectional area to obtain the volumetric flow rate (cf Equation 3).

Normally, the cross-sectional average velocity $\bar{v}$ would be obtained by integration of the measured velocity profiles over the flow cross section. However, detailed information about the flow profile is difficult to obtain (in particular close to the wall) and it is time-consuming and challenging to measure it in real time. The LDV technique is therefore based on measuring the flow velocity at the flow centreline (pipe axis) only. An empirical scaling factor (derived from a model function) is applied to obtain the average velocity from the axial velocity.

In this work, the model function, that is the relationship between the axial velocity and the cross section average velocity, is approximated by a linear function of the natural logarithm of the Reynolds number (designated later as A^*) :

$$\frac{v_{axis}}{\bar{v}} = a + b\ln(Re_d) + \epsilon = A^*. \quad (7)$$

Where a is the intercept of the model function, b is the slope of the model function and, ϵ is an error term introduced from assuming this particular relationship between $v_{axis}/\bar{v}$ and $\ln(Re_d)$.

Equation 3, Equation 4 and Equation 9 are combined to obtain the measurement function for the volumetric flow rate measured by the LDV instrument:

$$Q_v = \frac{v_{axis}\pi d^2}{4\left(a + b\ln\left(\frac{\rho v_{axis} d}{\mu}\right) + \epsilon\right)}. \quad (8)$$

The symbols are listed in Table 2.

Symbol	Explanation
Q_v	Volumetric flow rate obtained from the LDV system
v_{axis}	Measured axial velocity using the LDV system
d	Internal diameter of the LDV convergent throat
a	Intercept of the model function
b	Slope of the model function
ρ	Density of LNG at local conditions of pressure and temperature
μ	Viscosity of LNG at local conditions of pressure and temperature
ϵ	Model function error

Table 2 : Symbols used in the measurement function for the volumetric flow rate

In this article and for illustration purposes, the uncertainty budget will be presented for a randomly-chosen measurement with liquid nitrogen at NIST under laboratory conditions. In this case, the uncertainty on mass flow rate has been estimated at 0.6% (k=2) and the Table 3 shows the contribution of each component.

X_i	x_i	unit	$u(x_i)$	c_i	$u_i(y)$	Contrib
d	0.0398	m	1.510E-5	0.12581	0.000002	3%
A^*	1.015	-	0.00367	-0.00246	-0.000009	78%
V_{axis}	2.04	m/s	0.00365	0.00122	0.000004	19%
Y=Qv	0.0025	m^3/s				
				U(y)/y	0.31%	
				U(y)	7.7E-6	
				k=	2.06	
				U(95%)	1.6E-5	
				U(y)/y	**0.63%**	

Table 3 : Uncertainty budget for volumetric flow rate under cryogenic conditions

6. Cryogenic measurement in Montoir de Bretagne LNG terminal during a truck filling

Real life on-site calibration during truck filling requires obtaining accreditation from a notified body for explosive environments. The first task was to design a safe package that can be used in an LNG terminal (Ex IIGT6). Figure 6 below presents the diagram of our concept where both 'ATEX' (Explosive environment) enclosures (Laser and Vacuum), the flow meter and the frame can be seen:

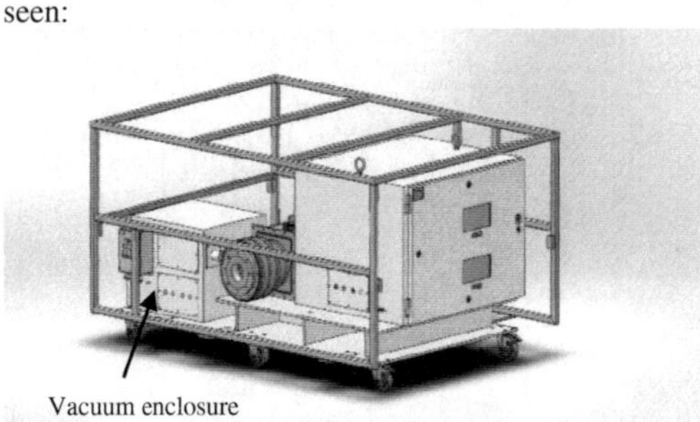

Figure 6 Sketch of the LDV Standard assembly (Laser and Vacuum enclosures, cryogenic mass flow rate standard and mobile frame).

The LDV standard was set up within an industrial facility to measure the axial velocity between the LNG tank and the truck. The aim of these experiments was to compare both the weighing technique and a Coriolis flow meter. Figure 7 shows the experimental setup:

Figure 7 LDV Standard installed in Montoir de Bretagne terminal during LNG truck filling.

During this test, the installation and the exploitation of the LDV package was transparent for the LNG terminal (from the operator's point of view). This equipment created no time delay for the truck refuelling. Cesame-Exadebit gained much useful experience on how to perform measurements in an industrial facility.

The natural micro-particles (micron-size particles) were detected in the LNG and the velocity measurements were consistent with the velocity calculated by the terminal output (truck scale, density etc.). There was no clear indication of the concentration, shape or numbers of these natural particles. Cesame-Exadebit is currently working to add an external seeding to maximize the capability of the LDV standard to be autonomic under any cryogenic setup.

7. Conclusions and perspectives

Industry's need to obtain traceability for cryogenic flowmeters has been outlined as an introduction to the work described in this paper. As a matter of fact, the economic impact of having accurate measurement of LNG is enormous since the global market is constantly increasing. The uncertainty on the volume of LNG is an important part of the overall uncertainty on the energy transfer from a carrier to a LNG terminal for example. Furthermore, current uncertainty assessments are rather optimistic and there is a lack of credibility from having non-representative conditions during flowmeter calibrations. Indeed, flowmeters are often currently calibrated in water at ambient conditions and calibration curves are then extrapolated to relevant Reynolds numbers for cryogenic application.

The work which has been done by Cesame-Exadebit within the Joint Research Program (JRP) on LNG, is to define a new route to the traceability chain. Within this framework, the Laser Doppler Velocimetry technique appears to be appropriate, since it is non-intrusive and the velocity can be traced back to SI unit by the fringe spacing and the Doppler frequency. The challenge to design suitable equipment for cryogenic conditions has been overcome (e.g. a vacuum required to avoid icing on the laser path, handling in an explosive environment). The set of experiments (in liquid nitrogen) has shown both promising results and the capability of the LDV standard to realise accurate velocity measurements. An exhaustive uncertainty budget in cryogenic conditions has been developed and it shows that the larger contribution can be attributed to the transposition function ($A*$).

Finally, the LDV standard has been used during daily rotation of LNG truck in a LNG terminal in Montoir de Bretagne. It is noteworthy that the carrying-out of the LDV experiments in a real-world environment during truck refuelling did not add difficulties or delays to the truck operations from an operator point of view at the LNG terminal in Montoir de Bretagne. The LDV standard offers a unique capability to perform online calibration of cryogenic flow meters under real conditions (temperature, pressure, piping and real flow disturbances) for end-users. The standard is traceable to SI units and the extended uncertainties have been determined and estimated to be lower than 0.6% (an on-going improvement to reduce the transposition function uncertainty which has a major impact on the uncertainty estimation). Indeed, Cesame Exadebit is currently working on an analytical model based on the boundary-layer theory (see Schlichting *et al.* [10] for further explanations).

8. References

[1] **GIIGNL**. "*LNG custody transfer handbook*". Technical report, 2015.

[2] **Kerkhof O.**, "*metrological support for LNG custody transfer and transport fuel applications*". Technical Report JRP-Protocol, 2014.

[3] **Strzelecki A., Ouerdani A., Lehot Y., Windenberger C., and Vallet J.P.**,"*pre-studying of laser Doppler velocimetry for LNG flow measurement*". Technical Report for Metrology for LNG - JRP, 2013.

[4] **Mickan B. and Strunck V.**, "*A primary standard for the volume flow rate of natural gas under high pressure based on laser Doppler velocimetry*". Metrologia, 51(5):459, 2014.

[5] **Strzelecki A., Ouerdani A., Lehot Y., Windenberger C., and Vallet J.P.**, "*LNG flowrate measurement using laser doppler Velocimetry*". 16th International Flow Measurement Conference, 2013.

[6] **Eder A., Durst B., and Jordan M.** "*Laser-Doppler Velocimetry—Principle and Application to Turbulence Measurements.*" Optical Measurements 117-138, (2001).

[7] **Scott J.L. and Lewis M.A.**, "*Uncertainty analysis of the NIST nitrogen flow facility*". National Institute of Standards and Technology Technical Note, 1364, 1994.

[8] **Span R., Lemmon E., Jacobsen R., Wagner W., and Yokozeki A.**, "*a reference equation of state for the thermodynamic properties of nitrogen for temperatures from 63.151 to 1000 k and pressures to 2200 mpa*". Journal of Physical and Chemical Reference Data, 29(6):1361–1433, 2000.

[9] **Thermeau J.P.**, "*propriétés des matériaux à basse température*". 5ème rencontre nationale des mécaniciens du CNRS, 7, 2004.

[10] **Schlichting, H., Gersten, K., Krause, E., Oertel, H.**, "*Boundary-layer theory*" (Vol. 7). New York: McGraw-hill, 1955.

9. Acknowledgements

The research leading to the results discussed in this paper has received funding from the European Metrology Research Program (EMRP). The EMRP is jointly funded by the EMRP participating countries within EURAMET

Cesame-Exadebit wants to thank Justervesenet – The Norwegian Metrology Service (and especially Åge Andreas Falnes Olsen and Gaël Chupin), for the inputs in building the cryogenic uncertainty budget.

V-shape nanotextured active surface of a Germanium photodiode and its role in enhancing the device electrical characteristics

I.Chaabane[1,2],O.Touayar[2],SG.Cloutier[1,*]

1 Department of Electrical Engineering, École de Technologie Supérieure, 1100 Notre-Dame Ouest, Montréal, Québec, QC H3C 1K3, Canada ; ibtihel.chaabane.1@etsmtl.net (I.C.);
2 Department of Physics and Instrumentation, National Institute of Applied Science and Technologies, Charguia, Tunis 1080, Tunisia; touayar.walid@planet.tn
* Correspondence: sylvaing.cloutier@etsmtl.ca; Tel.: +1-514-396-8897

Abstract. The performance of an optoelectronic device is evaluated by its sensitivity. This sensitivity can be expressed in one hand as a function of the reflectance and in another hand as a function of the output current. In this work, we succeeded to enhance the electrical response of a Germanium (Ge) PN junction photodiode. Indeed, we evaluated the impact of increasing the detector active surface/air ratio (by creating V-shape nanotexturing) on its electrical characteristics. To do so, all the device realization steps were carefully studied. First, we realized a shallow N-type layer by phosphorous ion implantation in a P-type substrate. The depth of the implanted layer was then studied to ensure that the V-shape created pores do not short-cut the PN junction and that their depths do not exceed the upper N-type layer. This V-shape nanotextured surface was created by a brief immersion in an aqua regia electroless etching bath. Finally, and to better take the measurements of the different electrical parameters, we optimised the form of the metallic electrodes. The resulting currents and voltages, in dark and under illumination were all studied as well as the device resistances and all the results were interpreted according to the nanotextured layer in terms of morphology and chemistry. Finally, it turned out that this brief aqua regia treatment can significantly enhance the device electrical characteristics. It is important to mention that it is possible to further enhance the device performance by enhancing the distribution and the depth of the upper implanted layer and by realizing deeper pores.

Keywords: spectral sensitivity, Germanium photodiode, nano-texturing, ion implantation, aqua regia.

1 Introduction

The sensitivity of an optoelectronic device such as photodiodes and solar cells depends on relectance factor in one hand, and on the electrical response which is the device output current in another hand.

The theoretical upper limits of the electrical characteristics that we can extract from a PN homojunction based solar cell can be determined based on the study of the detailed balance limit [1] known as the schockley and Queisser Limits. The maximum theoretical values corresponding to Eg = 0.67eV which is the bandgap energy of Germanium at room temperature are Isc equal to 60mA / cm^2, Voc approximately equal to 0.5V and finally the saturation current is arround 10^{-5}A / cm^2. These values illustrate an ideal case and cannot be achieved. In the cited study, the determination of these parameters assumes that only wavelengths that are greater than the material bandgap **are absorbed in totality by the material** and that the only phenomenon taken into account is radiative recombination of Electron-hole pairs. Shockley and Queisser have relied on other hypotheses such as infinite mobility of charge carriers assuming that all excited charges will reach the outer circuit and that both the light source (1SUN) and the cell are black bodies. Therefore, the energy absorbed is equal to the energy emitted. As these hypotheses are **experimentally unverified**, the authors of this report cited reasons leading to experimental values below these limits and justifying this discrepancy with the following arguments:

• Auger effect,
• Formation of complexes, donor or acceptor, which become recombination centers,
• In any junction manufactured at high temperatures, there are vacant densities and even dislocation loops.

Many are the works [2, 3] that focused on solving the problem of reflection and different are the solutions proposed to decrease the reflectance factor and thereby enhance the output current of the devices.

A first way to decrease the reflectance is to dispose several photodiodes in a configuration of a trap detector as represented in [4]. The design of the detector in this work is in a such a way that the specular reflection of the incident light is oblique and it is successively directed from one photodiode to another. The third photodiode is aligned at a normal incidence so that the light beam emerges from the detector after five reflections. In the visible, the residual overall reflectance of this detector is generally 0.3%, a value which is sufficiently small to allow interpolation between some reflection measurements with an uncertainty factor of less than 0.01% in the receptivity[5]. However, specular reflectance is not the only parameter that influences the sensitivity of the trap detector, because there is also the diffuse reflectance, the absorption of photons without generation of charge carriers, in addition to the load-bearing ratio (losses / gains), where the third effect is generally larger.

A second way to reduce photo-detectors reflection is to perform a surface treatment [6]. The criticism of Raut [6] constitutes a profound review on the subject. The basic concept of this method is to add a transparent layer in the studied wavelengths range which has a refractive index n intermediate between that of the air n_0 and that of the semiconductor n_2 of the device active surface such that:

$$n = \sqrt{(n_0 n_2)} \qquad (1)$$

By interference effects, the incident radiation undergoes some reflections before leaving the surface. The limitation of this transparent monolayer deposition technique is that this antireflection layer must be adjusted in thickness d to serve a particular wavelength λ_0 such that d is an odd multiple of $\lambda_0 / 4$. This monolayer is not effective throughout the whole range. The use of a multilayer film or the arrangement of several anti-reflection films whose refractive index is gradually reduced starting from the refractive index of the substrate to that of the air were also discussed in the cited study with their advantages and disadvantages.

A third way to reduce reflection is the surface treatment [2, 7-10] which aims to increase the surface-to-air ratio and thus making the surface rough in a micro- or nano-scopic scale to trap the incident flow. We can distinguish between physical dry etching [11], chemical dry etching [12], Reactive Ion dry etching [13], etching by ion implantation [14, 15], electrochemical wet etching [2, 7] and electroless chemical wet etching [16] which is the type of the etching we use in this study to realize the PN junction nano-textured Germanium photodiode that we characterize electrically.

It is obvious that the experimental conditions of published works that discuss the same topic are not identical to our investigation; the criterion of choice for papers whose the electrical results will be exposed in the following was posed on the design of the structure which must rely on Ge homo-junction.

Akkari et Al [17] have characterized a porous Germanium PN-junction photodiode etched using electrochemical etching. The junction was located at 400nm depth of the surface. The I-V curve in dark of this device reports Vs=0.45V which is very interesting and an important value of saturation current. However, the I-V curve under illumination reports a value of Voc=0.05V which is very low and doesn't concord with the Vs value recorded in dark and with Ge bandgap. The shape of the I-V curve is linear and reveals a resistive behavior rather than a rectifying one. The value of Isc reported despite this is equal to 6mA. Also, another group [17] realized a monojunction Germanium based solar cell, the junction is created by spin-coating with moderate doping and a short diffusion time. The junction was not subject of study in this report, but the impact of the antireflection layer and the passivation layer were studied. Several devices have been made and the results of Voc and Isc vary between 0.186V-0.244V and 13.3mA-45.8mA respectively. Finally, few years later, the same group [18] realized a solar cell with the same previous structure based on Germanium monojunction. The difference is that for all the achievements in this report they used a same anti-reflective and passivation layer, however their attention was devoted to three other important points which are the concentration of the doping, the formation of the transmitter and the realization of the contacts. The best values of the electrical parameters obtained under illumination are Voc=0.268V and Isc=46,4mA.

In this work, we discuss the integration impact of a V-shape nano-textured active surface on electrical parameters of a Germanium PN junction photodiode, going through the fabrication process of the latter. The V-shape nano-textured structures were achieved using an original electroless method of etching using aqua regia treatment by immersion in a brief bath. The I-V measurements in dark and under illumination were recorded using a keithley based setup and all the other electrical parameters were determined graphically.

2 Theoretical background

Germanium (Ge) as a semiconductor has a band gap equal to Eg=0.67 eV at room temperature (300K). This means that germanium is unable to absorb photons with energies less than its band gap [19]. As the band gap is conversely proportional to the wavelength, this means that Ge is unable to absorb long wavelengths higher than:

$$\lambda_{max} = \frac{hc}{E_g} = 1.85\ \mu m \qquad (2)$$

which makes it suitable for near-infrared (0.7-1.4 µm) based opto-electronic devices such as photodiodes and solar cells just like Silicon for visible range (0.4-0.7µm).

To take advantages of these functions, it is important to create at least one jonction. This jonction could be homo- or hetero-junction. For this case, let's focus on PN homo-junction. Starting from a P-type substrate in which positive charges are dominating, one need to dope the substrate surface to create negative charges, going through the neutrality of the material (intrinsic state by compensation) and till the charging type is inverted. The concentration of the free positive and negative charges are related by the law of Mass Action [19]:

$$n.p = ni^2 \qquad (3)$$

From the equation (2) and having the specification of the departure p-type substrate, one can determine the appropriate concentration to dope in order to have a top N-type layer.

To do so, the ion implantation process [19] was selected to realize the doping. It involves accelerating ionized impurities with an electric field in order to give them the energy necessary to penetrate the target material.

Once the PN junction is created, it is important to realize the front and back contacts in order to collect informations from the device. The front contact should respond to a compromise between conduction and transparency. So the form of the front contact should be studied. However, the role of the back contact,in addition to the connexion with the external circuit, is to protect the device from transmittance. Indeed, the sample for our case is opaque and thick enough to not allow the transmition through out the substrate. Also, even if we suppose that a small part of the flux will cross all the thickness of the substrate which is not the case and which is not desired, in Ge-based opto-electronic devices the back face is completely covered with a metal (back contact) and this metal will reflect back the flux toward the junction.

The equivalent electrical diagram of a PN homojunction Germanium based photodiode can be represented as it is shown in fgure 1:

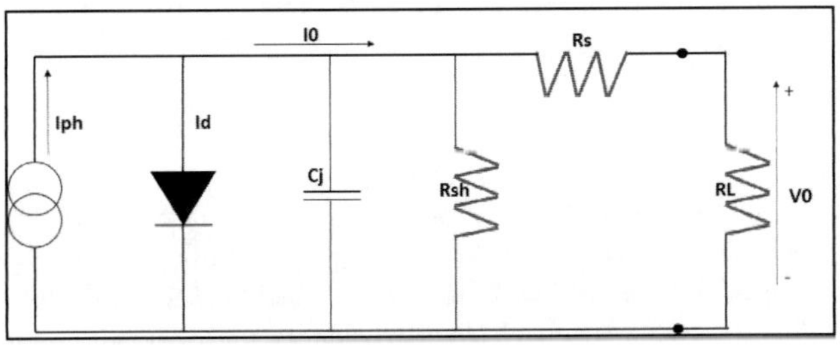

Figure 1 Electrical equivalent circuit of a photodiode

By the equivalent electrical circuit of a photodiode, we want to better represent its different components and their interactions in order to get as close as possible from the reality.Indeed, the behavior of a photodiode can be represented by a classic diode in parralel with a current source. This current source represents the generated current after an incident flux.On another side, the PN junction of the device is similar to two parrallel and very close metallic booklets of a capacitance between which the energy is infinite.Finally, the intrinsic defaults and the defaults generated by the ion implantation can be represented by R_{sh} (the more this valuer is high, the better it is) and the resistance of the metal-semiconductor and metal-metal contacts (the more this value is low, the better it is). The values of these two resistances can be determined graphically from the experimental I-V curve in the dark.

The current-voltage characteristic of a photodiode without incident light (in dark) is similar to a rectifying diode. When the photodiode is polarised, the current increases exponentially and when an inverted polarisation is applied, a small inverse current I_{sat} related to I_d appears :

$$I_d = I_{sat}\left(e^{\frac{qV_A}{K_BT}} - 1\right) \quad (4)$$

Where Id is the dark current of the photodiode, I_{SAT} is the inverse saturation current, q is an electron charge, V_A the applied voltage, k_B = 1,38 x 10-23 J/K, is the Boltzmann constant and T is the absolut temperature (273 K = 0 °C).

Now, when the photodiode is illuminated, this shifts the I-V curve by the amount of photocurrent (I_P) :

$$I_{TOTAL} = I_{sat}\left(e^{\frac{qV_A}{K_BT}} - 1\right) - I_p \quad (5)$$

Finally, the contribution of the nanotextured layer is essentially based on optical property.

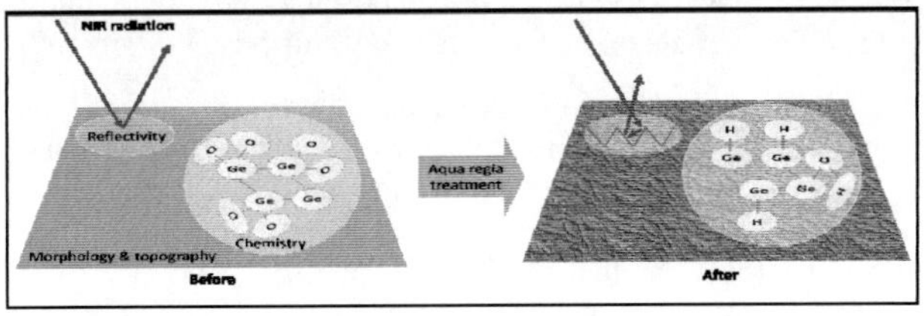

Figure 2 Graphical abstract of the chemical treatment results on the surface

Indeed, as shown in figure 2, a porous layer will trap the light and the flux will go up several reflections before leaving the surface. We believe that the decrease of reflectance will be useful to improve Ge-based optoelectronic devices because the junction will be at the level of the porous layer. What we want is that most of the photons (to not say all) will be absorbed at the level of this junction and never transmit further and even if it is the case the back contact will be there to reflect back what is transmitted.

3 Experimental setup

All the samples are produced using commercial Ga doped P-type Ge(100) wafers with resistivity ρ=0.23-0.25Ω purchased from MTI corporation.These wafers are 2" inch diameter, 500μm-thick and single side polished. These substrates were directly sent from MTI corporation (wafer supplier) to INNOVION (company that realizes the implantation) and opened for the first time in a clean room for the ion implantation process. The parameters of the implantation were selected and sent to INNOVION for execution.These parameters are the species to implant, the dose, the energy of implantation, and the tilt angle. Stopping Range of Ions in Matter (SRIM) simulation was done with taking into consideration the litterature to choose implantation parameters.

Once the ion implantation is done, the wafers were sealed in their containers and sent to our laboratory. First, the implanted Ge wafers with PN junction are cleaved into $1cm^2$ pieces using a diamond scriber. $1cm^2$ piece corresponds to the dimension of one device (photodiode) in progress. The device is then dipped for 1 min in 2% HF, rinsed with DI-water and blow-dried with ultra-high purity nitrogen (N_2) gas: This Cleaning Protocol (CP) will be repeated after each manipulation step. In order to activate the implanted species and cure the damages generated from the implantation, it is necessary to anneal the device. The annealing was done in a standard furnace for annealing using a quartz tube. The annealing was done at 525° for 30 min under N_2 ambiance.In order to characterise the depth of the phosphorus implanted layer, Secondary Ion Mass Spectroscopy-Time of Flight was done using ION-TOF SIMS before and after the annealing. Also, for metal deposition of the front and the back contacts, Plasminic SPT-H330 sputtering deposition was realized under vaccum.Aluminium was used for the front contact (Al-Ge typeN) and copper for the back contact (Cu-Ge type P). These metals were choosen based on litterature [20] and the available metal targets that we dispose.

For the case of porous Ge-photodiodes, the metallisation steps are preceded by the aqua regia electroless etching process. To do so, the samples are cleaned following the CP described above, then cleaned samples are immersed immediately in a fresh aqua regia mixture (HCl:HNO3 at 3:1). This 3:1 ratio refers to the respective volumes of HNO3 and HCl solutions as received from Aldrich: Nitric acid (HNO3) at 70%, hydrochloric (HCl) acid at 37%. After 4-5 minutes etching time, the samples are removed from the solution bath and rinsed with DI-water, followed by N_2 blow-drying. The nano-structured Ge samples are then sealed in clean closed containers for metallic deposition.

After the metal-contacts deposition, the devices becomes ready to be electrically characterized. The figure 3 describes the setup implemented for I-V measurements. The experimental setup for the I-V characterization as shown in figure 3 (a) is composed of 3 essential parts (the keithley, the computer and the lamp). We find the keithley which is the device containing the source of voltage and allowing not only the polarization of the photodiode, but also the reading of the device response which is the current. On the one hand, the keithley is connected to the photodiode using conductive wires and metal clips as shown in figure 3 (b), and on the other hand it is connected to a computer which allows the configuration of the inputs parameters and the representation of the IV curve via a LABVIEW interface.

In addition to the keithley and the computer, we find the lamp, which is an essential element to the manipulation, and which is calibrated so as to allow the illumination of the photodiode with a power of 1SUN.

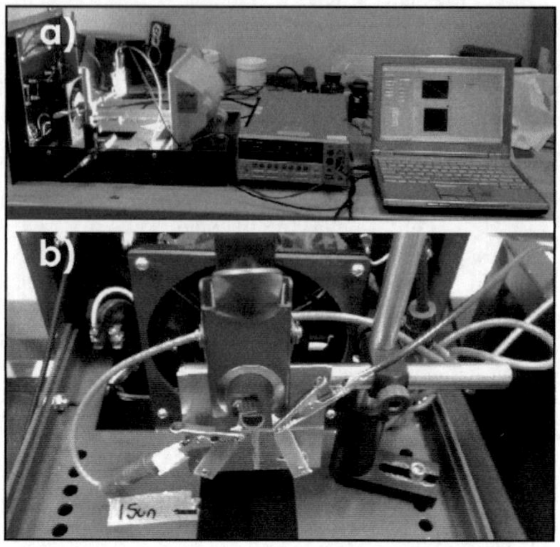

Figure 3 I-V measurements setup. (a) Setup parts, (b) Device probing.

4 Results and discussions

4-1 Ion implantation results by SRIM simulation and SIMS analyzis

Figure 4 represents the result of the SRIM simulation for phosphorous distribution in Germanium by ion implantation with an energy of 150KeV and a tilt angle of 7° (to avoid channeling effects). This simulation is useful because it informs, among others, about the stopping range of the implanted atoms and the dose of implantation.

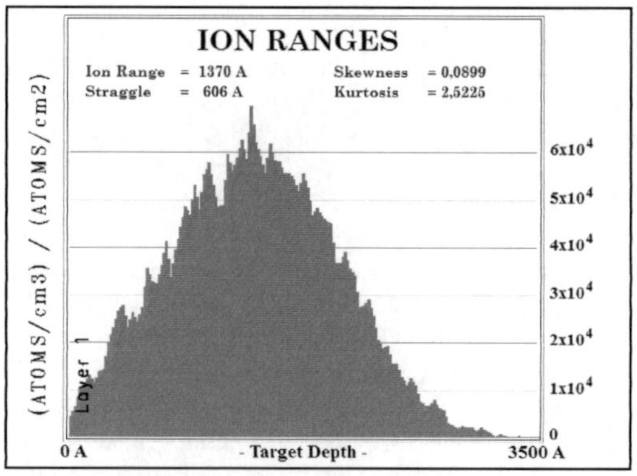

Figure 4 SRIM simulation for Phosphorous implantation in Germanium with an energy of 150 KeV and a tilt angla of 7°.

The energy is responsible of the stopping range in the material. For 150KeV, it is about 310nm as we can see from figure 4. The dose is determined from the peak of the distribution taking into account the maximum solubility of the implanted species in the target material. For this case, the maximum solubility of phosphorus in Germanium enabling to cure the damages and to recover the crystallinity of the material is about 2e20 at/cm3 [21]. From this datas we conclude that the maximum dose that can be used in the implantation is 3.10e15 at/cm2.

Now, to compare the simulation with the ion implantation actually realized, SIMS analyzes are essential. Figure 5 represents SIMS analyzes of two different samples, one as implanted and the other after implantation and thermal treatment. The thermal treatment for a such case is important to cure damages resulted by the ion implantation and to activate the implanted atoms.

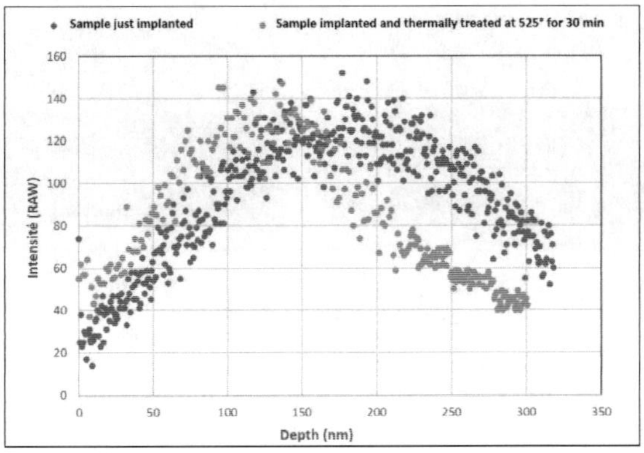

Figure 5 SIMS analyzes of the phosphorous implanted layer in Germanium before and after the annealing

The sample was annealed in a standard furnace in N_2 ambiance at 525 ° for 30min. If we compare the results of the two samples, the effect of the annealing is evident and it causes out-diffusion of the implanted atoms. Now, If we compare simulation and SIMS results, it is clear that both results have the same distribution peak and the same stopping range.

To summarize, the resulted N-type layer is shallow and the one shot ion implantation gives a distribution following a normal law. This is not the best when one wants to etch the surface. Ideally, the doping profile should be a square starting as close as possible from the surface. What we suggest for future ion implantation is a stepwise implantation with different energies.

Thus, instead of implanting with only 150KeV, it will be more interesting to sweep from 500KeV to 30 or 20KeV with a determined and fixed step as it is shown in figure6.

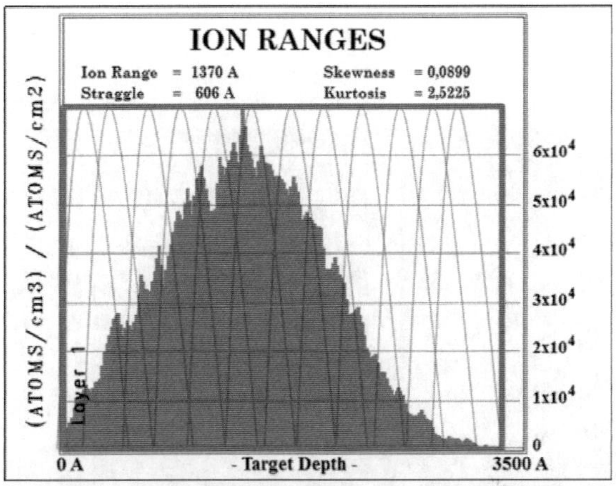

Figure 6 Representative shape of a Stepwise implantation

4-2 An Overview about the aqua regia etching under AFM

In this paper, we will not develop the method established to realize and understand the results of this original electroless etching using aqua regia. A detailed and complete investigation was published [22] in which we characterize the nanotextured surface for different immersion time baths in term of structure, morphology, topography, crystallinity, chemistry and reflectance.

The figure 7 represents an overview of the resulting surface morphology of the etched surface under AFM. Indeed, the resulting V-shaped nano-textured surface is homogeneous and a brief 5 minutes bath in aqua regia allows having a mean depth around 310nm according to the statistical calculation executed by the software Gwiddion. Unfortunately, this software doesn't give the different values that the variable (height) can take from each iteration between pixel 1 and pixel n. So, it becomes not possible for us to calculate the standard variation around the mean. However, it is important to precise that the mean height is calculated from the points defined by the pixels of the picture. For our measurements, we considered a picture of 512 by 512 pixels which result on n= 262.144 points. The mean height of 262.144 points is consequently very representative of the surface state.

In this same study mentioned above, we demonstrated that after aqua regia treatment, the nanotextured surface remains cristilline, becomes hydrogene passivated and that the reflectance decreases from 55% to 42% after this brief 5 minutes bath.

As we explained in the previous section, the doping profile we have is not perfect but we need to quantify in this work how much enhancement we can obtain from a such configuration. Better results with the same etching are expected using a better junction.

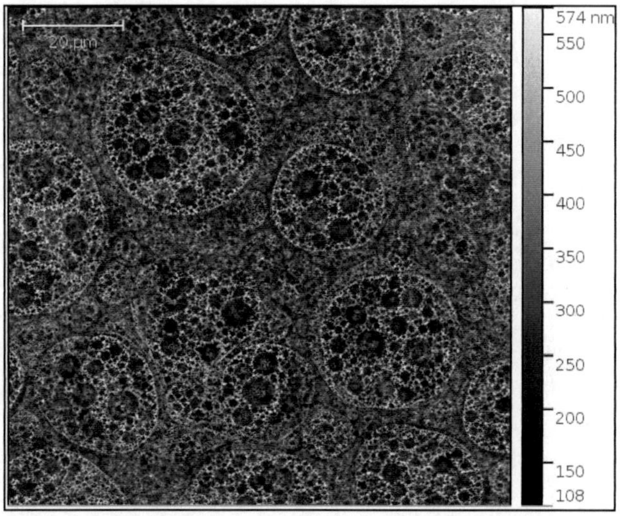

Figure 7 AFM image of an aqua regia etched surface in a 5minutes immersion bath

4-3 Metal deposition of the front contact: a compromise between conduction and transparency

While the back contact of the device is simple to realize because it consists to totally cover the back face with an appropriate metal, the front contact should respond to a compromise between conduction and transparency. The figure 8 shows the different evolution that the mask for the metal front contact deposition undergone to relieve the problems related to laser resolution, deposition quality and device-probes contacts.

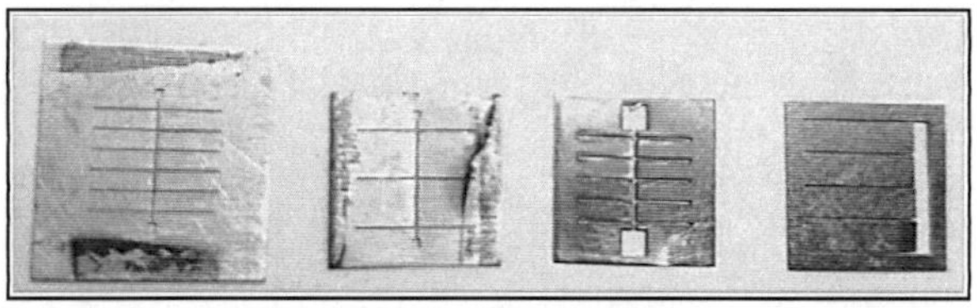

Figure 8 Evolution steps of metalic mask configuration

A grid mask [23] should at least have two components: the fingers and the bus. A third component is useful to contact the device with an external circuit is the pads. Electrons in surface will be attracted by the metal and will follow lower resistances. Consequently, they will join fingers to reach pads going through the bus. For experimental purposes, we choose to eliminate pads and to widen the bus to finish with mask parameters illustrated in table 1.

Table 1 Final parameters of the mask used for front metal contact deposition

Thickness of the stainless steel	Width of fingers (µm)	Width of the bus (µm)
As thin as possible	150	1000

A wide bus allows several measurement points to be taken without destroying the device, contrary to a pad that scratch rapidly while probing the device to take measurements.

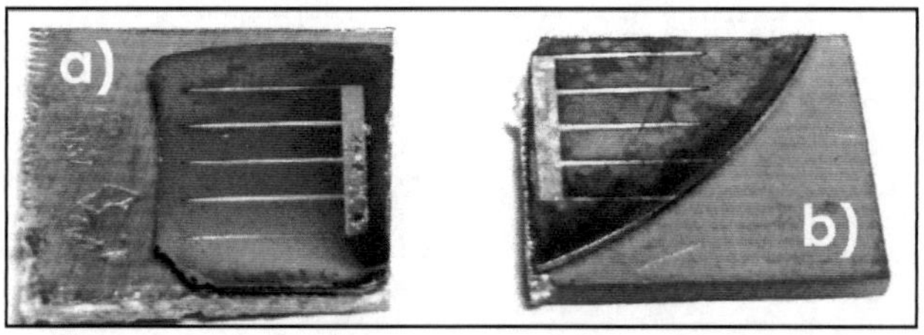

Figure 9 PN junction photodiode. (a) bulk Germanium based, (b) porous Germanium based

Figure 9 (a) and (b) represents a bulk Ge-photodiode and a porous Ge-photodiode respectively. As we can see, the bus is partially damaged after several points of electrical measurements.

4-4 I-V Electrical characterisation results using Keithley solar simulator:

While figure 10 (a) represents IV characteristic of a Ge photodiode in dark and under illumination, figure 10 (b) represents the same entity, but on a semi-logarithmic scale (logI-V). These two presentations are complementary and allow us not only to check the rectifying behaviour of the device through the shape of the curves but also to extract the different electrical parameters discussed in section 2. All of these parameters are summarized in Table 2.

Table 2 Electrical parameters of bulk Germanium photodiode

	V_S (V)	V_{oc} (V)	R_S (Ω)	R_{SH} (Ω)	Isc (mA)	Isat à 0V (A)	Iph at 1V (mA)	Isat at 1V (mA)
Ge	0.25	0.27	33	833	0.529	$1.2\ 10^{-5}$	10	4.8

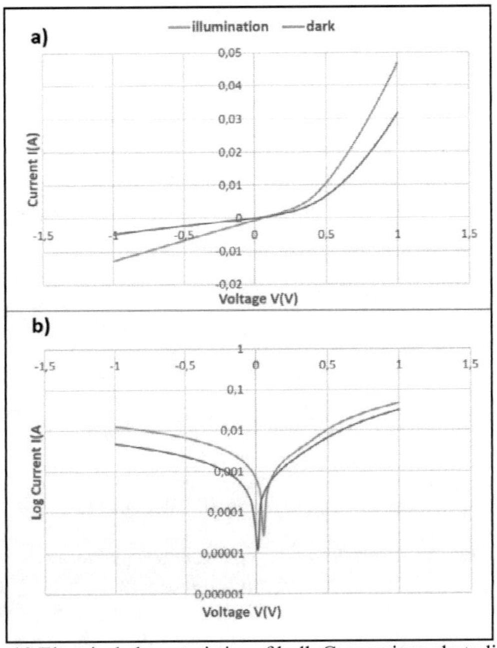

Figure 10 Electrical characteristics of bulk Germanium photodiode in dark and under illumination.(a) I-V curve, (a) logI-V curve

The I-V Curve in the dark is very important because it informs about the quality of the device and gives information about the values of Isc and Voc (through the values Isat, Vs , Rs and Rsh) that one hope to get after exposing the device to illumination. A device with a large saturation current value for example (such as the case of this device) will decrease both the values of Isc and Voc. Also, the value of Vs tells if the response of the device comes from the junction of the semiconductor or other barrier. It must always be checked whether the latter is proportional to the band gap energy of the semiconductor or not. The value of Rs informs on the quality of the contacts between the different materials of the device. This value must be small to ensure that the current easily reaches the external circuit. Finally, the high Rsh is the better it is because this resistance reflects the defects accumulated during the manufacturing process. As a result, a poorly derived solar cell will behave not as a rectifier, but rather as a resistance. The measurement of I-V on the bulk Ge photodiode (values shown in table 2) shows that the response of this device comes from Germanium since the values of Vs and Voc are 0.25V and 0.27V respectively. Also, the value of Rs is significantly smaller than Rsh. Regarding the current, the value of the Isat is important which contributes to the decrease of the resulting open-circuit current and which has a value of 0.529 mA

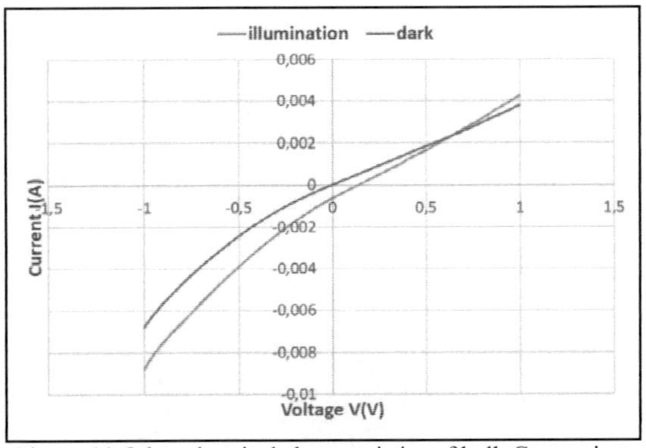

Figure 11 Other electrical characteristics of bulk Germanium photodiode in dark and under illumination.

These results represent the best values that we were able to obtain from the bulk Ge photodiode. However, we obtained other I-V responses with less encouraging paces. figure 11 is a typical example of the latter. Although the response of the detector remains in the same range I = 0.6mA, the values of the voltages Vs and Voc are very small which indicates either the probable presence of a metal-semiconductor schottky barrier resulting from manufacturing defects and preventing the proper functioning of the device or a low value of Rsh resulting from the defects accumulated during the manufacturing process: hence the domination of the resistive behavior against the degradation of the rectifying onc.

Table 3 Electrical parameters of porous Germanium photodiode

	V_s (V)	V_{oc} (V)	R_s (Ω)	R_{SH} (Ω)	Isc (mA)	Isat at 0V (A)	Iph at 1V (mA)	Isat at 1V (mA)
PGe	0.27	0.29	30	1499	2.08	$6.67\ 10^{-6}$	6.86	1.53

Now after analyzing the different I-V results obtained on bulk Ge photodiodes, it is interesting to analyze the results of porous Ge photodiodes. The curves of the I-V characteristics illustrated in figures 12 (a) and (b) represent a proper rectifying behaviour. If we compare the general shape of the curves obtained with the bulk Ge photodiode and this one, the first thing to notice is the considerable reduction of the saturation current and this allow having more constancy of the current on the reverse polarization interval. The second thing is the increase of the current in short circuit and the third thing is that the activation of the device (in the passing dipole) becomes more abrupt which reflects a better rectifier behavior, a better shunt resistance and therefore a better value of Voc. The different values obtained from the porous Ge photodiode are summarized in table3.

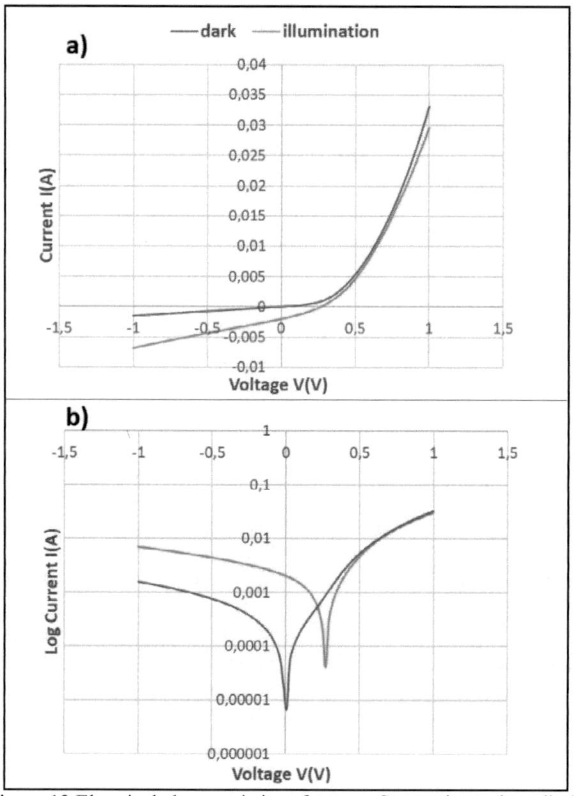

Figure 12 Electrical characteristics of porous Germanium photodiode in dark and under illumination.(a) I-V curve, (a) logI-V curve

In fact, if we go back to the previous principal measurement, we find that the values of Vs and Voc have increased from 0.25V-0.27V to 0.27V-0.29V respectively. The shunt resistance moves from 833 Ω to 1499 Ω and the serie resistance has decreased slightly from 33 to 30Ω. With regard to the current, the saturation current noted a very large decrease against the increase of the short-circuit current from 0.53mA to 2.08mA. Based on these preliminary results, we conclude that the small 5 minutes treatment with aqua regia improves all the parameters of the photodiode.

However, as for the case of the bulk Ge photodiode, for some tests we obtained almost linear responses. These results are illustrated in figure 13 and indicate, as for the previous case, either the presence of a schottky barrier, a low value of shunt resistance, or a combined effect of this two latter.

The major problem for this kind of results is the values of the activation voltage that are low compared to the activation voltage proportional to the germanium band gap energy, which suggests that the electrical response could come from a barrier other than that of Ge. If this distortion comes only from the low value of the shunt resistance and despite the fact that the value of the open circuit voltage is 0.18V, the answer could come from Germanium junction, then the values of the short-circuit current obtained for this case are more than 9 mA.

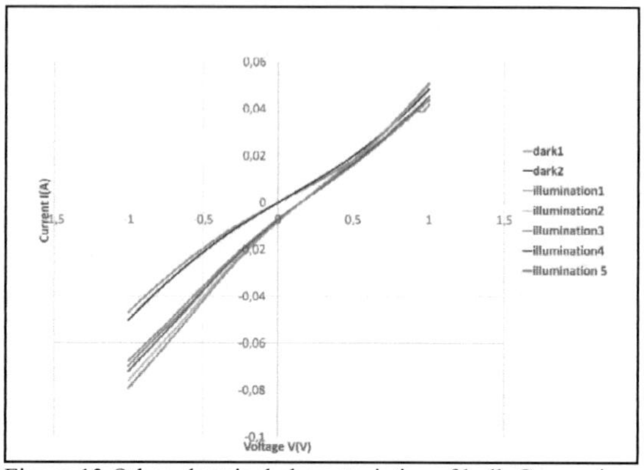

Figure 13 Other electrical characteristics of bulk Germanium photodiode in dark and under illumination

Now, if we go back to our two main results on which the responses are clearly proportional to Germanium band gap and with a clear rectifying behavior, it is important to link the improvement of the Isc and Voc values to the surface treatment we realized [22]. Indeed, we note that the improvement of the IV characteristic after the introduction of the porous layer on the front face of the device is primarily due to the increase of the surface to air ratio with the creation of the porous anti-reflective layer, and secondly due to the passivating effect of aqua regia used as an etching agent during chemical etching. Effectively, the hydrogenated termination of the surface passivates the pendant bonds of germanium thereby causing a decrease in the recombination rate and therefore an increase of the charge carriers life time in the surface and thus reducing the saturation current as shown in Figure 14.

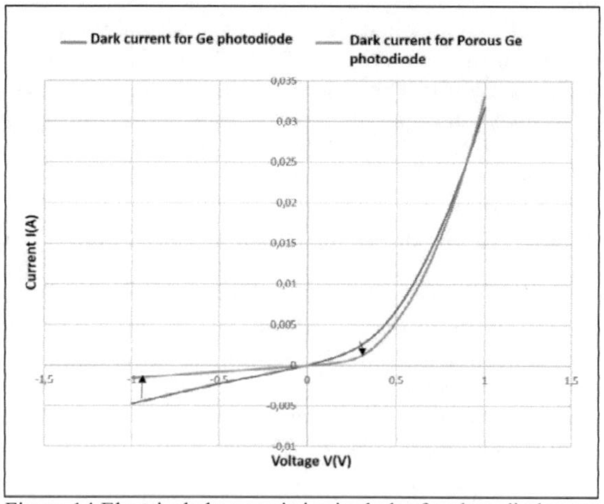

Figure 14 Electrical characteristics in dark of a photodiode; one bulk Germanium based and another porous Germanium based

Working on reducing the saturation current is therefore a key component for improving the overall performance of the device.

5 Conclusion

In this work, we evaluated the impact of surface nanotexturing on the electrical parameters of Ge photodiodes.Indeed, we exploited an original method of etching we developed recently in an ulterior work to realize a porous active surface of a Ge photodiode. The steps of photodiode design and realization were described and the quality of the realized junction was discussed. In the limits of the resulted doping profil, we quantify the electrical parameter inheancement recorded from photodiodes realized exactly in the same conditions except for the etching step.Hence, we have the flat active surface (bulk Ge) and the nanotextured active surface Ge based photodiodes.

Indeed, for the junction located in a depth of 310nm from the surface and a doping profil following normal law, also for an aqua regia treatment in an immersion bath of 4-5minutes giving a mean depth of pores that respects the junction location, it was possible to inheance voltage values, shunt resitance value, and short cut current value that moves from 0.53mA to 2mA, also the values of serie resistance and saturation current decrease.

This results could be widely improuved with a doping more deep and with a profil following a square law. This will allow the realization of pores more deep and will avoid the ponctual short-cut of the jonction that decrease considerably the performance of the device

References

1. Shockley, W., Hans J Queisser, Detailed balance limit of efficiency of p n junction solar cells Journal of applied physics, 1961. 32(3): p. 510-519.
2. Akkari, E., Z Benachour, S Aouida, O Touayar, B Bessais et J Benbrahim. , Study and characterization of porous germanium for radiometric measurements. physica status solidi (c), 2009. 6(7): p. 1685-1688.
3. Jung Woo Leem, Y.M.S., and Jae Su Yu, Broadband antireflective germanium surfaces based on subwavelength structures for photovoltaic cell applications optics express, 2011.
4. Zwinkels, J.C., Erkki Ikonen, Nigel P Fox, Gerhard Ulm, Maria Luisa Rastello, Photometry, radiometry and the candela: evolution in the classical and quantum world Metrologia, 2010. vol. 47(no 5): p. R15-R32.
5. Haapalinna, A., Petri Kärhä et Erkki Ikonen, Spectral reflectance of silicon photodiodes. Applied optics, 1998. 37(4): p. 729-732.
6. Raut, H.K., V Anand Ganesh, A Sreekumaran Nair et Seeram Ramakrishna, Anti-reflective coatings: A critical, in-depth review. Energy & Environmental Science, 2011. 4(10): p. 3779-3804.
7. Fang, C., H Föll et J Carstensen., Electrochemical pore etching in germanium Journal of Electroanalytical Chemistry, 2006. 589(2): p. 259-288.
8. Garralaga Rojas, E.H., J.; Carstensen, J.; Föll, H.; Brendel, R., Porous germanium multilayers. Phys. Status Solidi C, 2011. 8: p. 1731–1733.
9. Rojas, E.G.T., B.; Plagwitz, H.; Hensen, J.; Baur, C.; Strobl, G.F.; Brendel, R. , Formation of mesoporous germanium double layers by electrochemical etching for layer transfer processes. Electrochem. Commun., 2010. 12(231-233).
10. Rojas, E.G.H., J.; Baur, C.; Brendel, R., Sintering and reorganization of electrochemically etched mesoporous germanium layers in various atmospheres. Sol. Energy Mater. Sol. Cells, 2011. 95: p. 292-295.
11. Manos, D.M., et Daniel L Flamm, Plasma etching: an introduction. ELSVIER, 1989.
12. Kurogi, Y., Recent trends in dry etching Thin Solid Films, 1982. 92(1): p. 33-40.
13. Franssila, S., et Lauri Sainiemi, Reactive Ion Etching (RIE). In Encyclopedia of Microfluidics and Nanofluidics, 2008: p. 1772-1781.
14. Kaiser, R., S Koffel, P Pichler, AJ Bauer, B Amon, A Claverie, G Benassayag, P Scheiblin, L Frey et H Ryssel., Honeycomb voids due to ion implantation in germanium. Thin Solid Films, 2010. 518(9): p. 2323-2325.
15. Toinin, J.P., Alain Portavoce, Khalid Hoummada, Michaël Texier, Maxime Bertoglio, Sandrine Bernardini, Marco Abbarchi et Lee Chow. , Nanoporous Ge thin film production combining Ge sputtering and dopant implantation. Beilstein journal of nanotechnology, 2015. 6(1): p. 336-342.
16. Sioncke, S.B., D.P.; Meuris, M.; Uwamahoro, O.; Van Steenbergen, J.; Vrancken, E.; Heyns, M.M., Etch Rates of Ge, GaAs and InGaAs in Acids, Bases and Peroxide Based Mixtures. ECS Trans, 2008. 16: p. 451–460.
17. Akkari, E., Oualid Touayar, F Javier Del Campo et Josep Montserrat, Improved electrical characteristics of porous germanium photodiode obtained by phosphorus ion implantation. International Journal of Nanotechnology, 2013. 10(5-7): p. 553-562.
18. Posthuma, N.E., Johan van der Heide, Giovanni Flamand et Jozef Poortmans., Emitter formation and contact realization by diffusion for germanium photovoltaic devices IEEE transactions on electron devices, 2007. 54(5): p. 1210-1215.
19. LEE, S.M.S.a.M.K., Semiconductor Devices Physics and Technology. 3 ed. 2010: JOHN WILEY & SONS, INC.

20. Li, S.S., Semiconductor physical electronics. Microdevices physics and fabrication technologies. 2012.
21. Simoen, E., Alessandra Satta, Antonio D'Amore, Tom Janssens, Trudo Clarysse, Koen Martens, B De Jaeger, Alessandro Benedetti, Ilse Hoflijk et Bert Brijs. , Ion-implantation issues in the formation of shallow junctions in germanium Materials Science in Semiconductor Processing,, 2006. 9(4): p. 634-639.
22. Ibtihel Chaabane, D.B., Oualid Touayar and Sylvain G. Cloutier, Shallow V-Shape Nanostructured Pit Arrays in Germanium Using Aqua Regia Electroless Chemical Etching. mdpi, 2017. 10: p. 854.
23. E. Suresh Kumar, B.S., Optimization of finger sapacing in photovoltaic modules for minimum power loss. Asian Journal of Computer Science And Information Technology, 2013. 3(2): p. 13-18.

Hydrodynamic study of an electrocoagulation reactor and simulation of the flow by COMSOL software

M.K. Mbacké, C. Kane*, M. Ndoye, A. Paye, and C.G.M. Diop

Laboratoire d'Electrochimie et des Procédés Membranaires (LEPM), Ecole Supérieure Polytechnique, Université Cheikh Anta Diop de Dakar, B.P.5085 Dakar-Fann - SENEGAL

Abstract.
An electrocoagulation reactor operating continuously is designed for the treatment of industrial effluents in Senegal.
The optimization of the operating parameters such as the flow rate, the residence time, the conductivity and so on for the treatment of these effluents requires an understanding of the reactor hydrodynamics.
Thus, this hydrodynamic study based on the residence time distribution curve (DTS) showed the presence of dead zone in the reactor with a theoretical residence time of 607.76 s for an average residence time obtained from the residence time distribution curve of 554.85 s.
A comparison of the curve obtained experimentally with the curves for an ideal reactor of the piston type or of a perfectly stirred type, has shown that the electrocoagulation reactor behavior is like a cascade of two perfectly stirred reactors with a difference between them of 0.15%.
The numerical simulation with COMSOL allowed to illustrate the velocity fields and to highlight the preferential zones during the flow in the reactor and thus to confirm the results obtained with the hydrodynamics with a relatively low absolute error of 4.6% obtained with the least squares method.
Keywords: electrocoagulation, hydrodynamic, simulation

1 Introduction

In addition to technological and environmental aspects, cost-effective methods are required to treat a wide range of wastewater pollutants in a diverse range of conditions. Electrocoagulation (EC) is an emerging technology that combines the functions and advantages of conventional coagulation, flotation, and electrochemistry in water and wastewater treatment [1]. As compared with traditional treatment methods, electrocoagulation provides a relatively compact and robust treatment alternative in which sacrificial metal anodes initiate electrochemical reactions that provide active metal cations for coagulation and flocculation. The inherent advantage of electrocoagulation is that no coagulants have to be added to the wastewater and hence the salinity of the water does not increase after treatment [2].
The technology is most commonly used in the oil and gas, construction, and mining industries to treat emulsified oil, total petroleum hydrocarbons, suspended solids, heavy metals, and other difficult-to-remove contaminants.
Electrocoagulation is performed by applying an electric current across metal plates that are submerged in water. Heavy metals, organics, and inorganics are primarily held in water by electrical charges. By applying another electrical charge to the contaminated water, the charges that hold the particles together are destabilized and separate from the clean water.
Electrocoagulation can be used as a pretreatment for processes such as clarification, reverse osmosis, and ultrafiltration, or as a polish treatment at the end of traditional treatment processes.

* Correspondence: cheikhou.kane@ucad.edu.sn

The technology, typically, eliminates the need of chemicals or biological additives or demulsifies. Without chemicals, there is also no need for chemical mixing tanks.
Previous studies have made it possible to assess the impact of the operating parameters on the efficiency of the electrocoagulation process [3]. The study of the performance of an electrocoagulation reactor essentially consists of determining the degree of progress of the desired abatement reaction. The degree of progress of the reaction carried out by a reactor is the result of the combination of hydrodynamics and reaction kinetics.The residence time in the reactor, as well as the flow conditions have a significant influence on the purification performance. The understanding of the impact of these parameters requires an understanding of the hydrodynamic behavior of the reactor. In this study, the hydrodynamic behavior of an electrocoagulation reactor was tested with the residence time distribution method. The results obtained were compared to the ideal reactor models to understand the flows in the reactor. Comsol Multiphysics modeling software was used to simulate the reactor and confirm the experimental results.
The paper is organized as follows: in Section 1 we present the overall context of the study as well as the benefits of the electrocoagulation process. Section 2 presents the residence time distribution method and the principle of simulation with Comsol. Section 3 outlines our experimental setup and measurement procedures. Section 4 presents experimentally obtained results of the hydrodynamic measurements and simulation. Section 5 summarizes the hydrodynamic behavior of the reactor compared to the ideal reactor model.

2 Theoretical background

2.1. Résidence time distribution method

Residence time is an important parameter for performance evaluation used for characterizing, modeling, and optimizing a chemical reaction system. Continuous reactors, such as horizontal auger tubes, typically which have imperfect flow characteristics where undesired back-mixing and flow stratification lead to variations in residence time. This variation is characterized by the residence time distribution (RTD) curve, which describes the probability that a particle or chemical species will spend a specific time at desired reaction conditions. The variance about the mean time of this distribution is one indicator of how precisely the reactor is able to target a specific residence time [4].

The theory of residence time distributions generally begins with three assumptions: the reactor is at steady-state, transports at the inlet and the outlet takes place only by advection, and the fluid is incompressible.

The incompressibility assumption is not required always, but compressible flows are more difficult to work with. A further level of complexity is required for multi-phase reactors, where a separate RTD will describe the flow of each phase, for example bubbling air through a liquid. The distribution of residence times is represented by an external residence time distribution or an exit age distribution, E(t). The function E(t) has the units of time^{-1} and is defined such that:

$$\int_0^{\infty} E(t)\,dt = 1 \qquad (1)$$

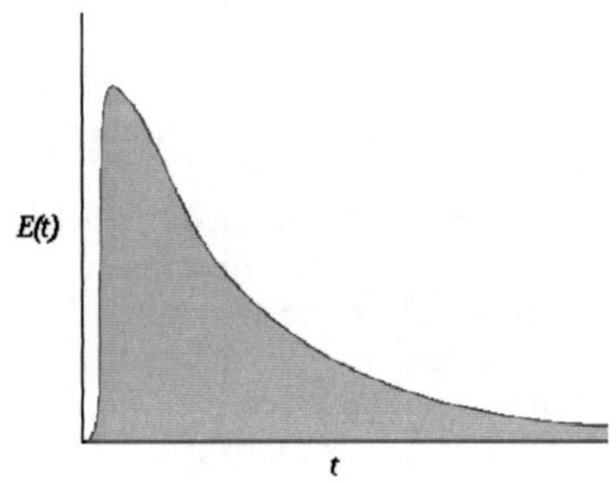

Fig. 1.: An RTD curve for a reasonably well-mixed reactor

The fraction of the fluid that spends a given duration, t inside the reactor is given by the value of E(t)dt. The fraction of the fluid that leaves the reactor with an age time less that t1 is:

$$F(t1) = \int_0^{t1} E(t)dt \qquad (2)$$

where F(t) is called “cumulative distribution”. Thus, the fraction of the fluid that leaves the reactor with an age greater that t1 is:

$$1 - F(t1) = \int_{t1}^{\infty} E(t)\,dt \qquad (3)$$

The average residence time is given by the first moment of the age distribution:

$$\mu_1 = \bar{t} = \int_0^{\infty} tE(t)\,dt \qquad (4)$$

If there are no dead, or stagnant zones within the reactor, then $\bar{t}$ will be equal to τ, the residence time calculated from the total reactor volume and the volumetric flow rate of the fluid: $\tau = V/v = \bar{t}$. The higher order central moments can provide significant information about the behavior of the function E(t). For example, the second central moment indicates the variance (σ^2), the degree of dispersion around the mean is as follows :

$$\sigma^2 = \int_0^{\infty} (t - \bar{t})^2 E(t)\,dt \qquad (5)$$

Residence time distributions are measured by introducing a non-reactive tracer into the system at the inlet. The concentration of the tracer is changed according to a known function and the response is found by measuring the concentration of the tracer at the outlet. The selected tracer should not modify the physical characteristics of the fluid (equal density, equal viscosity) and the introduction of the tracer should not modify the hydrodynamic conditions. A suitable tracer material for RTD-experiments should exhibit similar physical properties, i.e. viscosity, diffusion coefficient, density, to the flow medium and in particular the materials used should behave inertly, not adhere or adsorb on to the reactor walls and be easily detectable. The experimental determination of the residence time distribution requires a well-defined introduction of a tracer species into the reactor inlet and the detection of its transient concentration leaving the reactor outlet. In general, the change in tracer concentration will either be a pulse or a step. Other functions are possible, but they require more calculations to deconvolute the RTD curve, E(t). In this study the pulse was used [5].

This method required the introduction of a very small volume of concentrated tracer at the inlet of the reactor, such that it approaches the dirac delta function. Although an infinitely short injection cannot be produced, it can be made much smaller than the mean residence time of the vessel. If a mass of tracer, M, is introduced into a vessel of volume V and an expected residence time of τ, the resulting curve of C(t) can be transformed into a dimensionless residence time distribution curve by the following relation:

$$E(t) = \frac{C(t)}{\int_0^{+\infty} C(t)\,dt} \qquad (6)$$

The residence time distribution of a reactor can be used to compare its behavior to those of two ideal reactor models: the PFR and the CSTR (or mixed-flow reactor). This characteristic is important in order to calculate the performance of a reaction with known kinetics.

In an ideal PFR, there is no mixing and the fluid elements leave in the same order they arrived. One of the most frequently used models is a piston flow, on which is superimposed a dispersion mechanism. This model is sometimes called dispersive piston [6].

$$\frac{\partial C}{\partial t} = \nabla(D\nabla C) - \bar{u}\nabla C + \varphi(C) \quad (8)$$

With

D: dispersion coefficient [m^2s^{-1}],

u: average velocity of the flow [$m.s^{-1}$] (in the case of a flow in a porous medium, it is the average interstitial velocity),

φ (C): rate of production or consumption of the reagent.

In the case of incompressible flow in a cylindrical reactor, the axial symmetry makes it possible to define a longitudinal axis of ordinates z and a distance with respect to this axis r. In some cases, particularly when the radius of the reactor is small in front of the length, the effect of the radial dispersion can be neglect.

$$\frac{\partial C}{\partial t} = D_z\frac{\partial^2 C}{\partial z^2} - \frac{\bar{u}\partial C}{\partial z} + \varphi(C) \quad (9)$$

In dimensionless coordinates and considering that the tracer does not react therefore φ (C) = 0, the equation 9 becomes:

$$\frac{\partial C}{\partial \theta} = \frac{D}{\bar{u}L}\frac{\partial^2 C}{\partial x^2} - \frac{\partial C}{\partial x} \qquad x = \frac{z}{L} \quad (10)$$

This equation shows a dimensionless number called Peclet number:

$$Pe = \frac{\bar{u}L}{D} \quad (11)$$

The value of the number of Peclet gives indications on the type of flow:

1/Pe → 0 dispersion is negligible and the flow is piston type;

1/Pe → ∞ dispersion is important hence a mixed flow

If Pe <100 the dispersion is strong and the solution of the equation depends on the flow conditions at the entry and exit points of the tracer. When the entry point is a section throat, the tracer can not disperse upstream of the inlet section. On the other hand, if the input section of the tracer is identical to the section of the reactor, the tracer can disperse upstream. Similarly, if the exit section is strangled, the tracer can not return to the reactor by dispersion once it has passed the exit section. This is not the case if the output signal consists of a tracer sample in any section of the reactor.

In this study, the input and the output are opened to diffusion, which makes it possible to write the boundary conditions. Considering that the tracer is injected at z = 0 and its output concentration measured at z = L:

$$E(t) \approx \frac{1}{2\bar{t}}\sqrt{\frac{Pe}{\pi}}\exp\left[\frac{-Pe\left(1-\frac{t}{\bar{t}}\right)^2}{4*\frac{t}{\bar{t}}}\right] \quad (12)$$

The number of Peclet is obtained from the variance

$$\sigma^2_{(t)} = \left(\frac{2}{Pe} + \frac{8}{Pe^2}\right) * \bar{t}^2 \quad (13)$$

The variance of an ideal plug-flow reactor is zero. The RTD of a real reactor deviate from that of an ideal reactor, depending on the hydrodynamics within the vessel. A non-zero variance indicates that there is some dispersion along the path of the fluid, which may be attributed to turbulence, a non-uniform velocity profile, or diffusion. If the mean of the E(t) curve arrives earlier than the expected time τ, it indicates that there is stagnant fluid within the vessel. If the RTD curve shows more than one main peak, it may indicate channeling, parallel paths to the exit, or strong internal circulation.

An ideal CSTR is based on the assumption that the flow at the inlet is completely and instantly mixed into the bulk of the reactor. The reactor and the outlet fluid have identical, homogeneous compositions at all times. An ideal CSTR has an exponential residence time distribution[7]:

$$E(t) = \frac{1}{\bar{t}} * \frac{n^n}{(n-1)!} * \left(\frac{t}{\bar{t}}\right)^{n-1} * \exp\left[\frac{-nt}{\bar{t}}\right] \quad (14)$$

To identify the model with an experimental curve, the only parameter to be determined is n, the average residence time being in principle given by the volume of liquid and the flow rate.

Whatever the method, it usually leads to a non-integer n.

When n is not integer, the physical meaning of the model is lost. However, it is possible to calculate the distribution using the gamma function.

$$E(t) = \frac{1}{\bar{t}} * \frac{n^n}{\Gamma(n)}\left(\frac{t}{\bar{t}}\right)^{n-1} \exp\left[\frac{-nt}{\bar{t}}\right] \quad (15)$$

To estimate the gamma function, we can use the approximation of the Stirling formula[8]:

$$\Gamma(n) \cong e^{-n}n^{\left(n-\frac{1}{2}\right)}\sqrt{2\pi}\left(1 + \frac{1}{12n} + \frac{1}{288n^2} - \frac{139}{51840n^3} - \frac{571}{2488320n^4}\right) \quad (16)$$

When n is large, ie greater than 25, the SDRs calculated from the model of the n series reactors are superimposed on the SDRs calculated from the dispersive piston model, taking

$$Pe = 2(n-1) \quad (17)$$

The number of Peclet is obtained from the variance

$$\sigma^2_{(\theta)} = \frac{\bar{t}^2}{n} \quad (18)$$

2.2. Principle of simulation with Comsol

The COMSOL software is one of the industrial CFD codes, allowing the prediction of fluids flow. It is a software that allows, in addition to dealing with multi physical problems. Indeed, the Partial Differential Equations (PDEs) are represented with equations in general forms allowing to personalize them and to couple them.

This software uses the finite element analysis method which is the most complete one to effectively solve the Navier-Stokes, convection-diffusion equations. The Navier-Stokes equations, which express physical laws of conservation of momentum, are deduced from the Newtonian laws of motion. They combine speed and pressure at each point of the flow [9].

Conservation equation of mass:

$$\partial\rho/\partial t + \mathrm{div}(\rho V) = 0 \quad (19)$$

Conservation equation of momentum:

$$\partial(\rho V)/\partial t = \mathrm{grad}\rho + \mathrm{div}(\rho V) + \rho g \quad (20)$$

It is possible to solve them using the model of the predefined rotational equations in COMSOL. This model will be used for 2D simulation.

3 Experimental setup

To measure a distribution of the residence times, it is enough to "mark" the molecules to be able to detect them in the output stream for this the tracer used can be a radioactive body, a dye, or any substance with the same hydrodynamic properties as the fluid but detectable by a physical property such as electrical conductivity. A signal using the tracer is applied to the reactor inlet, so as not to disturb the flow regime, and the "response" to the output is examined.

The residence time distribution measurements were carried out by salt tracing with sodium chloride in a reactor with a volume occupied by the liquid of 6370 ml.

The sample taken to measure the concentrations at the outlet of the reactor must satisfy the conditions of representativeness of the concentration, in time and over the whole of the outlet section. The representativity with respect to the section is ensured either by a mixing device at the outlet of the reactor, or by adopting a small and small exit section with respect to the average section of the reactor. This option was chosen.

The choice of sampling frequency over time must be made accurately to prevent peaks or short circuits from being detected. To do this, preliminary tests with a maximum number of doses were made to set the frequency on the one hand and concentrate the catch in the vicinity of possible concentration peaks on the other hand.

The NaCl content at the outlet of the reactor is measured by a conductivity meter.

The reactor unit used at the pilot scale consists of four distinct zones. This is a first zone corresponding to the distribution chamber from which the effluent is distributed homogeneously in the cell. The second zone represents the electrocoagulation cell where the electrodes are housed. The third zone is a conical physical separation zone where the sludge is recovered allowing the flocs to be separated from the treated effluent. The fourth zone is used to recover the flocs that leave the cell under the effect of flotation.

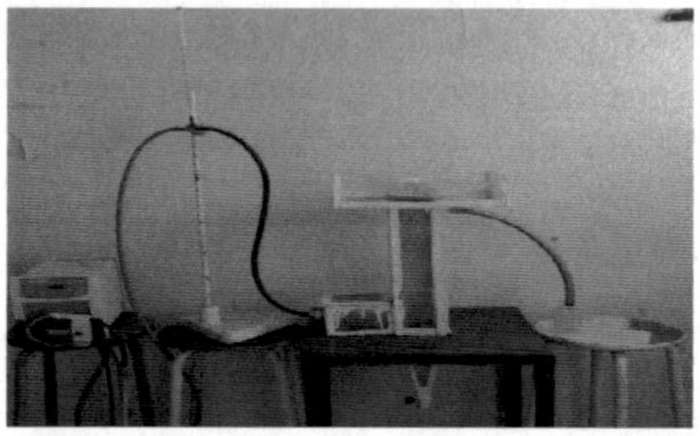

Fig. 2.: Experimental apparatus

A pump is used for the fluid flow in the reactor.

For simulation under COMSOL, a two-dimensional geometry is used with baffles to avoid preferential paths and to have a good time of stays. The simulation reactor is represented by the following figure 3.

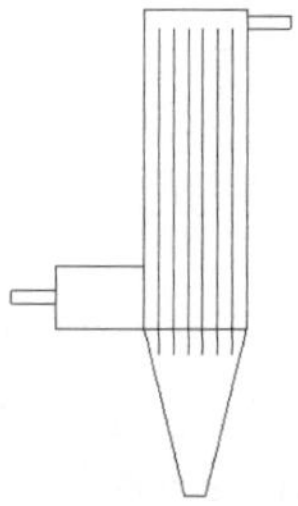

Fig. 3.: 2D reactor geometry

4 Results and discussions

Beforehand, the feed pump is calibrated to determine the actual flow rate (y) based on the flow rate displayed (x). The equation of the line reflecting the evolution of the conductivity(y) as a function of the concentration of sodium chloride (x) is also determined.

$$y = 100.290x - 12.952 \quad (21)$$

$$y = 0.369x - 0.002 \quad (22)$$

The tracing operation was carried out on the electrocoagulation reactor. The tracing being carried out with an injection of 1 g of NaCl in 5 ml of water with a flow rate of 10.48ml / s for a period of 5s, 98.48% of the mass of the tracer was restored.

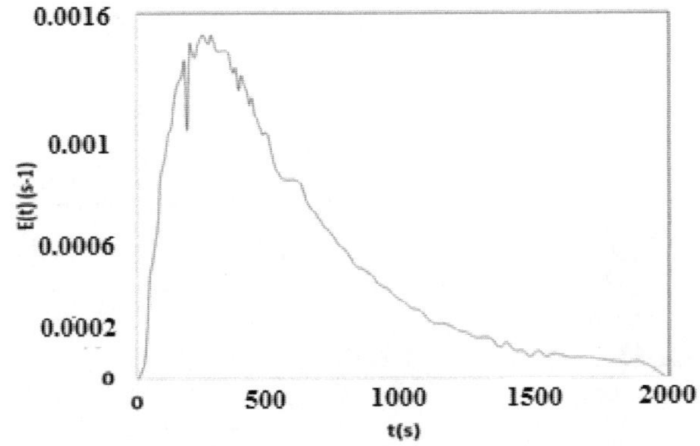

Fig. 4. Residence time distribution in the reactor

The experimental results make it possible to determine the mean residence time calculated from the moment of order 1 (equation 4) and the variance is calculated with equation 5.
The theoretical residence time is given by the ratio of the volume to the flow rate, the reactor volume being 6370 ml and the flow rate 10.48 ml / s.

Table 1. The parameters of the residence time distribution

Designation	Value
Flow rate (ml/s)	10.48
Theoritical residence time τ(s)	607.76
Mean residence time $\bar{t}$ (s)	554.85

The average residence time obtained is less than the passage time $\bar{t}<\tau$.
This result indicates a flow defect characterized by a short-circuit phenomenon. There is a preferential path in the reactor, which means that a fraction of the flow goes well before the rest. This corresponds to a large concentration peak in output just after the stimulation. The flow rate of fluid that then actually flows through the entire reactor is lower than that at the inlet.

Once the RTD curve has been obtained, its observation makes it possible to make some hypotheses. A peak or a large fluctuation of concentration in the first moments shows the presence of a short-circuit, an average residence time much lower than the passage time, the presence of a dead zone and a significant drag of the curve, the presence of stagnant zones.
The next step is to find a transfer function that is closest to the RTD curve, but not too complex to use in the future. This transfer function, coupled with the kinetic law of the reaction, makes it possible to evaluate the influence of the type of flow on the progress of the reaction at the outlet of the reactor.
The dispersive piston model (Equations 12 and 13) gave the following results with the variance and residence time obtained from the RTD curves.

Table 2. The parameters of the piston dispersive model

Designation	Value
Flow rate (ml/s)	10.48
Theoritical residence time τ(s)	607.76
Mean residence time $\bar{t}$ (s)	554.85
Peclet number	6.49

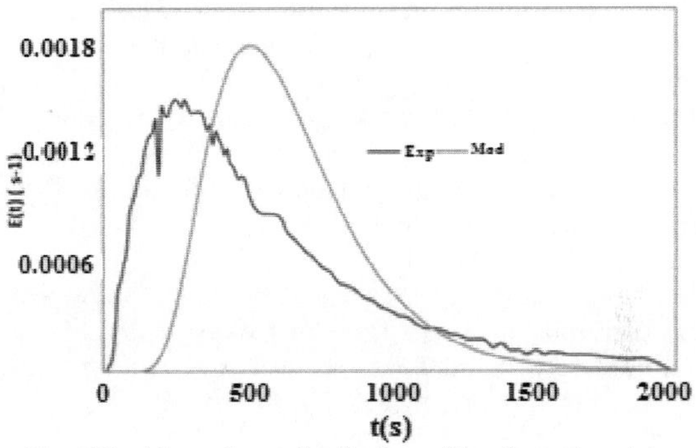

Fig. 5 Residence times distribution of the dispersive piston model

Figure 5 shows a phase shift in time of the two distributions as well as a loss of amplitude of the experimental curve. This can be due to a recirculation zone in the reactor.

The cascade reactor model was tested with determination of reactor number n. The number of reactors is obtained from the variance.

Table 3. Parameters of the n cascade reactor model

Designation	Value
Flow rate (ml/s)	10.48
Theoritical residence time τ(s)	607.76
Mean residence time $\bar{t}$ (s) 554.80	
$\Gamma(n)$	1.99
n	2

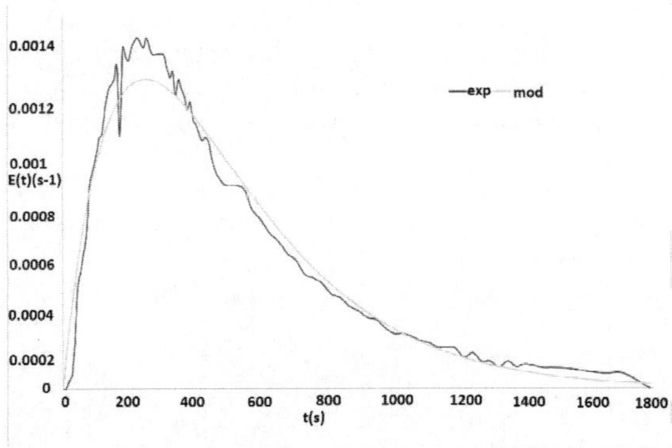

Fig. 6 Residence times distribution of the cascade model

Figure 6 shows the experimentally obtained RTD confrontation and the model of 2 cascaded reactors.
The results of the modelizations of the flow in a series of perfectly agitated reactors make it possible to draw different information on the hydrodynamic behavior of the reactor
The comparison of the experimental and model RTD curves shows the reproduction of the shape of the curve with a loss of amplitude of the curve of the cascade model. This loss is probably due to the recirculation phenomenon and the presence of dead zones.

The values of the measured concentrations are quite close to the calculated values, the difference calculated by the least squares method is 0.15% for all the points. The final tail of the two curves induces the existence of dead zones.
The experimental results and the comparison with the dispersive piston reactor and cascade reactor models show that the system corresponds to a cascade of two perfectly stirred reactors. Indeed, the distribution chamber and the reaction chamber is like a series of reactors.

Simulation of flow with Comsol showed velocity profiles with preferential paths.

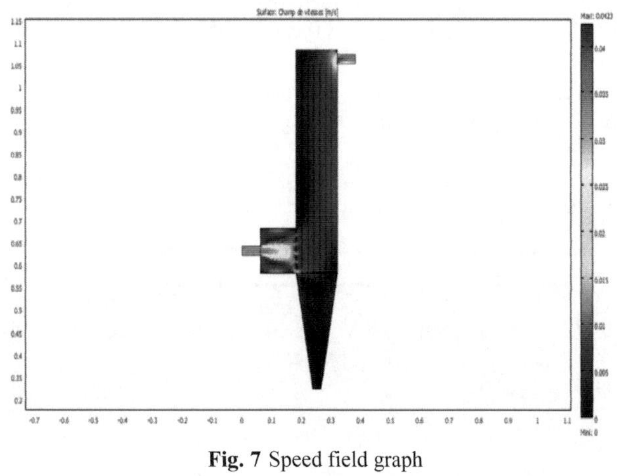

Fig. 7 Speed field graph

Figure 7 confirms the presence of the vortices generated by the recirculation zones after widening of the passage section at the entrance and therefore the existence of negative speeds. This speed field confirms that the flow is far from evolving into piston flow.
In order to identify the zones of reciculation, the velocity profiles are represented at the inlet, at the middle and at the outlet of the reactor.

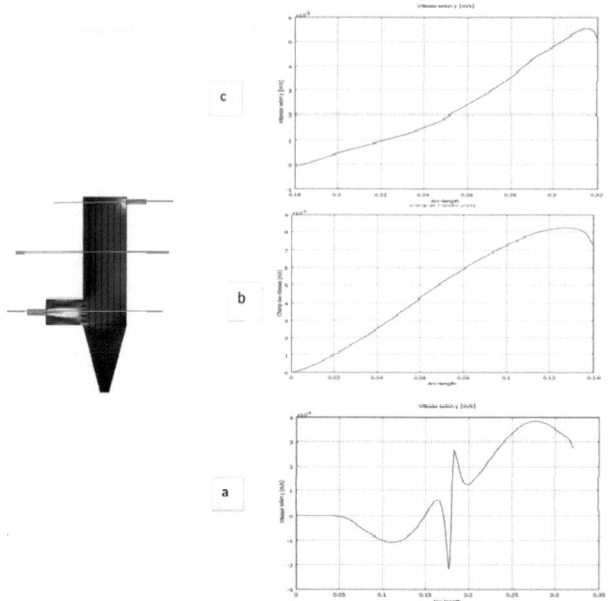

Fig. 8. Profiles at the inlet, the middle and the outlet of the reactor.

The profiles obtained do not indicate a negative value in the middle and at the exit. However, at the inlet of the reactor there are negative values of the speed, which shows that there is a recirculation zone.

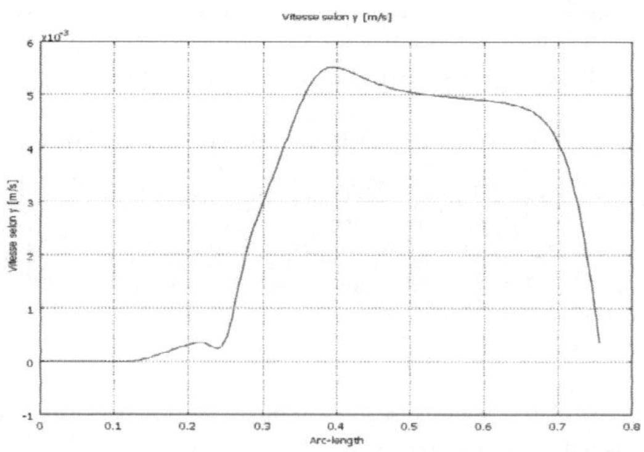

Fig. 9. Profile speed on a longitudinal plane

The velocity which is practically nil at the bottom of the reactor reaches a maximum value in the middle of the reactor then increases to approximately 3.10^{-4} m / s when tending towards the reactor outlet.
The velocity fields obtained are used for the simulation of passive transport in the reactor.
It consists of injecting a concentration step C and simulating the evolution of the concentration in the reactor as well as at the outlet. The results given by COMSOL represent the flow of concentration at the exit by the section. This approximation is

justified by the small diameter of the outlet compared to the diameter of the reactor.
The conditions of the simulations are the injection conditions of a step. At t = 0 the concentration in all the reactor is zero and then injected at the reactor inlet a concentration c which is equal to 3.42mol / l. At the output level a zero scalar flux is fixed.

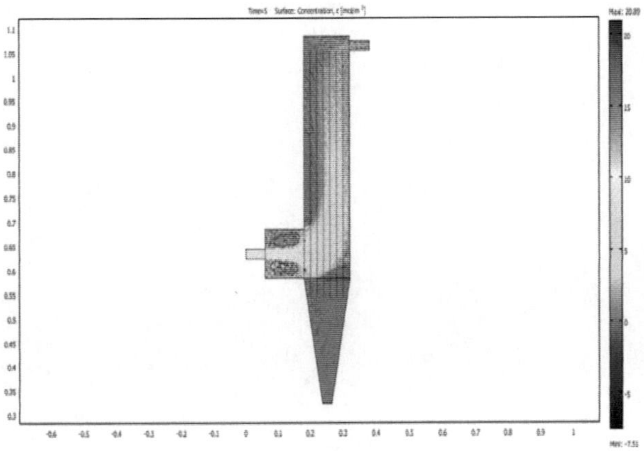

Fig. 10. Simulation of the evolution of the concentration

Figure 10 shows the evolution of the concentration in the reactor 1s after the step injection. Several simulations were performed at t = 50s, t = 100s, t = 200s, t = 500s, t = 750s, t = 1000s, t = 1500s and t = 1800s. From these simulations the concentration at the outlet was calculated for each case, which made it possible to trace the evolution of the concentration as a function of time in the reactor.

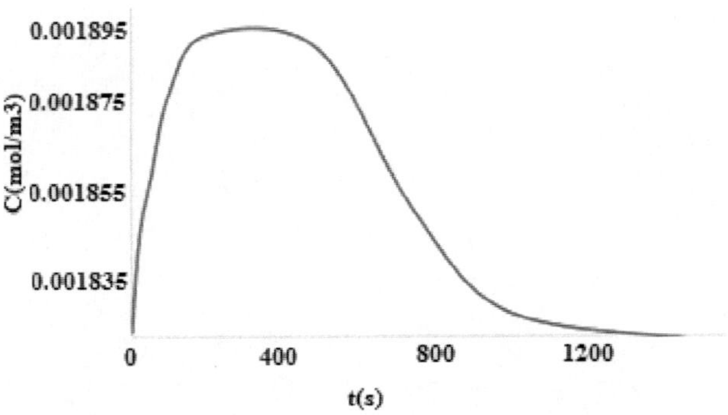

Fig. 11. Concentration profile obtained under COMSOL

The experimental curve of the evolution of the concentration as a function of time with the same time steps is given in the figure below.

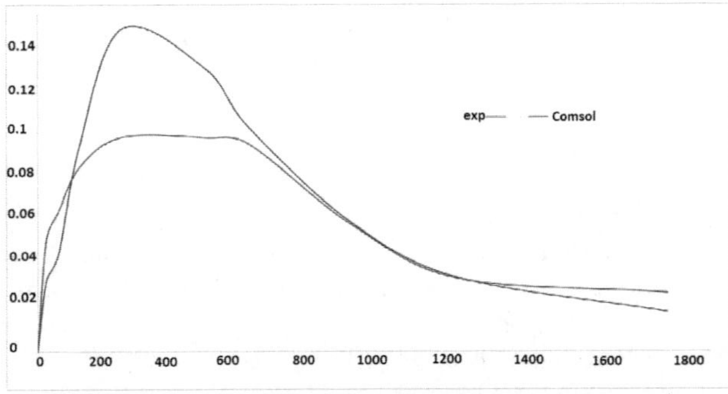

Fig. 12. Comparison of experimental RTD curves and simulation under COMSOL

The confrontation of RTD curves allows the comparison of calculations with experimental measurements. The evolution of the calculated concentrations regains the pace of the measurements (Figure 12) and the calculated values are in good agreement with the experimental values. However, there is a fairly large difference between the amplitudes. This difference is caused by the existence of dead zones confirmed by the simulation of hydrodynamics.

5 Conclusion

The study of the hydrodynamics of the electrocoagulation reactor, through the determination of the residence time distribution, is a valuable tool for various reasons. Its first contribution is to allow exploration and understanding of flow and measurements hydrodynamics can also diagnose the causes of the malfunction to remedy it.
Sodium chloride is used as an injection tracer with a short time (5s) to approach a Dirac and the RTD obtained is used to validate the simulation models.
First, the experimental curve of the RTD is compared with the dispersive piston model: a phase shift as well as a loss of amplitude between the two curves are noted.
Then, the RTD is used to approach the cascade model of n perfectly stirred reactor; for n = 2 the model reproduces the shape of the experimental curve with a loss of amplitude, probably due to the existence of recirculation zones and dead zones, and the difference calculated by is 0.15%. This induces that the reactor has the behavior of a cascade of 2 perfectly stirred reactors with short circuit and dead zones.
To validate these obtained results, the COMSOL code was used to simulate the hydrodynamics of the reactor using the turbulence model k-ε. This simulation confirmed the existence of a recirculation zone in the distribution chamber and also dead zones.
The simulation of the passive transport is carried out in turbulent regime and the concentrations at the exit were calculated then the curve of the evolution of the distribution of the residence times was drawn, this curve reproduces the pace of the experimental curve with a loss amplitude and an error of 4.6% for the entire value series.
RTD modeling has well represented the hydrodynamic

behavior of the reactor, the continuation of this study could improve the performance of this reactor: namely reduce dead zones and review the geometry to avoid recirculation of the fluid.

References

1. P. K. Holt, G. W. Barton and C. A. Mitchell, "The Future for Electrocoagulation as a Localised Water Treatment Technology," Chemosphere, Vol. 59, No. 3, 2005 355-367. doi:10.1016/j.chemosphere.2004.10.023
2. I.Kadabsli, I. Arslan Alaton,T.Olmez Hanci, O. Tunay, Electrocoagulation applications for industrial wastewaters: a critical review, J. of environmental technology reviews **1**,3,2012
3. M.K. Mbacké, C. Kane, I. Diouf, C.G.M.Diop Removal of crystal violet by electrocoagulation: Optimization and reaction mechanisms involved, J. Soc. Ouest-Afr.Chim. **39** ; 64- 76 (2015)
4. D. Sievers, E. Kuhn, M. Tucker, J. Stickel, and E. Wolfrum Residence Time Distribution Measurement and Analysis of Pilot-Scale Pretreatment Reactors for Biofuels To be presented at the 2013 AIChE Annual Meeting San Francisco, California November 3-8, 2013
5. P.V. Danckwerts. "Continuous flow systems. Distribution of residence times". *Chemical Engineering Science*. **2**: 1–13(1953)
6. Wen C.Y., Fan L.T. , M. Dekker. Models for flow systems and chemical reactors. New York, p. 570, (1975).
7. Levenspiel O. New York London p. 600, (1972).
8. Villermaux J. Génie de la réaction chimique : conception et fonctionnement des réacteurs. 2e édition. Paris : Lavoisier, Tec & Doc, p. 448, (1993).
9. COMSOL MULTIPHYSICS 3.5 "Tutorial Guide", 2008.

Dew-point temperature measurement effect on water vapour line in the near infrared

N. Khelifa*

Laboratoire Commun de Métrologie : LNE/ Cnam, 61 rue du Landy, la Plaine Saint-Denis, 93210, France.

Received:

Abstract. The HITRAN database (High-Resolution Transmission molecular absorption database) is an extremely helpful reference for selecting lines of molecular species. In the case of water vapour, a particular relative strong absorption line around $\lambda \approx 1392.5\,\mathrm{nm}$ is suitable for the detection of molecules because of its high strength but also because it is well separated from the neighbouring transitions thus avoiding any interference. Firstly, we present the optical system that uses a distributed feedback (DFB) laser diode, emitting around $1392.5\,\mathrm{nm}$ (power ≈ 3 mW and line width ($\leq 10\,\mathrm{MHz}$) to detect water vapour, in the moist air trapped in a sealed enclosure, by direct absorption spectroscopy. However, for metrology needs, we are looking for a means to control the water vapour concentration in ambient air in near real time and especially when optical chilled mirror hygrometer is used for its performance in both accuracy and repeatability of the measurements. The use of this type of instrument is then examined from the point of view of its impact on the measurement of relative humidity by exploiting the molecular absorption device.
This paper reports the measured frequency positions of the observed line at $\lambda \approx 1392.5337\,\mathrm{nm}$ for different air pressures and compares them with the values given in HITRAN database. In addition, we discuss the possibility of using water vapour detection by spectroscopy to observe the change of the shape and the position of the absorption line induced during measurements of the dew point temperature by the optical chilled mirror hygrometer.

Keywords: DFB laser diode; absorption spectroscopy; water vapour line; gas detection; dew-point temperature.

1. Introduction

La vapeur d'eau dans l'air, souvent exprimée en humidité relative, joue un rôle particulier dans de nombreux domaines, comme en métrologie des masses où ce paramètre doit être déterminé et contrôlé avec une grande précision lors des mesures d'une masse inconnue par comparaison à un étalon référencé au système international d'unités (SI) [1-2].
L'hygromètre optique à miroir refroidi est largement utilisé dans les laboratoires de métrologie ainsi que dans les applications industrielles nécessitant une grande exactitude et une bonne répétabilité des mesures d'humidité relative [3-4]. En effet, la précision et la stabilité à long terme de ce type d'instrument sont des atouts précieux comparés à ceux obtenus avec des dispositifs basés sur d'autres principes de mesure (psychromètre, hygromètre capacitif ou résistif,...). Dans ce travail, nous avons considéré un dispositif de détection de vapeur d'eau basé sur la technique de spectroscopie d'absorption [4-5]. La sensibilité de la mesure d'absorption est fondamentalement limitée par l'intensité de la transition d'absorption interrogée mais aussi de la longueur du trajet durant lequel la lumière interagit avec les espèces absorbantes.

Correspondance: naceur-eddine.khelifa@lecnam.net

Dans le cas de la vapeur d'eau, une raie d'absorption relativement intense, centrée autour de la longueur d'onde $\lambda \cong 1392{,}53$ nm, est soigneusement sélectionnée et enregistrée tout en évitant toute interférence avec des transitions voisines.

2. Contexte théorique et signal d'absorption

Dans le proche infrarouge, la molécule d'eau présente un très grand nombre de raies d'absorption avec des intensités relativement importantes dans la bande à 1,3 µm, comme le montre la figure 1. Les largeurs spectrales de ces raies peuvent aller de quelques mégahertz à plusieurs gigahertz, selon les conditions de pression et de température de la vapeur d'eau dans l'air mais aussi de celles des autres espèces auquelles elle est mélangée. En général, les diodes laser monomode de type DFB sont accordables en longueur, par variation de leur température ou de leur courant de fonctionnement, sans saut de mode que sur queques gigaretz. Ainsi, pour mesurer la longueur d'onde au centre de la raie observée , nous avons choisi de travailler à des pressions d'air humide relativement faibles, afin de pouvoir scanner entièrement la forme de la raie.

Dans le cas de notre expérience, la diode laser disponible permettait une accordabilité, sans saut de mode, sur un peu plus de 5 GHz par variation de son courant électrique

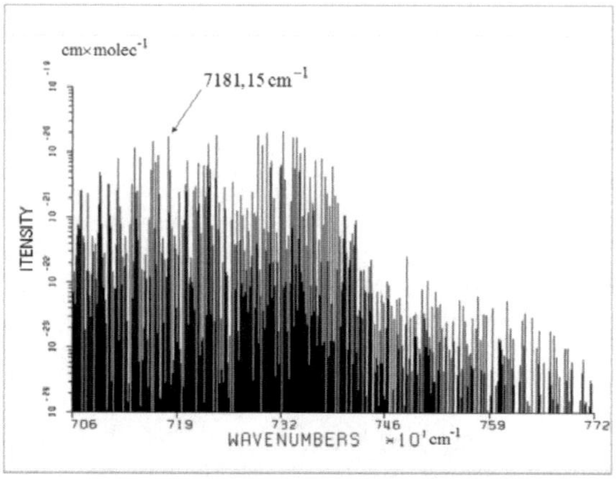

Fig. 1. Raies d'absorption de la vapeur d'eau dans la plage spectrale en terme de nombre d'onde $\sigma = 1/\lambda$ (7061 $\rightarrow$7720 cm^{-1}

Tous les résultats, qui sont reportés dans ce papier, ont été obtenus avec la raie d'absorption ayant pour nombre d'onde 7181,15cm^{-1} ou comme longueur d'onde 1392,53 nm .

La spectroscopie d'absorption directe est fondée sur la loi de Beer- Lambert. En effet, l'intensité $I_0(\nu)$ d'un rayonnement monochromatique de fréquence ν, traversant une cellule de gaz contenant une espèce absorbante, à la fréquence $\nu = c/\lambda$, subit une variation donnée par la relation :

$$I_t(\nu) = I_0(\nu)\exp[-S(T)g(\nu - \nu_0) \times P \times N \times \ell]$$

$I_t(\nu)$, est l'intensité du rayonnement après avoir traversé la cellule ; S(T) et g(ν – ν$_0$) sont respectivement l'intensité et la forme de la raie d'absorption ; P et N la pression et la fraction molaire du milieu absorbant et ℓ , la longueur de la cellule contenant l'espèce absorbante. Ainsi, la raie d'absorption est obtenue en faisant varier, de façon uniforme et sans saut de mode, la longueur d'onde du laser de telle sorte à couvrir toute la largeur de la raie. Quelques précisions sur cette procédure de mesure seront données dans la section 3.

La figure 2 montre des enregistrements simultanés, obtenus pour les signaux $I_t(\lambda)$ et $I_0(\lambda)$, pour la raie à 1392,53 nm. $I_0(\lambda)$, correspond à l'intensité du laser à l'entrée de l'enceinte et $I_t(\lambda)$, à celle observée après un parcours de l'ordre de ℓ=0,53 m dans l'enceinte, pour une pression d'air humide de 7 hPa.

Il faut noter que $I_0(\lambda)$ représente le fond laser engendré par le balayage du courant de la diode laser par une rampe de tension, nécessaire pour faire varier, sans saut de mode, la longueur d'onde de la diode laser.

Par la suite, nous présenterons les résultats des enregistrements ramenés au seul signal $I_t(\lambda)/I_0(\lambda)$, qui correspond à la raie d'absorption sans le fond du laser.

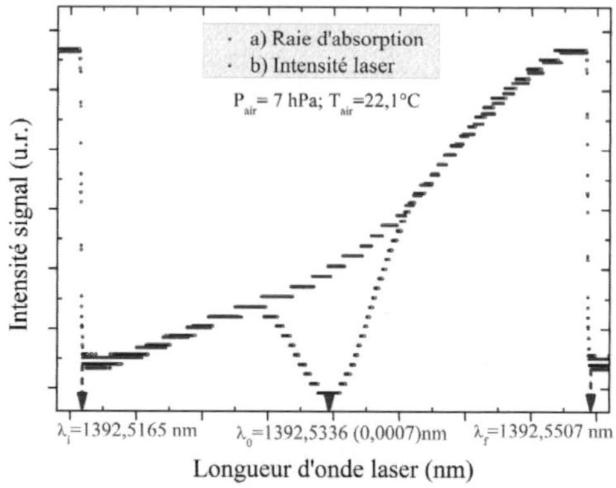

Fig. 2. Raie d'absorption à 1392,53 nm sur fond du laser. a) $I_t(\nu)$ et b) $I_0(\nu)$

Le sommet de la raie d'absorption est mesuré à l'aide d'un lamdamètre, fonctionnant sous vide primaire dans la plage de longueur d'onde allant de 1 à 1,5 µm, racordé au préalable sur un laser Nd-YAG à 1.064 µm du laboratoire. La résolution des mesures de la longueur d'onde de la diode laser, pour un point de fonctionnement donné (courant I_{DL} et température T_{DL} fixés), est à l'échelle de 10^{-4} nm.

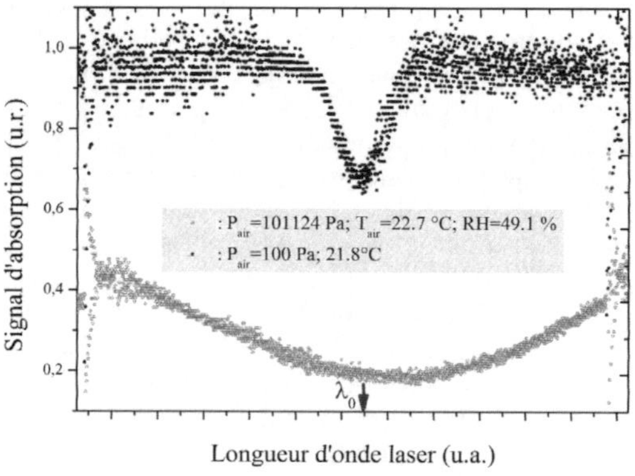

Fig. 3. Signal d'absorption sans fond laser pour la raie à 1392,53 nm de la vapeur d'eau pour deux pressions d'air humide.

Dans le tableu 1, sont reportés les résultats de calcul [7], ainsi que celle reportée dans HITRAN [8] après la mise à jour, des positions de raies de la vapeur d'eau entre 500 et 8000 cm^{-1} à partir des travaux de R.A. Toth [9]. Les valeurs indiquées correspondent à la longueur d'onde dans le vide, $\lambda_{vide} = 1/\sigma$, ou σ est le nombre d'onde en cm^{-1}.

Table 1. Quelques valeurs de la longueur d'onde associées à la raie d'absorption à 1992,53 nm de la vapeur d'eau à tempérture ambiante

Référence	longueur d'onde (nm) calcul	longueur d'onde (nm) mesure
[7]	1392,535	
Ce travail		1392,5336 (0,0007)
[8-9]		1392,5335 (0,0005)

En tenant compte de l'incertitude des mesures associée à la longueur d'onde centrale de la raie d'absorption à 1392,53 nm, la nouvelle mesure est en très bon accord avec la valeur considérée dans le HITRAN. Aussi, il n'est pas dit qu'un effet, de la pression de l'air humide que nous avons considérée (7 hPa), sur la position du centre de la raie ne soit pas présent.

3. Experience et procédures

Une diode laser monomode (type DFB) émettant autour de 1392,5 nm est utilisée comme source lumineuse (puissance de 3 mW, largeur de raie <6 MHz) pour détecter la vapeur d'eau, obtenue dans l'air sous une enceinte étanche, par la technique de spectroscopie d'absorption.
Le dispositif est muni d'une sonde de température, d'une jauge de pression (1- 800 hPa), d'un baromètre (800- 1150 hPa) et de deux sondes hygrométriques (capacitive et à miroir refroidi). Chacun de ces capteurs est placé directement dans une enceinte étanche vis à vis de l'extérieur. La sonde de température, de type Pt-100, permet de mesurer la température de l'air avec une incertitude de l'ordre de 10^{-2} °C.

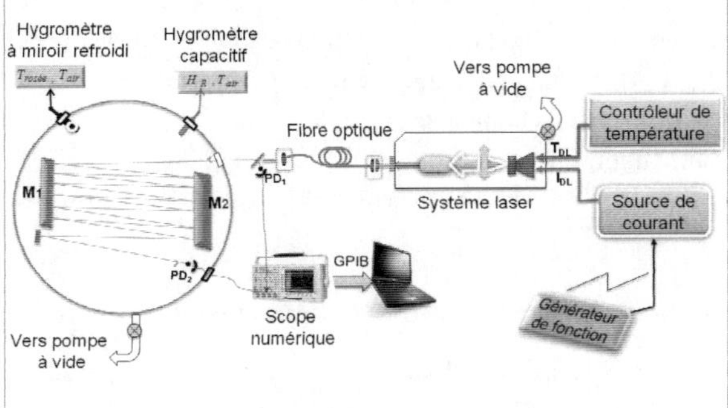

Fig. 4a. Dispositif expérimental (PD_1 et PD_2 sont des photodiodes. M1 et M2 sont des miroirs plans à couches diélectrique.

Le capteur de pression, modèle Druck, donne la pression atmosphérique à 5 pascals près. Ces capteurs sont au préalable étalonnés à partir de références se trouvant au laboratoire. Quant à l'hygromètre optique à miroir refroidi, il est ici utilisé uniquement pour observer l'effet de la methode de mesure, sur laquelle il est fondé, sur la forme de raie d'absorption de la vapeur d'eau. Le faisceau laser est acheminé à travers une fibre optique à l'intérieur de l'enceinte de mesure. Il subit des allers-retours entre deux miroirs plans, avec des traitements adéquats pour un R_{max} autour de 1392 nm.
Le parcours total ℓ du faisceau laser peut être ajuster entre 0,53 m et 1,40 m. L'intensité du faisceau laser $I_0(\lambda)$ est mesurée à l'entrée de l'enceinte (phodiode PD_1) et $I_0(\lambda)$ après un parcours ℓ à l'intérieur de l'enceinte (phodiode PD_2). La figure 2 montre les intensités, $I_0(\lambda)$ et $I_0(\lambda)$, observées lorsque la longueur d'onde du laser est balayée entre λ_i et λ_f en modulant le courant électrique à travers la diode laser à l'aide d'une rampe de tension. La température de la diode laser est fixée et maintenue constante à mieux que 0,02°C à l'aide d'un asservissement du type proportionnel-intégral-dérivateur (PID).

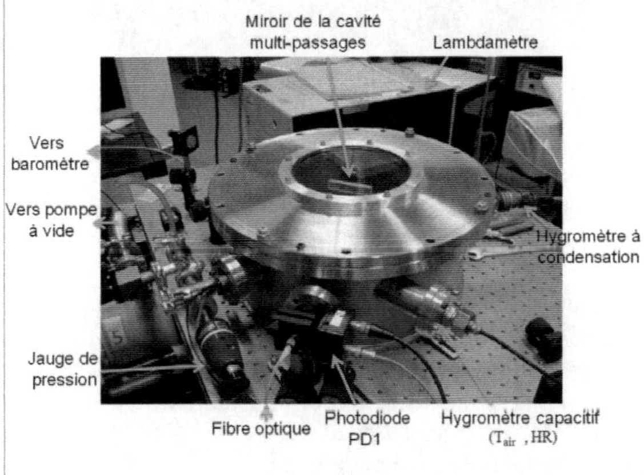

Fig. 4b. Photographie patielle de l'expérience montrant l'enceinte de mesure avec différents capteurs.

4. Expérience et résultats

– ***Mesure de la température du point de rosée***

Comme nous l'avons signalé, l'hygromètre optique à condensation, une fois raccordé à une référence gravimètrique, permet d'obtenir des mesures d'humidité performantes tout à fait satisfaisantes. Cependant, pour justifier le fait qu'un contrôle des variations d'humidité est nécessaire lors de son utilisation, nous avons évalué l'ordre de grandeur de la perturbation de l'air humide, engendrée par la condensation au niveau du miroir de l'instrument, pendant la mesure de la température du point de rosée. Le capteur d'humidité de l'hygromètre est installé à l'intérieur de l'enceinte en acier inoxydable amagnétique de 17 dm^3 de volume. Il est constitué d'un miroir de grande qualité optique de diamètre $\Phi = 5$ mm, asservi en température pour les mesures du point de rosée.

Nous avons mis en évidence l'influence de l'hygromètre à condensation sur la forme de la raie d'absorption lors de sa mise en route mais également lorsqu'il est mis à l'arret.

La figure 5a montre l'effet de la mise en route de l'hygromètre sur la forme de raie d'absorption à 1392,53 nm de la vapeur d'eau dans l'air à pression atmosphérique.

La surface comprise entre les deux courbes correspond à la quantité de molécules d'eau piégées sous forme de rosée sur le miroir de l'hygromètre. Pour interpréter ce résultats, nous avons, à partir d'une approche semi-empirique, evalué un ordre de grandeur de la quantité de vapeur d'eau dans l'enceinte qui se condense sur le miroir de l'hygromètre lorsque ce dernier est mis en fonctionnement.

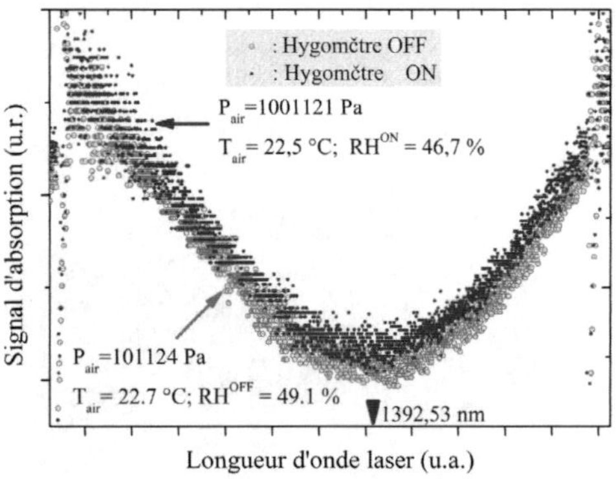

Fig. 5a. Effet de de la mesure de la température de rosée sur la raie d'absorption à 1392,53 nm pour une pression d'air de 1011,21 hPa.

Cette variation est également déterminée à partir des mesures de l'humidié relative relevées à l'aide d'un transmeteur capacitif d'humidité et de température.

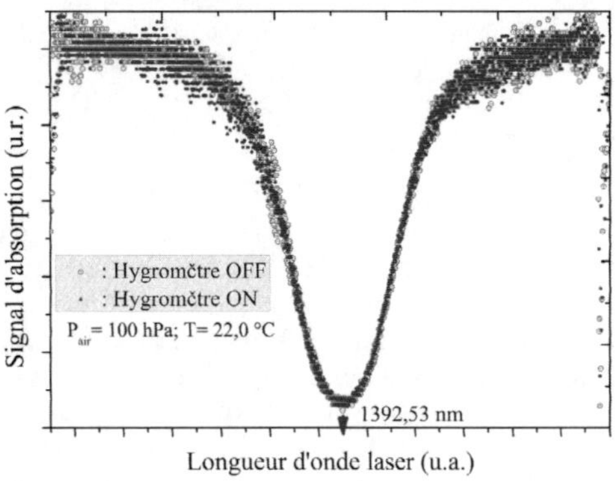

Fig. 5b. Effet de de la mesure de la température de rosée sur la raie d'absorption à 1392,53 nm à une pression d'air de 100 hPa.

Dans le cas d'une pression d'air humide de l'ordre de 100 hPa, comme le montre la figure 5b., cet effet de l'hygromètre sur la forme de la raie d'absorption est moins important.

Couche de rosée stabilisée sur le miroir de l'hygromètre

La variation du nombre de molécules d'eau dans l'enceinte, à la suite de la condensation d'une partie de ces molécules sur le miroir de l'instrument, est évaluée sur la base de quelques approximations.

- L'épaisseur de la couche de rosée (e_{ros}) est estimée à partir de la résolution de l'œil normal ($\Re_{oeil}$), qui est comprise entre $1{,}14\times10^{-4}$ et $4{,}55\times10^{-4}$ radians [10]. Par conséquent, un dépot de rosée stabilisé, qui est observé d'une distance de l'ordre de 0,25m, aura une épaisseur moyenne de l'ordre de:

$$e_{ros} = \overline{\Re_{oeil}} \times d_{obs} \cong 71\ \mu m\ .$$

- Pour la molécule d'eau, on considère la configuration et les dimensions indiquées sur la figure 6.

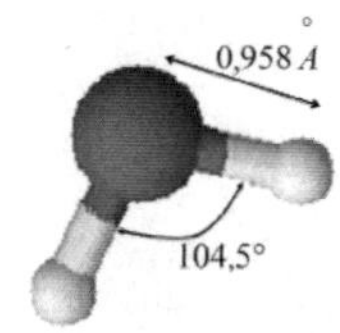

Fig.6. Géométrie de la molécule d'eau

- Pour établir l'encombrement d'une molécule d'eau, on l'assimilera à une sphère de diamètre égal à sa plus grande longueur, soit: $d = 1{,}51\ \mathring{A}$ et $V(H_2O) \cong 1{,}80\times10^{-30}\,m^3$

Le volume de la rosée, qui couvre le miroir de l'hygromètre, est alors estimé par :

$$V_{ros} = e_{ros} \times \frac{\pi \times \Phi^2}{4} \cong 1{,}39\times10^{-9}\ m^3$$

- Dans l'état liquide, les molécules sont proches les unes des autres en raison des liaisons hydrogène qui se forment et se rompent pour donner un agencement des molécules à la fois désordonnées mais compactées.

En admettant que cet arrangement moléculaires se retrouve aussi dans le cas de la rosée, le nombre de molécules qui y sont piégés est alors donné par:

$$n_{mol} \cong \frac{1}{5} \times \frac{V_{ros}}{V(H_2O)} = 1{,}6\times10^{20}\ \text{molécules}$$

Le facteur 5, correspond au taux moyen de remplissage en raison de l'arangement des molécules d'eau dans le volume que forme la rosée sur le miroir de l'hygromètre. Ce rapport est déduit à partir d'un calcul simple en considérant que la rosée a une masse volumique voisine de $1 g/cm^3$ et une masse molaire de 18,015 g. Traduit en termes de masse, ce nombre de molécule de vapeur d'eau correspond à une masse de rosée donnée par :

$m_{rosée} = n_{mol} \times \frac{18{,}015}{6{,}02 \times 10^{23}}$, soit: $m_{rosée} \cong 4{,}7 \times 10^{-3}$ g

Humidité relative et nombre de molécules d'eau dans l'air humide.

La pression partielle de la vapeur d'eau dans l'air humide sous l'enceinte à pression P_{air} est donnée par:

$$P_{H_2O} = x_V \times P_{air}$$

x_V est la fraction molaire de la vapeur d'eau dans l'air humide.

$$x_V = x_{vw}(P_{air}, T_{air}) \times HR$$

x_{vw} est la pression de vapeur saturante, elle est donnée par [11]:

$$x_{vw}(P_{air}, t_{air}) = \frac{e_w(T_{air})\, f(T_{air}, P_{air})}{P_{air}}$$

Avec : $\ln[e_w(T_{air})] \cong \frac{17{,}62 \times T_{air}}{243{,}12 + T_{air}} + \ln(611{,}2)$ ou T_{air} est en °C.

Pour $T_{air} = 22{,}7\,°C$, $e_w = 2752$ Pa, le facteur $f(T_{air}, P_{air})$ d'augmentation pour la vapeur d'eau dans l'air humide à $T_{air} = 22{,}7$ °C et $P_{air} = 1011{,}24\ hPa$ est $f \cong 1{,}0041$.

Soit: $x_{vw}(P_{air}, t_{air}) = 0{,}02733$ et $x_V = 0{,}02733 \times HR = 0{,}0134$

La masse volumique de la vapeur d'eau est calculée à partir de la relation :

$$\rho_V = \frac{18{,}015 \times P_{air} \times x_V}{Z \times R \times T_{air}}$$

Soit : $\rho_V \cong 9{,}9313\ \text{g} \times \text{m}^{-3}$

Ainsi, la masse de la vapeur d'eau dans l'air humide, occupant le volume de 17 dm^3 de l'enceinte, avant la mise en route de l'hyromètre est :

$$m_V = \rho_V \times 17 \times 10^{-3} = 0{,}169 \text{ g}$$

Lorsque la température du miroir de l'hygromètre atteint la température du point de rosée, le processus de condensation des molécules d'eau est stoppé en raison de l'asservissement de la température du miroir au point de rosée. La masse de la vapeur d'eau dans l'air sous l'enceinte se réduit alors à :

$$m_V^{eff} = 0{,}164 \text{ g}$$

De ce fait, la quantité de vapeur d'eau subit une diminution, qui correspond à la vapeur d'eau qui a été condensé sur le miroir. Soit :

$$\frac{m_V - m_V^{eff}}{m_V} = 2{,}9\%$$

Cela, signifie que dans les conditions de l'expérience, la mise en fonctionnement de l'hygromètre à condensation pour mesurer la température du point de rosée fait diminuer le taux d'humidité relative de l'ordre de 3 % . Compte tenu de l'exactitude des mesures qui est souvent recherchée, notamment en métrologie des masses, cette perturbation du taux d'humidité ne peut être ignorée.
Comme le montre la figure 7, cet effet sur la raie d'absorption à 1392,53 nm est tout à fait observable et mesurable en valeur relative à partir du signal intégré sur toute l'étendue de la raie d'absorption.

Les taux d'humidité relative (HR^{OFF}) et (HR^{OFF}), obtenus avec le transmetteur capacitif d'humidité et de température, sont respectivement de 49,1 % et de 46,7 %. Ainsi, l'écart expérimental, de l'ordre de 2,4 %, est tout à fait comparable avec le résultat du calcul qui a été developpé. Ceci, montre que l'approche que nous avons utilisée pour évaluer la pertubation de l'air humide, pendant le fonctionnement de l'hyromètre à point de rosée, est tout à fait réaliste.

5. Discussions

Pour présenter d'une autre façon l'effet de la mesure de la température du point de rosée sur la raie d'absoption de la vapeur d'eau, nous avons observé les variations de l'absorption, rapportée à toute la raie, au cours du temps et pour différentes conditions expérimentales et de pression d'air humide. La courbe de la figure 7 montre les deux phases de cette absorption, observées dans les mêmes conditions que celles des enregistrement de la figure 5 (comme reportées sur la figure 7). Présenté de cette manière, l'effet de la mise en route de l'hygromètre à condensation sur le signal d'absorption par la vapeur d'eau est plus significatif.

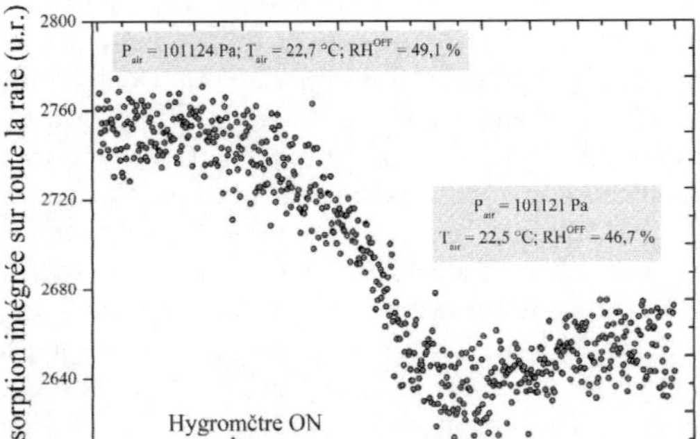

Fig. 7. Signal d'absorption intégré sur tout la raie d'absorption de la vapeur d'eau dans l'air humide à pression atmosphérique avec mise en route de l'hygromètre à condensation.

De la même manière, les resultats obtenus, dans les mêmes conditions que ceux de la figure 5b, concernant l'évolution du signal d'absorption au cours du temps sont indiqués sur la figure 8. Pour cette expérience, les indications du transmeteur capacitif d'humidité ne sont pas fiables et sont notés par HR^{OFF} et HR^{OFF} sur la figure 8. Les seules mesures sont celles de la température de l'air humide, qui est quasiment constante dans les deux situations de l'hygromètre à miroir refroidi, et la pression de l'air humide.

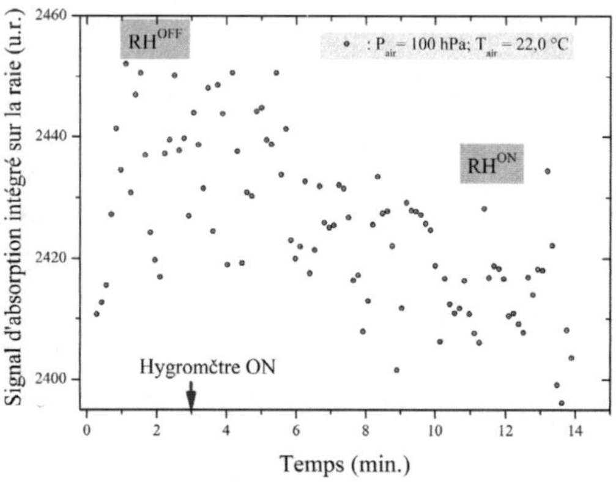

Fig. 8. Signal d'absorption intégré sur toute la raie d'absorption de la vapeur d'eau dans l'air à pression de 100 hPa.

6. Conclusion

La technique de détection optique, fondée sur l'absorption selective par des atomes et molécules, connait encore des applications dans différents domaines. En effet, le developpement de nouvelles sources lasers, permettant d'obtenir une émission laser, accordable sur des nouvelles plages de longueur d'onde, est rapidement exploité par cette technique pour la détection, par exemple de polluants sous forme de traces et autres dans des conditions extrêmes (haute température, haute pression, zone irradiée,...). Dans ce travail, nous avons utilisé une diode laser, type DFB monomode de faible puissance, pour sonder la vapeur d'eau dans une enceinte fermée pouvant être mise sous vide primaire. L'observation de la raie à 1392,53 nm a permis de faire une nouvelle mesure de la longueur d'onde centrale de cette raie à mieux que 10^{-3} nm.
Cette valeur est en bon accord avec notamment celle qui est reportée dans la base HITRAN. Ce résultat, nous a permis également de mettre en évidence et d'évaluer la variation, de la quantité de vapeur d'eau dans l'air humide, induite par la condensation d'une partie sur le miroir d'un hygromètre optique à point de rosée.
Le calcul qui a été developpé donne un ordre de grandeur tout à fait comparable à celui observé dans le cas de l'air humide à pression atmosphérique.

References

1. S. Davidson, Air density for mass calibration, XVI IMEKO World Congres, Viennz, AUSTRIA September 25-28 (2000).

2. A. Malengo and W. Bich, Buoyancy contribution to uncertainty of mass, conventional mass and force, Metrologia 53, p.762 (2016). http://dx.doi.org/10.1088/0026-1394/53/3/1010

3. R. S. Jachowicz , Dew point hygrometer with heat injection-principle of construction and operation , Sensors and Actuators B, Vol.7, p.455 (1992). https://doi.org/10.1016/0925-4005(92)80343-V

4. V.J. Dosoretz, S. Ronchinsky , Chilled mirror hygrometer with performance monitoring, US Patent 4,629,333, 16 déc 1986.

5. A. Hartmann, R. Strzoda, R. Schrobenhauser, R. Weigel. Ultra-compact TDLAS humidity measurement cell with advanced signal processing, Appl. Phys. B 115, p.263 (2014). https://doi.org/10.1007/s00340-013-5599-7

6. J. Holdgkinson and R. P. Tatam, Optical gas sensing: a review, Meas. Sci. Technol. 24, P.1 (2013).
http://dx.doi.org/10.1088/0957-0233/24/1/012004

7. J. Verges. Private communication, Université Paris XI, Laboratoire Aimé- Cotton (Orsay).

8. L.S.Rothman et al., The HITRAN 2008 molecular spectroscopic database, Journal of Quantitative Spectroscopy & Radiative Transfer vol. 110, p. 533 (2009). https://doi.org/10.1016/j.jqsrt.2009.02.013

9. R.A. Toth. Linelists of water vapor parameters from 500 to 8000 cm^{-1}. http://mark4sun.jpl.nasa.gov.data/spec/H2O/

10. M. Born & E. Wolf, Principles of Optics, 4th. edition, Pergamon Press (1970).

11. R.E. Bentley. Temperature and Humidity Measurement, vol.1, p.135, Springer (1998).

Calibration of surveying equipment: Case study of Tanzania.

A, Charles, angela.charles@tbs.go.tz

Tanzania Bureau of Standards (TBS), Metrology Laboratory, Dar es Salaam, Tanzania

ABSTRACT. Surveying is a science that is used to establish relative position of an object or area. A complete survey will give the relative position of an object in three dimensions. This includes the horizontal distance, vertical distance (elevation) and angle. Surveying is used in various fields throughout the country. It is used in the construction industry, mining industry, military and various government agencies. The objectives of surveying include determination of relative position of objects, distance and angle between objects. This information facilitates the preparations of plans, cross-section and quantities of various engineering and construction projects. The information is also used in establishment of boundaries, preparation of maps, establishment of control points and as one means for quality control during project execution. Various equipment are used to carry out surveying work. These ranges from a simple staple tape measure, to levelling staff and level machine, theodolite, odometer, total station and more advanced instruments such as the GPS and mirror stereoscope. The accuracy of these equipment and instruments is very important as the results affect the quality, safety, security and economics of projects, individuals and the nation. The accuracy of these instruments can be affected by events such as repairs after damage, improper transportation of new equipment or machine default during manufacturing and time which include over use in a given time or the equipment not being used in a prolonged time. To ensure that equipment is accurate and precise, calibration is very important. The accuracy and precision of surveying equipment has major significance in day to day activities and lives of people across the country. The accuracy of surveying equipment will greatly reduce boundary conflicts between individuals, villages and government with the people surrounding government properties such as game reserves. It will also assure that construction projects are constructed to detail as per plan.

Keywords: Surveying, Measurement, Calibration

1. Introduction

Land is all around us, and a universal need for every living thing. Without land there is no life. All three basic needs of the human being are supported by the land primarily. The food we eat is grown on the land, the shelter we need has to be established on the land, and the cloths that we wear pass through many processes from the cotton in fields to the industries that need land to be erected on. Over and above the basic needs we need land for transportation, commercial buildings, waste disposal and various other social economic activities. Without land life would not be as it is today.
Our day to day use of the land requires us to measure and locate point on, above or below the land or earth. From the simple fencing of an individual property to boundary between neighbors, and the complex establishment of right of way for roads, railways, pipelines and power lines, the underlining principle remains the same, measure and locate. This principle is called Surveying.

1.1 Surveying

Surveying is the art and science of measuring and locating points and angles in three dimensions on, above and below the surface of the earth. It is an art due to the creative and experience required to provide accurate information economically and in a timely manner. It is a science due to the mathematical and scientific methods employed. Basically the difference between one professional surveyor and the other is based on the art part of it, since that is not taught in schools

1.2 Survey measurement

There are three basic measurements for any complete land survey measurement.

a) Distance measurement: this is measurement carried out to determine the relative horizontal distance between two points. It can be carried out using the staple chain and link of know length, measuring tape (steel, fiber or invar) or the more advanced Electronic Distance Measuring devices.
b) Angle measurement: both the vertical and horizontal angels of and object or point can be measured in surveying. Horizontal angles have been measured using the historic Compass to provide arithmetic bearing or azimuth to more accurate theodolites.
c) Level measurement: the vertical distance (height) of point relative to another is determined by the leveling method. The simplest way to determine the height of a point is by using an altimeter, where air

pressure data is used to calculate the height. For more precise height measurement, a leveling machine and staff are employed.

1.3 Survey methods

Survey measurement can be classified into two types

a) Geodetic survey: this is type of survey where the true shape of the earth is considered. It is used when high accuracy is needed and covers a large area.

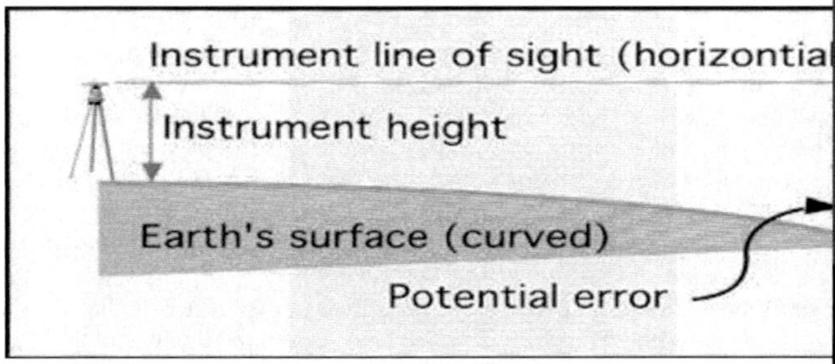

Fig 1: survey measurement classification

b) Plane survey: this method ignores the spherical shape of the earth and considers it a plane surface. It is useful for general construction survey and survey of small areas where the error can be ignored.

1.4 Uses of surveying

Data collected from land surveying has several applications including

a) Control surveying: for establishment of reference points for various uses
b) Topographic survey: for establishment of topographical map of an area
c) Boundary survey: for establishment of length and direction of land lines
d) Construction survey: used during constructing in engineering for layout, setting out, determining quantities of earth work, and for monitoring of engineering construction.

1.5 Accuracy and precision

Accuracy and precision are important parameter of any measurement and much so on a survey measurement.

Accuracy has been defined as closeness of the measured data to the true value. Mathematically, accuracy is defined by the number of point in a given measurement. A measurement of 5.74 mm is considered more accurate than that of 5.7 mm.

Precision is the closeness of the measured value. Data is more precise if they are closer together than when they are far apart.

Four scenarios are present in any measurement. It may be neither accurate or precise, accurate but not precise, precise but not accurate and both accurate and precise

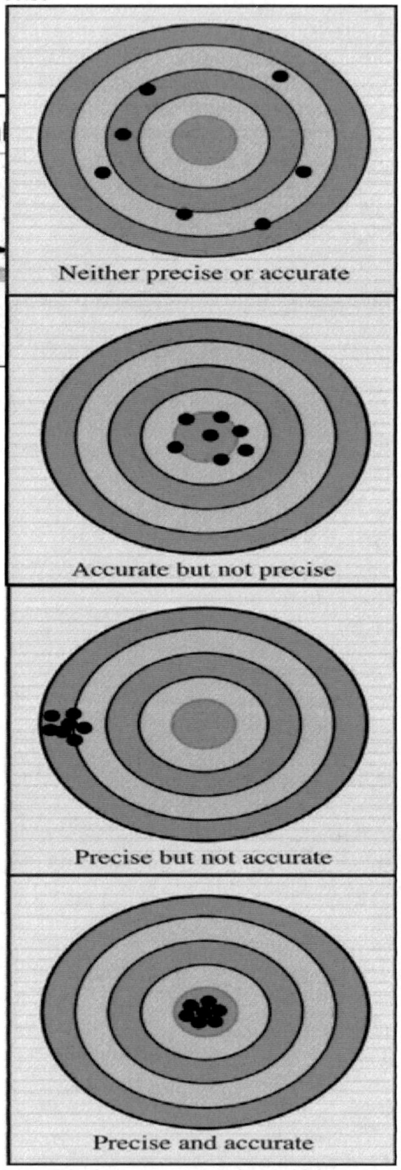

Fig 2: accuracy and precission

Survey data must be accurate to be useful. There are mainly two causes of inaccuracy of data

a) Random error: this error is not of known cause and hence can be very hard to control.
b) Systematic error: these are errors that are predictable and can be accounted for.

Wrong and inaccurate survey data can lead to wrong decision that can be very expensive. A wrong boundary set between the grazing and cultivating land can cause civil war between the users of the neighboring lands. A wrong setting out angle at a construction site can cause a 50 storey building to be out of allowable vertical deflections. Survey data can also be used in courts as part of evidence and hence should be very accurate to facilitate fair ruling.

2. Survey activities in Tanzania

The history of land survey in Tanzania dates as far back as 1893 during the Germany colonization. Surveying has been used to establish boundaries for villages, township, cities, regions and at a national level.

Currently the main stake holders of land surveying in Tanzania are the Government and the private sector. The government concentrates on regulation and establishment on control points, topographic, geodetic, hydrographic and triangulation surveys. The private sector plays a major role in cadastral surveys and construction surveying.

2.1 User group of land surveying

Surveying activities in the country are carried out by various organizations in the private and governmental level. These organizations include

a) The Ministry of Land, Housing and Human Settlement Development
b) Tanzania National Roads Agency: the agency that is responsible for management of all trunk and regional roads in the country
c) Regional and district land offices: these offices are responsible for allocation of land use and boundaries at their respective levels.
d) Teaching institutes: there are several institutes that teach courses in land surveying. These include University of Dar es Salaam (UDSM), University of Dodoma (UDOM), Aridhi Univerisity (ARU), Chuo cha Aridhi Morogoro and Chuo cha Aridhi Tabora.
e) Surveying companies: several privately owned companies exist in the country.
f) Construction Companies: Several construction companies (contractors) and Consultants employ professional land surveyors for their day to day activities

3. Calibration of survey equipment

Calibration has been defined as the comparison of two readings carried out in similar conditions, one with a known value or true value and one whose value is not known. The equipment whose value is not known is usually referred to as the unit under test (UUT).

Instrument error can be of different types, this includes

a) Span error: this occurs when the zero (or initial) reading of an equipment is correct but errors occur over the span of measurement
b) Zero error: this is a condition where an instrument has zero error and that error causes a constant error in all other span reading of the instrument.
c) Combined zero and span error: This is a combination of the two errors where an instrument has both zero error and span error
d) Linearization error: This is the condition where an instrument gives correct reading at the beginning and at the end but has errors in between the two points.

To detect these errors and correct them by adjustment or correction factor, calibration of the instrument is required. These errors can occur due to

i. Drift of instrument
ii. Change in environmental conditions
iii. Changes in electrical supply
iv. Improvement of the instrument by adding components or programs
v. Changes in the data acquisition process

Land surveying like any other equipment should be calibrate to ensure that the readings produced are accurate. The calibration of survey equipment should be done as per

a) Statutory need: the survey act should outline the necessity and frequency of calibration of survey equipment
b) Event: several event should warrant the need calibration of survey equipment, this include repaired equipment, new equipment, equipment subjected to shock, and improved equipment
c) Time: when equipment has been used heavily in a given time, or has not been in use over a long period of time it should be re calibrated before it is used for carrying out land surveys.

3.1 The survey equipment measurand

There are two basic measurements in any complete survey. These measurements are

i. Angle
ii. Length

Both of these measurements can be measured either horizontally or vertically. Their combination gives a complete and useful survey data.

3.2 Calibration standard

A calibration standard is an artifact whose value is known and can be compared to that of a unit under test. For the purpose of this paper four standards will be discussed. These standards have been found to be the foundation or start point for any organization in need of doing calibration of survey equipment.

i. Angle Standards: These are required for calibration of angle measuring equipment including theodolites and total stations.
ii. Tape Measure: A calibrated steel tape can be used to calibrate other measuring tapes whether they are steel or fiber tapes.
iii. Linear Laser Interferometer:The linear laser interferometer can be used in the calibration of leveling staff. The method is convenient for both conventional levels and bar coded levels. The method is used by comparators and the levels can be calibrated horizontally or vertically.
iv. Baseline:This is system of established points of a known value and accuracy that can be used for calibration of Electronic Measuring Devices and Total stations

3.3 Calibration of survey equipment in Tanzania

As a developing country Tanzania has enormous survey activities both for construction purposes, land allocation and mapping.

Metrology laboratory at Tanzania Bureau of Standards is the national physical laboratory, responsible calibration of equipment and instruments and act as a custodian for all physical standards in the country. The Laboratory also does calibration of equipment in different fields for private and public organaisation in various fields including mass, small volume, force, temperature, time and frequency, dimension and bulk volume.

Realising the importance of survey and role it plays in development, construction and alleanating land conflicts the bureau is in the process of procuring standards and capacity building for calibration of survey equipment.

Calibration of survey equipment is currently carried out by pricvate agencies of surveying equipment suppliers including Leica, Stonex and Sokia.

4. Effects of un-calibrated survey instruments

An instrument that is not calibrated and has unknown error affects safety, productivity and quality of any project. These effects may vary in intensity from one project to the other. Wrong data has many causes including knowledge of the operator and correct use of an instrument. For the purpose of this paper we will consider that these other factors are done correctly and do not cause any error in the measurement. Survey data with errors has many effects these include

i. Land conflicts. Land conflict has many causes; among those is the misallocation of boundaries as a result wrong data. This can be seen at individual levels (conflict between two people), at a village level and national wise e,g the boundaries of national reserves, conflicts between land for animal grazing and cultivation
ii. Wrong payment of contractor: if a survey instrument has unknown error, for every 1 mm of the error in the construction of 6.5m width road of 50 km length this could result in 325m3 of under paid or over paid work.
iii. Quality of work: an instrument that is not calibrated can result in poor quality of work as the consultant approves works that is of low quality due to wrong level data from surveying. This could also be seen at setting out high rise building. An error at setting out could results in deflections that are outside allowable range.
iv. Poor design: Survey forms the basis for design of most infrastructure. Wrong data will result in poor design and hence affects the value and quality of the project.

5. Conclusion

Most of our day to day activities depend on the use of land. To appropriately use the land, it must be measured and allocated for each and every use. For the engineers in any civil engineering project, land surveying form a very important part of the quality assurance, and design process. For all these functions to be executed effectively it is important that the instruments and equipment used in surveying are working according to manufacturer specification and there error is known and corrected. To correct this error calibration of these instruments and equipment is very important.

It is thus important to prepare and endorse a national survey calibration policy, to regulate the survey activities in the country. Tanzania Bureau of Standards should continue to facilitate and fastrrack where possible its capacity to calibrate survey equipment in the country. This will help in bringing harmony of survey activities carried out by different firms and will also improve most challenges and conflicts that are a result of using instruments and equipment that are not calibrated.

References

1. J.Mango, Aspects of surveying and equipment calibration for transport infrastructures (2017)
2. E.J.Liwa, 120 years of surveys and mapping in Tanzania (1983 - 2013) (2013)
3. Radiation safety manual for use of radioactive Materials, Survey instrument calibration (2017)
4. J.Jeziko, Calibration of surveying instrument and tools - means of quality increase of deformation measurement (2014)
5. H.C.Engler A.L.S, the Calibration of survey equipment (2012)
6. S.S.Katambi, Development of the new cadastral Survey System in Tanzania (2009)
7. D.Martin, G.G.France, Calibration of Total Stations Instruments at ESRF (2006)

Metrology in Solar Energy: an exemple of resealing of a pyranometer repaired by remplacing its external hemisphere damaged

S. Touré et M. Sidibé

Laboraatoire e'Energie Solaire, UFR SSMT, Université F. Houphoouët-Boigny Abidjan Cocody 22 BP 582 Abidjan 22. Email: siakaahtoure@yahoo.fr

Received:

Abstract Our Laboratory is very often involved in solar radiation measurements. Those measurements are made in order to assess the solar energy potential. Measurements are also made during the experimental study and tests of our built thermal conversion systems of solar energy such as solar cookers, solar water heaters, solar stills, and solar dryers. Measurements are also made during the experimental study of the photovoltaic systems we elaborate. This work concerns the reparation and the resealing of one of our pyranometers Eppley PsP which was accidentally damaged. The external hemisphere (dome) was cracked. Another dome was fabricated using the damaged one as model. With this new dome, a resealing of the pyranometer was made. The pyrometer yields under radiation, a voltage v in Volts. The radiation (W/m²) is expressed as E = v/k. Before the cracking of the pyranometer external dome, the value of the constant k was $k = 9.1.10^{-3}$. We have a second pyranometer Eppley, in a good state, whose constant is $k = 10.41.10^{-3}$; it has been considered as the normal pyranometer and used as standard. The measurements made simultaneously with the two pyranometers showed important discrepancies between the two radiations obtained. Hence we looked for a constant of the repaired pyranometer that gives accurate values of the radiation. The best agreement between the two measurements is obtained for $k = 8.2.10^{-3}$ .Two days of test were considered. For the first day one get for $k = 9.1.10^{-3}$, RMSE = 70. 6 W/m² and for $k = 8.2.10^{-3}$, RMSE = 22.14 W/m². For the second one gest for $k = 9.1.10^{-3}$, RMSE = 62.75 W/m² and for $k = 8.2.10^{-3}$, RMSE = 31.05 W/m².

Key words: Solar energy, radiation measurement , pyranometer; solar constant ; global radiation

1 Introduction

There is today a rapidly increasing of the population that leads to an increasing demand of energy everywhere in the world. The over exploitation of fossil fuel energy sources such as petroleum, wood fuel and coal is responsible of serious environmental problems. In front of such situation, renewable energy sources become attractive. Solar energy has multiple applications. The research works made in that field and also the evaluation of solar energy systems, require a good knowledge of the solar energy potential. This solar energy potential assessment must be carried out by means of reliable measurement instruments that measure the solar irradiance. One of the instruments very often used in that field is the pyranometer which measures the global irradiance.

2 Evaluation and measurement of the solar radiation

2.1 Solar constant and solar radiation estimation models

The solar constant is defined as the energy coming from the sun by unit time that reaches a unit surface perpendicularly to the direction of propagation of the solar radiation at the average distance earth-sun and outside the atmosphere. This solar constant, which is an average value, is $G_{sc} = 1367\ W/m^2$. Some models exist, that allow the assessment of the solar irradiance. The calculated radiations in those models are function of the extraterrestrial radiation E_{sc} which varies during the year. According to Spencer (1971), this extraterrestrial global irradiance is expressed as

$$E_{sc} = G_{sc}(1 + 0{,}033cos\frac{360n}{365D}) \quad (1)$$

Another relationship is the one of Iqbal (1983) [1] expressed as

$$E_{sc} = G_{sc}(1{,}000110 + 0{,}034221cos\frac{(n-1)360}{365} + 0{,}001280sin\frac{(n-1)360}{365} + 0{,}000719cos2\frac{(n-1)360}{365} + 0{,}000077sin2\frac{(n-1)360}{365}) \quad (2)$$

Several models are used to estimate the solar irradiance received on the ground; The estimated quantities are:

- The solar irradiance I_h due to the direct component of clear sky

- The solar irradiance D_h due to the diffused component;

- The global solar irradiance in the horizontal plan

$$G_h = I_h + D_h \qquad (3)$$

The different models generally take into account the transmission due to the Rayleigh diffusion, the transmission due to the absorption by gases (essentially O_2 et CO_2), the transmission due to the absorption by atmospheric ozone, the transmission due to the extinction by the aerosols.

One of those models is the model of Bird & Hulstrom [1, 2, 3, 4, 5]. Another one is the model of Capderou [6,7]

2.2 Measurement of the solar irradiance and the duration of sunshine

The direct irradiance is measured by means of a pyrheliometer. As for the global solar irradiance in a horizontal, plan, it is measured by using a pyranometer. The duration of sunshine is generally measured by means of a Campbell - Stokes heliograph [8]

Our study concerns the pyranometer, a schema of which is shown in Figure 1

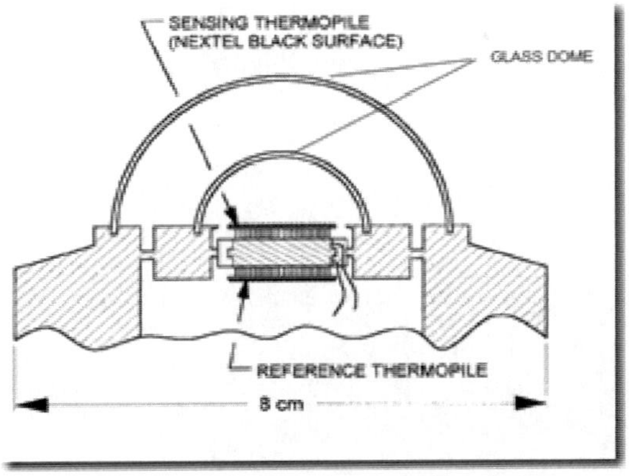

Fig. 1. Schema of a pyranometer sowing the two domes

The two pyranometers Eppley PsP involved in the present study are shown below. The pyranometer repaired is shown in Figure 2. As for the pyranometer used as standard, the one which was not damaged, it is shown in Figure 3.

Fig. 2. Pyranometer Eppley with its external dome renewed, whose initial coefficient before reparation was , $k = 9.1.10^{-3}$.

. **Fig. 3.** Pyranometer Eppley used as standard, in a good state, whose coefficient is $k = 10.41.10^{-3}$

In the principle, most of the pyranometers use the temperature difference that appears between a black surface which is a good absorbent of visible solar radiation, and a white surface which reflects it. [8]. The black surface grows warm more than the white one and the difference of temperature between the two surfaces is measured by means of a thermocouple which yields a voltage v en mV. The solar irradiance E (W/m²) is given by the following relationship

$$E = \frac{v}{k} \quad (4)$$

In equation (4), k (mV/W/m²) is a characteristic constant of the pyranometer. As it can be seen in Figures 2 and 3, the receiver (black surface) is protected against the bad weather (wind, rain dust…) by two transparent hemispheres or domes. The pyranometer measures, in a horizontal plan, the solar radiation coming from the demi-space [8]

3 Experimental study

During an experimentation, the external dome of the pyranometer shown in Figure 2 received a shock and was cracked.. Another dome was fabricated using the damaged one as model. It is shown in Figure 4.

Fig. 4. Glass hemisphere fabricated to replace the external dome of the pyranometer shown on Figure 2, which was cracked

After reparation, this pyranometer which had to be resealed is shown in figure 2. The normal pyranometer, which was used to make the sealing, is shown in Figure 3.Two days of experimentation were chosen: 04 April 2008 and 05 April 2008. For each of the two days, solar irradiance was simultaneously measured by the two pyranometers. Each pyranometer was connected to a multimeter and yielded a electromotive force v which was converted into solar irradiance by using equation (4). The irradiance yielded by the normal pyranometer is called Enor. The one which is yielded by the pyranometer to be sealed is called EEtalon1. The later pyranometer had a constant $k = 9.1.10^{-3}$ mV/W/m² before the cracking of its external dome. As for the normal pyranometer, its constant is different and is $k = 10.41.10^{-3}$ mV/W/m²

4 Results and discussions

The discrepancies between the values of Enor and EEtalon1 were important. As a consequence, we have recalculated EEtalon1 with the following values of k: $k = 9.1.10^{-3}$; $k = 8.7.10^{-3}$; $k = 8.5.10^{-3}$; $k = 8.2.10^{-3}$ mV/W/m². For each value of k, the values of EEtalon1 obtained are compared with the Enor values. Figure 5 shows the evolution curve with time of the irradiances obtained for 04 April 2008. The curves of Enor and EEtaalon1 for the different values of the constant k are shown. It can be seen that the lowest discrepancy between Enor and EEtalon1 is obtained for $k = 8.2.10^{-3}$ mV/W/m²

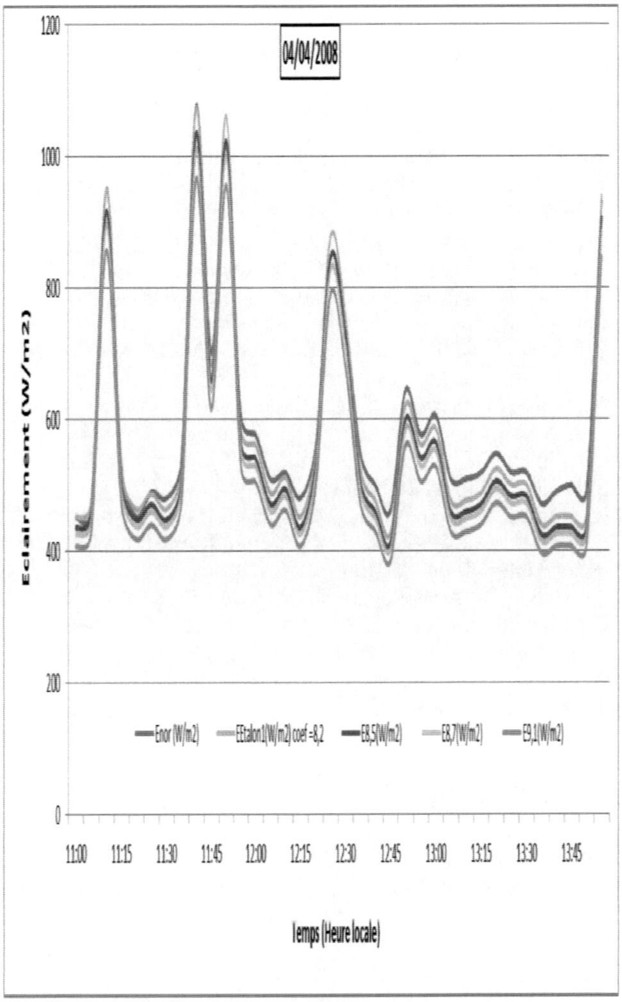

Fig. 5. Evolution Curves of Enor and EEtalon1 on 04 April 2008 for $k = 9.1.10^{-3}$; $k = 8.7.10^{-3}$; $k = 8.5.10^{-3}$; $k = 8.2.10^{-3}$ mV/ W/m².

In Figure 6 are shown the comparative evolutions with time of Enor and EEtalon1 for$k = 8.2.10^{-3}$. It can be seen that most of the time, a good agreement is observed between the two curves

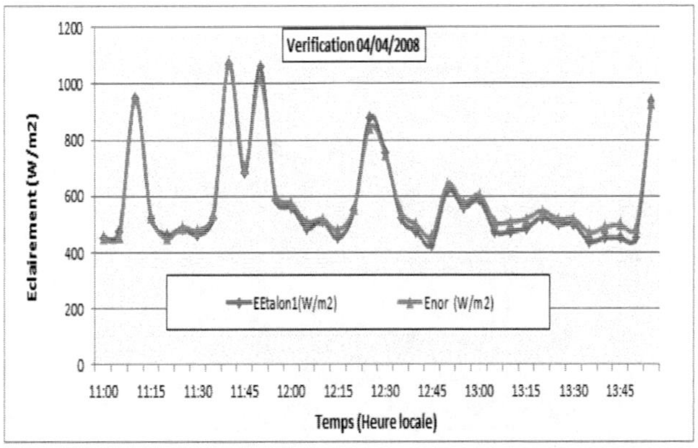

Fig. 6. Evolution Curves of Enor and EEtalon1 on 04 April 2008 for k $k = 8.2.10^{-3}$ mV/W/m².

The same experimentation was carried out on 05 April 2008. Figure 7 shows the evolution curve with time of the irradiances obtained for 05 April 2008. The curves of Enor and EEtaalon1 for the different values of the constant k are shown. Once again, the lowest discrepancy between Enor and EEtalon1 is obtained for $k = 8.2.10^{-3}$ mV/W/m²

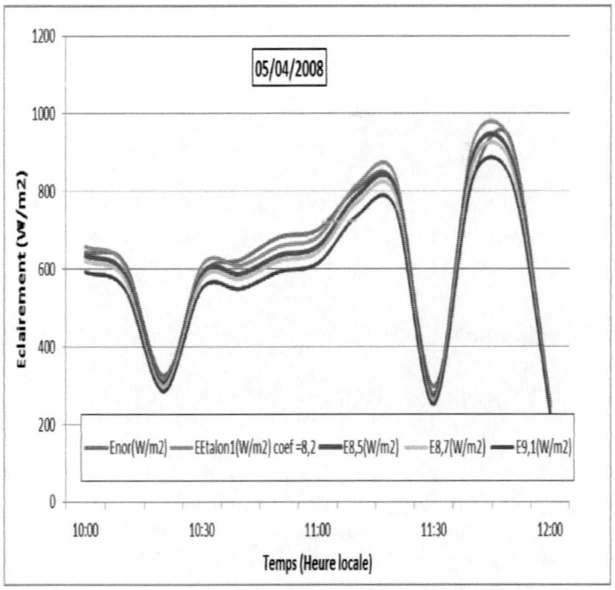

Fig. 7. Evolution Curves of Enor and EEtalon1 on 05 April 2008 for $k = 9.1.10^{-3}$; $k = 8.7.10^{-3}$; $k = 8.5.10^{-3}$; $k = 8.2.10^{-3}$ mV/W/m².

For this reason, like in the case of 04 April, the comparative evolutions with time of Enor and EEtalon1 for $k = 8.2.10^{-3}$ are shown in Figure 8. It can be seen again that most of the time, a good agreement is observed between the two curves

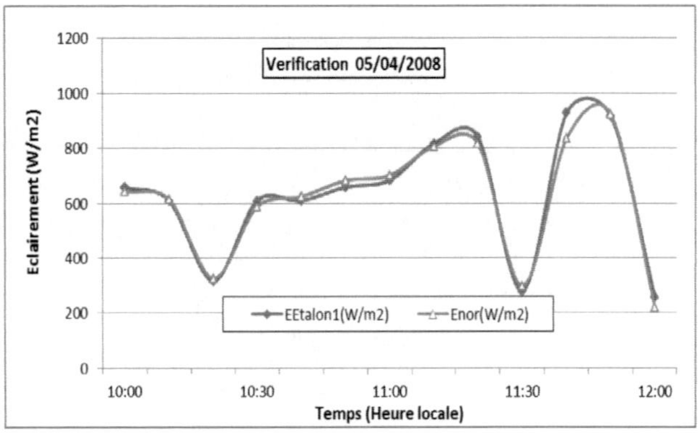

Fig. 8. Evolution Curves of Enor and EEtalon1 on 05 April 2008 for $k = 8.2.10^{-3}$ mV/W/m².

A statistical analysis was made by using the parameter RMSE which is defined as

$$RMSE = \left[\frac{1}{N}\sum_{i=1}^{N}(E_{Etalon1} - E_{nor})^2\right]^{1/2} \quad (5)$$

The following results were found. For the first day, for $k = 9.1.10^{-3}$ mV/W/m², RMSE = 70.62 W/m² and for $k = 8.2.10^{-3}$ mV/W/m², RMSE = 22.14 W/m².

For the second day, for $k = 9.1.10^{-3}$ mV/W/m², RMSE = 62.75 W/m² and for $k = 8.2.10^{-3}$ mV/W/m², RMSE = 31.05 W/m²

The statistical analysis confirms that the better goodness of fit Between Enor and EEtalon1 is obtained for $k = 8.2.10^{-3}$ mV/W/m².

5 Conclusion

The study showed that the irradiance evolution with time is the same for the normal pyranometer and the repaired pyranometer. As a consequence, one can say that the active part of the repaired pyranometer (the black surface), was not damaged. The discrepancies observed between the irradiances measured by the two pyranometers were due to the constant of the repaired pyranometer which had to be changed. It was shown that for $k = 8.2.10^{-3}$ mV/W/m², instead of $k = 9.1.10^{-3}$ mV/W/m² , a good agreement is obtained between the irradiance yielded by the two pyranometers.

References

1. M. Iqbal, An introduction to Solar Radiation, Academic Press, Department of Mechanical Engineering, University of British Columbia, Canada (1983)

2. M. Mesri-Merad, L. Hougab, A. Cheknane, N.L.Bachari Estimation du rayonnement solaire au sol par des modèles empiriques, Revue des Energies Renouvelables **4**, 451–463 (2012)

3. M. Koussa, A. Malek, M. Haddadi, Validation de quelques modèles de reconstitution des éclairements dus au rayonnement solaire direct, diffus et global par ciel clairRevue des Energies Renouvelables **9**, 307- 332 (2006)

4. R. Hanane, F.S. Mohammed, C. Mohammed, Estimation de la composante directe normale du rayonnement solaire à partir des données satellites-cas , de Rabbat, 16ème Journées Internationales de Thermique (JITH 2013) Marrakech (Maroc) 13 au 15 nov 2013

5. M. Sidibé., D. Soro , W.F.. Fassinou, S. Touré, Reconstitution of Solar Radiation on a site of the Littoral in Côte d'Ivoire, International Journal of Engineering Research and Technology ISSN 0974-3154 **Vol 10 Number 1**, 19–34 (2017)

6. A. Mefti, M.Y. Bouroubi, A. Khellaf, Analyse critique du Modèle de l'Atlas Solaire de l'Algérie, Revue des Energies Renouvelables. **2**, 69–85 (1999)

7. M. Capderou, Atlas Solaire de l'Algérie, Tome 1 Vol 1 et 2**:** Modèles théoriques et expérimentaux , Office des Publications Universitaires , Algérie (1987)

8. J.M.. Chassériaux, Conversion Thermique du Rayonnement Solaire, Dunod Paris **p 151** (1984)

Seasonal variability of the solar energy potential of the city of Abidjan : Experimental comparative study of two sunshine measurement techniques

A.P.A. KOUASSI[1*], S. TOURE[1], D. TRAORE[1], J.B. ACKAH[2,3] and F.O. MENEY[3]
[1]*Laboratoire d'Energie Solaire (LES), Unité de Formation et de Recherche des Sciences des Structures de la Matière et Technologie, Université Félix Houphouët Boigny 22 BP 582 Abidjan 22, Côte d'Ivoire*
[2]*Laboratoire de Physique de l'atmosphère et de Mécanique des Fluides (LAPA-MF), Unité de Formation et de Recherche des Sciences des Structures de la Matière et Technologie, Université Félix Houphouët Boigny 22 BP 582 Abidjan 22, Côte d'Ivoire*
[3]*Agence pour la Sécurité de la Navigation Aérienne (ASECNA) 15 BP 918 Abidjan 15, Côte d'Ivoire*

Abstract- Most countries have a national weather station. In Côte d'Ivoire, it is the Aeronautical and Meteorological Exploitation Company (SODEXAM) which is in charge of it through its databank. The inaccessibility of these data leads many solar energy entrepreneurs to move towards free sites that are often out of phase with the meteorological realities of the area considered. We propose in this paper, a comparative study of two sunshine measurement techniques, namely, the technique of the heliograph (national station) and that of the thermoelectric pyranometer (our laboratory), to discuss the reliability of the data provided by this structure. In addition, we analyzed the seasonal variations of the insolation of Abidjan from 1978 to 2017. The comparison of the results produced by these two approaches showed a discrepancy of up to 43%, with much higher values for the national station. The analysis of the solar field of this city over a period of 19 years has shown a great variability of the solar energy potential which starts from a decrease in energy, from 4447 Wh/m^2 (1978-1988) to 3303 Wh/m^2 (2003-2009), to achieve an energy increase up to 4782 Wh/m^2 (2016-2017). The characterization of the solar year allowed us to divide the months into three solar seasons depending on the irradiation : the big season regrouping the months whose average daily irradiation (Ir$_m$) is greater than 5 Kwh/m^2, the average season (4 Kwh/m^2<Ir$_m$<5 Kwh/m^2) and the short season (Ir$_m$<4 Kwh/m^2).
Keywords : Heliograph, pyranometer, daily global irradiation, solar energy potential, solar season.

1 Introduction

Global solar radiation is the most useful data to characterize the radiative climate of a region [1]. It is necessary to carry out an accurate evaluation of the average irradiation for the optimal sizing of a production system using solar energy. The distribution of the available solar energy can be obtained from the exploitation of the data of several techniques of collection of sunshine. The Campbell-Stokes heliograph is one of the most widely used measuring instruments in the field of sunshine climatology [2]. It gives approximations in the estimate of the real value of the global radiation [3]. In Côte d'Ivoire, a study in 2009 showed that there is a difference of 48% between the mean monthly sunlight values determined using a heliograph and the satellite data provided on the solar field [4]. In this work, we carry out an experimental comparative study of two solar data collection techniques. The first technique concerns the determination of solar irradiation from the direct measurement of the illumination by using a thermoelectric pyranometer. For the second, we use the insolation duration measured with a heliograph to determine solar irradiation.

2 Materials and methods

2.1 Materials

In this work, we determined the daily solar irradiation from the measurements of sunshine carried out with an Eppley thermoelectric pyranometer then with a Campbell-Stokes type heliograph.

The thermoelectric pyranometer delivers an electromotive force E (in mV) proportional to the illumination I (in W/m^2) received ($E=C.I$). The coefficient of proportionality C of the pyranometer we used is 10.41 10^{-3} mV.w^{-1}.m^2. The electromotive force between its terminals was measured with a voltmeter with an absolute uncertainty of ±0.001 mV. The measurements were recorded in steps of 1 minute.

We also calculated the global irradiation from the sunshine hours that were measured by SODEXAM (Aeronautical and Metéorological Exploitation Company) in 2017 at another site in Abidjan. These measurements were made using a Campbell-Stokes heliograph. It is an instrument that consists of a glass sphere with a diameter of about 10 cm inside and a strip of paper is placed (Figure 1). The concentrated rays on this paper burn part of it when the intensity of the radiation is greater than 120 W/m ^{2} [5]. The length of the burned part of the paper, called the heliogram, makes it possible to deduce the duration of sunshine in hours. The length of the burned part of the paper may depend on the moisture of the paper [6]. Measuring the length of the exactly burned part therefore leads to uncertainties in determining the duration of sunshine [3].

Fig. 1 – Measurement by the Campbell-Stokes heliograph

The two study sites are 20 kilometers apart. The location of the sites is shown in Figure 2.

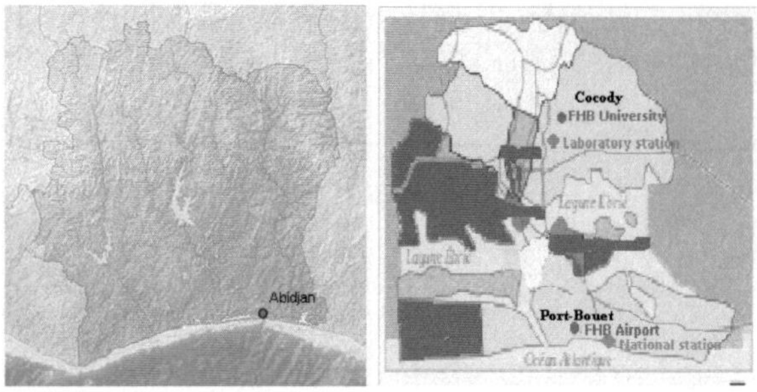

(a) Geolocation of the city of Abidjan (b) Geolocation of stations in Abidjan

Fig. 2 – Geolocation of the two sunshine collection sites

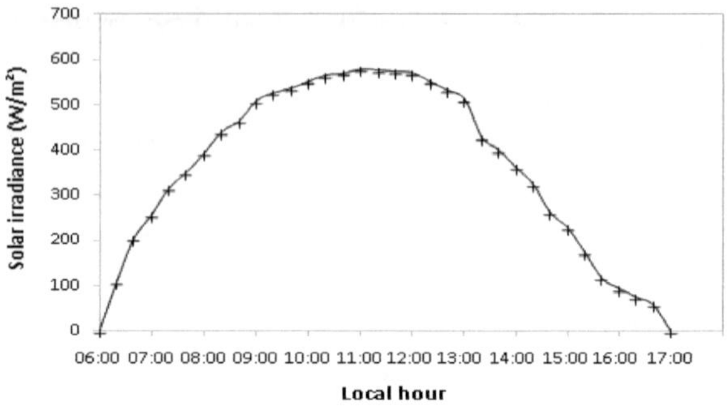

Fig. 4 – Variation of the solar irradiance for a clear day

2.2 Methods

2.2.1 Measurement of sunshine using the pyranometer and calculation of the global irradiation

The pyranometer was placed in the horizontal plane of the roof of the laboratory building 10 meters above the ground. The irradiation measurements were carried out throughout the year 2017 (from January 1 to December 31). The collected data was recorded every minute using a data logger connected to a computer. The schema of the acquisition system is shown in Figure 3.

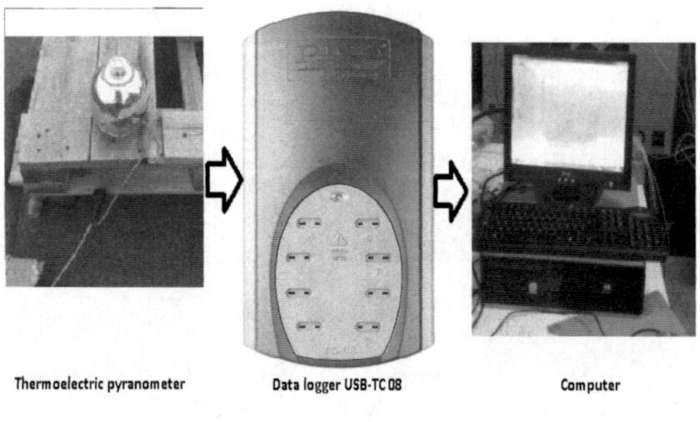

Fig. 3 – Eppley thermoelectric pyranometer coupled to an acquisition system

The solar irradiance I (W/m^2) was obtained from electromitive force E (mV) measured across the pyranometer. We used the following relation :

$$I = \frac{E}{C} \tag{1}$$

For each day (from 6 am to 6 pm), we calculated the global irradiation Ir_d (Wh/m^2) from the curve of variation of the irradiance over time . For sunny days, we obtained curves that have the same evolution as that shown in Figure 4.

Global irradiation was evaluated using Simpson's numerical integration method [7]. We get :

$$Ir_d = \frac{\Delta t}{2}[(I_1 + I_n) + 2\Sigma_{i=2}^{n-1} I_i] \tag{2}$$

In equation (2), Ir_d is expressed in Wh/m^2. The discretization step Δt is 1 minute (that is $\frac{1}{60}$ h), I_1 and I_n are the values of the irradiance respectively at sunrise and at sunset, and I_i is that corresponding to the ith measure. For each month, we calculated the average Ir_m value of the daily global irradiation.

2.2.2 Estimation of the global irradiation from sunshine duration

We used the Angström model [8] to determine global irradiation from the duration of sunshine. In this model, the global irradiation Q_S ($Wh/m^2.d$) is expressed by :

$$Q_S = Q_0(a + b\frac{H}{H_0}) \tag{3}$$

In equation (3), Q_0 (Wh/m^2) is the global average extraterrestrial irradiation of the locality. For the period concerned, a and b are constants that also depend on the locality. H represents the measured sunshine duration and H_0 the maximum sunshine duration of a clear day. We have determined the value H_0 from equation (4).

$$H_0 = \frac{2}{15}\cos^{-1}(-\tan\Phi\tan\sigma) \tag{4}$$

where Φ is the latitude of the place and σ the declination. The expression of σ according to the number n of the day is :

$$\sigma = 23.45\sin(360.\frac{284+n}{365}) \tag{5}$$

The extraterrestrial global irradiation Q_0 is expressed by :

$$Q_0 = \frac{24}{\Pi}I_{sc}(1{+}0.033\cos\frac{360n}{365})(\cos\Phi\cos\sigma\sin W_s{+}\frac{\Pi W_s}{180}\sin\Phi\sin\sigma) \tag{6}$$

$$W_s = \cos^{-1}(-\tan\Phi\tan\sigma) \tag{7}$$

In equation (6), I_{sc} represents the solar constant which is 1367 W/m^2.

The latitude for the locality of Abidjan is $\Phi = 5.2$°N. We used the universal values of the coefficients a (0.2336) and b (0.4987) established by Driesse and Thevenard [9]. For each month of the year 2017, we have calculated the daily average value of the global irradiation from the average daily value of the sunshine duration.

3 Results and discussions

3.1 Evaluation of the monthly average irradiation from the pyranometer and the heliograph

For each of the 12 months of the year 2017, we calculated the daily average irradiation (Ir_m) from the values of the illumination on the one hand and from the duration of sunshine (Q_S) on the other hand. The values obtained are summarized in Table 1.

Table 1 – Values of the global irradiation evaluated by the pyranometer and the heliograph during the year 2017 in Abidjan

Month	Q_0 (Wh/m^2)	H_0 (h)	H (h)	Q_S (Wh/m^2d)	Ir_m (Wh/m^2d)
Jan	9397	11.7	7.0	4993	3590
Feb	9974	11.8	6.5	5063	3680
Mar	10400	11.7	7.9	5924	4403
Apr	10439	11.9	6.5	5287	4153
May	10140	12.2	6.3	4971	3516
Jun	9847	11.7	3.3	3686	2351
Jul	9948	12.3	5.2	4425	2513
Aug	10254	12.2	4.3	4202	2507
Sep	10102	12.03	4.1	4077	3048
Oct	10061	11.9	5.8	4800	3344
Nov	9567	11.8	7.1	5117	3502
Dec	9985	11.9	5.9	4808	3369

The values of the duration of sunshine are those that have been measured by the national meteorological station. We calculated the values of Q_S from equation (3) with $a = 0.2336$ and $b = 0.4987$. The variations of Q_S and Ir_m are shown in Figure 5. In this figure, a clear difference is observed between the values obtained from the measurements made with the pyranometer and the heliograph. For the latter, the daily monthly irradiation is higher.

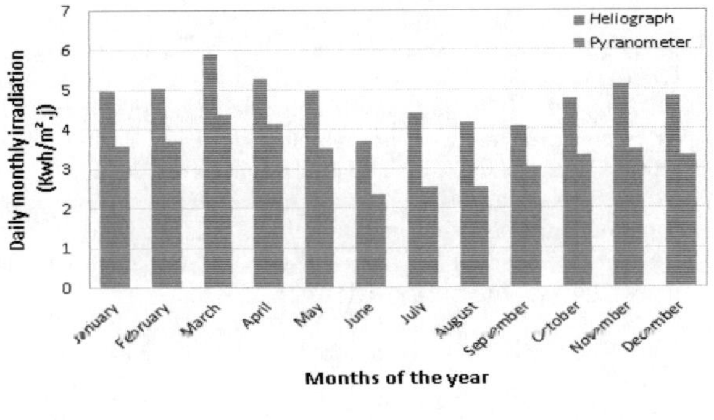

Fig. 5 – Monthly average irradiation determined using a pyranometer and a heliograph in Abidjan in 2017

The differences observed between the results of the two techniques are presented in Figure 6.

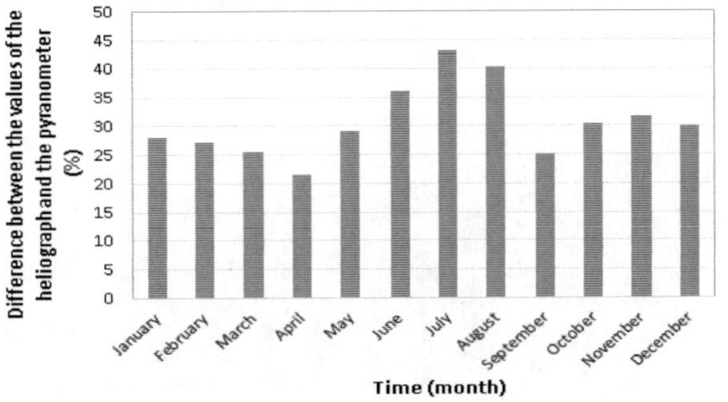

Fig. 6 – Difference between the values measured by pyranometer and the heliograph during the year 2017 in Abidjan

We are seeing a global variation of the order 27% except that of the months (June, July and August) of the great rainy season in Côte d'Ivoire with a value that reached 43% in July. The differences observed come from the fact that the pyranometer and the heliograph are not installed on the same site. The geographical position of two stations greatly influences the value of the sunshine collected. They are also due to the approximation related to the Angström adjustment coefficients a and b [10] and to the exact measurement of the duration of sunshine [3].

3.2 Monthly variation of average daily irradiation

For 2017, global irradiation varied from month to month as shown in Figure 7.

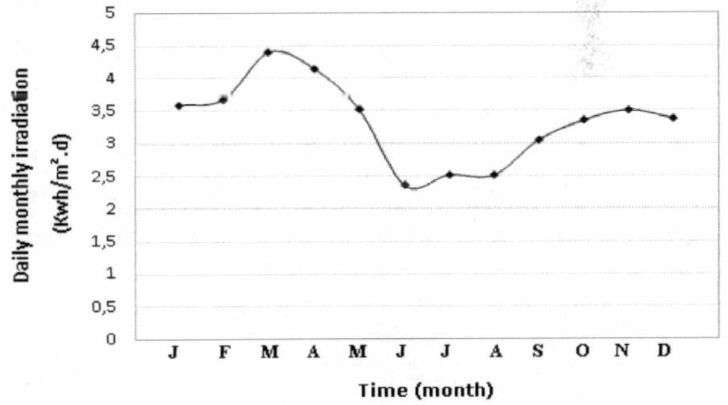

Fig. 7 – Annual variation of the global irradiation in Abidjan in 2017 obtained from the pyranometer

The highest value is observed in March (4403 $Wh/m^2.d$). The least sunny month is June (2351 $Wh/m^2.d$). In general, analysis of the data collected with the pyranometer showed that in 2017, there was a steady increase in global irradiation from January (3590 $Wh/m^2.d$) until March with 4403 $Wh/m^2.d$. Next, we observed a decay from April (4153 $Wh/m^2.d$) to August where we had 2507 $Wh/m^2.d$. Finally from September to November, the sunshine increases again and then decreases in December.

The solar energy potential in Abidjan has generally the same type of variation. We have shown in Figure 7, the variation of the average daily irradiation from 1978 to 1988 [11-12], from 2003 to 2009 [4] and from 2016 to 2017.

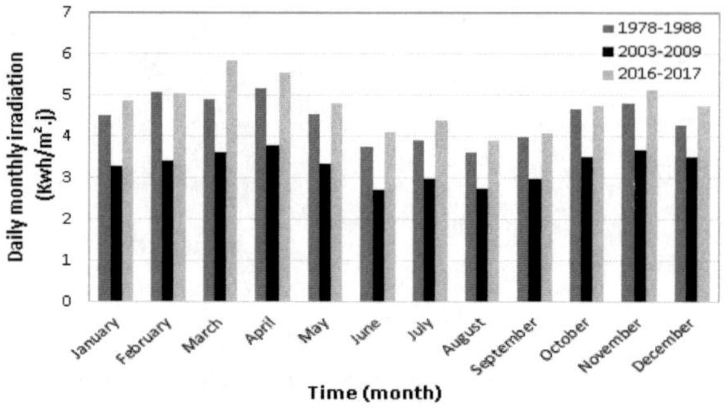

Fig. 8 – Daily monthly irradiation of the city of Abidjan from 1978 to 1988, from 2003 to 2009 and from 2016 to 2017

Figure 8 shows that the months with high average daily irradiation were generally the same from 1978 to 1988, from 2003 to 2009 and from 2016 to 2017. The daily values are different over the 3 periods considered. Nevertheless, for the same period, annual average irradiation varies little in tropical areas [13]. In the case of Abidjan, we have represented in Figure 9, the annual average values observed from 2003 to 2009.

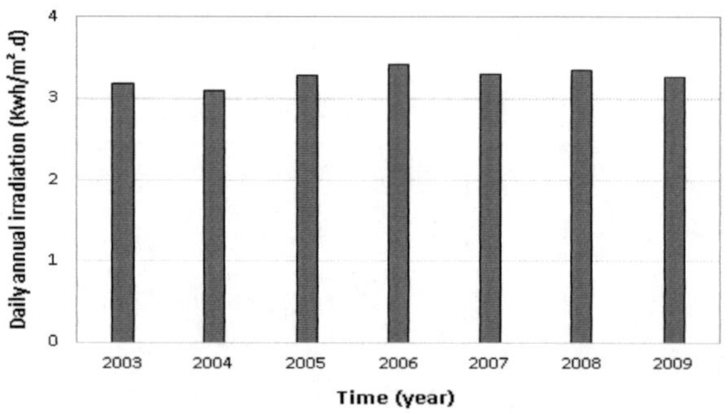

Fig. 9 – Annual average irradiation of Abidjan city from 2003 to 2009

4 CONCLUSION

This work made it possible to evaluate the daily global irradiation of the city of Abidjan in 2017, at two sites 20 kilometers apart, using two sunshine measurement techniques. On the one hand, we directly measured solar irradiance using an Eppley PSP type pyranometer, and on the other hand, we used sunshine durations collected from a Campbell-Stokes type heliograph. The study shows that the solar irradiation values obtained from the heliograph are high compared to those determined with the pyranometer. The maximum variation observed in July is 43% of the value measured by the heliograph technique. The two techniques of evaluation of the solar field show that in Abidjan, which is in tropical zone, the solar energy available on a horizontal plane varies from one month to another. For the year 2017, the maximum observed in March was 5924 $Wh/m^2.d$ with the heliograph and 4403 $Wh/m^2.d$ with the pyranometer. In that same year, the months of strong sunshine in Abidjan were February, March, April and November. For these months, the daily average irradiation evaluated from the data collected by the pyranometer is greater than 4000 $Wh/m^2.d$. The lowest value was obtained in June with an daily average irradiation of 2351 $Wh/m^2.d$.

References

1. B.A. Monteny, J.P. Lhomme, Etude du climat radiatif de la région sud-ouest de Côte d'Ivoire (zone Taï), Rapport de l'Office de la Recherche Scientifique et Technique Outre-Mer (ORSTOM), Centre ORSTOM d'Adiopodoumé, Côte d'Ivoire, (1981)
2. D. Matte, Climatologie de l'ensoleillement au Québec, Mémoire de Maitrise en Sci. Géo., Université Laval, Québec, (2011)
3. O.M.M, Guides des instruments et des observations météorologiques, Org. Météorol. Mond., 4e édition, Genève, (1973)
4. T. Brou, Etude technico-économique des technologies solaires en Côte d'Ivoire, Mém. en Mast. Spéc. Gén. Ener., Institut 2ie, Burkina Faso, (2010)
5. R. Leduc et C. Calvet, La mesure de la durée d'insolation, Atmosp. Océ. **4(19)**, 380-382, (1981)
6. J.A. Duffie and W.A. Beckman, Solar engineering of thermal processes, J. Wiley and sons, 4th Edition, (2013)
7. J. Verges, Détermination d'un pas optimum d'intégration pour la méthode de Simpson, Math. and Comp. in sim. (Elsevier) **3(22)**, 177-188, (1980)
8. A. Angström, Solar and terrestrial radiation, Utrecht : Report to international commission for solar research on actinometric investigations of solar and atmospheric radiation, (1923)
9. A. Driesse and D. Thevenard, A test of Suehrcke's sunshine-radiation relationship using a global data set, Ener. Sol. (Els. Sci.) **2(72)**, 167-175, (2002)
10. M. Drif et M. Chikh, Estimation de l'irradiation solaire par la logique floue, Rev. des Ener. Ren. (Chemss), 105-110, Algérie, (2000)
11. D.G.T.X., Plan national de l'énergie : Situation énergétique existante. Les énergies renouvelables, Direction et Contrôle des Grands Travaux, Vol. II-6, P. 9, Côte d'Ivoire, (1991)
12. W.F. Fassinou, Réfrigérateur solaire photovoltaïque à trois compartiments avec batterie de froid : Etude, réalisation et analyse des irréversibilités, Doct. 3me cyc. en Sc. (Ener. Sol.) **248**, Univ. Nat. de Côte d'Ivoire, P. 223, (1997)
13. S. Brigand, Les principes de l'énergie solaire photovoltaïque, Techn. de Cons., Editions le Moniteur, 17-35, (2008)

Wind parameters measurement to analysis the sectoral variation influence on the diurnal behavior of wind potential for a site: Application on the site of Nouakchott, Mauritania

E. Abdi[a], B. Bilal[a*], D. Nourou[a], M. Ndongo[a], CMF Kebe[b], P.A. Ndiaye[b]

[a]Laboratoire de Recherche Appliquée aux Energies Renouvelables de l'Eau et du Froid (LRAER)/FST/Université de Nouakchott, BP: 5026 Nouakchott, Mauritania
[b]Centre International de Formation et de Recherche en Energie Solaire (C.I.F.R.E.S), ESP BP: 5085 Dakar Fann, Senegal

Abstract. The aim of this paper is to analyze the influence of the sectoral and the diurnal variation on the available wind potential. The meteorological data collected in two localities in Nouakchott-Mauritania were used. These data cover the period of one year and were measured every second and averaged on ten minutes. The used approach allows determining the wind rose. Furthermore, the wind rose was classified into three main sectors characterized by frequencies between 0 and 10%, 10 and 20% and more than 20% respectively. For each sector, the diurnal variation of wind speed, power density, Weibull parameters, turbulence index, Power law exponent, air density, temperature and relative humidity were determined. The results showed that the dominant wind direction is the northwestern (330-359°). The domination direction (15% frequency) was observed for the sector (0-90°) and (300-330°). However, for the sector (90° -300°), the frequency of the wind remains lower (less than 7%). The calculated of the mean wind speed at the height 90 m for the three sectors was 8.15 m/s, 8.02 *m/s* and 6.10 *m/s* respectively. The corresponding power density was 465.37 *W/m²*, 542.63 *W/m²* and 239.14 *W/m²* respectively. The turbulence index (0.084, 0.087 and 0.068) indicated that the sectors (0-90°, 300-330° and 90-300°) were more turbulent than the sector (330-359°) and these turbulence indexes was more important for the day-time than for the night-time period.

Keywords: Wind potential; diurnal characteristics; sectoral characteristics; turbulence index.

1. Introduction

Renewable energy plays an interesting role for solving problems of energy and helps to reduce greenhouse gas emissions worldwide. To optimize the wind energy utilization, an accurate estimation of wind resources is needed. Most studies of wind energy in many countries [1-12] are often limited to the determination of mean wind speed and some statistical characteristics (e.g wind distribution, turbulence index and power low exponent) for a period of a year and / or for a month.
Jie Zhang et al. [13] and Santos-Alamillos [14] presented methods for characterizing wind potential based on the determination of power density and wind speed distribution. These studies did not take into account the influence of the wind direction variation on the diurnal variation of the potential.
Using wind data measured every hour, Jordi Mazon et al. [15] have presented a study on the contribution of sea breeze to the wind potential by determining wind distribution and power density.
Several other studies [16-24] have presented different approaches to characterize and to model the wind potential. These works have been interested to determine the monthly variation of mean wind speeds, modeling parameters of the wind speed distribution (e.g. Weibull parameters) and the resulting productible.
In Senegal, works [25-30] allowed to characterize the wind potential for several sites located in the northwest coast of Senegal (from Dakar to Saint-Louis). These works have focused particularly on the determination of the monthly mean wind speed, the distribution of wind speed and annual power law exponent.
In Mauritania, a study [31] allowed to identify the level of interest in wind potential on the Mauritanian coast and the need to estimate wind potential on the coast from Nouakchott to Nouadhibou using more and accurate measured data.
None of previously presented works has studied the analysis of the influence of the wind direction variation on the diurnal wind potential and on the wind speed vertical profile. So, the aim of this work is to analyze the influence of the directions variation on the diurnal behavior of the wind potential parameters (wind speed, turbulence index, power law exponent and air density).
The rest of this paper is structured as follows: Instruments of measurements and Mathematical models are presented in Sections 2 and 3 respectively. Section 4, presents the approach used for this study. Resultants and discussion are presented in Section 5. Finally, conclusion is drawn in Section 6.

2. Materials and Methods

2.1. Instruments of measurements

The data used in this study are collected in Nouakchott, Mauritania and are measured every second, averaged by 10 minutes and then recorded in the Datalogger memory (Table 1). The data were collected over a one-year period: from 1st January 2016 to 31th December 2016 and incorporate several parameters (wind-speed, wind-direction, pressure, temperature, humidity, air density). The data collected, every ten minutes for each of these parameters, consist of the average of 600 values measured every second during the ten minutes, the maximum, the minimum and the standard deviation of those values. The wind-speeds were measured at three different heights (10 *m*, 30 *m* and 90 *m*), while the wind-direction was measured at 28.5 *m* and 88.5 *m* (Figure 1). In the framework of its wind-farms project, the Mauritanian electricity company installed, since 2015, the measurement station used in this work. The project consists of 30 MW a wind-farm (15 wind-turbines of 2 MW each). Two measuring masts (mast 1 and mast 2) were installed near the wind-power generators to control their operation. The anemometers and the wind-vanes were installed in the north direction with respect to the tower position. The characteristics of the used anemometers and wind-vane are given in the tables 2 and 3.

Table 1. Geographic Coordinates of Measurement Towers

Measurement location	Longitude (°)	Latitude (°)	Altitude (°)	Measurement height (*m*)
Mast 1	-1796	15.98	2 m	20, 30 et 90
Mast 2	-17.92	15.99	2 m	20, 30 et 90

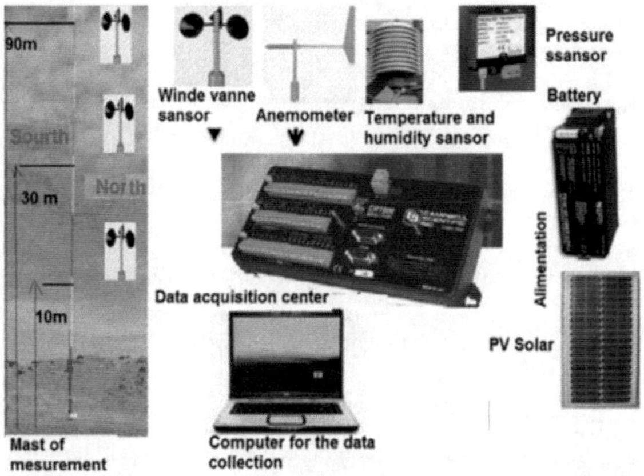

Fig. 1. Components of wind measurement systems installed in Nouakchott

Table 2. Technical Characteristics of Anemometers

Technology of Anemometer	Frist class
Measurement interval	0,3 à 75 *m/s*
Accuracy	De 0,3 à 50 *m/s* 1%
Resolution	0,05 *m/s*
Operating temperature	-50 à 80 *°C*
Signal Output	Frequency
Starting speed	Inferior to 0.3 *m/s*
Supply voltage	3,3–4,2 VDC, 0.3 *mA*

Table 3. Technical characteristics of the wind-vane

Technology of Wind-vane	Compact
Measurement interval	0-359°(0°refersto the north)
Resolution	0.5°
Accuracy	±3°
Measurement principle	Potentiometer
Output of the potentiometer	2 *kΩ*
Supply voltage	0V–24V DC with 20 *mA*
The survival speed	80 m/s during 30 minutes
Operating temperature	-40 to70*°C*

2.2. Mathematical models

1) *Mean wind speed:* In the present study, the wind speeds data measured every ten minutes for one year for each mast were used to calculate the wind potential. The mean wind speed values were calculated by using Eq. (1), [32].

$$v_m = \frac{1}{n} \cdot \sum_{i=1}^{n} v_i \tag{1}$$

Where n is the observation number and v_i is the wind speed in time stage *i*.

2) *Weibull distribution:* Weibull distribution has been commonly used in literature to express the wind speed distribution and to estimate the wind power density. The Weibull distribution is a good match with the experimental data. The probability density function of Weibull is given by Eq. (2) [17]:

$$f(v) = \frac{k}{A} \cdot \left(\frac{v}{A}\right)^{k-1} \exp\left(-\left(\frac{v}{A}\right)^{k}\right) \tag{2}$$

Where A and k are respectively the scale and the shape parameters of Weibull, which can be determined by using the Maximum likelihood method Eqs. (3) and (4) [33].

$$k = \left(\left(\frac{\sum_{i=1}^{n} v_i^k \ln(v_i)}{\sum_i v_i^k}\right) - \left(\frac{\sum_{i=1}^{n} \ln(v_i)}{n}\right)\right)^{-1} \tag{3}$$

$$A = \left(\frac{\sum_{i=1}^{n} v_i^k}{n}\right)^{\frac{1}{k}} \tag{4}$$

Smaller k values correspond to more variable (more gusty) winds and the higher A values correspond to a good potential.

3) *Wind power density:* The long-term wind speed distribution f (*v*) is combined with the available wind power to give the average wind power density, which can be expressed as follows [34]:

$$\overline{P} = \frac{1}{2} \cdot \rho \cdot A^3 \cdot \Gamma\left(1 + \frac{3}{k}\right) \tag{5}$$

Where Γ(x) is the gamma function of (x) given by:

$$\Gamma(x) = \int_0^{\infty} t^{x-1} e^{-t} dt \tag{6}$$

4) *Extrapolation of the wind speed with the height:* The wind speed was collected at 10 and 30 and 90 m of high. For wind projects, it is necessary to estimate the wind speed at the wind turbine hub height. According to the literature, the most commonly used method to adjust the wind speed from one level to another is the power law method [35] expressed by:

$$v = v_0 \cdot \left(\frac{h}{h_0}\right)^{\alpha} \tag{7}$$

Where v_0 is the reference wind speed (*m/s*), h_0 is the reference height (m), v is the wind speed (*m/s*) to be determined for the desired height *h*, and *α* is the power law exponent estimated by using the wind speed measurement at two altitudes.

5) *Turbulence index*

The turbulence index is defined as the ratio of the standard deviation to the wind-speed (equation 8) [**36**]. It provides information on the turbulence of the site and could be used to explain the effects of the tower on the quality of the measured wind-speed data.

$$I_n = \frac{\sigma}{v_m} \qquad (8)$$

σ: the standard deviation of the wind-speed (*m/s*)
V_m : mean wind-speed (*m/s*)

3. Approach of study

The proposed approach consists to:

- determine the wind rose and divide it into three directional areas which the frequency of occurrence is between (0 and 10%), (10 and 20%) and greater than or equal to 20%.
- for each areas, determine the average value of: wind speed, power density, Weibull parameters, power law exponent, air density, temperature, relative humidity and turbulence index.
- for each sector, determine the hourly behavior of each of the previously announced parameters

The approach was applied based on the mathematical models presented in the section 2.2 and using the data collected on the Nouakchott-Mauritania site. The average of wind speed, power density, Weibull parameters, turbulence index was calculated using the wind speed collected at 90 *m* of height. The power law exponent was calculated using the wind speed measured at the height of 10 *m* and 30 *m*.

4. Results and discussion

Meteorological data (wind speed, wind direction, standard deviation of wind speed, air density, temperature, relative humidity) collected on the two measuring masts are used.
The data of the wind direction allowed to determine the wind rose. The results are shown in Figure 2. It can be observed that the dominate wind direction is the northwestern (sector 330-359°). The frequency of occurrence in this sector was 25%. However for the sector from 0° to 90° and the sector from 300° to 330°, the frequency of occurrence was between 15% and 20%. For the sector from 90° to 300°, the frequency of occurrence is less than 5%.

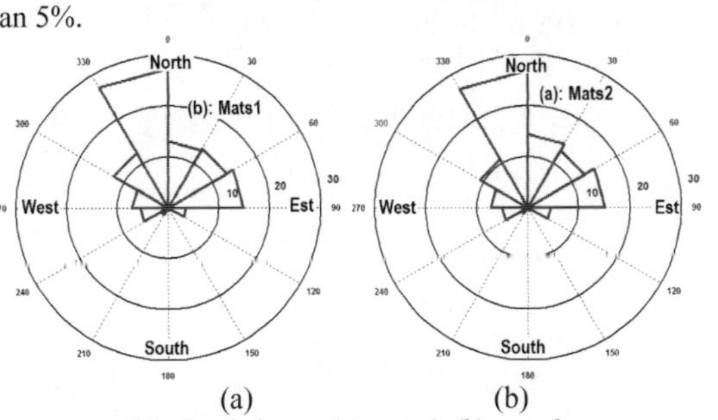

(a) (b)

Fig. 2. wind rose: (a) mast 1, (b) mats 2

According to the classification intervals, three sectors are identified for the two masts:

- The sector from 90 to 300° which the frequency of occurrence was between 0 and 10°;
- The sector from 0 to 90° and from 300 to 330° which the frequency was between 10 and 15%;
- And the sector from 330° to 360° which the frequency was greater or equal to 20%.

For the three sectors identified, the average value of: mean wind speed, Weibull parameters, power density, air density, temperature, relative humidity, power law exponent, and turbulence index ware calculated. The results are shown in Table 4. Figure 3 and Figure 4 illustrate the hourly variation of these parameters.
It can be seen (Table 4) that the sector 330-360° has the highest mean wind speed (8.19 *m/s* for the mast 1 and 8.16 *m/s* for the mast 2). The corresponding power density is 542.63 W/m^2 and 509.8 W/m^2 for the two masts respectively. This sector (330-360°) corresponds to the dominant direction of wind and is characterized by the turbulence index of 0.0926 for the mast 1 and 0.0731 for the mast 2). Generally, the turbulence index remains the lowest for the all three sectors and for the both masts. The power law exponent was the lowest (Table 4) compared to the literature which the power law exponent which was between 0.08 and 0.4 [**37**].
For example, for the sector 330-360°, the power low exponent was 0.068 and 0.085 for the two masts 1 and 2 respectively.
Figures (3-a) and (4-a) showed that the mean wind speed is greater during the period 15h to 23 for the sector 330-360° compared to 0-90°, that can be explained by the change of the wind directions of the sea and land breeze between the day and the night-time period. However, the average of the wind speed measured for the sector 90-300° remains the lowest compared to the other sectors for the both day and night-time periods.
Figures (3-d) and (4-d) show, for the all sectors, that the turbulence index is higher for the day-time (from 10 am to 08 pm) compared to period of the night-time. This remark is observed for the two locations. That can be explained by the intensity of the wind speed, which is greater during the day-time than during the night-time. Likewise, with the increase of the intensity of wind speed during the day-time, the power law exponent becomes smaller. Indeed, with a high wind speed, the effects of the obstacles become less felt by the sensors.
Figures (3-h and 4-h) and figures (3-i and 4-i) indicate that the ambient temperature is higher during the day-time than during the night-time period. While, the relative humidity was higher for the night-time compared to the day-time period. However, the air density remains relatively stable over the whole period (day and night-time period). It remains between 1.17 kg/m^3 and 1.19 kg/m^3 for the three sectors and for the two measuring masts.
It is interesting to note that the air density measured at the Nouakchott site is lower than the standard air density (2.225 *kg/m3*) widely used in the characterization of the available wind potential and to calculate the producible. Indeed, the use of the standard value of the air density can lead to an overestimation of the producible which generates an increase in the cost of system feasibility.

Table 4. Wind potential parameters calculated for the sector: 0-90 &300-330°, 90-300° and 330°-360°

Sector	Mast1			Mast2		
	0-90° & 300-330°	90-300	330-359	0-90° & 300-330°	90-300	330-359
Mean wind speed (*m/s*) at 90 *m*	8. 02	6.14	8.19	7.73	6.10	8.16
Scale parameter (-) at 90 *m*	8.85	6.80	9.03	8.54	6.83	9.02
Shape parameter (-)	3.75	3.25	3.79	4.02	3.31	3.77
Power density (*W/m2*) at 90 *m*	465,37	239,14	542.63	460.75	197.58	509.8
Turbulence index(-) at 90 *m*	0.0997	0.0934	0.0926	0.0817	0.0965	0.0731
Power law exponent (-) at 90 *m*	0.085	0.088	0.068	0.099	0.088	0.085
Air density (-)	1.18	1.176	1.183	1.18	1.18	1.18
Temperature (°C)	26.85	26.39	23.64	27.1	26.66	24.23
Relative Humidity (%)	29.92	74.57	76.91	33.25	82.02	86.54

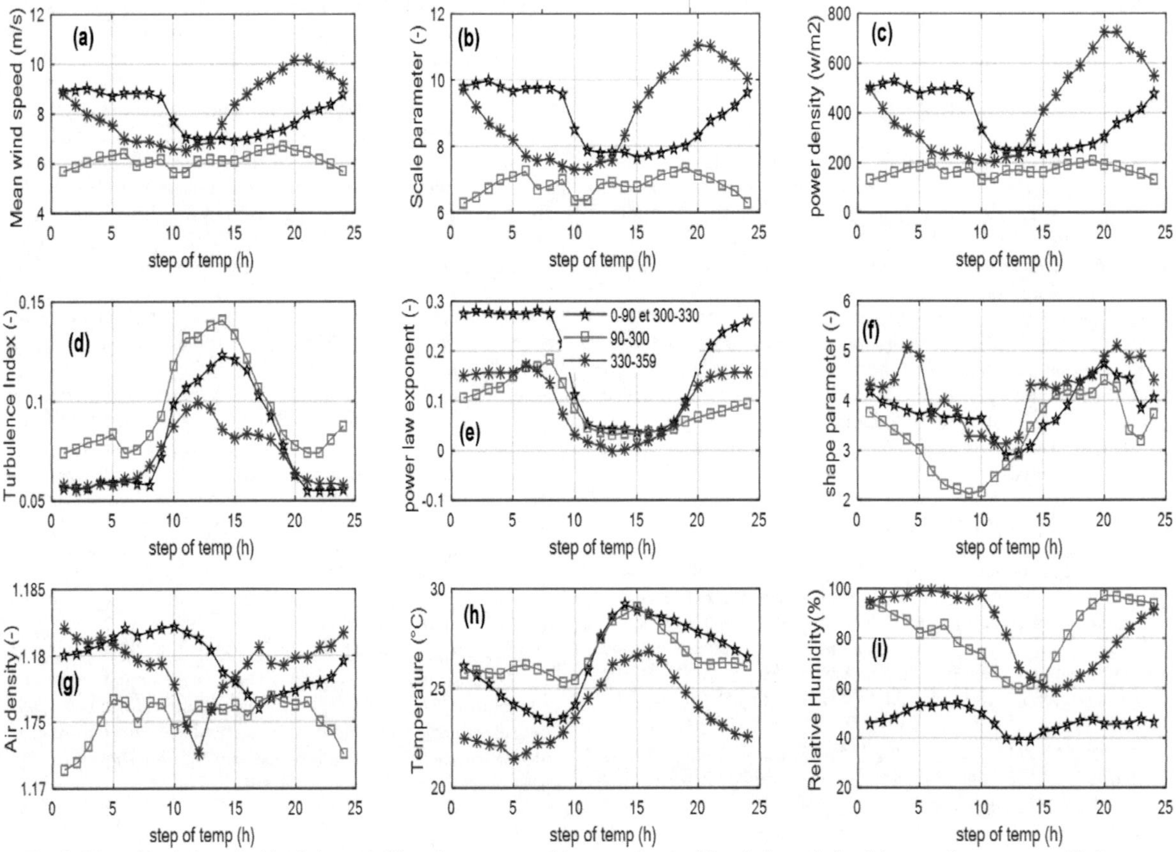

Fig. 3. Diurnal variation of : (a) wind speed, (b) scale parameter, (c) power density (d) turbulence index (e) power low exponent (f) shape parameter (g) air density (h) temperature, (i) relative humidity for the mast 1

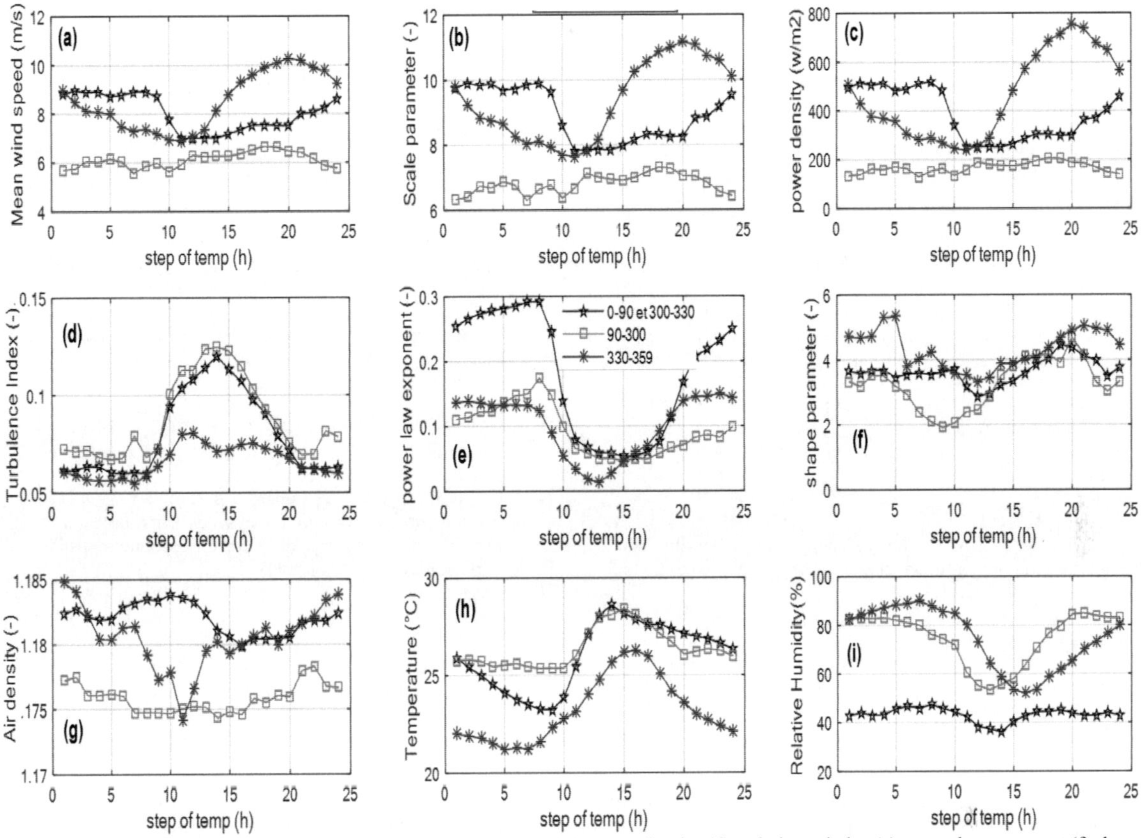

Fig. 4. Diurnal variation of : (a) wind speed, (b) scale parameter, (c) power density (d) turbulence index (e) power low exponent (f) shape parameter (g) air density (h) temperature, (i) relative humidity for the mast 2

5. Conclusion

The object of this study was to develop an approach allowed to analysis the sectoral variation influence on the diurnal behavior of wind potential for a site. The developed approach was applied to site of Nouakchott-Mauritania.

The meteorological data collected for one year in tow location in Nouakchott was used.

The results allowed to observe that, from one sector to another the intensity of the mean wind speed was different as well as its contribution to the available potential. Likewise, the turbulence of the site varies according to the wind direction.

The analysis of the diurnal variation influence on the available potential made it possible to observe that according to the period (day or night-time period), the mean wind speed varied from one sector to another as well as the turbulence of the site.

It is important to mention that the position of the measurements mast with respect to the dominant wind direction as well as the orientation of the sensors with respect to this dominate wind direction and with respect to the measurements mast could have a significant influence on the quality of the meteorological data and therefore on the feasibility analysis of the wind project.

It is, therefore, interesting in the rest of this work to analyze the influence of the presence of the measurements mast and the wind sensor orientation on the quality of the wind measurements.

References

1. L. Hamane et A. Khellaf. Evaluation des ressources énergétiques éoliennes de l'Algérie. Proc. CHEMSS 2000, Alger, pp. 74-379, (2000).
2. L. Hamane et A. Khellaf. Wind energy resources in Algeria. WREC 2000, Brighton, UK, pp. 2352-2355, (2000).
3. L. Aicha-Haman et A. Khellaf. Evaluation mensuelle de la ressource éolienne à travers l'Algérie. Rev. Energ. Ren. ICPWE, pp. 147-152, (2003).
4. H. NedjariDaaou, S. Haddouche et N. Merzouk. Amélioration de la carte des vents des données interpolées. Rev. Energ. Ren. ICPWE, pp. 119-24, (2003).
5. M. A. Tabet Helal et N. Ghellai. Le gisement éolien à Beni-Saf Région Côtière de l'Ouest Algérien. Rev. Enrg. Ren. ICPW, pp: 143-46, (2003).
6. O.A. Jaramillo, R. Saldan and U. Miranda.Wind power potential of Baja California. Renewable Energy. **29**, 2087-100, (2004).
7. A. N. Celik. A statistical analysis of wind power density based on the Weibull and Rayleigh models at the southern region of Turkey. Renewable Energy. **29**, 593-604, (2003).
8. J.D.K. Bishop and G. A.J. Amaratunga. Evaluation of small wind turbines in distributed arrangement as sustainable wind energy

option for Barbados. Energy Conversion and Management. **49**, 1652-61, (2008).
9. E. Migoya, A. Crespo, A. Jiménez, J. Garcia and F. Manuel. Wind energy resource assessment in Madrid region. Renewable Energy. **32**, 1467-83, (2007).
10. C. Wichser and K. Klink. Low wind speed turbines and wind power potential in Minnesota, USA. Renewable Energy. **33**, 1749-58, (2008).
11. J.K. Kaldellis. The wind potential impact on the maximum wind energy penetration in autonomous electrical grids. Renewable Energy. **33**, 1665-77, (2008).
12. A.S. Ahmed Shata and R. Hanitsch. Electricity generation and wind potential assessment at Hurghada, Egypt. Renewable Energy. **33**, 141-8, (2008).
13. J. Zhang, S. Chowdhury, A. Messac. A comprehensive measure of the energy resource: Wind power potential (WPP). Energy Conversion and Management. **86**, 388–98, (2014).
14. F.J. Santos-Alamillos, D. Pozo-Vázquez , J.A. Ruiz-Arias , V. Lara-Fanego, J. Tovar-Pescador .A methodology for evaluating the spatial variability of wind energy resources: Application to assess the potential contribution of wind energy to baseload power. Renewable Energy **69**, 147-56, (2014).
15. J. Mazon, J. Rojas, J. Jou, A. Valle, D. Olmeda, C. Sanchez. An assessment of the sea breeze energy potential using small wind turbines inperi-urban coast alareas. J. Wind Eng. Ind. Aerodyn.**139**, 1–7, (2015).
16. A.M. Makbul Ramli, S. Twaha, Z. Al-Hamouz. Analyzing the potential and progress of distributed generation applications in Saudi Arabia: The case of solar and wind resources. Renewable and Sustainable Energy Reviews **70**, 287–97, (2017).
17. A. Allouhia, O. Zamzouma, M.R. Islam, R. Saidur, T. Kousksou, A. Jamil, A. Derouich. Evaluation of wind energy potential in Morocco's coastal regions. Renewable and Sustainable Energy Reviews. **72**, 311-24, (2017).
18. L; Jiale, X.B Yu. LiDAR technology for wind energy potential assessment: Demonstrationand validation at a site around Lake Erie. Energy Conversion and Management. **144**, 252–61, (2017).
19. A. Nouri, M.A. Babram, E. Elwarraki, M. Enzili. Moroccan wind farm potential feasibility. Case study. Energy Conversion and Management. **122,** 39–51, (2016).
20. S.M Boudia, A. Benmansour, N. Ghellai, M. Benmedjahed, M. Abdellatif T. Hellal. Temporal assessment of wind energy resource at four locations in Algerian Sahara. Energy Conversion and Management. **76**, 654-64, (2013).
21. N. Nawri, Guðrún N. Petersen, H. Bjornsson, A.N. Hahmann, K. Jónasson, C.B Hasager, N. Clausen. The wind energy potential of Iceland. Renewable Energy. **69**, 290-99, (2014).
22. K. Mohammadi, O. Alavi, J.G. McGowan. Use of Birnbaum-Saunders distribution for estimating wind speed and wind power probability distributions: A review. Energy Conversion and Management. **143**, 109–22, (2017).
23. F. Fazelpour, E. Markarian, N. Soltani, Wind energy potential and economic assessment of four locations in Sistan and Balouchestan province in Iran. Renewable Energy. **109**, 646-67, (2017).
24. J. Wang, J.H. KailiangMa. Wind speed probability distribution estimation and wind energy assessment. Renewable and Sustainable Energy Reviews. **60**: 881-99, (2016).
25. P.A. Ndiaye. Etude et modélisation du potentiel éolien sur le site de Dakar. Application à la conception d'aérogénérateurs optimisés sur ce site. Thèse de Docteur Ingénieur, ENSUT, UCAD, 141 p, (1988).
26. I. Youm, J. Sarr, M. Sall, A. Ndiaye and M. Kane. Analysis of wind data and wind energy potential along the northern coast of Senegal. Rev. Energ. Ren. **8**, 95-108, (2005).
27. C.M.F. Kebe, V. Sambou, B. Ould Bilal, P.A. Ndiayeet M. Los. Evaluation du potentiel éolien du site de Gandon dans larégion nord du Sénégal. International Metrology Conference CAFMET (2008).
28. P.Ndiaye, C.Kraif, L.Protin et G.Fleury. Study and modelling of the wind power potential on the site in Dakar by a microcomputer. Electrical And Power Systems Modelling And Simulation, p. 95-8, (1989).
29. B. Ould Bilal, P. A. Ndiaye, C. M. F. Kébé, V. Sambou. Evaluation du potentiel éolien des sites de Kayar et de Potou Application au choix d'une éolienne adaptée au site. Casamancesun (2010).
30. B. Ould Bilal, P. A. Ndiaye, C. M. F. Kébé, V. Sambou, M. Ndongo. Méthodologie de caractérisation d'un site éolien Application à deux sites dans la côte nord du Sénégal. DMD-(2009).
31. B. Ould Bilal, C.M.F. Kébé, V. Sambou, M. Ndongo et P.A. Ndiaye. Etude et modélisation du potentiel éolien du site de Nouakchott. Journal des Sciences Pour l'Ingénieur. n° 9, pp. 28-34, (2008).
32. M. Gokcek, A. Bayulken, S. Bekdemir,''Investigation of wind characteristics and wind energy potential in Kirklareli, Turkey'', Renew Energy. **32,** 1739–52 (2007)
33. J.V. Seguro, T.W, ''Lambert. Modern estimation of the parameters of the Weibull wind speed distribution for wind energy analysis'', Journal of Wind Engineering and Industrial Aerodynamics. **85**, 75-84 (2000)
34. W. Zhou, H. Yang, Z. Fang, ''Wind power potential and characteristics analysis of the Pearl River Delta Region'', Renew Energy. **31**, 739–53 (2006)
35. A.M. Omer, ''On the wind energy resources of Sudan'', Renewable and Sustainable Energy Reviews, **12**, 2117–39 (2008)
36. Measnet. ''Evoluation of site specifique wind condition.'' Version april 2016, 56p.
37. Sathyajith M. Wind Energy Fundamentals, Resource Analysis and Economics. Springer-Verlag Berlin Heidelberg (2006).

Minotoring and evaluation of photovoltaic module characteristics using imaging techniques

Ababacar Ndiaye [a,b,*], Cheikh M. F. Kébé [b], Abdérafi Charki [c], Boudy Ould Bilal [d,c], Vincent Sambou [b], Papa A. Ndiaye [b]

[a] Université Assane Seck de Ziguinchor, UFR – Sciences et Technologies, Département de Physique, BP 523 Ziguinchor, Sénégal.
[b] Centre International de Formation et de Recherche en Energie Solaire (CIFRES), Ecole Supérieure Polytechnique-UCAD, BP 5085 Dakar-Fann, Sénégal
[c] Université d'Angers-ISTIA-LARIS, 62 Avenue Notre Dame du Lac 49000 Angers, France
[d] Ecole des Mines de Mauritanie (EMiM), BP 5259, Nouakchott, Mauritanie

Received:

Abstract. The effects of a sub-Saharan coastal climate on PV modules degradation was studied in this paper. A Mono and a polycrystalline-silicone solar PV module exposed in Dakar, dry and coastal climate, at the extreme West of Senegal was studied. As first inspection in this region, the electrical parameters of two PV modules A and B operated during about 10 years, are measured under standard testing condition(STC) and their I-V characteristics were fitted. The initial I-V characteristics was performed under real conditions and translated to STC and compared to the measured I-V characteristics at standard test conditions (STC) obtained in PV Laboratory after exposition. After the operating years, the main important parameters of the studied PV modules: short-circuit current I_{SC}, open circuit voltage V_{OC}, maximum power P_{MPP}, nominal current I_{MPP} and Voltage V_{MPP} are evaluated and then compared to the initial parameters obtained during initial exposition to estimate their degradation.
Moreover, the defects that affected the PV module are explored by visual inspection, Electroluminescence (EL) and thermography (IR) imaging methods. The results show absolute degradation of maximum power (ΔP_{MPP}) nearing -5.35 % and -2.92% for the mono and polycrystalline silicon operating about 10 years. The inspection reveals many degradations in both modules. Most of the degradations due to the climate are found in the mono and a very advanced I_{SC} mismatch is found with the IR image. The polycrystalline has many mechanical defects that's does not too much affect the performance characteristics.

Keywords: photovoltaic, degradation, performance, electroluminescence imaging, thermography imaging

1 Introduction

The use of Renewable Energies becomes more and more necessary for the satisfaction of the world Energy demand, with less negative effects on the environment. Global warming and fossil fuels depletion force the world to seek for solutions to ensure our survival and those of future generations. Africa in particular is facing a critical energy scenario. According to the World Bank, 25 countries in sub-Saharan Africa are in energetic crisis. Only 32% **[1]** of the population has access to electricity in 2012 with a very high average price of US $ 0.13 **[2]** per kilowatt hour.
However, the continent can rely on its significant renewable energy resources to improve its situation. Several renewable energy sources are available in different localities. East Africa is known for its large geothermal deposit. The extremities are marked by the presence of remarkable wind potential with an estimated power of 1,300 GW. Hydropower with an available capacity of 238 GW is the most exploited clean energy in the continent. But solar energy remains the most abundant source on the continent. Africa is the sunniest continent of the world. An average radiation of 2650 kWh / m^2 / year, with an estimated sunshine duration of 3500 hours / year could enable the continent to satisfy its energy needs.
Several energy projects based on solar photovoltaic are planned or executed on the continent. Nevertheless, for better exploitation of solar resources, adaptation of technologies to the African environment is essential. The technical characteristics of the existing solar panels are given under the standard testing conditions (STC) corresponding to a mild climate of 25 ° C and a sunshine of 1000W / m^2. These conditions are totally different from the ambient exposure conditions of panels in Africa. In this context, it is pertinent to identify, quantify and compare the major defects or expected modes of failure for the various climates that can be encountered in sub-Saharan Africa (arid, continental, wet or coastal monsoon) and which are Very different from the climate of central Europe.
The study is about degradation of the performance of mono and polycrystalline solar panels after about ten (10) years of exposure in a coastal climate precisely at the Polytechnic superior school of Dakar (ESP).
The analysis focuses on data collected using electroluminescence (EL) and infrared imaging methods.

2 Location and platform test presentation

2.1 Presentation of the experimental environment

2.1.1 Temperature

The photovoltaic platform shown in Fig. 2 is used in this study. It is installed at Dakar in Senegal. Dakar is located on the extreme western Africa with geographic coordinates 14.61° North latitude and 17.37° West longitude. In Senegal, the climate is of sub-desert tropical type punctuated by damp summers and dry winters. On the other hand, the DAKAR region, which has an advanced position in the Atlantic Ocean, is characterized by a coastal microclimate. This is strongly influenced by the trade winds and the monsoon coming from the sea. On average, the temperatures are always high. the average daily maximum temperature is 24°C from January to March and between 25 and 27°C in April, May and December. From June to October, temperatures reach 30°C (Fig. 1) **[3]**.

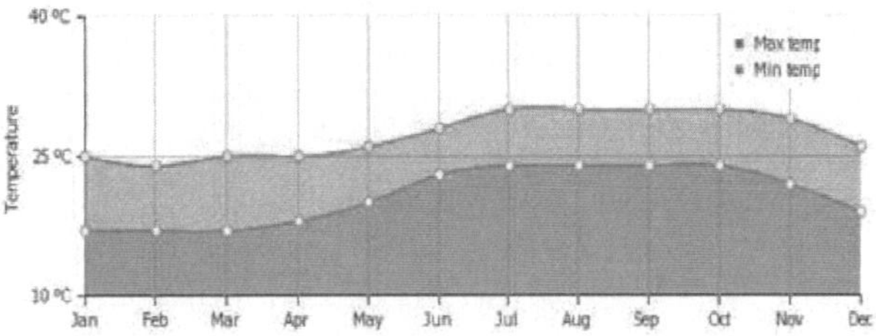

Fig.1. Average min & max temperature in Dakar.

2.1.2 Radiation and insolation

Radiation and insolation are key parameters, among others, in the quantification of the producible energy but also of the effects of radiation on the photovoltaic material. The radiation is expressed in kWh / m^2 while the insolation is expressed in hours. High radiation and insolation values correspond to very high temperatures and low values at low temperatures and vice versa. The average sunshine varies from 7.3h/d during the rainy season when the sky is always cloudy at 9 h / d during the dry season when the sky is clear **[4]**. The highest average monthly value for radiation is 6,92kWh/m^2 /d and is in the period from March to June, while the lowest is 4.57kWh/m^2/d corresponding to the months from July to February.

2.1.3 Humidity

Variations in relative humidity depend in part on the air temperature and the hygrometric characteristics of the air masses. The annual evolution of the relative humidity of the air is also tempered by the maritime influence and the annual average is around 70%. The highest values coincide with the heart of the rainy and low season in the months of April-May and October-December January. Main climatic characterics are presented by Table 1**[5]**.

Table.1. Main climatic characteristics of Dakar.

Months	Temperature	Relative Humidity	Daily solar radiation - horizontal
	°C	%	kWh/m²/d
January	20.7	70.2%	4.89
February	20.7	74.9%	5.80
March	21.0	78.5%	6.57
April	21.4	83.0%	6.92
May	22.8	82.9%	6.71
June	25.6	82.3%	6.21
July	27.1	79.7%	5.60
August	27.4	83.0%	5.34
September	27.6	84.7%	5.34
October	27.6	81.8%	5.53
November	25.8	73.8%	4.98
December	23.4	68.6%	4.57
Annual	**24.3**	**78.6%**	**5.70**

2.2 Platform and modules presentation

The platform used is composed of four (4) modules. Two monocrystalline manufactured by WAAREE in the left. The Two polycrystalline modules in the left are BP Solar products. One module on each technology have been chosen (A & B) to evaluate and analyze the degradation affecter about 10 years of operation. The two modules A & B fielded have been installed in same period 2007. The PV modules initial characteristics have been measured using the analyzer IV-400. The obtained IV curve initially designed and the characteristics obtained in exposition location and translated to STC are detailed for each module.

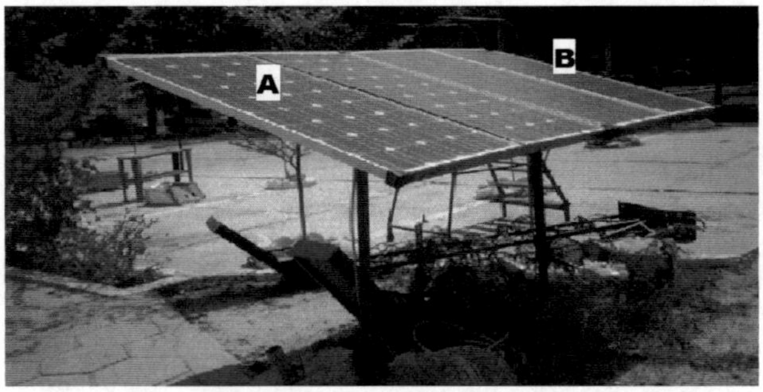

Fig.2. Photovoltaic platform installed in Dakar University.

A monocrystalline solar panel of 106 WP (given by manufacturer) was used as a reference model for experimentation and simulation. However, the data used for degradation assessment are those measured on-site. The measurement cared out just after the installation of the system on the site, have been done under local conditions and automatically "translated" to the standard testing conditions (STC). The main performance characteristics are extracted are gathered in following table. The maximum current and voltage have been used to obtain the PMPP. The maximum power obtained initially is equal to 114W_P.
The second module used (B) is a polycrystalline also of 110 W_P

according to the data given by the constructor. Like the module A, the initial measurements were established using the IV-400 analyzer. These measurements on site and "translated" to the STCs determine the different performance parameters grouped in Table3. With its 36 polycrystalline cells connected in series, the measured power on site for the poly is equal to 114 W_P.

Table.2. Technical characteristics of the PV modules.

Modules	Technology	Manufacturers	References	Characteristics	Values
Module A	Monocrystalline Silicon	WAAREE	WS-110	Maximum power (P_{MPP})	114 W
				Nominal voltage (V_{MPP})	16.22 V
				Nominal current (I_{MPP})	7.04 A
				Open circuit voltage (Uoc)	21.41 V
				Short-circuit current (Isc)	8.56 A
				Fill factor (FF)	62.20%
Module B	Polycrystalline Silicon	BP Solar	WS-110	Maximum power (Pmax)	114 W
				Maximum voltage (Vmax)	17.31 V
				Maximum current (Imax)	6.59 A
				Open circuit voltage (Voc)	21.76 V
				Short-circuit current (Isc)	7.43 A
				Fill factor (FF)	70.50%

3 Data acquisition and analysis methodology

3.1 Data acquisition

The main objective of this work is to evaluate and analyze the degradation on two crystalline modules exposed for about 10 years. But the main element in all that being to have the effects of the environment on the panel and the consequences generated on the electrical characteristics. For this, the main data used are: the electrical characteristics initially obtained and after the years of exposure, the EL and IR images.

- The initial Electrical performance characteristics are obtained using the analyzer IV-400. Photovoltaic module analyzer I–V 400 carries out the field measurement of the I–V characteristic and of the main characteristic both of a single module and of module strings. The acquired data are then processed to extrapolate the I–V characteristic at standard test conditions (STC). Output current or voltage from the module is measured with the 4-terminal method, which allows extending the measurement cables without requiring any compensation for their resistance, thus always providing accurate measures.

- IV curve and electrical characteristics obtained after exposition, have been measured using a lab solar simulator. The PASAN solar simulator is equipped with 4 Xenon flash tubes that generate a pulsed, calibrated and time-steady light. The light travels through a black tunnel and illuminates the module, which is positioned 8 meters away on a uniformly illuminated 3x3 meters surface. Different irradiance levels can be reproduced, however in our case the teste was carried out under STSs. A tracer records the electrical response of the module measuring up to 4000 points of the I-V curve, along with other electrical parameters.

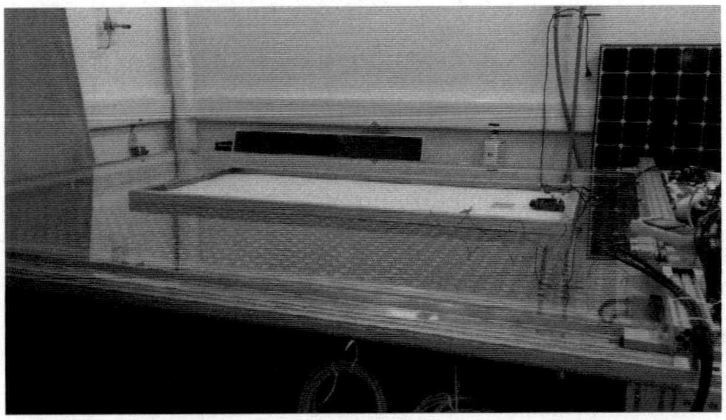

Fig. 3. IV measurements on the module.

- The set-up for PV EL Imaging is simple, consisting of: shortwave infrared (SWIR) camera with lens darkened enclosure solar cell / module Power Supply. An SWIR camera with In GaAs sensor and a spectral range from 0.9 to 1.7 µm was used in this study for capturing the EL image. Two different EL images have been made using different current. The first with a current equal to I_{SC}, the second was made with just I= 10% I_{SC} which allows to clearly identify the most affected surfaces.

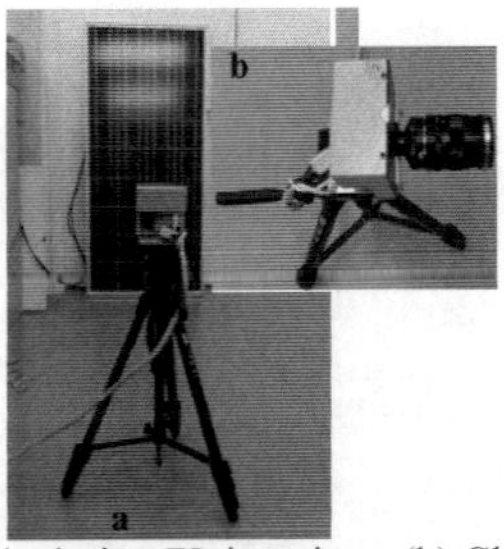

Fig. 4. (a) Module during EL imaging - (b) Close-up of the EL camera.

- For IR Imaging, the measuring device is a thermal imaging camera with a surface temperature measurement range of -20°C to 250°C and a 31° x 22.5° field of view, the user can view and save a quick snapshot of temperature patterns in any given area, thus quickly identifying unusual hot or cold spots. With ≤80mK thermal sensitivity, temperature differences of just 0.8°C are visualized on the 3.5" cooler screen via the 160 x 120-pixel thermal sensor. Three different color palettes give added functionality whilst hot and cold spots can be activated to immediately highlight hot and cold spots in the field of view. A digital read out of the surface temperature at the measurement point is shown alongside both the thermal image and the visible-light picture from the camera.

Fig. 5. (a) Module during IR imaging - (b) Close-up of the IR camera.

- The percentage of the surface affected by the different types of degradation is obtained with the GeoGebra software. GeoGebra is a dynamic mathematics software that combines geometry, algebra, spreadsheet, graph, statistics and infinitesimal calculus into a single easy-to-use software. It allows, according to a chosen scale, to quantify the selected surfaces and to put them in color. Thus, these surfaces in comparaison with the total surface gives the percentage of the surface affected by the degradation [46].

3.2 Analysis approaches

In this study, degradation phenomena observed in PV modules operating in the field for about 10 years are presented. Nondestructive diagnostic techniques including I-V curve analysis, infrared (IR) thermography and electroluminescence (EL) are employed here to assess PV performance and identify the defects. And the software Geogebra with the EL image give important information on the percentage of affected surface. Two Modules that have undergone different stages of degradation, from mechanical and manufacturing defects to severe visual degradation phenomena due to environmental effects, are analyzed, and performance characteristics degradation estimates are given for the 2 different technologies tested, revealing the need for a deeper understanding of PV degradation phenomena that occur under real conditions of operation. The diagnostic methodology of degradation is presented in Fig. 6.

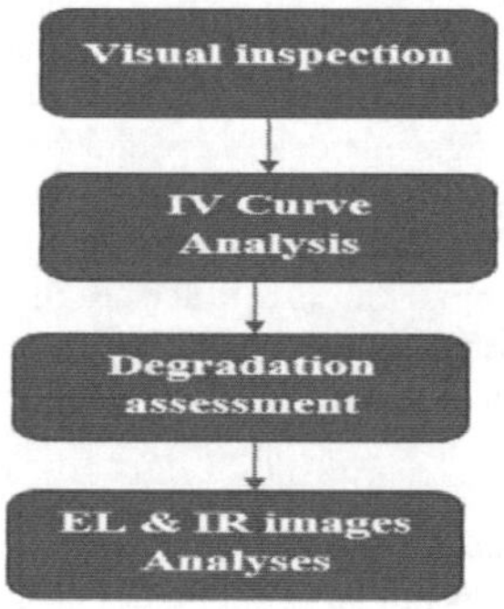

Fig. 6. Degradation Diagnostic methodology.

4 Analysis of electrical characteristics

In this section, the aim is to assess, quantify and analyze the degradation of the two PV modules that operated during nearly ten (10) years in the tropical climate of Dakar located at the extreme west of Senegal. This locality, as described in chapter 3 is marked by a tropical and semi-arid climate. We investigated the degradation of the main important electrical parameters (PMPP, ISC, UOC, IMPP, UMPP and the FF) of two PV modules installed in the University of Dakar.
For further details in addition to the visual inspection, both modules were analyzed by Electroluminescence(EL) and Infrared(IR) imagery. This inspection allows to identify the different defects in the module, quantify the affected surface and analyze the temperature distribution to understand the different performance characteristics degradation that affected the two PV modules.

4.1 Photovoltaic modules degradation assessment

4.1.1 Monocrystalline module (A)

4.1.1.1 Characteristics after 10 years of exposure

After using the module for about 10 years, the performance characteristics were again measured. These measurements obtained at PV LAB in Switzerland are carried out directly in the STC with a simulator. The PASAN tester TC 1.1.3 used, is a pulsed solar simulator, for current-voltage (IV) characterization of photovoltaic modules. The results obtained are plotted in the curve IV in blue in Fig. 7.

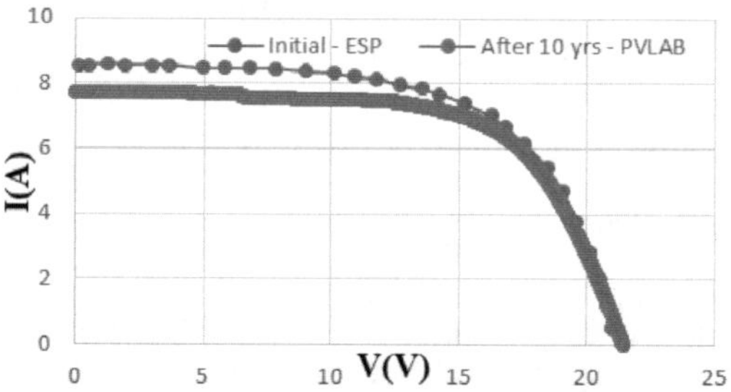

Fig. 7. I-V characteristics of monocrystalline module (A).

Table 3. Performance characteristics comparison after about 10 years.

Measurements	P_{MPP} [W]	Uoc [V]	U_{MPP} [V]	Isc [A]	I_{MPP} [A]	FF [%]
Initial - Measured at ESP	114	21.405	16.24	8.56	7.020	62.2
After 10yrs - Measured at PVLAB	107.905	21.44	16.178	7.750	6.670	**64.9**

The realization of this curve IV in comparison with the initial curve already shows degradation of certain performance characteristics. The short-circuit current ISC from 8.56A to 7.75A is the most affected characteristic. Therefore, the maximum power current IMPP is affected. Initially the maximum power of 114 W obtained with IMPP of 7.02A decreases by 6.095 W. The maximum power current thus becomes 6, 67 A.

4.1.1.2 Degradation assessment

The measurements initially carried out with the natural sunlight and translated back to the STC with the IV400 analyzer; and those using a simulator in the STC conditions at PV LAB made are used to evaluate the different variations that occurs during the module exposition. The nominal (IMPP) and short circuit

(Isc) current, the nominal (UMPP) and the open-circuit (Uoc) voltage, and the PV module maximum power (PMPP) degradation are evaluated by comparing each measured value after 10 years with the reference value obtained with the initial measurements given in table 2. The degradation of these different parameters is expressed in percentage as a function of the difference between the initial normalized values and the obtained after exploitation **[3]**.

The results obtained from the degradation calculations are summarized in the following graph (Fig. 8).

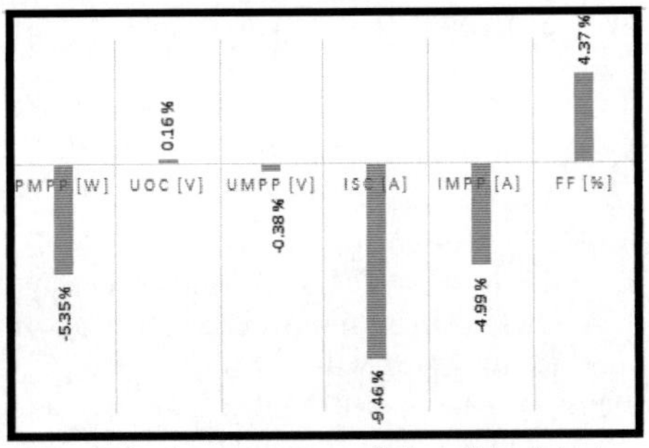

Fig. 8. Performance Degradation of module A.

From Fig.8, it can be seen that the open-circuit voltage is not affected because the calculated degradation is positive. The UMPP also expresses a very slight degradation of just -0.38%. However, the nominal and short circuit current degradation is striking and equal to -4.99% and -9.46% respectively, which is generally caused by mismatched cells and increase sometimes series resistance increase. Such kind of IV distribution and Isc reduction refer to irradiation decreases or shaded cells. In general, this is the consequences of operating area reduction or cells properties inhomogeneity. Also, a non-homogeneous temperature distribution could be expected by thermal imaging to confirm the aging of this module. The considerable degradation of IMPP particularly affects the maximum power which is degraded by -5.35%. The fill factor degradation rate is also positive, meaning that the theoretical power degradation is more important than the maximum power diminution.

4.1.2 Polycrystalline module (B)

4.1.2.1 Characteristics after 10 years of exposure

After 10 years of operation in hot and semi-arid climatic conditions, the PV module I-V curve were measured using pulsed solar simulator the comparison between measurements made initially and after exposition (Fig. 9) showed that, the short circuit current (I_{sc}) and the open circuit voltage(U_{OC}) did not change too much. However, the trend of the IV curve obtained after the operation years shows a slight decrease in the maximum power. In the literature **[6, 7]**, such a change on curve IV is due to an increase in the series resistance R_S. This variation in resistance mainly affects the PV module operating voltage.

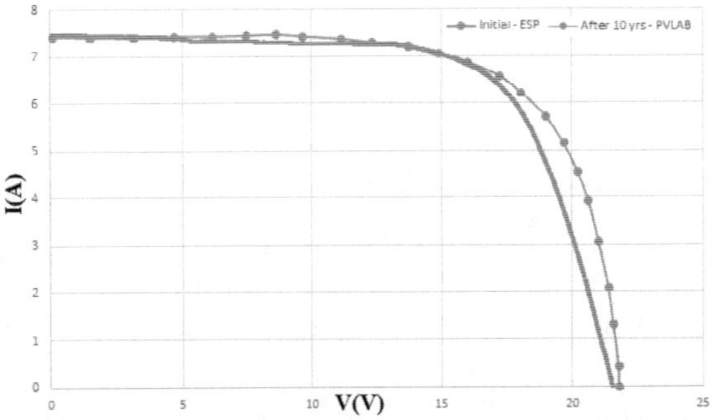

Fig. 9. I-V characteristics of monocrystalline module (B).

The comparison between the performance characteristics initially measured and that after the years of operation clearly shows that the nominal(IMPP) and short-circuit (ISC) current have not been affected. However, even if the variation is not too great, among all the parameters, voltage was the only electrical characteristic that deteriorated. The open-circuit voltage goes from 21.765 V to 21.5 V. The maximum power voltage has experienced the greatest variation, with an initial value equal to 17.3V, it becomes 16.73V, ie an absolute reduction of 0.6V.

Table 4. Performance characteristics comparison after about 10 years.

Measurements	P_{MPP} [W]	Uoc [V]	Umpp [V]	Isc [A]	Impp [A]	FF [%]
Initial - Measured at ESP	114.01	21.765	17.311	7.429	6.586	70.5
After 10 yrs - Measured at PVLAB	110.686	21.502	16.726	7.480	6.618	68.8

4.1.2.2 Degradation assessment

The results obtained are summarized in figure 10. As expected with series resistance increase visible in the IV curve (Fig. 10), the maximum power voltage is the most affected characteristic, its absolute deterioration is -3.38%. Indeed, for a PV module exposed for almost 10 years, a degradation of only -2.92% of the maximum power is a good compatibility sign of this technology within the climate. However, it is always necessary to evaluate the different types of defects that affected the module to verify the material defects caused by the tropical climate. The Fill factor (FF) degradation is mainly due to the degradation nominal voltage degradation.

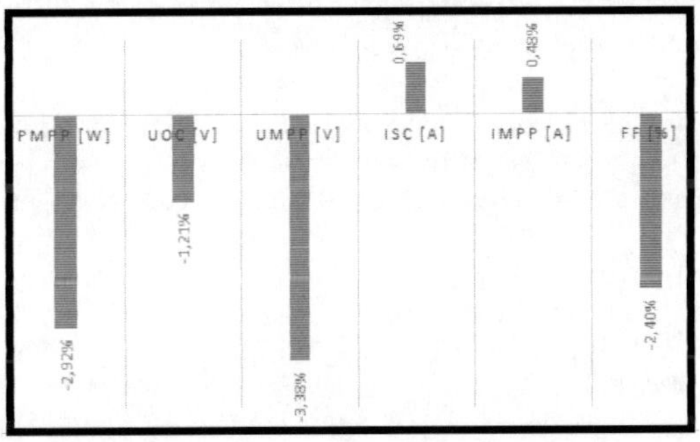

Fig. 10. Performance Degradation of module B.

4.1.3. Comparative study

The comparison between calculated degradation of the different characteristics for the two PV modules are summarized in table 5. For the monocrystalline PV module (A), the short circuit current is the most affected characteristic with a degradation equal to -9.46%. The polycrystalline module(B) characteristics are slightly affected, but it is important to mention that the nominal voltage is the most affected parameter. This is to say that the drop in the maximum power output in the two PV modules does not have the same causes. The two modules than have different defects leading to such reduction of the maximum power.
The PMPP degradation is equal to -5.35% for module A, and just -2.92% for module B. thus, electrically the monocrystalline is more affected under such a climate.

Table 5. Performance characteristics degradation for the two PV Modules.

	P_{MPP} [W]	U_{OC} [V]	U_{MPP} [V]	I_{SC} [A]	I_{MPP} [A]	FF [%]
PV module A	**-5.35%**	**0.16%**	**-0.38%**	**-9.46%**	**-4.99%**	**4.37%**
PV module B	**-2.92%**	**-1.21%**	**-3.38%**	**0.69%**	**0.48%**	**-2.40%**

5 Analysis by imaging techniques

5.1. Module A: monocrystalline

5.1.1. Electroluminescence analysis (EL)

5.1.1.1. Degradation types identification

Defects in the material of the cell, micro-cracks, broken metallization, shunts, inactive regions are detected via Electroluminescence imaging in figure 11 (Fig. 11). This El used to identify the defects is made under ISC current. The fault types present in the modules are identified with different colors.

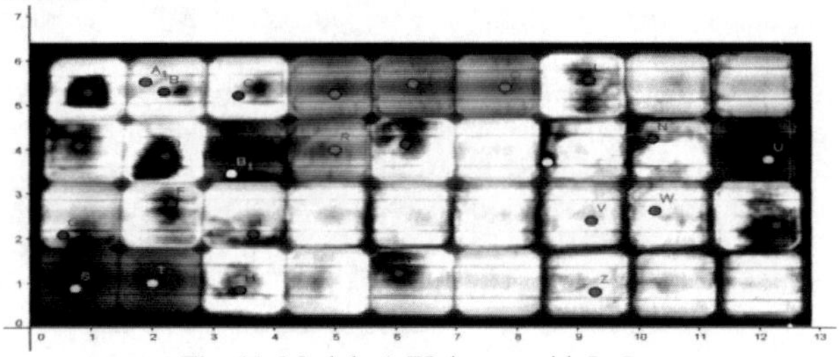

Fig. 11. Module A EL image with I= Isc.

• 15 cells (blue) have visual impairments such as discoloration and corrosion identified during visual inspection. These types of defects are directly related to climatic conditions mainly humidity.

2 cells with breakages which often occur during transport, packaging or installation of the modules. These types of mechanical damage are caused by insufficient packaging and vibration / shock.

• 4 cells with casting defects better known by the Contact finger interruptions. These types of defects are usually caused by insufficient screen printing during manufacturing. Because of their significant presence and non-uniform distribution, their remarkable effects on cells productivity are clearly evident.

• 4 other cells have microcracks, these types of defects such as breaks often occur during transport of the modules. The variation of the intrinsic manufacturing process can also be the cause of cells microcracks. But they are less serious and mostly invisible during visual inspection. However, they may cause deterioration in performance after several years of operation.

• 3 cells have unspecified dark areas. Several assumptions can be made about the origin of the dark shade: it may come from a local modification of the efficiency favoring non-radiative recombination of the charges, modification of optical proprieties of this zone and therefore the number of photons collected by the detector, or a modification of the contact resistance.

These assumptions mean that it is not possible to identify all the types of degradation present in an EL image on the simple visual criterion **[8, 9]**.

In summary (Table. 5), most of the defects identified on the module are due to the effects of the exposure climate conditions. 14 cells suffer from material degradation due mainly to contact of water with the cells. This water often present in moist air causes discoloration and corrosion. Given the climatic conditions of the operating site, it is evident that the high humidity of the hot location has effects on the cells. Indeed, Dakar is a very wet place with an annual average of 78.6%.

Table 5. Defects observed in module A.

Degradation type	**Number of effected cells**	**Percentage relative to the total number of cell**
Micro cracks	2	5.56%
Visual degradation	14	38.89%
Contact finger interruption	5	13.89%
Dark area	3	8.33%
breakages	5	13.89%

The rest of the defects are for the most part mechanical. 6 cells have either microcracks or breaks due to poor handling during transport or laying. Manufacturing defects are fairly present. 4 cells with metallic hits severely affected are identified. 3 other cells have unidentified defects but often come from manufacturing.

5.1.1.2. Affected area Evaluation

The use of the GeoGebra dynamic mathematics software allowed to quantify the total area affected by the different degradation types. The EL image used to determine the surfaces is the one supplied with a current equal to 10% of ISC. An EL image taken at about 10% of the rated current of the photovoltaic module is more suitable for isolated cell parts quantification.

The maximum power(PMPP) that the PV module can produce depends strongly on its productive surface as described in Chapter 1. Thus, the evaluation of the affected surface by the different types of degradation makes gives the opportunity to analyze the effects of productive surface decrease on the characteristics.

According to the chosen scale on the figure 25, the panel's total area is 75 cm2. The fifteen (15) degraded areas evaluation gives a total dark surface of 20.97 cm2 affected by the different types of defects cited above. Thus, 27.96% of the module's surface has been deteriorated. This materiel degradation of the surface leaded to a degradation of -5.35% in the maximum power (P_{MPP}). Then, the degradation of 1% of the surface causes a reduction of about 2% in the maximum power. Nevertheless, the black areas should not be interpreted as a totally zero emission, a black zone emits very little compared to the rest of the cell. And this is what causes electrical mismatches and reduce the I_{SC}.

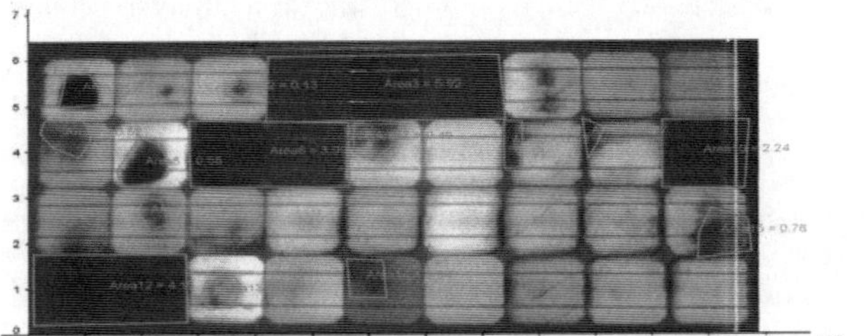

Fig. 12. Module A EL image with I= 10%Isc.

5.1.2. Analysis by infrared imaging (IR)

In a normal PV module, all the cells are considered identical. For a defect less module, the temperature distribution is homogeneous because all the cells have the same characteristics. Thus, PV module thermography image visualization is a very useful tool to state a PV module. Infrared imagery specifically identifies hot spots and cold spots. Hot spots indicate a decline in productivity in these areas, which dissipates the surplus current from other parts as heat. This occurs when the cell is totally or partially shaded, fractured or electrically defective. The severity of this degradation is directly related the cell's the temperature. The cold zones highlight the visual degradations. The areas affected by these types of degradation act as insulators. The monocrystalline module IR image in figure 26 shows a striking thermal disparity. Temperatures range from 0 ° C to 62 ° C. Several hot points or surfaces are visible; Which proves that the different types of degradations identified previously decrease the electrical current. The cold parts identified represent the visual defects highlighted in the EL image. This photovoltaic module exposed for about ten (10) years shows a great thermal inhomogeneity, meaning an advanced electrical mismatch. This justifies the significant ISC degradation and the decrease of the I_{MPP}.

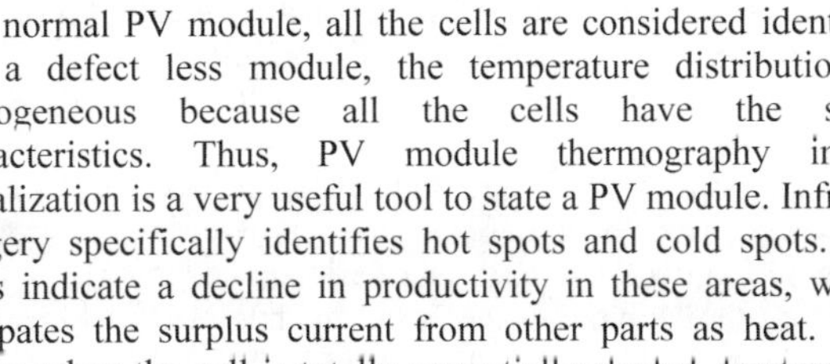

Fig. 13. Module A IR Image

5.2. Module B: Polycrystalline

5.2.1. Electroluminescence analysis (EL)

5.2.1.1. Degradation types identification

The EL image for polycrystalline module was realized under the same conditions as the previous analyzed monocrystalline. For defects identification, the EL image used is realized under the short circuit current (I_{SC})with different colors pointing fingers at the types of degradation present in the module.

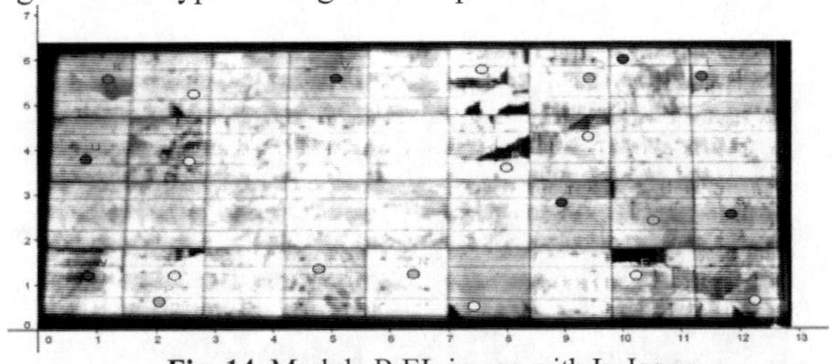

Fig. 14. Module B EL image with I= Isc.

9 cells of the polycrystalline module experienced fairly extensive breaks which isolated the broken cell parts.

- 6 cells have visual defects due to the effects of the environment. During visual inspection, delamination of PV module's encapsulat has been identified. Which probably justifies the presence of these dark surfaces indicating visual degradation.
- 5 cells have localized shunts. This type of defects is generally due to problems during cell's manufacturing (a particle, an anomaly in growth, etc.). It may also be a consequence of an external event such as electrostatic discharge or mechanical stress.
- 2 cells have micro cracks which elongated the list of mechanical defects.

for the polycrystalline module, mechanical defects due to physical constraints are the most present defects. Nine (9) cells in total have breakages often very advanced, and 2 others have micro cracks.

Table 6. Defects observed in module B.

Degradation type	Number of effected cells	Percentage relative to the total number of cell
micro cracks	2	5.56%
visual degradation	6	16.67%
localized shunt	5	13.89%
broken cells	9	25.00%

Concerning the material or visual defects often due to the effect of the environment, they are present on 6 cells which are not nevertheless very affected. Indeed, since a polycrystalline module is not homogeneous in nature, it is sometimes difficult to identify the photoelectric effect. Manufacturing defects also are still present with many localized shunts.

5.2.1.2. Affected area Evaluation

Using the same software, and with the EL image of the polycrystalline at I = ISC, the results obtained show that the isolated surface is not very important. Seven (7) zones are isolated, representing a total area of 6.38 cm2. So only 8.5% of the module's surface was severely affected, causing a degradation of -2.92% of the maximum power (PMPP) . Thus 3.5% of the power decreased to 1% of affected area.

However, it has always been pointed out that these isolated areas represent the consequences of all the defects identified. Similarly, they are not totally eliminated from the module, even if their participation is weak they slightly participate in the functioning of the module.

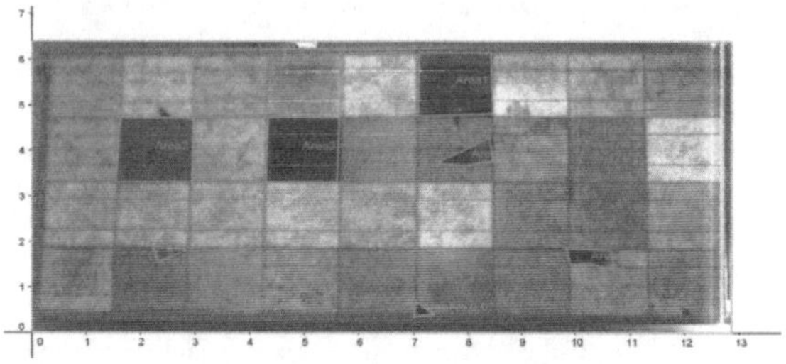

Fig. 15. Module B EL image with I= 10%Isc.

5.2.2. Analysis by infrared imaging (IR)

The IR image of the polycrystalline module shows a more homogeneous thermal distribution compared to the mono. Temperatures range from 29 to about 39 ° C. The maximum temperature is not then so critical because it is less than the NOCT of 45°C. the biggest part of the surface has a temperature of about 30 ° C. Apart from 3 hot spots identified and some cold areas, the thermal disparity is not significant enough. Thus, the passage of the electric current is not too disturbed hence the low degradation of the current compared to the initial characteristics.

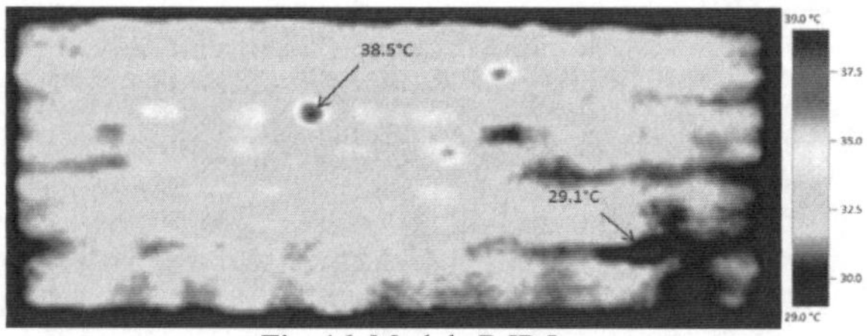

Fig. 16. Module B IR Image

5 Conclusion

The evaluation of the degradation already proves that the modules were affected after the years of exposure. The P_{MPP} degradation is equal to -5.35% for module A, and just -2.92% for module B. But it should be noted that the modules did not have the same degradation behavior. Module A experienced a significant drop in its short-circuit current (ISC), while module B had a slight decrease in its nominal voltage UMPP.

In this way, the visual inspection, EL and IR imaging allow to identify the different defects leading to such kind of degradation for the two modules. Even if there is not enough information on the degradation effects of each type of climate on the different crystalline technologies; defects due to the environmental conditions found in this study are much more present in the monocrystalline module than on the polycrystalline. The mechanical defects on the polycrystalline module are too advanced and will obviously be at the origin of most of the consequences on performance characteristics. The surface monocrystalline module isolated surface by the identified defects is much more important (27.96% of total area), compared to the poly (only 8.5% total area). finally, EL images of the two PV modules in this study show that with the technology used, the environmental effects have been much more felt on the single-crystalline one. However, the affected surface analysis shows that the effect of percentage of affected surface on the PMPP are more important for the polycrystalline than the mono.

The IR image for the monocrystalline module well justifies extensive degradation of the short circuit current and maximum power. The Module Isc mismatch clear shown in the thermography with many hot spots means that those parts can no more produce the short circuit current. So, the damage previously identified as corrosion and discoloration decreased the electrical output of several cells. Indeed, in the IR image analysis with a current equal to ISC shows a large rise in temperature which reached 60 ° C. This means that a big part of the module no longer produces enough power and transforms the surplus current coming from the healthy cells into heat. For the poly, the IR image shows that productivity is not too affected. The temperature distribution is almost homogeneous. We can then say that; the important mechanicals defects identified with the EL image do not affect too much the cells' production. Thus, by comparing the analyzes of the IR and EL images of the two modules it can be concluded that the defects caused by the climate on the mono module affect much more the production than the numerous mechanical defects on the poly.

References

1. AIE, African Energy Outlook : focus on Sub-saharan Africa countries, International Energy Agency, Paris, 2014.

2. The world Bank and Energy in Africa, World Bank, [Online].Available: http://web.worldbank.org/WBSITE/EXTERNAL/COUNTRIES/AFRICAEXT/0,,contentMDK:21935594~pagePK:146736~piPK:146830~theSitePK:258644,00.html.

3. A. Ndiaye, C.M.F. Kebe, A. Charki, P.A. Ndiaye, V. Sambou, A. Kobi, Degradation evaluation of crystalline-silicon photovoltaic modules after a few operation years in a tropical environment, Solar Energy, vol. 103, 70-77(2014).

4. ANAMS: National Agency for Meteorology of Senegal, 2012. http://WWW.meteo-senegal.net.

5. R. Beate, S. Jan and K. Michael, Fluorescence imaging for analysis of the degradation of PV modules, IEEE-Journal of photovoltaics, Vol. 3, 2013.

6. F. D. S. Freire, "Performance and Degradation Analysis of Operating PV Systems," Rochester Institute of Technology, 2016.

7. A. Virtuani, H. Müllejans, E. D. Dunlop, Comparison of indoor and outdoor performance measurements of recent commercially available solar modules. Prog. Photovolt: Res. Appl., 19: 11–20. doi:10.1002/pip.977.

8. E. Kaplani, Degradation in Field-aged Crystalline Silicon Photovoltaic Modules and Diagnosis using Electroluminescence Imaging, in 8th International Workshop on Teaching in Photovoltaics, Prague, 2016.

9. R. Beate, S. Jan and K. Michael, Fluorescence Imaging for Analysis of the degradation of PV modules, IEEE Journal of photovoltaics, vol. 3, 2013.

Accuracy evaluation of two different pyranometers used in resource assessment for PV applications

Azouzoute Alae[1], Alami Merrouni Ahmed[1,*], Bennouna El Ghali[1], Ghennioui Abdellatif[1]

[1] Institut de Recherche en Energie Solaire et Energies Nouvelles - IRESEN, Green Energy Park, Km 2 Route Régionale R206, Benguerir, Morocco.

Received:

Abstract. To accelerate the PV integration, assessment, with high accuracy, of the technology performances before installation is crucial. This can be performed by measuring the solar irradiance at ground level in the selected areas. A variety of irradiance sensors is available in the market, however, the selection of the most suitable and adaptable one for the local conditions is a hard task. The aims of this study is to evaluate the difference between the existing two devices used in the PV market such as thermopile pyranometer and reference cell. The experiment has been done at Green Energy Park in Benguerir. The SR11 pyranometer and the ISET reference cell was the chosen devices, installed and monitored side by side at the selected site. The results show, for two months of period test with different climate conditions (June represent the summer season, and December that represent the cold season), that the daily absolute deviation between the plan of array irradiance measurements of the chosen devices can reach 30 W/m² in June and it range between -6 W/m² and 2 W/m² in December. The monthly average deviation was found to be -4.8% and -0.7% in June and December respectively. The present results underline that to guarantee good resource assessment, the measurements of solar irradiance need to be corrected such that the reference cell underestimate the irradiations values.

Keywords: Plane of array Irradiance, Radiometry, Solar resource.

1 Introduction

The integration of Photovoltaic into the electricity network has increased during the last decade [1]. To ensure an optimal integration and to face the intermittence of this technology, the solar irradiance variation should be measured with high accuracy, to enable the power plants operators to plan and forecast the electricity production during the day, therefore, to maximize the benefits.

To measure the amount of solar irradiance, thermopile pyranometer and Photovoltaic (PV) reference cell are the most used devices. The pyranometers are the most trusted in scientific community for the PV system monitoring. However, reference cells are less expensive and they have the same response, to the irradiance, as the PV modules. Therefore, in the last few years a large spot light has been oriented to the evaluation of the reference cells the accuracy especially for PV applications.

Dunn et al. [2] conducted a comparison study between the PV reference cell and thermopile pyranometer; they found that under specific conditions (clear sky at 1000 W/m²) the typical irradiance measurement uncertainty (for a confidence interval of 95%) is in around of ±2.4 and ±5.3% for the PV reference cell and pyranometer respectively.

* Correspondence: *alami@iresen.org

Similarly, Meydbray et al. [3] calculated the deviation of the two devices in four different locations. The authors considered only spectral effect, and they found that the daily solar irradiation deviation can reach up to 3%. Besides, even for the broadband irradiance measurement and under other conditions, the PV reference cell can have the same or better measurement uncertainties than the pyranometer.

In the present work, a comparison between the Plane of Array irradiance (POAI) data, measured at tilt plan of 32° by a first class (ISO 9060) thermal sensor and an ISET reference cell (with a relative measurement uncertainty <±4%) will be evaluated and presented for different time resolution.

Results show that the reference cell instruments can be useful for the solar PV resources assessment in comparison to the thermopile pyranometer. We found that the monthly deviation between the solar irradiation measurements from the chosen devices was around -4.8% and -0.7% in June and December respectively.

2 Materials and Methods

In this section, we will discuss the characteristics of the thermopile pyranometer and the photovoltaic (PV) reference cell used in this study. Furthermore, the statistical metrics used for the accuracy check of the reference cell will be defined and discussed.

a) The SR11 Pyranometer:

The irradiometer used as reference in our study is the Hukseflux thermal sensor SR11 (as shown in Fig.1). This sensor is classified as a first-class specification sensor with the ISO 9060 standard and the WMO guide (see Table 1). According to the American Society Testing Materials ASTM E2848 standard, the SR11 is the favorite tool for outdoor PV system performance monitoring [4].

Fig. 1. SR11 Pyranometer and ISET reference cell Installed at GEP.

Table 1. Characteristics of Hukseflux SR11 pyranometer.

Pyranometer specification ISO 9060 classification	First class
Response time (time to reach 95% response)	< 30 sec.
Zero offset –A: response to 200 W/m² net thermal radiation (Ventilated)	+ 7 W/m²
Zero offset –B: response to 5 K/h ambient temperature change.	± 2 W/m²
Non-stability (percentage change per year)	± 1.5%
Non-linearity (percentage deviation of the responsivity at 500 W/m² due to any change of irradiance in the interval of 100 to 1000 w/m²).	± 1%
Directional response of beam radiation (the range of errors caused by assuming that the normal incidence responsivity is valid for all directions when measuring from any direction, a beam radiation whose normal incidence irradiance is 1000 W/m²).	± 20 W/m²
Spectral sensitivity: percentage deviation of the product of spectral absorbance and transmittance from the corresponding mean, within the range 350 to 1500 nm.	± 5%
Temperature response: percentage deviation due to any change of ambient temperature within an interval of 50 K (e.g. -10 to +40 °C typical).	4%
Tilt response: percentage deviation in responsivity relative to 0° tilt horizontal due to change in tilt from 0° to 90° at 1000 W/m² beam irradiance.	± 2%

Table 1 presents the ISO 9060 classification for the first-class category of the pyranometers [5]. This category is referred by the WMO as "Good quality". Regardless the classification, there is no big difference between the ISO and WMO specifications. In fact, the WMO standard specifies a spectral range of 300 to 3000 nm [6], while the ISO standard's spectral range is from 350 to 1500 nm. Furthermore, the WMO specifies two other classification: "Resolution" (the smallest detectable change, 5 W/m² for the First class) and "Achievable uncertainty" (8% hourly totals, and 5% Daily totals correspond to the Good quality category), which are not mentioned in the ISO specifications standard.

The SR11 is specifically designed to measure the solar radiation within a 180° (hemispherical) field of view angle. The pyranometer absorb all sunlight transmitted due to the thermopile sensor with a black coting. It is known that the pyranometer response to the beam radiation change with the cosine of the angle of incidence, thus, will be in a full response when the solar radiation is perpendicular to the sensor's surface, (i.e., 0° angle of incidence, or in other words, when the sun is at zenith) and with no response when the sun is at horizon (90° angle of incidence, especially during the sunrise and sunset).

Additionally, the SR11 first class pyranometer has a light sensitivity or a spectral response in the range of 285 to 3000 nm. Consequently, it covers the whole solar spectrum. Besides, this device was designed to treat equally all the type of wavelength regardless the direction it comes from, as presented in Fig.2.

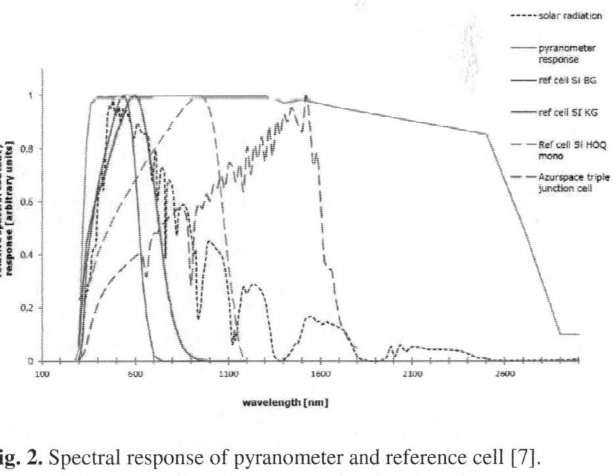

Fig. 2. Spectral response of pyranometer and reference cell [7].

b) The ISET Reference Cell:

In our study, we have selected the ISET sensor 02581 solar radiation sensor manufactured by the IKS Photovoltaik GmbH Company (as shown in Fig.1). This sensor is a mono-crystalline solar cell having an aluminum powder-coated in facade quality with an operating temperature range of - 25 °C to + 80 °C. This device has an integrated Pt100 temperature sensor to allow the monitoring of the device temperature. The irradiation measurement process is very easy, the coming solar radiation is eventually converted into a proportional current by a specific solar cell, and then the measured voltage is determined through a special shunt resistor with thermal connection to the casing. This voltage is then converted to irradiation by multiplication of a sensitivity value pre-defined by the manufacturer.

Contrarily to the pyranometer, the reference cell has a limited response to the solar spectrum. Indeed, as illustrated in Fig.2, the reference cell do not respond to the entire coming wavelength equally and they have a non-flat spectral response. This is one error source that can influence the irradiation data measured by those devices.

c) Statistical metrics for the RC accuracy check:

As mentioned above, the objective of this paper is to assess the accuracy of the reference cells and to check its performances against the thermopiles and there suitability for PV applications. For this reason, both devices were installed side by side at Green Energy Park (GEP) research facility, in Benguerir. In this paper, we will present the results of two months with different climate conditions: June with high temperature values and December with low temperature and high humidity values. The irradiation data of the two sensors were monitored each 10 sec then collected and carefully checked. For our comparison, the pyranometer has been selected to be the reference device and the reference cell records will be checked against it.

To do so, the call for statistical performance indicators, like the root mean square error, mean bias error, the normalized root mean-square error, the Standard deviation of the residual, the coefficient of determination, and t-statistic is the best way and the most used in the literature [8,9].

In what follow, the *i*th value of the pyranometer will be noted x_i and the *i*th value of the reference cell will be noted y_i. The mean value of each distribution (totaling N points) will be noted X_m and Y_m respectively for the pyranometer and reference cell.

The root mean square error (RMSE) can be calculated using this formula:

$$RMSE = \sqrt{\frac{\sum(x_i - y_i)^2}{N}}$$

The Mean bias error (MBE) is obtained using the formula bellow:

$$MBE = \frac{\sum(x_i - y_i)}{N}$$

The normalized root mean-square error (NRMSE) is the non-dimensional forms of the RMSE and it can be calculated by normalizing RMSE to the mean of the reference data.

$$NMRSE = \frac{RMSE}{X_m}$$

The standard deviation (SD) is an indicator used specially to quantify the amount of variation or dispersion of the reference data set compared to that of the pyranometer. It can be obtained through the equation:

$$SD = \sqrt{\frac{N(RMSE^2 - MBE^2)}{N-1}}$$

The coefficient of determination (R^2) or R-squared is similar to the correlation coefficient, R. The coefficient can be obtained by:

$$R^2 = \left(\frac{\sum(x_i - X_m)(y_i - Y_m)}{\sum(x_i - X_m)^2(y_i - Y_m)^2}\right)^2$$

The t-statistic (TS) is obtained by the equation bellow:

$$TS = \sqrt{\frac{(N-1)\,MBE^2}{RMSE^2 - MBE^2}}$$

In our paper, these indicators were calculated for three different time resolutions: 1-minute, 1-hour, daily.

3 Results and discussion

In order to evaluate the performance of the selected reference cell, we have analyzed the dataset for two different exposition periods, June and December. Fig.3 presents the irradiation measurements of the two devices under clear sky condition on different journey from June and December. As we can see, the difference between the irradiance measured by the reference cell and the pyranometer is typically significant in June. The difference can be clearly marked in the hot season (June as an example) where the temperature influence dramatically the performances of the PV panels. Whereas in December the difference between the two curves is not distinguishable.

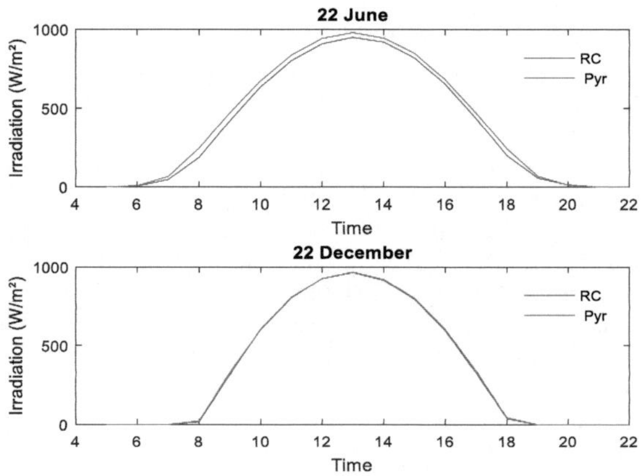

Fig. 3. The hourly irradiation (W/m²) for both, reference cell and pyranometer during 22 June and 22 December (sunny day).

Fig.4 shows an in-depth comparison between the thermopile and the reference cell for hourly data. We can easily see that the two datasets are in very good correlated for the two periods, but in December the R^2 is higher than the one in June. That means that, generally, there is no remarkable difference between the GHI measurements from the pyranometer and the reference cell.

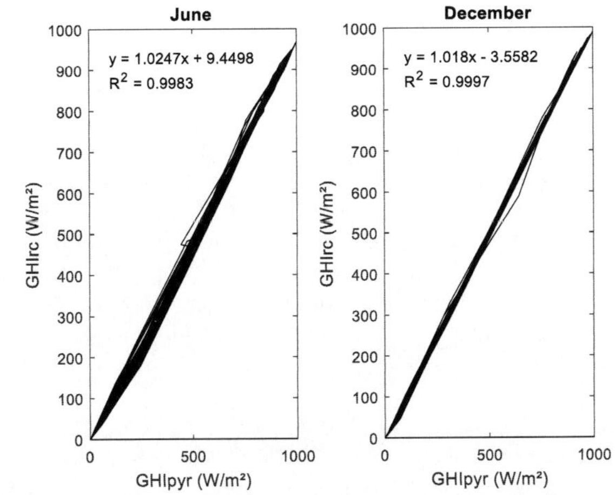

Fig. 4. Comparison of the hourly measured dataset from reference cell and thermopile pyranometer.

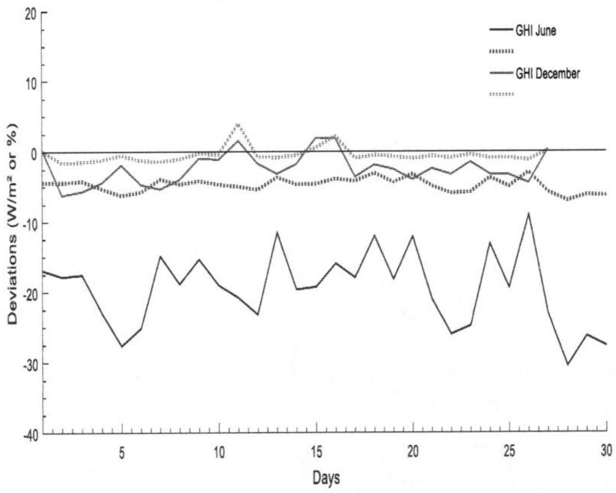

Fig. 5. The daily irradiation deviations (in W/m², solid lines) and relative deviations (in percent, dotted lines) in June and December.

In order deeply understand the difference between the two devices; a statistical approach has been used to analyze their irradiation measurements data. Fig.5 shows the daily deviation of POAI records for the chosen test period. As it can be seen, and in accordance to the previous measurements, in December the deviation exhibits more stability in comparison to June and for both absolute (in W/m²) and relative (in percent %) errors. Furthermore, the deviation for all the test period seems to be negative, that means underestimates the irradiations values. Indeed, the POAI deviation in December it ranges between -6 W/m² and 2 W/m² while it reaches -30 W/m² in June.

Table 2. Data comparison summary.

	MBE (W/m²)			RMSE (W/m²)			NRMSE (%)		
	Minutes	Hourly	Daily	Minutes	Hourly	Daily	Minutes	Hourly	Daily
June	-19.57	-18.50	-19.57	45.946	24.977	20.273	11.292	6.492	4.982
December	-2.398	-2.264	-2.396	13.027	6.546	3.247	3.913	2.077	0.975
	TS			**SD**			**R^2**		
	Minutes	Hourly	Daily	Minutes	Hourly	Daily	Minutes	Hourly	Daily
June	82.381	26.599	19.944	41.569	16.975	5.375	0.993	0.999	0.994
December	30.975	8.093	5.577	12.804	6.149	2.232	0.999	1	1

In order to deeply evaluate the deviation of the reference cell, Table 2 summarizes the statistical errors of the irradiation measurements. As it can be noticed, in June, the POA irradiance had a large, negative daily average bias (up to -19%), which confirms that the reference cell underestimates the POAI values. This bias difference is, however, much smaller (up to -2%) in December, which is mainly due to the low temperature values during the testing period.

In accordance with the previous results, the daily NRMSE error in June is higher in comparison to the one in December with 5% and 1% as error values respectively.

Finally, to obtain a quantitative evaluation of the difference between the two sensors, the monthly deviation has been calculated. As illustrated in Table 3, the monthly deviation average is around -0.7% in December and is evaluated as -4.8% in June.

Table 3. Monthly deviation difference between the reference cell and pyranometer.

	(POAIpyr - POAIrc)/POAIpyr %
June	**-4.8**
December	**-0.7**

With these results, we can say the reference cells underestimates the POAI values. This underestimation is much higher in the summer than the winter, which is completely understandable, since the PV cells are highly affected by the high temperature values.

4 Conclusion

Considering the importance of accurate measurements of the POAI for the deployment of photovoltaic solar plants. The most trustful sensor to use is thermopile pyranometer. In this work, a comparison study between the reference thermopile pyranometer and a mono-crystalline reference cell has been done to evaluate the accuracy of the last one under different climate conditions. Results show that, generally, the measurements of the two sensors are in good agreement with an R^2 of 99.97 %. However, in high temperature periods, the relative deviation decrease reaches -4.8%. This deviation decreases significantly in December to reaches -0.7%. Additionally, we concluded that the reference cells underestimate the irradiation values, which requires the correction of the values if this device is used in the resource assessment

References

1. A. Alami Merrouni, A. Amrani, A. Mezrhab. Electricity production from large-scale PV plants: Benchmarking the potential of Morocco against California, US. Energy Procedia, 119C (2017) pp. 346-355.
2. L. Dunn, M. Gostein, K. Emery, Comparison of Pyranometers vs. Reference Cells for Evaluation of PV Array Performance, in, Proceedings of the 38th IEEE Photovoltaic Specialists Conference (PVSC), 2012 Austin, USA.
3. J. Meydbray, E. Riley, L. Dunn, K. Emery, S. Kurtz. Pyranometers and reference cells, what makes the most sense for PV power plants? NREL/JA-5200-56718; 10 October 2012.
4. ASTM E2848-11, Standard Test Method for Reporting Photovoltaic Non-Concentrator System Performance, ASTM International, West Conshohocken, PA, 2011, www.astm.org.
5. Solar Energy - Specification and Classification of Instruments for Measuring Hemispherical Solar and Direct Solar Radiation, ISO 9060, Ammonit Measurement GmbH 2018, http://ammonit.com/en/products/sensors/solar-sensors-pyranometers/368-iso-9060-specification [last Access 1/10/2018].
6. Guie to Meteorological Instruments and Methods of Observtion, WMO- No. 8, World Meteorological Organization, 2014.
7. Hukeflux Thermal Sensors B.V., 2011. "Outdoor PV performance monitoring: pyranometers versus reference cells".
8. C.A.Gueymard, A review of validation methodologies and statistial performance indicators for modeled solar radiation data: Towards a better bankability of solar projects. Renewable and Sustainable Energy Reviews (2014)39:1024–1034.
9. A. Alami Merrouni, A.Ghennioui., F. Wolfertstetter, A. Mezrhab. (2017, June). The uncertainty of the HelioClim-3 DNI data under Moroccan climate. In AIP Conference Proceedings (Vol. 1850, No. 1, p. 140002). AIP Publishing.

Calibration and Verification of small parallel coordinate measuring machine

R. Furutani[a,]* and M.Ozaki[b]

[a]Tokyo Denki University, School of Engineering, Department of Precision Machinery Engineering, Japan
[b]Nippon Institute of Technology, Faculty of Engineering, Department of Mchanical Engineering, Japan

Received:

Abstract. The parallel mechanism is used for high precision positioning. The 2D small coordinate measuring machine is developed based on the parallel mechanism. This small coordinate measuring machine can move at x-y coordinates in three degree of freedom. In order to improve the accuracy of this system, the kinematic parameters should be calibrated. In this article, the kinematic calibration method and its result are shown. After that, the performance of this system is verified.

Keywords: Parallel mechanism, Coordinate Measuring Machine, Calibration, Verification

1 Introduction

The mechanism with two or more degree of freedom is referred to as mechanism with multi-degree-of-freedom. They are categorized into two types. One is the parallel mechanism of which the actuators are disposed in parallel and the other is the serial mechanism of which the actuators are disposed in series. Serial mechanism has been used in many industrial robots because it can take the wider attitude angle and work area. However, it is known that the serial mechanism has a problem that the errors are accumulated. On the other hand, as the actuators in parallel mechanism are arranged in parallel, it is considered to be more accurate than a serial mechanism. Therefore, it is expected to be used in precision positioning device[1,3].

However, the kinematic parameters of the prallel mechanism has a large relation with the other parameters. So, in self-calibration method based on the kinematic equations, the kinematic parameters were not estimated enough well[2].

In this paper, the kinematic parameters are estimated on the polinominal equations which don' t have any physical and mechanical relation. The polinominal order is limitted until 3rd order. After estimation, there are some small values in polinominal parameters. But it is proved that some small values are neccesary to estimate the position of the parallel mechanism to remove these small parameters.

3 Self-calibration method

Self-calibration method is a calibration method that does not use the artifact. Calibration is performed by determining the kinematic parameters (element angle and dimensions of the part) using the model equation of the mechanism and the length and orientation of the actuators and stylus coordinates. The self-calibration process is shown following. At the first, the model formula can be expressed as equation (1), where *C* is the coordinates of the stylus parallel mechanism, *L* is the deviation of actuator length and *K* is kinematic parameters.

* Correspondence:ryo@cck.dendai.ac.jp

$$f(C, \quad L, \quad K) = 0 \tag{1}$$

Then, when n number of the measured value are obtained, n-th stylus coordinates and n-th deviation of the actuator lengths is expressed as C_n and L_n. In this case, the kinematic parameters K is expressed as in equation (2).

$$f(C_n, L_n, K) = 0 \tag{2}$$

Equation (2) can not be solved analytically. Therefore, the estiomation of the kinematic parameters $\hat{K}$ is carried out by least squares method. It is possible to obtain the coordinates of the stylus using the estimated kinematic parameters including the errors of the poisitioning device. Then the paralell stage could estimate the highly accurate positioning of the stylus coordinates $\hat{C}$ by using the estimated kinematic parameters $\hat{K}$ and the deviation of the actuator lengths L_n .

$$\hat{C} = g(L_n, \hat{K}) \tag{3}$$

3 Model of paralell mechanism and kinematic paraemters

The model of parallel mechanism of this research is shown in Fig.1. This parallel mechanism has three actuators and the end effecor is supported at the rotational joints of the elastic hinges by three actuators.

The definition of the kinematic parameters are shown here. (wx1, wy1), (wx2, wy2) and (wx3, wy3) are one end of the actuator to the base plate and are represented by the world coordinate system. (px, py) is the stylus coordinates of the triangle stage and is represented by the world coordinate system. (Δpx, Δpy) is the displacement of the stylus. (sx1, sy1), (sx2, sy2) and (sx3, sy3) are the coordinates of the vertex of triangle stage and are represented by a local coordinate system with the origin of the stylus location. L1, L2 and L3 are actuator length. ΔL1, ΔL2 and ΔL3 are actuator amount of expansion and contraction. θ is the rotation angle and is positive when the stage rotates in clockwise.

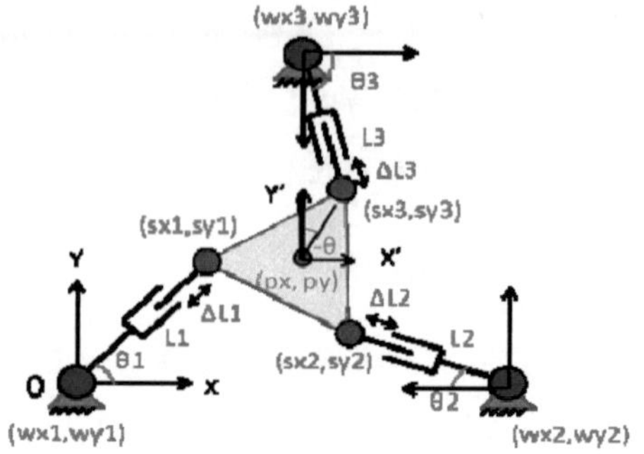

Fig. 1. Definition of models and parameters of the mechanism

4 Model equations

The model equations are built based on the kinematics of the paralell mechanism. The equeation is shown as (4)

$$\sqrt{(wxi-uxi)^2+(wyi-uyi)^2} = Li + \Delta Li \quad (4)$$

,where uxi and uyi are the coordinates of the vertex of triangle stage represented in the world coordinate system.

The kinematic parameters were estimated in [2] based on the quation (4) using least squares method. However, the estimated kinematic values are so different from the nominal values.

Because the some implicit assumption were introduced.

(1) The end-effector, triangle stage, is rigid.

(2) the displacement of the actuator is proportional to the applied voltage.

These assumptions looked incorrect in this parallel mechanism.

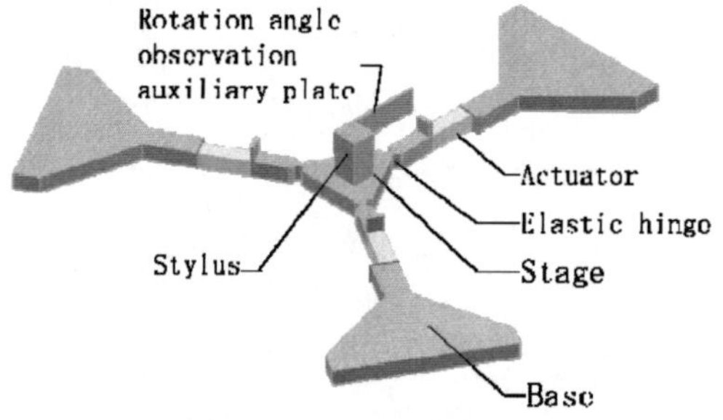

(a) 2D parallel mechanism consists of the bases, actuators and stage. Stage is supported with three actuators.

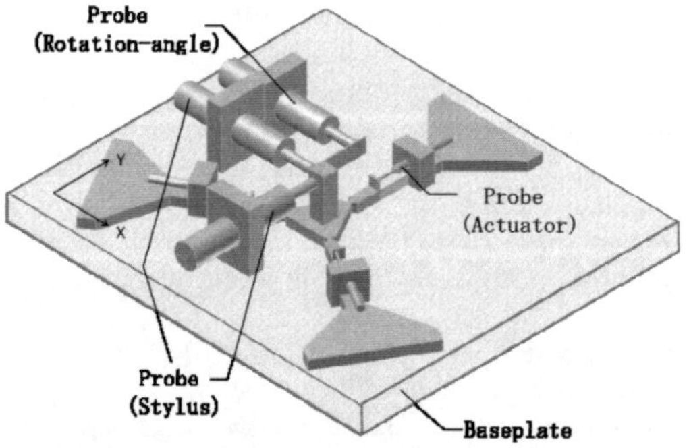

(b) 2D parallel mechanim is set on the baseplate. six measureing instruments are set up.

Fig. 2. 2D parallel machanism and measuring instruments for calibration

In this article, the physical and kinematic relations of parameters are ignored. The model equations are assumed as just polinominal forms of the applied voltages and the deviations of the acuator lengths. The relationship between the applied voltage and the deviation of the actuator lengths is assumed as also polinominal form.

$$x = \sum_{i=0}^{n}\sum_{j=0}^{n}\sum_{k=0}^{n} p_{xijk}(v_1)^i(v_2)^j(v_3)^k$$
$$y = \sum_{i=0}^{n}\sum_{j=0}^{n}\sum_{k=0}^{n} p_{yijk}(v_1)^i(v_2)^j(v_3)^k \quad (5)$$

$$x = \sum_{i=0}^{n}\sum_{j=0}^{n}\sum_{k=0}^{n} q_{xijk}(d_1)^i(d_2)^j(d_3)^k$$
$$y = \sum_{i=0}^{n}\sum_{j=0}^{n}\sum_{k=0}^{n} q_{yijk}(d_1)^i(d_2)^j(d_3)^k \quad (6)$$

$$d_i = \sum_{i=0}^{n}\sum_{j=0}^{n}\sum_{k=0}^{n} r_{ijk}(v_1)^i(v_2)^j(v_3)^k \quad (7)$$

,where v_i are appliend voltage, d_i are the deviation of the actuator lengths.

5 2D parallel mechanism with three degree of freedom

2D parallel mechanism is shown in Fig.2(a). Three bases are fixed on the world coordinate system. Three actuators are disposed between the base and the stage. The stage are supported by three actuators and can move in x and y direction and rotation according to the variations of three actuator lengths.

2D parallel mechanism is fixed on the baseplase as shwn in

Fig.2(b) and the coordinate system of this device is related with the world coordinate system, which is sometimes called the machine coordinate system.

The used actuators are laminated piezoelectric element (made NEC Tokin, AE0505D16F) of which the maximum amount of displacement is 17.4 ± 2.0 [μm] and generating force is 850[N] at the time of applying DC150V.

In addition ,since the amount of displacement of the stacked piezoelectric element is up to 17μm, it is enlarged displacement by designing to be shifted from the center of gravity of the stage hinge come arcuate notches(See Fig.3). The rotation angle of stage and the amount of displacement of stage are measured at the stylus point by the capacitive displacement gauge (Iwatsu Electric Co., Ltd., ST-3511, ST-0532A) as shown in Fig.2(b).

The stage rotation angle is calculated from the difference between the stage displacement of the coaxial direction of displacement and rotation angle observation auxiliary plate as shown in Fig.2(b), and the distance between the axes of two capacitive displacement gauges.

Fig.3 shows the situation that the parallel mechanism is set up and the measuring gauges are set up for experiments.

6 Estimation result of parameters

The deviation of the actuators, the location of stage, the rotational angle of stage are measured simultaneously. In experiments, the applied voltage to the actuators are independently varied from 0 to 150[V]. So, the deviations, the coordinates of stage, the rotational angle, the applied voltage are collected.

Three model equations(5-7) are applied to these collected data.

Equation (5) are equations to determine the relationship between the coordinates of stage and the applied voltage. The coordinates of stage can be estimated applying the estimated parameters to equation (5). The differences between the measured coordinates of stage and the estimated coordinates are calculated. The minimum and maximum differences in xy-cooridnates are (-0.44, -0.57) and (0.38, 0.64).

Equation (6) are equations to determine the relationship between the coordinates of stage and the deviations of the actuators. The coordinates of stage can be estimated applying the estimated parameters to equation (6). The differences between the measured coordinates of stage and the estimated coordinates are also calculated. The minimum and maximum differences in xy-cooridnates are (-0.16,-0.24) and (0.19,0.19).

Equation (7) are equations to determine the relationship between the deviation of the actuator length and the applied voltage to the actuator. The deviation of the actuator lengths are estimated applying the estimated parameters to equation (7).

7 Consideration

The result of equation (6) is better than that of equation (5). This means that the deviation of the Piezo actuator is not

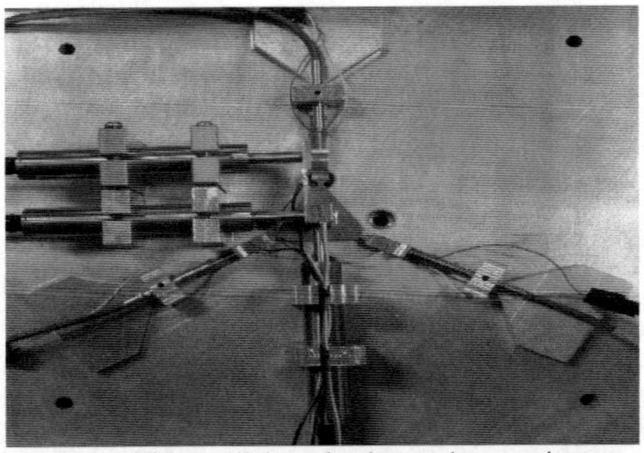

Fig. 3. Picture of the parallel mechanism and measuring gauges.

proportional to the applied voltage. Because the forces of Piezo actuators are sometimes against the other forces. Each equation (5) to (7) fits the collected data well. The relationship among these equations should be explained. As the equation (1) is just a kinematic model, the mechanical model should be considered.

After that, the model parameters could be estimated not only kinematically and also mechanically.

8 Conclusion

The small size paralell stage was develped. The kinematic parameters of the parallel mechanism was estimated based on the assumption that the stage was rigid and the deviation of the actuator length were proportional. This estimated parapmeters could not estimate the coordinates of the parallel stage. As it was impossible to determine the deformation of the stage and the relationship between the deviation and the applied voltage at this moment, the model equation was assumed as the polinominal function.

By the estimation result based on the polinominal model, it is proved that the stage is not rigid and the deviation of the actuator length is not proportional.

In future, the kinematic and mechanical model of the parallel mechansim should be determind comparing the rigid kinematic model and the polynominal model.

References

1. Yukio Takeda, parallel Mechanism(Introduction to Precision Engineering), J of JSPE ,**71**(11), 1363-1368 (2005)

2. S.Yokouchi, H.Takazawa, T.Tanaka, M.Ozaki, R.Furutani, Self calibration of 2D parallel mechanism with three degree of freedom, Proc. of ICPE 2014, **B35**, 267-270 (2014)

3. Akihira Torii Masaaki Banno Akiteru Ueda Kae Douki, A Study on the Small-size Self-propelled Stewart platform, IEE Trans EIS ,**130**(4),660-667(2010)

Estimation of the Measurement Uncertainty of the Stiffness Modulus: Test case of Indirect tensile on cylindrical specimens

Hicham Mezouara [(1)], Latifa Dlimi [(1)], Abdelouahhab Salih [(2)], Mohamed Afechcar [(3)]

[1]Faculty of Science Department of Physics Ibn Tofail University Kenitra, Morocco
[2]PES Génie Mécanique LMD- E.N.S.E.T. B.P. 6207 Rabat – Maroc Responsable de l'Equipe de Recherche Instrumentation, Mesures et Essais Auditeur Technique attaché au MCI, Consultant de l'ANPME
[3]National Center for Studies and Road Research CNER/DRCR BP 6226, Rabat-Instituts Rabat, Morocco

hicham_dess@yahoo.fr

Abstract: This study treaty the uncertainties of measure that we can meet in the essay of the stiffness modulus of bituminous. We present all the sensors installed on chains of measure of module of rigidity as well as their uncertainty ranges, Several parameters influence on the value of the module of rigidity of one coated such as the parameters related in the conditions of essay and others are rather connected to the specification of the equipment are the speed, the level of load are, the temperature, the dimension of the tested sample and the acquisition of the data, all these factors have a great influence on the value of the modulus of rigidity.
To qualify the uncertainty factors we used two approaches: Approche1 is made by following the approach described by the GUM (Guide to the expression of uncertainty in measurement), the approach 2 by the numerical simulation of the Monte Carlo. The two results are then compared for an interval of confidences of 95%.

Keywords: Stiffness modulus, uncertainty, Propagation of variances, GUM, Monte-Carlo.

1 Introduction

In the laboratories of the essays, the realization of the essays implies the use of the more and more successful ways as well in the production as in the control.
The use of machines to measure became widespread in the essay of the stiffness modulus of bituminous.
However, knowledge of measurement uncertainties in control and metrology operations remains a major problem that is still poorly understood.
The parameters that can modify the results of these rigidity modulus tests are multiple such as the parameters related to the test conditions and others, rather, related to the specification of the equipment which are the speed and the level of loading, the temperature, the size of the sample tested and the data acquisition… . All these factors have a great influence on the value of the modulus of rigidity.
To qualify the uncertainty factors we used two approaches: Approche **1** is made by following the approach described by the GUM (Guide to the expression of uncertainty in measurement), the approach **2** by the numerical simulation of the Monte Carlo. The two results are then compared for an interval of confidences of 95%.
The indirect tensile test on cylindrical test specimens of the stiffness module is based on standardization EN 12697-26 « Bituminous mixtures - Essay methods for hot hydrocarbon mixtures - Part 26: Rigidity modulus », appeared in 2004 [1-2-3]... Of the five annexes corresponding to as many test methods, we are interested here in Appendix C (Indirect tensile essay on cylindrical specimen IT-CY).

2 Testing machine and sensors:

For the realization of the essays, a hydraulic press of capacity 50 kN is used. The main Characteristics are the following ones:

- To define the various test parameters is made by means of specific software.
- Create the desired solicitation signals. The control of the press and the thermal enclosure as well as all the elements necessary for the programming of an essay.

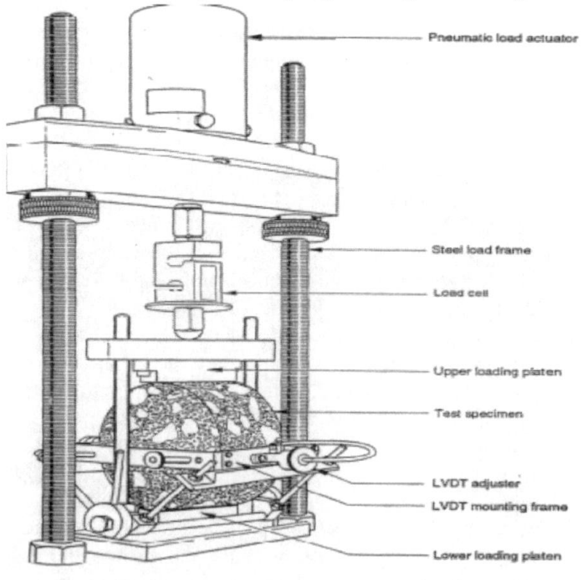

Fig 1: Test equipment of the rigidity modulus (EN 12697-26)

The command of the press is made by means of the software. This program allows you to define the different parameters and create the desired solicitation signals: The command of the press and the thermal enclosure wall as well as all the elements necessary for the programming of an essay.

3 Instrumentation :

The measures will take place in a room, internal of the test laboratory, identified under "Room" and maintained in the ambient weather conditions.
The module test machine housed in a thermoregulated enclosure calibrated /verified in extern, in which a constant test temperature between 0 and 40 ° C can be maintained near the specimens with an accuracy of ± 0,5 ° C.
The machine is tracked metologically by control charts obtained from the tests on a working etalon (Etalon Ring).

- The deformation measuring system consisting of two linear sensors (LVDT : Linear Variable Differential Transformers), capable of measuring the transient diametral deformation of the specimen during the application of a charge pulse with an accuracy better than 1μm.
- A load cell (or force sensor) for measuring the applied load with an accuracy of 2%. The two force sensors and displacement are calibrated separately by an external organization.
- Adapted thermocouples, calibrated externally, able to measure at ± 0.1 ° C the temperature of the specimen and the conditions of storage and testing.
- The calibrated caliper externally, allows to measure the thicknesses and diameters of the specimens with an accuracy of ± 0.1mm.

4 Measure of module of rigidity [4-5-6-7-8]

According to standard NF EN 12697-26: 2004, on compacted specimens, diameter Φ100mm, thickness 53mm and density 2451kg / m^3, indirect tensile tests were made.

The rigidity module was determined using a pneumatic press (fig. 1) located in a thermostatic chamber to control the temperature.

The essay consists of applying a cyclic compression load diametrically on the specimen. We measure the variation of the horizontal diameter.

The pulse duration of the applied load shall be 124 milliseconds, followed by a rest period of 3 seconds. The magnitude of the charge is necessary to produce a transient increase of 4 microns in the horizontal diameter of the specimen.

During the test, 10 pulses of conditioning charge are first applied to allow the press to calibrate the magnitude of the charge and the duration. Then 5 more charge pulses are applied for each direction, the variation of the diametral deformation is measured horizontal and applied load. The modulus of rigidity is calculated using the measurements of the 5 charging pulses according to the following formula:

$$E = \frac{F*(\upsilon + 0.27)}{(Z*H)} \qquad (1)$$

Or :

E is the modulus of stiffness measured, expressed in MPa;
F is the value of the vertical load applied, expressed in N;
Z is the amplitude of the horizontal deformation obtained during the charge cycle, expressed in mm;
H is the thickness of the test piece, expressed in mm;
υ is the poisson's ratio a value of 0.35 was taken;

Table 1 summarizes the conditions of the essays:

Horizontal deformation referred to	5 ± 2 μm
Frequency in Hz	10
Number of pulses	10
The pulse repetition period	3 ± 0,1 s
Load rise time	124 ± 4ms
Poisson's ratio	0,35
Essay temperature	15 C

Table 1

The results of the essays:

Module of Rigidity Mean measured (E in Mpa)	6503,125
Module of Rigidity Mean corrected (E ' in Mpa)	6696

With,
Corrected module of rigidity given by the following formula

$$E' = E \times [1 - 0{,}322 \times (\log(E) - 1{,}82) \times (0{,}6 - K)] \qquad (1)$$

5 Calculation of uncertainties by method GUM [9-10] :

We will structure the calculation of uncertainty in four steps:

- Specify the measurand:
The definition of the measurand with the writing of the mathematical model representing it of each input quantity of the model is estimated and the value of the result (measurand) is determined.
Before starting the measurements, it is important to define what we are going to measure, we have based on the standard NF EN 12697-26: 2004 and the rigidity modulus essay technical file:

- Force F

- Longitudinal Z displacement
- The thickness of the test specimen h
- The Poisson's ratio
- The load factor k

- Identify sources of uncertainty:
Sources of uncertainty were identified by the 5M method and are presented in the following diagram.
The factors that can influence the value of the modulus of rigidity of the asphalt are mainly: temperature, loading speed and stress level, frequency or loading time, sample size tested and repeatability of the test process. All of these factors are of paramount importance to the value of the module.

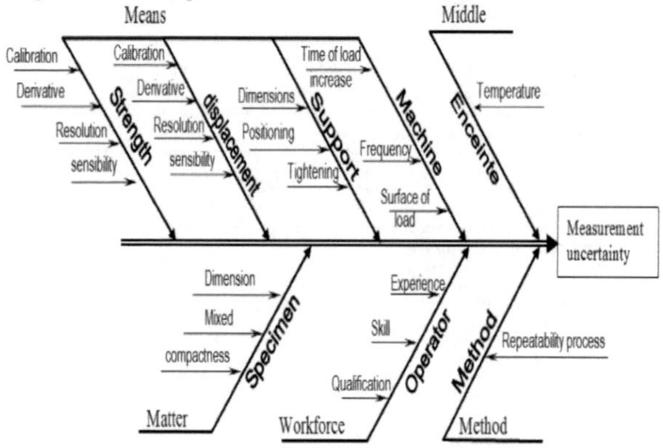

The method of the 5M

- Quantify the sources:
Uncertainty type A: Repeatability of the essay process (U_{PA}):
The complete process of determination of the module (E) of the material is made n time in a independent way, The result is automatically obtained by the software of piloting of the machine.
The measurement process is characterized by the estimate S_X (experimental standard deviation) of the repeatability of E : $u_A = S_X$

Où $S_X = \sqrt{\frac{\sum_i^n (E_i - \bar{E})^2}{n-1}}$ (3) avec $\bar{E} = \frac{\sum E_i}{n}$

Uncertainty type of the type B : (u_{B1})

$$u_{B1} = \sqrt{\left(\frac{0,62 \times u_F}{Z \times h}\right)^2 + \left(\frac{0,62 \times F \times u_Z}{Z^2 \times h}\right)^2 + \left(\frac{0,62 \times F \times u_h}{Z \times h^2}\right)^2} \quad (4)$$

Uncertainty obtained from the law of propagation of Uncertainties on the measurand equation of the modulus of rigidity we obtain the following equation (MPa) :
Avec

$$u_{B1}^2(y) = \sum_{i=1}^{n} \left[\frac{\partial f}{\partial x_i}\right]^2 . u^2(x_i) \quad (5)$$

The correlation between the variables is negligible.

or each sensor, the measurement uncertainty u is given by:

$$u = \sqrt{u_{ET}^2 + u_{der}^2 + u_{res}^2 + u_s^2} \quad (6)$$

The standard uncertainty u comes from:
u_{ET} : Uncertainty related to peson calibration (force sensor)
u_{der} : The uncertainty related to drift over time,(For 1st calibration we shall take ($u_{der} = u_{ET}$)
u_{res} : Uncertainty related to the resolution of the measured value,
u_s : The uncertainty related to the sensitivity of temperature, the essays were realized only between 0 and 40°C, at constant temperature. At fixed temperature, there is no drift of sensor measurements with temperature.
To determine these uncertainties, we refer to all the information (observed data, verification findings, calibration certification, expert opinion, data sheets, manufacturer's data ...) and in particular the following guides [JCGM -100-2008 et GUM 1995].

- Summary of standard uncertainties: see Table 2

- Determination of expanded uncertainty:
The expanded uncertainty corresponds to a quantity defining an interval, around the result of a measurement; it can be expected to include a large fraction of the distribution of values that could be reasonably attributed to the measurand.

$U(E') = k.u(E')$ Or K is the enlargement factor, we can take as an enlargement factor K=2 to have a level of confidence from 95% The final result expressed with two significant figures, by using the rule of rounding of Gauss.
Expanded uncertainty on the corrected module:

$$U(E') = 2u(E')$$

$$U(E') = \pm 39,06 Mpa$$

If all sources of uncertainty are taken into consideration, then there will be greater uncertainty [11] :

$$U_{GUM} = 2u_{GUM}$$

With $u_{GUM} = \sqrt{u_A^2 + u_F^2 + u_Z^2 + u_h^2 + u_K^2 + u_{B_2}^2 + u_{B_3}^2}$
= 382 ,0085 Mpa

So we have an expanded uncertainty:
$U_{GUM} = \pm 764,0170$ Mpa

histogram.

Code u_i	Sources of uncertainty components		Law	Standard uncertainty u_i (Half extended)	Sensitivity coefficient $Si = \frac{\partial E}{\partial x_i}$	Uncertainty (Si*ui)	Contribution (sensitivity indices) Si en (%)
u_F	Force sensor (in N)	Peson :u_{ET} (Calibration)	Normal law	1	/	/	/
		Peson :u_{Der} (Derivative)		1	/	/	
		Peson :u_{Res} (Resolution)	Uniform Law	2.88675135	/	/	
		Peson :u_s (Sensitivity)	Arc-sine Law	0	/	/	
		u_F	Normal law	**1.914854216**	**2.924528302**	**5.600045347**	**0.03**
u_z	Displacement sensor LVDT : deformation (in μm)	LVDT :u_{ET} (Calibration)	Normal law	0.00890956	/	/	
		LVDT :u_{Der} (Derivative)		8.9096E-06	/	/	
		LVDT :u_{Res} (Resolution)	Uniform Law	4.0825E-05	/	/	
		LVDT :u_s (Sensitivity)	Arc-sine Law	0	/	/	
		u_z	Normal law	**0.00840008**	**1674.292453**	**14.064191**	**2.15**
u_h	Thickness of the test specimen (in mm)	Caliper :u_{ET} (Calibration)	Normal law	0.001266144	/	/	
		Caliper :u_{Der} (Derivative)		0.001266144	/	/	
		Caliper :u_{Res} (Resolution)	Uniform Law	0.002106028	/	/	
		Caliper :u_s (Sensitivity)	Arc-sine Law	0.000163379	/	/	
		u_h	Normal law	**0.180165144**	**0.126361695**	**0.022765973**	**0.00254**
u_k	Load area factor	u_k	Uniform Law	**0.01**	/	**0.003**	**0.00143**
Calculation of Uncertainty Composite type on the equation $u_{B1} = u_E$ (en Mpa)							**15.13811397**
Calculation of Uncertainty Composite type on the equation $u_{E'}$ (en Mpa)							**19.53299021**
u_{B2}	Load rise time (in ms)		Uniform Law	155.4919745	1	155.4919745	23.72
u_{B3}	Temperature (in C°)		Arc-sine Law	183.9361515	1	183.9361515	28.06
u_A	Repeatability		Type A	296.507257	1	296.507257	45.23

Tableau 2

6 Analysis of contribution of the parameters:

The analysis of contribution consists in identifying among all the parameters of the model those who have an influence on the essays of the module of rigidity.

To determine the most influential parameters, the contribution analysis is used to identify the input parameters that contribute the most to the uncertainty of the final results. They are characterized by uncertainty and high sensitivity. However, a parameter with excessive sensitivity and small uncertainty, or vice versa, can be a significant contributor. The contributions of the parameters are represented in the form of a

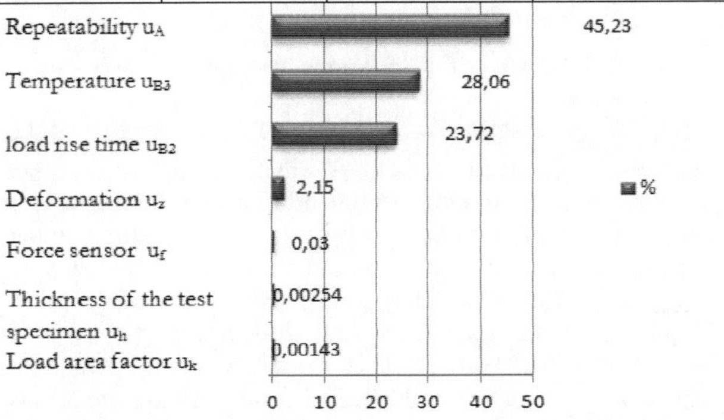

We selected 3 factors (Time of load increase 23 %, temperatures 28 % and Repeatability 47 %), those with the

highest index percentages are the bills with the most influence in their range of variation on rigidity modulus tests. It can be noted that the three factors having first-order percentage indices higher than the factors (force sensor, LVDT displacement sensors and the thickness of the specimen), this is explained by the values of the uncertainties of these factors. which are negligible in the face of uncertainties due to factors such as load time, temperature and repeatability.

7 Calculation of the uncertainties according to the method Monte Carlo :

The Monte Carlo numerical [12-13-14] then is a necessary alternative. To implement it, we must first define the influence factors of the output quantity and associate them via an analytical or numerical model. It may be noted that this step was already necessary for the linear method. Each factor of influence is associated with a statistical distribution.

A random generator is then used to generate prints of each influence factor

Selection of distributions for the input variables.
The probability densities of each input quantity are defined in Table 3 of the GUM method. The standard deviations of each variable are obtained by taking the standard uncertainties calculated by the GUM approach.

Source of uncertainty	Type of distribution	standard uncertainty
Force sensor (N) u_F en N	Normal law	2,5648
Deformation u_z en μm	Normal law	0,034567
Thickness of the test specimen u_h in mm	Normal law	0,04359
Load area factor u_K	Uniform Law	0,25
Load rise time u_{B2} (in ms)	Uniform Law	149,65767
Temperature u_{B3} (in C°)	Arcsine law	184,6527
Repeatability u_A	Type A	297,56

Table 3 : density of distributions for the input variables

When all the distributions of the input quantities have been defined, we can then generate 10^6 realizations of each input quantity by drawing in their probability density function, it is necessary to have a sufficiently powerful random number generator, the calculation is carried out in a specific software (MC-Ed) It allows to define a module for each module size (load, strain, specimen thickness, load surface factor, etc.) and then assemble them into a metamodule. Finally, he chooses the numerical value of each term of the model, its associated uncertainty and the probability function.

The Monte Carlo simulations of 10^6 values obtained from the output quantity, which makes it possible to construct the empirical distribution of the measurand Fig 2

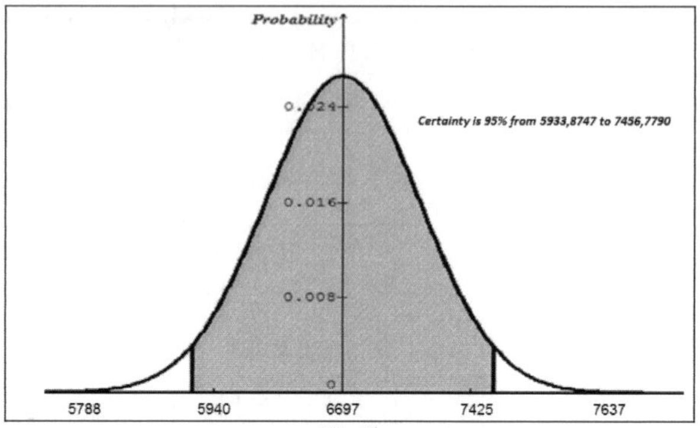

Fig 2

We notice that the distribution of shape Gaussienne, The maximum stiffness modulus value (7456.7790Mpa) and the minimum (5933.8747 MPa) define an interval that contains 95% of the values attributable to the measurand. The Mean value is 6697.02 MPa and the standard deviation is 380.8446 MPa.

with ,

$$u_{Monte\ carlo} = \sqrt{u_A^2 + u_F^2 + u_Z^2 + u_h^2 + u_K^2 + u_{B_2}^2 + u_{B_3}^2}$$

Finally, the result is given with a confidence interval
I_p (E') = [E'_{low} , E'_{high}] corresponding to a probability p of 95 % (Fig 2) :

- Standard deviation = 380,8446 Mpa
- Extended interval, $I_{(95\%)}$ (E') = [5933,8747 ; 7456,7790]Mpa

8 Comparative study between the two methods (GUM and Monte Carlo)

The results obtained by the GUM method and by the Monte-Carlo method for the evaluation of measurement uncertainties of the modulus of rigidity.

Grandeur	Method GUM	Method Monte-Carlo
E'	6696 Mpa	6697,02 Mpa
U	382,0085 Mpa	380,8446 Mpa
Extended interval in Mpa	[5931,9830 ; 7460,0170] (K=2)	[5933,8747 ; 7456,7790] (à 95%)

We note that the difference between the two confidence intervals obtained is very small and that the interval calculated by numerical simulation of Monte-Carlo is included in that of the propagation of the uncertainties. Moreover, these results are quite in agreement with each other and we can consider that the results given by the numerical simulation of Monte Carlo validate the law of propagation of the uncertainties.

We also applied the comparison criterion described in document (BIPM JCGM 10). Indeed, it is advisable to apply the law of propagation of the variances (GUM) by adding terms of higher degree if necessary, and to give a confidence interval of 95% for the output variable. Then, to validate the law of propagation of the variances, it is necessary to apply the numerical simulation of Monte Carlo in order to provide a standard uncertainty and a confidence interval of 95%. It must then be determined whether the confidence intervals obtained by the Monte Carlo method and the law of propagation of the uncertainties are in agreement with a degree of approximation calculated as follows :

We express the standard deviation in the form $a \times 10^r$ or a is an integer of 2 numbers (corresponding to the number of significant digits, here 2) and r an integer. The precision of the comparison is then : $\delta = 0{,}5.10^r$.

The expanded uncertainties obtained by each method are compared. We form the differences:

$d_{low} = \left| E' - \text{EMBED Equation.3} - E'_{low\,(MONTE-CARLO)} \right|$

$d_{high} = \left| E' + \text{EMBED Equation.3} - E'_{high\,(MONTE-CARLO)} \right|$

If these differences are both less than the previously determined tolerance, then the results obtained by the GUM method are validated.

If we take 2 significant figures for, $u_{Monte-Carlo}$ we have: E'=6696 Mpa

$u_{Monte-Carlo} = 380\ \text{Mpa} = 38.10^1\text{Mpa}$

Donc $\delta = 0{,}5.10^1 = 5$

$d_{low} = 1{,}89173$

$d_{high} = 3{,}23795$

The results obtained show that the two quantities d_{low} and d_{high} are not bigger than δ , so the analytic approach GUM is validated by the approach Monte-Carlo.

Comparison of two variances $u^2_{(Monte\_Carlo)}$ and $u^2_{(GUM)}$ (Fisher's test):

The Fisher comparison test compares the variances of two uncertainty calculation approaches (GUM) and the numerical simulation of Monte Carlo under populations, and confronts the following hypotheses:

$$H_0 : u^2_{(Monte\_Carlo)} \approx u^2_{(GUM)}$$

$$H_1 : u^2_{(Monte\_Carlo)} \neq u^2_{(GUM)}$$

The statistic of the test F is thus defined by:

A risk of α=0,05 (5%)

In our case $F = \dfrac{u^2_{(GUM)}}{u^2_{(Monte\_Carlo)}}$;

The Degrees of freedom :

– $n_{GUM} - 1 = 6$

– $n_{Monte\ Carlo} - 1 = 6$

We calculate:

$$F = \frac{u^2_{(GUM)}}{u^2_{(Monte\_Carlo)}} = \frac{(382{,}0085)^2}{(380{,}8446)^2} = 1{,}00612 \quad ;$$

We compare this value to the tabular value of the F in the table of the law F :

$F^{n_{GUM}-1}_{n_{Monte\ Carlo}-1} = F^6_6 = 4{,}284$

Extract of the table F

$F_{.05}(\nu_1, \nu_2)$

ν_2 \ ν_1	1	2	3	4	5	6	7	8
1	161.448	199.500	215.707	224.583	230.162	233.986	236.768	238.882
2	18.513	19.000	19.164	19.247	19.296	19.330	19.353	19.371
3	10.128	9.552	9.277	9.117	9.013	8.941	8.887	8.845
4	7.709	6.944	6.591	6.388	6.256	6.163	6.094	6.041
5	6.608	5.786	5.409	5.192	5.050	4.950	4.876	4.818
6	5.987	5.143	4.757	4.534	4.387	4.284	4.207	4.147
7	5.591	4.737	4.347	4.120	3.972	3.866	3.787	3.726

It is concluded that the observed ratio is smaller than the reference ratio: F < F^6_6 and so we do not reject the hypothesis H_0 .

9 Conclusion and recommendation

The analytical method (GUM) makes it possible to easily perform a complete analysis of uncertainty: it makes it possible to calculate the uncertainty of the impact scores, their sensitivity to the variation of the input parameters and the contribution of the uncertainty of the test. The modulus of stiffness according to GUM the greatest uncertainty comes from the three factors (Load rise time 23%, temperatures 28% and Repeatability 47%).

The comparison between the uncertainty calculated using the analytical method and the results of the Monte Carlo method showed no significant difference, it is because of the linearity of the measurement models used for each of the tests and the independence of the effects of the contributions to uncertainty considered.

The Monte Carlo simulations carried out made it possible to show that the modulus of rigidity is Gaussian so it is easy to give a confidence interval, with the maximum value of modulus of rigidity (7456.7790 Mpa) and the minimum (5933, 8747 Mpa) define an interval that contains 95% of the values attributable to the measurand. The Mean value is 6697.02 MPa and the standard deviation is 380.8446 MPa.

Certain functionality of Monte Carlo are reduction of the effort of analysis required for the complex or not linear models, in particular since the partial by-products of the first one(night) or the upper order used to supply coefficients of

sensibility for the law of distribution of the uncertainty (GUM) are not necessary.
The analytical method remains very relevant as far as the cases of not linearity are rare in the practical order of magnitude of the sources of uncertainties and in the complex processes.
Both methods are thus feasible and it is interesting to make these two calculations in parallel to verify his result.
Mainly, for the evaluation of the uncertainties of test measurements of stiffness modulus. It is recommended to proceed with the GUM approach. The ease of use, speed and the amount of information essential to the analysis of the uncertainty it provides. Making this method available would allow the uncertainty analysis to gain popularity, improving the interpretation of rigidity modulus test results.
The use of the analytical method (GUM) would, in addition, improve the quality of the uncertainty analyzes, since the sensitivity quickly reveals the incoming parameters likely to contribute a lot to the uncertainty of the impact scores.

References

[1] NF EN 12697-26- Annexe C, Méthodes d'essai pour mélange hydrocarboné à chaud : module de rigidité .

[2] Huet C. représentation de module et complaisances complexes arithmétique et logarithmique. Crope fr Rgéole tome 1-5. Nov 1947 page 237.

[3] Cornil P. détermination du module de rigidité et Essais de fatigue en flexion sur éprouvettes de matériaux hydrocarbonés encastrées à une extrémité Rapp rech. CRR Bruxelles, 1968.

[4] JCGM, « Vocabulaire international de métrologie - Concepts fondamentaux et généraux et termes associés (VIM) », BIPM, JCGM 200:2008 (E/F)

[5] Di Benedetto, H., M. N. Partl, et al. (2001). " Stiffness testing for bituminous mixtures." Materials and Structures 34: 66-70.

[6] Kim, Y. R., Y. Seo, et al. (2004). "Dynamic modulus testing of asphalt concrete in indirect tension mode." Transportation Research Record 1891: 163-173.

[7] Nunn, M. E. et T. M. Smith (1997). Improvements to the indirect tensile stiffness modulus test. 2nd European Symposium - Performance and durability of bituminous materials, Leeds.

[8] JCGM , Evaluation of measurement data-supplement 1 to the Guide to the expression of the measurement _propagation of distributions using a Monte-Carlo method , BIPM . JCGM 10.

[9] NF ENV 13005 Guide pour l'expression de l'incertitude de mesure. Afnor 1999.

[10] PLATEL F., « Mise en pratique de la méthode de Monte-Carlo Projet Monte-Carlo Editor (MC-Ed) », MetGen, Dossier métrologie 25

[11] ISO/CEI Guide 25 :1990 Prescriptions générales concernant la compétence des laboratoires d'étalonnage et d'essais.

[12] James E. GENTLE, (2003). "Random Number Generation and Monte Carlo methods" – Springer, Statistics and Computing, second Edition.

[13] H. SCHWENKE, B.R. L. SIEBERT, F. WÄLDELE, H. KUNZMANN, (2000). "Assessment of Uncertainties in Dimensional Metrology by Monte Carlo Simulation: Proposal of a Modular and Visual Software" – Annals of the CIRP Vol. 49/1/2000.

[14] ISO/IEC Guide 98-3/Suppl.1:2008(E) Uncertainty of measurement - Part 3: Guide to the expression of uncertainty in measurement (GUM:1995) Supplement 1: Propagation of distributions using a Monte Carlo method. Geneva (Switzerland): ISO, December 2008, 98 p.

*** Formatting Issue - Best Available Paper/Graphic ***

7th International Metrology Conference – CAFMET 2018

Minimizing the Undercut Condition in On-Machine Measurement Using Weighted Total Least Squares Fitting

C. Berry and A. Barari*

University of Ontario Institute of Technology, Faculty of Engineering and Applied Science, Oshawa, Ontario, Canada

Received:

Abstract. In the on-Machine Measurement (OMM) process, the machined part is inspected using a coordinate metrology sensor without being removed from the machine tool. The result of this inspection process can be used to plan for additional machining phase correcting the undesired geometric deviations of the machined surface that are caused due to the inherent errors of the machining process. This approach can be conducted in a closed-loop manner leading to full conformance of the final product to the design tolerance zone. The geometric deviations on a machine surface can be classified to overcut and undercut regions. These involve both excess leftover material, undercut, and excess removed material, overcut. Although an overcut cannot be corrected by additional cutting of the corresponding region, the overall surface can be corrected by wise removal of the material from the undercut regions. This paper presents a new fitting algorithm that minimizes the undercut region material to be removed to achieve the conformance to tolerance zone of the planar surfaces. The developed fitting algorithm uses a weighted total least square approach that not only eliminates any overcut region, but also minimized the volume of all the undercut regions which need additional machining operation. This algorithm is developed for various inspection systems when the data points are captured from the surface of the work piece using any coordinate metrology sensor including the tactile inspection probes, laser scanner, or other types of optical sensors. The developed algorithm is implemented and practiced for various validation case studies and satisfactory results are observed.

Keywords: On-Machine Measurement, Coordinate Metrology, Laser Scanner, Geometric Tolerance Zone, fitting process, Overcut and Undercut regions, Weighted Total Least Square

1 Introduction

Metrology is an essential part of any manufacturing effort. In any process, regardless of the size or shape, there will always be inconsistencies in the manufactured surface quality. These errors can be caused by many different factors, such as machine error or tool error. As the manufacturing industry gets more advanced, the customer requirements for surface quality and dimensional accuracy has also increased in tandem. While the machines used to produce parts become more and more advanced, they still cannot produce perfectly smooth surfaces. To verify that these surfaces are within the bounds defined by the client, coordinate metrology is used.

The simplest case that can be dealt with is that of planar surfaces. For these surfaces, an ideal plane can be fit to a set of points obtained from the manufactured surfaced. Once this plane has been fit to the points, the distance of each point to the fit plane can be determined and the surface quality can easily be calculated. Generally, an error bound is set for this plane, and the sampled points are meant to lie inside it if the part has been manufactured correctly. While in the past there were a few different was to fit this plane, the total least squares method has become something of an industry standard. It is easy to determine for planar surfaces, and provides a simple way to quickly determine if the sampled part is within acceptable

* Correspondence: ahmad.barari@uoit.ca

parameters without causing too many false rejections. If a part is rejected by this method however, it can be put through another manufacturing process to correct the errors. Depending on the error geometry, this could lead to milling or additive manufacturing procedures needing to be used. Total least squares as it currently exists does not take into account the cost of these operations, or the availability of these operations, and can cause parts to be fully rejected because of this. To solve this problem, we propose the use of weighted total least squares.

2 Theoretical background

van Huffel [1] conducted a review in errors in variables modeling techniques. While the book focused on the mathematical fitting strategies, there were also papers on the fitting of idealized geometry to point clouds for coordinate metrology. Zwick [2] did a comparison between total least squares, linear least squares, and minimax fitting. He showed that linear least squares and minimax fitting had efficient solutions in two-dimensional space, but had inefficient solutions in three-dimensional space. Total least squares, however, had efficient solutions in both spaces.

This meant that it was more applicable for a wider variety of problems, especially when computing power was limited. Zwick did note that linear least squares and minimax fitting were gaining interest again due to the properties of the techniques, linear least squares being less aggressive and minimax fitting being very aggressive. This led to different results after fitting that could affect how a part is treated.

Nielsen [3] introduced a refinement to the least squares estimation using Lagrange multipliers. During this time, the least squares problem was still an optimization problem, and Nielsen wanted to determine a way to solve both linear and nonlinear constrained problems. The Lagrange optimization algorithm he proposed allowed for these solutions without affecting the results of the estimation.

Nassef and ElMaraghy [4] conducted a comparison between total least squares and minimax fitting with a focus on point selection for different feature geometries. Their main concern was the effect of the sampling strategy on the error found by the fitting algorithm. They initially discussed the differences of TLS and minimax fitting, and go over some past criticisms. The major criticism of TLS fitting was its apparent overestimation of the geometric deviations and so, minimax fitting gained popularity because of its more aggressive approach. However, after further research they determined TLS fitting was reporting deviation values closer to the true values than minimax fitting. Nassef and ElMaraghy found that the geometric features of the part should determine the sampling method used.

Krystek and Anton [5] proposed a TLS method involving weighted points in two dimensions. They tested their method against known datasets and determined that it functioned similarly to other TLS methods. The main advantage over other implementations was the ability to perform regression on all data sets. Before this, TLS suffered when the result was a vertical line as there were discontinuities in the equation. This made TLS fitting more robust while maintaining the same quality of results found in other studies.

Malengo and Pennecchi [6] extended the weighted total least squares algorithm to curves as well as straight lines. They also wanted to incorporate straight-line fitting so that one package would be able to solve for both curves and straight lines. The algorithm they developed was good at dealing with both uncertain and correlated variables while minimizing uncertainties in the measurements. They verified their results against a Monte Carlo method and determined their algorithm maintained much lower uncertainty values while the Monte Carlo method had increased uncertainty as the models' nonlinearity increased.

Shakarji and Srinivasan [7] looked at tolerance standards involving TLS fitting of lines, planes and parallel planes. Their goal was to provide algorithms for each of the geometries that were simple and easy to implement, and did not need optimization algorithms to solve. They presented and proved these algorithms, and verified that the algorithms gave the same or better results than the traditional method of solving TLS fits. Shakarji and Srinivasan showed that the iterative method was no longer necessary and instead, by solving a few equations, you could find the TLS fit.

Shakarji et al. [8] produced a review of TLS fitting and its role in coordinate metrology. They discuss why TLS fitting has remained an attractive option over the years, the ease of use of the algorithm, and its applications for nonlinear problems. One of their main points is that ISO standards are beginning to use TLS fits, which means they will need to be used to check for standards. Near the end of the paper, they look at the uses of weighted total least squares in fitting. They state that by weighting points in low-density areas higher than those in high-density areas, the discrepancy of data sets will be removed as a source of error.

Considering fitting to a tolerance zone instead of fitting to an ideal geometry was introduced in [9, 10]. This consideration increases the nonlinearity of the optimization problem during the SGE process, however the results of this fitting can be much more practical and efficient to avoid rejecting an acceptable part. Complexity resulting from nonlinearity of the objective function in the fitting process can cause trapping in local minima which produces false results for inspection [11-13]. [11] presents an iterative approach for SGE that avoids this issue by re-energizing the current solution to check for other minima in the area.

3 Experimental setup

Total least squares fitting takes a plane and fits it to a set of points to minimize the square of the orthogonal distance from each point to the plane. To do this, the plane and point set will be defined. The plane will be represented by where α β and γ are the principal angles defining the plane, and r is the orthogonal distance from the plane to the origin. The point set will be, where x, y and z are the coordinates of each point. Once these are defined, the objective function to minimize is as follows.

Where is the orthogonal distance of a point to a plane, as shown in the equation below.

Where x_i, y_i, and z_i are the coordinates of a single point. Substituting this equation into Equation 1, the minimization problem becomes the following.

As this is a minimization problem, the first derivative of the equation is taken and set to zero. This is used to determine the point where the function is smallest. The second derivative of the equation is also found in order to determine if the function has global minima or maxima.

*** Formatting Issue - Best Available Paper/Graphic ***

The second derivative is a positive constant, so the function is always convex. This guarantees that there is a minimum value. Now, r is isolated so that it can be replaced in the minimization function.

Where ,, and are values the represent the average x, y, and z values for the whole data set. At this point, a simple partial differential equation cannot be done to determine the minimum values of the three principal angles of the plane. Instead, the minimization problem is redefined it is as follows.

Where π is the plane, is a vector containing the coordinates of the current point, and represents the centroid. To determine the minimum of this function, the Lagrange multiplier method is used. For this, is set, which becomes the following.

Where is the gradient of and is a stationary point that minimizes the function. This breaks down into the following equations.

Equation Error: Reference source not found shows that the vector that minimizes the function is the smallest eigenvector of . Weighted total least squares follows this pattern almost exactly, with a few modifications. The minimization problem is defined again, however, a weight factor is added.

Here, is a set of weights, each associated with a point, where each weight is a positive value. The partial derivative is then taken with respect to r in order to determine whether the centroid is still a required point on the TLS plane.

Equation Error: Reference source not found shows that the weighted centroid is a point on the fit plane. The rest of the solution follows the same path as the non-weighted version, however, the value of needs to be determined. The following also represents the minimization problem as redefined in Equation Error: Reference source not found, but with added weights.

Where is the vector that defines the principal angles of the plane. M then becomes the following.

If we use this to find the new we get, it becomes the following.

Solving for the smallest eigenvector of provides the orientation of the fit plane. However, this problem can be solved without having to calculate . The singular value decomposition of any mxn matrix A is the following.

Therefore, the following equation can be found.

Where V is the right singular vectors of A, U is the left singular vectors of A and S is the singular values of A. The eigendecompostion of a matrix B that is an nxn square matrix with n linearly independent variables is the following equation.

Where Q contains the eigenvectors of B and Λ contains the corresponding eigenvalues of B. If is set, when B is a symmetric positive definite matrix, equations Error: Reference source not found and Error: Reference source not found are equal, and *V* is equal to *Q*. Thus, because *V* contains the eigenvectors of A, we can simply choose the vector associated with the smallest singular

value, and this will be the vector that determines the principal angles for the fit plane. By removing the need for a transpose and multiplication, the numerical accuracy of the method is increased.
This weighted method can then be used to modify the fit plane. After calculated the TLS fit plane, the distance of each point to the plane can be calculated using the following equation.

Where d is the distance from the point to the plane, x, y, and z are the coordinates of the plane, A, B, C, and D are the values defining the plane. With this data, weights can be calculated. As an example, the simplest way to minimize the undercut condition is to examine the points below the fit plane. As these points are in the overcut condition, they are not as important as those above the plane. This is because they cannot be repaired by removing more material. For these points, a very small weight is applied. This causes the fit plane to consider these points as "closer" to the fit plane, and thus they will influence the fit plane less. For those points above the plane, the fit plane has to be such that they bring all the points within some tolerance zone. For this paper, this weight will be based on the distance of the point to the plane. If the point is a large distance from the plane, it needs to influence the plane positioning more, and thus needs a higher weight. Using a scalar multiple of the distance of the point to the plane is an easy solution to this. If the scalar multiple is uniformly applied to each weight, then the distance the plane moves can be calibrated.

4 Results and discussions

Two case studies will be examined. The first case will be purely 2D, in order to clearly show the effects of the developed method. The second case will be for a 3D surface scan.
The 2D case is simply 10 random points. In the figure below, the TLS fit line for this data set is shown.

Fig. 1 Unweighted Case for 2D data set

In the above figure, the TLS fit line is shown. The points below the fit line are in the overcut condition, and the points above the line are in the undercut condition. In order to minimize the number of points in the undercut condition, the developed method is applied, and the weights required to skew the TLS fit plane properly are determined. The results of the method are shown in the figure below.

Fig. 2 Weighted Case for 2D data set

It can be seen in the figure above, that when compared to Fig. 1 the fit plane has shifted up dramatically. Now, instead of having 5 points in the undercut condition, there are only three. This drastic shift is due to the Undercut points being far from the fit plane. This causes the points to have a very high weight, and to have a greater effect on the location of the new fit plane under WTLS. This shows that using WTLS can provide a significant shift in the fit line for 2D problems, and minimizes undercut in those situations. In the next case, a 3D problem will be examined. The piece to be examined is shown in the figure below.

Fig. 3 3D Test Piece

The chosen work piece is an exaggeration of some manufacturing defect. With large sloping curves and no clear planar area, it is a difficult piece to work with. The scan data was obtained with a high density laser scanner. In the figure below, the data set is shown with the TLS fit plane.

Fig. 4 Unweighted Case for 3D data set

With this configuration, there are 1488 points are above the plane, and 1514 points are below. This is consistent with how a TLS fit should be applied. There is a large bump in this dataset that would be considered an undercut area. After weighting, the following fit plane is found.

Fig. 5 Weighted Case for 3D data set

With the WTLS fit plane, 707 points are above the fit plane, and 2295 points are below. This is a 47.5% decrease in the number of points in the undercut condition.

5 Conclusion

In this paper, a system to minimize the undercut condition in on-machine measurement was presented. By using a weighted total least squares method, the fitting process is conducted to minimize the undercut conditions on the best fitted surface. The developed methodology was then verified and tested against a two dimensional and three dimensional case. In both cases studies, the method successfully shifted the fit plane to achieve the desired minimization. For the tested piece, the undercut condition was reduced by 47.5%. This shows that the developed methodology may be used to minimize the undercut condition for planar surfaces in on-machine measurement systems. The developed methodology can be employed in various industrial applications including correction of the machining errors in closed-loops of inspection and machining, intermittent inspection and machining, repair of dies and tools, and post processing of products for precision manufacturing.

References

1. S. van Huffel, Recent advances in total least squares techniques and errors in variables modeling. SIAM (1997).
2. D.S. Zwick, Applications of Orthogonal Distance Regression in Metrology. Recent Adv. Total Least Squares Tech. Errors-in-variables Model. 93, 265–272 (1997).
3. L. Nielsen, Least-squares estimation using Lagrange multipliers. Metrologia. 35, 2, 115–118 (1998).
4. A.O. Nassef, H.A. ElMaraghy, Determination of Best Objective Function for Evaluating Geometric Deviations. Int. J. Adv. Manuf. Technol. 15, 2, 90–95 (1999).
5. M. Krystek, M. A Anton, weighted total least-squares algorithm for fitting a straight line. Meas. Sci. Technol. 18, 11, 3438–3442 (2007).
6. A. Malengo, F. Pennecchi, A weighted total least-squares algorithm for any fitting model with correlated variables. Metrologia. 50, 6, 654–662 (2013).
7. C.M. Shakarji, V. Srinivasan, Theory and Algorithms for Weighted Total Least-Squares Fitting of Lines, Planes, and Parallel Planes to Support Tolerancing Standards. J. Comput. Inf. Sci. Eng. 13, 3, 31008-1-31008–11 (2013).
8. V. Srinivasan, et al., On the Enduring Appeal of Least-squares Fitting in Computational Coordinate Metrology. (2013).
9. A. Barari, et al., Integrated Inspection and Machining Approach to Machining Error Compensation: Advantages and Limitations. Proc. FAIM. 563–572 (2004).
10. A. Barari, A Best-Fit Method to Maximize Conformance to Tolerance in Surface Coordinate Metrology. J. C. 7, 1, 20–27 (2012).
11. H. Gohari, A. Barari, A Quick Deviation Zone Fitting in Coordinate Metrology of NURBS Surfaces Using Principle Component Analysis. Measurements. 92, 352–364 (2016).
12. A. Barari, Inspection of the machined surfaces using manufacturing data. Journal of Manufacturing Systems 32, Issue 1, 07-113 (2013)
13. A. Barari, Sources of Uncertainty in Coordinate Metrology of Automotive Body. Proceedings of 2nd CIRP International Conference on Assembly Technologies and Systems, 21-23 (CATS 2008)

Uncertainty estimation of an auto-compensated laser interferometer systems calibration

Bousselham Samoudi*

National School of Applied Sciences of Safi, Cadi Ayyad University
Sidi Bouzid's Road, BP 63, Safi 46000, Morocco

Received:

Abstract. The purpose of this article is to overview the art's state of laser interferometer systems calibration, including a theoretical background measurement of length, as a power technique widely used in industry for direct precision measurement of length and displacement. Such essential periodic laser interferometer calibration confirms the traceability measurement chain to the absolute standard for the metre. The measurement method and modelequation, which serves as the basis for the uncertainty evaluation, is described. The uncertainty evaluation is performed in accordance with the document JCGM 100:2008-Evaluation of measurement data – Guide to the expression of uncertainty in measurement (GUM).

Keywords: Uncertainty, Length standard, Laser interferometer systems, Edlèn formula, GUM

1 Introduction

A Laser interferometer systems is any optical instruments used for displacement measurement based on laser light interference [1]. It is used for very small linear measurements and have taken over from gauge blocks as the most useful dimensional metrology devices in many applications [2]. Lasers are now used in a wide variety of measuring instruments and systems from range finders that can measure the distance to the moon to a fraction of a millimetre to xy wafer steppers for the semiconductor industry that control the position of a silicon wafer to a fraction of nanometre [3]. Lasers have been utilised for many years, mainly for the assessment of a diverse range of physical properties but principally for precise distance-measurement.

Laser measurement is fundamentally based on the principle of optical interferometry a basic beam and its return beam, which carries certain dimensional information. This return beam is normally reflected from a specially manufactured matched-optic such as an accurately positioned reflective mirror which is placed on an observed object, via an interferometric optical source. The main problem during laser measurement assessment is the–laser beam stability. From the time when laser beam wavelength is utilised as a measuring-length, the influence of the environmental conditions, such as ambient temperature; humidity; thermal air-flow; plus other contributory factors; must be effectively and consistently controlled [4].

* Correspondence: b.samoudi@uca.ma

Calibration can define the accuracy, precision, as well as the quality of measurements being recorded utilising specific plant and equipment. Hence, over time, there is a tendency for these results and its attendant-accuracy and precision to drift. This drifting is particularly noticeable when utilising certain levels of high technologies, or measuring particular parameters such as exacting dimensional measurements, in association with changes in the local ambient temperature, humidity and to a lesser extent, by air-movement—typically by drafts and/or thermal air-currents.

Accordingly, to be confident in the metrological results being measured, there is an on-going need to both service and maintain the calibration of equipment throughout its lifetime for reliable, accurate, and repeatable measurements [4].

The calibration of a laser interferometric system that will be used in the air consists first in determining the value of λ_0, and in checking the calculation of the refractive index (equal to the inverse of the correction factor) provided by the automatic compensator , as well as the calibration of the environment and material temperature sensors, and the checking of the system counter

The paper is organized as follows: in Section 2 we briefly describe the state of the art of laser interferometer systems calibration, including an overview of theoretical background measurement of displacement. Section 3 outlines the principle and calibration procedures based on beat frequency technique for the determination of wavelength in vacuum. According to Edlén equation, the refractive index of air affects the wavelength of laser. To overcome this difficulty, air refractive index will be compensated. Finally, Section 4 summarizes most of sources contributions to uncertainty of measurement according to GUM approach.

2 Theoretical background

A laser interferometer measures displacement using interferometry. Most laser interferometers have the same configuration as the Michelson interferometer. One of the reflecting mirrors of the Michelson interferometer is attached to the object whose displacement is to be measured. The two main types of laser interferometers are the homodyne type and the heterodyne type, being the latter take advantage in terms of measurement accuracy.

Consider two linearly polarized light waves on photodetectors $\vec{E}_1$ and $\vec{E}_2$, whose polarizationdirections are the same and optical frequencies are E_{01} and E_{02}, respectively. These waves are expressed by [5].

$$\vec{E}_1 = E_{01} e^{i(2\pi f_1 t + \Phi_{01})} \vec{e}_1 \tag{1}$$

$$\vec{E}_2 = E_{02} e^{i(2\pi f_2 t + \Phi_{02})} \vec{e}_2 \tag{2}$$

where E_{01} and E_{02} are the amplitudes of reference and measurement signal respectively; Φ_{01} and Φ_{02} are the phases of the waves.

The interference signal between the two light waves is expressed by

$$I(t) = \langle |\vec{E}_1 + \vec{E}_2|^2 \rangle \tag{3}$$

$$I(t) = E_{01}^2 + E_{02}^2 + 2E_{01}E_{02}\cos[2\pi(f_1 - f_2)t + (\Phi_{01} - \Phi_{02})] \tag{4}$$

The detected signal of this first detector is proportional to:

$$I_r = 2E_{01}E_{02}\cos[2\pi(f_1 - f_2)t + (\Phi_{01} - \Phi_{02})] \tag{5}$$

This first beating signal is called the reference signal, I_r, its frequency, being very stable and equal to the frequency difference of the beams, which is precisely that generated by the Zeeman effect in one case or that of the AOM excitation in the other.

Each beam travels with different paths in the interferometer, one towards the fixed reflector and another towards the mobile reflector. After passing through a polarizer, both beams are physically joined together, detecting their beating in a second photodetector, I_m

$$I_m = 2E_{01}E_{02}\cos[2\pi(f_1 - f_2)t + (\Phi_{01} - \Phi_{02}) + [(\Phi]_m - \Phi_r)] \tag{6}$$

I_r and I_m differ only in a phase that is proportional to the difference of paths traveled by each beam. This second signal, I_m, is called a measurement signal, its phase and instantaneous frequency are variable during the displacement of the mobile reflector. When the moving reflector moves, this phase difference depends on time, generating a Doppler shift of the frequency of the second beam that is proportional to the speed, v so,

$$\Delta f = \frac{2vf_2}{v_1} = \frac{2vnf_2}{c} \tag{7}$$

The phase difference between the reference and measured signals at the points of rest of the moving mirror will be the temporal integral of the frequency variation between the corresponding instants,

$$\Delta\Phi = \int_{t_1}^{t_2} 2\pi\Delta f dt = \int_{t_1}^{t_2} \frac{2vnf_2}{c} dt \tag{8}$$

$$\Delta\Phi = 2\pi\frac{nf_2}{c}\int_{t_1}^{t_2} v\, dt = 4\pi n\frac{f_2}{c}\Delta l \tag{9}$$

That is, to determine the displacement of the mobile reflector, it is necessary to measure the phase difference between both signals. Displacements in opposite directions cause negative or positive phase increases, being his discernment very simple.

$$\Delta l = \frac{\Delta\Phi \lambda_2}{4\pi n} \tag{10}$$

For precise interferometry, the stability of the laser frequency is important. The two frequencies are usually generated by a two-mode stabilized laser, a Zeeman laser, an acousto-optic modulator (AOM). The beat frequency is ~600 MHz in the case of a He–Ne two-mode stabilized laser, f_1 and f_2, (linearly polarized in quadrature) in the range of a few hundred kilohertz to a few megahertz in the case of a Zeeman laser and several tens of megahertz in the case of an AOM [6]. A higher beat frequency means a faster measurable movement speed.

3 Laser interferometer systems calibration method

The frequency beat is a heterodyne technique that allows the measurement of the unknown frequency in comparison with frequency standards [7-8]. In previous studies, this technique is used for the absolute frequency measurement of an iodine-stabilised He–Ne laser operated according to the current international recommendations at 633 nm; by optical frequency comb generator are published [9]. Recently we used the same method to measure the absolute frequency of Zeeman-stabilized He–Ne lasers operating at 633nmby an optical frequency comb generator [10]. Due to the detector response used, the optical frequency measurement requires that the frequency difference between the reference and the measurand does not exceed some GHz.

Fig. 1 shows the heterodyne-type laser interferometer method used to measure the displacement of a corner reflector [11-13]. Light beams with different frequencies, f_1 and f_2, are linearly polarized, and the directions of polarization are orthogonal to each other.In order to make the reference beat signalwith a

frequency of $|f_1 - f_2|$, portions of the light beams are refl ected by a beam splitter (BS). These light beams pass through a polarizer with a direction of 45° and generate the beat signal on a photodetector. The remaining light beams are incident on a polarization beam splitter (PBS). The reflected light by PBS, whose optical frequency is f_1, traverses the fixed path with a stable corner reflector and is reflected by the PBS again. The transmitted light with an optical frequency of f_2 traverses the changing path with a moving corner reflector and is transmitted to the PBS. These two beams interfere and generate a beat signal on another photodetector after passing through a polarizer.
The phase difference between the measurement beat signal and reference beat signal indicates the displacement of the moving corner reflector.
A corner reflector is useful because it reflects the light beam back in the same direction without feedback to the laser light source. However, some applications require the use of a plane mirror instead of a corner reflector. In this case, the measurement beam traverses a measurement path twice. As a result, the resolution is doubled compared to that of a corner reflector [6].

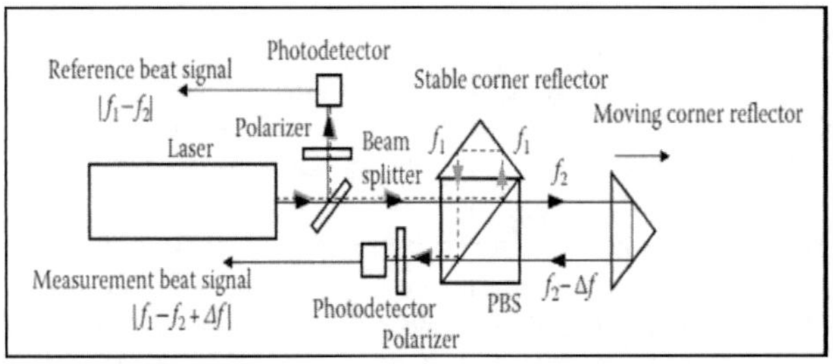

Fig. 1. Heterodyne-type laser interferometer method for the displacement measurement of a corner reflector and PD: photodetector (Image © [6]).

For the calibration of a complete laser measurement system it is necessary to follow these steps:

a) Calibration of the wavelength in the vacuum of the laser, as well as its variation during several hours of operation, which gives an idea of its stability over time.
b) Verification of the refractive index (inverse of the correction factor of the wavelength provided by the automatic compensator), including at this point the calibration of the ambient sensors.
c) Calibration of material temperature sensors.
d) Verification of the system counter.
e) Assessment of the complete system.

Taking into account the previous approach, the calibration can be divided into three parts:

3.1 Determination of the wavelength in the vacuum, λ_0.

It is carried out by means of the technique of beat frequency, which is the beating frequency between the laser to be calibrated and the reference laser. The latter being usually a He-Ne laser stabilized by an ion absorption cell, emitting at 474 THz. The Iodo cell is located inside the resonant cavity. The design complies with the 1983 recommendations of the International Committee of Weights and Measures, later revised in recommendation 1 (CI-1997) [14].
The measurements are taken for more than ten hours of operation, counting after the calibration laser has stabilized according to the manufacturer's specifications.
One of the fundamental limitations is that they are susceptible to variations in the speed of light due to variations in the refractive index of the air. Therefore, in any interferometry measurement, environmental conditions must be measured to calculate the wavelength compensation factor.
Once the wavelength of the laser in calibration is obtained, the calculation of the refractive index (inverse of the correction factor of the wavelength provided by the automatic compensator) is verified, including at this point the calibration of the ambient sensors. The pressure sensor will be calibrated in the pressure laboratory and according to the appropriate procedures.
The determination of the refractive index can be obtained in the medium by measuring the factors on which the refractive index depends and by applying mathematical approximations to the calculation of the refractive index. For the measurement of habitual interferometric distances the formula of Edlén is used [15-17].

$$(n-1)_{tp} = \frac{\left(\frac{p}{\mathrm{Pa}}\right)(n-1)_s}{96\,095{,}43}$$
$$x\,\frac{\left[1+10^{-8}\left(0{,}601-0{,}00972\frac{t_{90}}{°\mathrm{C}}\right)\frac{p}{\mathrm{Pa}}\right]}{\left(1+0{,}0036610\frac{t_{90}}{°\mathrm{C}}\right)} \quad (11)$$

where $(n-1)_{tp}$ is the refractivity of air at atemperature t and atmospheric pressure p and $(n-1)_s$ is given by the revised dispersion equation:

$$(n-1)_s \, x\, 10^8 = 8342{,}54 + 2406147x\left[130-\left(\frac{\sigma}{\mu\mathrm{m}^{-1}}\right)^2\right]^{-1} \quad (12)$$

For the difference in the refractive index of moist air, containing a partial pressure f of water vapour, anddry air at the same total pressure the following revisedexpression has been obtained:

$$\left(n_{tpf}-n_{tp}\right) = -\left(\frac{f}{Pa}\right)$$
$$x\left[3{,}7345-0{,}040-\left(\frac{\sigma}{\mu\mathrm{m}^{-1}}\right)^2\right]^{-1} x10^{-10} \quad (13)$$

The 3σ uncertainty associated with these equations is 3×10^{-8} (mainly due to uncertainties in pressure, temperature and humidity measurement) and appliesto ambient atmospheric conditions over the range of wavelengths 350 nm to 650 nm [17].

3.2 Assessment of the calculation of the refractive index, n

It will be studied from the results contained in the certificates issued for the different sensors, taking the errors that contribute most to the error in the calculation of the refractive index. It is not necessary to calibrate the humidity sensor, since it has a minimal influence on the refractive index; it is enough to verify by comparison with the laboratory's standard sensor that the values are within a reasonable range. In addition, in some equipment there is no such sensor, but a fixed value of humidity is selected through a switch.
The refractive index is calculated by the interferometric system from the values indicated by the sensor or ambient sensors. In order to determine the deviation of the values obtained by the equipment with respect to conventionally true values, the difference between the results calculated by the equipment and those obtained by the Edlèn equation [17] for the same input data is studied, on the one hand, the contributions to the error derived from the results contained in the calibration certificates of the different sensors, taking the errors that most contribute to the error of the calculation of the refractive index. Usually the range of temperatures goes from 10 °C to 30 °C and the one of pressures of 650 mmHg to 750 mmHg, but these ranges can vary.

3.3 Verification of the counter, N

It is carried out by comparing the system in calibration with a laser-reference system. For this purpose, the reference laser and the calibration laser are aligned in the path configuration and common optical elements, both arranged for distance measurement. Distance measurements are taken every meter with each of the equipment, using the same compensation factor in the two systems.

Finally, an assessment of the complete measurement system is made, where the values indicated by an interferometric system with laser and reference sensors are compared with those of the interferometric system that we are calibrating, with its laser and calibrated sensors. The difference between these values must be close to the error evaluated in the calibration together with its associated uncertainty.
The calibration will be carried out provided that the environmental conditions of the laboratory usually are kept within the following limits: Temperature: (20 ± 0,5) °C and Humidity: (45 ± 10) %.

4 Evaluating measurement uncertainty

The measurement uncertainty is evaluated following the rules of the Guide to the Expression of the Uncertainty in Measurement or GUM [18]. In the terminology of the GUM, statistical evaluation of the uncertainty groups the uncertainty components as type A and all others as type B.
The combined standard uncertainty is the sum of squared standard uncertainty components. Each component represents the standard uncertainty associated to each factor that has influence on the measurement results.
For the distances measurement, a laser system interferometric is usually configured in such a way that the length measured in the medium is a multiple of the half-wavelength, that is,

$$L = \frac{N\,\lambda_0}{2\,n} \qquad (14)$$

where, L is conventionally true length, N the number of reference system accounts, n the refractive index seen by the reference system, and λ_0 the wavelength in the vacuum of the reference system.

The mathematical model associated to the measurement of distances by means of laser interferometric systems, reflects the deviation of the distance measurement results of the interferometric system in calibration with respect to the reference standards used, and can be expressed in the form,

$$\Delta L = L_0 - L + C_{cos} = f(N_c, N, n_c, n, \lambda_c, \lambda_0, C_{cos\square}) \qquad (15)$$

where L is the nominal length, N_c is the number of system counting at calibration, N is the number of counting of the reference system, n_c is the refractive index seen by the system in calibration, n is the refractive index seen by the reference system, λ_c is the wavelength in the vacuum of the system at calibration, λ_0 is the wavelength in the vacuum of the reference system and $C_{cos\square}$ correction for misalignment between the beams.

$$\Delta L = L \times \left(\frac{N_c - N}{N} - \frac{n_c - n}{n} + \frac{\lambda_c - \lambda_0}{\lambda} \right) + C_{cos\square} \qquad (16)$$

Applying the law of propagation of uncertainty, the corresponding expression is obtained by using combined standard uncertainty $u_c(\Delta L)$ (assuming the absence of correlations)

$$u_c^2(\Delta L) = \left(\frac{\partial f}{\partial N_c}\right)^2 u^2(N_c) + \left(\frac{\partial f}{\partial N}\right)^2 u^2(N) + \left(\frac{\partial f}{\partial n_c}\right)^2 u^2(n_c) + \left(\frac{\partial f}{\partial n}\right)^2 u^2(n) + \left(\frac{\partial f}{\partial \lambda_c}\right)^2 u^2(\lambda_c) + \left(\frac{\partial f}{\partial \lambda}\right)^2 u^2(\lambda) + u^2(C_{cos\square}) \qquad (17)$$

That is,

$$u_c^2(\Delta L) = \left(\frac{L}{N}\right)^2 u^2(N) + \left(-\frac{L}{n}\right)^2 u^2(n) + \left(\frac{L}{\lambda}\right)^2 u^2(\lambda_0) + \left(\frac{L}{N_c}\right)^2 u^2(N_c) + \left(-\frac{L}{n_c}\right)^2 u^2(n_c) + \left(\frac{L}{\lambda_c}\right)^2 u^2(\lambda_c) + u^2(C_{cos\square}) \qquad (18)$$

Each of the contributions to uncertainty is analyzed below.

4.1 Wavelength of the reference laser, λ_0

The wavelength of the laser is determined by comparison with a reference laser; that is, using the following equation

$$\lambda_0 = \frac{c}{f_{ref} + \delta f_0} \qquad (19)$$

where c is the speed of light in the vacuum, f_{ref} is the frequency of the reference laser, and δf_0 is the measured values of the frequency differences between the two lasers. Following the propagation law of uncertainty, the combined standard uncertainty $u_c(\lambda_0)$ of the measured standard wavelength λ_0 is

$$u_c^2(\lambda_0) = \left(\frac{\partial \lambda_0}{\partial f_{ref}}\right)^2 u^2(f_{ref}) + \left(\frac{\partial \lambda_0}{\partial \delta f_0}\right)^2 u^2(\delta f_0) \qquad (20)$$

$$u_c^2(\lambda_0) = \left(\frac{\lambda_0^2}{c^2}\right)\left[u^2(f_{ref}) + u^2(\delta f_0)\right] \qquad (21)$$

One of the most important recommended radiations, as the reference laser, in the field of length metrology and worldwide precision measurements is that at 474 THz (633 nm) from a He–Ne laser, stabilized on an absorbing hyperfine component in $^{127}I^2$. The relative standard uncertainty of its frequency is estimated at $2{,}1 \times 10^{-11}$ [19]; thus, its contribution to the uncertainty in the determination of the wavelength is negligible. However, if another type of reference laser is used, the value of its uncertainty must be quantified and taken into account in the calculation of the final uncertainty value.
The speed of light is considered constant and without associated uncertainty, in what refers to the definition of the unit of length.

The uncertainty associated to the mean value of the frequency differences between the two lasers is estimated using a type B evaluation of uncertainty. To do so, we consider a type of rectangulardistribution, with an amplitude $(f_{max} - f_{min})$, where the firstis the maximum value and the second is the minimum oneof the frequencies found

$$u(\delta f_0) = \frac{(f_{max} - f_{min})}{2\sqrt{3}} \qquad (22)$$

The coefficient of sensitivity, c_{λ_0}, according to the expression (18)

$$c_{\lambda_0} = \frac{L}{\lambda_0} \qquad (23)$$

Assigning a number of degrees of freedom $v_i = 100$, this is a conservative approach by which the rectangular distributions are associated with an effective number of degrees of freedom equal to 100, to avoid an "infinite" number of degrees, which would suppose a total security as regard to the limit's values of distribution.

4.2Wavelength of the calibration laser λ_c

The wavelength of the laser in calibration is a value given by the manufacturer, and introduced in the calculation of the distance measured by the interferometric system. It is assumed without associated uncertainty

$$u(\lambda_c) = 0 \qquad (24)$$

4.3Evaluation of the refractive index , n

The conventionally true refractive index n is calculated by the Edlén's formula [17] with the data obtained from the calibration certificates of the environmental conditions sensors. Then we must consider the calibration uncertainties of the sensors for the determination of the uncertainty of the value of the refractive index. Taking into account that

$$n = F(\sigma, t_{90}, p, f) \qquad (25)$$

$$u_c^2(n) = \sum_{i=1}^{N}\left[c_i u(x_i)\right]^2 = \sum_{i=1}^{N} u_i^2(n) \qquad (26)$$

$$u_c^2(n) = u_{\lambda_0}^2(n) + u_p^2(n) + u_t^2(n) + u_f^2(n) \qquad (27)$$

For usual working conditions in many laboratories, such as $\lambda_0 = 632{,}999\,354$ nm ; $t = 20\,°C$; $P = 93{,}325$ kPa ; and $f = 1{,}172\,5$ kPa
The following sensitivity coefficients are obtained

$$c_p = \frac{\partial n}{\partial p} = 3 \times 10^{-9}\,\mathrm{Pa}^{-1} \qquad (28)$$

$$c_f = \frac{\partial n}{\partial f} = 3{,}63 \times 10^{-9}\,\mathrm{Pa}^{-1} \qquad (29)$$

$$c_{\lambda_0} = \frac{\partial n}{\partial \lambda_0} = -1{,}14 \times 10^{-6}\,\mu\mathrm{m}^{-1} \qquad (30)$$

Since u_{λ_0} is a very low value in this type of measurements, they have almost no weight in the calculation of the uncertainty associated with the refractive index .In addition, the uncertainty of Edlén's formula must be taken into account, which, according to the reference [17] is 3×10^{-8} for 3σ .It results

$$u^2(n) = \left[3 \times 10^{-9} \times u(p)\right]^2 + \left[8{,}86 \times 10^{-7} \times u(t)\right]^2 + \left[3{,}63 \times 10^{-10} \times u(f)\right]^2 + \left(1 \times 10^{-8}\right)^2 \qquad (31)$$

The coefficient of sensitivity, c_n, according to the expression (19)

$$c_n = \frac{L}{n} \approx L \qquad (32)$$

The degrees of freedom are obtained using the Welch-Satterthwaite formula [18] from the values obtained from the partial uncertainties,

4.4 Evaluation of the refractive index by the system under calibration, n_c.

Due to the fact that the interferometric system in calibration uses a different formula than Edlén to calculate the refractive index, normally a simplified version, the difference observed by this fact is studied. To do this, ten measurements are made and the value of n is evaluated for the same values of environmental conditions.

One of the contributions to uncertainty will be obtained as type-A evaluation

$$s^2 = \frac{1}{N' - 1}\sum_{j=1}^{m}\left(x_j - \bar{x}_j\right)^2 \qquad (33)$$

$$u(n_{c1}) = \frac{s}{\sqrt{10}} \qquad (34)$$

Another contribution is due to the resolution, in many cases it is of the order of 10^{-7}. Considering a rectangular distribution

$$u(n_{c2}) = \frac{10^{-7}}{2\sqrt{3}} \qquad (35)$$

$$u^2(n_c) = u^2(n_{c1}) + u^2(n_{c2}) \qquad (36)$$

The coefficient of sensitivity, c_{n_c}, according to the expression (19)

$$c_{n_c} = \frac{L}{n_0} \approx L \qquad (37)$$

4.5Number of accounts of the reference system N

The counter is calibrated by comparison with a reference, aligning the two beams, in such a way that they travel the same optical path, using common optical elements and the same values of environmental conditions. The uncertainty associated with this process is the uncertainty of the reference counter. Taking into account that in this type of equipment the minimum resolution is usually $0.01\ \mu m$, is obtained:

$$Resol. = \frac{0.01\ \mu m}{\frac{\lambda}{2}} = 3.13\ x10^{-2}\ \text{fringe fraction} \qquad (38)$$

$$u^2(N) = \frac{3.13\ x10^{-2}}{2\sqrt{3}}\text{fringe fraction} \qquad (39)$$

The coefficient of sensitivity, c_N, according to the expression (18)

$$c_N = \frac{L}{n} = \frac{\lambda_0}{2} \qquad (40)$$

4.6 Number of accounts of the reference system under calibration, N_c.

Analogously to the previous section, the uncertainty due to the number of accounts of the system under calibration depends on the resolution of the instrument. Taking into account that in this type of equipment, the minimum resolution is normally $0.01\ \mu m$. Considering a rectangular distribution

$$Resol. = \frac{0.01\ \mu m}{\frac{\lambda}{2}} = 3.13\ x10^{-2}\ \text{fringe fraction} \qquad (41)$$

$$u^2(N_c) = \frac{3.13\ x10^{-2}}{2\sqrt{3}}\text{fringe fraction} \qquad (42)$$

The coefficient of sensitivity c_{N_c} according to the expression (19)

$$c_{N_c} = \frac{L}{n} = \frac{\lambda}{2} \qquad (43)$$

4.7cosine error, C_{cos}

When the measurement axis is not parallel to the moving axis, a cosine error is induced [6]. Alignment of the measurement and moving axes should be performed by moving the corner reflector or reflecting mirror as much as possible in order to minimize the cosine error. If a misalignment of 3 mm in 25 meters is assumed, the cosine error of $7\ x10^{-9}L$. Considering a rectangular distribution

$$u(C_{cos}) = \frac{7\ x10^{-9}L}{2\sqrt{3}} = 2.02\ x10^{-9}L \qquad (44)$$

By collecting everything and substituting, we end up with the model equation

$$u_c^2(\Delta L) = \left(\frac{\lambda_0}{2}\right)^2 u^2(N) + (-L)^2 u^2(n) + \left(\frac{L}{\lambda_0}\right)^2 u^2(\lambda_0) + \left(\frac{\lambda_0}{2}\right)^2 u^2(N_c) + (-L)^2 u^2(n_c) + u^2(C_{cos}) \qquad (45)$$

$$u_c^2(\Delta L) = [L^2((\Delta u(f_s(ref))/f_{ref})^2 + (((f_{max} - f_{min}))/(2\sqrt{3}))^2 + (3\ x\ 10^{(-9)}\ x\ u(p))^2 + (8,56\ x\ 10^{(-7)}\ x\ u(t))^2 + (3,63\ x\ 10^{(-10)}\ x\ u(f))^2 + (1\ x\ 10^{(-8)})^2 + (s/\sqrt{10})^2 + (10^{(-7)}/(2\sqrt{3}))^2 + (2,02\ x\ 10^{(-9)})^2)$$

The influence parameters and the associated standard uncertainties have been listed in Table 1.

Table 1. The uncertainty budget

Input			Probability	Uncertainty	sensitivity	Contribution	Degrees

quantities X_i	Symbol	Value	distributions	$u(x_i)$	coefficient $\|c_i\|$	uncertainty $u_i(L)$	of freedom ν
Vacuum wavelenght	λ_0				1	$4.88 x 10^{-9} L$	100
Frequency variation	δf	8 MHz	Rectangular	2.31 MHz	$2.11 x 10^{-9} \lambda_0$		100
Wavelength of the calibration laser	λ_c			0			
Refraxive index n	$n = F(t_{e0}, p, f)$	$2.8 x 10^{-7}$	Normal	$1.4 x 10^{-7}$	$1 L$	$1.4 x 10^{-7} \lambda_0$	135
Refraxive index n_c	n_c			$2.89 x 10^{-8}$	$1 L$	$2.89 x 10^{-8} L$	100
Repeatability	$s(n_c)$	$5.0 x 10^{-9}$	Normal	$2.041 x 10^{-9}$			9
Resolution	$r(n_c)$	$1.0 x 10^{-7}$	Rectangular	$2.88 x 10^{-8}$			100
Reference counter number	N	0.0316 fringe	Rectangular	$9.12 x 10^{-3}$ fringe	$0.32\ \mu m$	$2.89 x 10^{-3} \mu m$	100
Number of counter of system under calibration	N_c	0.0316 fringe	Rectangular	$9.12 x 10^{-3}$ fringe	$0.32\ \mu m$	$2.89 x 10^{-3} \mu m$	100
cosine error (up to 25 m)	C_{cos}	$7.0 x 10^{-9}$	Rectangular	$2.02 x 10^{-9}$	1	$2.02 x 10^{-9} L$	100

4.8 Calculation of the expanded uncertainty

The expanded uncertainty, U, is obtained by multiplying the combined standard uncertainty $u_c(\Delta L)$ to the coverage factor k

$$U = k \, . \, u_c(\Delta L) \qquad (47)$$

where k is a function of the effective degrees of freedom obtained by Welch–Satterthwaite formula [18], from the values and the degrees of freedom of the partial uncertainties, for the desired confidence value, typically 95 %. If it can be assumed a normal distribution the factor $k = 2$ is often used.

5 Conclusion

The laser interferometry is an efficient tool for length and displacement measurement. A detailed procedure to calibrate laser interferometer systems is given. The uncertainty evaluation is performed by taking the most sources contributing to standard uncertainty, in accordance with the document JCGM 100:2008-Evaluation of measurement data – Guide to the expression of uncertainty in measurement (GUM).

References

1. N.V. Raghavendra and L. Krishnamurthy, Engineering Metrology and Measurements", Oxford University Press, p. 192 2013.
2. V. Zivkovic, S. Zelenika, and G. Stefanovic, Uncertainty evaluation for the gauge blocks calibration using the modified DMDM gauge block interferometer, Int. J. Metrol. Qual. Eng. **3**, 19–27 (2012).
3. D.Flack and J. Hannaford, Fundamental Good Practice in Dimensional Metrology, Edit. Queen's Printer and Controller of HMSO, 2012.
4. G.T. Smith, Laser Instrumentation and Calibration. In: Machine Tool Metrology. Springer International Publishing Switzerland, p. 204-205 (2016)
5. Eugene Helcht, Optics, Pearson Education, 2017.
6. A. Hirai, M. Kajima, and S. Telada, Displacement. In: Handbook of Optical Metrology: principles and Applications, CRC Press, p. 394-395, 2008.
7. P. Hariharan, Basics of interferometry. Elsevier (2007).
8. W. R. C Rowley, Analysis of laser frequency stability by heterodyne measurement, NPL Report MOM 78, 1986.
9. B. Samoudi, M. Mar Pérez-Hernández, S. Ferreira-Barragáns, E. Prieto,Absolute optical frequency measurements on iodine stabilized He–Ne at 633 nm by using a femtosecond laser frequency comb, Int. J. Metrol. Qual. Eng. **3**, 101–106 (2012).
10. BousselhamSamoudi, Realisation of the metre by using a femtosecond laser frequency comb: applications in optical frequency metrology, Int. J. Metrol. Qual. Eng. **8**, 16- (2017).
11. Laser and Optics User's Manual, Chap. 7A, Linear interferometers and retroreflectors, Agilent Technologies, 2002 (available on Agilent's Web site).

12. L.J. Wuerz, and R.C. Quenelle, Laser interferometer system for metrology and machine tool applications, Prec. Eng., **5**, 111, (1983).
13. F.C. Demarest, High-resolution, high-speed, low data age uncertainty, heterodyne displacement measuring interferometer electronics, Meas. Sci. Technol., **9**, 1024 (1998).
14. T.J. Quinn; Practical realization of the definition of the metre (1997), Metrologia, **36**, 211-244 (1999).
15. B. Edlèn ; The Refractive Index of Air, Metrologia, **2**, 71-80 (1966).
16. K.P Birch and M.J.Downs, An Updated Edlén Equation for the Refractive Index of Air, Metrologia, **30**, 155-162 (1993).
17. K. P. Birch and M. J. Downs, Correction to the Updated Edlèn Equation for the Refractive Index of Air, Metrologia, **31**, 315-316, (1994).
18. BIPM, Evaluation of measurement data – Guide to theexpression of uncertainty in measurement, JCGM 100 (2008)
19. T.J. Quinn, International report: Practical realization of the definition of the metre, including recommended radiations of other optical frequency standards (2001), Metrologia **40**,103–133 (2003).

Towards a High-accurate Metrology for Optical Asphere and Freeform Surfaces

Y. Arezki (1,2*), C-M. Souzani (2), N. Anwer (3), and H. Nouira (1*)

[1]Laboratoire Commun de Métrologie, Laboratoire National de Métrologie et d'Essais (LNE), 1 Rue Gaston Boissier, 75015 Paris, France
[2]LURPA, ENS Cachan, Université. Paris-Sud, Université Paris 13, Sorbonne Paris Cité, Université Paris-Saclay, 94235 Cachan, France
[3]LURPA, ENS Paris-Saclay, Univ. Paris-Sud, Université Paris-Saclay, 94235 Cachan, France

Abstract. Aspheric and freeform (non-symmetric features) surfaces are a very challenging class of optical elements. Their applications have grown considerably in the last few years in areas such as imaging systems, lithography, automotive, etc. The reason for this growth is that aspheres and freeform surfaces are superior to classical spherical optics due to their additional degrees of freedom of geometry. Unlike standard optical surfaces such as spherical lenses, aspherical lenses and freeform provide superior optical performances especially for aberration control at multiple locations.

In this context, the European project "15SIB01-FreeFORM", lunched in 2016, aims at developing traceable metrology for asphere and freeform optical surfaces with accuracy less than 30 nm. The proposed topics include the development of reference minimum zone fitting algorithms, traceable measurement machines and original optical thermo-invariant standards.

Regarding its complicated description, freeforms metrology is challenging either during the process of measurement or data fitting. Data fitting complication increases when adopting infinite norm (L_∞) instead of Least Squares (L_2) to determine the Minimum Zone (MZ). In this context, a new algorithm named "Hybrid Trust Region method (HTR)" was implemented for Minimum Zone fitting of aspheric surfaces. HTR was applied and validated on generated specific reference data. The newly introduced algorithm was also applied to analyse data obtained by measuring a specific standard using an enhanced ultra-high precision profilometer directly traceable to the SI meter definition. The newly introduced method proved to be more efficient than existing methods.

Keywords: Dimensional metrology, Aspherics, Freeform, Data fitting, Minimum Zone, Optimization, Thermo-invariant standard, Ultra-high precision measuring machine

1 Introduction

In the context of optical design, an aspheric lens is defined as a rotationally symmetric surface with a radius of curvature that varies gradually from the centre of the lens. This class of optical elements represents various advantages over classical (spherical lenses) especially for their ability to eliminate spherical aberrations [1].

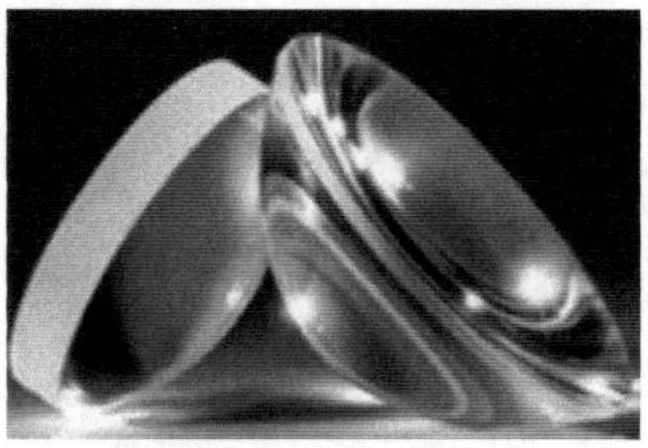

In recent decades, fields of application of aspherical lenses become wider (lithography, medical imaging, metrology, automotive, lasers, etc.) [2]. This fact is due to advancements in different manufacturing techniques especially glass and plastic moulding as well as grinding and polishing methods.

Minimum zone (MZ) determination is a crucial issue in metrology, its value indicates about form deviation of components. Form deviation plays an essential role in the function the aspheric must satisfy. To determine the Minimum Zone, form deviations, which are orthogonal distances between measured data and the reference surface, must first be determined. Peak-to-valley (PV) is the difference between the maximum and minimum deviations. MZ is the least value of peak-to-valley (PV). Two approaches exist to determine the so-called reference surface: Least Squares (LS) (also called Gaussian or L_2 fitting) and Minimax (Chebyshev, L_∞ fitting). The use of the formal method is widespread and most of industrial software consider LS fitting because of its simplicity. However, the MZ value given by LS is overestimated in approximately all cases. On the other hand, Chebyshev fitting gives more accurate value of MZ since it directly minimizes PV. Nevertheless, the mathematical handling of this method is more challenging since it results in the minimization of a non-smooth objective function [3, 4].

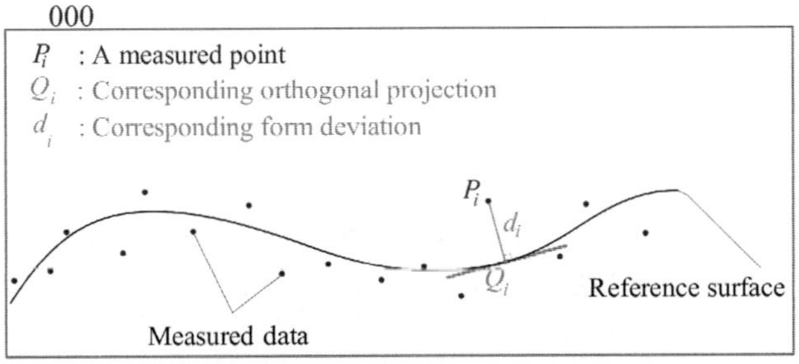

Fig. 1. Definition of form deviations

2 Aspherical representation

Various mathematical formulations exist to describe an aspherical lens, (splines, Zernike polynomials, Chebyshev polynomials, etc.). However, the one given by ISO 10110-12: 2007 (called monomial formulation) is the most used [5].

This formulation is given as an explicit equation. In cylindrical polar coordinates, the formulation is expressed as $z = f(r, \theta)$. Since aspheric shapes are rotationally symmetric, there is no angular dependence. Then $z = f(r)$ is applied instead.

$$z(r) = \frac{r^2}{R\left(1 + \sqrt{1 - (1+\kappa)\frac{r^2}{R^2}}\right)} + \sum_{m=0}^{M} a_{2m+4}\, r^{2m+4} \qquad (1)$$

Where:

z	:	sag of surface parallel to the optical axis
r	:	radial distance
R	:	radius of curvature at the vertex
κ	:	conic constant
a_{2m+4}	:	monomial coefficients

The aperture size of the lens (R_{max}) defines the domain of r : $0 \leq r \leq R_{max}$ for which equation (1) is valid. The number of monomial terms (M) depends on the desired accuracy.

Despite its simplicity, monomial formulation represents several drawbacks especially numerical instabilities resulting from heavy cancellations that occur because of high order polynomials. Moreover, LS fitting gives a seriously ill-conditioned Gram matrix. Besides, coefficients used in this formulation lack from physical meaning.

To cope with these drawbacks, further formulations were proposed. Most of them describe aspherical lenses using orthogonal polynomials, which gives a nearly diagonal Gram matrix, resulting in a more stable system and consequently more accuracy [6]. A detailed comparison of different formulations was established by Gross et al. in [7].

3. Minimum zone determination

Suppose given are a set of m measured data points $\{P_i\}_{1 \leq i \leq m}$ and their corresponding orthogonal projections $\{Q_i\}_{1 \leq i \leq m}$ onto a surface described by the mean of an implicit equation $f(q, s) = 0$, with $q = (x, y, z)$ are the coordinates of a given point on the surface and s are the surface' shape parameters. The minimum zone fitting problem could be formulated as in eq. (1).

$$\min_{x} \phi(x) \quad \text{where} \quad \phi(x) = \max_{1 \leq i \leq m} f_i(x) \qquad (2)$$

f_i denotes the Euclidean distance between the point P_i and its corresponding orthogonal projection Q_i , $x \in R^n$ could be either the set of intrinsic shape parameters s , or the motion parameters m : rotation and translation applied to $\{P_i\}$. Unlike LS fitting, the objective function to optimize is not smooth, which makes the minimax fitting more challenging.

3.1 Initial solution selection: L-BFGS algorithm

To find a solution for the optimization problem given in (2), iterative methods are used. In this case, an initial solution should be carefully chosen. Since LS solution is close to MZ one in most cases, LS is taken as an initial alignment.

To determine LS fitting, a quasi-Newtonian method: Low memory Broyden-Fletcher-Goldfarb-Shanno (L-BFGS) is convenient [8]. Similar to Newtonian method, L-BFGS aims to find a descent direction based on information incorporated in the Hessian matrix and the gradient vector with one difference: At each iteration, the Hessian is approximated using information from the last K iterations, where K is a user-defined parameter. With each time, the new approximation replacing the oldest one in the queue. In [4] El-Hayek et al show that this method has linear time complexity with respect to the number of points, run faster and provides similar or better results that the Levenberg-Marquardt (LM) method. It should be mentioned that one of the results investigated in this work is to verify the impact of initializing the MZ fitting with LS solution.

3.2 Review of literature

Different classes of methods such as computational geometry techniques [9], linear/nonlinear programming, smoothing techniques or free derivatives methods like downhill simplex search methods were used to determine the MZ for straightness, flatness, roundness and cylindricity tolerance [10]. The use of most of the cited methods could not be extended to complex geometries.

Only few works were conducted especially for aspherical shapes. In [11] L_p-norm is used to approximate L_∞ by gradually increasing p. The resulting objective function is smooth and the classical optimization techniques could be used. However, when p becomes high, numerical instabilities rise and the system becomes highly ill-conditioned. A heuristic nondeterministic optimization method called Differential Evolution algorithm (DE) is given in [12]. This method performs poorly for large clouds of points (>100.000). Other methods could be used for the same aim, namely, Exponential Penalty Function (EPF) and Primal-Dual Interior Points method (PDIP) detailed in [13] and [14] respectively. The formal method is a smoothing technique; the non-differentiable objective function is approximated via a parametrized objective function and optimized at each iteration until a termination criterion is satisfied. In the latter, the problem given in (2) is formulated as a constrained nonlinear optimization problem and the corresponding Lagrangian function is solved using Newtonian method.

4. The Hybrid Trust Region Algorithm (HTR)

The main idea of the Hybrid Trust Region algorithm consists of performing either trust region step, line search step or curve search step according to the specific situation faced at each iteration. This enables to avoid solving the trust region problem many times. For each iteration, a first point consists of obtaining a trust region trial step d_k by solving the quadratic problem $QP(x_k, B_k)$ given in (2).

$$\begin{aligned} &\min_{(d,z)\in\mathbb{R}^{n+1}} \frac{1}{2} < d, B_k d > + z = M_k(d,z) \\ &s.t. < \nabla f_i(x_k), d > - z \leq \phi(x_k) - f_i(x_k) \qquad i = 1,\dots,m \\ &\|d\|_\infty \leq \Delta_k \end{aligned} \tag{3}$$

Where B_k is n by n symmetric positive definite matrix, Δ_k is the parameter defining the trust region domain, z is an introduced parameter depending on the first derivative of the objective function ϕ , ∇f_i is the gradient of the function f_i and $<.,.>$ defines the dot product.

The trust region domain is defined using L_∞ instead of L_2 so as (QP) becomes an easily-solved quadratic problem. It should be mentioned that the proposed (QP) in (2) is always feasible since $(0,0)$ is a feasible solution. This problem could be solved using classical methods adapted to quadratic problems such as interior point method [15].

If the resulting trust region trial step d_k could not be accepted, a corrected step $d_k + \tilde{d}_k$ is determined by solving the problem $\widetilde{QP}(x_k, B_k)$ given in (3).

$$\begin{aligned} &\min_{(\tilde{d},z)\in\mathbb{R}^{n+1}} \frac{1}{2} < d_k + \tilde{d}, B_k(d_k + \tilde{d}) > + z = \tilde{M}_k(\tilde{d},z) \\ &s.t. < \nabla f_i(x_k), \tilde{d} > - z \leq \phi(x_k + d_k) - f_i(x_k + d_k)\; i = 1 \dots \\ &\|d_k + \tilde{d}\|_\infty \leq \Delta_k \end{aligned} \tag{4}$$

If neither the initial trust region step d_k nor the corrected step $d_k + \tilde{d}$ could be acceptable in trust region scheme, a line search along d_k or a curve search is performed if the d_k is a descent direction. If it is not the case, a curve search is used to find a step length t_k that verifies (4) where $\alpha \in \left(0, \frac{1}{2}\right)$.

$$\phi(x_k + t_k d_k + t_k^2 \tilde{d}_k) \leq \phi(x_k) - \alpha t_k < d_k, B_k d_k > \tag{5}$$

Where d_k is the solution of (2) and $\tilde{d}_k$ is the solution of (3). In the case $\|d_k\| \leq \|\tilde{d}_k\|$, $\tilde{d}_k$ should be taken to be 0.

For B_k update, the Powell's modification of BFGS formulas is used [16]. A detailed implementation of the algorithm is given in [17].

5. Application on reference data

The HTR algorithm was tested on reference data generated using Forbes method [18]. Reference data generation is based on the idea of stating optimality conditions and then deriving data sets for which optimality conditions are automatically satisfied. This method is able to generate only vertex solutions for the aspheric shapes Minimum Zone fitting problem. Only transformation parameters are sought, shape coefficients are supposed given (table 1). Data with a predefined number of points (N={121, 1024, 10404 and 100489}) and a previously known Minimum zone value MZ_{ref} ($MZ_{ref}=10^{-4}$) are generated. In order to assess the performance of the proposed algorithm in regards to Exponential Penalty Function algorithm (EPF) [13], each generated dataset were submitted at the same time to both algorithms: EPF and HTR. The corresponding PV values respectively PV_{EPF} and PV_{HTR}, as well as execution time, respectively T_{EPF} and T_{HTR}, are compared.

Table 1. Surface nominal coefficients used for reference data generation

	R (*mm*)	κ	a_4 (*mm*$^{-3}$)	a_6 (*mm*$^{-5}$)	a_8 (*mm*$^{-7}$)	a_{10} (*mm*$^{-9}$)
I	101.58	-1	-1.70 10^{-13}	-8.51 10^{-14}	-4.25 10^{-14}	-2.12 10^{-14}
II	19.79	-0.9	-1.51 10^{-17}	-7.55 10^{-18}	-3.77 10^{-18}	-1.88 10^{-19}
III	8.88	-0.8	-1.94 10^{-12}	-9.72 10^{-13}	-4.86 10^{-13}	-2.43 10^{-13}
IV	4.14	-0.9	-4.17 10^{-12}	-2.08 10^{-12}	-1.04 10^{-12}	-5.21 10^{-13}
V	0.77	-1	-2.22 10^{-11}	-1.11 10^{-11}	-5.56 10^{-12}	-2.78 10^{-12}

Table 2. : Values of $PV\text{-}MZ_{ref}$ and execution time for HTR and EPF (configuration III)

N	PV_{HTR}-MZ_{ref} (mm)	PV_{EPF}-MZ_{ref} (mm)	T_{HTR} (s)	T_{EPF} (s)
121	4.24 10^{-15}	1.13 10^{-14}	2.18	2.48

1024	2.18 10^{-16}	2.61 10^{-16}	4.32	4.47
10404	1.41 10^{-15}	3.08 10^{-15}	4.27	36.50
100489	6.73 10^{-15}	6.78 10^{-15}	20.52	255.06

Tables 2 illustrates obtained values of PV-MZ_{ref} as well as execution time for both algorithms (for configuration III). Concerning PV values, both algorithms give enough accurate results with superiority of HTR for all test cases. In fact, for approximately all generated data points, HTR returns PV values ten times more accurate than EPF. In regards to execution time, HTR clearly overcomes EPF. For the later algorithm, execution time is five times higher than the formal, especially for data points that exceed 1 000 points.

6. Experimental investigation

6.1 Overview

Freeforms are defined as surfaces with no axis of rotational invariance. Nowadays, freeform optics application has exponentially grown in various areas (energy, aerospace, illumination, medical systems, optical measurement systems etc.), offering new opportunities to optical designers and new challenges for optics manufacturing and measurement. Freeform optics enable a significant enhancement of optical devices' performance, such as simultaneously correcting aberrations, expanding field of view and increasing depth of field. As consequence, it leads to simplify system structure to fewer surfaces, lower mass, lower cost, smaller package-size and reduced stray-light, as well as to easily system integration and assembly [19].

Aspheric optics can be considered a special case of freeform optics with an axis of rotational invariance. In various applications, spherical lenses were used to replace several spherical lenses, as for example the objective lens from Schneider Optics where the use of one asphere led to half the size and weight and increased image quality [19]. More complex freeform surfaces may perform better. Olympus Corporation replaced all spherical lenses by only one freeformto implement the optical function leading to ever more reduced size and weight, as well as to better increase the image quality.

Freeform mirrors, including aspheres, have been used to solve the problem of astigmatism in traditional CTS (Czerny-turner spectrometer). It results in a reduction in sagittal spot size to around 10 mm.

Furthermore, aspherical lenses were used in green laser systems and gave appropriate energy concentration of the Gaussian distribution of laser source [20]

6.2 Optical elements design

In literature, two main strategies for optical design of optical components can be distinguished: multi-parameter optimization and direct mapping [21].

In multi-parameter optimization the optical requirement is defined as a quantitative merit function that is to be minimized.. The direct mapping method is called source-target mapping, which defines a truly accurate freeform solution that takes the light from the source distribution to the desired target distribution. The surface feature points are obtained using this method, and then modelled by fitting or interpolation to get freeform surfaces. Several important direct mapping methods are: (**I**) Partial differential equations method, (II) Point-to-point mapping method and (III) Simultaneous multiple surface (SMS) method.

(I) Partial differential equations method is based on establishment of a relationship between the three normal vectors of incident surface, target surface and optical surface by solving partial differential equations.

(II) Point-to-point mapping method is based on iterative solve of equation between the lighting energy emitted by the source and the lighting energy obtained by the target in order to get the surface form. This method is applied specially for general illumination tasks.

(III) Simultaneous multiple surface (SMS) method is based on ‘‘bundle coupling’’ and ‘‘prescribed irradiance’’. Optical components calculated by SMS method have the features of compactness, efficiency and simplicity.

6.3 Developed thermo-invariant material standard

Several material standards were designed and developed within the running project 15SIB01-FreeFORM [22], but in this paper, only one optical material standard made of Zerodur® material is selected and presented.

Zerodur® is a glass-ceramic produced by Schott AG, especially for a number of very large and also some smaller telescope mirrors in spatial applications. Zerodur® material is considered as a thermo-invariant material with a very low thermal expansion coefficient of less than $0.005\times10^{-6}\ K^{-1}$. Thus, it can be used to produce mirrors that retain acceptable figures in extremely cold environments such as deep space. Although, it has advantages for high-precision applications requiring low thermal expansion coefficient, which is the case in metrology. Further relevant characteristics of Zerodur® material are:

- high 3D homogeneity with few inclusions, bubbles and internal striae,
- hardness similar to borosilicate glass, so that it can be ground and polished easily,
- high affinity for coatings,
- low helium permeability,
- non-porous ceramics,
- good chemical stability.
- fracture toughness approximately 0.9 $MPa{\cdot}m^{1/2}$.

The strategy adopted to develop the thermo-invariant material standard is different from what presented in the previous section. Its design is selected such as to enable the validation and comparison of implemented minimum zone

(MZ) fitting algorithms. It consists of a traditional aspheric optical surface, as specified in ISO 10110-12:2007, combined with nine steps projected along orthogonal directions. The theoretical amplitude of the steps is equal to 7 µm, this value is selected with respect to the adopted manufacturing process. The final obtained optical surface presents neither axis of symmetry nor degree of invariance (figures 3, 4 and 5). The aspherical shape parameters are illustrated in table 3.

The role of the added steps is twofold. First, it is an added form error to illustrate departure from the ideal aspheric shape. Second, during the fitting of data points resulting from the measurement of the material standard, significant points defining the minimum zone lie exactly at the top of the steps and then the value of MZ could be previously known.

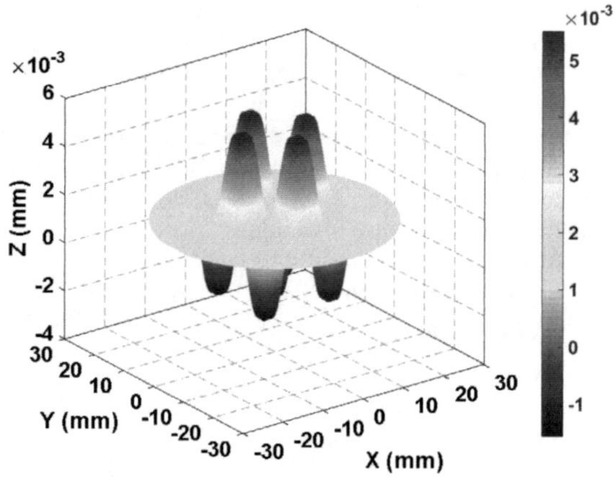

Fig. 3. Aspherical material standard design

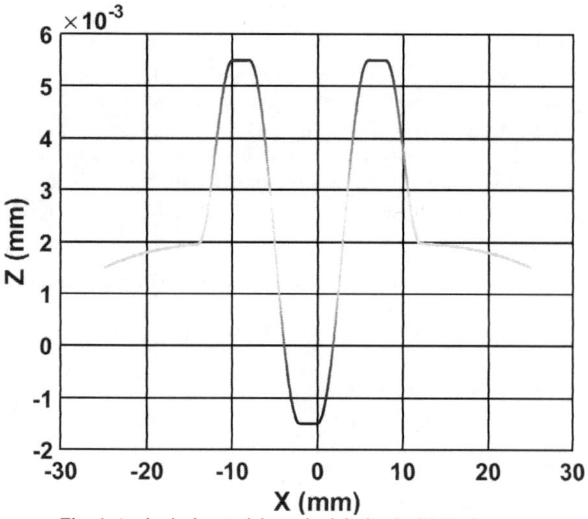

Fig. 4. Aspherical material standard design in (X,Z) plane

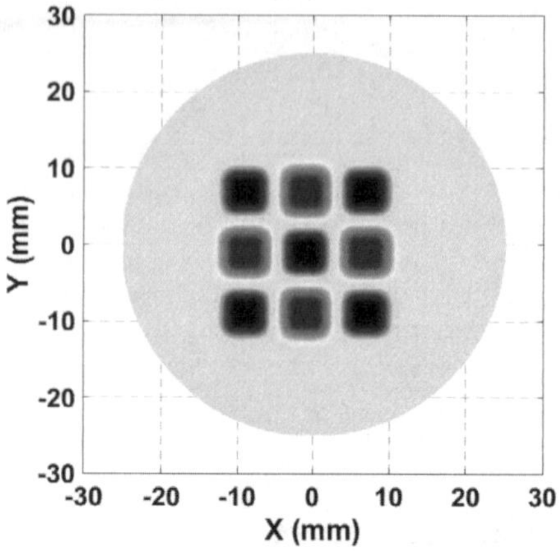

Fig. 5. Aspherical material standard design in (X,Y) plane

Table 3. Material standard shape parameters values

Parameter	Value
R_{max}	9.127e+40
κ	-1
a_4	1.278e-09
a_6	7.922e-16
a_8	-1.859e-18
a_{10}	1.733e-21

Zerodur material is selected for several reasons:

- optical components are widely used in many applications,
- machinability of optical material is better investigated and understood
- optical application growth requests more and more accurate optics
- thermal stability

6.4 Manufacturing of the thermo-invariant material standard

An original approach to processing (material removal) optical lenses with magnetic fluids is the magnetorheological finishing (MRF). This technology was initiated by William Kordonski in 1990 [23].The fundamental element of MRF is MR polishing fluid. It consists of a liquid composition that undergoes a change in mechanical properties and converts into plastic material in presence of a magnetic field. Generally MR fluid contains very small ferromagnetic particles (0.1 µm). These particles become magnetised in the presence of magnetic field and organised into chains of particles, forming then a spatial structure. The spatial structure provokes a change in mechanical properties. Without magnetic field, the particles return progressively to a disorganised state, while the initial condition of the overall material is restored.

In theory, MR polishing fluid contains four mains constitutes: magnetic particles, polishing abrasive, chemical additives and water. Nevertheless, water is almost used as a carrier fluid for polishing glasses and silicon substrates without any additional chemical agent.

The schema presented in figure 6 shows the concept of the Q22 multiple-axis, computer-controlled MRF machine for the manufacturing of the material standard described previously. The lens is fixed such as a converging gap can be formed between the lens and the rotating spherical wheel. One litre of MR polishing fluid is loaded into the closed-loop fluid delivery system, where fluid properties such as temperature and viscosity can be continually monitored and controlled.

The fluid is drawn out of the conditioner and extruded onto the rotating wheel in a thin ribbon that will contact the optical surface. The ribbon is then removed by a suction cup and fed back into the conditioner. An electromagnet, located below the polishing wheel, has specially designed pole pieces that extend up to the underside of the apex of the wheel rim. These pole pieces exert a strong local magnetic field gradient over the upper side of the wheel rim. When the magnetorheological fluid passes through the magnetic field, it stiffens in milliseconds, then returns to its original fluid state as it leaves the field, again in milliseconds. This precisely controlled zone of magnetised fluid becomes the polishing tool. When the optical surface is placed into the fluid, the stiffened fluid ribbon is squeezed from its original thickness, which results in significant shear stress and subsequent polishing pressure over that section of the optical surface.

The Q22 MRF process is carried out by specific software and requires two main input functions:

- to describe the shape distribution and removal rate of the MRF polishing tool
- to describe the initial surface error of the optic to be polished and corrected.

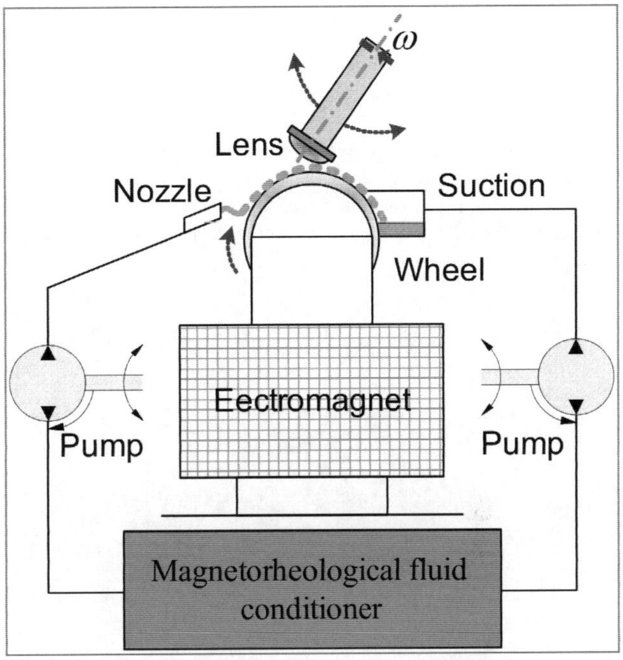

Fig. 6. Concept of the Q22 multiple-axis computer-controlled MRF machine

Fig. 7. Manufacturing of an aspheric lens using a MR process

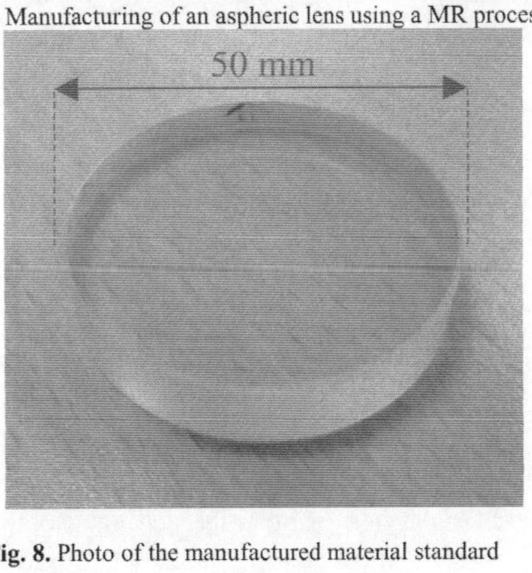

Fig. 8. Photo of the manufactured material standard

6.5 Measurement and analysis

The manufactured material standard was evaluated using a specific accurate aspheric metrology systems developed by QEDTechnologies. This system is the Subaperture Stitching Interferometry (SSI), which enables manufacturers to measure a wide range of aspheres with up to 1000 waves of departure, without relying on dedicated, expensive null-optics. The SSI has been designed such as to accurately test mild to steep aspheres with one fast.

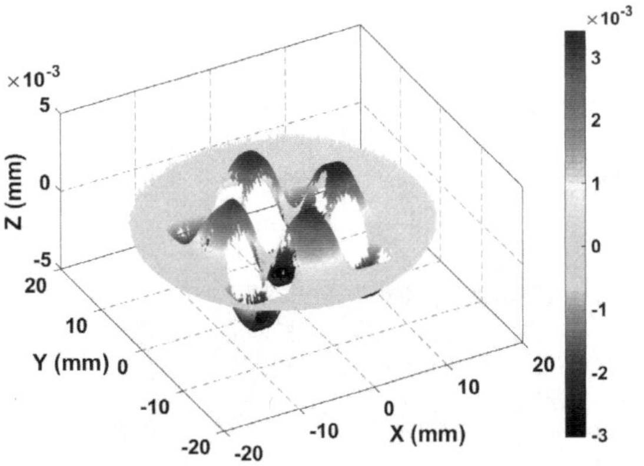

Fig. 9. The Subaperture Stitching Interferometry (SSI) measured data

The stitching process reconstructs the full-aperture map of the surface from a collection of sub-aperture, each covering only a portion of the whole surface. The QED's stitching algorithms enable, with high accuracy, an automated, reconstruction of the full-aperture. It is based on the use of an advanced optimization method to minimize the discrepancies between overlapping regions of subapertures caused by several sources of systematic and random measurement error. Through its integrated calibration capability, the system can deliver better accuracy than a standard full-aperture test.

A large cloud of points (~500 000 points) were collected and analysed thanks to the developed HTR algorithm presented previously. The recorded dataset is illustrated in figure 9. The PV is equal to 6.28µm. Calculation time was completed in less than 5min using Matlab®.

The resulting PV value is approximately 720 nm from the one specified in the design. This deviation is due essentially to the manufacturing process duration of 9 hours, while a normal MR process cycle take 15 to 45min.

7. Conclusion

In this paper, high accuracy metrology of freeform and aspheric optical elements is discussed. This includes the development of reference minimum zone fitting algorithms, traceable measurement machines and original optical thermo-invariant standards.

A new method called Hybrid Trust Region algorithm was developed for the Minimum Zone fitting of aspherical shapes. This method was tested using reference data, obtained results show that the introduced method provides superior performances compared to existing methods. In a related work, this method was also applied on measured and benchmark data. Resulting PV values and calculation time are better than for existing methods.

A design for a thermo-invariant material standard was also suggested. It consists of an aspheric shape to which a well-defined form error was added. The resulting artefact had a well-known PV value.

The material standard was manufactured using a Magnetorheological (MR) finishing process and measured using a Subaperture Stitching Interferometry (SSI) system. The Hybrid Trust Region algorithm was used to analyse the obtained data. The resulting PV value was compared to the one specified in the design. Results show that the obtained PV value is approximately 720 nm from the one specified in the design. This deviation is due to the long manufacturing process duration of 9 hours. In fact, a normal MR process cycle must take 15 to 45min.

In a future work, the developed algorithm will be applied on more complex shape. The development of corresponding artefacts is also considered.

Acknowledgement

The authors sincerely thank the EMPIR organization. The EMPIR initiative is co-funded by the European Union's Horizon 2020 and innovation programme and the EMPIR participating states within EURAMET and the European Union (15SIB01: FreeFORM).

Reference

[1] J. M. Geary, Introduction to Lens Design: With Practical ZEMAX Examples. Willmann-Bell, 2002.

[2] H. H. Karow, Fabrication Methods for Precision Optics. Wiley, 2004.

[3] N. El hayek, "Contribution à la reconstruction de surfaces complexes à partir d'un grand flot de données non organisées pour la métrologie 3D.," Paris, ENSAM, 2014.

[4] N. El-Hayek, H. Nouira, N. Anwer, O. Gibaru, and M. Damak, "A new method for aspherical surface fitting with large-volume datasets," Precis. Eng., vol. 38, no. 4, pp. 935–947, Oct. 2014.

[5] ISO 10110-Part12, "Optics and photonics - Preparation of drawings for optical elements and systems - Part 12: Aspheric surfaces." 2007.

[6] G. W. Forbes, "Shape specification for axially symmetric optical surfaces," Opt. Express, vol. 15, no. 8, pp. 5218–5226, Apr. 2007.

[7] H. Gross et al., "Overview on surface representations for freeform surfaces," in SPIE, 2015, vol. 9626.

[8] D. C. Liu and J. Nocedal, "On the limited memory BFGS method for large scale optimization," Math. Program., vol. 45, no. 1–3, pp. 503–528, Aug. 1989.

[9] S. T. Huang, K. . FAN, and J. H. WU, "A new minimum zone method for evaluating flatness errors," Precis. Eng., vol. 15(1), pp. 25–32, 1993.

[10] T. S. R. Murthy, "A comparison of different algorithms for circularity evaluation," Precis. Eng., vol. 8(1), pp. 19–23, 1986.

[11] Y. G. Shi, "Weighted simultaneous Chebyshev approximation," J. Approx. Theory, vol. 32(4), pp. 306–315, 1981.
[12] X. Zhang, X. Jiang, and P. J. Scott, "A minimax fitting algorithm for ultra-precision aspheric surfaces," J. Phys. Conf. Ser., vol. 311, no. 1, p. 012031, 2011.
[13] X. Zhang, H. Zhang, X. He, M. Xu, and X. Jiang, "Chebyshev fitting of complex surfaces for precision metrology," Measurement, vol. 46, no. 9, pp. 3720–3724, Nov. 2013.
[14] X. Zhang, X. Jiang, A. B. Forbes, H. D. Minh, and P. J. Scott, "Evaluating the form errors of spheres, cylinders and cones using the primal–dual interior point method," Proc. Inst. Mech. Eng. Part B J. Eng. Manuf., vol. 227, no. 5, pp. 720–725, May 2013.
[15] S. P. Boyd and L. Vandenberghe, Convex Optimization. Cambridge University Press, 2004.
[16] M. J. D. Powell, "How bad are the BFGS and DFP methods when the objective function is quadratic?," Math. Program., vol. 34, no. 1, pp. 34–47, Jan. 1986.
[17] F. Wang and K. Zhang, "A hybrid algorithm for nonlinear minimax problems," Ann. Oper. Res., vol. 164, no. 1, p. 167, Nov. 2008.
[18] A. B. Forbes and H. D. Minh, "Form Assessment in Coordinate Metrology," SpringerLink, pp. 69–90, 2011.
[19] Henselmans, R (Rens), "Non-contact measurement machine for freeform optics." Technische Universiteit Eindhoven, 2009.
[20] Y.-C. Cheng, W.-Y. Hsu, Y.-H. Chen, G.-D. Su, and P. J. Wang, "Design and Fabrication of Free-Form Shaped Lens for Laser Leveler Instrument," in Frontiers in Optics 2010/Laser Science XXVI (2010), paper FThX2, 2010, p. FThX2.
[21] P. Benítez and J. C. Miñano, "The Future of Illumination Design," Opt. Photonics News, vol. 18, no. 5, pp. 20–25, May 2007.
[22] "FreeFORM: Home." [Online]. Available: https://www.ptb.de/empir/freeform-home.html. [Accessed: 19-Jun-2017].
[23] W. Kordonski and S. Gorodkin, "Material removal in magnetorheological finishing of optics," Appl. Opt., vol. 50, no. 14, pp. 1984–1994, May 2011.

Thermal conductivity experimental measurement of different building materials

M. Boumhaout[1,2]*, L. Boukhattem[1,3], H. Hamdi[2], B. Benhamou[1,2], F. Ait Nouh[1]

[1]EnR2E, National Center of Studies and Research on Water and Energy, CNEREE, Cadi Ayyad University, Marrakesh, Morocco
[2]Energy Process Research Group, LMFE, CNRST Associated Research Unit (URAC 27), Faculty of Science Semlalia, Cadi Ayyad University, Marrakesh, Morocco
[3]LMPEQ, National School of Applied Sciences, Safi, Cady Ayyad University, Marrakesh, Morocco

Abstract. An experimental study was conducted to determine the thermal conductivity of different building materials using the boxes method (device EI700) as well as the hot wire method (device FP2C). The characterized materials are the expanded polystyrene (EP), the extruded polystyrene (XPS), the wood (W), the reference mortar (sand + cement) (RM) and a bio-composite material (reinforced mortar with date palm fibers mesh) (RFM). After calibrating these two experimental devices, a comparison of thermal conductivity obtained by the two devices has been performed and measurement uncertainties were also evaluated. Thus, the results found are satisfactory with an acceptable relative difference.

Keywords: Temperature, thermal conductivity, boxes method, hot wire method, uncertainties.

1 Introduction

Thermophysical characterization of building materials, by different experimental devices, has been the subject of numerous studies. Thus, most of the thermal conductivity measurements have been made by the box method. For this reason, [1-6] have measured the thermophysical properties of some local materials namely: cork, plaster, hollow brick, olive pomace and cork concrete, stabilized earthen bricks and tropical wood. Recently, the same method has been used by several authors [7-13] for measuring the thermal conductivity of materials such as: soil from Agadir region, expanded and extruded polystyrene, Chad soil, reinforced mortars by wood chips, polystyrene beads and date palm fibers respectively.

In this work, different steps taken to control the measurement results obtained by the EI700 device using the box method are presented.

Firstly, different temperature probes were calibrated, and determined the heat losses coefficient of boxes method was determined. Afterwards, this device had been installed in an air-conditioned room before it was calibrated using the standard materials whose thermal conductivity values were presented in the literature.

At the end of this work, the thermal conductivity values of some materials obtained by two studied methods: the box method and the hot wire method were compared.

* Corresponding author: mustapha.boumhaout@edu.uca.ac.ma

2 Boxes method

The boxes method, device EI700 (Figure 1), allows the creation of an "ideal" experimental environment for measuring the thermal conductivity of two identical or different materials.

The thermal conductivity measurement principle is based on achieving a permanent unidirectional heat flow through the sample placed in the first box, between the isothermal cold capacity (A) of the device and the heat source with constant heat flow ($Q = \frac{U^2}{R}$) regulated using a rheostat (R) in order to adjust the temperature inside the box, T_B at a level slightly higher than the outside temperature (ambient temperature). Once the permanent regime is achieved, i.e. when the values of temperatures remain constant for more than approximately half an hour, the temperature gradient in the centre of the sample and the heating voltage are recorded by acquisition software. Then the following expression is used to deduce the value of thermal conductivity:

$$k = \frac{e}{A\,\Delta T}\left[Q - C(T_B - T_a)\right] \quad (1)$$

With:
U: Potential difference (V).
R: Electrical resistance (Ω).
T_B : Ambient temperature inside the box B_1 (°C).
T_a : Ambient temperature of room (°C).
k : Thermal conductivity ($W.m^{-1}.K^{-1}$).
e: Thickness of sample (m).
A: Area of the sample faces, normal to heat flow.

C: Heat losses coefficient (W/K).

T_H : Temperature of hot surface (°C).

T_C : Temperature of cold surface (°C).

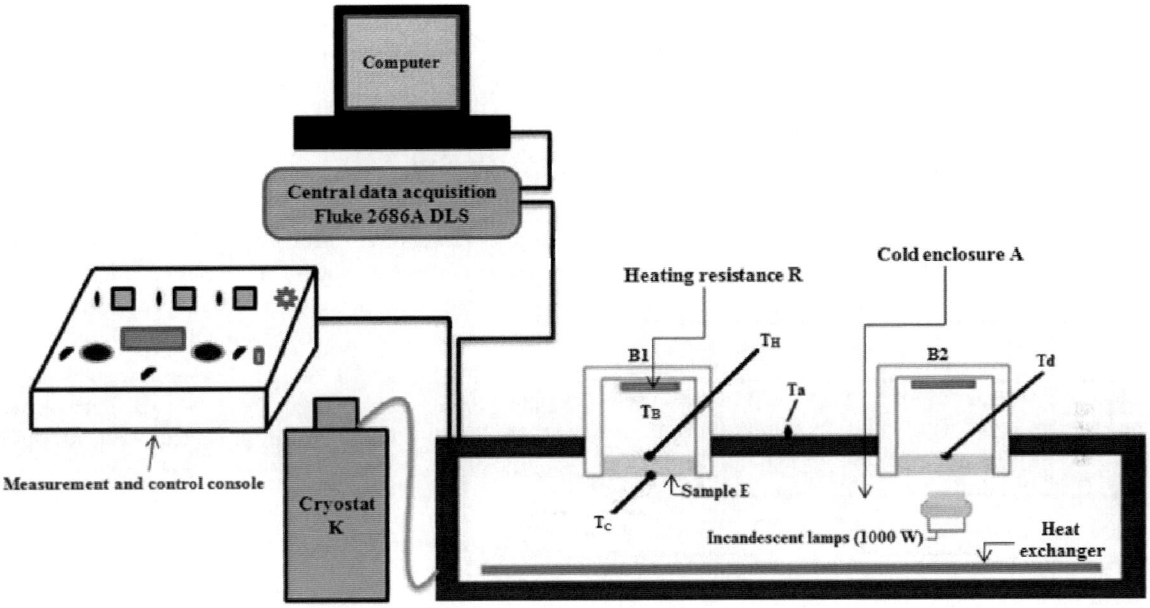

Fig. 1. EI700 device schematic sketch (Boxes method).

3 Calibration of device EI700

3.1 Calibration of temperature probes PT100

The calibration of different temperature probes PT100 (Room temperature probe and contact temperature probe) of the EI700 device, consists in fixing various surface temperature probes on a small piece of Expanded Polystyrene and collect them next to the temperature sensor of the room then cover these probes with the box B_1 (Figure 2).

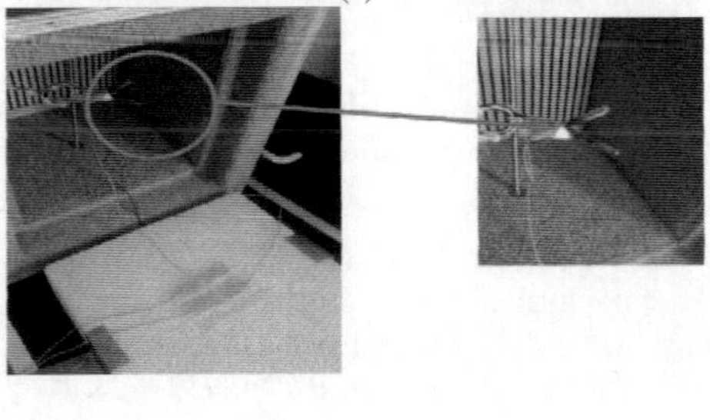

(a)

(b)

Fig. 2. Calibration of temperature probes PT100 (a). Probes fixed on Expanded Polystyrene (b).

After 2 or 3 hours, temperature stabilization time, the temperatures indicated by each of the temperature probes are recorded through the data acquisition unit (FLUKE 2686A DLS). The calibration results of different temperature probes are presented in Table 1.

Table 1. Calibration results of temperature probes.

	Ta (°C)	T_B (°C)	T_H (°C)	T_C (°C)	T_B–Ta (°C)	T_H–T_C (°C)
t_1	26.73	26.76	27.94	29.34	0.03	-1.40
t_2	26.78	26.82	27.98	29.36	0.04	-1.38
t_3	26.72	26.76	27.92	29.30	0.04	-1.38

3.2 Evaluation of the heat loss coefficient *C*

To determine experimentally the heat losses coefficient *C* of box B_1, we imposed two different flows Q and Q' for the Expanded Polystyrene thickness *e* and thermal conductivity k and we obtained the following system of equations (Eqs (2)):

$$\begin{cases} Q = k/_e(T_H - T_C) \times A + C(T_B - T_a) \\ Q' = k/_e(T'_H - T'_C) \times A + C(T'_B - T_a) \end{cases} \quad (2)$$

By resolving this system, the value of constant C is found to be: $C = (0.19 \pm 0.01)$ W/K for the box B_1.

3.3 Calibration of the box (B_1) for thermal conductivity measurement

We have determined the value of the concerning thermal conductivity (k_{lit}) presented in the literature for each material as a function of its density. After that, we determined the thermal conductivity value measured for each material (k_m) by the EI700 device (Table 2).

Table 2. Calibration of the box (B_1).

Materials	k_m (W/m.K)	k_{lit} (W/m.K)
Extruded Polystyrene (XPS)	0.037	0.033
Expanded Polystyrene (EP)	0.040	0.047
Cork board	0.06	0.055
Mortar	0.79	0.80

The thermal conductivity values measured (k_m) are in the obedience with those presented in the literature (k_{lit}). So, we can say that box B_1 is calibrated.

The different temperatures are recorded when the difference between the ambient temperature of the box B_1 (T_B) and the ambient temperature of the room (Ta) is less than 0.1°C.

4 Comparison of the thermal conductivity results measured by two experimental devices

To ensure the reliability of the boxes method for thermal conductivity measurement, results obtained by this method were compared to the ones obtained by hot wire method (calibrated using a rock wool sample) for some building materials namely: the expanded polystyrene (EP), the extruded polystyrene (XPS), the wood (W), the reference mortar (sand + cement) (RM) and a bio-composite material (mortar reinforced with 48% of date palm fibers mesh) (RFM). The obtained results are resumed in Table 3.

Table 3. Comparison of the thermal conductivity measured by box and hot wire methods for some building materials.

Materials	*k* (W/m.K) Box method	*k* (W/m.K) Hot wire method	*Relative difference (%)*
EP	0.040±0.002	0.042±0.003	5
XPS	0.037±0.001	0.038±0.003	3
W	0.19±0.01	0.21±0.02	9
RM	0.794±0.048	0.728±0.005	8
RFM48%	0.312±0.028	0.342±0.026	9

The measurements have been repeated three times for a better estimation of measurement error. These thermal conductivity measurements by the two methods are obtained with a relative difference which does not exceed 9% (Table 3) for all the tested materials. And the methods accuracy is approximately 3 to 9% for the box method and 1 to 9% for the hot wire method.

5 Conclusion

In this work, we calibrated the temperature probes PT100 of the device EI700 and we also calibrated the box B_1 of the same experimental device allowing the measurement of the thermal conductivity using some standard materials whose thermal conductivity values were presented in the literature.

The results of thermal conductivity measurement for some building materials obtained by two experimental devices (EI700 and FP2C) are also presented with measurement uncertainties.

Acknowledgment

This study is a part of the RafriBAT project financially supported by a grant from the Hassan II Royal Academy of Sciences and Techniques, Morocco.

References

[1] H. Ezbakhe, S. Bousad, and A. El Bakkour, "Etude Thermique de la Terre Stabilisée au Ciment Utilisée en Construction au Nord du Maroc," *Rev. Energ. Ren.*, vol. **69**, pp. 69–72, 2001.

[2] A. EL Bakkouri, "Caractérisation hygroscopique, thermophysique et mécanique des matériaux allégés : cas du béton allégé avec du liège ou avec des grignons d'olive" , Thèse de DES, Université Abdelmalek essaadi Faculté des Sciences Tétouan, Maroc, Décembre., 2004.

[3] I. Aboubou, L. Diabaté, and G. Mengy, "Détermination de la conductivité thermique de matériaux de construction à Bamako," *Journal des Sciences Pour l'Ingénieur*, N° **4**, pp. 1-6, 2004.

[4] P. Meukam, A. Noumowe, Y. Jannot, and R. Duval, "Caractérisation thermophysique et mécanique de briques de terre stabilisées en vue de l'isolation thermique de bâtiment," vol. **36**, no. September, pp. 453–460, 2003.

[5] P. Meukam, Y. Jannot, a Noumowe, and T. C. Kofane, "Thermo physical characteristics of economical building materials," *Constr. Build. Mater.*, vol. **18**, pp. 437–443, 2004.

[6] P. S. Ngohe-Ekam, P. Meukam, G. Menguy, and P. Girard, "Thermophysical characterisation of tropical wood used as building materials: With respect to the basal density," *Constr. Build. Mater.*, vol. **20**, no. 10, pp. 929–938, Dec. 2006.

[7] L. Boukhattem and A. Hamdi, "characterization of variation of thermophysical properties of soil with moisture : silty soil samples from agadir region in morocco," *Phys. Chem. News*, vol. **66**, no. October, pp. 34–39, 2012.

[8] M. Boumhaout, L. Boukhattem, H. Hamdi, B. Benhamou, F. Ait Nouh, "Energy efficiency in buildings: Thermophysical characterization of building materials", in: Int. Renewable and Sustainable Energy Conf. IRSEC'2013, Ouarzazate, 07 March 07–09, 2013, doi: 10.1109/IRSEC.2013.6529675. **http://ieeexplore.ieee.org/document/6529675/**

[9] M. Boumhaout, L. Boukhattem, H. Hamdi, B. Benhamou, F. Ait Nouh, "Thermomechanical characterization of composite materials : mortar reinforced by date palm fibers mesh of Marrakesh", Int. Renewable and Sustainable Energy Conf. IRSEC2015, Marrakesh, December 10-13, 2015, doi: 10.1109/IRSEC.2015.7455035. **http://ieeexplore.ieee.org/document/7455035/**

[10] M. Ahmat-Charfadine, M. Barka, A.M. Tahir, M. Soultan, S. Gaye, A.C. Beye, Thermo-physical properties of local materials used in the construction of chad, Am. J. Civ. Eng. **3** (5) (2015), pp. 140-141.

[11] A. Adili, M. Lachheb, A. Brayek, A. Guizani, and S. Ben Nasrallah, "Estimation of thermophysical properties of lightweight mortars made of wood shavings and expanded polystyrene beads using a hybrid algorithm," *Energy Build.*, vol. **118**, pp. 133–141, 2016.

[12] M. Boumhaout, L. Boukhattem, H. Hamdi, B. Benhamou, and F. Ait Nouh, "Thermomechanical characterization of a bio-composite building material: Mortar reinforced with date palm fibers mesh," *Constr. Build. Mater.*, vol. **135**, pp. 241–250, 2017.

[13] L. Boukhattem, M. Boumhaout, H. Hamdi, B. Benhamou, and F. Ait Nouh, "Moisture content influence on the thermal conductivity of insulating building materials made from date palm fibers mesh," *Constr. Build. Mater.*, vol. **148**, pp. 811–823, 2017.

Collusion and falsification of results in proficiency testing

P. Briggs

Proficiency Testing Australia, Sydney, Australia

Abstract. Proficiency testing is used internationally to provide objective evidence of testing laboratories testing competence. This paper covers the requirement in ISO/IEC 17043 regarding preventing collusion between participants and falsification of results in a proficiency testing program. Collusion between participants and falsification of results if this does occur will diminish the confidence from other participating laboratories and their customers and also other interested parties such as regulators and laboratory accreditation bodies in the proficiency testing process. This paper outlines some practical examples that a proficiency testing provider can use to reduce the chance of collusion between program participants and falsification of results.

Keywords: Collusion, Falisification, Proficiency

1 Introduction

Interlaboratory comparisons are widely used for a number of purposes and their use is increasing internationally. The main purpose for an interlaboratory comparison for proficiency testing is to provide an evaluation of the performance of laboratories for specific tests or measurements and to monitor laboratories' continuing performance.

By the very nature of the design of proficiency testing these comparisons involve the participation in a short space of time by multiple laboratories working in the same scientific field. Where common samples are sent by the proficiency testing provider to the participating laboratories in the form of a 'test' then this may lead to a change in laboratory operations. To provide a true evaluation and monitoring of performance then the overall design of the programs should be to encourage the participating laboratories to treat the proficiency testing samples as routine samples received from a commercial client.

2 ISO/IEC 17043 Technical requirements

ISO/IEC 17043 [1] details the technical requirements for the design of proficiency testing programs including details for information to be included in the documented plan before the commencement of the program. Section 4.4.1.3 j) states - "*reasonable precautions to prevent collusion between participants or falsification of results, and procedures to be employed if collusion or falsification of results is suspected.*"

This requirement may be considered to place an unfair load of responsibility on the proficiency testing provider to attempt control the ethical and professional behaviour of organisations that have registered to participate in their proficiency testing programs.

3 Collusion

Collusion in proficiency testing may be considered to mean a form of cheating from the participating laboratory. There may be a situation where two or more people from two or more participating laboratories work together in a deceitful way to submit results for their benefit in the evaluation of their testing performance.

When a proficiency testing program is planned the aim is to provide an evaluation for the individual participating laboratory testing or measurement performance. Within the individual laboratory there may be one or multiple staff involved in the sample preparation, testing and submission of the results to the proficiency testing provider. In this case, this is quite acceptable as proficiency testing programs do not generally restrict participation to one staff member from the laboratory. So therefore collusion cannot be considered if all people involved in the participation are from the one individual laboratory.

In proficiency testing programs there may be multiple laboratories from the same organisation participating in the same round of the program. In this case the participating laboratories from the same organisation would likely to be using the same quality system and laboratory procedures. Therefore if two or more people from two or more laboratories from the same organisation are working together to submit results should this be considered as collusion?

In another case there may be two or more people from two or more laboratories from different organisations working together to submit results. As each laboratory are from different organisations they would unlikely to be sharing any staff and also each organisation would be using a separate quality management system and laboratory procedures. Can this case then be considered as collusion?

4 Falsification of results

The falsification of results in proficiency testing may be considered to mean the submission of results are stated untruthfully or are being misrepresented as being from the participating laboratory.

The detection of falsification of results in a proficiency testing program may be quite difficult to detect by the organiser of the program. Results from programs are commonly submitted by the participant to the proficiency testing provider either in hard copy or electronically. The submitted results are identified by the laboratory code issued by the proficiency testing provider to ensure confidentiality of results. The submitted results may also include either a signature from the laboratory staff and/or some form or unique laboratory identification such as address or organisation logo. So the assumption taken by the proficiency testing provider is that the results are from the laboratory identified.

If the falsification of results is due to collusion then this may be detected quite easily if the results are identical. If the results reported were similar to other participants reported results then the falsification of results in this case would be quite difficult or impossible to detect.

A way that a participating laboratory be involved in falsification of results is to sub-contract the testing to another laboratory and then to submit these results as their own to the proficiency testing provider. In this case this would be impossible for the proficiency testing provider to detect unless he was advised of this practice by a third party.

5 Detection of suspect results

A typical proficiency testing program involves many laboratories reporting many test and measurement results in a defined range of quantified values.

To detect suspect results due to collusion or falsification of results then the main feature could be identical results reported by two or more laboratories. The physical location of the laboratories may also be considered as it would be unlikely that participants operating in different economies would be sharing information.

If there is a narrow range of expected values for a test then there is a high probability that results reported between some participants may be identical. The probability of identical results being reported as coincidence lessens when the reporting accuracy increases and lessens further upon replicate reporting for single or multiple samples. In addition to the reported value other reported information may also be considered such as measurement uncertainty and methods to check if this is common between the suspected results.

Suspect results may be quite easier to detect if in the form of duplicated results between laboratories in a small data compared to a large data set.

If there is obvious duplication of reported results between participants in a published proficiency testing program final report then if identified by the proficiency testing provider then this would surely also be noticed by the other program participants which would seriously diminish the credibility of the final report and also could damage the reputation of the proficiency testing provider's services.

6 Program design to prevent collusion and falsification of results

Proficiency testing programs may be designed to prevent collusion or falsification of results if there has been evidence of suspect results in completed rounds of the program.

If there are a large number of participants in a program then the participants could be randomly divided into two or more groups with each group receiving a unique set of samples. Each group in the program would need to have a minimum number of participants to allow the reported results to be statistically evaluated for testing performance. The samples could be labelled the same between each group or the samples could be labelled differently between each group. If it was suspected that participants from within one organization were in collusion to report results then the proficiency testing provider could purposely decide to split the participants into different groups that would receive the unique sample set.

For programs were there are a small number of participants the program design could be to provide unique sample identification for common samples in the program that are sent to each participant. This design could apply to programs involving either single program samples or multiple program samples sent to participating laboratories for testing.

7 Action for suspect results

The reported results produced in an established proficiency testing program can usually show by the historical data if suspect results have been reported. If there has been no evidence of collusion or falsification of results in an established program then the program design would not need to be changed to prevent this future possibility. At the time of a current program is there was evidence the challenge faced by the proficiency testing provider is what actions should be undertaken. This is quite a difficult process as it could involve the proficiency testing provider incorrectly accusing the participant of dishonest reporting.

A subtle approach could be to highlight the suspect reporting in the commentary in the published final report.

In an extreme case the proficiency testing provider could refuse request for participation in the program by the suspected laboratory.

However in most cases where the proficiency testing provider may believe that there is enough not evidence to suggest that suspect results have been reported that there has been no action taken.

8 Conclusion

The requirement as stated in ISO/IEC 17043 remains a challenge for the proficiency testing provider to identify evidence of collusion or falsification of results have actually occurred in the program. The immediate actions following detection of the suspect results are limited and the prevention may be restricted to changes in the design of the program.

References

1. ISO/IEC 17025: 2005 General requirements for the competence of testing and calibration laboratories

Assessing interlaboratory comparison data adjustment procedures

Kavya Jagan and Alistair Forbes

Data Science Group, National Physical Laboratory

Abstract

Interlaboratory comparisons are one of the key activities in metrology. The inputs to the exercise are estimates $\mathbf{x} = (x_1, \ldots, x_n)^{\mathrm{T}}$ of a measurand α along with their associated standard uncertainties $\mathbf{u} = (u_1, \ldots, u_n)^{\mathrm{T}}$, $u_j = u(x_j)$. Employing a model of the form

$$x_j \in \mathrm{N}(\alpha, u_j^2), \quad j = 1, \ldots, n,$$

we may wish to find a consensus value for α. A χ^2 test can be used to assess the degree to which the spread of the estimates $\mathbf{x}$ are consistent with the stated uncertainties $\mathbf{u}$. If they are judged to be inconsistent, then an adjustment procedure can be applied to determine $\tilde{u}_j \geq u_j$ so that $\mathbf{x}$ and $\tilde{\mathbf{u}}$ represents better consistency. The underlying assumption behind this approach is that some or all of the laboratories have underestimated or neglected some uncertainty contributions, sometimes referred to as 'dark uncertainty', and the adjusted $\tilde{\mathbf{u}}$ provides an estimate of this dark uncertainty derived from the complete set of laboratory results. There are many such adjustment procedures, including the Birge and Mandel-Paule procedures.

In implementing an adjustment procedure, a desirable objective is to make as minimal adjustment as necessary in order to bring about the required degree of consistency. In this paper we discuss the use of relative entropy, also known as the Kullback-Leibler divergence, as a measure of the degree of adjustment. We evaluate how different adjustment procedures compare in terms of this relative entropy measure, and how they compare with a procedure that is designed to minimise relative entropy subject to achieving the desired degree of consistency.

1 Introduction

Interlaboratory comparisons (ILCs) are one of the key activities in metrology, and are undertaken for a number of reasons, e.g., i) to determine a consensus value for a quantity by combining experimental results from a number of laboratories, ii) to assess the degree of equivalence of different laboratories or measurement methodologies. In this paper we are primarily interested in finding a consensus estimate for the quantity being measured. The starting point for the analysis of ILC data is usually a model [4] of the form

$$x_j \in \mathrm{N}(\alpha, u_j^2), \tag{1}$$

where α is the value of the measurand, x_j is the estimate of α produced by the jth laboratory and u_j its associated standard uncertainty. Given the model (1), the distribution for α is derived from the weighted least squares estimate

$$a = a(\mathbf{u}) = (C^{\mathrm{T}}C)^{-1}C^{\mathrm{T}}\mathbf{y}, \quad y_j = x_j/u_j, \quad C_j = 1/u_j,$$

involving the $n \times 1$ observation matrix C. If the data is regarded as a sample from Gaussian distributions as in (1), then a is a sample from the Gaussian distribution $\mathrm{N}(\alpha, V_a)$, $V_a = (C^{\mathrm{T}}C)^{-1}$.

Under the model (1), the sum of the squares

$$R^2 = R^2(\mathbf{u}) = \mathbf{r}^{\mathrm{T}}\mathbf{r}$$

of the weighted residuals $\mathbf{r} = \mathbf{r}(\mathbf{u}) = \mathbf{y} - Ca$ is a sample from a χ^2_{n-1} distribution with $n-1$ degrees of freedom. The degree of consistency of the data $\mathbf{x} = (x_1, \ldots, x_n)^{\mathrm{T}}$ and $\mathbf{u} = (u_1, \ldots, u_n)^{\mathrm{T}}$ can be assessed by evaluating $\Pr(\xi^2 \geq R^2)$ where $\xi^2 \sim \chi^2_{n-1}$. If $\Pr(\xi^2 \geq R^2)$ is less than 5 %, say, then there is doubt about consistency of the data [4]. If data is judged to be inconsistent, the weighted least squares estimate a might not a reliable estimate of α in the sense that the variance matrix V_a may underestimate the uncertainty associated with this estimate. In the presence of inconsistency, an adjustment procedure can be applied to adjust the uncertainties to achieve a better consistency; see, e.g., [1, 5, 6, 3, 7, 9, 13, 15, 16]. The underlying assumption behind these approaches is that some or all of the laboratories have underestimated or neglected some uncertainty contributions, sometimes referred to as 'dark uncertainty', and the adjusted uncertainties implicitly provides an estimate of this dark uncertainty derived from the complete set of laboratory results.

We assume that the original data supplied is $\mathbf{x}$ with associated uncertainties $\mathbf{u}_0$. The least squares analysis involves C_0, $\mathbf{y}_0$, $\mathbf{r}_0$, R_0^2 and $V_{a,0}$, quantities that correspond to those above evaluated for $\mathbf{x}$ and $\mathbf{u}_0$. We assume that R_0^2 indicates inconsistency and we look for adjusted uncertainties $\tilde{\mathbf{u}}$ that lead to better consistency.

We look for adjustment schemes that determine $\tilde{\mathbf{u}}$ for which the consistency constraint $R^2(\tilde{\mathbf{u}}) = c^2$ is satisfied. The choice of c^2 needs to be considered. Let

$$\hat{\sigma}^2(\tilde{\mathbf{u}}) = \frac{R^2(\tilde{\mathbf{u}})}{n-1}. \quad (2)$$

Given the model $x_j \in \mathrm{N}(\alpha, \sigma^2 \tilde{u}_j^2)$, where σ^2 is unknown, the term $\hat{\sigma}^2(\tilde{\mathbf{u}})$ can be regarded as a posterior estimate of σ^2. For this reason, it is common to choose $c^2 = n-1$ so that the adjusted $\tilde{\mathbf{u}}$ corresponds to $\hat{\sigma}^2(\tilde{\mathbf{u}}) = 1$, indicating that the $\tilde{\mathbf{u}}$ so determined are 'fully adjusted'. However, tests of consistency usually will indicate inconsistency if the observed sum of squares is greater than the 95 percentile, say. If $c^2 = n-1$, a set of input data that has a sum of squares at the 96th percentile will be adjusted to achieve $\hat{\sigma}^2 = 1$ while one achieving the 94th percentile will remain unadjusted. Hence, a relatively small change in the input data can result in a large change in inferences about α. Thus it can be argued that c^2 should be set to the same value used to test consistency.

Our main concern is to derive the adjusted $\tilde{\mathbf{u}}$ that represents a minimal departure from the stated $\mathbf{u}_0$ according to some measure. In this paper we discuss adjusted uncertainty measures derived by minimising the relative entropy or Kullback-Leibler divergence [11, 12] a measure of how far $\tilde{\mathbf{u}}$ is from $\mathbf{u}_0$. Section 2 describes a number of single parameter adjustment schemes in which the degree of adjustment is determined by the consistency constraint. Section 3 defines the relative entropy of an adjustment and section 4 describes adjustment through minimising relative entropy. A comparison of adjustment procedures in terms of the degree of adjustment of ILC data is presented in section 5. Our concluding remarks are given in section 6.

2 Single parameter adjustment schemes

In this section we use the notation $\mathbf{u}^2$ to denote the vector $\mathbf{u}^2 = (u_1^2, \ldots, u_n^2)$, the vector of variances derived from $\mathbf{u}$. We consider adjustment schemes that produce adjusted uncertainties $\tilde{\mathbf{u}}$ according to

$$\tilde{\mathbf{u}}^2 = \mathbf{u}_0^2 + \lambda \mathbf{v}^2, \quad \lambda \geq 0$$

where $\mathbf{v}^2$ is a fixed vector specifying the direction in which the variances are to be adjusted and λ is a single parameter specifying the degree of adjustment and is chosen so that the consistency constraint is satisfied. We can write the consistency constraint as $R^2(\lambda) = c^2$, indicating the dependence on the single parameter λ. Once λ is specified, a consensus value for α along with its associated uncertainty can then be determined from the adjusted uncertainties $\tilde{\mathbf{u}}$ and $\mathbf{x}$. The advantage of a single parameter adjustment procedure is that the adjustment is determined by solving a single (nonlinear) equation. The specific procedures below relate to different choices for the direction vector $\mathbf{v}^2$.

2.1 The Birge procedure

The Birge procedure [1] corresponds to a choice of $\mathbf{v}_0^2 = \mathbf{u}_0^2$ i.e. it scales all the input uncertainties by the same factor, usually $\hat{\sigma}_0^2$,

$$\mathbf{u}_B^2 = \hat{\sigma}_0^2 \mathbf{u}_0^2, \quad \hat{\sigma}_0^2 = R_0^2/(n-1).$$

With this adjustment, the sum of squares of the weighted residuals R_B^2 derived from the data $\mathbf{x}_0$ and $\mathbf{u}_B$ is equal to its expected value, $n-1$, i.e., the mean of the associated distribution χ_{n-1}^2. Alternatively, adjustment could made to the c^2 percentile.

2.2 The Mandel-Paule procedure

The Mandel-Paule procedure [13] corresponds to a choice of $\mathbf{v}_0^2 = \mathbf{e}$, where $e_j = 1$, $j = 1, \ldots, n$. The same additive adjustment is made to each variance component $\mathbf{u}_0^2$ which can be motivated by a model in which all the participants have omitted the same additive influence factor from their uncertainty budget. As before, the parameter λ is chosen so that the sum of squares of the weighted residuals R_{MP}^2 derived from the data $\mathbf{x}_0$ and $\mathbf{u}_{MP}$ is equal to c^2.

2.3 A steepest descent procedure

Inconsistency is indicated if the sum of squared residuals $R_0^2 = R^2(0)$ is too high and we require that $R^2(\lambda) < R^2(0)$ so that $\mathbf{v}_0^2$ represents a descent direction for $R^2(\lambda)$. Since we are interested in determining $\tilde{\mathbf{u}}^2$ that achieve consistency with an adjustment of $\mathbf{u}_0^2$ that is minimal in some way, we can set $\mathbf{v}_0^2$ to be the steepest descent direction:

$$\mathbf{v}_0^2 = \nabla_{\mathbf{u}^2} R^2(\mathbf{u}) \Big|_{\mathbf{u}^2 = \mathbf{u}_0^2}$$

A small step in the direction of $\mathbf{v}_0^2$ will bring about the swiftest reduction in $R^2(\mathbf{u}_0)$.

2.4 Solving for λ

Estimating λ involves solving the nonlinear equation $R^2(\lambda) = c^2$ for λ. The Birge procedure has the advantage that the solution can be determined directly. For other procedures, an iterative approach, such as Newton's algorithm [10], is required.

3 Relative entropy as a measure of degree of adjustment

Relative entropy, or Kullback-Leibler divergence, [11, 12], is a measure of the difference between two distributions. For continuous distributions it is given by

$$D_{\mathrm{KL}}(p||p_0) = \int p \log(p/p_0).$$

For any p and p_0, $D_{KL}(p||p_0) \geq 0$ and $D_{\mathrm{KL}}(p||p_0) = 0$ only if $p = p_0$. Note that $D_{\mathrm{KL}}(p||p_0) \neq D_{\mathrm{KL}}(p_0||p)$ and therefore relative entropy is not a norm. It is usually the case that p_0 is an approximate distribution of p and the relative entropy is a measure of information gained using p over p_0.

For multivariate Gaussian distributions,

$$D_{\mathrm{KL}}(\mathrm{N}(\mathbf{x}, V)||\mathrm{N}(\mathbf{x}_0, V_0)) = D + S,$$

where

$$D = \frac{1}{2}\left[\log\left(|V_0 V^{-1}|\right) + \mathrm{Tr}\left(V V_0^{-1}\right) - n\right]$$

and

$$S = \frac{1}{2}(\mathbf{x} - \mathbf{x}_0)^{\mathrm{T}} V_0^{-1}(\mathbf{x} - \mathbf{x}_0).$$

In the above $|A|$ is the determinant of a square matrix A and $\mathrm{Tr}(A)$ is the trace of A, the sum of its diagonal elements. For our application with $\mathbf{x}$ the same for both distributions and diagonal variance matrices, the relative entropy is a function of $\tilde{\mathbf{u}}$ and $\mathbf{u}_0$:

$$D_{\mathrm{KL}}(\tilde{\mathbf{u}}||\mathbf{u}_0) = \frac{1}{2}\left[\sum_{j=1}^{n} \log\left(\frac{u_{0,j}^2}{\tilde{u}_j^2}\right) + \sum_{j=1}^{n} \frac{\tilde{u}_j^2}{u_{0,j}^2} - n\right].$$

4 Adjustment procedure based on minimising relative entropy

We are interested in adjustment procedures that represent as small a change as necessary, as measured by the relative entropy, to bring about consistency. This problem can be formulated as

$$\min_{\tilde{\mathbf{u}}} D_{\mathrm{KL}}(\tilde{\mathbf{u}}||\mathbf{u}_0)$$

subject to

$$R^2(\tilde{\mathbf{u}}) = c^2.$$

The problem can also be parametrized in terms of weights

$$w_{0,j} = 1/u_{0,j}^2, \quad \tilde{w}_j = 1/\tilde{u}_j^2,$$

with

$$D_{\mathrm{KL}}(\tilde{\mathbf{w}}||\mathbf{w}_0) = \frac{1}{2}\left[\sum_{j=1}^{n} \log\left(\frac{\tilde{w}_j}{w_{0,j}}\right) + \sum_{j=1}^{n} \frac{w_{0,j}}{\tilde{w}_j} - n\right].$$

In terms of weights $\tilde{\mathbf{w}}$, the consistency constraint in equation (2) can be written explicitly as

$$E(\tilde{\mathbf{w}}) = c^2 S_w - S_w S_{wxx} + (S_{wx})^2 = 0,$$

where

$$S_w = \sum_{j=1}^{n} \tilde{w}_j, \quad S_{wx} = \sum_{j=1}^{n} \tilde{w}_j x_j, \quad S_{wxx} = \sum_{j=1}^{n} \tilde{w}_j x_j^2.$$

Thus $E(\mathbf{w})$ is a quadratic function of the parameters $\tilde{\mathbf{w}}$. In terms of the weights $\tilde{\mathbf{w}}$, we arrive the adjustment procedure

$$\min D_{\mathrm{KL}}(\tilde{\mathbf{w}}||\mathbf{w}_0)$$

subject to

$$E(\tilde{\mathbf{w}}) = 0, \quad 0 \leq \tilde{w}_j \leq w_{0,j}, \quad j = 1, \ldots, n.$$

The last set of inequalities imposes the constraint that we only look for an adjustment that increases the input uncertainties.

4.1 Newton scheme to determine $\tilde{\mathbf{w}}$

If we assume that if $E(\mathbf{w}_0) < 0$, that is, $R^2(\mathbf{u}_0) > c^2$, the optimal $\tilde{\mathbf{w}}$ automatically satisfies the constraints $\tilde{w}_j \leq w_{0,j}$, then the optimal $\tilde{\mathbf{w}}$ is a critical point of the Lagrangian function

$$\mathcal{L}(\tilde{\mathbf{w}}, \kappa) = D_{\mathrm{KL}}(\tilde{\mathbf{w}}||\mathbf{w}_0) + \kappa E(\tilde{\mathbf{w}}).$$

This leads to a square system of $n + 1$ equations

$$\begin{aligned} \nabla_{\tilde{\mathbf{w}}} D_{\mathrm{KL}} + \kappa \nabla_{\tilde{\mathbf{w}}} E &= \mathbf{0}, \\ E &= 0 \end{aligned}$$

that can be solved iteratively using Newton's method, for example [10]. A starting estimate $\tilde{\mathbf{w}}$ could be the Birge solution with κ defined by the least squares solution of the first n equations above. The Newton scheme can be implemented in stages for decreasing values c_k^2 of c^2, starting with a value of c^2 close to c_0^2 determined by the input $\mathbf{u}_0$, and ending up with the desired value for c^2. The staged approach may help issues with divergence of a simple Newton scheme if the starting point is far from the solution.

5 Example calculations

We present calculations for data derived from the Consultative Committee for Length key comparison CCL-K1, calibration of gauge blocks by interferometry. The measured results x_j and associated standard uncertainties $u_{0,j}$ are from eleven participating laboratories measuring nine tungsten carbide gauge blocks of nominal lengths ranging from 0.5 mm to 100 mm [14, Table 5].

The analysis of the data for the 100 mm gauge block found that the χ^2 value was 0.98 indicating inconsistency of the data. Figure 1 shows the estimates $\mathbf{x}$ and the uncertainty bars $x_j \pm 2u_j$ for the input uncertainties $\mathbf{u}_0$ and the adjusted uncertainties $\tilde{\mathbf{u}}$ for the Birge, Mandel-Paule (M-P), steepest decent (S-D) and minimum relative entropy (DKL) procedures. The adjustment schemes determined consistency for c^2 set at the 80 percentile value. The Birge and Mandel-Paul (M-P) schemes each apply the same adjustment to the uncertainties from all the laboratories, either multiplicatively or additively. The degree of adjustment for the steepest descent (S-D) approach depends on how far the laboratory estimate is from the consensus value a_0 determined from the initial weighted least square (WLS) analysis . If x_j is close to a_0, then $\tilde{u}_j$ remains close to $u_{j,0}$. For laboratories 6, 7 and 11, the steepest descent approach makes a larger adjustment to the uncertainties as the respective estimates are further away from a_0. Visually, there is evidence that the steepest descent method brings about minimal adjustment compared to the other two single parameter adjustment schemes. The extent of adjustment using each of these methods can be quantified using the Kullback-Leibler divergence, the lower the divergence, the smaller the adjustment. Table 1 shows that among the single parameter adjustment schemes, the steepest descent method has the lowest Kullback-Leibler divergence. It is next only to the minimum relative entropy adjustment scheme. Like the steepest descent scheme, the minimum relative entropy method only makes a substantial adjustment to the uncertainties of laboratories 6, 7, and 11. However, the extent to which the uncertainties are adjusted is such that the relative entropy is minimised.

As discussed above, with the steepest descent approach, if the estimate x_j provided by the jth laboratory happens to be very close to the consensus value a_0 determined by the WLS approach (using the input $\mathbf{u}_0$), then the steepest descent vector will have only a very small component in the direction of increasing u_j so that u_j remains essentially unadjusted. If the consensus value $\tilde{a}$ given by the adjusted $\tilde{\mathbf{u}}$ is significantly different from the initial consensus value, there may be evidence the u_j should also undergo some adjustment as x_j is no longer so close to the new consensus value. This suggests implementing a staged approach determining steepest descent adjustments for a sequence of values c_k^2 descending from c_0^2 down to the desired c^2.

Consensus values and their associated uncertainties are shown in table 2. All the adjustment schemes result in a larger uncertainties around the consensus value which is a direct consequence of adjusting each laboratory's estimates of uncertainty $u_{0,j}$. The minimum relative entropy adjustment method yields the smallest uncertainty around the consensus value as a result of the minimal adjustment to $u_{0,j}$.

There are a number of points of interest associated with tables 1 and 2. In table 1, we see that the steepest descent method makes a smaller change to the input distributions as measured by the relative entropy compared to the Birge and Mandel-Paule procedures. Both the Birge and Mandel-Paule procedures provide and adjustment direction $\mathbf{v}^2$ that does not depend on how the input estimates x_j relate to the consensus value a_0, whereas the steepest descent procedure does reflect this information with the uncertainties associated with estimates further from the consensus value undergoing more adjustment. Of course, the fact that there is inconsistency means that use of the initial consensus estimate a_0 to determine the decree of adjustment has to be undertaken with caution. An advantage of the relative entropy approach (as well as guaranteeing a minimal adjustment according to the criterion) is that the initial consensus estimate plays a significantly lesser role in the adjustment procedure. A feature of table 2 is the spread of the consensus estimates from -73.2 nm to -76.4 nm, a range of 3.2 nm that can be compared to standard uncertainty of the order of 4 nm. This shows that the method of adjustment can have a significant impact in the reported consensus value.

The adjustment procedures we have considered so far have the feature that the input uncertainties are adjusted to achieve a desired degree of consistency and the adjusted uncertainties are then treated as known exactly as far as the determination of the consensus value is concerned. It seems more reasonable to regard the input uncertainties as estimates of the true uncertainties and then use the ensemble of information provided by the ILC to update these estimates in a Bayesian framework. Such an approach recognises that the updated estimates are not known exactly and this lack of complete knowledge about them will contribute an uncertainty to the consensus value derived from them. A Bayesian version of the Birge and Mandel-Paule procedures is considered in [2], for example, and leads to t-distributions associated with the consensus value. The Bayesian approach can be developed further [8] in a hierarchical model that leads to a consensus distribution that is a mixture of t-distributions (in the same way that a t-distribution is a

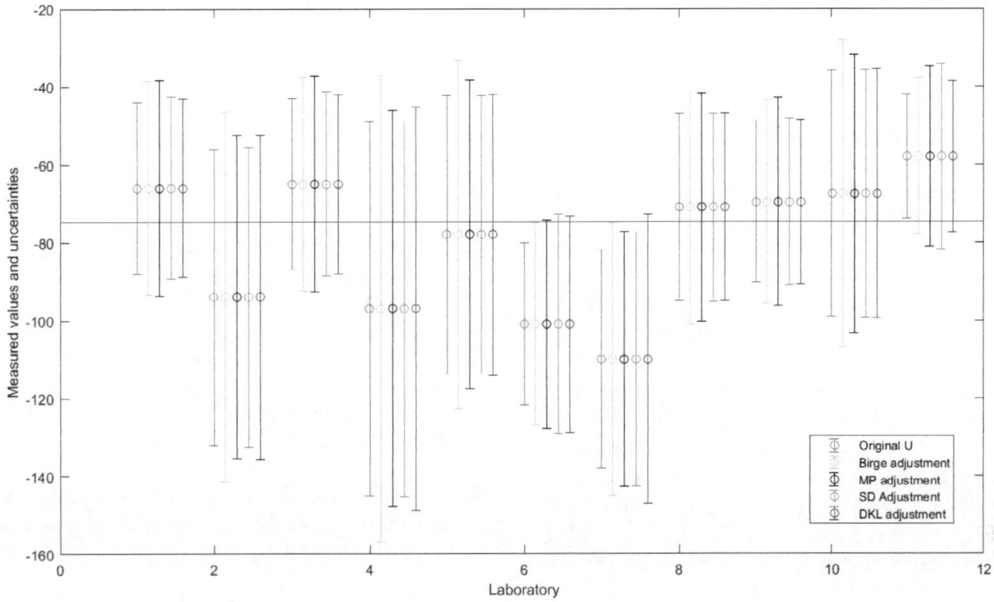

Figure 1: Estimates and 95% confidence intervals of a 100 mm gauge block for various adjustment procedures.

mixture of Gaussians). The analysis of the gauge block data in [8] led to a consensus estimate of −73.3 nm with associated standard uncertainty of 3.8 nm which is more in line with the relative entropy estimate in table 2. We must bear in mind that the relative entropy approach associates a Gaussian distribution to the consensus estimate while the Bayesian approaches assign heavier-tailed distributions.

Table 1: $D_{\mathrm{KL}}(\tilde{\mathbf{u}}||\mathbf{u}_0)$ for various adjustment schemes

	$D_{\mathrm{KL}}(\tilde{\mathbf{u}}\|\|\mathbf{u}_0)$
Birge	0.64
Mandel-Paule	0.56
Steepest descent	0.36
Relative entropy	0.27

Table 2: Consensus values along with their associated uncertainty.

	Estimate/nm	Uncertainty/nm
WLS	-74.8	3.7
Birge	-74.8	4.6
Mandel-Paule	-76.4	4.6
Steepest descent	-75.0	4.2
Relative entropy	-73.2	4.1

6 Concluding remarks

This paper has been concerned with the analysis of inter-laboratory comparison (ILC) data and approaches to resolving inconsistency in such data. When data is judged to be inconsistent, the weighted least squares estimate of the consensus value of the quantity being measured might not reliable. Several adjustment schemes have been discussed in this paper. The underlying assumption behind adjustment procedures is that some or all of the laboratories have underestimated or neglected some uncertainty contributions, sometimes referred to as 'dark uncertainty', and the adjusted uncertainties provide an estimate of this dark uncertainty derived from the complete set of laboratory results. We have been interested in adjustments procedures that make minimal adjustments to the input uncertainties. One way of quantifying the extent of adjustment is the Kullback-Leibler divergence or relative entropy. We have compared adjustment schemes such as the Birge and Mandel-Paule methods with a steepest descent adjustment and relative entropy adjustment that are specifically designed to minimise the degree of adjustment. The Birge and Mandel-Paule methods tend to make large adjustments compared to that that can be achieved using a minimal relative entropy adjustment. The steepest descent method tends to compare well with the relative entropy adjustment and is not as numerically demanding as it involves only solving a single nonlinear equation.

Acknowledgement

This work was supported by the UK's National Measurement System programme for Data Science.

References

[1] R. T. Birge. Probable values of the general physical constants. *Rev. Mod. Phys*, 1:1–73, 1929.

[2] O. Bodnar, C. Elster, J. Fischer, Possolo A., and B. Toman. Evaluation of uncertainty in the adjustment of fundamental constants. *Metrologia*, 53(1):S46–S54, 2016.

[3] A. G. Chunovkina, C. Elster, I. Lira, and W. Wöger. Analysis of key comparison data and laboratory biases. *Metrologia*, 45(2):211–216, 2008.

[4] M. G. Cox. The evaluation of key comparison data. *Metrologia*, 39:589–595, 2002.

[5] M. G. Cox, A. B. Forbes, J. Flowers, and P. M. Harris. Least squares adjustment in the presence of discrepant data. In P. Ciarlini, M. G. Cox, F. Pavese, and G. B. Rossi, editors, *Advanced Mathematical and Computational Tools in Metrology VI*, pages 37–51, Singapore, 2004. World Scientific.

[6] M.G. Cox. The evaluation of key comparison data: determining the largest consistent subset. *Metrologia*, 44(3):187–200, 2007.

[7] C. Elster and B. Toman. Analysis of key comparisons: estimating laboratories' biases by a fixed effects model using Bayesian model averaging. *Metrologia*, 47(3):113–119, 2010.

[8] A. B. Forbes. A hierarchical model for the analysis of inter-laboratory comparison data. *Metrologia*, 53:1295–1305, 2016.

[9] A. B. Forbes and C. Perruchet. Measurement systems analysis: concepts and computational approaches. In *IMEKO World Congress, September 18–22, 2006, Rio de Janeiro*, 2006.

[10] P. E. Gill, W. Murray, and M. H. Wright. *Practical Optimization*. Academic Press, London, 1981.

[11] S. Kullback and R. A. Leibler. On information and sufficiency. *Ann. Math. Statist.*, 55:79–86, 1951.

[12] D. J. C. MacKay. *Information Theory, Inference and Learning Algorithms*. Cambridge University Press, 2003.

[13] R. C. Paule and J. Mandel. Consensus values and weighting factors. *J Res. Natl. Bur. Stand.*, 87:377–385, 1982.

[14] R. Thalmann. CCL key comparison: calibration of gauge blocks by interferometry. *Metrologia*, 39:165–177, 2002.

[15] K. Weise and W. Woeger. Removing model and data non-conformity in measurement evaluation. *Measurement Science and Technology*, 11:1649–1658, 2000.

[16] R. Willink. Statistical determination of a comparison reference value using hidden errors. *Metrologia*, 39:343–354, 2002.

Assesment of predictive capability

A. Bourdim, M. Bourdim, and B. Bloul*, F. Hacizade

Eole laboratory, Department of Mechanical Engineering, University of Tlemcen Algeria
*Reliability laboratory of petrolium equipment & Materials - Boumerdes, Bougara Algeria
Received:

Abstract: The current economic problems seem to affect a world that is increasingly reactive, companies are evolving very quickly in an atmosphere of increased competitiveness, so we have to be able to distinguish very quickly from our competitors by optimization of the Quality-Costs-Development Time. Quality is therefore a requirement to be met in order to satisfy the customer's needs. The study of the predictive capability of measuring devices, methods and production systems is a very important means of quality control. Operations associated with the characteristics of the used measuring that can have a significant effect on product quality should be identified. Appropriate control should be established to ensure that these characteristics remain within the specification. In this study a simple methodology is proposed for the rapid determination of the predictive capability of the measuring devices based on the R & R statistical method (repeatability and reproducibility).

Key words: predictive capability, quality, repeatability, reproducibility, interval of tolerances, measurement uncertainty.

1 Introduction

Standardization system requires organizations to ensure that the equipment used is capable of carrying out appropriate controls and measures. These, together with their uncertainties, lead to a justified decision to accept or refuse the produced products. Care must therefore be taken to monitor and optimize the manufacturing process and to ensure that the control and measurement devices are still reliable and capable of satisfying the required specifications made by the manufacturer.

To put under control a manufacturing or control process it is necessary to evaluate its capability, in other words, evaluate if it is capable to produce under best conditions.

All measurement systems, integrating instrument, methods and the environment in which the measurement is carried out determine the control of manufacturing processes.

To carry out studies of measurement systems, the objectives and limits of the analysis must be defined in order to determine the necessary information. And for this, often short method is used to determine the capability of measuring instruments.

2 Predictive capability of measuring devices

The predictive capability of a measuring devices is the ability of the measurement process to satisfy customer specifications [1]. Its determination is part of a prevention strategy and allows a company to verify that it is able to comply with specifications in order to satisfy the customer's needs. Since the capability is calculated statistically by measurements, which are generally affected by dispersions corresponding to the maximum variation t hat could be observed by measuring the same object. The measurement uncertainty IM results from the properties of the instrument, the operator, the environment of measurement (temperature, vibration,...), the measurement procedure,…

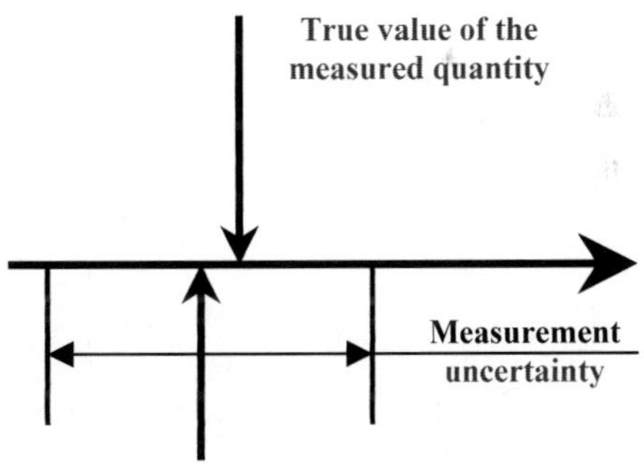

Fig.1: **Measurement uncertainty**

In figure.1, the read value on the measuring instrument may be located over the whole area of measurement uncertainty and therefore be more or less close to the true value of the measured quantity.

Repeatability and Reproducibility requirements must therefore be made.

We must therefore make measurements following conditions of Repeatability and Reproducibility.

Measured variance (R&R) = operator Variance + Measurement chain variance

$$\sigma^2_{R\&R} = \sigma^2_{instrument} = \sigma^2_{repeatability} + \sigma^2_{reproducibility} \quad (1)$$

Correspondence: bourdim56@yahoo.fr

2.1. Compliance criteria

Standard NF-E 02-204 (1987) prescribes that the measurement uncertainty IM must be less than or equal to1/4 of the IT tolerance interval. This gives a minimum capability Cmc equal to 4 [2], ie.**4IM≤IT**. This means that if a measuring instrument has a capability of 4 for a dimension to be checked, it will be ensured that the dimension is conforms only if the read value is within the conformity zone which is equal to 3/4 of the tolerance (Fig.2).

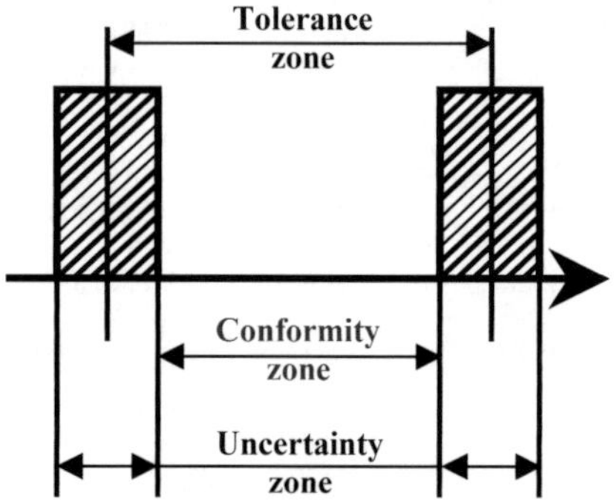

Fig.2: Conformity zone

2.2 Calculation assumptions

The measurements made by the controlled instrument must follow a normal Gaussian distribution with a lower natural limit LNI and an upper natural limit LNS (fig.3), defined by convention by the following equations:

LNI = $\mu - 3\sigma$ = Pr ($x \leq$ LNI) = 0,00135.

LNS = $\mu + 3\sigma$ = Pr ($x \leq$ LNS) = 0,99865

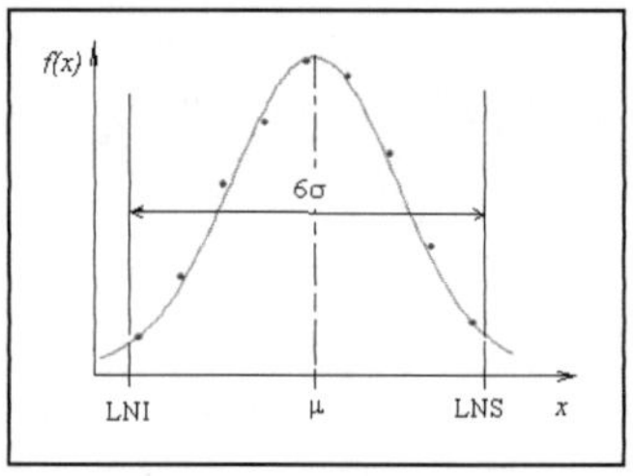

Fig.3: Gaussian distribution of measurements

According to AFNOR X06-030, a control process will be declared "fit" if it has demonstrated, for the selected characteristics that it is capable of producing for a sufficiently long period, with a theoretical rate of non-Conformities lower than the internal requirements of the company. This rate is frequently fixed at 0.27% (method 6σ)[3].

That is, the controlled limits are within ± 3σ so that 0.135% of the measurements are below the NLI and 0.135% are above the LNS.

Dispersion = Measurement Uncertainty IM = 6 $\sigma_{instrument}$

$$\frac{Tolerance\ Interval}{Measurement\ Uncertainty} = \frac{IT}{IM} = \frac{IT}{6\sigma_{instrument}} \qquad (3)$$

Tolerance interval IT = Higher deviation (ES) - Lower deviation (EI)

In order to meet the standards and minimize measurement dispersions, it is recommended to take measurements under conditions of repeatability and reproducibility, since all the modalities for carrying out the repeatability conditions are constant, whereas the reproducibility conditions Incorporate most sources of variation.

$$\sigma^2_{instrument} = \sigma^2_{repeatability} + \sigma^2_{reproducibility}$$

$$\sigma_{repeatability} = \frac{\overline{R}}{d_2} \qquad \text{With} \qquad \overline{R} = \frac{\sum R_i}{k}$$

Where k is the number of operators (k = 2)

N = number of measurements / parts / operator	**2**	3	4	5
d_2	**1.128**	1.693	2.059	2.36

2.3 Calculation of reproducibility dispersion

The reproducibility is composed of the variability due to the operator to which the repeatability that it contains is subtracted to avoid redundancy when calculating the Cmc.

$$\sigma_{reproducibility} = \sqrt{\sigma^2_{operator} - \frac{\sigma^2_{repeatability}}{N}}$$

Where:

N = the total number of measurements per piece and per operator

$$\sigma_{operator} = \frac{\sqrt{(X_i - M)^2}}{\sqrt{k}} = \frac{R_M}{d^*_2}$$

With: $R_M = M_{max} - M_{min}$

In this relation d_2* is the divisor used for the estimation of the dispersion or of the standard deviation.

According to [3], for two measurements per piece and per operator (N = 2), we obtain d_2* = 1.414.

N = number of measures/piece/operator	**2**	3	4	5
d^*_2	**1,414**	1,693	2,059	2.36

Finally, the measurement uncertainty (IM) must be compared with the tolerance of the measurement (IT) in order to verify that the capability of the measuring device is acceptable, it is then necessary to check the inequality: **4IM ≤ IT**

2.3 Procedure

The main steps of this method are as follows:

a) 10 representative pieces of the entire dispersion of the measured characteristics must be selected.

b) Several operators (from 2 to 5) must make two sets of measurements for each of the 10 pieces. These measurements must be carried out at the control station under normal conditions.

c) In a metrological laboratory it is necessary to determine the actual dimensions of each part, generally with a better order of precision.

d) The results of the measurement shall be presented in a table (Table 1).

Table 1:

	OPERATOR A				OPERATOR B			
Samples	Set1	Set2	m	r	Set1	Set2	m	r
part1	xA11	xA21			xB11	xB21		
part 2	xA12	xA22			xB12	xB22		
part 3	xA13	xA23			xB13	xB23		
part 4	xA14	xA24			xB14	xB24		
part 5	xA15	xA25			xB15	xB25		
part 6	xA16	xA26			xB16	xB26		
part 7	xA17	xA27			xB17	xB27		
part 8	xA18	xA28			xB18	xB28		
part 9	xA19	xA29			xB19	xB29		
part 10	xA110	xA210			xB110	xB210		
	M =		R =		M =		R =	

m= average of the measured values for a part and by an operator

r = measuring range – x_{max}-x_{min}

M = average of measured values by an operator for all the tested parts

R = average of ranges. It concerns all measured parts by an operator.

2.4 Application

We have applied this method to the method of calibrating a system to measure vibration accelerations. The calibration device produces a vibratory motion with a constant acceleration a = $10^{\pm 0.1}$ ms^{-2}. The 10 parts in this application were KD35 piezoelectric sensors are used to measure the acceleration produced by the calibration device. The results obtained after the measurement are shown in Table 2.

2.4 Application

Based on the values in the table above, the results are as follows: d_2= 1,128 (tabulation)

- d_2*= 1,414 (tabulation)
- R = 1,95
- $\sigma_{\mathbf{repeatability}}$ = 1,729
- R_M = 2,25
- $\sigma_{\mathbf{operator}}$ = 1,591
- $\sigma_{\mathbf{reproducibility}}$ = 1,976
- $\sigma_{\mathbf{instrument}}$ = 2,625
- $6\sigma_{\mathbf{instrument}}$ = IM (measurement uncertainty) =15.75
- If IT = 10 (specification)

Then, Cmc = 4,44, where 4 IM > IT, We can consider that this system is not capable for this measurement accuracy.

7. CONCLUSIONS

This summary reflects the importance and impact of computing predictive capability in business, throughout our study we addressed the capability calculations using a very simple and quick statistical approach. This will allow us to validate our approach, by repositioning the different standards using the case studies.

The assessment of predictive capability is therefore an indispensable tool, and is widely used in large companies. Using the statistical tool, the capability was able to bring a more rigor in the respect of the quality. It is certain that this tool will be deployed more and more in the future in all companies.

REFERENCES

1. D.R Bothe, Measuring Process Capability: Techniques and Calculations for Quality and Manufacturing Engineers. McGraw Hill, 1997

2. J.L Vachette, Amélioration continue de la qualité Les Editions d'Organisation - Paris, 1990

3. Manual on the Presentation of Data and Control chart Analysis" - publication ASTM STP - 150, New York, 1986

4. ISO 9004:1987 Gestion de la qualité et éléments de système qualité - Lignes directrices -1987

5. L. Wisweh, M. Sandau, R. Ichimiya, S. Sakamoto, Determination of the Measuring Uncertainty and its use for quality assessment and quality control, in: Research Report of Faculty of Engineering, Niigata University, Japan, No. 47; 1998, Page 1–15.

Research on the achievement of a primary standard for air kerma

S. Patrascu[1], E. Iliescu[1], S. Bercea[1], D. Dusciac[1], A. Celarel[1], A. Ostrowsky[2], C. Cenusa[1], I. Cenusa[1], M. Donois[2], V. Blideanu[2], J-M Bordy[2]

[1] "Horia Hulubei" National Institute for R&D in Physics and Nuclear Engineering (IFIN-HH), Magurele, Romania, [2]CEA, LIST, Laboratoire National Henri Becquerel (LNE-LNHB), France

Received:

Abstract. This paper deals with the research performed by scientists of CEA-LNHB and IFIN-HH/ CMRID in the frame of project 14 RPT 04 ABSORB. One of the scientific and technical objectives of this project is to study the design of cavity chamber primary standard, to establish a research capability in measuring the air kerma for photon energies such as those of ^{60}Co or/and ^{137}Cs used in radiotherapy. A cavity-ionization chamber is dedicated to the absolute measurement of the air kerma (K_{air}) or the air kerma rate ($\dot{K}_{air}$). Therefore, the value of the sensitive volume of the chamber is a quantity involved in the relation used for K_{air}. In this way, the participating laboratories will be able to build and operate primary standards with a harmonized target uncertainty budget of 0.5 %, and to elaborate and apply harmonized calibration procedures.

Keywords: air kerma, cavity ionization chamber

1 Introduction

The collaboration between IFIN-HH/CMRID and CEA/LNHB in the field of the metrology for dosimetry was intensely developed during the last 10 years. An example of this collaboration is the participation of the two laboratories in several international projects regarding the development of secondary and primary standards for the dosimetry of the environment as well as for medical applications of the ionizing radiation. In this way, the participating laboratories will be able to build and operate primary standards with a harmonized target uncertainty budget of 0.5 %, and to elaborate and apply harmonized calibration procedures. In the framework of this project, a cavity ionization chamber was designed.

2 Theoretical background

The verification of the components of the cavity ionization chamber included measurements of linear dimensions of pieces provided by the manufacturer, accordingly to the technical specifications shown in Figure 1 to 5 here below. The preparation of the components included polishing of contact surfaces (polystyrene components), in order to ensure excellent insulation properties. A cavity-ionization chamber is dedicated to the absolute measurement of the air kerma (K_{air}) or the air kerma rate ($\dot{K}_{air}$). Therefore, the value of the sensitive volume of the chamber is a quantity involved in the relation used for K_{air}. The quantity kerma (Kinetic Energy Released in Material) is the sum of the initial kinetic energies of all the ionizing charged particles liberated by uncharged ionizing particles, to a unit of mass of matter.

$$K = \frac{dE_{tr}}{dm} \qquad (1)$$

$[K] = 1$ Gy $= 1$ J/kg

Where: dE_{tr} is the sum of the initial kinetic energy of all the ionizing charged particles; dm is the mass of matter element, in which the energy was released.

The Absorbed Dose (D) is the mean energy imparted by the radiation to a unit mass of matter,

$$D = \frac{d\varepsilon}{dm} \qquad (2)$$

$[D] = 1$ Gy $= 1$ J/kg

The absolute measurement of the air kerma (K_{air}) and air kerma rate ($\dot{K}_{air}$), as well as for absorbed dose to air (D_{air}) and absorbed dose to air rate ($\dot{D}_{air}$) can be performed with an ionization chamber of a special type, namely the cavity-ionization chamber. This is the reason for which, the value of the sensitive volume and its shape and geometry are very important for a correct operation of the detector.

3 Experimental setup

The cavity ionization chamber designed and manufactured within the CATRAS project has a spherical shape. The chamber's wall is made of graphite. The inner surface of the wall is one of the polarizing electrodes. The chamber's wall is made up of two components (Figure 1) forcedly assembled, and are irremovable after assembly (Figure 1). The collecting electrode (Figure 2) is made also from graphite. It is mounted on an aluminium (DURAL) rod, by screw. The surfaces of these components (coloured in blue) were very polished, in order to reduce, as much as possible, the leakage currents. The wall material for such a cavity ionization chamber, for air kerma measurement, is graphite. As the mechanical processing of the graphite is a very complicate task, the only company that assumed it was ABT SORIME (France). The components of the ionization chamber were processed of different materials, according to their role in the chamber assembly. Therefore, the material for the chamber wall (Figure 1), as well as the central (collecting electrode) (Figure 2) was graphite (carbon Lorraine 5890PT); the insulating components of the chamber (some of them presented in Figure 3 and Figure 4) are made of cross-linked polystyrene (provided by CEA-LNHB).

The central component (collecting electrode) is installed in a metal stem made of aluminium (DURAL) (Figure 5). The set-up technology for the ionization chamber had several steps: checking of all the components provided by the manufacturer; technologies for polishing and cleaning of all components; assembling of the components; tests regarding the correct assembling; electrical and radiological tests, to determine some of the parameters of the ionization chamber. All these operations were performed in the laboratories of CEA-LNHB.

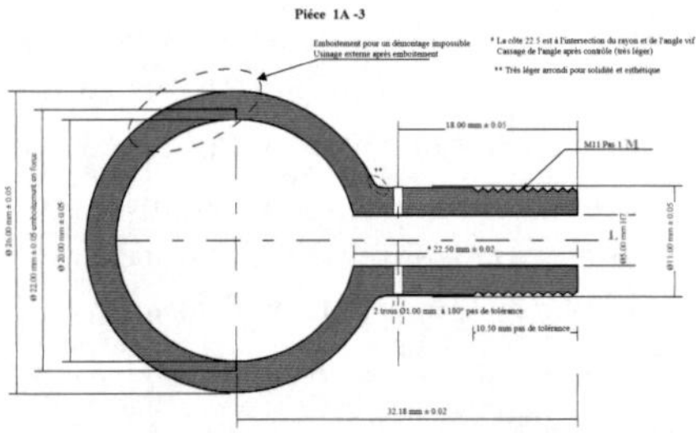

Fig. 1. Component 1A-3: spherical electrode (graphite)

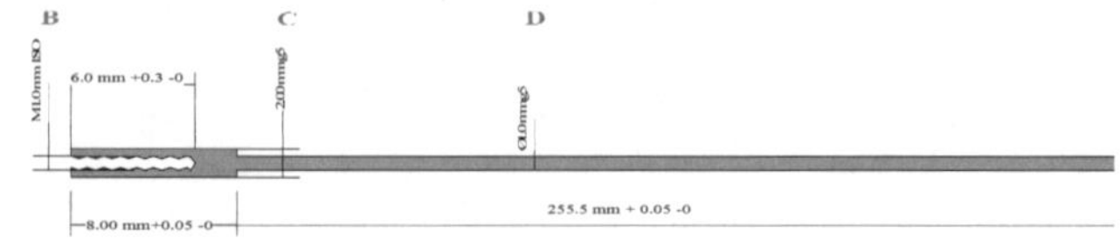

Fig. 2. DURAL

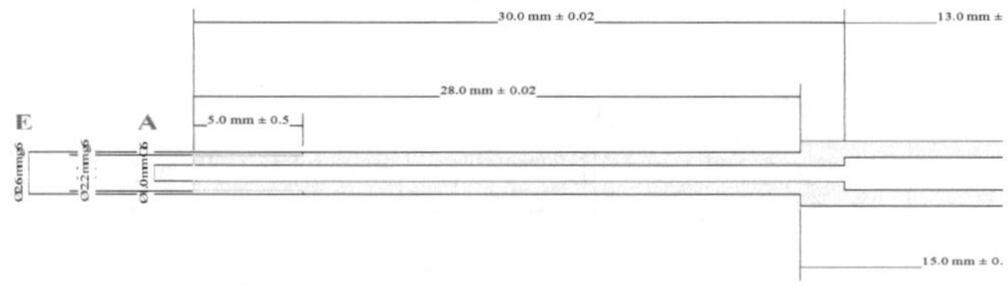

Fig. 3. Cross-linked polystyrene

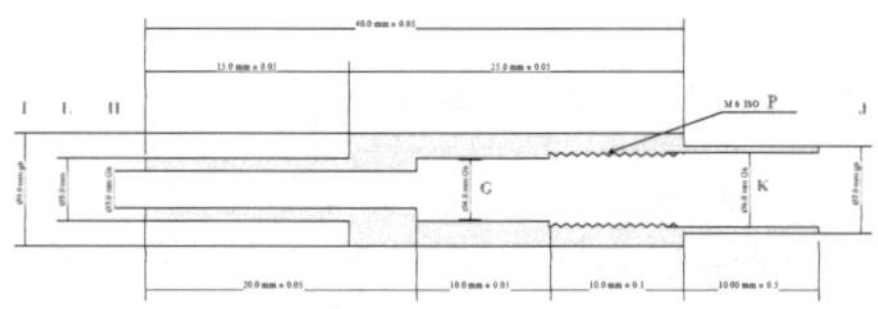

Fig. 4. Cross-linked polystyrene

All the components presented above were assembled in such a way to obtain the cavity ionization chamber (Figure 5).

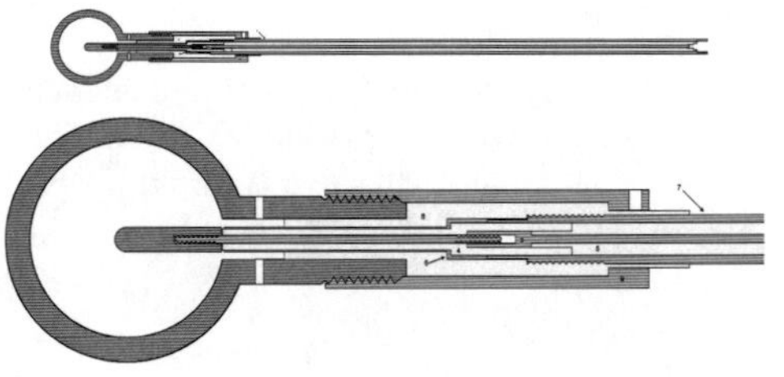

Fig. 5. Assembled ionization chamber (scheme)

In order to check whether the positioning of the components is correct (according to the design), a radiography of the assembly was made. For the radiography, a L 7901-01 HAMAMATSU PHOTONICS X-ray machine was used. (The parameters of the X-ray machine were: U=100kV, I_{max}=250 μA). The image of the chamber was captured by a C7942SK-05 HAMAMATSU PHOTONICS sensor and then, was digitally recorded in a computer. The first radiography is shown in Figure 6. In this figure, it can be seen that the position of the central electrode is not correct in relation to the spherical cavity (the central electrode does not enter enough into the volume of the chamber).

4 Results and discussions

The distance between the correct position and the actual position of the central electrode was of 0.1 mm, in relation to the interior surface of the chamber's wall.

Fig. 6. First version of the assembled ionization chamber (radiography)

In the next stage, the chamber was disassembled. All the pieces made of polystyrene were examined using a microscope, in order to observe if and where, major imperfections exist on their surface and to insist to polish these areas. The conclusion after this examination was that there were no such areas. The finishing technology had also two stages. In the first stage, a polishing cream with diamond granulates of 6 μm was used. After cleaning with isopropyl alcohol and drying with compressed air, the polishing process continued, by using diamond granulates of 3 μm. All the components made of polystyrene and aluminum were finally cleaned with ultrasound in ultra-pure water and isopropyl alcohol. Then, the pieces were dried out for 90 min at 60^0C. The graphite collecting electrode was screwed on the aluminum rod and the electrical contact between the two components was tested using a Fluke 89 multi-meter.

In Figure 7, a photo of the final assembled ionization chamber is shown.

Fig. 7. Final version of the assembled ionization chamber (radiography)

5 Conclusion

The materials used for manufacturing the components of the cavity-ionization chamber are suitable for the aim of the project. The technology used assured the necessary quality of the components of the detector, in order to fulfil all the requirements, supposed by its destination as primary standard for air kerma measurements.

References

1. ICRU Report No. 85: "Fundamental Quantities and Units for Ionizing Radiation (Revised)", Journal of the ICRU, Volume 11, No 1, 2011

Automatic Registration and Evaluation of Point Clouds Data Measured from Multi-sensor

F. Li*, C. Hitchens

Nuclear Advanced Manufacturing Research Centre (Nuclear AMRC), The University of Sheffield, Advanced Manufacturing Park, Brunel Way, Rotherham, S60 5WG, United Kingdom

Received:

Abstract. A new automatic registration algorithm is proposed to solve the rigid registration problem of scattered point clouds measured from multi-sensors; specifically for those artefacts are lack of abundant features. The existing techniques exhibit significant limitations to deal with this type of registration problems. The first step is to automatically perform a coarse registration of the multi-sensor point data by estimating principal pose of point datasets. In the second step, the translation matrices obtained from coarse registration algorithms are used to provide correct trend for fine registration and the optimal translation matrices are solved using an iterative algorithm. The third step, the accuracy of registered surfaces, which are measured from multi-resolution sensors, is evaluated using a new method which is based on the normal vectors of points. A Matlab toolbox has been developed to verify the proposed algorithms. Experimental results show that the proposed methods are effective and robust. The tool box can be used to register multi-sensor point data and evaluate the accuracy of matched surfaces.

Keywords: Multi-sensor; Optical measurement; Registration; ICP algorithm

1 Introduction

Since the requirements on the accuracy, complexity and of measurements are increasing, various techniques including tactile method for example coordinate measuring machine (CMM) [1] and optical methods such as photogrammetry [2], fringe projection [3] and laser scanner [4] are used for acquiring surface points from an object. Even though tactile methods and optical sensing technologies have been widely used in data acquisition in dimensional metrology, it has been shown that each technique is applicable to different scenarios and has its own advantages and drawbacks. Therefore multi-sensor techniques have been developed to achieve holistic geometrical information and improve reliability or reduce measurement uncertainty [5].

As the point cloud data is captured in respective sensor's coordinate system, these coordinate systems have to be registered to one common coordinate system to produce correct results after measurement. The same surface measured by different sensors can be considered as a rigid body movement, the geometric transformation method can be used to deal with data registration. The transformation parameters can include a 3×3 rotation matrix and a 3×1 translation vector. The transformation parameters can commonly be determined by the Least Square Criterion. This can be calculated by minimisation of the variance of distance of corresponding points in overlapping areas of point clouds. Registration is one of the most decisive steps in three dimensional (3D) modelling.

A new framework to automatically register pairwise point clouds captured from different sensors has been presented in this paper. The point datasets are first automatically registered using principal pose estimation methods and then evaluated by own-developed algorithm, which is based on the normal vectors of points. This framework can register and evaluate the unordered point clouds measured from multi-sensor without any initial pose information of point clouds.

* Correspondence: feng.li@sheffield.ac.uk

The main contribution of this paper is the following:

- A new coarse registration method is proposed to align 3D rigid point data measured from different sensors.
- A full automatic framework is presented for registration of unordered points datasets without any initial estimation or manual operation.
- A new approach based on the normal vectors of points is introduced to evaluate the registration accuracy of point clouds.

The rest of this paper is organised as follows. Section 2 reviews previous work on the field of 3D data registration. Section 3 presents the overall structure of the proposed method. Section 4 describes the relevant mathematical formulations and specific registration method which includes coarse registration and fine registration steps. Section 5 introduces a new methodology for the evaluation of point clouds after registration. Section 6 gives the experimental results and compares the proposed approach with other registration methods. Section 7 concludes with some discussions.

2 Literature review

The goal of registration is to find the minimum Euclidean transformation between a set of point clouds. The application of markers [6] onto the object is one common method used in many commercial systems. Other solutions may use the knowledge about the sensors positions to transform the datasets into one common coordinate system; for example calibrating the movement between two measurements in advance [7] or exploiting mechanical devices such as turntables [8]. In addition, the numerical methods are another type of solutions and numerous algorithms have been developed to solve the registration problems, which may be divided into coarse and fine registration processes. If previous information of the motions of point clouds is unknown, a coarse registration is needed to obtain the initial estimations. Coarse registration is followed by fine registration to obtain the most accurate solution as possible. After fine registration, the point clouds are combined to form a complete 3D model.

The goal of coarse registration is to find the correspondences between both 3D surfaces and compute an initial estimation of the rigid motion between two point clouds. The coarse registration can be performed manually or automatically; for automatic coarse registration, extensive research has been explored and discussed. The existing techniques, for example Spin Image Matching [9], Ransac-based Darces [10] and the method of Genetic Algorithm [11], have been developed for coarse registration. Gelfand, et al. [12] presented a technique to constrain unstable transformations by finding the common sample features in the pairwise point cloud, which can be exploited to minimise registration uncertainty and roughly register point clouds. Mian, et al. [13] presented a novel feature matching algorithm for automatic pairwise registration of range images, which is based on the normal vector of the points. Their algorithm used a novel tensor representation which represents semi-local 3D surface patches of a range image by third order tensors. Tensors of two range images are matched to identify correspondences between them. In this way correspondences can be verified and then used for pairwise registration of the range images. In addition, He, et al. [14] proposed an automatic registration algorithm based on the curvature feature. In their method, the feature points that have the maximum local curvature variations are extracted and then the initial matching points can be acquired by computing the Hausdorff distance of curvature.

After coarse registration, the iterative algorithm is exploited to obtain the best registration result possible. These methods use an initial estimate of the motion, which may be obtained from the coarse registration process, and the refine the transformation matrix by minimising the distance between temporal correspondences, for example using the Iterative Closest Point (ICP) algorithm [15-17] and its variants [18-21].

As most coarse registration methods are based on 'feature-matching'. This type of methods usually needs abundant features to identify and extract to align point clouds. However, in many applications, there is a demand to register point clouds scanned from artefacts that are lacking in rich features, such as the samples discussed in this paper. The techniques based on feature-matching are tested but do not seem to work properly for the cases discussed in the paper. Therefore, a new approach is introduced to solve this problem and the method is applied to register the point datasets measured from multi-sensors.

3 Framework of the proposed method

The aim is to register 3D point clouds captured from different sensor sources, which include the CMM, structured light scanner, laser scanner and confocal microscope. These sensors have different working principles. In addition, the scans may contain large missing regions; for example when using structured light scanner to measure the metal surfaces due to reflections. This paper presents a novel method to register point clouds measured from multi-sensors; it mainly includes three modular components – first coarse registration of point clouds; then the fine registration; final evaluation of the matching accuracy of overlapping surfaces, based on normal vector method. The systematic framework of the proposed method is show in Fig. 1.

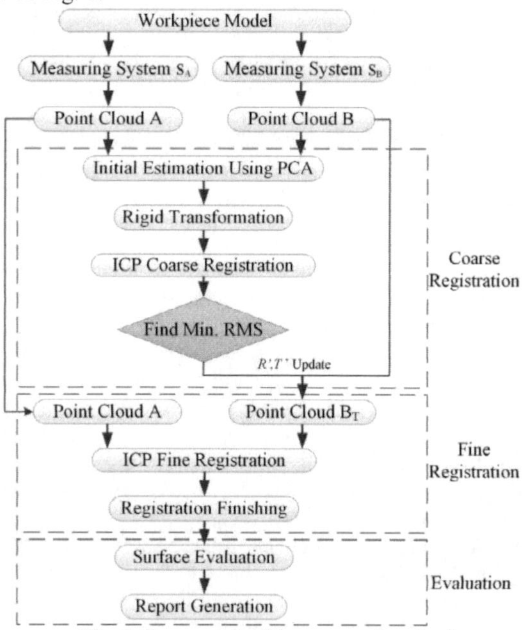

Fig. 1. Framework of the proposed method

As shown in Fig. 1, A and B are two 3D point clouds datasets acquired from measuring system S_A and S_B, respectively. The aim of the first step is to roughly register the pairwise point clouds. Then point cloud B_T can be obtained from B using the rotation matrix R' and translation vector T', which are calculated from coarse registration result. In the second step, point clouds A and transformed B_T are reregistered using ICP algorithm to obtain the final rotation matrix R and translation vector T. This step is a fine registration process. In the third step, the registered surfaces are evaluated using own-developed method which is based on normal vectors of points. The detailed technologies are elaborated in the Section 4 & 5.

4 Registration of point clouds data from multi-sensors

As discussed above, the point dataset generated from different sensors with respect to their own reference system. No initial transformation information can be exploited to register pairwise point clouds. Therefore the registration method involves two steps: first a coarse registration then followed by a fine registration.
The purpose of coarse registration is to roughly align the two datasets according to their overlaps and provide a correct trend for the fine registration. It includes two basic steps: principal poses alignment and overlapping alignment. The fine registration is an iterative approach to obtain the most accurate solution as possible.

4.1 Coarse registration of point clouds

If we suppose A and B are two 3D point clouds datasets acquired from measuring system S_A and S_B, respectively; then both A and B are N×3 matrices. A N-points sub-dataset $A_C\ \{m_i \mid m_i \in A, i = 1,2,\ldots,N\}$ is taken from A; if we can find its semantically corresponding N-points sub-dataset $B_C\ \{m_i' \mid m_i' \in B, i = 1,2,\ldots,N\}$ from B, then the point clouds registration is to find the 3×3 rotation matrix R' and a 3×1 translation vector T' between local coordinates from measuring system A and B. The R' and T' can be computed by minimising the object function

$$J_o = \sum_{i=1}^{N} \|m_i' - (R' \times m_i + T')\|^2 \qquad (1)$$

The main challenge in point cloud registration is the automatic establishment of correspondences between overlapping views of the point clouds to be registered. Fig. 2 (a) shows an example of point clouds scanned from different sensors. Magenta points are measured from a CMM and the sky blue points are scanned from a structured light scanner. In this example, the magenta points are fixed and the sky blue points are moved to find the optimal transformation matrix. In computer graphics and computer vision, the simplest and most widely accepted method for the determination of location and orientation of an 3D shapes is based on the principal axes of the object [22], which completely consists of its orientation and position with respect to an orthogonal frame or coordinate system. In this paper, the statistical technique, principal component analysis (PCA) has been used to evaluate the location and orientation of the point clouds to guide coarse registration.
The specific coarse registration algorithm follows these logical steps:
1) Two point clouds A (magenta) & B (sky blue) are measured from different sensors with their respect coordinate system (Fig. 2 (a)); then calculate the principal axes of the point clouds A & B, separately (Fig. 2 (b)); take matrix A as the example;

a) Compute the 3×3 covariance matrix M_A from A;
b) Compute the eigenvalues and eigenvectors estimation of M_A;
c) The first principal axis is the eigenvector corresponding to the minimum eigenvalue. The other two principal axes are obtained from the remaining two eigenvectors.
d) The first principal axis is defined as X-axis. The Y-axis and Z-axis of the principal coordinate system are defined along the second and the third principal axes, respectively.

2) Calculate the centroids (centre of mass) of point clouds A & B and translate point cloud B into A using the centroids (Fig. 2 (c)); then rotate and align them using the calculated principal axes (Fig. 2 (d));
3) Execute ICP coarse algorithm to register the point clouds and calculate the root mean squares RMS (equation (15));
4) Clockwise spin point cloud B π/4 rad along the first principle axis of A and execute Step 3 (Fig. 2 (e)); totally carry on spinning seven times;
5) Find the minimum RMS and output its corresponding transformation parameters R' & T' (Fig. 2 (f)).
In coarse registration algorithm, the maximum number of iterations is set to 25 for each registration attempt to save computation time.

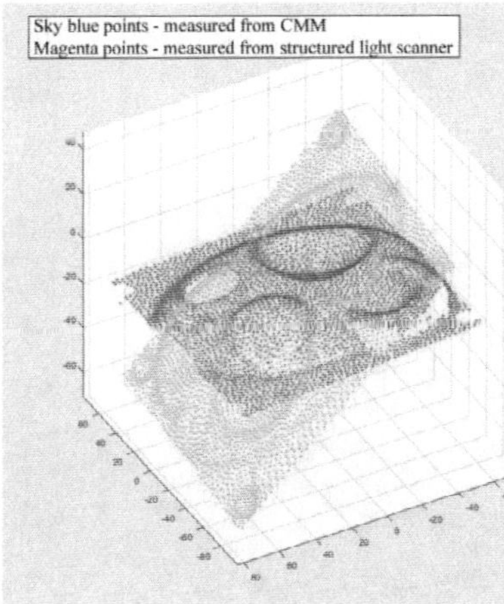

(a) Point clouds before registration

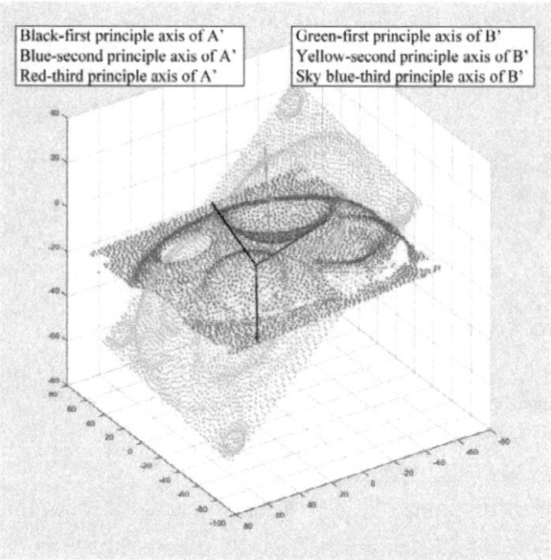

(b) Point clouds principle pose estimations

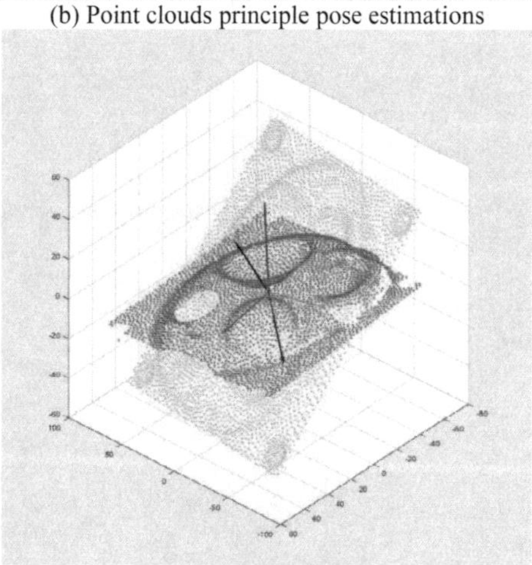

(c) Origin alignment

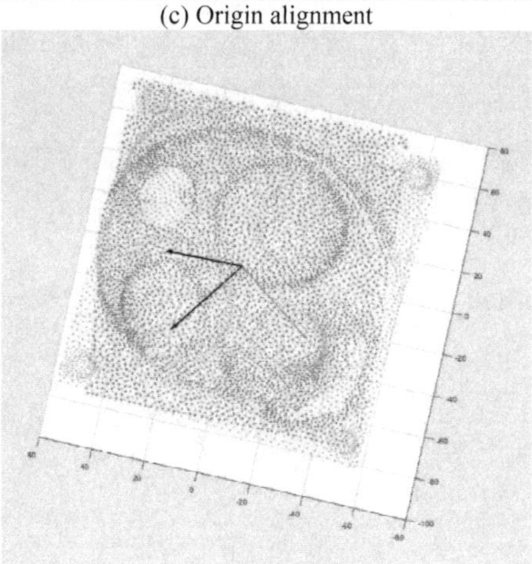

(d) Axes alignment

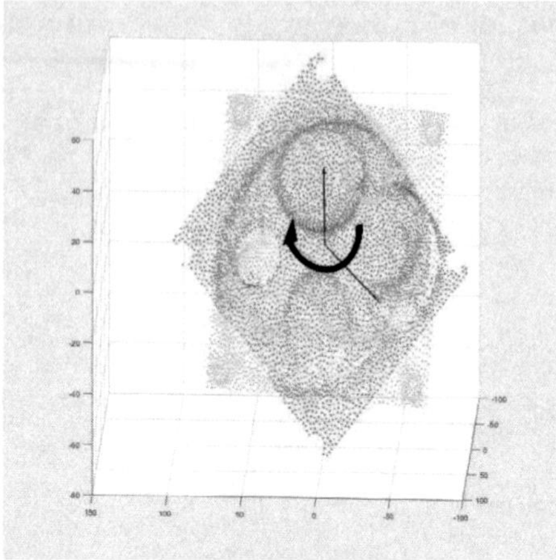

(e) Spin point cloud

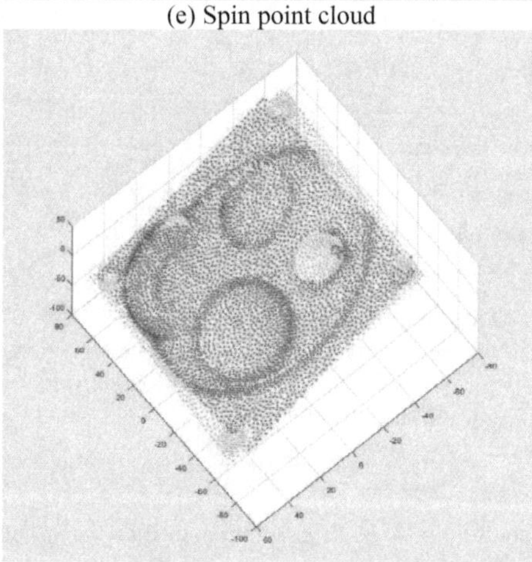

(f) Coarse registration result

Fig. 2. Point clouds coarse registration process

4.2 Fine registration of point clouds

After the coarse registration, the transformation matrices R' and T' can be used to adjust the location and position of original point cloud B.

$$B_T = B \times R' + T_N' \quad (2)$$

where T_N' is a N×3 matrix created from T'.

Then the original point cloud A and updated point cloud B_T can be fine registered to obtain the optimal solution using ICP algorithm. In this paper, $k-d$ tree [23] is used to seed up the algorithm in order to improve the efficiency of searching speed of neighbour points.

After finding the dataset $A_C \{a_i \mid a_i \in A, i = 1,2,\ldots,N\}$ in point cloud A and its corresponding dataset $B_C \{b_i \mid b_i \in B, i = 1,2,\ldots,N\}$ in point cloud B, the singular value decomposition (SVD) method [24] can be exploited to solve the rotation matrix R. The algorithm is described as follows:

1) Calculate the centroid of A_C & B_C;

$$\begin{cases} c_A = \frac{1}{N}\sum_{i=1}^{N} a_i \\ c_B = \frac{1}{N}\sum_{i=1}^{N} b_i \end{cases} \quad (3)$$

2) Define object function

$$J = \sum_{i=1}^{N} \left\| A_i - (B_i \times R + T) \right\|^2 \quad (4)$$

If the least squares solutions to equation (4) is $\overline{R}$ & $\overline{T}$, then $A_i'\left\{A_i' = B_i \times \overline{R} + \overline{T}\right\}$ and A_i have same centroid, which is

$$c_A = c_{A'} \quad (5)$$

3) Suppose c_B is the centroid of B and let

$$\begin{cases} d_i = b_i - c_B \\ d_i^* = a_i - c_A \end{cases} \quad (6)$$

4) Then object function can be rewrite as

$$J' = \sum_{i=1}^{N} \left\| d_i^* - R \times d_i \right\|^2 \quad (7)$$

5) J' can be decomposed as

$$\begin{aligned} J' &= \sum_{i=1}^{N} (d_i^* - Rd_i)^T (d_i^* - Rd_i) \\ &= \sum_{i=1}^{N} (d_i^{*T} d_i + d_i^T R^T R d_i - d_i^{*T} R d_i - d_i^T R^T di^{*T}) \quad (8) \\ &= \sum_{i=1}^{N} (d_i^{*T} d_i + d_i^T d_i - 2 d_i^{*T} R d_i) \end{aligned}$$

Therefore minimising J' is equivalent to maxing fuction J'', where

$$J'' = \sum_{i=1}^{N} d_i^{*T} R d_i = tr(\sum_{i=1}^{N} R d_i^{*T} d_i) = tr(RH) \quad (9)$$

$$H = \sum_{i=1}^{N} d_i^{*T} d_i \quad (10)$$

6) Calculate the SVD of H

$$H = U \Lambda V^T \quad (11)$$

7) Let $X = VU^T$, then

$$XH = VU^T U \Lambda V^T = V \Lambda V^T \quad (12)$$

Obviously, XH is a symmetrical and positive definite matrix. Thus, for any 3×3 orthonormal matrix R, we have

$$tr(XH) \geq tr(RXH) \quad (13)$$

8) Therefore, X maximises J'' in function (9) among all 3×3 orthonormal matrices; if $det(X) = 1$, X is the desired rotation matrix. Translation matrix can be calculated by:

$$T = c_B - R \times c_A \quad (14)$$

In the fine registration, the algorithm will stop iterating when the difference between two adjacent RMS results is less than 10^{-5}.

5 A new method to evaluate registered point clouds based on the normal vector

The traditional method to evaluate the registration results is to calculate the RMS of the corresponding points. The RMS can be calculated by

$$RMS = \sqrt{\frac{\sum_{i=1}^{N} \left[d(p_i^A, p_i^B) \right]^2}{N}} \quad (15)$$

where p_i^A is a point in point cloud A, p_i^B is the corresponding point in dataset B. $d(p_i^A, p_i^B)$ is the distance between p_i^A and p_i^B, and N is the number of those sampled points.

As the point clouds measured from various sensors which have different resolution, the traditional method is not suitable for surfaces matching accuracy evaluation in such cases. To address this issue, a new evaluation method, which is based on the normal vectors of point clouds, is used to evaluate matching accuracy of surfaces measured from the multi-sensors after registration.

5.1 Normal vectors calculation

Many measuring systems support to output polyhedral surfaces directly, which is also called mesh file, such as STL file or PLY file. These files are composed of polygon meshes (see Fig. 3) from which the local neighbour information of each vertex can be found.

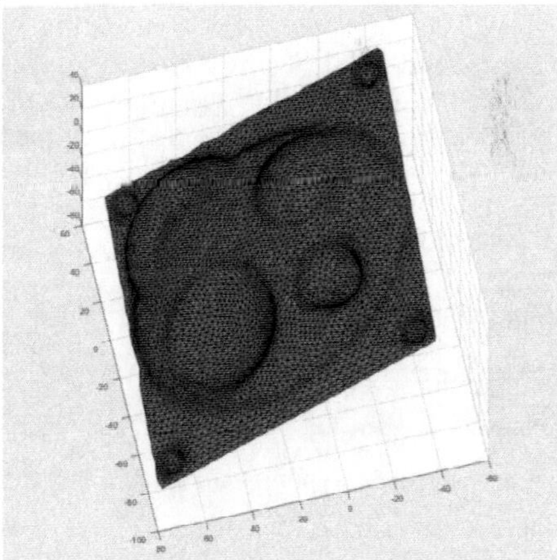

Fig. 3. An example of triangle mesh

The structure of an ASCII STL file can be described as below:

solid *name*
…
facet normal n_x n_y n_z
outer loop
vertex a_{1x} a_{1y} a_{1z}
vertex a_{2x} a_{2y} a_{2z}
vertex a_{3x} a_{3y} a_{3z}
endloop
endfacet
…
endsolid *name*

While a typical structure of PLY file can be described as:
Header
Vertex list
Face list
(lists of other elements)

In this case, the facet normal $\vec{n}$ can be obtained directly or calculated from the vertices of triangle (Fig. 4 (a)):

$$\vec{n} = \frac{(\vec{a_2} - \vec{a_1}) \times (\vec{a_3} - \vec{a_1})}{\left|(\vec{a_2} - \vec{a_1}) \times (\vec{a_3} - \vec{a_1})\right|} \quad (16)$$

If the data acquired from scanning system are point cloud format, the scattered point sets are needed to approximate the proper polyhedral surfaces in order to build the topology structures. The method developed by Alliez, et al. [25], is one of the most popular methods for surface reconstruction of scattered point, which can be exploited to approximate polyhedral mesh. However, any other efficient algorithm can be used as long as it can construct the satisfying mesh from unorganized point clouds.

5.2 Projection principle

We suppose the existence of three non-collinear points a_1, a_2 and a_3 in dataset A, then the plane $\alpha: \overline{A}x + \overline{B}y + \overline{C}z + \overline{D} = 0$ can be defined by these three points; $\vec{n}$: $(\overline{A}, \overline{B}, \overline{C})$ is the normal vector of plane α (see Fig. 4 (b)). If $b_1(x_o, y_o, z_o)$ is one point in dataset B and α is the closest plane to b_1 in terms of Euclidean distance, we can draw a line through the point b_1 and perpendicular to α and intercept α at a_1'; a_1' is the projection of b_1 on α.

The distance d between b_1 and α can be calculated by

$$d = \left\| \vec{b_1}, \vec{a_1'} \right\| = \frac{\left|\overline{A}x_o + \overline{B}y_o + \overline{C}z_o + \overline{D}\right|}{\sqrt{\overline{A}^2 + \overline{B}^2 + \overline{C}^2}} \quad (17)$$

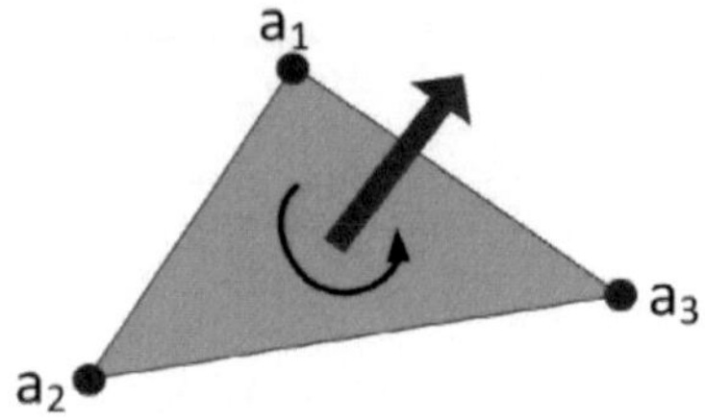

(a) Normal of triangle facet

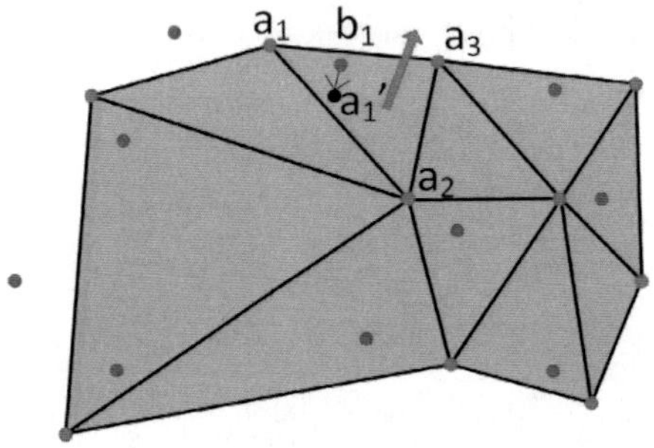

(b) Evaluation method

Fig. 4. Facet normal and registration error evaluation method

5.3 Algorithms description

The specific algorithm is described as follows:

1) Find the projections from the vertices of a source surface on a target surface;
   a) Define a line along the normal direction that passes through vertex on the source surface;
   b) Compute the intersection point of the line and the target surface; the intersection is the projection of vertex from the source surface on target surface;
   c) If multiple intersections have been found then choose the closest one to the source vertex;
   d) If no intersection then return a null value.

2) Calculate the standard deviation (SD) between vertices on source surface and its corresponding projection on target surface using equation (18);

$$SD = \sqrt{\frac{\sum_{i=1}^{N}\left[d(p_i^A, p_i^B) - \overline{d}\right]^2}{N-1}} \quad (18)$$

where $\overline{d}$ is the average of distances and can be calculated by

$$\overline{d} = \frac{\sum_{i=1}^{N} d(p_i^A, p_i^B)}{N} \quad (19)$$

3) Remove erroneous points if the distance values are bigger than five times of the SD; then calculate registration error based on the normal vector method.

6 Experimental implementation

6.1 Equipment & testing samples

The CMM used in this paper is the Hexagon Metrology Global Silver 7107 (see Fig. 5 (a)) with maximum permissible error of length measurement (MPE) = (1.5+3×L/1000) μm (L in mm) and probing error (1.5 μm) according to ISO 10360-1 [26] and ISO 10360-2 [27]. The Hexagon Lecia T-Scan 5 laser scanner (LS) (Fig. 5 (b)) and GOM ATOS III Triple Scan structured light scanner (SLS) with two 8 megapixel cameras (Fig. 5 (c)) have also been used for data acquisition. In addition, the KEYENCE 3D Laser Scanning Confocal Microscope (CM) VK-X260K (Fig. 5 (d)), with height accuracy of 0.2+L/100 μm or less [28], has also been exploited to compare with data scanned from structured light scanner.
The artefact used for test is FreeForm reference standard WP-150 (see Fig. 5 (e)) which is developed by National Physical Laboratory (NPL). The characteristics of this standard can be found in [29]. The Diode Laser Cladding Sample (Fig. 5 (f)) has also been selected as the testing artefact.

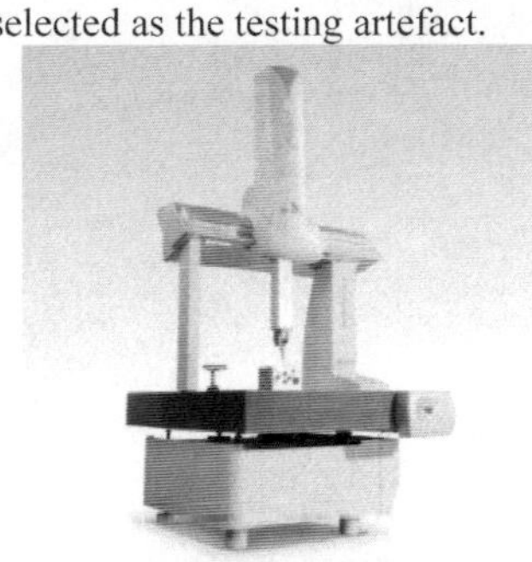

(a) Hexagon Global Silver 7107 CMM

(b) Hexagon Lecia T-Scan 5 Laser Scanner

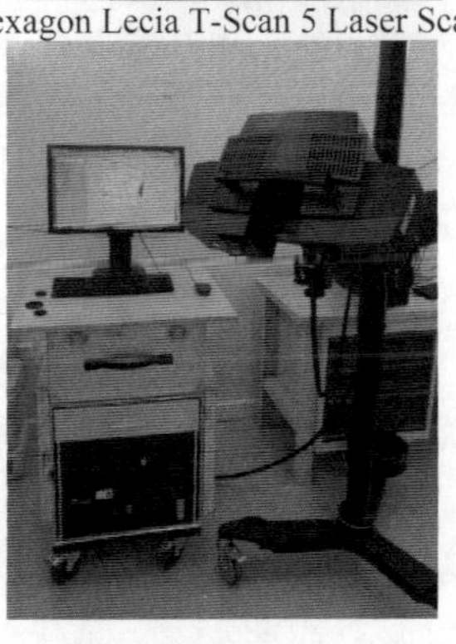

(c) GOM ATOS III Triple Scan

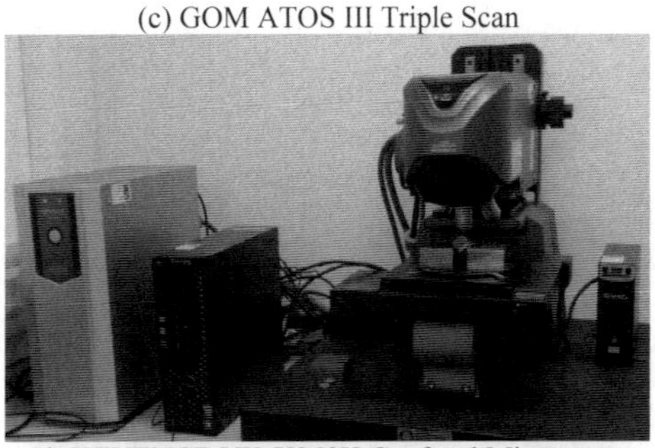

(d) KEYENCE VK-X260K Confocal Microscope

(e) NPL Freeform Standard

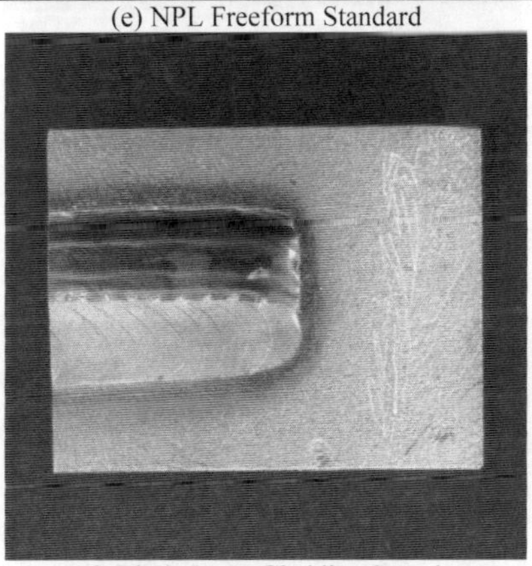

(f) Diode Laser Cladding Sample

Fig. 5. Elements of the test

6.2 Experiment results and analysis

In this paper, three cases have been tested to validate the proposed method: case one – one data totally encapsulates another; case two – two data sets full overlap; case three – partial overlap. In these three cases, the point cloud data are obtained using different equipment with differing numbers of points. This information is listed in Table 1.

Table 1. The data acquisition method and number of points

	Case One		Case Two		Case Three	
Equipment	CMM	SLS	SLS	CM	LS	SLS
Number of points	15309	17419	11825	28476	17014	14867

The point clouds of Artefact are first aligned using PCA then spun a $\pi/4$ rad, ICP algorithm is executed after each spinning. The RMS of registration of each pose is shown in Fig. 6. In this example (Case one), the magenta point is scanned by GOM structured light scanner while the sky blue point is measured from by Hexagon CMM, the left image in each figures is the initial pose of point clouds before registration and the right one is its corresponding coarse registration result.

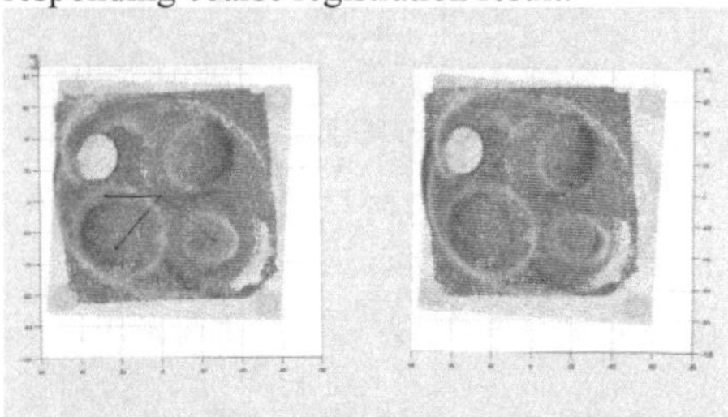

(a) 0 rad

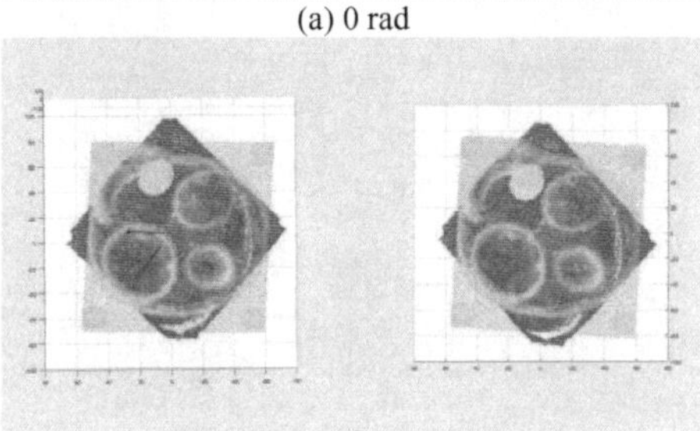

(b) $\pi/4$ rad

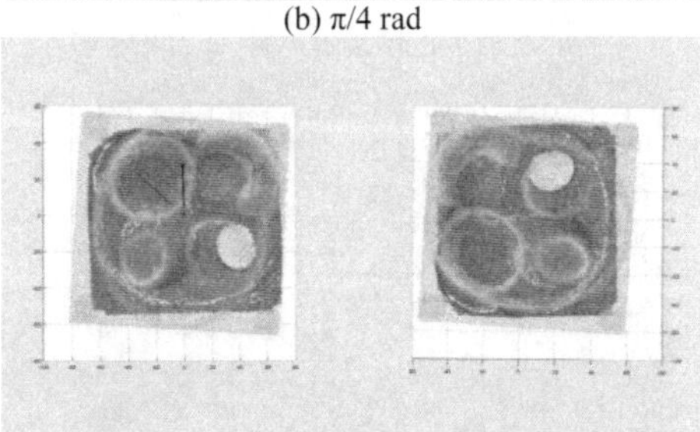

(c) $\pi/2$ rad

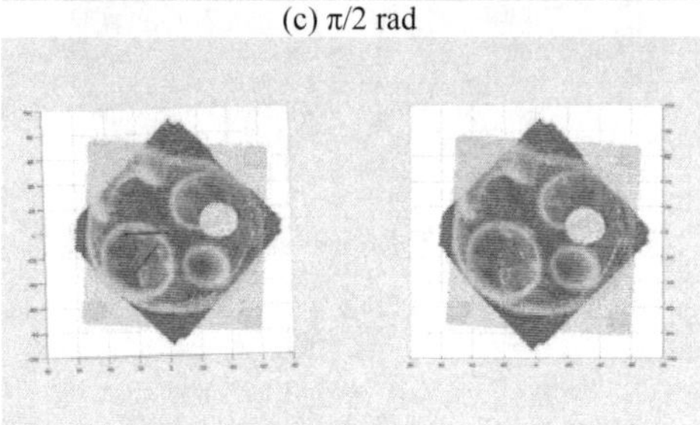

(d) $3\pi/4$ rad

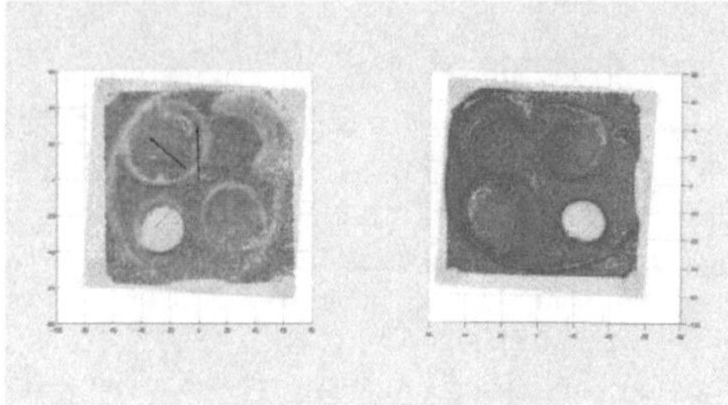

(e) π rad

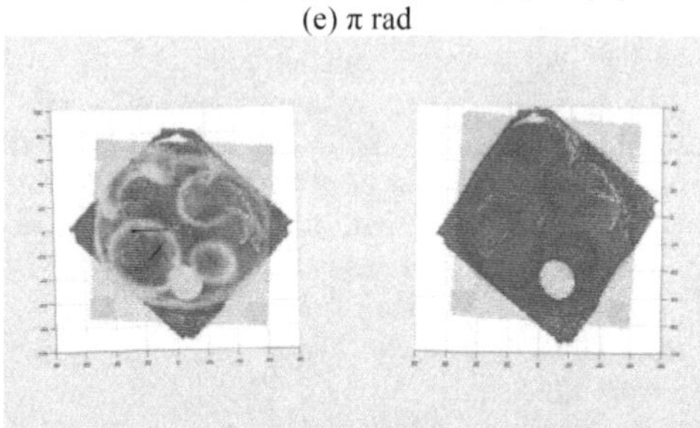

(f) $5\pi/4$ rad

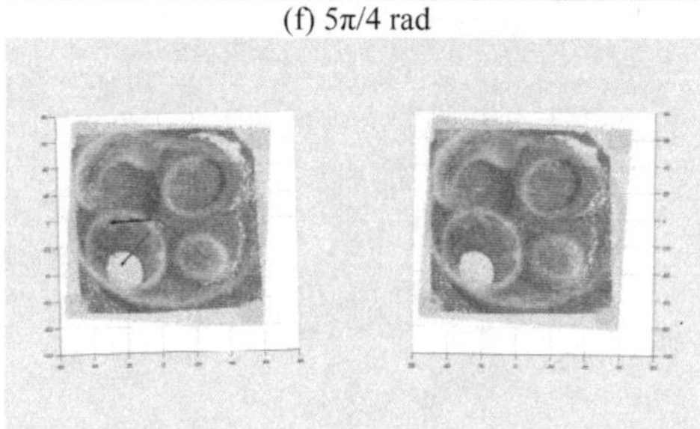

(g) $3\pi/2$ rad

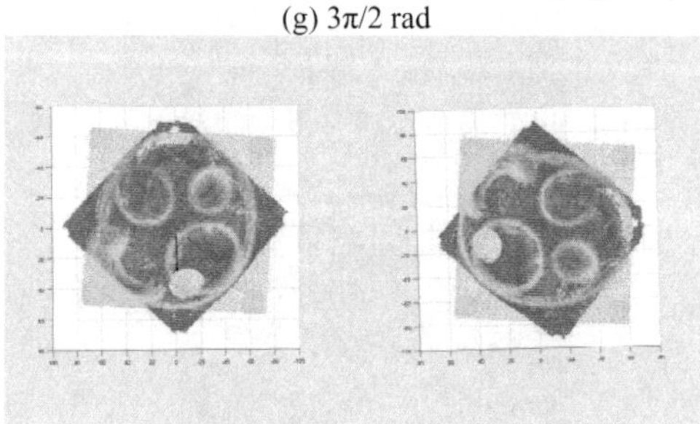

(h) $7\pi/4$ rad

Fig. 6. Pose of point clouds before registration and after coarse registration (Case one)

Fig. 6 shows the π rad provides the best registration result (bold fonts in Table 2) for Case one. The RMS and computation time of coarse registration for each position of three cases are listed in Table 2.

Coarse registration		0	$\pi/4$	$\pi/2$	$3\pi/4$
Case One	RMS (mm)	5.1437	5.0630	4.4183	4.4277
	Time (s)	1.966	1.836	1.270	1.316
Case Two	RMS (mm)	1.4739	0.7098	0.4586	1.504
	Time (s)	1.680	1.362	1.308	1.533
Case Three	RMS (mm)	4.2325	6.0778	5.4734	6.1518
	Time (s)	0.951	1.368	1.348	1.312
		π	$5\pi/4$	$3\pi/2$	$7\pi/4$
Case One	RMS (mm)	**0.6839**	3.754	4.7677	4.9365
	Time (s)	0.619	1.240	1.379	1.289
Case Two	RMS (mm)	1.4574	1.4574	**0.2426**	1.5100
	Time (s)	1.675	1.675	1.005	1.559
Case Three	RMS (mm)	5.6094	6.2836	5.6119	**1.1988**
	Time (s)	1.261	1.533	1.425	1.118

Table 2. Coarse registration results

From both Fig. 6 and Table 2, we can conclude that the registration results heavily depend on the initial pose of the point cloud. From Table 2, we can also see that the computing speed is fast and satisfied since the iterations have been set up to 25 for coarse registration.

The rotation and translation matrices of the minimum RMS obtained from coarse registration can then be used to update the original point cloud B to provide correct trend for find registration. After updating, the original point clouds have already been roughly aligned, as shown in Fig. 6 (e). The point clouds before registration and the final registration results of three cases are shown in Fig. 7. The point clouds have been precisely registered after fine registration.

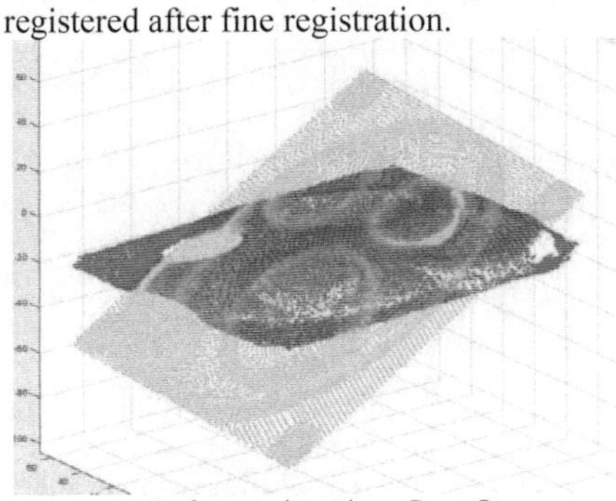

(a) Before registration: Case One

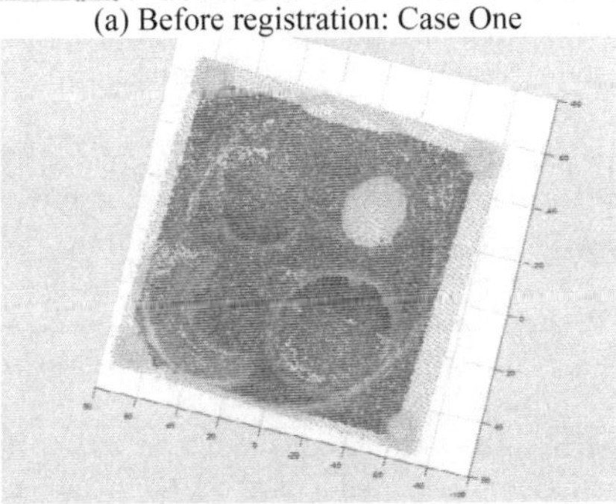

(b) Fine registration: Case One

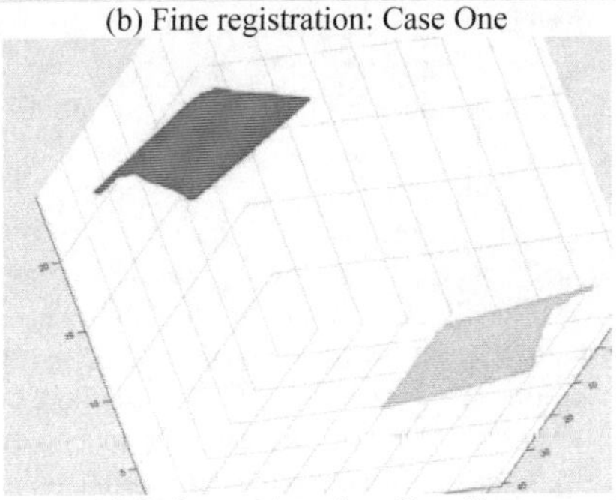

(c) Before registration: Case Two

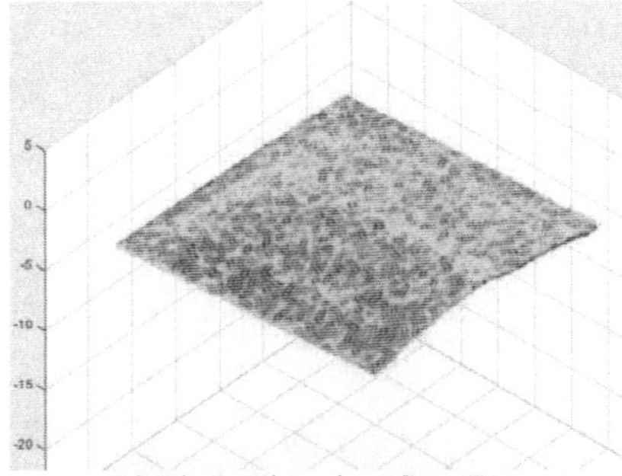

(d) Fine registration: Case Two

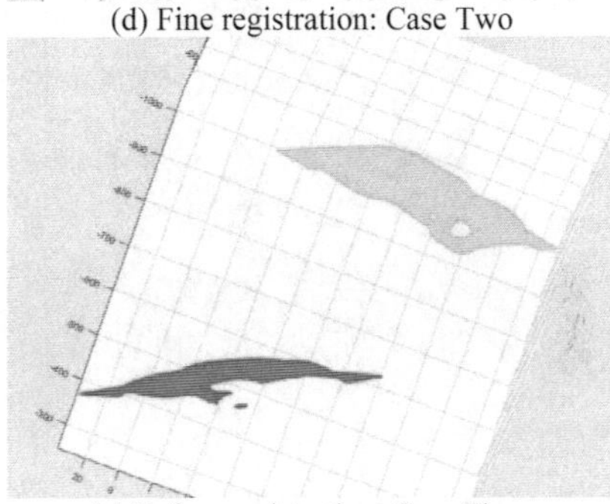

(e) Before registration: Case Three

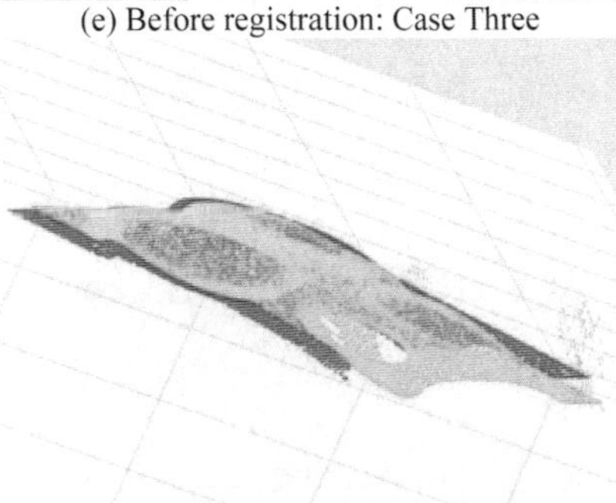

(f) Fine registration: Case Three

Fig. 7. Point clouds before and after fine registration

The RMS trends of fine registration are shown in Fig. 8 and the results are listed in Table 3.

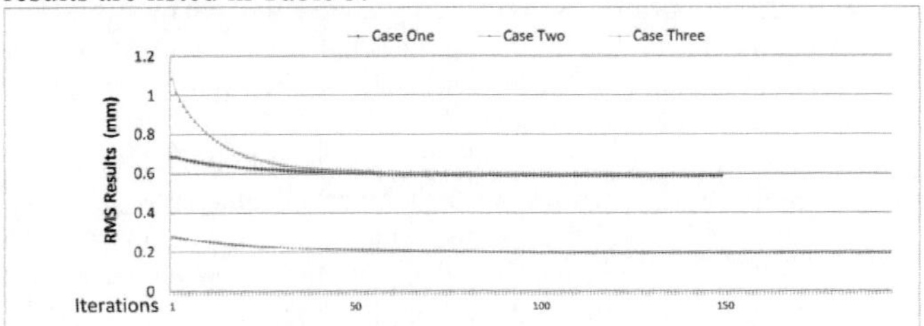

Fig. 8. RMS of fine registration

Fig. 8 indicates that the fine registration algorithm can converge quickly to calculate of the accurate solution if the coarse registration provides a correct trend.

From Table 2 and Fig. 8, we can conclude that the fine registration results are decided by the coarse registration, which greatly depend on the initial pose of the point clouds. A good coarse registration plays a vital role in generating the satisfactory final.

6.3 Performance comparison using different methods

Then the method introduced in Section 5 is used to evaluate the registration accuracy. The registered mesh surfaces and the projections on the reference surface for Case One are shown in Fig. 9 (a) and (b), respectively.

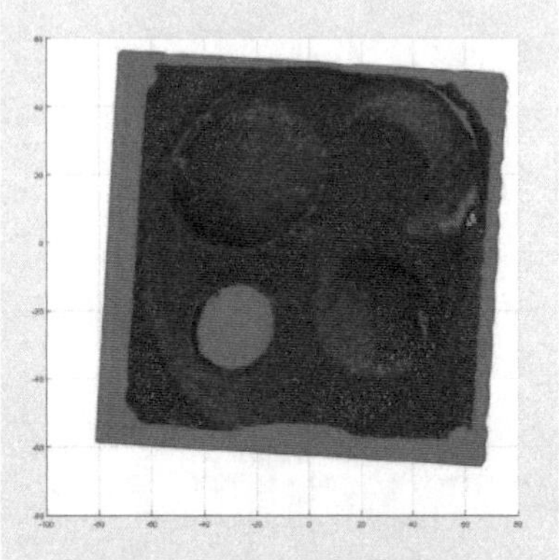

(a) Registered mesh

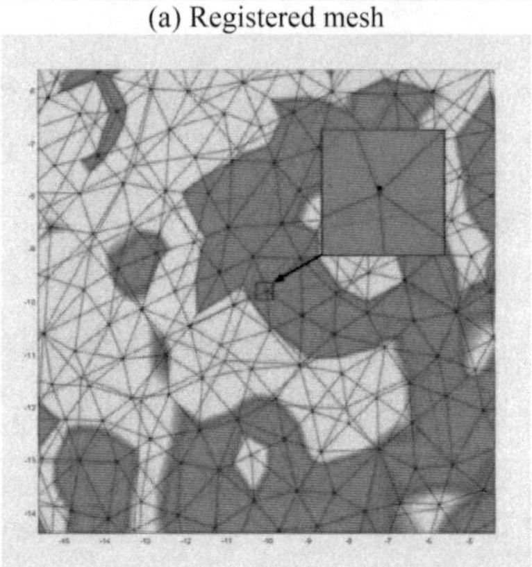

(b) The projections of vertices on the reference surface

Fig. 9. Point clouds evaluation (Case one)

The ICP algorithms, introduced by Besl and McKay [16] and Zhang [17], are the most classic methods to register point clouds and obtain an accurate solution by finding the minimum distance between point-correspondences, known as closest point. Every point in the first image is taken into consideration to search for its closest point in the second image, so that the Euclidean distances between the temporal corresponding points in the datasets can be minimised and the process is iterated until convergence. Bergström and Edlund [21] improved the ICP algorithm. Their work used robust M-estimation techniques to limit the influence of outliers and iteratively re-weighed least squares to incorporate the robustness. The correspondences of above two methods are based on finding the minimum distance between point-correspondences. In this paper, these three popular methods are selected to finely align the point clouds after coarse registration and compare with proposed approach.

It is worth mentioning, all these fine registration methods including the fine registration approach cannot reach accurate results without execution of coarse registration step. The alignment errors and computation time using different methods for three cases are listed in Table 3.

Table 3. Fine registration results comparison using different methods

Fine registration	Besl's method		Zhang's method	
	Error (mm)	Time (s)	Error (mm)	Time (s)
Case one	0.8493	105.73	0.3263	2.96
Case two	0.1598	82.43	0.1485	2.38
Case three	2.0852	122.26	0.4372	6.37
	Bergström's method		Proposed method	
	Error (mm)	Time (s)	Error (mm)	Time (s)
Case one	0.0506	33.84	0.0267	4.26
Case two	0.0645	124.69	0.0236	7.62
Case three	1.0967	30.70	0.4529	5.57

From Table 3 we can see that the presented approach obtain satisfactory results in terms of both accuracy and speed in comparison to other methods.

7 Discussion & conclusion

Multi-sensor data fusion techniques are employed to achieve more holistic geometrical measurement information since the requirements on the complexity of dimensional metrology are increasing. When applying the multi-sensor techniques for data acquisition, the datasets acquired from individual sensor have to be registered into a common coordinate system. The main challenge for the registration of point clouds scanned from different sensors is the automatic establishment of correspondences between overlapping views of the point data.

In this paper, a new automatic registration method has been proposed to align the two surfaces acquired from multi-sensors according to their overlapping sections. It can provide reliable alignment results for the multi-sensors data registration, especially when the point clouds have a lack of abundant features. Firstly, the principal poses of point clouds scanned from different sensors are estimated using PCA method, and aligned using centroids and principle axes. Secondly, the initial estimations for transformation matrices are computed by coarse ICP registration algorithm, then one point cloud is fixed and another one is spun $\pi/4$ incrementally and the RMS is recalculated. Thirdly, all eight RMS are compared to find the minimum RMS; its corresponding rotation matrix and translation vector will be output as the coarse registration results. Finally, the transformation parameters obtained from coarse registration are used as good initial estimations to provide correct trend for fine registration to converge to calculate the optimal rotation and translation matrices.

While evaluating the matching accuracy of surfaces measured from different sensors, characteristic such as sensor resolution has to be considered. A new method based on the normal vectors of points is presented and exploited to assess the matching accuracy of the overlapping sections of two surfaces. The proposed evaluation method further proves the accuracy

and feasibility of the automatic registration approach.
A Matlab tool box has been developed to verify the algorithms proposed in this paper. This tool box can be used to automatically align point data measures from homogenous and inhomogeneous sensors into a common coordinate system. It can also be employed to evaluate the accuracy of different measuring systems, and can even be further exploited to compare the different registration techniques.

Acknowledgment

The authors gratefully acknowledge the support of the High Value Manufacturing (HVM) Catapult.

References

1. Weckenmann, A., et al., Probing Systems in Dimensional Metrology. CIRP Annals - Manufacturing Technology, 2004. 53(2): p. 657-684.
2. Summan, R., et al., Spatial calibration of large volume photogrammetry based metrology systems. Measurement, 2015. 68: p. 189-200.
3. Zhang, Z., C.E. Towers, and D.P. Towers, Robust color and shape measurement of full color artifacts by RGB fringe projection. Optical Engineering, 2012. 51(2): p. 021109-1-021109-7.
4. Wang, Y. and H.-Y. Feng, Effects of scanning orientation on outlier formation in 3D laser scanning of reflective surfaces. Optics and Lasers in Engineering, 2016. 81: p. 35-45.
5. Weckenmann, A., et al., Multisensor data fusion in dimensional metrology. CIRP Annals - Manufacturing Technology, 2009. 58(2): p. 701-721.
6. Ahn, S.J., W. Rauh, and M. Recknagel. Ellipse fitting and parameter assessment of circular object targets for robot vision. in IEEE/RSJ International Conference on Intelligent Robots and Systems. 1999. IEEE
7. Li, F., et al., A practical coordinate unification method for integrated tactile–optical measuring system. Optics and Lasers in Engineering, 2014. 55: p. 189-196.
8. Li, L., et al., A reverse engineering system for rapid manufacturing of complex objects. Robotics and Computer-Integrated Manufacturing, 2002. 18(1): p. 53-67.
9. Johnson, A.E. and M. Hebert, Using spin images for efficient object recognition in cluttered 3D scenes. IEEE Transactions on pattern analysis and machine intelligence, 1999. 21(5): p. 433-449.
10. Chen, C.-S., Y.-P. Hung, and J.-B. Cheng, RANSAC-based DARCES: A new approach to fast automatic registration of partially overlapping range images. Pattern Analysis and Machine Intelligence, IEEE Transactions on, 1999. 21(11): p. 1229-1234.
11. Chow, C.K., H.T. Tsui, and T. Lee, Surface registration using a dynamic genetic algorithm. Pattern recognition, 2004. 37(1): p. 105-117.
12. Gelfand, N., et al. Geometrically stable sampling for the ICP algorithm. in 3-D Digital Imaging and Modeling, 2003. 3DIM 2003. Proceedings. Fourth International Conference on. 2003. IEEE.
13. Mian, A.S., M. Bennamoun, and R.A. Owens, A novel representation and feature matching algorithm for automatic pairwise registration of range images. International Journal of Computer Vision, 2006. 66(1): p. 19-40.
14. He, B., Z. Lin, and Y.F. Li, An automatic registration algorithm for the scattered point clouds based on the curvature feature. Optics & Laser Technology, 2013. 46: p. 53-60.
15. Chen, Y. and G. Medioni. Object modeling by registration of multiple range images. in Robotics and Automation, 1991. Proceedings., 1991 IEEE International Conference on. 1991. IEEE.
16. Besl, P.J. and N.D. McKay. A Method for registration of 3-D shapes. in Robotics-DL tentative. 1992. International Society for Optics and Photonics
17. Zhang, Z., Iterative point matching for registration of free-form curves and surfaces. International journal of computer vision, 1994. 13(2): p. 119-152.
18. Almhdie, A., et al., 3D registration using a new implementation of the ICP algorithm based on a comprehensive lookup matrix: Application to medical imaging. Pattern Recognition Letters, 2007. 28(12): p. 1523-1533.
19. Xie, Z., S. Xu, and X. Li, A high-accuracy method for fine registration of overlapping point clouds. Image and Vision Computing, 2010. 28(4): p. 563-570.
20. Boughorbel, F., et al., A new method for the registration of three-dimensional point-sets: The Gaussian fields framework. Image and Vision Computing, 2010. 28(1): p. 124-137.
21. Bergström, P. and O. Edlund, Robust registration of point sets using iteratively reweighted least squares. Computational Optimization and Applications, 2014. 58(3): p. 543-561.
22. Ezquerra, N. and R. Mullick, An approach to 3D pose determination. ACM Transactions on Graphics (TOG), 1996. 15(2): p. 99-120.
23. Simon, D.A., Fast and accurate shape-based registration. 1996, Carnegie Mellon University Pittsburgh.
24. Arun, K.S., T.S. Huang, and S.D. Blostein, Least-squares fitting of two 3-D point sets. IEEE Transactions on pattern analysis and machine intelligence, 1987(5): p. 698-700.
25. Alliez, P., et al. Voronoi-based variational reconstruction of unoriented point sets. in Symposium on Geometry Processing 2007.
26. QS 9000, Measurement System Analysis—Reference Manual. 1995.
27. EN ISO, 10360-2:2009. Geometrical Product Specifications (GPS), Acceptance and Reverification Tests for Coordinate Measuring Machines (CMM) Part 2: CMMs used for measuring linear dimensions, 2009.
28. KEYENXE, (2017). Retrieved from http://www.keyence.com/ss/products/microscope/vkx/.
29. NPL high precision traceable FreeForm reference standard, (2017). Retrieved from http://www.npl.co.uk/upload/pdf/freeform-high-precision.pdf. 2017.

7th International Metrology Conference – CAFMET 2018

Quality and Metrology Components in Laboratories

A. Ibrahim

Kenya Bureau of Standards,Nairobi, Kenya

Received:

Abstract. Effective and efficient laboratories run based on a customized or standard quality system. Components of such a system are describes in this paper. the metrological aspects of the system are also enumerated. Lastly, various conformity assessment schemes to ascertain the quality system are mentioned.

Keywords: Quality system, components of a quality system, measurement traceability, intercomparisons, conformity assessment.

1 Introduction

Defining quality, an abstract term and making it verifiable is a challenge to many. However, quality can simply be defined as the attribute(s) or characteristic(s) that provide the degree to which products or services comply with existing requirements. The quality features are objective and measurable. An institution can easily achieve offering quality goods and services by having a quality system in place. Thereafter, proving compliance of products to national and international specifications requires a consistent network, known as quality infrastructure (Annex 1). This consists of various institutions that provide conformity assessment services for states, industries and consumers. An internationally recognized quality infrastructure serves objectives in terms of safety, environment, health and consumer protection furthermore, it contributes to sustainable economic, ecological and social development.

Conformity assessments are based on a recognized quality management system. Some examples are industrial production that requires measurement devices whose accuracy has been verified by metrology laboratories. Test laboratories competence needs to be verified in all aspects for the results to be widely accepted. Those who offer calibration, inspection and certification services as well as those who grant accreditation must also prove their abilities. This all forms a complex system that is firmly linked to international standards with different international bodies paying their specific roles (Annex 2)

The importance of quality can never be over emphasized. This applies for small and medium-sized enterprises just as much as for internationally operating corporations across all sectors. Businesses must rely on services of the institutions that provide quality infrastructure. Existing protective regulations and standards support the quality of goods produced. This is essential for wider market access and competitiveness. When processes and interfaces are improved, efficient processes are created. A recognized quality infrastructure lowers production costs and promotes innovation through continual improvements to the quality systems.

2 Quality System Components

A quality system can be defined as the interrelated processes that together deliver the overall organization quality objectives. For such a system to work, there has to be a quality management system that is established, documented (though not a prerequisite), implemented, maintained and with room for continual improvement. A quality management system has four basic components as enumerated below.

2.1 Quality Management System Planning and establishment

It involves coming up with a plan on how the quality management system should be including the scope. The next step is setting up the quality policy and objectives. Finally, it is the actual implementation of the quality system.

2.2 Quality Control

These are the ongoing efforts to maintain the integrity of a process to maintain the reliability of achieving an outcome. A perfect example in a quality system is method validation. Another example would be the use of statistical control charts like the Shewhart control charts Below.

Shewhart Control Chart

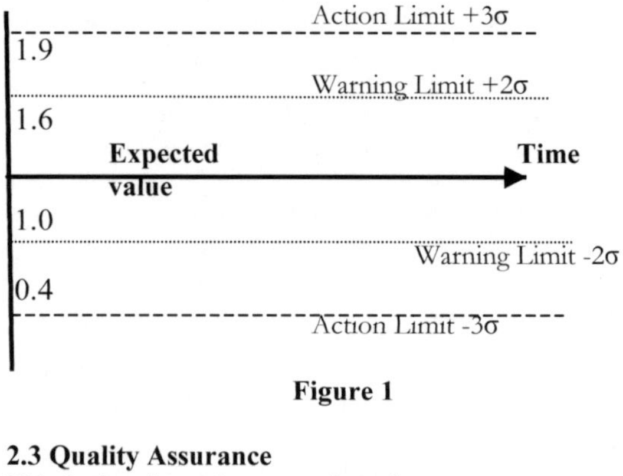

Figure 1

2.3 Quality Assurance

This is the planned systematic actions necessary to provide enough confidence that a product or service will satisfy the given requirements. In testing laboratories an example would be the use of certified reference materials while in calibration labs exemplified by interlaboratory comparisons.

2.4 Quality Improvement
This is the purposeful change of a process to improve the reliability of achieving an outcome. In the quality system, the reduction of uncertainty of measurement would fit the category.

However, the last three usually overlap most of the time and it may be difficult for one to distinguish between them. These shall be discussed later as one as monitoring and maintenance of the quality system.

3 Establishment of a Laboratory Quality System
The laboratory is at the frontline when it comes to the quality infrastructure for testing quality of products. There are two types of laboratories; those that offer testing and verification of consumer products, medical, forensics etc and those in metrology for the measurement or calibration services. Both share common basic requirements to establish and implement a quality system as discussed below.

3.1 Quality Documentation
If a laboratory adopts a formal quality management system, there's bound to be documentation emanating from the established quality management system. These may include a quality policy, a quality manual, operating procedures for various processes and records from the implementation of the system.

Documentation is important but it is critical to realize that it is not, in itself, the quality system but a tool of the system. The documentation plays two key roles. First, it is a mechanism for defining the quality system so that there is a consistent and secure basis for monitoring the system; in short, unless the system is clearly specified it is difficult to monitor whether it is being used. It is also a means of communication within the laboratory so that all staff are aware of their responsibilities and the procedures to be adhered to.

The key piece of quality documentation is the quality manual. This is the document which describes in detail the policy on quality and the quality management structure and describes or refers to the procedures which constitute the working quality system. The quality manual is, typically, prepared and checked by laboratory management, usually under the overall co-ordination of the quality manager. It should, however, be formally authorized for issuing from as high a point in the management hierarchy as possible. This ensures that the manual has the strongest authority and also shows a commitment on the part of the senior management to the quality system. The quality manual may be completely comprehensive and self-contained or it may make reference to subsidiary documents such as operating procedures. Whatever the case, the quality manual must be the primary source for all aspects of the operation of the quality system and must either contain all necessary information or must explain clearly where such information is to be found.

Laboratories also have subsidiary documentation in the form of operating procedures a key among them being the calibration and testing methods. Others are procedures that describe processes such as handling of test and calibration items how to conduct some quality based processes such as audits etc. The level of detail for these procedures should be such as to enable a trained practitioner to carry out calibrations and tests in a proper and consistent fashion. There are three types of methods used by laboratories. The first is standard methods published as standard procedures by standards bodies like ISO, ASTM, national standards or published in scientific literature. If these are adopted, they must be followed strictly without violation of the publications. The second is the adapted in house methods that are developed based on standard procedures. The last is the in house methods developed exclusively by a laboratory for its exclusive internal use. Lastly, there are work instructions that may be separate from procedures with descriptions such as operation of equipment, cleaning or maintenance. These may be derived from manufacturer's manuals and need not be copied or can be developed in house.

3.2 Quality System Records
A laboratory should keep two sets of records; technical records and quality records. Records must be kept in such a way that they can easily be retrieved if necessary and they must be secure, held in confidence and reasonably protected from destruction. There should be a documented policy on the period of retention of records. Any records which are relevant to ongoing issues need to be kept for at least the duration of that issue. An example is records that should be kept until an assessment/ audit cycle is dispensed of and may be disposed if necessary.

(i) Sample Technical Records

- All original observations, raw data, calculations and derived data in the form of worksheets, notebooks, instrument output, etc
- Records of installation, maintenance, calibration and checks carried out on instruments and other equipment
- Copies of all reports/certificates issued by the laboratory
- Intercomparison/ proficiency test reports etc

(ii) Sample Quality Records

- Records of staff qualifications, training and review of training in the form of a staff register

- Records of all audits and reviews of the quality system, including records of corrective and preventive action taken.
- Records of all customer complaints and response to non-conforming work, and details of follow-up and any corrective action taken
- Records of suppliers and sub-contractors etc

3.3 Accommodation

For laboratories to offer quality services, they must be set up in suitable structures. The working area should be adequate and comfortable for staff. This is also important for clear separation of calibration/testing items such as those waiting to be worked on, those being worked on and those awaiting dispatch avoiding mix-up and improving efficiency. Adequate space also avoids cross contamination for items like chemicals that should not be kept near each other. The laboratories should be spaced such that there is separation between neighbouring areas with incompatible activities. For instance, a temperature calibration lab should be far from length and mass laboratories to avoid the effect of expansion. For testing laboratories, a microbiology laboratory should be far from a chemistry lab with chemicals that kill.

The laboratories should have reliable utilities like electricity, water and provisions for back up sources where necessary. They should have proper ventilation/ air conditioning, lighting and heating. All these are necessary for the health and safety of laboratory personnel and visitors as well as proper laboratory operations. In most cases, access to the laboratories has to be controlled for safety and security purposes. This protects customer samples from loss or contamination. It also protects unauthorized visitors from harm in areas with hazards such as radiation/dosimetry laboratories.

3.4 Environment

The environmental conditions should be conducive for a particular laboratory application. For instance, dust is not expected in a photometry or electrical laboratories but due to nature of a civil materials testing laboratory there's bound to be dust. Laboratories that do radio frequency measurements should be shielded from electromagnetic interference. Laboratories with radiation sources should be adequately protected/shielded. Extreme sound and vibrations should be avoided for laboratories conducting acoustics and vibration measurements. Direct heat and humidity is unwanted in most calibration and testing laboratories. All environmental conditions that affect measurements and tests directly or indirectly must be monitored and records maintained.

3.5 Personnel and Management

The management structure of a laboratory is supposed to be formally described in the quality manual or other document within the organization if the laboratory is part of a larger organization. The management is composed of the technical management and quality management. The technical management's role and scope has to be specified. Technical management has an obligation to ensure that technical activities are conducted in accordance with the requirements of the quality system.

Technical management structure must also make clear how supervision arrangements work. Typical laboratory structures include technical staff and professional staff. The general division of labour is that professional staff have the responsibility for method selection, development of new methods and for interpretation of data etc, whereas the actual bench work is done by technical staff, although professional staff may also be involved. Overall, the professional staff are responsible for the ultimate quality of the data so the structure must show how they discharge this responsibility by supervision of the technical staff.
The quality management structure must be headed by a quality manager, however named in the organization. The manager is responsible for the quality system through monitoring and advising and not managing quality control and assurance. The manager is responsible for administering the controlled documents, compiling the quality manual and organizing audits and reviews of the quality system. The quality manager is responsible for effective enforcement of the quality system and advises top management on quality issues by virtue of close familiarity with the quality system.

There should be provision for deputies for all key positions especially those of the quality manager and laboratory manager, for continuity in discharge of their functions in their absence. Staff may of course operate at more than on level so long as they are qualified for the positions. For each level of structures, there should be descriptions of qualifications and experience necessary to fill the post. There should also be clear job descriptions describing the duties to be carried out and the level of responsibility to be accepted, including responsibility for supervision.

3.6 Equipment

Equipment are the cornerstone for measurement of quality of products and the environment. They form the foundation for the metrological component in the quality system since without measurement it would be impossible to quantify quality. Equipment includes all items that may affect the validity of measurements or calibrations including reference measurement standards, working standards etc. Each laboratory should acquire equipment that is fit for purpose to meet the intended measurement specifications and tolerances.

4 Monitoring and Maintenance of the Quality System

A laboratory must take active actions to check that its quality system is being operated properly and that it is achieving the required standard of quality. Quality control provides some feedback on these issues but this is not, in itself, sufficient to meet all the r requirements. The system must be pro-active and provide quality assurance. Moreover, the quality system itself must be under continual scrutiny. A laboratory should have the following:

- A mechanism for checking that the quality system is being implemented on a day to day basis
- A mechanism for taking corrective action to ensure that a negative situation is remedied to prevent recurrence
- Mechanism to monitor trends in quality performance so that failures can be anticipated and dealt with before they become critical
- A review of the performance of the quality system to determine whether it is delivering the objectives associated with it.
- A means to improve the quality system.

Here are the most important quality control and quality assurance schemes.

4.1 Equipment Maintenance

All new equipment must be checked for correct functioning before being put to service. The starting point is the details of verifications and calibrations carried out before commissioning of new equipment. The next phase is the periodic calibrations based on recommended intervals. This should also include routine maintenance of such as cleaning, oiling, service etc. When equipment malfunctions are detected, repairs are supposed to be conducted immediately and subjected to performance checks as per the manufacturer's recommendations. Equipment are supposed to be subjected to intermediate checks in between calibrations for quality control.

It is recommended that all equipment's record be available since being put to service. The best way to keep these records is to institute an equipment log for each item which is, ideally, kept in the laboratory next to the appropriate equipment. In some cases, it may not be practical to keep the log next to the equipment, but it should be close by and readily accessible. That way, the records become a complete history of the equipment so that its state of calibration and performance at any given time can be demonstrated.

4.2 Measurement Traceability

Measurement traceability refers to the unbroken chain of comparisons which starts with a unit under calibration to a recognized international standard of measurement. This may be the International Systems of measurement (SI) or any other system like industry or consensus standard where traceability to SI is not possible. An example is the measurement of colour fastness (Annex 3)

The most cost effective means to achieve international traceability is through national metrology institutes (NMIs) who are the custodians of the national measurement standards. The NMIs establish a link to the international measurement system by periodically checking its standards against those of other countries and at times the BIPM (for member states). Additionally, NMIs and the lower laboratories can achieve measurement traceability through interlaboratory measurement comparisons. There are three major categories, key, supplementary and bilateral comparisons.

Laboratories and industries requiring calibration can then go to NMIs and have their equipment calibrated in the knowledge that the calibration is internationally traceable. Countries without NMIs can import measurement traceability from neighbouring countries or ship their measurement standards to other countries with NMIs. Where it's not possible to ship bulky measurement standards, the personnel and reference standards are brought to the calibration site.

4.2 Audits

These are conducted to check compliance to the quality system. They may be internal or external (third party such as accreditation bodies or customers). The quality manager is responsible for organizing the audits, ensuring that corrective actions to remedy the non conformities are adequate, carried out and effective. Ideally, all aspects of the quality system should be audited at least annually. The audits must be conducted by competent personnel

4.3 Customer Complaints, Quality Incidents and other Feedback.

All laboratories are not ideal and at times receive queries or complaints from customers. They are required to record all customer complaints, investigate them systematically starting with the root cause, and finally record the results of the investigation and the corrective action taken. This provides a valuable source of feedback on the operation of the quality system; ultimately, the main objective of a quality system is to ensure excellent customer service.

Proactive soliciting of both positive and negative feedback from customers is recommended. One can use annual customer surveys or use feedback forms accompanied with calibration/test reports. The two methods may also be extended to cover processes outside the technical area but affecting the customer such as TAT, pricing etc.

Staff can detect and relay information about quality deterioration. There can also be internal or external detection of non conforming work and other quality failures. All these require corrective actions be initiated to rectify the non conformities.

Below is a list of some common quality assurance methods used in a quality system

- Use of certified reference materials(CRM) - a sample for which the test results are firmly established and agreed, ideally on an international basis

- Interlaboratory intercomparisons - exchanging samples/aretefacts with other laboratories and comparing results.
- Use of spikes- This, at the very least, demonstrates that the laboratory would detect the material or organism being sought if it were present.
- Quality control samples- They are samples for which the laboratory has established values and acceptance limits
- Consensus standards – these are specific industry standards for tests and measurements that have no traceability to SI
- Reference methods - In the case of some tests and measurements, different methods may give different results. In these cases, the 'correct' result is defined in terms of a reference method which is tightly specified, and traceability effectively means traceability to the reference method.
- Statistical quality control – this mainly uses control charts such as the Shewhart chart that gives a general plot between the expected values against measured values over time to guide on drift from expectations

4.4 Accreditation and Technical Peer Review

Accreditation is the formal recognition that an organization is competent to perform specific processes, activities or tasks in a reliable, credible and accurate manner. From an accreditation body point of view, it is a third party attestation that a conformity assessment body fulfils specified requirements and is competent to carry out specific conformity tasks. Accreditation remains at the apex of conformity assessment. Most testing and calibration laboratories are accredited to the famous international standard ISO/IEC 17025 standard. The laboratories must comply with all the key requirements of the standards for their services to be accredited. However, there are some countries who have established high reputation in calibration and are self declared to comply to the standard, eg NIST of USA, PTB of Germany etc. If a laboratory is not accredited, one is to seek clarification on the policy to accept the laboratory services.

Another acceptable route for third party recognition is technical peer assessment so that measurement results are acceptable. The assessment involves assessment of the entire quality system with emphasis on technical aspects like measurement traceability, intercomparisons, including the publishing of calibration and measurement capabilities in the BIPM database.

4.5 Management Reviews

A quality management review is a management function where key members of laboratory management examine the performance of the quality system as a whole. The objective is to determine whether the system is delivering what is required as per the standard and may also include other local/policy requirements perceived to be relevant by management. Management reviews also consider audit reports to check for weaknesses in the system that needs remedial preventive and corrective action.

5 Conclusion

All these structures and activities lay emphasis on learning from experience and strengthening the future position of the quality system.

References

1 **United Nations Industrial Development Organization,** *Complying with ISO 17025: A practical guidebook for meeting the requirements of laboratory accreditation schemes based on ISO 17025:2005 or equivalent national standards*, 2009

2 **PTB,** *First we take measurement, then we take measures*, 2016

3 **DAkkS,** *News and Developments from DAkkS, 2017*

4 Michael Lombardi, *Traceability In Time And Frequency Metrology, 1999*

5 **Wikipedia**, *Components of a Quality System*

Annex 1

Quality Infrastructure

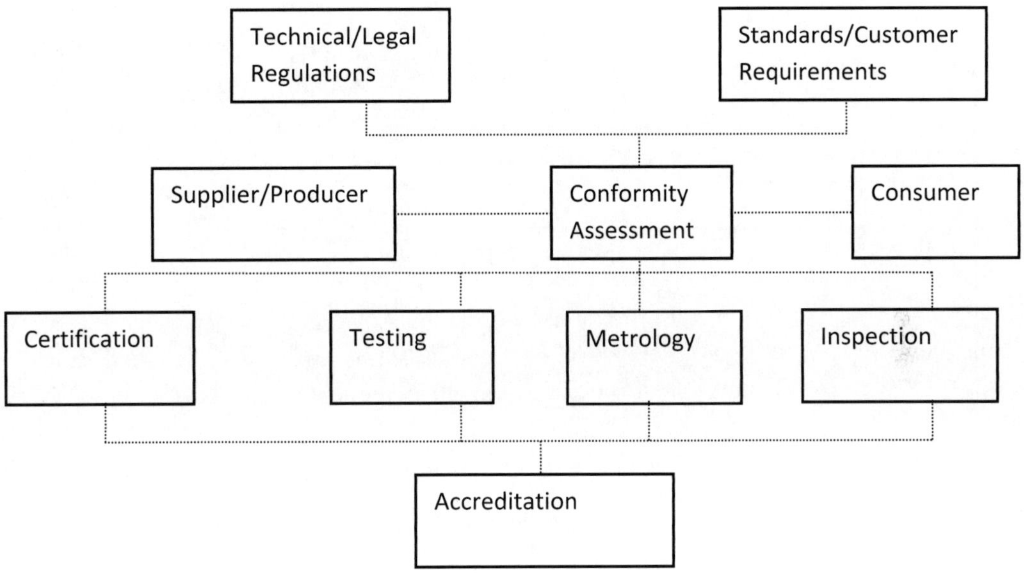

Annex 2

International Conformity Assessment System

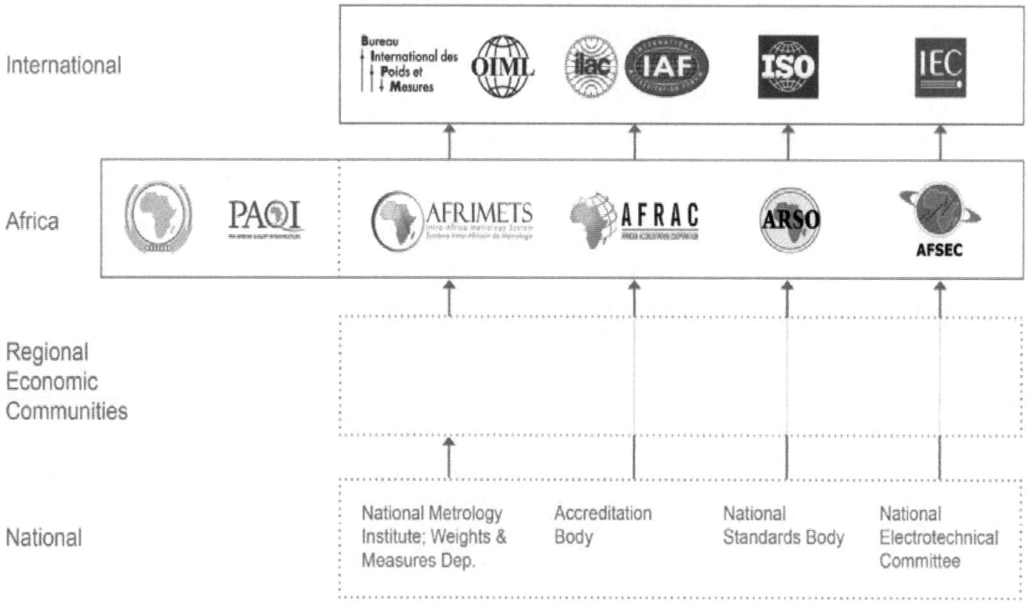

Annex 3

Measurement traceability to International System of Units (SI)

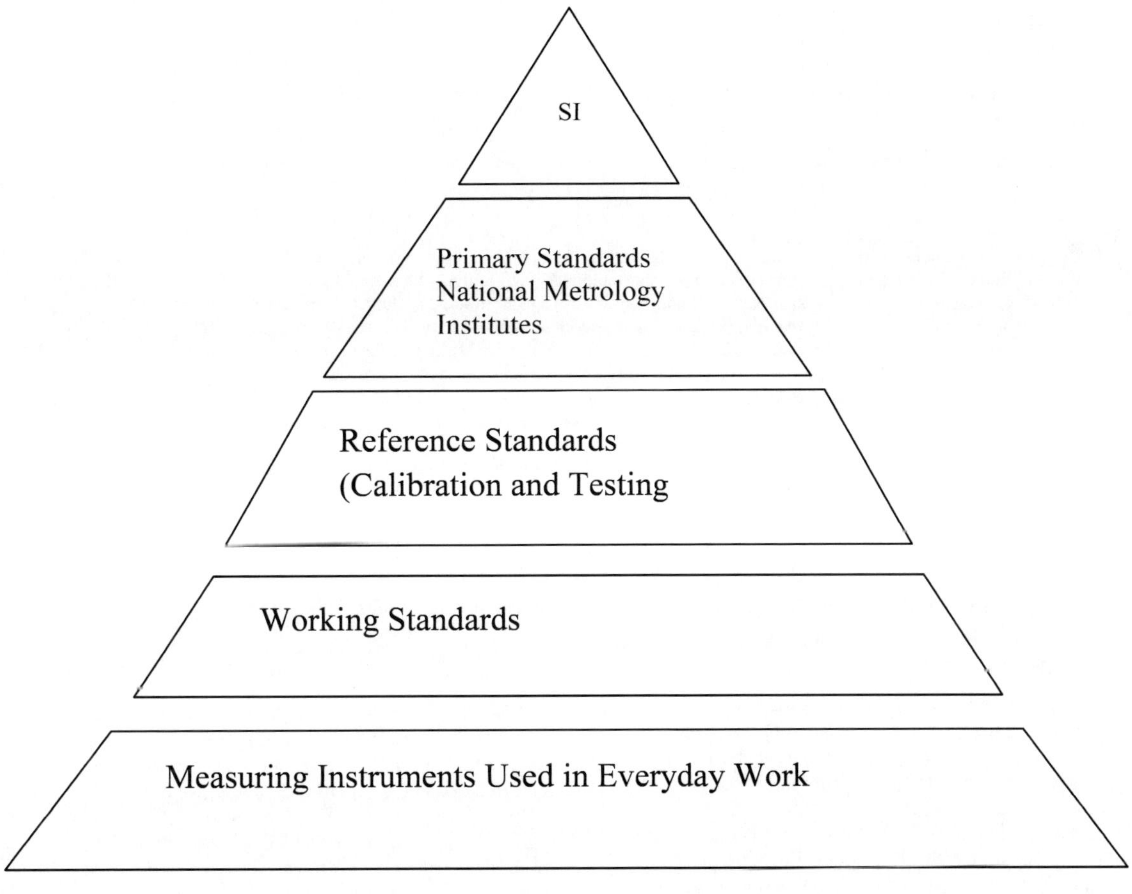

Mutualisation of metrological practices in research laboratories: IRD Senegal

M. Gueye1,2*, H. Bassene3, M. Cissoko4, E-J. Diatta5,2

1LEMSAT, Laboratory of Microbial Ecology of Soils and Tropical Agroecosystems, IRD-Bel air hydrocarbon road, Dakar, Senegal; 2LMI IESOL, Ecological Intensification of Cultivated Soils in West Africa, IRD-Bel Air Hydrocarbon Road, Dakar, Senegal; 3URMITE, Research Unit on Infectious and Tropical Emerging Diseases, IRD-Hann Road of the Marist Fathers, Dakar, Senegal; 4LCM, Joint Microbiology Laboratory IRD-Bel Air Hydrocarbon Road, Dakar, Senegal; 5LAMA, Laboratory of Analytical Means, IRD-Bel Air Hydrocarbon Road, Dakar, Senegal.

Summary. The quality approach is an indispensable tool in research structures where measurement is ubiquitous. Metrology is one of them and is one of the factors making it possible to ensure the relevance of the scientific results obtained. Providers in metrology are rare and the decline in budgets allocated to research laboratories requires to optimize the management of measuring instruments. The metrology managers of the various laboratories certified ISO 9001: 2015 at IRD Dakar (URMITE, LEMSAT, LAMA, LCM) are committed to setting up mechanisms for sharing instruments and harmonizing metrological practices for better management. in charge of this activity. To do this, we organized ourselves into a working group and identified the devices that we have in common under metrological oversight or that must be. Common procedures and instructions are drafted according to the standards in force. Standards and some control devices are pooled under controlled access and used by authorized persons. For some regulatory audits, a contract is established between our institute and the inspection body specifying our requirements for the same inspector to carry out the same procedures for all laboratories. We have also put in place tools that allow us to verify the compliance of the results of certain devices for which we do not have verification standards or service providers at the national level. This allowed us to optimize calibration intervals and reduce the cost of services. Some instruments are now calibrated internally by standards connected to the IS using internal skills. This approach allowed the improvement of the quality of the work, which resulted in a saving of time for the realization of certain activities and a motivation of the actors. In addition, it has made it possible to establish new scientific and technical collaborations because of the recognized reliability and relevance of the measures.

Keywords: Research, quality approach, mutualization, harmonization, ISO 9001

1 Introduction

The Laboratory of Microbial Ecology of Soils and Tropical Agroecosystems (LEMSAT), the Research Unit on Emerging Infectious and Tropical Diseases (URMITE), the Joint Microbiology Laboratory (LCM), the Analytical Resources Laboratory (LAMA), implanted in Dakar, have engaged in a quality approach for a decade. This approach aims to contribute to the quality of our research through good organization, appropriate documentation, traceability and reliability. We are among those who have dared to take the ISO 9001 [1] certification in research in Africa and introduce quality management in the practice of research. The certification attests that the structure has a quality management, that is to say that it organized its work according to the requirements of the ISO 9001 standard [2].

In research such an approach aims at satisfying a request that it is from the carrier of the project or from the research financier, or to answer a research objective. The process of producing results involves a series of steps to verify the validity of the results and to ensure their reproducibility [3].

All the activities that ensure the control of the quality of measurement results is metrology. It is necessary on the one hand to calibrate the instruments, on the other hand to check the stability of their performances. The laboratory shall define and apply a calibration and verification procedure to ensure that any equipment involved and used during an analysis process has accuracy qualities such that the result is of value as close as possible to the true value, with controlled uncertainty. It is therefore important that the calibration and verification operations are carried out, that their results have been validated and recorded and that users have access to this information when using the equipment [4]. However in Senegal the providers of metrology are rare. For example there is only one provider involved in the fields of masses and temperatures. The demand being strong it is often difficult that it can ensure all the benefits in time. These services also have a cost and with the decrease of the budgets allocated to the research laboratories it is a strong constraint for the directors of laboratory and actors

* Correspondence: mariama.gueye@ird.fr

of metrology. For a better support of this activity, the metrology managers of the various laboratories certified ISO 9001: 2008 at the IRD Dakar (URMITE, LEMSAT, LAMA, LCM) are therefore committed to the mutualisation of instruments and the homogenization of metrological practices.

2 Organization

We organized ourselves into a working group led by one of the metrological managers (that of LEMSAT) under the responsibility of the Quality and Safety Environment Engineer (QSE) of the IRD in Senegal. However, other metrology managers also participate in ensuring the state of their measurement and analysis equipment. The unit directors set the policy and objectives of their respective laboratories and allocate the necessary means of action for its smooth running. The QSE engineer provides the relay between the metrology and representation managers (Figure 1). The coordinator prepares and leads periodic meetings. Needs are discussed in order to share, raise awareness and act together. An objective needs analysis is performed. After each meeting of the working group, a report is sent to the directors of the laboratories so that they become aware of the progress of the objectives and can adjust them if necessary, be alerted of the problems encountered and be informed of the actions to be taken. Take to remedy this, and more broadly to improve the management system.

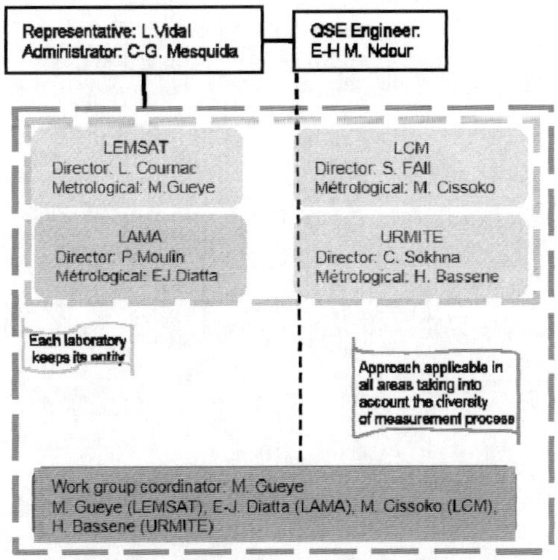

Fig. 1. organization chart of the working group

Choice of work equipment

From the knowledge of the needs of each one to have relevant scientific results, to leave as much as possible of the providers and to reduce the costs, the inventory of fixtures at the level of each structure was made. To do this the inventory of equipment was carried out by the corresponding metrology manager. Each unit based on its activities has identified the instruments that affect its analysis results. Then for each equipment was decided whether it was necessary to monitor metrology or not and if so the type of monitoring to be performed (internal or external). Then we selected the devices we have in common under metrological monitoring. Following this we defined our mission and analyzed our strengths and weaknesses for its realization. Finally, we have identified our objectives.

4 Equipment Management

Each unit continues to take charge of the management of its equipment under the responsibility of the corresponding Metrology Manager. However, it becomes accessible if necessary to other teams depending on its availability and respecting the rules put in place at the level of each structure.

A comparative study of the procedures or instructions used at the level of each laboratory for each device under metrological monitoring is carried out. In order to better structure our action, we proceeded to the homogenization of the procedures by apparatus. For that after census and study of the procedures set up in the various laboratories we took the procedure which seemed to us the best and improved it based on the standards in force [5]. Each laboratory adopts it by putting its logo and header and integrates it into its system. The verification or calibration intervals are managed by each laboratory according to its needs for some devices and are common for others. However the procedures are not fixed because the members of the group realize feedbacks to identify the necessary improvements to be made after validation by all.

The standards and control devices of each laboratory are collected and stored with the coordinator to coordinate their archiving and updating. It also ensures their connection to the International System of Units (SI) by authorized organizations. This is done with the financial participation of each laboratory. The external documents, the equipment life record, which is used to record all uses or interventions, the calibration, verification, maintenance and use procedures [6] as well as the registration certificates. Calibration of these instruments are made available to the members of the working group. The entry and exit flows of the stallions are traced and their proper functioning is checked each time before each exit and on their return to the borrower who must be an authorized person. A written procedure that explains the whole process is put in place.

5 Regulatory Audits

A service contract is established between our institute and the inspection body, under the direction of the QSE Engineer and the administrator, after validation by the metrology managers. Our requirements are specified in the contract so that the same inspector does the checks by following the same procedure for all the laboratories. Each laboratory bears the cost of its services and manages its documents and receives its inspection report (s). A copy of each report is given to the QSE Engineer for a better follow-up.

6 Verification of devices in the absence of standards and service provider

In some cases there is no local service provider to cover certain services and we do not have access to stallions in order to carry them out ourselves. We then set up ad hoc tools that allow us to verify as much as possible the conformity of the results generated. For example for extractor hoods we do periodic tests with the smoke test (visual check) to check the absence of air outlet from the inside of the working volume to the outside of it, at the level of workplan.

With regard to laminar flow hoods our main objective is that the hood is sterile, that there is no contamination of the samples. We do a bacteriological control of the air of the volume of work. To do this we put boxes of nutrient medium under the hood at different times of exposure. These boxes are sealed and incubated in the oven. It follows observation phases for 72h. If nothing pushes on these boxes we say that the hood is sterile if there is one or more colonies that grow on the boxes then the hood is not sterile. In this case it is necessary to decontaminate the hood and the verification process is redone. This step is usually sufficient to remove any contamination. However in case the contamination persists it is not possible to call on the technical service and we will try to clean the filter. The verification process must be resumed.

With respect to thermocyclers we introduce 1 or 2 positive controls during PCR that we position at different locations at the wells of the thermal cycler, all depends on the number of sample. If one of the positive witnesses does not work one can say that there is a "worry" about the well because it could be a manipulative effect. Then a pcr is resumed with delivery of the positive control in the same place for verification This after having taken all the precautions during the PCR preparation to eliminate any manipulative effect. As a result of this, if there is still problem with the positive witness then we can say that there is a problem with this well. The latter will be identified and will no longer be used and adjacent wells will also be verified.

7 Using a self-assessment tool

The study of the pooling process and its control factors induces the use of a self-assessment tool allowing the monitoring and the progression of the practices. The tool is based on an automated spreadsheet that allows a quick assessment of the process put in place by the main actors. The evaluation grid includes 7 good practices [1- Group management by the Unit Directors 2- Group management by the coordinator 3- Management of human resources in the laboratory 4- Document management of equipment 5- Availability of equipment 6 - Metrological confirmation of equipment 7- Environmental conditions of use and storage of equipment] which are detailed each with 5 to 7 performance criteria. User responds to proposals on a six-level truthfulness scale: Unanimous False (0%), False (20%), Fairly False (40%), Mostly True (60%), True (80%), True Proven (100%). The set of results is then presented in real time, in a 7-branch synthetic 'radar' diagram (Figure 2). These results can therefore be printed and capitalized in the process of setting up the pooling of practices [7].

8 Résultats et discussion

The members of the working group proceeded to the application of the self-assessment tool, ie 4 people. According to their evaluation, the pooling process is 91% assured. Standard deviations range from 0% to 3%. Figure 2 summarizes the percentage of average proficiency obtained for each good practice. Three of the factors achieve less than 90% of mastery, namely: group management by unit managers (84% ± 0%), the Group's human resource management (75% ± 2%) and environmental conditions use and storage of equipment (86% ± 3%).

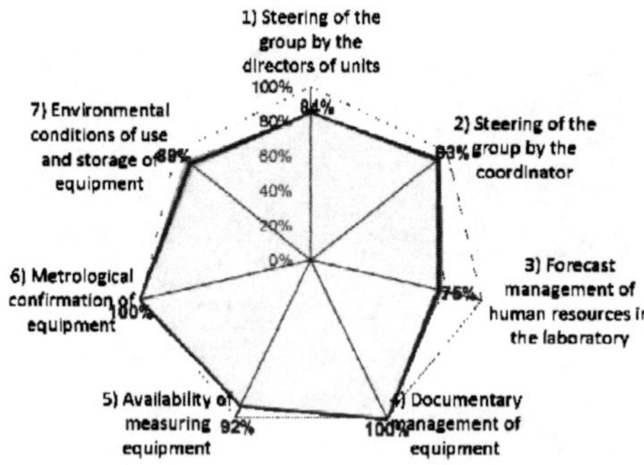

Fig. 2. Result of the self-assessment of the mutualisation of metrological practices

The system put in place is quite robust. However, to identify areas of improvement in processes with mastery rates below 90%, we looked at the responses to each criterion.

It appears that despite the assumption of the means for the metrological confirmation of the equipment by the unit directors and their good will we have not yet the means to buy some verification standards to be more autonomous. We have planned to make a comparative study of the costs of external services compared to the purchase of standards for the internal connection of certain services as is already the case for scales, pipettes, pH meter, and spectrophotometer.

Points for improvement are also needed in the process of the management of human resources. In fact, despite the fact that the HR division has provided training, it turns out that the staff is not sufficiently trained, especially for taking care of certain services internally. It also appears that the staff is not sufficient for the work requested because not all members of the group are just metrology managers. They have other activities within their respective laboratories. This slows down our dynamics of pooling and homogenization of practices and this also results in the holding of very distant meetings. The identification of equipment maintenance personnel is lacking in the process of equipment use and storage. However it should be noted that each person using equipment has the responsibility to make it clean and in good condition; this is checked after each equipment return.

The use of a self-assessment tool has made it possible to quantify the level of pooling and homogenisation of practices in our research laboratories, and to target critical points. Proposals for improvement have been made. Their realization will be a first step in solving these problems.

9 Conclusion

The implementation of the pooling process allowed us to optimize calibration intervals and reduce the cost of services. Some instruments are now calibrated internally by standards connected to the IS using internal expertise. This approach allowed the improvement of the quality of the work, which resulted in a saving of time for the realization of certain activities and a motivation of the actors. In addition, it has made it possible to establish new scientific and technical collaborations because of the recognized reliability and relevance of the measures. The use of the self-assessment tool, developed as part of the quality approach in the research and analysis laboratories, enabled us to quantify the level of control of the processes implemented, to identify the critical points and priorities for improvement.

References

1. NF EN ISO 9001, Quality Management System - Requirements, Ed. Afnor® 2008,

2. E. Giesen, Quality approach and ISO 9001 standard, A managerial culture applied to research IRD editions (2013)

3. J-P. CHIPPAUX, La Paz, July (2008)

4. NF EN ISO 10012: 2003, Quality management system - Essential principles and vocabulary

5. Managing and Controlling Measurement Processes and Equipment, Volume 1, Ed. Afnor® (2005)

6. E. Fargier, M. Priel, Organization of a calibration laboratory, Techniques of the engineer (2007)

7. S. Bousbiat, quality approach in research, UTC, (2010)

University training in metrology and skills development in quality assurance for the export sector

Mounir Ben Achour*[1], Asma El Hamzaoui[2], Iris Nadolny[2], Nada Lachaal[3], Walid Touayar[1]

1) Ministry of Higher Education and Scientific Research (MESRS - Tunisia)
2) Physikalisch-Technische Bundesanstalt (NMI - Germany)
3) Ministry of Industry and Small and Medium Campanies (MIPMC - Tunisia)

Received:

Abstract. The bilateral cooperation project between Tunisia (Ministry of Industry and Small and Medium Campanies) and Germany (PTB: German National Institute of Metrology), entitled "Developing expertise in quality assurance for the export sector" aims at providing Tunisian companies with a whole range of calibration services offered by qualified local service providers. In the scope of this project, various diagnoses have been made. Promoting the integration of metrology in the Tunisian university curriculum, they identify the needs of universities in terms of training programs and equipment, technical skills as well as the training of trainers.

Keywords: Metrology, Teaching, University Teacher, Academic Training, Industrial, etc..

1 Introduction

As part of the bilateral cooperation project between Tunisia (Ministry of Industry and Small and Medium Campanies) and Germany (PTB: German National Institute of Metrology), entitled "Developing expertise in quality assurance for the export sector", diagnoses identifying the universities' needs in terms of training programs and equipment, technical skills as well as the training of trainers have been made.
Their objective is to promote the integration of metrology in the universities' curriculum and to adapt the academic training according to socio- economic requirements. [1].

Most training courses in the field of organizational, theoretical and practical metrology are not acquired, even basic knowledge has insufficient acquisition rates. Consequently, companies consider trainings in all areas of metrology as necessary.

On the one hand, 65% of companies have already made use the specific training provided in the field of metrology. On the other hand, the offer's inadequacy is deplored, since the training is limited to theoretical basics so far.

Concerning the academic training in metrology, more than 40% of companies are not aware of its existence in Tunisia. Only a third of them recruited [IN1]metrologists having acquired higher education. Their satisfaction with these recruitments is only positive in half of the cases, not only the lack of practical training but also the poor application of their knowledge was criticized. The companies' demand mainly concerns technicians (professional training) and metrological technicians.

In the years to come, the majority of them is planning recruitments in this field which are however limited to at most two persons. In addition, two thirds of the companies consider an engineer with an advanced training in metrology as sufficient. According to them, there is no need to hire a specialized metrologist.

An action plan has been drawn up on the basis of the diagnoses' results. Its main objective is to adjust the already existing offer to the companies' requirements and to promote the use of metrology within them, thereby facilitating their access to export markets.
Today, university professors working in the field of metrology are generally teachers in academic disciplines. Even though they already have a more or less theoretical and profound knowledge, the results clearly showed their need and request to refresh and deepen it on a practical basis. In view of the new demands in metrology and the current development towards a general harmonization of training programs on all levels, it appears necessary to adapt their expertise accordingly.

* Correspondence: benachourmounir@gmail.com

2 Theoretical background [2]

Having examined the offer of academic training in the field of metrology has highlighted several areas for improvement.

Inadequate training: Further education courses in metrology are almost absent yet, hence the idea to promote a corresponding offer in universities and to facilitate administrative procedures for training institutions and the industry. As a result, the qualification and skills of the companies' staff would be maintained and even improved. The offer of training in metrology mainly focuses on "Applied License" (Figure 1). This invites us to reconsider its distribution and to create new and more targeted learning opportunities.

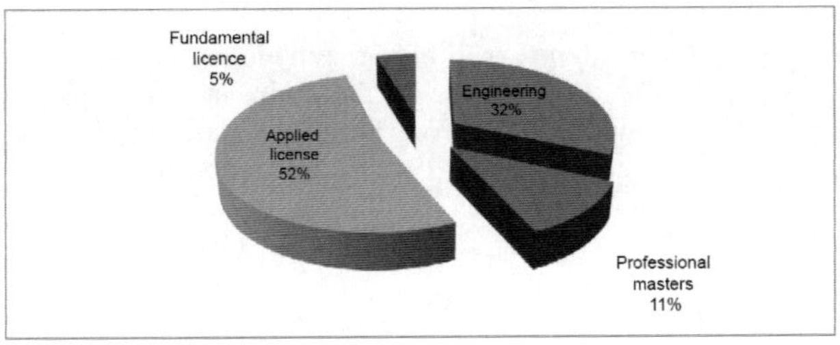

Figure 1: Distribution of the offer of initial academic training

For all the courses listed, at all levels, the share related to metrology teaching does not exceed 7% of the total hourly volume of academic teaching (Figure 2). Consequently, these indications on hourly volumes reveal that the teaching of modules directly related to metrology is limited to raising awareness in the majority of training institutions. If we link this quantitative analysis with the stakeholders' opinions (training institutions, learners, industrialists) on the training's quality, we can explain why Tunisian companies are dissatisfied with the offer of academic and professional training and therefore hesitate to employ metrologists having graduated from local universities.

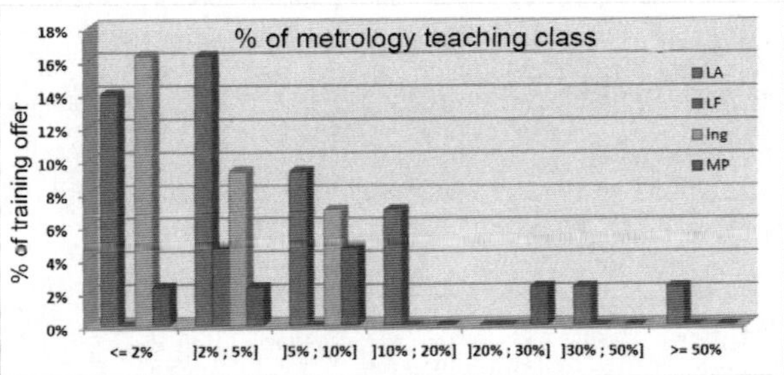

Figure 2: Part of metrology education by level of academic training

Insufficient resources (Figure 3): The proportion of teaching responsibles in metrology being dissatisfied with the amount of time reserved for courses in their field of study is 15%. In addition, the division of time between lectures, tutorials and labs should be revised since a significant percentage of teachers and learners are not content with it. Due to the lack of equipment, practical parts are indeed reduced to a minimum or at least restricted in most of the cases. As result, also the tutorial parts are limited in terms of quantity and quality.

Finally, the named shortcomings (lack of equipment and low number of industrial teachers) result in a theoretical training often criticized by companies afterwards. A large number of teaching managers and learners consider the equipment's condition and performance as not satisfactory. Apart from that, the state of metrology spaces is often criticized. For this reason, a general inventory is clearly necessary.

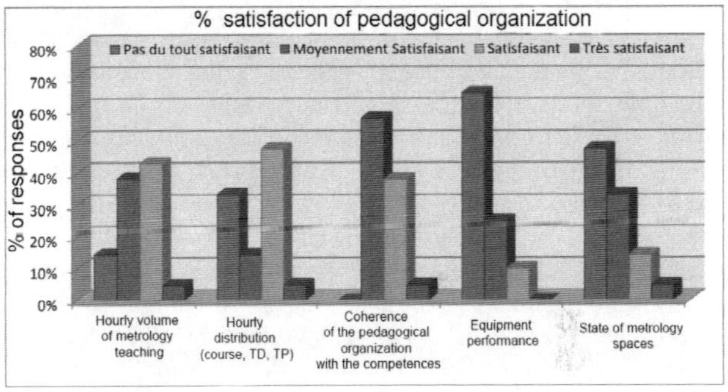

Figure 3: Educational organization of academic training in metrology

Training programs are not fully available and only partially applied, requiring a thorough review (Figure 4).

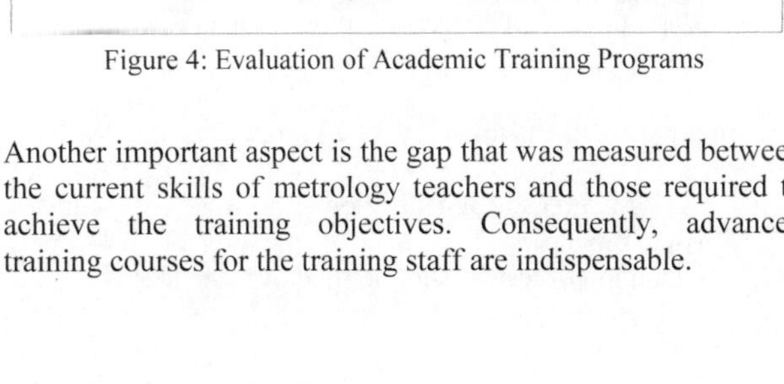

Figure 4: Evaluation of Academic Training Programs

Another important aspect is the gap that was measured between the current skills of metrology teachers and those required to achieve the training objectives. Consequently, advanced training courses for the training staff are indispensable.

Insufficient results (Figure 5): The almost complete lack of learner satisfaction surveys does not allow us to estimate the training's quality. Indeed, an evaluation on part of the learners can be very useful in order to determine actions for a continuous improvement of training offer systems. Furthermore, the lack of a database measuring the integration rate of graduates in companies hampers an assessment of the companies' requirements.

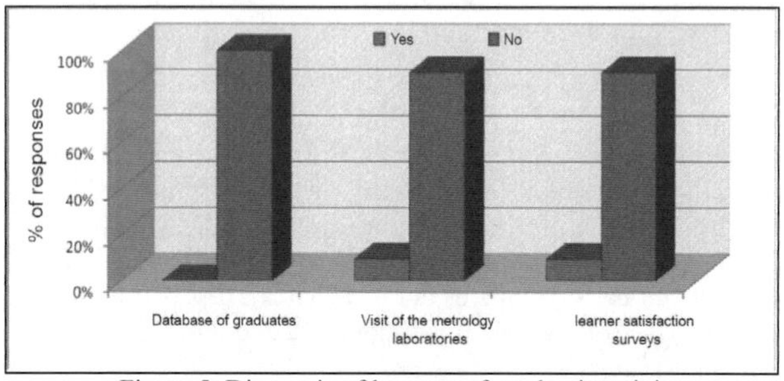

Figure 5: Diagnosis of learners of academic training

As already mentioned, there is a remarkable discrepancy between the graduates' actual competences and those required by manufacturers. Thus, it should be considered problematic that the manufacturing industry is practically excluded from the teaching of metrology modules. As a consequence, training methods applied in metrology should be reviewed in order to harmonize them with economical needs.

In this context, a regular and well-adapted alternation between the university and the company is an effective tool for transmitting knowledge and know-how to the learner. University- business partnerships are essential for the promotion and recognition of the environment, making the described exchange possible.

3 Practical context

An action plan [3] has been drawn up on the basis of the diagnosis' conclusions. It was validated by the ad hook committee, constituted by the Ministry of Higher Education and Scientific Research. Its objective is to adjust the existing offer to the corporations' needs and to promote the use of metrology within them, thereby facilitating their access to export markets.

Indeed, the diagnosis clearly showed the need of university teachers whose knowledge should be refreshed and deepened on a practical basis. Due to the new demands in metrology and the current development towards a general harmonization of training programs on all levels, it appears necessary to adapt their expertise accordingly.

The action plan contains three types of action:

- Information and sensitization
- Training upgrade
- Training of teachers in the field of metrology

Information and sensitization

On the one hand, the diagnosis reveals that the manufacturers consider metrology as important. They are as well conscious that metrology will allow not allow ensure their companies' competitiveness but also the penetration of foreign markets, particularly of those with highly developed legislations and regulations.

On the other hand, the diagnoses have determined that the main shortcomings of academic training concern the insuffiency of practical units and the inadequacy of the topics studied. The named problems make a training in conformity with the requirements of the Tunisian market difficult. Therefore, it is strongly recommended to organize an information and sensitization day each for the southern, northern and central region of Tunisia. The target group would be teaching responsibles who already have experience in teaching metrology or show a possible interest in it

Upgrading the academic training in metrology

According to the study of needs, the main shortcomings in terms of academic training concern the practical trainings' insuffiency and the inadequacy[IN2] of the studied subjects. As a consequence, it is recommended to act at two different levels in parallel:

- Harmonize basic training in metrology at all academic levels (Bachelor, Engineer and Master) and integrate teaching modules related to metrology
- Establishment of pilot laboratories for academic training in metrology

Revision of basic training in metrology:

The companies stated that graduates are, apart from few exceptions, not well prepared to work in the field of metrology (superficial and theoretical training). In addition, the vast majority prefer to hire a professional engineer with profound knowledge rather than a specialist in metrology without expertise in their industry

Consequently, it is recommendable to integrate adapted metrology teaching modules into already existing training programs rather than developing further targeted metrology training courses. For this purpose, the improvement of training offer systems for higher education should involve the creation of an enlarged sectoral committee, bringing together university teachers and a representative of the Ministry of Industry and Small and Medium Campanies (MIPMC) as well as the National Agency of Metrology (ANM). The committee would focus on updating the training programs through an ambitious, diversified and targeted content.

The members of this sectoral committee will have the following tasks:

- set goals for the teaching units
- detail the teaching units' constituent elements
- develop lesson plans for the teaching units
- develop a teaching module dedicated to the popularization of industrial metrology; integrate it into the program during the

first year of training, with the main objective of making learners aware of the notion of metrology
• incorporate topics such as "methods of calibration and measurement", "use of calibration results", "managing a range of measuring instruments", "estimation of measurement uncertainties", "Optimization of the cost of metrology" and "knowledge and implementation of the reference system 17025" in training programs.
• establish a reliable evaluation system for teaching units
• set an adequate hourly volume for the metrology modules
• divide the hourly volumes between lectures, tutorials and practical work
• develop teaching kits presenting the basics of metrology for academic institutions and select appropriate training equipment, technically comparable to that of professionals.

A further recommendation would be to support this committee or a small committee with a study visit abroad (to recognized higher education institutions in the field of metrology) in order to allow the revision of the trainings' content for different academic fields.

From a practical point of view, it is proposed that:

- The revision of basic metrology programs is done at two different levels. First at the level of the LMD system and then at the level of engineering and professional masters courses.
- The revision is performed gradually over two to three years
- Entrust this study to experts with significant experience at the university level.

At the same time, it appears necessary to strengthen the relationship with the business world (to introduce more "co-constructed" alternated academic training).

Establishment of university reference centers for training in metrology

The necessity of upgrading metrology training is based on the fact that the laboratories in higher education institutions are under-equipped in terms of quantity and quality. Because of insufficient budgets, these laboratories have problems not only concerning maintenance but also the availability of consumables. Their needs are too important to be fulfilled in the near future. But it is necessary to act. Therefore, it is proposed to start by strengthening at least one reference center for academic training in metrology for the main industrial sectors.

The state would concentrate its resources on selected laboratories. Certain of this size already exist but they are often reduced to the strict minimum. For this reason, it is recommended to concentrate efforts on the reference poles. The distribution of these reference centers can be made on the basis of the universities' sectoral specialities, as it was the case for the national metrology chain in the support institutions of the Ministry of Industry of Small and Medium-sized Campanies (mechanical / dimensional building materials / mass and weighing ...). However, the implementation of this concept is not unproblematic given the increase of universities at regional level and the lack of coherence concerning the setting up of their metrology laboratories. Besides, the actual condition of their equipment and the issue of regional distribution have to be taken into account.
For this purpose, the following university reference centers have been identified:

- Mechanics: ENISo (sousse), ENIS Sfax (Sfax) and ENIT (Tunis)
- Electrical and electronic: ENI-CARTHAGE (Tunis) and FSS (Sfax)
- Agrifood: INAT (Tunis) and ESIAT (Tunis)
- Chemistry: FST (Tunis), ISBAT (Tunis) and ISET Gabes (Gabes)
- Textile and clothing: ISET (Ksar Hellal) and ENIM (Monastir)
- Pharmaceutical production: ISBST (Ariana) and Faculty of pharmacy in Monastir
- Energy field: FSB (Bizerte) and ENIM (Monastir)
- Building materials (temperature): INSAT (Tunis) and ISSAT (Mateur)

In the long term, it is recommended to equip each large region (North, Center and South) with a complete metrology infrastructure (the various sizes) at the university level.
In fact, the recommendation to distribute pilot laboratories is established according to establishments' activity sector, but this does not impede that all sectors of activity can be covered in the academic institutions of the three major regions (North, Center and South).
Once these institutions have been selected and the quantities assigned to them, it is proposed to provide them with the necessary technical assistance to constitute the centers of excellence:

- Visits of similar model institutions world wide
- Definition of needs (identification of necessary equipment, quantification of needs ...)
- Preparation of the specifications
- Technical assistance for staff (teachers and technicians) responsible for the operation and maintenance of the laboratory in the areas of managerial and technical management

Training of university teachers in the field of metrology

University teachers in the field of metrology are generally teachers in academic disciplines with more or less extensive and theoretical knowledge of metrology, what affects their performance negatively. The survey clearly showed their need and requires them to refresh and deepen their knowledge. Given the current orientation towards the harmonization of metrology training for all academic levels, teachers' knowledge should be harmonized accordingly and adapted to new needs.

In the survey concerning academic institutions, most of the

teachers interviewed expressed a request to retrain and strengthen their skills. Consequently, a further recommendation would be to offer a general training followed by specific course units responding to the requests made by the different areas defined in the needs study report.

4 Results and discussions

Implementation of the first action: Information and sensitization (figure 6) to metrology in academic institutions in three regions distributed geographically north, center and south (FSB: May 3rd, 2017; ENISo: April 6th, 2017; FSS: March 16th, 2017) and include academics, researchers, students and industry from each region. The objective of these days is to make academics aware of the importance of metrology and to analyse the current state of teaching. In addition, they should be compared to the economy's needs in terms of skills. This aims at improving the quality of programs and teaching methods in order to better meet the labor market's demands.

The 1st Metrology Sensitization Day for the southern region takes place at the Faculty of Sciences of Sfax (FSS) on March 16th, 2017, followed by the second one for the central region at the National School of Engineers of Sousse on April 6th, 2017. The same event for Tunisia's northern region takes place at the Faculty of Sciences of Bizerte on May 3rd, 2017. These days were organized by the Ministry of Higher Education and Scientific Research and the Ministry of Industry and Small and Medium Campanies in collaboration with "PTB"; Germany's National Institute of Metrology. Further partners are the National Metrology Agency as well as, UTICA, INRAP, CNCC, FST, INSAT, IEAQA, LCAE, CBS, CETIME and TUNAC.

The organization of sensitization days for academics was carried out in collaboration with civil society organizations such as the Tunisian Association of Metrology (ATMET) on the subject "Metrology as portal of knowledge to employability". On the one hand, this allowed to bring universities closer to their socio-economic environment and, on the other hand, to bring together the various actors in the field of metrology.

Figure 6: Sensitization Days.

Implementation of the second action: Training of university teachers in the field of metrology. In order to put into practice the action plan's recommendations, two training sessions were conducted by two university experts: Pr Marc HIMBERT and Pr Walid TOUAYAR as international and national experts, respectively. These two sessions were intended for university trainers in charge of teaching metrology in their institutions.

Thus, two groups, each consisting of twenty teachers, participated in these training workshops that took place in Hammamet-Tunis from July 18 to 22 and July 25 to 29, 2017. The session's last days were devoted to a study visit of INSAT's pedagogical laboratories of practical work in metrology.

Previously, the participants were selected by the technical committee. The selection criteria were agreed with the members of the ad hoc committee and the representatives of the PTB. Not only the offer but also the participants' diverse disciplinary fields reflect the conformity of the expressed need for metrological training in different university courses with the educational content thereupon provided.

The approach used to achieve the expected objectives was progressive, since the experts modulated their interventions, thereby taking into account the assimilation of the statistical bases and the methods of determination of the global uncertainty balance sheets. Supported by basic applications in the field of metrology, they were applied in many fields, for example the electrical, mechanical or agricultural sector.

The participation of members of the Ad'hoc Committee at the first session facilitated the formulation of recommendations for further actions. Their presence was highly beneficial, because they are all either presidents or members of national commissions and therefore responsible for program reforms and validations.

The two training sessions provided a great opportunity to bring together people who are in charge of teaching instrumentation and measurements, quality control and metrology. The participants' evaluation of these two courses showed considerable satisfaction (Figure 7).

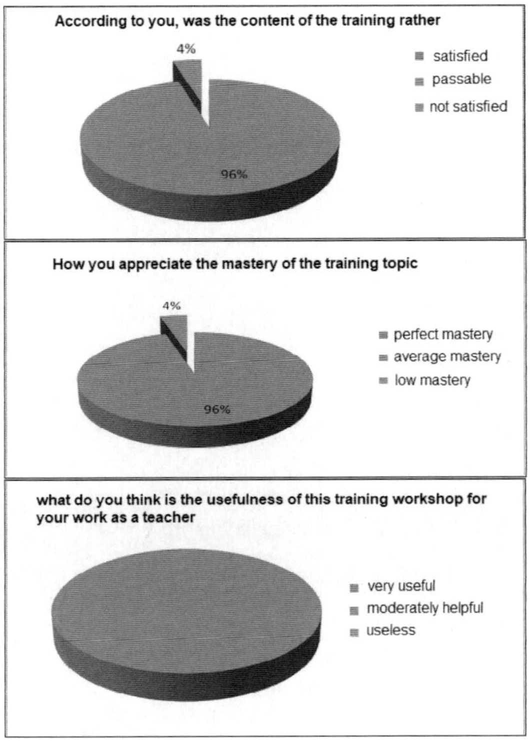

Figure 7: Evaluation by participants

Following these two training sessions, a sheet for improvement of the teaching modules relating to metrology has been made available. It will eventually allow to propose a harmonization of the existing educational contents that will be ensured from this academic year (2017 / 2018) onwards.

At the end of these two training sessions, the participants:

- have worked with the fundamental concepts defined in the texts relating to the International Vocabulary of Metrology (VIM). The results of the rapid assessment questionnaire, developed by the PTB highlighted, that 96% of the participants' considered the training's content as satisfactory. Apart from that, the evaluation questionnaire emphasizes the usefulness of this training for the university trainers. The percentage of people considering it as very useful is 100% for the first and 74% for the second session.

- At the end of the fourth day, after having worked with the examples proposed by both experts, the participants have become more familiar with the concepts developed during the two training sessions. Even though the performance indicator of the derived benefits is not quantifiable, analysing the questionnaire reveals the participant's interest in updating the content of their courses and this taking into account new acquired concepts. The new program sheets they proposed gave an idea of the participants' involvement in updating the existing educational offer according to their extended knowledge. These improvements will be applied from the current academic year onwards. At the end of each session, participants felt much more familiar with the compilation of error source balances and the topic of uncertainty and associated standard uncertainties.

5 Conclusion

After having finished the training, improvements in knowledge, particularly in terms of the international vocabulary of metrology, have been noted among the participants; unassisted teachers have been able to develop curriculum sheets based on new concepts not taken into account previously; implementation of the sheets proposed from the beginning of the academic year (September 2017) onwards; the proposed sheets have brought out fundamental notions of metrology common to all the specialties which are currently taught; Establishment of a circle of academics teaching metrology not knowing each other beforehand.

6 Perspective

These activities will be followed by other specific training sessions meeting the requirements of the different fields of metrology. After the training sessions, university teachers having participated in these training sessions should share their know-how with their colleagues. In addition to that, it would be necessary to support the eight pilot laboratories that were already identified.

References

1. Strategic Plan for the Reform of Higher Education and Scientific Research 2015 - 2025 (validated by the Council of Universities on 19 January 2015).
2. Report of "Diagnosis on the needs of the Tunisian industry in services in the field of industrial metrology and the potential of the supply of academic and professional training in this field" Project no.: 95096 (2016) .
3. MESRS action plan validated by the ad hoc committee (2017).

La mesure de la performance de la qualité des soins: Point de vue du personnel exerçant dans les Etablissements des soins de santé primaires au Maroc.

Zaadoud B [1,2], Chbab Y[1,3], El Ghaza S [1]. Chaouch A[1].

[1] : Laboratoire d'agro physiologie, Biotechnologie, Environnement et Qualité, Faculté des Sciences, Université Ibn Tofail, BP : 14000, Kenitra, Maroc
[2] : Cellule Qualité, Délégation provinciale du Ministère de la Santé, Moulay Yacoub, Maroc
[3] : Cadre Unité qualité, DHSA Ministère de la Santé Maroc.

Correspondent : Zaadoud Brahim
Hôpital Ibn Alkhatib, Fès, Maroc.
Zaadoud@gmail.com
Tel: 21261624913

Received:

Résumé

Objectifs : L'objet de notre recherche porte sur la mesure et l'évaluation de la performance dans les Etablissements de Soins de Santé Primaires (ESSP). Evaluer la perception des acteurs des ESSP de la performance de la qualité des soins des établissements de soins.

Méthode : Le recueil de données s'est effectué à travers un questionnaire pour le personnel qui exerce dans les ESSP ce questionnaire comporte 3 parties adapté selon le modèle de Donabedian (Structure, processus et résultats), comprenant sept domaines. La première partie concerne la Structure consacrée pour la planification de la qualité et le leadership et la gestion des ressources humaines. La deuxième partie concerne les processus consacrée à la gestion des processus, le monitorage et l'analyse. La troisième partie traite les résultats de la qualité et la satisfaction des usagers. Chaque domaine comporte 4 à 9 questions traitant un aspect avec un total de 46 questions. Le questionnaire a été adressé aux concernés de façon individuelle soit directement, soit à travers les emails, en assurant aux répondants une confidentialité totale, en soulignant l'indépendance du chercheur de la direction, et en proposant un droit de révision sur les propos tenus, afin d'instaurer un « climat de confiance relatif ». Les réponses sont classées entre 'pas du tout d'accord' avec un score de (1) et 'tout à fait d'accord' avec un score de (5). Ce type de question offre l'avantage de faciliter le recueil et le dépouillement de l'information.

Résultats : On note des différences significatives dans la perception de la qualité des soins du personnel de santé en général. Les démarches d'ACQ restent un bon outil pour améliorer la qualité des soins. La satisfaction de la population reste élevé avec une performance de (74%), les démarches d'ACQ sont des outils efficaces du changement organisationnel, L'impact sur le changement de pratiques professionnelles pour notre cas (68%) ont cette image qui varie entre moyen et faible sur le CQ. La continuité et l'intégration des soins ne sont assurées que dans 34% des cas, La fragmentation des services, l'utilisation inefficace des fournisseurs de soins, la mauvaise qualité de la collecte et de la gestion de l'information, le manque de coordination, un manque d'importance accordée à la prévention, ainsi que des déficits dans l'accès aux soins ressortent comme les problèmes principaux.

Conclusion : Même si les liens ne sont pas encore suffisamment établis dans le cadre d'une recherche scientifique, les démarches qualités sont généralement reconnues comme outil essentiel pour aider les établissements à améliorer la qualité et la sécurité des patients. Les outils proposés dans les démarches qualités restent un levier essentiel pour la promotion des démarches qualité. Elles ont démontrés des effets positifs sur la qualité des soins, mais certain contraintes freinent leur évolution. Il n'est pas encore courant d'effectuer des évaluations de la qualité des soins dans les ESSP afin d'obtenir les informations pertinentes sur la valeur ajoutée. D'où, la nécessité d'avoir des outils de mesure de performance qui mettent en cohérence le pilotage du niveau opérationnel avec la stratégie, intégrer les objectifs organisationnels dans les mesures de performances opérationnelles et faire évaluer ses structures vers un réel management par la qualité qui passerait par l'appropriation par tous les personnels des outils de gestion par la qualité.

Mots clés : Qualité des soins, Mesure de la Performance, Amélioration continue de la qualité, Perception

1 Introduction

Au cours de ces dernières années, l'amélioration de la qualité des soins de santé est devenue une priorité absolue et un objectif principal pour tout système de santé dans le monde entier (Berwick. D. M 2004), (Belghiti A., 2008), (OCDE, 2011). En effet, en 2000, l'organisation Mondiale de la Santé (OMS) dans son rapport sur la santé dans le monde 2000 a mis l'accent sur l'amélioration des performances des systèmes de santé des pays afin d'atteindre les trois Objectifs du millénaire pour le développent (OMD) liés à la santé (OMS, 2000). Dans ce contexte la mesure de performance en soins de santé qui est essentielle pour améliorer la qualité, réduire les erreurs, favoriser une plus grande efficience devient primordiale (Sharon J., 2008).

Cependant, le système de santé est un système complexe, sa complexité est caractérisée par : 1) des processus nombreux, en partie non standardisables et d'évolution rapide. 2) des métiers multiples et en évolution permanente. 3) une sociologie particulière, notamment en ce qui concerne la répartition des pouvoirs de décision, 4) une qualité des produits (résultat des soins délivrés) difficile à appréhender pour les professionnels et les patients, 5) une difficulté à identifier et à valoriser l'effet des démarches qualité (Grimmer et al, 2014).

De plus, les systèmes de soins de santé sont actuellement confrontés à plusieurs défis redoutables : l'augmentation de la demande de soins, l'émergence d'un paysage économique dans lequel les systèmes de soins doivent faire plus avec moins (OCDE, 2011), une mauvaise utilisation des services de santé, le manque de conscience de l'importance de la mesure des erreurs dans la pratique des soins de santé (IOM, 2000).

Dans les pays en développement et surtout en Afrique, les systèmes de santé peinent à remplir efficacement leurs fonctions, du fait de leur faiblesse et de leur fragmentation (OMS, 2005). La faiblesse des systèmes de santé s'explique par un certain nombre de facteurs, à savoir : des insuffisances au niveau de la planification et de la prévision, la pénurie des ressources humaines, financières et matérielles, l'insuffisance des données pour informer de manière éclairée la prise de décision, les lacunes des processus institutionnels, et les faiblesses du suivi de la performance et de l'impact des interventions (Amadou. B. M. et al. 2007).

La mesure, l'évaluation et la comparaison des performances de la qualité des soins a trois objectifs principaux : 1) responsabiliser les prestataires de santé, 2) élaborer des politiques mieux adaptées et 3) permettre aux prestataires et aux autres parties prenantes d'échanger leurs connaissances (Veillard. J. et al, 2010). Cependant, la qualité des soins est un concept difficile à saisir d'où la complexité de son évaluation (Zaneta. P. et al, 2008). Il faut veiller à ce que la dynamique complexe de la prestation des soins de santé, les différents niveaux d'évaluation des soins et les différentes perspectives des intervenants clés du système soient adéquatement représentés.. Puisque la qualité des soins revêt des dimensions multiples et peut être appréhendée selon différents points de vue (OCDE, 2011).

La qualité des soins revêt des dimensions multiples et peut être appréhendée selon différents points de vue. D'où La question sur le consensus entre les différents points de vue sur la qualité des soins de santé est-il toujours possible ? Les démarches qualites sont articulées autour de deux grandes dimensions de la qualité : D'une part l'objectivation d'un déficit de qualité grâce à la mesure des écarts par rapport à des référentiels préalablement définis. D'autre part la mise en œuvre d'initiatives d'amélioration continue de la qualité reposant sur les outils et les approches qui ont fait preuve sur le terrain (Accréditation, certification, audit et Concours et prix qualité).

Le Maroc, comme tous les pays du monde, n'a pas échappé à cette vague de la qualité des soins qui a accompagné des réformes politiques, institutionnelles, économiques et sociales durant les années quatre-vingt-dix (Belghiti, 2013). Plusieurs projets ont mis en œuvre les activités d'Assurance Qualité par les différentes structures du ministère de santé, tels que l'audits clinique , l'approche d'équipe pour la résolution des problèmes, l'élaboration des standards et des normes, l'accréditation des hôpitaux , la certification des laboratoires d'analyses et l'instauration de cycles qualité selon l'approche de gestion intégrée de la qualité qui focalise ses interventions sur le processus d'amélioration continue de la qualité. Tout ceci a été conclu par une conférence sur la qualité de santé en 2002 ou un certain nombre de recommandations ont été émises : 1) afficher une volonté politique et apporter le soutien nécessaire pour la mise en place d'un système d'accréditation. 2) Identifier et uniformiser les mécanismes de normalisation existants et mettre en place de nouveaux mécanismes. 3) Créer un organe national d'accréditation. 4) Renforcer le système d'information et de documentation sur la qualité de soins. 5) Élaborer, adapter, réviser, diffuser les référentiels nationaux. 6) Implanter, soutenir, généraliser les démarches d'Assurance Qualité dans les structures sanitaires. 7) Former, informer, sensibiliser les acteurs de santé et partenaires sur le système d'accréditation (Ministère de santé Maroc, 2002).

La gouvernance axée sur la qualité exige l'évaluation des systèmes de santé pour savoir s'ils sont en mesure de fournir des soins efficaces, surs et centrés sur le patient. Cette gouvernance est tributaire des informations sur la qualité des soins de santé qui visent à : 1) améliorer la cohérence et la coordination des soins, 2) prévenir la maladie, 3) faire en sorte que les malades reçoivent les soins dont ils ont besoin. 4) Garantir l'efficacité des soins, 5) garantir la sécurité des soins, 6) récompenser les prestataires de santé qui dispensent des soins de qualité, et 7) faire évoluer les systèmes de santé vers un mode de gouvernance basé sur les résultats et régi par la qualité (OCDE, 2011).

Malgré les efforts fournis en matière de recherche sur la qualité des soins un certain nombre de questions restent poser :

- Comment améliorer la qualité des soins ?
- Comment mesurer la performance en matière de qualité des soins ?
- Comment introduire les stratégies d'amélioration de la qualité des soins dans les politiques publiques ?
- Les démarches qualités (CQ) améliore-t-elle la performance dans les établissements de soins ?

2. METHODOLOGIE DE L'ETUDE:

En nous basant sur le cadre théorique du Concours Qualité et les autres Démarches Qualités, nous avons évalué le Systéme de Santé Marocain à l'aide d'indicateurs qui ne sont pas directement liés au volume, tout en documentant les aspects qualitatifs de l'utilisation. Ces indicateurs relèvent de l'accessibilité, la continuité, la globalité, et la productivité des soins, l'efficacité et l'efficience, nous avons proposé un cadre multidimensionnel d'évaluation de la performance des services de santé.

Dans notre recherche, on a opté pour la méthode qualitative basée sur l'approche interprétative, cette approche est utilisée de plus en plus dans la recherche sur les services de santé.

Quatre questions principales se posent dans le contexte de la collecte de données sur la Mesure de la Performance dans les soins de santé primaires. Il s'agit de la complexité, du cout, du type de données à collecter et de la qualité des données collectées (Adair C., 2003).

A. Hypothèses

H1. Les démarches qualités (CQ) favorisent l'amélioration de la performance de la qualité des soins. Il existe une relation très étroite entre les démarches qualités (CQ) et la performance de la qualité des soins.

H2. La mesure de la performance de la qualité des soins ne pose aucuns problèmes et les cadres conceptuels de mesure de la performance de la qualité des soins sont uniformes et facile à utiliser.

B. Les objectifs

Évaluer les systèmes de mesure et de gestion de la performance dans le domaine de soins au Maroc surtout l'approche Concours Qualité comme démarche générique de Systémique Qualité Improvisent Germany, en analysant les différentes dimensions et perspectives de la qualité des soins de santé, et les différents aspects de mesure de la performance dans les établissements des soins de santé primaires.

Evaluer l'impact des démarches qualités sur la qualité des soins dans ESSP ainsi que le niveau de performance. Les démarches qualités (CQ) améliore-t-elle la performance dans les établissements de soins ? Comment est mesurée la performance de la qualité des soins dans les ESS ?

Éclaircir un certain nombre de questions sur le CQ : Est-ce que le CQ est le plus appropriée pour le système de santé Marocain ? Permet de bons résultats sur la qualité des soins ? Peut améliorer les processus et représentent une DQ pérenne ?

C. Le questionnaire :

On a fait appel à un questionnaire qui comporte 3 parties adapté selon le modèle de Donabedian (Structure, processus et résultats), comprenant sept domaines. La première partie concerne la Structure consacrée pour la planification de la qualité et le leadership et la gestion des ressources humaines. La deuxième partie concerne les processus consacrée à la gestion des processus, le monitorage et l'analyse. La troisième partie traite les résultats de la qualité et la satisfaction des usagers. Chaque domaine comporte 5 à 9 questions traitant un aspect avec un total de 46 questions.

Le questionnaire a été adressé aux concernés de façon individuelle soit directement, soit à travers les emails, en assurant aux répondants une confidentialité totale, en soulignant l'indépendance du chercheur de la direction, et en proposant un droit de révision sur les propos tenus, afin d'instaurer un « climat de confiance relatif ». Les réponses sont classées entre 'pas du tout d'accord' avec un score de (1) et 'tout à fait d'accord' avec un score de (5). Ce type de question offre l'avantage de faciliter le recueil et le dépouillement de l'information.

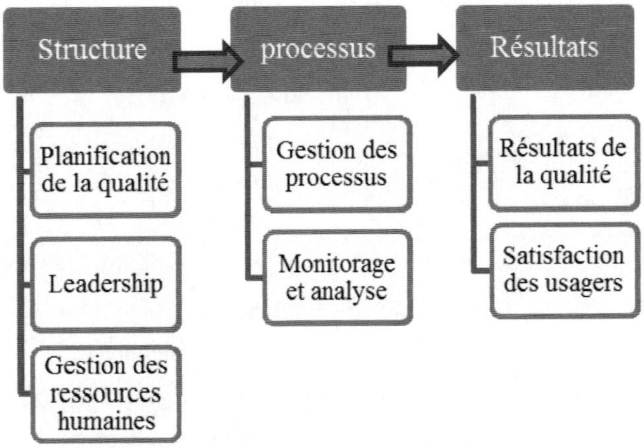

Figure 1. Cadre conceptuel du questionnaire

D. L'échantillonnage :

La population cible est le personnel de santé qui exercent dans ces établissements qui ont participé à la mise en œuvre d'une démarche qualité au sein de leur établissement sanitaire. Notre échantillon a été choisi par tirage aléatoire parmi le personnel. Les critères d'inclusion sont la participation au 'CQ' ou autres démarches qualités et le volontariat. Le questionnaire est adressé pour 70 personnes exerçant dans les 'ESSP' de 05 régions du Maroc, 62 questionnaires ont été récupéré remplis. Les profils des répondants sont comme suit 24 médecins dont 12 sont médecins chef de des ESSP et 38 infirmiers dont 18 sont des infirmiers chefs des centres de santé qui ont initié une démarche qualité. (Tableau.1)

Tableau 1. Répartition de personnes enquêtées selon le profil et le statut vis avis de la responsabilité.

Profil	Médecin		Infirmier		Total	
	Avec Responsabilité	Total	Avec Responsabilité	Total	Avec Responsabilité	Total
Nombre	12	24	18	38	30	62

Tableau 2. Répartition de personnes enquêtées selon l'ancienneté dans le système de santé et le sexe

		Années d'ancienneté dans le système			
		0-10 ans	10 - 20 ans	20 ans et +	Total
sexe	M	4	14	8	26
	F	6	24	6	36
Total		10	38	14	62

3.PRÉSENTATION ET ANALYSE DES RESULTATS

A. La perception globale

Le personnel des ESSP de notre échantillon (57%) qualifie la qualité dans les établissements de soins de santé comme moyenne, alors que 9 % ont une mauvaise perception de la qualité des services, tan disque 34% ont une bonne perception sur la qualité de leur système de santé. (Graphique. 1)

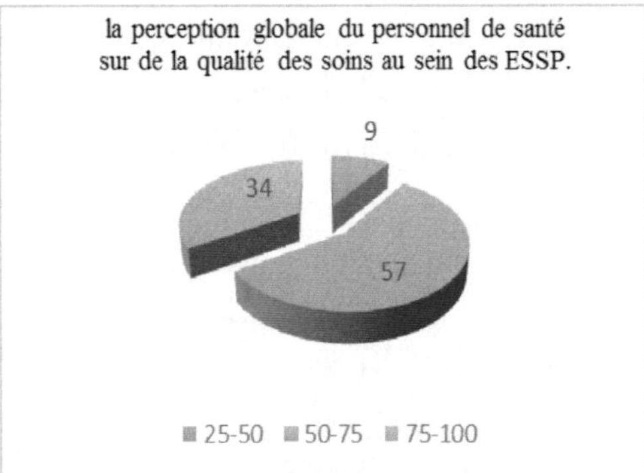

Graphique 1. Répartition du score global de la perception de la qualité des services de santé par le personnel de santé.

Les réponses du personnel sont très variées selon les dimensions, et l'étendu entre le score min et le score max est très réduit (10 points) pour la dimension résultat de la qualité, alors qu'il est très large (37 points) pour la dimension planification de la qualité. Pour les principes de la gestion de la qualité selon le programme Nationale d'assurance Qualité qui sont : Planification de la qualité et gestion de la qualité, le leadership et la satisfaction des usagers les scores moyens dépassent les 70%. (Tableau. 3).

Tableau 3. La perception du personnel des ESSP de la qualité des services de santé selon les dimensions du questionnaire.

Dimensions	Min	Moy	Max	Ecart
Planification de la qualité	42	65	77	37
Monitorage et analyse	52	60	67	15
Leadership	52	71	83	31
Gestion des ressources humaines	47	58	72	25
Gestion des processus	42	56	67	25
Résultats de la qualité	73	79	83	10
Satisfaction des usagers	63	74	80	17
Moyenne générale	53	66	75	22

B. La perception de la qualité du personnel des ESSP par dimension et par aspects :

Les dimensions sont décortiquées en aspects.

1.Planification de la Qualité :

Le score moyen de cette dimension est de (65%), Trois aspects sont performants à savoir : Le maintien des objectifs spécifiques pour améliorer la qualité des services et des soins, l'implication dans le développement de plans d'amélioration de la qualité des services et des soins et la participation de dans l'élaboration des plans d'action et la priorisation des activités ont un score de (77%). Le score pour la disposition de temps nécessaire pour planifier et tester les améliorations, la participation à l'établissement des priorités pour l'amélioration de la qualité des services et des soins est de (65%). Alors que la participation des partenaires (autres centres de santés, groupes communautaires, hôpitaux, organismes divers, etc.) à l'établissement des priorités pour l'amélioration de la qualité des services et des soins reste très faible avec un score de (42%). (Tableau. 4)

Tableau 4. Le niveau de perception du niveau de performance de la dimension "planification de la qualité" par le personnel

La planification de la qualité	Score en %
La disposition du temps nécessaire pour planifier et tester les améliorations.	**65**
Le maintien des objectifs spécifiques pour améliorer la qualité des services et des soins.	**77**
L'implication dans le développement de plans d'amélioration de la qualité des services et des soins.	**77**
l'établissement des priorités pour l'amélioration de la qualité des services et des soins par le personnel	**65**
Les partenaires (autres centre de santé, groupe communautaires, hôpitaux, organisme divers, etc.) Participent de façon significative à l'établissement des priorités pour l'amélioration de la qualité des services et des soins.	**42**
Moyenne du domaine	**65**

2.Monitorage et analyse des données :

Le score moyen de cette dimension est de (60%). Les scores les plus élevés pour cette dimension sont représentés par les aspects : La collecte de données sur la qualité des services et des soins et l'implication du personnel dans l'identification des données à collecter pour l'amélioration de la qualité des services et des soins par un score de (67%). L'utilisation de données sur la qualité des services et des soins, l'amélioration de l'utilisation des données et des informations sur la qualité des services et des soins et la vérification et l'amélioration de la fiabilité des données sur la qualité des services et des soins avec un score de (60%). Le centre de santé compare ses données sur la qualité des services et des soins avec d'autres centres de santé avec un score de (58%). Le score le plus bas est pour

l'amélioration de la pertinence de ses données sur la qualité des services et des soins (52%). (Graphique. 2)

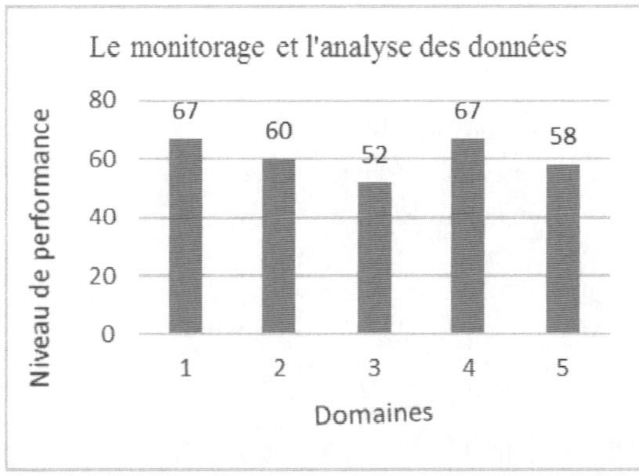

1. La collecte de données sur la qualité des services et des soins.
2. L'utilisation de données sur la qualité des services et des soins.
3. Chercher la pertinence des données sur la qualité des services et des soins.
4. L'implication active dans la collecte de données pour l'amélioration de la qualité des services et des soins.
5. La notion de comparer les données sur la qualité des services et des soins avec d'autres centres de santé.

Graphique 2. Le niveau de perception du niveau de performance de la dimension " monitorage et analyse " par le personnel.

3.Résultats de la qualité :

Le score moyen de cette dimension est de (79%). Les aspects les plus performants qui composent cette dimension sont les améliorations constantes et mesurables de la qualité des services et des soins avec un score de (83%). Des améliorations constantes et mesurables des résultats de la satisfaction des usagers avec un score (82%). Pour la notion de mesure des améliorations de la qualité de son organisation de façon constante est de (77%). Le maintien de cette amélioration de la qualité malgré les contraintes multiples est de (73%). (Tableau. 5)

Tableau 5. Le niveau de perception du niveau de performance de la dimension " résultats de la qualité " par le personnel.

Résultats de la qualité	% score
Les améliorations sont constantes et mesurables de la qualité des services et des soins.	83
Les améliorations sont constantes et mesurables des résultats de la satisfaction des usagers.	82
Les améliorations sont constantes et mesurables de la qualité de l'organisation	77
un maintien de l'amélioration de la qualité malgré les contraintes multiples.	73
Moyenne du domaine	**79**

4.Gestion des processus de la qualité :

Le score moyen de cette dimension est de (56%). Les performances de cette dimension restent moins performants en général : Pour le contrôle régulièrement des équipements et matériels pour s'assurer qu'ils satisfassent aux normes de qualité et la recherche d'amélioration de l'approche qualité et de (67%). L'encouragement de l'utilisation des indicateurs pour mesurer la qualité est de (62%). La coordination des efforts du personnel avec les autres pour améliorer la qualité des services offerts par le centre de santé est de (58%). L'utilisation des données issue des partenaires, (autres centre de santé, groupes communautaires, hôpitaux, organisme divers.) pour l'élaboration du plan d'amélioration de la qualité du centre de santé est de (57%). L'évaluation de la qualité avant d'être mis en place est de (50%). Le centre de santé dispose de politique efficace pour soutenir le développement de la qualité des services et des soins avec un score de (45%). La collaboration avec les partenaires (autres centre de santé, groupe communautaires, hôpitaux, organisme divers, etc.) pour améliorer la qualité de leurs produits et services est de (42%).

5.Le Leadership :

Le score moyen de cette dimension est de (71%). Les scores de cette dimension sont très élevés. Le leadership contribue à l'amélioration de la qualité des services et des soins ont eu le score le plus élevé de (83%). Les responsables font preuve d'un leadership visible en créant un environnement favorable à l'amélioration de la qualité des services et des soins (80%). Le personnel encourage les efforts pour améliorer la qualité des services et des soins et participe activement aux activités pour améliorer la qualité des services et des soins avec un score de (77%). Le personnel recueille de l'information auprès des usagers et des familles (besoins, suggestions) pour améliorer la qualité des services et des soins (72%). Le personnel fait des suggestions pour améliorer la qualité des services et des soins (70 %). La vision claire pour améliorer la qualité des services et des soins avec un score de (63%). Le personnel montre une habileté à gérer les changements (organisationnel, technologique) nécessaires pour améliorer la qualité des services et des soins (62%). Le personnel a une connaissance approfondie de la manière d'améliorer la qualité des services et des soins (52%). (Tableau. 6)

Tableau 6. Le niveau de perception du niveau de performance de la dimension " leadership " par le personnel.

Leadership	% score
Maintenir un environnement favorable à l'amélioration de la qualité des services et des soins	80
La participation active aux activités pour améliorer la qualité des services et des soins.	77
Avoir une vision claire pour améliorer la qualité des services et des soins	63
Avoir l'habileté à gérer les changements (organisationnel, technologique) nécessaires pour améliorer la qualité des services et des soins	62
Avoir une connaissance approfondie de la manière d'améliorer la qualité des services et des soins.	52
Encourage les efforts pour améliorer la qualité des services et des soins	77
Moyenne	71

6.Satisfaction des usagers :

Le score moyen de cette dimension est de (74%). Les aspects de cette dimension sont : L'étude des plaintes des usagers est utilisée pour prévenir la répétition des mêmes problèmes (80%), la contribution à résoudre rapidement les plaintes des usagers (78%). L'utilisation des données issues des usagers pour améliorer les services (77%). L'évaluation de manière satisfaisante les besoins des usagers et leurs attentes ainsi que les données sur les usagers sont largement diffusées auprès des personnels du centre de santé avec un score de (73%). L'évaluation de manière satisfaisante de la satisfaction des professionnels du centre de santé l'égard des services (63%). (Tableau.7)

Tableau 7. Le niveau de perception du niveau de performance de la dimension " satisfaction des usagers " par le personnel.

Satisfaction des usagers	% score
L'évaluation les besoins des usagers et leurs attentes.	**73**
La contribution à résoudre rapidement les plaintes des usagers.	**78**
la prévention de la répétition des mêmes problèmes.	**80**
La diffusion des données auprès des personnels du centre de santé.	**73**
L'évaluation de la satisfaction des professionnels du centre de santé à l'égard des services.	**63**
Moyenne	**74**

7.Gestion des ressources humaines :

Le score moyen de cette dimension est de (58%). Les aspects de cette dimension : La motivation pour améliorer la qualité des services et des soins avec un score de (73%). La disposition d'un système efficace pour que le personnel fasse des suggestions aux responsables sur la manière d'améliorer la qualité des services et des soins (72%). La formation en d'autres méthodes qui appuient l'amélioration de la qualité des services des soins. « Communication, gestion de la CS ….. » (58%). La coopération inter services pour améliorer la qualité est soutenue et encouragée (55%). L'organisation de la formation sur la gestion de la qualité des services des soins et l'autonomie professionnelle pour améliorera la qualité des services et des soins avec un score de (50%). l'organisation de la formation nécessaire pour améliorer les habiletés professionnelles et la performance (47%). (Graph. 3)

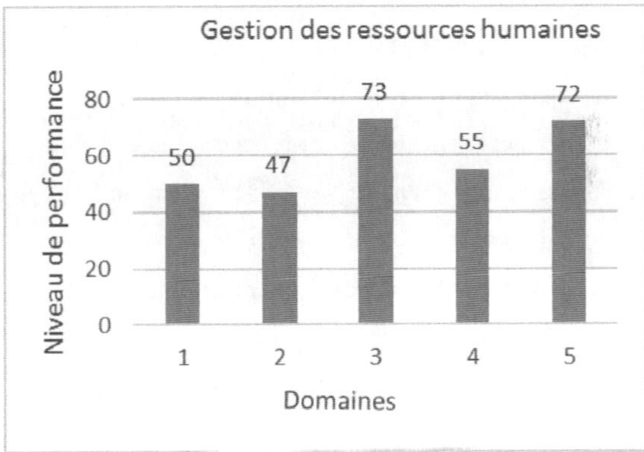

1.La formation du personnel sur la gestion par la qualité des services des soins.
2.La formation nécessaire pour améliorer les habiletés professionnelles et la performance.
3.La motivation du personnel pour améliorer la qualité des services et des soins.
4.La coopération inter services pour améliorer la qualité est soutenue et encouragée.
5.Un système efficace est implanté pour que le personnel fasse des suggestions aux responsables sur la manière

Graphique 3. Le niveau de performance de la dimension " gestion des ressources humaines' par le personnel.

4.DISCUSSION ET CONCLUSIONS :

Notre plan de discussion des résultats sera organisé en 3 niveaux : Discussion de la méthodologie, discussion des objectifs et discussion des résultats.

1. Discussion de la méthodologie de l'étude

Plusieurs études se sont intéressées par la recherche sur l'efficacité de la certification et la mesure de performance (Ovretveit et al. (2002), Braithwaite et al. (2006), Pomey et al. (2004), Shaw (2001, 2003), Walshe et al. (2001), Øvretveit

(2005)) d'autres études ont explorées l'impact de ces programmes sur les organismes accrédités (Pomey et al. 2004) (Devkaran. S, 2014), d'autres ont tenté d'analyser la performance de la certification en examinant leur structure et leur processus (Greenfield D et al. 2008), (Devkaran. S, 2014). Ce qui témoigne de la complexité du problème et le non unification des méthodes de recherche sur la qualité des soins et la mesure de performance.

Le cadre d'évaluation de cette étude repose sur une Synthèse (une sommation) entre le paradigme de la qualité de soins de Donabedian, qui lie la structure, le processus et les résultats, sur un cadre conceptuel d'évaluation de la performance des soins de santé primaires fondée sur le cadre du CQN, associé à une synthèse d'autres cadres cités dans la littérature (Cadre de Starfield B. Megaret E.).

Cependant, même si ces études tiennent compte de nombreux indicateurs pour analyser les systèmes de santé, elles les utilisent en sommant tout simplement les scores obtenus dans chacun des indicateurs. Cette agrégation des indicateurs réduit l'information disponible à un seul et unique score global, sans réellement tenir compte de l'interdépendance entre les indicateurs et les relations qui peuvent exister entre eux (Silva. B., 2011). Par ailleurs, en utilisant un score global pour analyser la performance des systèmes de santé, il n'est pas possible de savoir dans quels indicateurs on obtient les meilleurs et les moins bons scores (Silva. B., 2011).

2. Discussion selon les objectifs de l'étude

La gestion de la performance est composée de formulation d'objectifs de performance, d'établissement de stratégies d'amélioration, d'évaluations par rapport à l'atteinte de ces objectifs, de mesures individuelles de la performance et de système de rétroaction (Rolland K., 2011). La mise en place d'une mesure transparente de performance à tous les niveaux du système de santé, avec une correspondance étroite entre les objectifs d'une intervention et les résultats suivis, des indicateurs appropriés de progrès et d'impact et des mesures qui tiennent compte des éléments de performance susceptibles d'être gérés par la direction (Figueras. J. et al. 2008).

Notre étude partage les objectifs de l'étude menée par El Jardali et al. (2014), qui vise à mieux comprendre : 1) l'impact de l'accréditation/Certification/ CQ sur la qualité des soins tel que perçu par les membres du personnel des soins de santé primaires. 2) comment l'accréditation/ Certification/ CQ ont touché le personnel et la satisfaction des patients. 3) Identifier les principaux catalyseurs et défis pour la mise en œuvre de l'accréditation/ Certification/ CQ. 4) Elaborer les stratégies possibles pour améliorer la mise en œuvre de l'accréditation / Certification et CQ dans les soins de santé primaires. Se focaliser sur l'évaluation des SSP comme objectif du SS confirmé par les expériences en Amérique latine visant à élargir les services de soins primaires en milieu rural à de larges segments de la population (Margaret E. et al, 2008). La mise en œuvre des soins de santé primaires (SSP) pourrait bien être l'une des réformes sanitaires systémiques les plus importantes des temps modernes, les pays dont les systèmes de soins de santé primaires sont plus solides ont manifestement des soins de santé plus efficaces, plus efficients et plus équitables (Timothy A. et al, 2013). En se basant sur la preuve qu'un système de soins de santé primaires réduit les inégalités en matière de santé entre les populations, et peut aussi contribuer davantage à améliorer la santé de la population que les services de santé spécialisés. Les centres de santé communautaire sont spécialement conçus pour offrir des soins de santé primaires (Sabrina W, 2010). Il est évident que, bien qu'il existe une relation entre l'offre de soins primaires et une meilleure santé, il y a des exceptions à la règle. Aux États-Unis par exemple, il existe une relation forte et solide entre l'offre de SSP et une meilleure santé, une plus grande équité et des couts plus faibles (Starfield, 2009).

3. Discussion des performances des ESSP

3.1. L'impact sur le système de soins en général :

Il existe des opinions divergentes et contradictoires quant à l'incidence des démarches qualités sur les résultats des clients. Les recherches existantes ne comportent pas d'analyse rigoureuse et approfondie du processus d'Accréditation /

certification et de sa relation avec la performance, les résultats, l'amélioration de la qualité et la sécurité des patients (Greenfield D et al. 2008). Ovretveit et al. (2002), ont révélé que la recherche documentaire contenait relativement peu de preuves concernant l'efficacité globale des interventions de qualité et des normes de qualité dans les soins de santé (Devkaran. S, 2014).

3.2. L'impact sur les Démarches Qualités (Accréditation / Certification/ CQ).

Plusieurs organismes d'accréditation/ Certification ont introduit, développé, incorporé et contrôlé des indicateurs de qualité clinique dans les organisations de soins de santé. En conséquence, des améliorations ont apparemment été observées dans les résultats de ces organisations en matière de soins sur l'infrastructure et la performance de contrôle des infections des hôpitaux (Devkaran. S, 2014). Les résultats des soins décrivent les effets et les conséquences des services sur la santé des personnes (Pineault R. et al, 2008). Les résultats pertinents pour les systèmes de soins de santé primaires sont liés à l'état de santé, à l'équité, à la satisfaction des patients et des prestataires, aux couts et à l'efficacité. Les études ont révélé des liens avec la gouvernance, l'accès, la continuité, la coordination, l'efficacité, la santé de la population et la vigueur des soins primaires (Kringos. D et al. 2010). Dans le cadre des soins de santé primaires les mêmes avantages sont rapportés entre notre étude et la littérature (Bueton S A, 2003): 1) Un meilleur contrôle de la qualité par l'atteinte d'un niveau minimum de qualité du service. 2) Une meilleure règlementation en respectant les normes juridiques et de sécurité. 3) L'amélioration continue et durable de la qualité. 4) La fourniture d'informations aux patients, ce qui confère une confiance dans les services fournis et leur permet de prendre des décisions éclairées. 5) Etablir une image positive des normes de pratique et de service dans les centres de soins de santé primaires. Selon Pomey et al. (2004), les résultats de la recherche sur la certification tendent à démontrer que c'est une forme efficace de contrôle professionnel qui peut avoir un impact positif sur les valeurs et la culture organisationnelle (Paccioni A. et al, 2009).

Les résultats de notre étude ont révélé une corrélation statistiquement significative entre les résultats de la qualité et les autres dimensions (le leadership, la planification stratégique de la qualité, la gestion de la qualité). Ce résultat est cohérent avec les recherches précédentes effectuées par Pomey et al. (2010), qui ont indiqué que la variable dépendante (résultats de qualité) était positivement corrélée au leadership, à l'engagement et au soutien, le développement du personnel, l'utilisation des variables de données. En outre, ils ont ajouté que le leadership, l'engagement et le soutien étaient significativement associés à des résultats de qualité qui indiquent que la haute direction était fortement engagée à l'accréditation dans leurs hôpitaux (Seada. A. M., 2012), ce qui n'est pas le cas pour notre étude ou l'engagement de la direction figure parmi les points faibles du CQ.

5. CONCLUSION

Malgré les défis que connait le système de santé marocain, on note que la perception de la performance chez le personnel de soins reste relativement élevée (dépasse en grande partie les 60%). les démarches d'ACQ sont un bon outil pour améliorer la qualité des soins, le score élevé des variables « résultats de qualité» indique que le personnel ont perçu une amélioration de la qualité pendant et après la mise en œuvre des démarches qualités. Même si les liens ne sont pas encore suffisamment établis dans le cadre d'une recherche scientifique, les démarches qualités sont généralement reconnues comme outil essentiel pour aider les établissements à améliorer la qualité et la sécurité des patients. Les outils proposés dans les démarches qualités restent un levier essentiel pour la promotion des démarches qualité. L'approche actuelle en matière de mesure de la performance de la qualité est loin de constituer un système national efficace de mesure de la performance et de production de rapports pour les raisons suivantes : - les objectifs ne sont pas bien définis et ne sont pas accessibles. -

Les approches existantes produisent des mesures qui sont incohérentes, complexes et instables, imposant aux prestataires de soins l'incertitude et le fardeau des mesures contradictoires. - Les soins primaires font également face à certains défis importants, dont la transition épidémiologique aux maladies chroniques, la décentralisation du système de santé et l'érosion du financement de la santé.

References

1. Alastair McColl, H. S. (1998, January). General practitioner's perception of the route to evidence based medicine: a questionnaire survey. BMJ, pp. 361-365.
2. Amadou B. (2007). Renforcement des systèmes de santé dans les pays de la région africaine de l'OMS : Répondre au défi. Brazzaville: Bureau régional de l'OMS pour l'Afrique, Health Systems and Reproductive Health, Special Issue 14.
3. Belghiti A. (2008). La réforme hospitalière au Maroc. Revue Gestions hospitalières, N° 472, Paris (France). pp. pp.52-55.
4. Belghiti, A. (2013). L'assurance qualité en santé pour une vision intégrée. 38e conference de l'INAS.
5. Berwick. D. M. (2004). Lessons from developing nations on improving health care. 328 (7448). BMJ, pp. 1124–1129.
6. Bolsin S, Colson M. (2000). The use of the cusum technique in the assessment of trainee competence in new procedures. Int J Qual Health Care 2000; 12:433-8.
7. Braithwaite et al. (2006). Health sector accreditation research: a systematic review David Greenfield , Jeffrey Braithwaite 2008 International Journal for Quality in Health Care 2008; Volume 20, Number 3: pp. 172–183
8. Bueton SA, W. J. (2003). Accreditation of general practices: challenges and lessons. Qual saf Health Care, Apr; 12(2), pp. 129-135.
9. charron-latour, J. (2014). Facteurs clés d'une démarche d'amélioration continue durable dans les établissements de santé du Québec ». Université de Montréal.
10. Devkaran, S. (2014). International Healthcare Accreditation: an Analysis of Clinical Quality and Patient Experience in the UAE. FACHE, MScHCM, BSc (Physiotherapy), CPHQ. Edinburgh Business School, Heriot-Watt University.
11. Donabedian A. (1982). *Explorations in Quality Assessment and Monitoring : the citeria and standards of quality». Tome II, p.504.* Health Administration press.
12. El Jardali F. et al, R. H.-S. (2014). The impact of accreditation of primary healthcare centers: successes, challenges and policy implications as perceived by healthcare providers and directors in Lebanon.
13. Figueras. J. et al. (2008). Health systems, health and wealth: Assessing the case for investing in health systems. World Health Organization.
14. Frenk, C. J. (2000,). A framework for assessing the performance of health systems. Bulletin of the World Health Organization.
15. Geyndt, D. (1995). Managing the quality of health care in developing countries. Washington DC : World Bank.
16. Grawitz. M. (1996). Méthodes des sciences sociales, 10ème édition, Paris, Dalloz.
17. Greenfield David, J. B. (2008). Health Sector Accreditation Research: A systematic review. International Journal for Quality in Health Care, Volume 20, Number 3; pp. pp. 172–183.
18. Grimmer et al. (2014). An evidence-based framework to measure quality of allied health care. Health Research Policy and Systems.
19. IOM (2000). To err is human: building a safer health system. Kohn LT, Corrigan JM, Donaldson MS, editors. :. Washington, DC : National Academy Press.
20. IOM. (2005). Improving the Quality of Health Care for Mental and Substance-Use Conditions: Quality Chasm. National Academy Press, Washington D.C.
21. Kohn LT, C. J. (2000). To err is human: building a safer health system. A report of the Committee on Quality of Health Care in America, Institute of Medicine. Washington, DC: National Academy Press.
22. Kringos DS, B. W. Boerma W, Hutchinson A, van der Zee J, Groenewegen P (2010). The breadth of primary care: a systematic literature review of its core dimensions. , 10 (1): BMC HSR, pp. 65-78.
23. Lanteigne, G. (2008). Etudes de cas sur l'impact de l'intégration du programme d'agrément canada sur le changement et l'apprentissage organisationnel : la Health authority of anguilla et la ca' foncella ospetale di treviso. Université de Montréal.
24. Leggat, M. S. (2009). A guide to performance management for the Health Information. Health Information Management Journal. Vol 38 No 3.
25. Margaret E. et al, K. l. (2008). Assessing health system performance in developing countries. University de Michigan.
26. Ministère de santé Maroc. (2002). Conférence Qualité Maroc. Marrakech.
27. OCDE. (2011). Améliorer la performance des soins de santé : Comment mesurer leur qualité, Éditions OCDE.

28. OMS. (2000). Rapport mondial sur la santé dans le monde 2000 – pour un système de santé performant. Oms, Genève, suisse, 2000. Oms, Genève, suisse.
29. OMS. (2005). Discours inaugural du directeur régional OMS. AFRO News • Vol. 6, No. 1.
30. Ovretveit et Gustafson (2002) Evaluation of quality improvement programmes. Qual Saf Health Care. Sep 11(3): 270–275.
31. Ovretveit J. (2005). Leading improvement. *Journal of Health Organization and Management. Vol. 19.*
32. Paccioni, A. S. (2009, No 76). L'accréditation des services de santé de première ligne : l'amorce d'une nouvelle culture organisationnelle ?,. Revue Sciences de la société,, pp. 117-133.
33. Pineault R, L. J. (2008). L'accessibilité et la continuité des services de santé : une étude sur la première ligne au Québec. Rapport de recherche. Montréal (Qc).
34. Haggerty Jl, Pineault R, Beaulieu Md, Brunelle Y, Gauthier J, Goulet F, et al. Practice features associated with patient-reported accessibility, continuity, and coordination of primary health care. Ann Fam Med. 2008; 6:116-23.
35. Pomey et al, (2010), Does accreditation stimulate change. A study of the impact of the accreditation process on Canadian healthcare organizations Marie-Pascale Pomey et al. Implementation Science. Pomey et al. (2004), Pomey MP, Contandriopoulos AP, François P, Bertrand D. Accreditation as a tool for organizational change. Int J Health Care Qual Assur. 2004; 17:113–24.
36. Rolland K. (2011). Exploration des conceptions de la performance privilégiées par des infirmières et des membres de l'équipe d'encadrement impliqués dans l'offre de services infirmiers : Une étude qualitative exploratoire.
37. Sabrina W, e. a. (2010). Developing a Performance Measurement Framework and Indicators for Community Health Service Facilities in Urban China . *BMC Family Practice.*
38. Seada, A. M. (2012). Impact of Hospital Accreditation on Quality of Care as perceived by Nursing Staff in King Khaled Hospital in Najran at Kingdom of Saudi Arabia. J Am Sci, pp. 308-315. 8(7)
39. Shah, L.-A. (2012). Value-risk based performance evaluation of industrial systems. Arts et Métiers Paris Tech.
40. Sharon J. (2008). Mesure du rendement en soins primaire. Canadian Family Physician. vol. 54 no. 9.
41. Shaw, 2001, External assessment of health care Charles Shaw, BMJ. Apr 7; 322(7290): 851–854.
42. Shaw, 2003, Evaluating accreditation Charles D. Shaw International Society for Quality in Health Care and Oxford University Press 2003; 455-456
43. Silva, A. d. (2015). A FRAMEWORK FOR MEASURING RESPONSIVENESS GPE Available from: Amala de Silva, May 05, WHO Discussion Paper Series: No. 32.
44. Silva. B. (2011). Pour une approche globale de l'évaluation de l'utilisation des services de santé : concepts et mesures. Pratiques et Organisation des soins volume 42 n° 1.
45. Starfield et al. (2010). Comparison of primary care experiences among adults in general outpatient clinics and private general practice clinics in Hong Kong. BMC Public Health.
46. Starfield, B. (2009). Primary Care and Equity in Health: The Importance to Effectiveness and Equity of Responsiveness to Peoples' Needs. Humanity & Society, 33, pp. 56-73.
47. Timothy A Carey John Wakerman, J. S. (2013). Core" primary health care services. . BMC Health Serv Res. May.
48. Veillard. J. et al, S. G.-A. (2010). International Health System Comparisons : From Measurement Challenge to Management Tool », in L.M.E. Smith (dir. pub.), Performance Measurement for Health System Improvement : Experiences, Challenges and Prosperity.
49. Benson L, Boyd A, Walshe K. (2001). Learning from CHI: the impact of healthcare regulation
50. Wendy, N. (2009). The Value and Impact of Accreditation in Health Care: A Review of the Literature.
51. Wheeler ds, G. m. (2011). Wheeler Ds, Giaccone Mj, Hutchinson N, et al. A hospital-wide quality-improvement collaborative to reduce catheter-associated bloodstream infections. Pediatrics 2011; 128:995-1004.
52. Wood J, L. M. (2011). Charts for monitoring clinical practice quality using primary care prescribing data: a case study of an initiative to encourage generic prescribing of proton pump inhibitors. . J Clin Pharm Ther, pp. 680-6.
53. Zaneta Piligrimienė et al. (2008). Different perspective on Health care quality is the consensus possible. No 1. Engineering Economics.

Processus et supports harmonisés pour la gestion des compétences au sein d'un laboratoire multi-domaines et activités.

C. CECCONI, A. CHAUSSE

Université Paris-Est, Anses, Laboratoire de sécurité des aliments, F-94700 Maisons-Alfort, France94706 Maisons-Alfort cedex
Mission qualité

Résumé.
Les laboratoires de Sécurité des Aliments (LSAl) et de Santé Animale (LSAn) de l'Anses (Agence nationale de sécurité sanitaire) exercent principalement des missions de référence et de recherche dans le domaine de l'alimentation et de la santé animale en utilisant des techniques d'analyses diverses et variées (exemples : microbiologie et physico-chimie des aliments, immuno-sérologie, bactériologie, virologie et parasitologie en santé animale). Ces activités sont caractérisées par des exigences de compétences scientifiques et technologiques, une très grande réactivité, opérationnalité et transparence.
Dans ce contexte, la gestion des compétences des agents est donc essentielle et indispensable pour la réalisation des activités. Cet article décrit le processus et les supports d'enregistrement développés pour suivre, de façon harmonisée, la qualification et l'habilitation des agents au sein des deux laboratoires.

Mots clés : Compétences, Qualification, Habilitation, Risques, Points critiques Méthodes, Traçabilité

1 Introduction

Le LSAl et le LSAn sont répartis sur deux sites géographiques, l'un basé à Maisons-Alfort (neuf unités/missions scientifiques du LSAl et trois unités scientifiques du LSAn) et l'autre à Boulogne-sur-Mer (deux unités scientifiques du LSAl).

Ces deux laboratoires (désignés par le sigle LSA dans la suite de l'article) exercent principalement des missions de laboratoire de référence (national, européen et international) et de recherche dans les domaines de l'alimentation et de la santé animale.

La particularité des missions du LSA est double ; d'une part, par la diversité de la nature de ses activités, d'autre part, par la multiplicité des domaines scientifiques/techniques analytiques.

Les activités du LSA consistent à :

- Réaliser des analyses officielles en première intention et en confirmation,
- Développer/adapter/valider des méthodes d'analyses,
- Organiser des essais interlaboratoires d'aptitude (EILA),
- Animer/former des réseaux de laboratoires,
- Surveiller et analyser les risques sanitaires,
- Produire des connaissances,
- Participer à l'expertise scientifique et technique.

La réalisation de ces activités s'exerce dans le champ de compétence scientifique suivant :

- Le LSAL intervient sur des dangers dus à la présence de contaminants microbiologiques (bactéries, parasites et virus) ou chimiques (toxines, pesticides, métaux) dans la chaîne alimentaire.
- Le LSAn intervient sur des maladies animales (exemples : Brucellose, Tularémie, Tuberculose, West-Nile, Fièvre catarrhale ovine, fièvre aphteuse, trichine, toxoplasmose, etc.) constituant des risques sanitaires épizootiques pluri espèces ou zoonotiques majeurs. Ainsi le laboratoire travaille sur des parasites, des virus et des zoonoses faisant intervenir diverses techniques analytiques telles que la biologie moléculaire, la bactériologie, l'immuno-sérologie, etc.

Les orientations stratégiques de l'Agence régissant les missions exercées au LSA sont définies dans un contrat quadriennal d'objectifs et de performances (COP). Ce COP, validé auprès des différentes tutelles de l'Agence, fixe les enjeux et objectifs à atteindre pour assurer la qualité de ses activités dont :

- **l'excellence scientifique**, par la robustesse de ses processus et la **compétence de son personnel**,
- **la réactivité et l'efficience** de son action et de ses travaux, en respectant les engagements contractuels et en s'adaptant à l'urgence en situation de crise,
- **la confiance de toutes les parties prenantes**, en respectant les exigences d'indépendance, de transparence et d'ouverture,
- **la capacité à anticiper les besoins**, notamment au travers de ses activités de veille, de vigilance, de recherche et d'études, en vue d'identifier les risques émergents.

La réalisation de ces activités est donc caractérisée par des exigences de compétences scientifiques et technologiques, une très grande réactivité et opérationnalité et de transparence. Dans ce contexte, il est donc essentiel d'assurer la fiabilité des résultats produits et ainsi inspirer confiance auprès de nos prescripteurs et nombreux collaborateurs.

La gestion des compétences est donc essentielle, indispensable et constitue un des éléments majeur permettant de garantir la fiabilité des résultats produits.

Ainsi, un processus commun et des supports d'enregistrement harmonisés ont été mis en place pour la qualification et l'habilitation des agents au sein du LSA.

Dans le présent article, le terme "processus d'habilitation" désigne l'ensemble de la démarche pour habiliter un agent : définition des besoins en compétences, parcours de formation, évaluation de la qualification, décision d'habilitation.

2 Contexte

Le LSA organise son fonctionnement en s'appuyant sur un système commun de management de la qualité afin d'assurer la réalisation de ses différentes activités dans une organisation d'ensemble cohérente et efficace (cf. Figure 1). Pour cela, il s'appuie sur plusieurs référentiels permettant de couvrir les missions réalisées :

- La norme NF EN ISO/CEI 17025 [1] pour la réalisation des prestations analytiques et pour la validation des méthodes d'analyses.
- la norme NF EN ISO/CEI 17043 [2] pour l'organisation des essais inter-laboratoires d'aptitude.
- les lignes directrices "recherche" de l'agence ANSES/PG/0073 et les prescriptions de la norme NF X50-553 [3] pour la réalisation de ses projets de recherche.

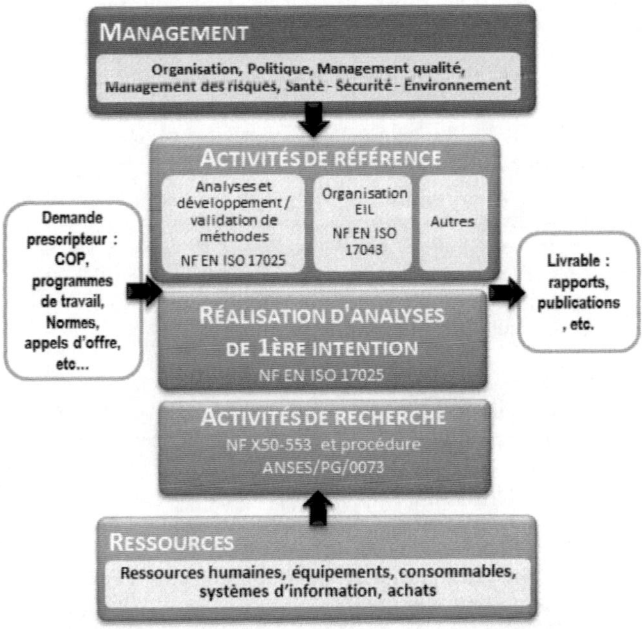

Figure 1 : Représentation synthétique du système de management de la qualité du LSA

L'objectif de ce système commun est d'harmoniser au maximum les pratiques afin de pouvoir répondre de façon uniforme aux exigences des référentiels appliqués, de réduire le nombre de documents gérés et d'avoir une cohérence dans l'organisation du LSA.

Etant donné la multiplicité des missions, diverses pratiques et organisations pour le processus d'habilitation des agents ont été mis en place au sein des unités techniques au fil du temps. Cette diversité dans les dispositions a engendré un système complexe dans sa gestion et redondant dans sa documentation. L'élément déclencheur pour la mise en place d'un processus harmonisé a été l'augmentation du nombre d'écarts relevés en évaluation externe en termes de dispositions et de preuves attestant la compétence d'un agent.

Ainsi, il a été décidé en action corrective de mettre en place des dispositions et outils communs avec comme objectif principal la prise en compte de la diversité des missions et des pratiques. Ce système est appliqué, aujourd'hui, quel que soit la nature de l'activité, la thématique étudiée ou l'organisation définie au sein de l'unité.

Note : Cet article traite uniquement du processus d'habilitation. Il est néanmoins nécessaire que ce dernier s'inscrive dans une démarche plus globale de gestion des compétences incluant par exemple la définition des métiers/fonctions et la gestion de fiches de postes. Ainsi, le processus d'habilitation du LSA s'inscrit dans la démarche globale de gestion des compétences de l'Agence, représentée par la figure 2 :

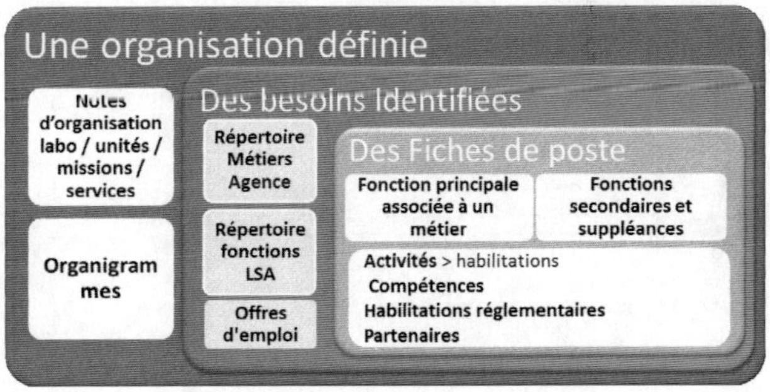

Figure 2 : organisation globale de gestion des compétences au LSA

3 Description du processus

3-1 Définitions

La première étape a été de définir un langage commun pour l'ensemble du LSA. En effet, les notions de compétence, qualification, habilitation, formation n'étaient pas toujours utilisées à bon escient. Une terminologie a donc été définie à partir de l'établissement des grandes étapes du processus d'habilitation (cf. Figure 3).

Si le terme "Compétence" est défini dans la norme NF EN ISO 9000 [4], les notions de "qualification" et "habilitation" ne sont pas définies dans les normes françaises. Ainsi, des définitions internes sont proposées :

- Compétence (NF EN ISO 9000 [4]) : aptitude à mettre en pratique des connaissances et savoir-faire pour obtenir les résultats escomptés.
- Qualification : ensemble des compétences acquises par un personnel : connaissances (formation initiale et continue), expérience antérieure et aptitude à réaliser la ou les actions définies.
- Habilitation : autorisation formelle d'un personnel à réaliser une ou plusieurs actions après vérification de sa qualification.

3-2 Le processus d'habilitation

A partir des définitions établies, l'organisation et la cohérence des étapes du processus d'habilitation ont pu être affinées (cf. Figure 3) :

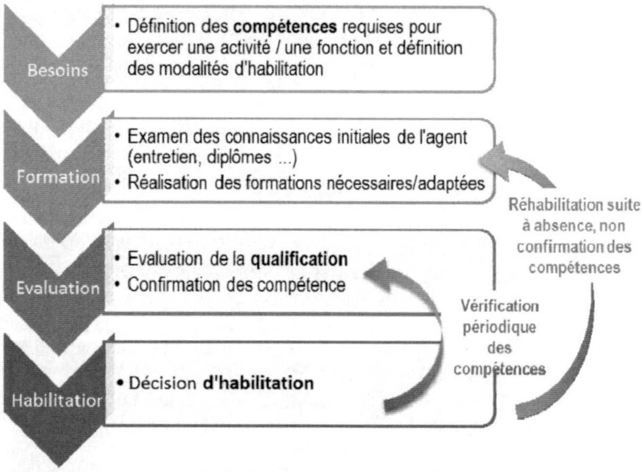

Figure 3 : processus d'habilitation au LSA

Une attention particulière a été portée sur la distinction entre les étapes de réalisation (formation, évaluation de la qualification) et l'étape de décision (habilitation) car des amalgames entre ces dernières ont souvent été constatés sur le terrain.
Cette différenciation est d'autant plus importante qu'elle permet de distinguer les acteurs responsables de chaque étape. En effet, il arrive que ces responsabilités soient différentes d'une étape à une autre (cf. 3-4).

3-3 Le domaine d'application

Le processus établi s'applique à tout type d'agent (personnel permanent ou temporaire, stagiaire, doctorant) et à toutes les activités du laboratoire (recherche, réalisation d'analyses, organisation d'EILA, etc.) y compris les activités supports (qualité, métrologie, etc.).

Par conséquent, deux types d'habilitation ont été définies afin de distinguer d'une part, la réalisation d'activités et d'autre part, l'exercice d'une fonction pour laquelle la réalisation des tâches associées nécessite une habilitation. Voici les définitions et exemples donnés pour ces deux types d'habilitation :

L'habilitation à une « activité » : elle concerne des activités de type technico-administratives, techniques, qualité, métrologie pour lesquelles une autorisation préalable d'exercer l'activité est requise.
Exemples d'activités : préparation des milieux de culture et réactifs, autoclavage de stérilisation ou de décontamination, travail en zone de sécurité (ex : laboratoire de niveau de sécurité biologique 3 ou biologie moléculaire), réalisation d'analyses (ex : réception/stockage/préparation des échantillons, analyse, calcul et saisie des résultats...), validation et signature des rapports d'analyses, émission d'avis et interprétation, vérifications métrologiques, réalisation d'audit interne.

Dans ce cas, la formation à délivrer et les critères de qualification pour être habilité à une activité sont définis dans un document intitulé "programme d'habilitation" et dont la trame d'enregistrement est commune (cf. 4-1).

L'habilitation à une « fonction » : elle concerne une nomination à une fonction pour laquelle la réalisation des tâches associées nécessite une habilitation.
Exemples de fonctions : correspondant qualité, correspondant métrologie, fonctions liées à l'organisation d'un EILA (coordonnateur, responsable du traitement des données, etc.), chef de projet de « validation de méthode ».

Dans ce cas, la formation délivrée et les critères de qualification pour être habilité à une fonction sont définis dans un document intitulé "formulaire d'habilitation à une fonction" et dont la trame est également commune (cf. 4-2).

Note : toutes les fonctions ne sont pas soumises à habilitation. Par exemple, les fonctions d'encadrement sont exercées après nomination par la direction et ne donnent pas lieu à habilitation (ex : chef d'unité, responsables d'équipe, chef de service, responsable technique, responsable qualité, etc.). Les compétences requises sont définies et vérifiées lors du processus de recrutement ou de nomination d'un agent. Des entretiens annuels d'évaluation permettent de vérifier le bon exercice des fonctions conformément aux fiches de poste.

La pertinence de délivrer une habilitation pour une activité ou l'exercice d'une fonction est définie sur la base de plusieurs facteurs de risque comme la criticité sur la qualité des résultats/de l'activité, la difficulté de mise en œuvre de l'action, la sécurité des agents, les impacts sur la société et l'image de l'agence (émission des livrables), etc. Elle est aussi largement guidée par les référentiels appliqués qui imposent l'habilitation de certaines tâches considérées comme critiques pour la qualité des résultats.

3-4 Les acteurs

Comme précisé dans le paragraphe 3-2, les différentes phases du processus d'habilitation sont disjointes afin d'associer pour chacune des responsables potentiellement différents. Pour simplifier l'intervention de ces acteurs, deux responsabilités ont été définies :

Le responsable d'habilitation : il organise l'habilitation initiale et le maintien des compétences des personnels en réalisant les actions suivantes : il participe à la définition des critères de qualification, désigne les formateurs, veille au respect des périodicités pour le maintien des compétences et prend la décision finale d'habilitation. Il s'assure ainsi que la personne à habiliter possède les compétences requises pour exercer l'activité ou la fonction selon les critères définis dans les programmes d'habilitation ou formulaires d'habilitation à une fonction.

Le formateur : il forme les personnels à habiliter en fonction des connaissances initiales de chacun. A l'issue de la formation, il émet un avis au responsable d'habilitation sur la compétence du personnel à partir des résultats obtenus lors de l'évaluation de la qualification.

4 Les supports d'enregistrement

Les supports d'enregistrement ont un rôle essentiel dans l'harmonisation du processus. En effet, ce sont eux qui permettent de donner un cadre commun et ainsi d'harmoniser les pratiques.

4-1 Habilitation à une activité - programme d'habilitation

Il a été mis en place un formulaire intitulé "Programme d'habilitation" permettant de définir les points suivants :

- le périmètre : technique d'analyses, méthode d'analyse, opération(s) métrologique(s), signature des résultats, etc.
- les objectifs (acquis attendus),
- la documentation nécessaire à la réalisation de l'activité,
- les étapes nécessitant une attention particulière (points critiques de l'activité - cf. exemple en Figure 4),
- la formation à délivrer en fonction des points critiques/sensibles listés,
- les modalités d'évaluation de la qualification (ex : questionnaire, analyse en double, analyse d'un matériau de référence, etc.) et les critères d'acceptation associés (souvent exprimés de façon quantifiée - cf. exemple en Figure 4)
- les modalités de maintien des compétences dans le temps : périodicité, fréquence nécessaire de pratique de l'activité, modalités d'évaluation (ex : participation à un EILA) et critères d'acceptation,
- les modalités de réhabilitation en cas d'absence prolongé ou de non-confirmation du maintien des compétences.

Ces programmes peuvent être découpés en actions lorsque l'habilitation ne peut pas être prononcée systématiquement pour la totalité d'une activité (ex : préparation des milieux de culture, préparation des échantillons, réalisation des analyses, lecture des résultats, etc.). Ainsi chaque action comportent, de façon spécifique, des modalités de formation, des épreuves pour l'évaluation de la qualification, des critères d'acceptation et des modalités de maintien des compétences (cf. Figure 4). Les actions pour lesquelles une personne est habilitée sont ensuite précisées sur une matrice des compétences (cf. 4-3).

Etapes nécessitant une attention particulière

- Préparation des échantillons : analyser la masse adéquate de muscle (sans gras ni tendon) selon l'espèce animale,
- Broyage des échantillons,
- Préparation du liquide de digestion et réalisation de la digestion artificielle dans les conditions adéquates (température et agitation),
- Filtration et décantation du liquide de digestion : utilisation d'un tamis et d'une ampoule à décanter conformes,
- Lecture du liquide de digestion : lire correctement le bassin de lecture (intégralement et à une mise au point correcte) et savoir détecter et identifier les larves de *Trichinella*.

N° Action	Description des actions	Formation / démonstration envisagée	Critères d'acceptation pour l'habilitation
01	Détection de larves de *Trichinella* par digestion artificielle (digestion + lecture)	Démonstration par le formateur et observation de larves. Mise en œuvre de la méthode sous tutorat	100% de résultats satisfaisants (cf. § épreuves d'habilitation initiale) + Attestation de stage externe
02	Détection des larves de *Trichinella* dans les bassins de lecture (lecture seule)	Observation de larves au microscope avec le formateur, comptages puis lecture autonome de bassins de lecture	100% de résultats satisfaisants (cf. § « épreuve d'habilitation initiale »)

Epreuves d'habilitation initiale

Action 1 (*Digestion artificielle + lecture*)
Epreuve : analyse autonome de 4 échantillons de référence
Critères : 1 échantillon négatif : pas de faux positif, 2 échantillons faiblement contaminés contenant 3 à 5 larves : pas de faux négatif (détecter au moins une larve), 1 échantillon fortement contaminé contenant 9 à 15 larves : détecter au moins 50% des larves (arrondi à l'entier inférieur)
Action 2 (*Lecture*)
Epreuve : lecture autonome de 4 bassins de lecture
Critères : 1 échantillon négatif : pas de faux positif, 2 échantillons positifs : détecter le nombre initial de larves dans le bassin +/-1 larve.

Figure 4 : Extrait du programme d'habilitation "Détection par digestion artificielle et identification de larves de *Trichinella sp.*" - Points sensibles, actions et épreuves d'habilitation initiale.

Les éléments de preuve (ex : échantillons analysés, résultats d'analyses, résultats de QCM, entretien, etc.) permettant de prouver que les compétences requises sont acquises (conformément aux critères établis dans le programme d'habilitation) sont conservés ou référencés dans le dossier d'habilitation de l'agent.

Une synthèse des résultats obtenus et la décision d'habilitation sont enregistrées sur un formulaire dont la trame est commune au LSA ou sur un formulaire spécifique à l'unité technique dès lors que les rubriques de la trame commune sont présentes.

4-2 Habilitation à une fonction

L'approche utilisée pour l'habilitation à une fonction est légèrement différente de l'habilitation à une activité puisqu'elle ne repose généralement pas sur des critères de qualification techniques souvent quantifiables (cf. §4-1). Les fonctions soumises à habilitation n'étant pas associées à des tâches techniques, l'approche est plutôt basée sur une appréciation des connaissances et du niveau d'expérience requis. Ainsi les habilitations à une fonction sont plutôt gérées au cas par cas. Pour certaines fonctions standards, la trame de formulaire est tout de même pré-remplie (cf. Figure 5).

Le formulaire d'habilitation à une fonction permet ainsi de définir :

- le périmètre de la fonction à exercer (projet, activité, fonction)
- les compétences et connaissances nécessaires à la réalisation de la fonction (cf. exemple en Figure 5)
- la formation reçue
- les moyens de vérification des connaissances mis en œuvre (cf. exemple en Figure 5)
- la date d'habilitation
- la validation de l'habilitation par le responsable
- la prise de connaissance par l'agent habilité

La rubrique "compétences" est découpée en deux parties : les compétences générales liées à la fonction et les compétences spécifiques liées au domaine scientifique (cf. Figure 5).

Compétence ou connaissances nécessaires	Moyen de vérification des connaissances et compétences*
Compétences générales -Conduite de projet : méthodologie et rigueur -Animation/pilotage de l'équipe projet -Capacité rédactionnelle scientifique et technique en français et/ou anglais -Connaissance du processus de développement et validation de méthode (selon la procédure interne) - Connaissance du système de management de la qualité (SMQ)	Entretien avec le chef d'unité réalisé. Niveau de compétence évalué sur la base des éléments suivants : -5 ans d'expérience dans la conduite de projets -Bon niveau rédactionnel : rédaction régulière de publications scientifiques, de comptes rendus -Bonne connaissance de la procédure validation de méthodes et du SMQ
Compétences spécifiques au domaine - Connaissance de la réglementation relative au domaine concerné - Connaissances générales et expérience scientifique en rapport avec le domaine (techniques / principes d'analyses, domaine d'application) concerné - Connaissances des statistiques dans le domaine concerné (ex : V.03-110, NF EN ISO 16140)	Entretien avec le chef d'unité réalisé. Niveau de compétence évalué sur la base des éléments suivants : - 3 ans d'expérience dans le domaine - Participation à des formations externes en statistique - Manipulation régulière de calculs statistiques en lien avec le domaine

Figure 5 : Exemple de critères de qualification pour la fonction "Chef de projet de validation de méthodes"

Contrairement au programme d'habilitation qui fixe uniquement les dispositions pour l'habilitation, le formulaire d'habilitation à une fonction à l'avantage de tracer sur un même document les dispositions, les éléments de preuve et la décision d'habilitation.

L'habilitation fonction est valide pour la durée d'exercice de la fonction pour un périmètre défini (projet, activité, fonction). Des entretiens annuels d'évaluation permettent de vérifier le bon exercice des fonctions conformément aux fiches de poste.

4-3 Suivi des compétences

Le LSA ne disposant pas d'outil commercial, une matrice des compétences, dont la trame est commune au LSA, a été mise en place afin de récapituler les compétences disponibles au sein de chaque unité technique (cf. Figure 6). Celle-ci est au format excel, ce qui permet, à l'aide de filtres, de visualiser simplement et rapidement les personnes habilitées à un programme ou une fonction, ainsi que les dates effectives d'habilitation ou de maintien.

Programmes et actions	LSA-INS-0112 - Act.1	LSA-INS-0113 - Act.1
Intitulé (mots clés)	P-MS - multi contaminar	Spéciation Arsenic
Responsable(s) d'habilitation	XXXXX	XXXXX
Périodicité de reconduction	1 an +/- 2 mois	1 an +/- 2 mois
M. X	23/05/17- Reconduction	
Mme Y	17/05/17- Reconduction	23/05/17- Reconduction
Mme W	06/10/17-Initial	17/05/17-Annulé

Figure 6 : Exemple d'une matrice de compétence

Ces matrices sont stockées, de façon partagée, sur le réseau informatique. Ainsi en cas de recherche de compétences, sur une technique d'analyses particulière par exemple, des possibilités de mutualisation peuvent être mises en évidence aisément. Cette fonctionnalité peut notamment être utilisée dans le cas d'un surcroît d'activité (par exemple en cas de crise sanitaire avec surplus d'échantillons à analyser).

5 Retour d'expérience

Quelques années ont été nécessaires pour stabiliser cette démarche et pour répondre complètement aux attentes initiales. En effet, le contenu des programmes d'habilitation n'était pas toujours conforme aux attentes et les premiers supports d'enregistrement établis étaient complexes et peu intuitifs à renseigner. Cette phase d'amélioration continue a permis d'aboutir à un système qui, d'une part satisfait aux référentiels et d'autre part satisfait les utilisateurs.

Les diverses évaluations externes ont permis de faire évoluer ce système mais aussi de prouver son efficacité. A ce jour, très peu d'écarts sont relevés en évaluation externe et la gestion des compétences constitue désormais un point fort du laboratoire.

6 Perspectives

Deux démarches qui peuvent être mises en corrélation avec la gestion des compétences ont récemment émergé au sein de l'agence :

Une démarche pour la gestion des ressources humaines qui consistent à avoir une gestion unique pour l'établissement des fiches de poste basé sur un référentiel "métier" commun à l'agence (ex : directeur de laboratoire, chef d'unité, technicien de laboratoire, responsable qualité, etc.). Chaque métier faisant référence à une liste d'activités définies également dans un répertoire commun (ex : manager une unité, construire et animer un projet scientifique, réaliser un protocole d'analyse, réaliser des vérifications métrologiques, valider et signer les rapports d'analyses, etc.).

A terme, il sera intéressant de faire le lien entre les activités affectées à l'agent et les habilitations correspondantes, par exemple via la matrice des compétences.

Une démarche risque dans laquelle la gestion des compétences est souvent citée comme moyen de maîtrise des risques identifiées.

La démarche d'habilitation devra donc, à terme, être entreprise au regard des risques identifiées dans le cadre de l'exercice des missions de l'agence. Ceci permettra également de répondre à la nouvelle version de la norme NF EN ISO/CEI 17025:2017 [5] dont la notion de risques et opportunités est largement introduite.

Références

1. Norme NF EN ISO/CEI 17025 - Exigences générales concernant la compétence des laboratoires d'étalonnages et d'essais - septembre 2005
2. Norme NF EN ISO/CEI 17043 - Évaluation de la conformité - Exigences générales concernant les essais d'aptitude - avril 2010
3. Norme NF X50-553 - Management des activités de recherche - juillet 2014
4. Norme NF EN ISO 9000 - Systèmes de management de la qualité - Principes essentiels et vocabulaire - octobre 2015
5. Norme NF EN ISO/CEI 17025 - Exigences générales concernant la compétence des laboratoires d'étalonnages et d'essais - novembre 2017

L'intégration de l'Internet des Objets dans le développement d'un processus de mesure dédié à la surveillance des températures lors du transport intersites des échantillons biologiques au sein des Laboratoires de Biologie Clinique du CHU de Charleroi (Belgique)

R. Lequeu[1], D. Govaerts[1], J.P. Binon[2], and L. El Hiki[3]

[1]Laboratoire de Biologie Clinique du CHU de Charleroi, Hôpital Civil Marie Curie. 140, Chaussée de Bruxelles, 6042 Lodelinsart, Belgique.
[2]Technologies de l'Information et des Communications, Hôpital André Vésale. 706, Route de Gozée, 6110 Montigny-le-Tilleul, Belgique.
[3]UMONS-Faculté Polytechnique, Institut des Sciences et du Management des Risques. 56, Rue de l'Epargne, 7000 Mons, Belgique.

Abstract. Force est de reconnaitre que l'un des déterminants de la Qualité des résultats des Laboratoires de Biologie Clinique (LBC) est le délai s'écoulant entre la prescription du clinicien et la transmission des résultats. La maîtrise de ce délai dépend directement de l'intégrité des prélèvements mais aussi du délai et des conditions de transport. Notre ambition est de relater, dans ce papier, un projet qui porte sur l'automatisation d'un processus de mesure intégrant l'internet des objets pour le suivi en temps réel des températures et la géolocalisation des prélèvements. Ce projet s'est développé au sein du LBC au CHU de Charleroi (Belgique) en collaboration avec la Direction des systèmes d'information. Il prend en considération les contraintes liées à la réalité multisitique des hôpitaux et à la répartition géographique des points de collecte des prélévements dans une zone urbaine.

Keywords: ISO 15189 ; Processus de mesure ; Internet des Objets ; Surveillance des températures

1 Introduction

D'après le CLSI (CLSI, 2007) [1], 70% des décisions médicales se basent sur les résultats d'analyses du Laboratoire de Biologie Clinique (LBC). Cette interdépendance soulève l'importance de la Qualité et de la fiabilité des résultats fournis par le LBC. Force est de reconnaitre que l'un des déterminants de cette Qualité est le délai s'écoulant entre la prescription du clinicien et la transmission du bilan de ces résultats. La maîtrise de ce délai dépend directement de l'intégrité des prélèvements/échantillons mais aussi du délai et des conditions de transport. Dans cette perspective, l'ensemble des étapes du processus pré-analytique, en aval de l'enregistrement des demandes d'examens qui se réalise lors de la réception des échantillons au LBC, doivent être sous contrôle. Ce constat se justifie par les exigences de la norme d'Accréditation ISO15189 concernant le délai de transport de l'échantillon (en fonction de la nature des examens) et le respect d'un intervalle de température spécifique : un dépassement significatif de la température exigée lors du transport pourrait conduire à la non réalisation de l'examen demandé.

2 Contexte

Quotidiennement, le LBC organise des tournées de ramassage de prélèvements dans les sites hospitaliers, auprès des médecins généralistes et dans plusieurs centres de prélèvements ambulatoires. Les échantillons doivent être maintenus dans des conditions optimales de conservation au niveau de la phase pré-analytique. Des critères sont définis par le LBC concernant l'acceptation ou le rejet des échantillons. Si des échantillons altérés sont acceptés, le compte rendu final doit indiquer la nature du dysfonctionnement et, le cas échéant, les réserves qui en résultent pour l'interprétation des résultats. Il est donc impératif de garantir l'intégrité de l'échantillon entre le moment où celui-ci est prélevé chez le patient et le moment où l'examen sera réalisé.

L'objectif poursuivi in fine est d'assurer une prise en charge fiable et optimale des examens de manière à rendre des résultats conformes reflétant l'état symptomatique du patient et permettant une prise en charge optimale diagnostqiue et thérapeutique par le médecin.

Le LBC du CHU de Charleroi s'est inscrit depuis de nombreuses années dans un processus Qualité et dans un processus d'amélioration continue. Le LBC est certifié ISO 9001 et est accrédité ISO 15189 pour l'ensemble des analyses des secteurs de biochimie et de microbiologie. Toutes les étapes du processus pré-analytique doivent garantir la traçabilité des conditions des prélèvements, de leurs transports et de leurs conservations. Les modalités de transport doivent permettre d'assurer selon la norme ISO 15189 que les échantillons ont été transportés au LBC en respectant un délai optimal en fonction du prélèvement à une température appropriée de manière à ne pas détériorer le prélèvement.

3 Problématique

Le transport des échantillons au sein des LBC du CHU de Charleroi s'effectue par l'organisation de cinq tournées journalières de ramassage auprès de 70 points de collecte. Les tournées peuvent avoir différents circuits en fonction des plages horaires et de la demande des médecins généralistes : (1) Les chauffeurs du LBC réalisent le ramassage des prélèvements auprès des médecins généralistes de la région de Charleroi. (2) Les LBC du CHU de Charleroi possèdent plusieurs centres de prélèvements situés dans l'hinterland géographique de la région de Charleroi. Les prélèvements réalisés dans ces centres sont acheminés vers le LBC principal (CORELAB) situé à l'Hôpital Civil Marie Curie. (3) Le Laboratoire de l'Hôpital André Vésale (Laboratoire d'urgence) réalise uniquement les examens urgents de son entité. Les examens non-urgents sont acheminés vers le Laboratoire central à l'Hôpital Civil Marie Curie.

Auparavant, le dispositif qui était mis en place permettait uniquement, via un tag de température (thermomètre électronique), l'enregistrement des températures dans des boîtes de transport thermiques. Le chauffeur assurant le transport ne vérifiait la température qu'à l'arrivée au LBC. Tout dépassement de température était signalé au personnel du LBC et selon son étendue, l'analyse pouvait être rendue non-conforme. Si un écart était significatif, cela pouvait engendrer un prélèvement non-conforme qui était répondu soit sous-réserve ou bien celui-ci n'était pas réalisé. Le délai était difficilement mesurable dans la pratique car le logiciel utilisé ne prévoyait pas une analyse des données qui étaient enregistrées et transmises par le tag.

La complexité de cette organisation logistique des flux soulève deux problématiques : (1) Le suivi des températures des prélèvements dans les phases de collecte (sur des sites géographiquement distribués), de transport et de la livraison au LBC . (2) L'estimation du délai de transport. Afin d'implémenter une solution intégrée à ce problème, la Direction du Laboratoire s'est renseignée auprès du Service Informatique de l'Institution afin d'analyser la situation et d'étudier la faisabilité de mise en œuvre d'une solution proactive intégrant conjointement la surveillance des températures lors du transport des échantillons et la géolocalisation des prélèvements.

Dans cette perspective, l'objectif de ce projet, réalisé au sein du LBC, vise la mise en place d'un processus de mesure combinant le suivi en temps réel des températures et la géolocalisation des prélèvements. Ce processus, automatisé dans une application informatique, se subdivise en trois phases : le captage, l'enregistrement et l'affichage.

Ce système doit être doté de quatre caractéristiques principales : (1) Permettre de suivre en temps réel la température des frigos box, de déterminer les alertes de température et de transmettre aux chauffeurs tout dépassement avant l'arrivée au LBC pour le dépôt des prélèvements. (2) Prévenir les acteurs du terrain avant le franchissement du seuil acceptable. (3) Permettre au responsable des centres de prélèvements extérieurs de géolocaliser le chauffeur concerné sur une carte afin de l'orienter vers le centre de prélèvements le plus proche. (4) Permettre le calcul des délais des différentes tournées.

4 Vers un processus de mesure intelligent

Le développement de notre processus de mesure projeté intègre l'internet des objets (IdO) dont l'utilisation est en plein essor [2] notamment dans le secteur de la Santé [3], [4]. Il se traduit à l'heure actuelle par l'accroissement du nombre d'objets connectés, c'est-à-dire d'appareils possédant une identité propre et des capacités de calculs et de communication de plus en plus sophistiquées : téléphones, montres, appareils ménagers, etc. Ces objets embarquent un nombre grandissant de capteurs et d'actionneurs leur permettant de mesurer l'environnement et d'agir sur celui-ci, faisant ainsi le lien entre le monde physique et le monde virtuel [5].

En fait, le paradigme de l'IdO vise à introduire une interconnexion intelligente des objets dans le monde physique à l'aide de dispositifs de détection d'information, tels que les puces RFID (Radio Frequency Identification) et les capteurs communicants connectés en utilisant des protocoles d'Internet et des systèmes d'information [6]. L'IdO se base sur un large pannel de technologies liées à l'identification et à la traçabilité (RFID), le web sémantique, les nanotechnologies, la mobilité, l'ébiquité et le crowdfunding [7].

Afin d'atteindre notre objectif, nous avons adopté le diagramme de déploiement proposé par Sehgal et al. [8]. Ce diagramme propose un cadre logique d'identification des objets ainsi que les interfaces virtuelles avec lesquelles ils doivent communiquer. Et ce, des capteurs jusqu'à l'utilisateur.

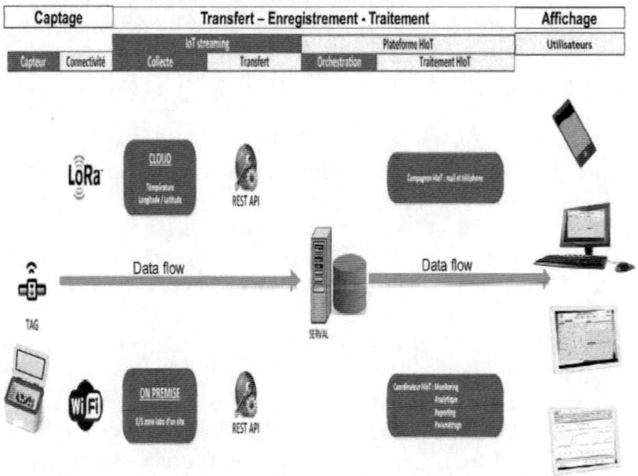

Fig. 1. Architecture du système

En fait, le système conçu s'articule sur les quatre étapes du processus de mesure envisagé dans ce projet (Fig.1) : Captage, Transfert, Enregistrement/Traitement et Affichage graphique des données. Par ce processus de mesure, la surveillance des températures, lors du transport intersites de prélèvements sanguins et microbiologiques, sont assurés en temps réel grâce à l'IdO.

Sur le plan de dimensionnement du système, les technologies IdO intégrées optimisent l'interconnexion de ces étapes par les flux de données qui vont du captage jusqu'à l'affichage auprès de l'utilisateur. Au niveau du captage, nous avons utilisé les tags, les réseaux public LORA (Long Range low power wireless plateform) et WIFI (Wireless Fidelity) privé pour la connectivité, l'IoT Streaming (Internet of Things), la collecte et le transfert des données vers le Cloud de l'hôpital. Enfin, la plate-forme HIoT (Healthcare Internet of Things) est utilisée pour l'orchestration, le traitement et l'affichage pour le suivi des températures et la géolocalisation des prélévements.

Sur le plan physique, des capteurs placés dans les frigos box permettent de remonter à fréquences régulières la température relevée à l'intérieur de ceux-ci ainsi que leurs géolocalisations. Pour cela, ils utilisent à la fois les réseaux LORA et WIFI.

LORA est un réseau orienté IdO qui couvre quasiment toute la Belgique et qui transmet de manière parfaitement sécurisée de petites quantités d'informations entre des objets et des systèmes avec une consommation électrique ultra faible, ce qui assure une durée de vie plus longue des batteries. Les informations transitent brièvement par le Cloud privé de l'opérateur du réseau LORA avant d'être redirigées vers notre Cloud interne (On Premise) afin d'être traitées par notre application. A chaque fois qu'une température interne est transmise, nous interrogeons en parallèle une application dans le Cloud qui nous renvoie la température extérieure correspondant à l'endroit où la mesure a été prise.

Notre réseau WIFI interne permet la détection en temps réel de l'entrée ou de la sortie d'un frigo box dans un site de notre institution hospitalière.

Le système est doté de deux modules d'alerte et d'alarme : le premier pour le suivi des températures et le deuxième pour le délai de transoprt des prélévements:

1- Concernant les températures, deux seuils sont définis au niveau de l'application : un pour l'alerte et l'autre pour l'alarme. Les valeurs seuils déterminées pour l'alerte sont [14°C, 23°C] et pour l'alarme [15°C, 24°C]. Une fois que la température dans le frigo box atteint les seuils d'alerte avant le dépassement des seuils d'alarme fixés, le système engendre et envoie une alarme au chauffeur ou à tout autre membre du personnel (secrétariat, reponsable du LBC). Cette alerte est envoyée via un message vocal sur le téléphone mobile du chauffeur qui doit confirmer la réception. Sinon le message est retransmis jusqu'à notification de celui-ci. Lorsqu'un frigo box en alerte ou en alarme température pénètre dans un site, le secrétariat concerné reçoit le même message vocal sur son téléphone fixe ou mobile. Il est à signaler que les alertes et les alarmes peuvent être notifiées aussi par mailing.

2- Concernant le délai de transport, une durée maximale de deux heures est fixée pour un circuit complet qui transite par plusieurs sites. Si un circuit n'est pas encore terminé après 1h45, une alerte via message vocal sur un téléphone mobile est également envoyée au chauffeur.

5 Résultats

Dans la solution proposée, l'application « Transport intersites de prélèvements sanguins et microbiologiques " offre aux utilisateurs un accès ergonomique et un accès rapide aux informations recherchées en terme de traçabilité.

Au niveau de l'affichage par les objets (téléphone mobile, écran de PC, tablette...), les utilisateurs (secrétariat et responsable du LBC) peuvent activer le début et la fin d'un circuit, réaliser le suivi de la température en combinant plusieurs circuits et notifier tout évènement lié à la tournée.

L'écran d'accueil permet d'accéder au menu du "Monitoring", "Analytique", "Reporting" et "Paramétrage" tout en géolocalisant la position du capteur et donc du frigo box. Cet affichage permet une visualisation "Global" (Fig.2) qui reprend tous les capteurs, ce qui permet d'afficher la température de l'enceinte thermique, la température extérieure ainsi que les derniers événements anormaux :

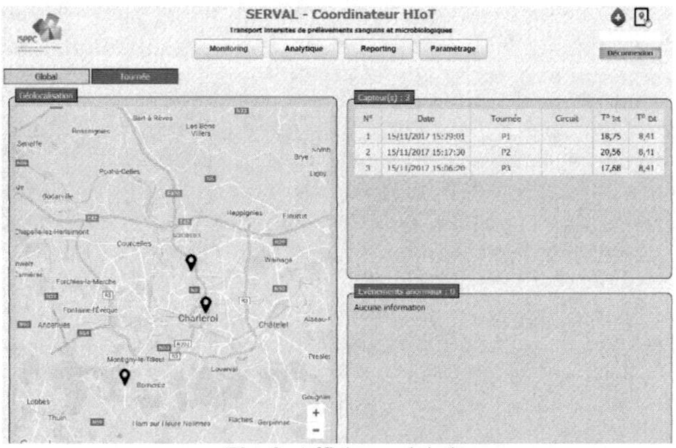

Fig. 2. Affichage global

Concernant l'affichage en "tournée" (Fig.3) : la tournée est toujours liée à une même enceinte thermique de transport et à son capteur. Sur une journée, plusieurs circuits aller/retour sont réalisés. L'affichage de couleur permet de signaler une alerte (orange) et une alarme (rouge).

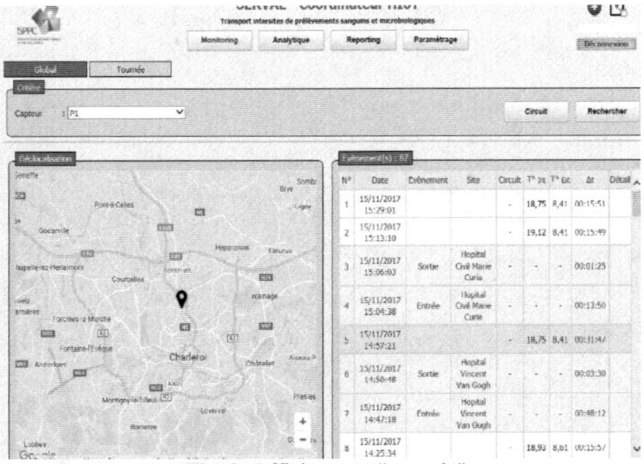

Fig. 3. Affichage en "tournée"

Dans cet écran (Fig.3), on peut sélectionner la tournée souhaitée, activer le début et la fin d'un circuit, réaliser le suivi de la température en combinant plusieurs circuits et signaler toutes les anomalies liées à la tournée.

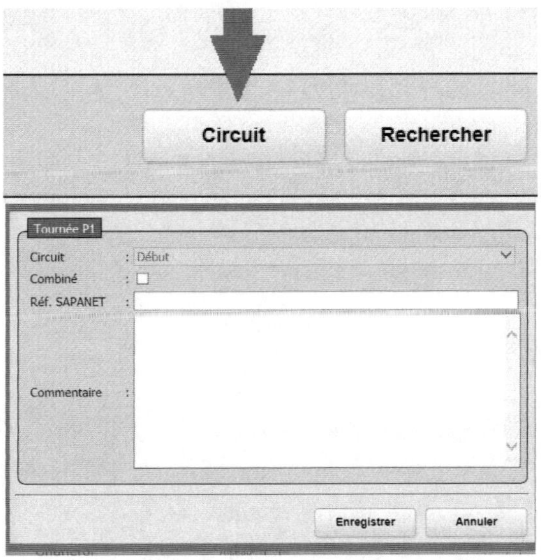

Le bouton "Analytique" de l'écran d'affichage global (Fig.4) permet, pour une tournée donnée, de prendre le chemin le plus court. Si le chauffeur reçoit une alerte, le système propose le trajet optimal afin de se diriger vers le site du LBC le plus proche et de prendre ainsi les mesures nécessaires afin de ramener la température dans les seuils définis.

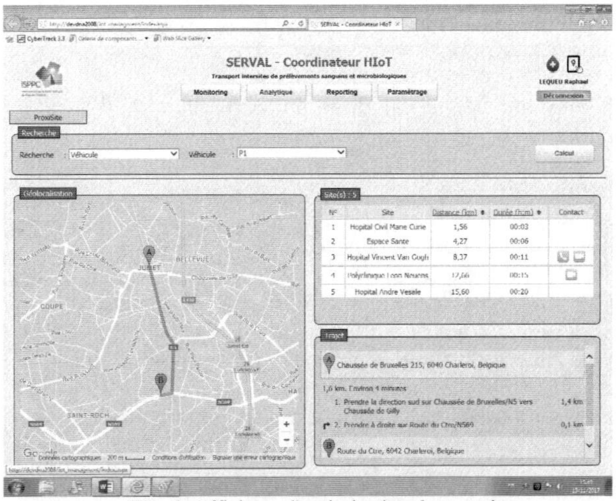

Fig. 4. Affichage d'optimisation de tournée

Concernant le reporting, la Figure 5 affiche l'écran qui permet d'obtenir toutes les données nécessaires à la traçabilité du transport des échantillons et permet de mesurer le délai de transport.

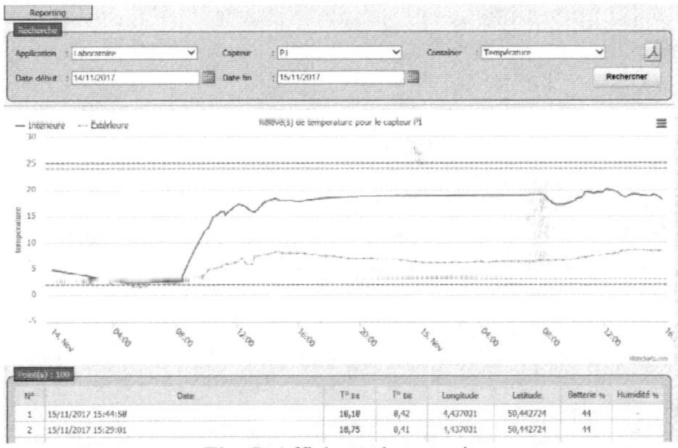

Fig. 5. Affichage du reporting

6 Conclusion et perspetives

Une des perspectives de la mise en place d'une solution permettant une gestion proactive du transport des échantillons, sera à terme, d'évaluer les performances de ce système par des Indicateurs Qualité liés à la température et au délai de transport. Ces indicateurs doivent être croisés avec les TAT (Turn Around Time) mis en place pour chaque analyse et chaque échantillon au LBC.

A travers ce projet relaté dans ce papier, nous soulignons que le déploiement de ce processus de mesure nécessite une réorganisation de la coordination logistique. Cette nouvelle organisation doit satisfaire aux exigences de la norme ISO

15189 mise en place au sein du Système de Management de la Qualité du LBC.

Une deuxième perspective de ce projet en cours est d'intégrer dans le système informatique de surveillance, un algorithme de planification des tournées de collecte des échantillons s'articulant sur le "Pickup and delivery problem" [9] avec la visualisation de fenêtres de temps. L'usage de cet algorithme nécessite un historique de données.

A l'heure actuelle, la solution informatique va se généraliser à l'ensemble des tournées et des activités de transport du LBC. A l'état actuel, il est trop tôt pour se prononcer sur le bilan du projet. Néanmoins, Il faudra, comme pour tout système, auditer et mesurer l'impact d'évolution de la solution proposée afin de progresser vers une dynamique intégrée d'amélioration continue.

Réferences

1. Clinical and Laboratory Standards Institute, Risk Management Techniques to Identify and Control Laboratory Error Sources, Proposed Guideline. Second Edition, EP18. Vol. 27. 23 (2007).
2. R. H. Weber, Internet of things – Gouvernance quo vadis ? Computer Law & Security Review. 29, 341–347 (2013).
3. A. Labrique, The Digital Revolution in LMICs: "Leapfrog" Opportunities for Global Health, In: e-Health Research 2016 International Congress, Paris, France (2016).
4. H. Servy, L, Gossec, e-santé et médecine : révolution ou évolution ? Lettre Rhumatol. 24, 412–413 (2016).
5. B. Billet, Système de gestion de flux pour l'Internet des objets intelligents, Thèse soutenue à l'Université de Versaille (INRIA), 19 mars2015.
6. Y. L. G. Zhou, Key Technologies and Applications of Internet of Things. Fifth International Conference on Intelligent Computation Technology and Automation (ICICTA), Zhangjiajie, Hunan (2012).
7. L. Tan, N. Wang, Future internet: The Internet of Things, Advanced Computer Theory and Engineering (ICACTE), 3rd International Conference on Advanced Computer Theory and Engineering, 5 (2010).
8. V.K. Sehgal, A. Patrick, L. Rajpoot, A Comparative Study of Cyber Physical Cloud, Cloud of Sensors and Internet of Things: Their Ideology, Similarities and Differences, IEEE International Advance Computing. Conference (IACC) (2014).
9. Y. Dumas, J. Desrosiers, F. Soumis, The pickup and delivery problem with time windows. European Journal of Operational Research, 1, Vol.54.7-22 (1991).

L'erreur médicamenteuse : manque de fiabilité humaine ou organisationnelle?

S. Filali El Ghorfi* , N. Meskens, F. Riane.

Faculté polydisciplinaire de Larache, département de sciences économiques et de gestion, Larache, Maroc.

Résumé. Les événements indésirables liés au soins sont très nombreux. la revue de la littérature montre que ces derniers constituent des mesures d'efficience et d'efficacité de l'organisation hospitalière. La qualité des soins et la sécurité du patient constituent des défis importants auxquels font face les acteurs de l'hôpital.
L'erreur médicamenteuse est parmi les événements indésirables. Elle est marquée par sa fréquence, sa gravité et son évitabilité. Cette problématique est à l'évidence celle d'un sous-système complexe (circuit hospitalier du médicament) intégrant la complexité du comportement humain et du fonctionnement du système hospitalier dans son ensemble.
l'objectif de ce papier est de montrer que les causes de l'erreur médicamenteuse sont à la fois humaines et organisationnelles. Notre contribution consiste à mettre l'accent sur la notion de la fiabilité globale et de proposer une mesure de celle-ci.

Keywords: événement indésirable, erreur médicamenteuse, fiabilité humaine, fiabilité organisationnelle.

1 Introduction

Les soins de santé présentent un paradoxe difficile en jumelant le postulat de « ne pas nuire » au patient et la réalité frappante qui montre que les soins ne sont pas sécurisés et que ce patient n'est pas à l'abri des événements indésirables survenant au moment de la prestation de soins [1, 2].

Ces événements indésirables liés au processus de prise en charge du patient sont nombreux et leurs conséquences sont parfois graves.

La survenue de ces événements indésirables parmi lesquels on trouve l'erreur médicamenteuse, constitue un thème de préoccupation majeure, à la fois pour les usagers, les professionnels de santé et les pouvoirs publics [3].
Alors quelle place occupe l'erreur médicamenteuse dans la littérature? s'agit-il d'un manque de fiabilité humaine ou organisationnelle.?, quelle mesure propose-t-on pour la fiabilité humaine.

2 L'erreur médicamenteuse quelques éléments de la littérature

Le repérage et la mesure des événements indésirables ont fait l'objet d'études nationales dans plusieurs pays. L'initiative la plus ancienne est celle qui a été menée aux Etats Unis[4].

Le tableau 1 constitue un résumé des résultats de ces études menées entre 1990 et 2012[1].

Tableau 1. résultats des études menées dans six pays sur le risque iatrogène

	États-Unis	Australie	Royaume-Uni	Canada	Belgique	France
Auteurs/Année	Brennan *et al.* (1991)	Wilson *et al.* (1995)	NHS, 2000 ; Vincent *et al* (2001)	Baker *et al.* (2004)	Van den Heede *et al.* (2006)	Michel *et al.* (2010)
Etude	HMPS	QAHCS	AOWM	CAES	AOBAH	ENEIS 2
Nombre d'hôpitaux	51	28	2	20	123	81
Fréquence	3,7%	16,6%	10,8% (10.000) (NHS, 2000)	7,5%	7,12% (en médecine)	15.5 %
(médicaments)	(19%)	(10,8%)		(23%)		(42%)
Gravité	13,6%	4,9%	8%	20,8%	2000 décès (Budget & Droit, 2007)	54.3%
Evitabilité	51,3%	70%	48 %	36,9%	-	47.3%
Coût	29 billions $	-	2 billions £ (NHS, 2000)	-	20 Millions € (Budget & Droit, 2007)	-

Ce tableau nous permet de retirer deux points importants :
Le premier est que les événements indésirables constituent une réalité nuisible pour les patients et pour les hôpitaux. La fréquence du risque iatrogène est importante. Elle peut atteindre jusqu'à 16.6% des patients admis à l'hôpital (voir tableau 1). Dans l'étude ENEIS 2 menée en France, les auteurs ont estimé, dans un service de 30 lits, l'occurrence d'un événement indésirable tous les cinq jours d'hospitalisation soit 6.2 événements pour 1000 jours d'hospitalisations [5].

* Correspondence: souadfilali@hotmail.com

[1] Une étude nationale ENEIS 3 est proposée pour 2017 en France.

Le deuxième, la place qu'occupe l'erreur médicamenteuse dans la survenue de ces événements. Elle est commune à toutes les études. Elle a pris une importance particulière vu les caractéristiques de fréquence, de gravité et d'évitabilité qu'elle réunit et vu les conséquences financières qu'elle engendre [6]. C'est une facette inéluctable du risque iatrogène.
En Europe, le groupe d'experts chargé de la sécurité des pratiques médicamenteuses [7] a constaté que l'incidence de l'ensemble des événements indésirables médicamenteux (EIM) varie entre 2,1% et 19,8% pour les patients hospitalisés en médecine interne et entre 2,6 et 21,5% en pédiatrie. Une proportion de 18,7 à 56% de ces EIM sont évitables. En France, l'étude ENEIS 2 a montré que 1,6 % des séjours causés par des événements indésirables graves évitables ont été associés à des produits de santé et notamment aux médicaments [3].
En Belgique, on estime en 2006, à 2000 le nombre de décès chaque année suite à l'erreur médicamenteuse et aux aléas thérapeutiques engendrant un coût annuel de 20 millions d'euros [8].
Aux Etats-Unis Une estimation récente indique que les coûts liés à la mortalité et la morbidité causée par des problèmes de médicament est passé de 76.6 billions de dollars en 1995 [9] à 177.4 billions de dollars en 2000 [10].

Aussi bien en Europe qu'aux USA, des études [11, 12, 13, 14, 15] ont montré que ces événements indésirables médicamenteux (EIM) sont fréquents, graves, évitables et touchent tous les types d'organisations hospitalières y compris celles accréditées.

L'erreur médicamenteuse à laquelle nous nous intéressons peut donc être à l'origine d'une perte d'efficacité thérapeutique et de préjudices tels qu'une aggravation de la pathologie, un handicap prolongé voire d'une mise en jeu de pronostic vital. Elle se produit au sein du circuit hospitalier du médicament.

3 Les caractéristiques du circuit hospitalier du médicament

Le circuit hospitalier du médicament est défini par la société Française de la pharmacie clinique comme « un processus de prise en charge thérapeutique médicamenteuse d'un patient, hospitalisé dans un établissement de santé, résident d'un établissement médico-social ou en soins ambulatoires. Ce processus interdisciplinaire est constitué des étapes de prescription, de dispensation, d'administration et de suivi thérapeutique, et comprend le traitement de l'information » [16].

Le circuit hospitalier du médicament est un sous-système marqué par les caractéristiques suivantes :

- il est transversal : il croise les unités cliniques et pharmaceutiques, il dote l'ensemble des services de soins présents dans un centre hospitalier par les médicaments nécessaires ;
- il est régi par une réglementation stricte. Chaque étape du circuit doit respecter le cadre réglementaire et législatif ;
- il est marqué par une forte composante humaine : divers professionnels de santé avec chacun sa spécialité, son périmètre de travail, son processus décisionnel, son fonctionnement et son niveau de responsabilisation.
- il est centré sur le patient ;
- il est critique (risqué): il est le maillon essentiel de la sécurité du patient ;
- il est hétérogène : l'organisation du circuit du médicament n'est pas standard dans tous les hôpitaux (informatisation, automatisation, distribution globale/individuelle) ;
- il est mal géré : son fonctionnement n'est pas optimal (les risques sont nombreux).

Les erreurs médicamenteuses liées à ce circuit

Le circuit du médicament est marqué par une grande interdépendance entre les professionnels de santé et par une interaction entre les unités cliniques et pharmaceutique.
La prescription est un acte médical, la dispensation est acte pharmaceutique et l'administration et le suivi thérapeutique est un acte infirmier. Chaque étape de ce circuit est une source d'erreurs potentielles qui peuvent engendrer des risques pour la santé du patient.
On distingue les erreurs principales des erreurs secondaires. Les erreurs principales sont liées aux différentes phases du circuit on cite : les erreurs de prescription, de transcription, de dispensation, d'administration et de suivi thérapeutique.
Une revue de la littérature montre qu'aucune étape du circuit n'a échappé à l'erreur (voir tableau 2) et que les variations entre ces erreurs s'expliquent par trois choses : la définition donnée à l'erreur médicamenteuse, la méthode de collecte des données, les critères d'exclusion et d'inclusion et l'unité de soins étudiée.

Tableau 2 : Estimation de l'erreur médicamenteuse principale dans la littérature

Auteur/ Année	Le taux d'erreur en %				
	Prescription	Transcription	Dispensation	Administration	Suivi thérapeutique
Leape *et al.*, 1995	39	12	11	38	-
Bates *et al.*, 1995	56	6	4	34	-
Kaushal *et al.*, 2001(a)	74	10	0.94	13	0.65
Cowley *et al.*, 2001	29	25	8	36	1
Fortescue *et al.*, 2003	77.8	5.8	1	12.8	0.5
Hicks *et al.*, 2004	22.5	10.7	5.9	59.5	1.2
Lisby *et al.*, 2005	39	56	4	41	76
Duthie *et al.*, 2005	34	3	18	41	Exclu du circuit
Stheneur *et al.*, 2006	28	-	-	60	-
Hicks *et al.*, 2007	28.4	12.2	7.3	50.3	1.8
Otero *et al.*, 2008	11.4	-	-	17.3	-
	7.3	-	-	9.2	-
Engum & Berckler, 2008	23	-	-	-	-
Fahimi *et al.*, 2008	-	-	33.6	66.4	-
Bundy *et al.*,2009	11	10	4.1	70	0.82
Ghaleb *et al.*, 2010	13.2	-	-	19.1	-
Pham *et al.*, 2011	29	25	8	36	1

Les erreurs secondaires sont celles qui détaillent et expliquent l'erreur principale à savoir : erreur d'omission, erreur de dose, erreur de posologie ou de concentration, erreur de médicament, erreur de forme galénique, erreur de technique d'administration, erreur de voie d'administration, erreur de débit d'administration, erreur de durée d'administration, erreur de moment d'administration, erreur de patient.

Tableau 3 : Erreurs médicamenteuses secondaires issues de la littérature

Types d'erreurs en (%) \ Auteurs/année	Kaushal *et al.* (2001a)	Fortescue *et al.* (2003)	Cowley *et al.* (2001)	Barker *et al.* (2002)	Hicks *et al.* (2004)	Handler *et al.* (2004)	Pham *et al.* (2008)	Engum et Breckler (2008)	Bundy *et al.* (2009)
Dose	28	28.4	25	17	24	17	18	72	25
Omission		10.9	27	30	20		11	5	4.4
Fréquence	9.4	12.5						2.2	
Préparation			6		5		4.7		8.4
Voie d'administration	18	17.7	1		1	2	2.5	2.2	0.49
Technique d'administration			2		5		2.3		2.6
Transcription/documentation	14	15.9							
Médicament (/non autorisé)	1.3		11	4	14		11	2.7	
Patient	0.16		3		2	5	4.4		
Allergie	1.3	1.8						4	4.1
Prescription	2.3		4		15	10	-	3	6.8
Poids	3.7								
Moment	12		13	43	3	26	3.7		7.9
Over dose		6.5							
Under dose		2.3							
Extra dose		0.7	7		6		4.3		25
Dose manquante		8.1							
Erreur de forme			1		1			5	1
Autres	9.9	23.1							0.33

Les erreurs secondaires qui contribuent le plus à toutes les erreurs médicamenteuses principales, calculées dans le tableau 2, sont les erreurs de dose et d'omission. Elles sont signalées dans la majorité des études.

Ce tableau 3 montre l'existence d'une hétérogénéité des données collectées et l'absence d'une classification standardisée des erreurs secondaires. Ainsi, la redondance est très remarquable. On trouve : erreur de dose, d'over dose, d'under dose, d'extra dose, ... Ces catégories, peuvent selon notre point de vue, être reprises sous l'angle de « l'erreur de dose ». En plus, les erreurs calculées par les auteurs sont de toute nature confondue. On ne peut pas savoir si les types d'erreurs calculées (ex : les erreurs de dose) sont liés à la prescription, à la dispensation ou à l'administration.

3 Les causes de l'erreur médicamenteuse

Dans cette partie nous désirons répondre à la question suivante :
L'erreur médicamenteuse est-elle due à un manque de fiabilité humaine ou organisationnelle ?

L'erreur médicamenteuse et la fiabilité humaine

Les principaux intervenants sont: le médecin, le pharmacien et l'infirmier. Dès qu'une erreur se produit, ces acteurs sont mis en cause. Le tableau 4 montre que la contribution des acteurs dans l'erreur médicamenteuse est différente. Se sont souvent les opérateurs de première ligne (les infirmières et les médecins) qui sont accusés le plus

Tableau 4: La contribution des acteurs dans l'erreur médicamenteuse

	Médecins	Pharmaciens	Infirmières	Secrétaires
Fortescue *et al.* (2003)	71.9%	1%	24.4%,	0.7%.
Duthie *et al.* (2005)	50%	18%.	77%	-
Pham *et al.* (2011)	24%	-	54%	-

L'erreur humaine a plusieurs aspects dont :

- Les ratés et les lapsus de mémoires étaient à l'origine de 57% des erreurs de prescription [17] et de moins de 12% pour les erreurs d'administrations[18].
- La négligence a contribué par 86% à l'erreur médicamenteuse dans les unités de soins intensives [19]. Elle est définie comme « tout soin qui n'arrive pas à atteindre les standards prévus par les médecins dans leur communauté »[4].
- Le déficit de performance a contribué à l'erreur médicamenteuse par une proportion comprise entre 29 et 50% [20, 21, 22]. La base des données MEDMARX définit le déficit de performance comme « toute erreur n'ayant pas de cause claire ». C'est-à-dire que les professionnels de soins ont toutes les compétences et les connaissances pour exécuter convenablement leurs tâches mais ils ont raté l'occasion de le faire [21].
- Le non respect des procédures est une cause très fréquente [18, 20, 21, 22, 23]. Elle a contribué par plus de 23% à l'erreur médicamenteuse [21].

- Le manque de connaissance du médicament concerne tous les acteurs et il est une cause commune à toutes les étapes du circuit du médicament [18, 24, 22, 25] . Il est à l'origine de 60% des erreurs de prescription, 15% des erreurs d'administration et 15% pour la transcription [18]. Ce manque de connaissance est dû à la croissance spectaculaire du nombre de médicaments sur le marché au cours des dernières décennies [26]. Ainsi, plus de la moitié des traitements prescrits par un médecin n'apparaissent pas dans le contenu de sa formation initiale qui requiert une mise à jour permanente [27]. Les médecins sont obligés par les codes de déontologie médicale, d'entretenir et de perfectionner leurs connaissances en participant à des formations continues et à l'évaluation des pratiques professionnelles. Ainsi, tout décalage entre l'évolution de la science et les pratiques des acteurs crée certainement des erreurs.
- Certains auteurs [22] ont montré que le manque d'expérience contribue à l'erreur médicamenteuse. Les médecins juniors font plus d'erreurs de prescription que les médecins habilités. Cependant, [28] ont constaté que les infirmières qui ont plus d'expérience sont celles les plus occupées dans leurs activité et donc ne peuvent réaliser tous les contrôles nécessaires et commettent plus d'erreurs que les jeunes infirmières. Pour [29, 30] il n'y a aucune relation entre l'expérience et l'EM.
- Les erreurs de calcul [20, 31] et la confusion de forme du dosage [32, 33] sont souvent attribuées à l'infirmière. L'exemple le plus cité est l'administration de 20 ml au lieu de 20 mg prescrite ou 0.8 mg au lieu de 0.08 mg. Une revue de la littérature sur les erreurs de calcul réalisée par [34] montre que l'administration de la mauvaise dose ne signifie pas qu'elle est nécessairement due à l'erreur de calcul et pas obligatoirement attribuable aux infirmières et à leurs compétences mathématiques.
- Le manque d'information essentielle sur le patient [18] et l'absence de pratiques basées sur les preuves [35] (qui se basent sur les données récentes issues de la recherche clinique et de la revue de la littérature) dans la prise en charge de chaque patient ont été aussi cités dans la littérature.

L'ensemble de ces erreurs humaines sont généralement liées à la mémoire et la vigilance humaine. Ces erreurs auraient dues avoir plus de chance d'échouer dans des systèmes qui sont désignés pour promouvoir la défaillance humaine. Selon [20]Cowely et al. (2001) parler d'une performance humaine est irréaliste dans ce type de système. Ainsi, tout signalement d'erreur reflète la présence d'une défaillance dans le processus qu'il a généré.
Ceci nous pousse à intégrer la deuxième partie de la question. qu'on est-il de la fiabilité de l'organisation hospitalière ?.

L'erreur médicamenteuse et la fiabilité organisationnelle

L'hôpital est un système complexe et à risque. Les défaillances de système sont dans 78% des cas à l'origine des erreurs médicamenteuses [18]. Ces défaillances se manifestent à différents niveaux :

- L'interruption de professionnel dans sa tâche est le principal facteur contribuant à l'erreur. Des études signalent une fréquence de 6 à 15 interruptions par médecin par heure [30]et en moyenne 8.4 par infirmière [54]. L'interruption entraîne d'une part, la distraction du professionnel de santé, qui est à l'origine de 50% d'erreurs [32]. [37] estime une erreur toutes les 74 minutes. D'autre part, l'interruption augmente le taux de déviation par rapport aux procédures [30]. Elle augmente l'erreur médicamenteuse de dispensation [36] et d'administration [30] et engendre des coûts qui s'élèvent à 27 millions de dollars2 chaque année [37].

- La charge de travail y contribue à 20.5% [22] et elle est souvent associée au manque d'effectif [32] et à la rotation fréquente du personnel. Selon [38], le taux de rotation (turnover) de l'équipe infirmière est souvent très élevé. Il dépasse 50% annuellement ce qui entraîne une perte de la mémoire organisationnelle concernant les politiques et les procédures et contribue donc à l'augmentation de l'erreur.

- Le transfert du patient (de la salle d'opération à la salle de réveil et puis à la chambre d'hospitalisation) contribue aux erreurs de dose. Souvent les infirmières oublient de noter la bonne information en temps réel[21, 33].

- La communication entre les acteurs est aussi un élément important. Le manque d'explication et le manque de confirmation de l'information entre les infirmières et leurs superviseurs, ont été cités comme des causes d'erreurs d'administration par [28]. Selon [31] , 15% des erreurs de prescriptions sont dues à des ordres oraux et 74% sont dues à une ordonnaces incomplète. La communication asynchrone, c'est-à-dire guidée par le système (ex : CPOE ou basée sur la documentation), entre le médecin et l'infirmière peut être une cause d'erreur puisqu'elle crée des ambiguïtés et exige un grand effort d'interprétation de l'information par l'infirmière [39].

- La formation des acteurs au niveau de la pharmacologie. Le manque de connaissance de médicament est certainement un facteur humain mais lorsqu'il est lié à la politique du gouvernement ou de l'hôpital il devient un problème du système. [40] ont montré que le programme de formation des infirmières de premier cycle ne doit pas se baser seulement sur les connaissances théoriques mais doit contenir des programmes liés à la sécurité du patient et à la réduction de l'erreur. D'autre part, [18] ont montré que les méthodes mises en place dans un hôpital pour la diffusion de l'information relative au médicament et à son bon usage sont aussi contributives à l'erreur.

---

[2] Selon [37], une erreur humaine, suite aux défaillances opérationnelles, peut coûter entre 0, 33 et 177 $ par patient.

- Le manque de standardisation des procédures, des doses et de la distribution des médicaments entre les unités ont été cités par [18]comme cause systémique de l'EIM. Cependant, aucune proportion n'a été calculée pour ces éléments.

- Les heures de pics peuvent aussi contribuer à l'erreur. Ces heures sont instables et différentes selon les unités de soins étudiées. [41] estiment que 19.8% des erreurs se produisent le matin à 9h dans les unités de soins intensifs. Pour [42], 67.6% des erreurs en pédiatrie et néonatologie se produisent l'après midi. Alors que pour [43], 42% de ces erreurs apparaissent entre 15h et 23h dans les services d'urgence.

- Les médicaments à risque : selon [44], la catégorie des médicaments pouvant être à l'origine d'une erreur médicamenteuse et créer un EIM potentiellement grave est celle liée à des maladies infectieuses, cardiaques et neurologiques. [45] trouvent que 50% des erreurs détectées dans leur étude sont engendrées par l'usage des médicaments liés au système nerveux comme la morphine. Les anti-infectifs et les vitamines K sont les plus impliqués dans l'erreur médicamenteuse dans les unités de soins de longue durée [38]. Les liquides à usage intraveineuse sont les produits les plus critiques en pédiatrie [20]. Ils nécessitent une grande performance humaine et de bonnes pratiques que ce soit au niveau de la préparation (dilution, calcules, manipulation) ou de l'administration (difficulté liée aux corps des nouveaux nés, les veines..). Les anticoagulants, les antibiotiques, l'insuline sont autant d'exemples de médicament à risque.

- Les abréviations : il existe plus de 10.000 abréviations utilisées en médecine avec plus de 16.000 significations. Ces abréviations sont souvent utilisées pour économiser du temps, alors qu'en réalité elles créent une perte du temps pour ceux qui les interprètent. Si ces abréviations sont mal interprétées alors le patient reçoit le mauvais médicament [47].

- L'organisation du circuit hospitalier : il est clairement admis que le système de délivrance globale des médicaments génère beaucoup plus d'erreur qu'un système de dispensation à délivrance nominative des médicaments [48,6]. Le premier se contente d'approvisionner les services cliniques, les personnels soignants étant responsables de préparer les doses à administrer. Le second consiste à délivrer pour chaque patient la dose exacte de chaque médicament, les différents produits étant regroupés par prise [49].

- Le conditionnement et le label : presque 53% des problèmes signalés dans la base des données MER sont dus à des médicaments ayant un label ou un conditionnement similaire [47]. Les problèmes de look-alike et du sound-alike sont les plus fréquents et ce aussi bien pour les génériques que pour les originaux [32 ,50]. En anesthésie, l'échange de seringue cause 70.4% des erreurs et la mauvaise identification des étiquettes cause 46.8% [51].

- Les préparations non centralisées : lorsque le pharmacien ne contribue pas à la préparation des médicaments, se sont les infirmières qui le font en ne possédant qu'une formation minimale dans la préparation de certains médicaments (ex : des médicaments intraveineux). Si cette préparation n'est pas contrôlée alors la probabilité d'erreur est grande [41].

- Les techniques de travail : En anesthésie les médicaments sont souvent pré remplis dans des seringues avant qu'ils soient utilisés. Ce qui crée la possibilité d'erreur en choisissant la mauvaise ampoule (14%) ou la mauvaise seringue (44%) surtout celles ayant des tailles similaires [52] .

On peut conclure que l'erreur médicamenteuse est une combinaison de défaillance humaine et organisationnelle.

4 Quelle mesure pour la fiabilité humaine et organisationnelle ?

Pour répondre à cette question, nous avons développé un cadre conceptuel qui met en exergue la notion de la fiabilité globale. Nous définissons celle-ci comme « toute interaction réussie entre les capacités de l'individu et celles de l'organisation permettant la réalisation d'une tâche sécurisée».
Notre contribution dans ce cadre conceptuel consiste à mettre en exergue une nouvelle classification des causes d'un événement indésirable (l'erreur médicamenteuse). Nous proposons une taxonomie de l'erreur humaine. Nous suggérons que l'erreur médicamenteuse puisse être la conséquence d'une non fiabilité humaine (causes directes), d'une non fiabilité organisationnelle (causes indirectes) et aussi d'une conjonction des deux non fiabilités (que nous appelons causes intermédiaires).
Nous avons développé donc une méthode d'analyse des causes de l'erreur médicamenteuse basée sur la fiabilité que nous avons nommé « MAC-F » [53]
Cette méthode se base sur un outil très simple à savoir la matrice de fiabilité. Dans laquelle nous classons en colonne les étapes du circuit de médicaments et leurs acteurs et en ligne nous classons les facteurs de fiabilités.
Nous avons utilisé les signes suivants pour mesurer la contribution de chaque facteur dans l'erreur médicamenteuse :

- Signe (-) lorsque le facteur de fiabilité ne fonctionne pas de façon optimale et contribue donc à l'erreur médicamenteuse (il n'empêche pas l'erreur de se produire).

- Signe (0) lorsque le facteur est neutre quant à l'apparition de l'erreur (il n'est pas en lien directe avec elle ou il n'a aucun effet)
- Signe (Ø) lorsque le facteur est inexistant (ce signe concerne spécialement les FI)
- Signe (+) lorsque le facteur contribue à récupérer et à corriger l'erreur.

Nous calculons ensuite par ligne et par colonne les indices de fiabilité correspondants.
Par ligne, nous obtenons les indices de fiabilité par variable (Σ- ; Σ+ ; Σ0 ; ΣØ). Ils reflètent la contribution de chaque variable dans l'EM le long du circuit clinique du médicament. C'est à dire au niveau de toutes les étapes du processus.
Par colonne, on calcule les indices de fiabilité par facteur. Ces indices nous donnent pour chacun des 5 cas, la contribution de chaque type de facteur dans l'apparition de l'EM (Σ(FS) ; Σ(FI) ; Σ(FC)).
La matrice permet ainsi de voir la contribution positive, négative, neutre ou inexistante de chaque facteur et de voir si ces indices sont spécifiques à un seul type d'EM ou s'ils ont un caractère répétitif, commun à tous les acteurs et s'ils sont impliqués dans toutes les EM du circuit du médicament.
Elle permet de distinguer les facteurs qui freinent la fiabilité et contribuent à l'erreur (ceux ayant les signes (- ; 0 ; Ø)) et les facteurs fiables qui permettent de récupérer l'erreur (ceux ayant le signe (+). Nous allons donc calculer les indices de fiabilité globaux pour chaque facteur (FS, FI et FC) en utilisant la formule suivante :

$$\Omega = \left(\frac{\Sigma +}{(\Sigma -) + (\Sigma 0) + (\Sigma \emptyset)}\right).$$

Étant donné la rareté des études sur le domaine de la fiabilité dans le milieu hospitalier, il n'existe pas un seuil nous permettant de séparer la fiabilité de la non-fiabilité. Nous désirons contribuer dans ce domaine en partageant notre réflexion.

Nous considérons que cet indice (Ω) doit être compris entre 1 et ∞ ($1 \leq \Omega \leq \infty$) pour avoir un circuit clinique fiable et sécurisé. Dans ce cas, on dit que le niveau de fiabilité est acceptable, lorsque Ω de chaque facteur est ≥ 1. Cependant, ce niveau de fiabilité est performant (compétitif), lorsque Ω tend vers l'infini (∞). C'est-à-dire lorsque le dénominateur tend vers 0. Ceci signifie que l'effet positif est prédominant et que les facteurs sont fiables et couvrent la défaillance des autres facteurs (faillibles, neutre ou inexistants).

Cependant si $0 \leq \Omega < 1$ la non fiabilité des facteurs est prédominante et l'EM sera de plus en plus fréquente (voir grave). Il faut mener des actions sérieuses d'amélioration afin de réduire l'erreur.

Les résultats de cette méthode montrent en détaille la contribution de chaque facteurs dans l'apparition de l'erreur médicamenteuse. Elle donne la possibilité de mettre le doigts sur le facteur critique et de proposer ainsi des actions d'améliorations adéquates. Cette méthode constitue un outil d'aide à la décision aux professionnels de santé.

5 Conclusion

L'erreur médicamenteuse est le résultat de combinanison de manque de fiabilité humaine et organisationnelle. catte fiabilité est difficilement mesurable. nous avons essayé de développer un cadre conceptuel celui de la fiabilité globale et de le valider en élaborant la méthode MAC-F[53]. l'objectif était de faire doter les professionnels de soins d'un outil simple d'analyse et de mesure afin de les aider à la prise de décision.

References

1. T.J.Vogus, K.M. Sutcliffe, et K. Weick, Doing no harm: enabling, enacting, and elaborating a culture of safety in health care. Academy of management perspectives; **24**, 4: 60-78 (2010).
2. L.T. Kohn, J.M. Corrigan, M.S. Donaldson , To err is human: building a safer health system. Washington, D.C.: National Academy Press(1999).
3.P.Michel, C. Minodier, M. Lathelize, C. Monnereau, S. Domecq, M. Chaleix, M. Kret, R.B. Sonnet, J.L. Quenon, L. Olier, Les événements indésirables graves associés aux soins observés dans les établissements de santé. Résultats des enquêtes nationales menées en 2009 et 2004. Dossier solidarité et santé n° 17(2010).
4. T.A. Brennan, L.L. Leape, N.M. Laird, L. Hebert, A.R. Localio, A.G. Lawthers, J.P. Newhouse, P.C. Weiler and H.H. Hiatt, Incidence of adverse events and negligence in hospitalized patients, results of the Harvard Medical Practice Study, NEJM; **324**: 370-376(1991).
5. P.Michel, C. Minodier, C. Monnereau, M. Lathelize, S. Domecq, M. Chaleix, M. Kret, T. Roberts, L. Nitaro, R.B. Sonnet, B. Quintard, J.L. Quenon, L. Olier, Les événements indésirables graves dans les établissements de santé : fréquence, évitabilité et acceptabilité. Etudes et Résultats n° 761(2011).
6.E. Schmitt, Le risqué médicamenteux nosocomial: circuit hospitalier du médicament et qualité des soins. Masson, Paris (1999).
7. Conseil de l'Europe Groupe d'experts charges de la sécurité des pratiques médicamenteuses (P-SP-PH/SAFE), Creation of a better medication safety culture in Europe: building up safe medication practices. Document disponible sur le site www.coe.int/t/e/social_cohesion/soc-sp/medication safety culture report e.pdf (2006).
8. Budget et Droit, Erreur médicale: l'indemnisation bientôt facilitée. Revue bimestriel Mars/avril. (2007).
9. J.A. Johnson et J.L. Bootman, Drug-related morbidity and mortality: a cost of illness model. Arch Intern Med; **155**: 1949-1956. (1995).
10. F.R Ernst et A.J. Grizzle, Drug-related morbidity and

mortality: updating the cost-of-illness model. J Am Pharm Assoc; **41**:192-199. (2001).

11. D.W. Bates, J. Teich, J. Lee, D.L. Seger, G.L. Kuperman, N. Maluf, D. Boyle, L.L. Leape, The impact of computerized physician order entry on medication error prevention. J. Am Med Inform Assoc; **6:** 313-321(1999).

12. T.K. Gandhi, S.N. Weingart, L.L. Leape, Medication errors and potential adverse events among outpatients. J. Gen Inter Med; **15**:1-16 (2000).

13.F. Fasting et S.E. Gisvold, Reports of investigation: Adverse drug errors in anaesthesia and the impact of coulerd syringe labels. Canadian Journal of Anaesthesia; **47**, 11: 1060-1067(2000).

14. G. Neale, M. Woloshynowych, C. Vincent, Exploring the causes of adverse events in NHS hospital practice. J R Soc Med; **94**,7: 322-330 (2001).

15. K.N. Barker E.A. Flynn, G.A. Pepper, D.W. Bates, RL. Mikeal, Medication errors observed in 36 health care facilities. Arch Inter Med; **162**: 1897-1903 (2002).

16. SFPC, La société française de la pharmacie clinique. Le dictionnaire Français de l'erreur médicamenteuse.1ière édition (2005).

17. Dean B., M. Schachter, C. Vincent, N. Barber, Causes of prescribing errors in hospital inpatients: a prospective study. Lancet ; **359**: 1373-1378. (2002).

18. L.L. Leape, D.W. Bates, D.J. Cullen, J. Cooper, H.J. Demonaco, T. Gallivan, Systems analysis of adverse drug events. JAMA; **274**, 1: 35-43. (1995)

19. Capuzzo N., L. Nawfal, M. Campi, V. Valpondi, M. Verri, R. Alvisi, Reporting of unintended events in an intensive care unit: comparison between staff and observer. BMC Emerg Med; **5**, 1: 1-7(2005).

20. E. Cowley, R. Williams, D. Cousins, Medication errors in children: a descriptive summary of medication error reports submitted to the united states Pharmacopeia. Current Therapeutic Research; **62**, 9: 627-640 (2001).

21 R.W. Hicks, C.S. Becker, C.S. Beya, Medication Errors in the PACU: A secondary Analysis of MEDMARX Findings. Journal of PeriAnesthesia Nursing; **19**, 1:18-28(2004).

22. J.C., Pham, J.L. Story, R.W. Hicks, A.D. Shore, L.L. Morlock, D.S. Cheung, G.D. Kelen, P.J. Pronovost, National study on the frequency, types, causes and consequences of voluntarily reported Emergency Department medication errors. Original contributions. The Journal of Emergency Medicine; **40**, 5: 485-492. (2011).

23. C.Stheneur, J.B. Armengaud, C. Castro, G. Chéron, B. Chevallier, Erreurs de prescription médicamenteuse en pédiatrie hospitalière : enquête prospective multicentrique. Implications pour la prévention. Archives de pédiatrie ; **13** . 1294-1298 (2006).

24. L.L. Leape, D.J. Cullen, M.D. Clapp, E. Burdick, H. Demonaco, J.I. Erickson, D.W. Bates , Pharmacist participation on physician rounds and adverse drug events in the intensive care unit. JAMA; **282**: 276-270 (1999).

25. K. Page et A. Mckinney Addressing medication errors: the role of undergraduate nurse education. Nurse education today; **27**,3: 219-224 (2007).

26. OMS, Elargir la pratique pharmaceutique : Recentrer les soins sur les patients. Document de travail. www.fip.org consulté le 30/4/2012(2006).

27. C. Baillard, Mauvaises prescription, mauvaises habitudes. MAPAR 2009. Document disponible sur : www.mapar.og. (2009).

28. T.Kazaoka, K. Ohtsuka, K. Ueno, M. Mori , Why nurses make medication errors: a simulation study. Nurse Education Today; **27**: 312-317(2007). .

29. F.Fahimi, P. Ariapanah, M. Faizi, B. Shafaghi, R. Namdar, M.T. Ardakani, Errors in preparation and administration of intravenous medications in the intensive care unit of a teaching hospital : an observational study. Australian critical care; **21**, 110-116 (2008).

30. J.I. Westbrook, A. Woods, M.I. Rob, W.T.M. Dunsmuir, R.O. Day, Association of interruptions with an increased risk and severity of medication administration errors. Archives of Internal Medicine; **170**, 8: 683-690 (2010).

31. E.Duthie, B. Favreau, A. Ruperto, J. Mannion, E. Flink, R. Leslie, Quantitative and qualitative analysis of medication errors: the New York experience. Advances in patient safety: from research to implementation; **1**: 131-144. Document sur le site: www.ncbi.nlm.nih.gov. (2005).

32.K.M Stratton., M.A. Blegen, G. Pepper, T. Vaughn, Reporting of medication errors by paediatric nurses. Journal of pediatric Nursing; **19**, 6: 385-392 (2004).

33. Hicks R.W., C.S. Becker, P.E. Windle, D.A. Krenzischek, Medication Errors in the PACU. Journal of PeriAnesthesia Nursing; **22**, 6: 413-419(2007).

34. K. Wright, Do calculation errors by nurses cause medication errors in clinical practice? A literature review. Nurse Education Today; **30** : 85-97 (2010).

35. M. Lisbey, L.P. Nielsen, J. Mainz, Errors in the medication process: frequency, type, and potential. International Journal for Quality in Health Care; **17**,1: 15-22 (2005).

36.E.A. Flynn K.N., Barker, J.T. Gibson, R.E. Pearson, B.A. Berger, L.A. Smith, Impact of interruptions and distractions on dispensing errors in an ambulatory care pharmacy. American Journal of Health system pharmacists; **56**: 1319-1325 (1999).

37. A.L Tucker, The impact of operational failures on hospital nurses and their patients. Journal of Operations Management; **22**: 151-169. (2004).

38. S.M. Handler, D.A. Nace, S.A. Studenski, D.B. Fridsma, Medication error reporting in Long Term Care. The American Journal of Geriatric Pharmacotherapy; **2**, 3 : 190-196 (2004).

39. M.C. Beuscart-Zéphir., S. Pelayo, F. Anceaux, D. Maxwell, S. Guerlinger, Cognitive analysis of physicians and nurses cooperation in the medication ordering an administration process. International Journal of Medical Informatics: S65-S77(2007).

40. K. Page et A. Mckinney, Addressing medication errors: the role of undergraduate nurse education. Nurse education today; **27**,3: 219-224 (2007).

41. F.Fahimi, P. Ariapanah, M. Faizi, B. Shafaghi, R. Namdar, M.T. Ardakani, Errors in preparation and administration of intravenous medications in the intensive care unit of a teaching hospital : an observational study. Australian critical care; **21**,

110-116 (2008).
42. P .Otero, A. Leyton, G.Mariani, J.M.C. Cerandas and the patient safety committee Pediatrics, Medication errors in pediatric inpatients: prevalence and results of prevention program. Pdiatrics, official journal of the American Academy of Pediatrics; **122**, 3 : 737-743. (2008).
43. J.C. Pham J.L. Story, R.W. Hicks, A.D. Shore, L.L. Morlock, D.S. Cheung, G.D. Kelen, P.J. Pronovost, National study on the frequency, types, causes and consequences of voluntarily reported Emergency Department medication errors. Original contributions. The Journal of Emergency Medicine; **40**, 5: 485-492 (2011).
44. M. Lisby, L.P. Nielsen, J. Mainz, Errors in the medication process: frequency, type, and potential. International Journal for Quality in Health Care; **17**,1: 15-22 (2005).
Lisby M., L.P. Nielsen, B. Brock, J. Mainz (2010). How are medication errors defined? A systematic literature review of definitions and characteristics. International Journal for Quality in Health Care; 22, 6: 507 – 518.
45. Hicks R.W., C.S. Becker, P.E. Windle, D.A. Krenzischek, Medication Errors in the PACU. Journal of PeriAnesthesia Nursing; **22**, 6: 413-419(2007).
46.S.M. Handler, D.A. Nace, S.A. Studenski, D.B. Fridsma, Medication error reporting in Long Term Care. The American Journal of Geriatric Pharmacotherapy; **2**, 3 : 190-196 (2004).
47.S. Becker, Common causes for medication errors identified. International Journal of Trauma Nursing. Pharmacy Notes: 113-115(1999).
48. A.D. Rambourg., C. Roux-Marson, J.M. Kinowski, Sécuriser la délivrance des médicaments : organisation et équipements. Risque & Qualité en milieu de soins ; **3**, 2 : 115-121(2011).
49. M.Dahan et J. Sauret, Sécurisation du circuit du médicament à l'assistance Publique-Hôpitaux de Paris (AP-HP). Rapport de l'inspection générale des affaires sociales (2010).
50. D.G. Bundy, A.D. Shore, L.L. Morlock, M.R. Miller, Pediatric vaccination errors: application of the "5 Rights" framework to a national error reporting database. Vaccine; **27**: 3890-3896 (2009).
51. B.A. Orser, R.J.B. Chen, D.A. Yee, Medication errors in anaesthetic practice: a survey of 687 practitioners. Canadian Journal of Anesthesia: 139-146 (2000).
52. F. Fasting et S.E. Gisvold, Reports of investigation: Adverse drug errors in anaesthesia and the impact of coulerd syringe labels. Canadian Journal of Anaesthesia; **47**, 11: 1060-1067 (2000).
53. S. Filali El Ghorfi ,N. Meskens et F. Riane, Méthode qualitative d'analyse des causes des erreurs médicamenteuses, GISEH, 11-13juillet Casablanca, Maroc(2016).
54. A.L Trucker et S.J Spear, Operational Failures and interruptions in Hospital Nursing, Health Services Research , **41**, 3 PArt I: 643-662(2006).

Gestion des non-conformités laboratoire dans un système de management intégré

A. Chausse[1], O. Pierson[2]

1. Université Paris-Est, Anses, Mission Qualité des Laboratoires de sécurité des aliments et de santé animale, F-94700 Maisons-Alfort, France
2. Anses – Direction de la Qualité et de l'Audit Interne

Résumé. L'Agence nationale de sécurité sanitaire de l'alimentation, de l'environnement et du travail (Anses) assure des missions de veille, d'expertise, de recherche et de référence sur un large champ couvrant la santé humaine, la santé et le bien-être animal ainsi que la santé végétale.
L'Anses est certifiée ISO 9001 dans ses champs de compétence : la production d'expertises scientifiques selon les prescriptions de la norme NF X 50-110, le pilotage de programmes de recherche, l'autorisation et le contrôle d'intrants du végétal, l'autorisation de produits biocides, la coordination d'activités de vigilance et le pilotage des activités scientifiques et techniques de ses laboratoires (au nombre de 11, accrédités* selon la norme NF EN ISO/CEI 17025).
Chaque entité de l'Agence possède son propre système de management de la Qualité. En 2015, le projet PETAL (Partage Et Transversalité pour l'Accréditation des Laboratoires) visant à harmoniser les dispositions générales de management a été initié. Plusieurs chantiers associés à ce projet ont été créés dont la mise en œuvre de dispositions communes à l'ensemble des entités de l'Anses pour le traitement des non-conformités. Ce chantier comprend également le déploiement d'un outil permettant de dématérialiser les enregistrements.

** portées disponibles sur www.cofrac.fr*

Mots clés : Qualité; Laboratoire; Certification; Accréditation; Non-conformité; Administration; Multi domaines; Multi activités

1 Introduction

L'harmonisation des dispositions dans une structure telle que l'Anses est un enjeu crucial. En effet ses activités sont variées et le nombre de référentiels augmente avec le nombre croissant de missions régaliennes qui lui sont confiées. Cette harmonisation permet :

- des gains d'efficience grâce à une articulation plus lisible pour les agents et la limitation des redondances dans les systèmes qualité spécifiques ;
- de renforcer les possibilités de partage, de construction et de valorisation d'une culture commune ;
- de consolider les dispositions de l'organisation ;
- de prétendre répondre aux critères de définition d'un système qualité commun dans la perspective d'évaluations externes optimisées ;
- d'anticiper les évolutions normatives, notamment les parutions de la NF EN ISO 9001 : 2015 [3] et de la NF EN ISO /CEI 17025 [2].

La gestion des actions correctives et préventives est particulièrement stratégique au regard de ces enjeux : elle traduit en grande partie les activités d'amélioration, qu'elles soient issues d'audits, de revues, de retours clients ou de déclarations spontanées. Le partage des pratiques et la visibilité sur les mesures correctives et préventives donne à la fois une opportunité d'échanges sur des actions ayant trait aux processus d'analyse et au pilotage du système de management.

2 Contexte

Le réseau des laboratoires de l'Anses s'est constitué par rapprochements successifs de laboratoires d'entités différentes, le dernier étant l'intégration au 1er janvier 2011 des unités du Laboratoire National de la Protection des Végétaux (LNPV). Avant même la création de l'Anses, chacun des sites laboratoires était doté d'un système de management propre, avec un manuel qualité, une structure documentaire, des procédures spécifiques. Des initiatives avaient été menées pour rapprocher les pratiques avant 2011, notamment dans le domaine des essais inter-laboratoires d'aptitude. Elles avaient donné lieu à des guides et modèles partagés.

Néanmoins, la convergence des pratiques était freinée par les facteurs suivants :

- il n'existait pas de système souple de partage de documents entre les différents sites ;
- sur le plan national, les dispositions du système de management n'étaient pas suffisamment matures et stabilisées en 2011 pour pouvoir porter des dispositions applicables aux laboratoires ;
- dans la mesure où les accréditations des laboratoires sont accordées par site, sur la base d'évaluations spécifiques, l'intérêt de partager des dispositions n'était pas perçu comme un bénéfice. Par ailleurs la mise en commun (effectuée dans d'autres réseaux) a pu être considérée comme un risque compromettant l'accréditation de l'ensemble des sites en cas de non-conformité ;
- on peut souligner enfin la réticence au changement et la nécessité d'un investissement supplémentaire de la part des responsables qualité des sites qui avaient développé avec leurs équipes des systèmes de management éprouvés.

Début 2014, la situation était plus propice :

- le siège de l'Anses venait d'obtenir la certification ISO 9001, ce qui validait par la même son système qualité et ses

pratiques documentaires ;
- le système de gestion électronique des documents était en cours de réception pour le siège et ouvrait des possibilités de partage plus importantes entre sites ;
- des échanges avec le Comité français d'accréditation (Cofrac) nous encourageaient, non pas à viser un système de management commun pour un audit spécifique, mais plutôt à prévoir l'intervention d'un même évaluateur qualiticien sur un cycle d'évaluation, de façon à croiser les observations d'un site à l'autre.

Dès lors, le bénéfice de dispositions partagées devenait plus clair sur le périmètre commun à tous les sites : celui des outils du système de management.

Sept ateliers ont donc été créés pour définir des pratiques communes par thématique (dont les actions correctives et préventives). Ces ateliers ont été animés en priorité par un responsable qualité d'un laboratoire. Des réunions d'échange et des points d'avancement réguliers avec le réseau des responsables qualité ont été planifiés. Le nom du projet d'ensemble a été défini à l'issue d'un concours : PETAL, pour Partage Et Transversalité pour l'Accréditation des Laboratoires. Dès le départ, il a été convenu que chaque livrable devait tenir compte des spécificités des sites pour permettre des adaptations, sans bien sûr transiger sur la conformité aux référentiels applicables.

3 Référentiels applicables

La lecture des différentes normes et référentiels opposables aux activités de l'agence montre que les orientations de leurs exigences en matière de traitement des non-conformités sont proches. Parfois, elles s'appuient l'une sur l'autre. Ainsi, le paragraphe "Système de management de la qualité de l'expertise" de la norme NF-X 50-110 [6] indique que "*Les exigences sont réputées satisfaites si l'organisme d'expertise dispose d'un système de management de la qualité incluant des activités d'expertise conforme à la norme NF EN ISO 9001:2000 ou s'il fait partie d'une entité qui [...] réalise par ailleurs des essais ou des étalonnages et répond aux exigences de la norme NF EN ISO/CEI 17025*".

Cette première étude a permis de considérer que la pluralité ou multiplicité des référentiels applicables ne serait pas un frein à ce projet d'harmonisation des pratiques.

Le tableau 1 liste exhaustivement les textes de référence sur lesquels s'appuie le projet. Il servira de référence pour son audit lors de sa validation, avant le déploiement.

Périmètre	Référentiel	
Laboratoires	NF EN ISO/CEI 17025 [1]	**4.8.** Réclamations **4.9.** Maîtrise des travaux [...] non conformes **4.11.** Actions correctives **4.12.** Actions préventives
	NF EN ISO/CEI 17025 [2]	**7.9.** Réclamations **7.10.** Travaux non conformes **8.5.** Actions à mettre en œuvre face aux risques et opportunités **8.6.** Amélioration **8.7.** Actions correctives
	NF EN ISO/CEI 17043 [3]	**5.8.** Réclamations et recours **5.9.** Maîtrise des travaux non conformes **5.11.** Actions correctives **5.12.** Actions préventives
	LAB REF 02 [8]	**8.** Eléments de lecture de la norme NF EN ISO/CEI 17025
	FD ISO 10006 [7]	**4.1.4.** Processus de management de projet **7.2.4.** Management des modifications **8.1.** Processus relatifs à l'amélioration
	NF EN ISO 9001 [3]	**0.3.3.** Approche par les risques **8.7.** Maîtrise des éléments de sortie non conformes **10.2.** Non-conformité et action corrective
Dir. Générale Pdts règlementés Expertise	NF EN ISO/CEI 17020 [5]	**7.5.** Réclamations et appels **8.7.** Actions correctives (Option A) **8.8.** Actions préventives (Option A)
	NF X 50-110 [6]	**8.3.** Maîtrise du produit de l'expertise non conforme **8.4.1.** Actions correctives **8.4.2.** Actions préventives

Tableau 1: Gestion des non conformités dans les référentiels opposables de l'Agence

4 Dispositions existantes

4.1 Vocabulaire

L'étude des dispositions existantes présentée dans le tableau 2 a permis de constater que le vocabulaire utilisé dans le système de management de la qualité de chacune des entités était globalement homogène. Ce constat était prévisible puisque les référentiels appliqués sont eux-mêmes complémentaires.

Les différences qui ont été notées concernaient en fait plus spécifiquement les pratiques que le vocabulaire. Par exemple, le système de management de la qualité du siège et des entités certifiées associées au siège préconise la mise en place d'actions curatives en deux temps :

1. une ou plusieurs action(s) décidée(s) et mise(s) en place par les agents opérationnels, sans validation documentée. On parle d'action(s) à chaud.

2. une ou plusieurs action(s) curative(s) décidée(s) et validée(s) par le niveau de responsabilité approbateur de l'exigence non-respectée.

Entité(s)	Situations non-conformes aux dispositions ou référentiels			Gestion des situations
Entité de Fougère	Non-conformité	Dérogation	Réclamation	Actions : . Immédiate . Corrective
Entités de Nancy ***Hydrologie*** **Niort Lyon**	Non-conformité	Dérogation	Réclamation	Actions : . Curative . Corrective . Préventive
Entité de Sophia Antipolis	Non-conformité	Dérogation	Réclamation	Actions : . Immédiate . Corrective
Entités de La Réunion Montpellier	Non-conformité	Dérogation	Réclamation	Actions : . Curative . Corrective . Préventive
Entité de Clermont Ferrand	Non-conformité	Dérogation	Réclamation	Actions : . Corrective immédiate . Corrective . Préventive
Dir. générale et entités certifiées associées	Ecart	Dérogation	Réclamation	Actions : . A chaud . Curative . Corrective . Préventive
Entité de Nancy ***Santé des végétaux***	Ecart	Dérogation	Réclamation	Actions : . Curative . Corrective . Préventive
Entités de Maisons Alfort Boulogne sur Mer Dozulé	Ecart Anomalie	Ecart Dérogation	Ecart Réclamation	Actions : . Immédiate . Corrective . Préventive
Entité de Nancy ***Rage et Faune sauvage***	Anomalie	Dérogation	Réclamation	Actions : . Curative . Corrective Proposition d'amélioration
Entité de Rennes	Anomalie Non-conformité audit	Dérogation	Réclamation	Correction Actions : . Corrective . Préventive
Entité d'Angers	Anomalie Non-conformité audit	Dérogation	Réclamation	Actions : . Curative . Corrective . Préventive
Entité de Ploufragan	Non-conformité Ecart audit	Dérogation	Réclamation	Actions : . Curative . Corrective . Préventive Fiche progrès

Tableau 2 : Vocabulaire utilisé par entité

4.2 Responsabilités

Les responsabilités et le niveau d'intervention de chaque agent peut varier d'une entité à une autre car chacune s'est adaptée à son organisation propre et à la taille de son effectif (de 6 à 200 agents). Chaque laboratoire possède un référentiel qualité qui répond aux exigences de la norme Afnor NF EN ISO/CEI 17025 [1]/[2]. La fonction responsable de chaque périmètre accrédité est donc la même, en la personne du responsable technique des activités. Dans la majeure partie des entités laboratoires, c'est lui qui est responsable de la mise en place des actions et qui valide le traitement technique d'une situation non conforme aux dispositions. Cependant, chaque laboratoire a adopté sa propre politique concernant le traitement des non-conformités : pour certains c'est le responsable technique qui décrit et valide les actions mises en place. Pour d'autres la personne qui enregistre la non-conformité décrit les actions (proposition) avant validation éventuelle du responsable technique. Cette responsabilité technique est confiée au chef d'unité (petites entités), à un chef d'équipe (entité moyenne possédant plusieurs équipes dans une même unité) ou à un chargé de projet scientifique (responsable d'une thématique et généralement d'un mandat de référence associé à cette thématique). Au niveau du siège de l'Anses et dans ses entités certifiées NF EN ISO/CEI 9001 [3], ces responsabilités incombent aux directeurs (approbateurs des dispositions non respectées). Les dispositions à déployer doivent donc avoir une certaine souplesse au niveau des responsabilités.

4.3 Processus

Les processus (au sens de flux ou séquences d'activités) de gestion des produits et situations non-conformes initialement déployés dans les différentes entités possèdent de nombreuses similarités. Néanmoins, les exigences du référentiel des laboratoires possèdent des spécificités non applicables dans les entités certifiées, comme la gestion de la marque Cofrac. La forme harmonisée à développer doit donc prendre en compte le caractère non applicable d'un certain nombre d'exigences d'une entité par rapport à une autre. Ainsi, le dispositif doit avoir un nombre, si possible limité, de champs dont la valeur n'est pas systématiquement exploitée.

5 Développement du projet

5.1 Choix du vocabulaire et description du processus

Sur la base du vocabulaire des différents systèmes qualité des entités (tableau 2) et des référentiels opposables dans chacune (tableau 1), un vocabulaire commun a été élaboré pour définir un nom à chaque processus et pour définir les différentes étapes de leur traitement. Ces étapes ont été définies principalement à partir des dispositions mais aussi des référentiels en vigueur. Les processus de réclamation et de non-conformité relevé lors des audits internes sont intégrés dans un seul processus permettant la traçabilité des non-conformités. La gestion est ainsi allégée pour plusieurs entités. Leur origine est consignée dans un champ permettant de caractériser chaque non-conformité, parmi les choix d'une liste déroulante.

En ce qui concerne les actions mises en place, le groupe de travail a proposé de créer deux processus de gestion des actions. Un processus permettant de caractériser les actions dites "*curative*" et les actions dites "*correctives*". Son paramétrage informatique permet de mesurer l'efficacité de chaque action corrective conformément aux exigences des référentiels. Un second processus nommé "Plan d'amélioration" permet de regrouper un ensemble d'actions *correctives* dont chacune est enregistrée sous la même forme qu'une action *curative*. L'efficacité de l'ensemble des actions peut ainsi être mesurée une seule fois, au niveau du plan d'amélioration.
La notion d'action *préventive* n'étant plus abordé dans les référentiels normatifs révisés, il a été décidé de traiter les améliorations spontanées au travers d'un processus où toute suggestion pourra être décrite et associé à des actions correctives (ou un plan d'amélioration).
Les processus de non-conformité et de dérogation ont été construits sous la même forme. L'objectif est de faciliter l'adaptation des agents aux différents formulaires.
Un logigramme des étapes principales a été construit pour chaque processus et présenté aux responsables qualité des entités afin d'obtenir un consensus. L'exemple du traitement des non-conformités et des dérogations est présenté en figure 1.

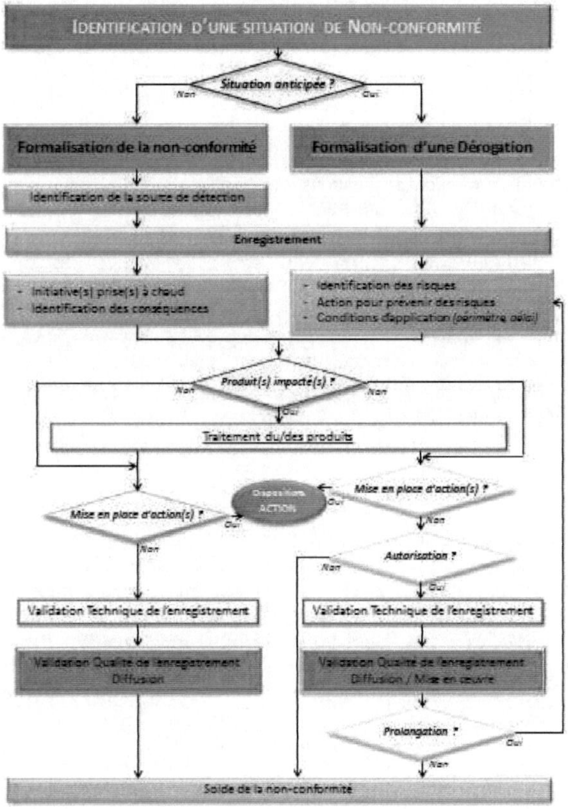

Figure 1 : Processus Non-conformités et Dérogations

5.2 Responsabilités

Deux niveaux de responsabilité ont été définis. Le premier est celui de la validation globale de l'enregistrement attribué aux agents en charge du management de la qualité du périmètre concerné par l'enregistrement. Ce niveau sert, d'une part, à valider la complétude et l'exactitude des informations décrites et caractérisées. D'autre part, il permet de s'assurer que les dispositions en vigueur sont bien respectées pour limiter la prise de décisions contradictoires avec d'autres processus du système de management de la qualité. Le second niveau est celui de la validation technique en rapport avec le cœur de métier concerné.
Pour que les dispositions soient applicables dans toutes les entités, quelle que soit leur organisation, les agents en charge de ces validations sont identifiés par leur nom (et non leur fonction) lors de l'enregistrement. En amont, chaque entité met à la disposition un récapitulatif des fonctions chargées de ces validations sur son périmètre. Les organigrammes en vigueur permettent en outre d'identifier chaque agent par rapport à ses fonctions.

5.3 Développement d'un outil dématérialisé

En 2014, l'Anses a déployé un outil de Gestion Electronique des Documents (GED) qui permet également de gérer les enregistrements liés au management de la qualité au moyen d'un module appelé Process, avec un circuit de signature électronique associé à des étapes clefs définies. Cette GED n'a pas de solution commerciale qui corresponde aux besoins de l'Anses. Cependant, l'utilisateur est libre de paramétrer selon ses propres besoins.
Le siège et les entités certifiées associées utilisent déjà cette GED Process depuis 2015 pour la gestion des non-conformités. Ce déploiement a servi de base pour dématérialiser les différents processus définis.
Les référentiels normatifs opposables dans les entités et principalement la norme NF EN ISO/CEI 17025 [1]/[2] imposent une validation des outils informatiques critiques. Dans le cas de ce projet, cette exigence est une opportunité pour vérifier indirectement la robustesse des dispositions sur chaque périmètre.

5.4 Validation des dispositions

Les processus définis ont été présentés et discutés avec les responsables qualité (RQ) des entités de l'Agence. Les désidératas de chacun ont été confrontés aux référentiels normatifs et pris en compte en fonction des possibilités de l'outil développé.
Dans un premier temps, l'outil GED Process a été paramétré par les chargés du projet. Puis il a été amélioré et validé informatiquement par un groupe de travail composé de RQ représentant l'ensemble des types d'organisations de l'Agence : 3 RQ d'entités certifiées 9001, 1 RQ d'un laboratoire de plus de 200 agents, 2 RQ de laboratoires de taille moyenne (entre 30 et 50 agents) et 1 RQ d'un laboratoire de petite taille (12 agents).

6 Déploiement du projet

Le déploiement des dispositions issues des travaux PETAL a été lancé dans les entités des RQ du groupe de validation de l'application puis dans chaque entité selon un calendrier laissé libre. Chaque entité devant planifier la période de déploiement comme suit :

- validation des performances de l'outil à l'échelle de l'entité ;
- enregistrement des fonctions responsables des processus au travers d'un formulaire d'enregistrement associé à la procédure générale de l'agence ;
- formation des agents à l'outil.

7 Discussion

Ce projet permet de répondre à plusieurs objectifs de la démarche PETAL. Il prend en compte l'ensemble des activités et référentiels (internes ou normatifs) de l'agence dans un seul outil intégré. Cette harmonisation des pratiques permet de consigner aisément des enregistrements impactant plusieurs entités et domaines. Ce projet est né d'un consensus de l'ensemble des entités et les perspectives d'amélioration suivent aussi ce principe d'unanimité. Ainsi, les dispositions sont portées et argumentées par un groupe d'experts dans le domaine du management de la qualité et au plus près du terrain. Enfin, le projet a validé un outil informatique connu et à la portée de tous les agents. Au-delà de cette valorisation, la connaissance de cet outil permet une adaptation plus rapide. Son développement a été simplifié puisque la base de données utilisée a été entièrement reprise (comptes utilisateur, thèmes de caractérisation des sujets, bibliothèque des référentiels…).

Plusieurs limites ont été néanmoins constatées par le groupe de travail en charge de la validation de l'application :

La dématérialisation de ces processus est susceptible d'entraîner des délais de gestion plus longs en particulier dans les structures à faible effectif. Une évaluation est prévue après une année d'utilisation.

- Dans quelques entités, un accompagnement des agents a été proposé pour adapter les équipes à ce nouveau vocabulaire ce qui a permis de refaire un point sur la terminologie, les définitions et les attentes exigées par les référentiels.
- Les deux possibilités d'enregistrement des actions correctives (un formulaire par action corrective ou bien un plan d'action d'amélioration) peuvent rendre l'exploitation des indicateurs difficile. C'est la raison pour laquelle il a été conseillé d'utiliser une seule option par entité.

La réussite d'une telle démarche dépend de la volonté « politique » de mutualiser. Elle doit être partagée par tous, pour que le déploiement ait de bonnes chances d'être réalisé dans un temps raisonnable. Il est par ailleurs essentiel d'obtenir l'adhésion des équipes, de les former, de les écouter en amont, et de faire preuve de pédagogie pour obtenir leur entière implication. Enfin, la planification du projet doit être irréprochable. Il est indispensable de prendre le temps et de faire preuve de pragmatisme (commencer par des concepts simples).

8 Conclusion

Le déploiement de ces dispositions est un levier d'amélioration, d'harmonisation et de cohérence sur l'ensemble du périmètre de l'agence. Par ailleurs cette mutualisation des supports permet de gagner en efficacité de traitement, par exemple dans le cas des non-conformités multi entités ou multi-sites.

Ce projet ouvre des perspectives sur de nouveaux objectifs qui permettront de faire face aux contraintes concernant notamment les effectifs. Le suivi des indicateurs clefs associés aux processus de non-conformité pourra par exemple être effectué plus aisément au travers d'extractions des données consignées dans l'application.

Cette expérience met en évidence la nécessité d'anticiper ce mode d'organisation par l'analyse des divergences entre les différentes entités : d'effectif, de domaine, de référentiel et enfin de maturité de leur propre système de management de la qualité. Cette analyse permet de fixer des objectifs quant aux livrables de ce type de projet qui doivent faire preuve d'adaptabilité.

Références

1. Norme Afnor NF EN ISO/CEI 17025 - Exigences générales concernant la compétence des laboratoires d'étalonnages et d'essais - Mai 2005
2. Norme Afnor NF EN ISO/CEI 17025 - Exigences générales concernant la compétence des laboratoires d'étalonnages et d'essais - Version projet 2017
3. Norme Afnor NF EN ISO 9001 - Systèmes de management de la qualité - Exigences - Octobre 2015
4. Norme Afnor NF EN ISO/CEI 17043 - Evaluation de la conformité - Exigences générales concernant les essais d'aptitude - Avril 2010
5. Norme Afnor NF EN ISO/CEI 17020 - Évaluation de la conformité - Exigences pour le fonctionnement de différents types d'organismes procédant à l'inspection - Octobre 2010
6. Norme Afnor NF X 50-110 - Qualité en expertise - Prescriptions générales de compétence pour une expertise - Mai 2003
7. Fascicule de documentation Afnor FD ISO 10006 - Systèmes de management de la qualité - Lignes directrices pour le management de la qualité dans les projets - Janvier 2005
8. Document de référence Cofrac LAB REF 02 - Exigences pour l'accréditation des laboratoires selon la norme NF EN ISO/CEI 17025 - Révision 10

Facteurs influençant la pérennisation de la démarche qualité dans les établissements de soins de santé primaire de la ville de Fès, Maroc

M. Hmidani[1], S. Maniar[2], B. Zaadoud[3], A. Charki[4], A. El Ouali Lalami[1*]

1- Institut Supérieur des Professions Infirmières et Techniques de Santé de Fès. Hôpital El Ghassani, Fès 30000, Maroc.
2- Service de la Santé publique, Direction Régionale de la Santé Fès-Meknès, Hôpital El Ghassani, Fès 30000, Maroc.
3- Cellule Préfectorale d'Epidémiologie, Délégation Médicale de My Yacoub, Hôpital Ibn EL Khatib, Fès 30000, Maroc.
4- Institut des Sciences et Techniques de l'Ingénieur d'Angers – Université de Angers, France.

* Correspondant auteur email : eloualilalami@yahoo.fr

Résumé

La démarche qualité telle qu'elle a été implantée depuis l'année 2000 au niveau des sites pilote de la Préfecture Médicale de Fès, avait comme but de se généraliser à tous les établissements de soins de santé primaire (ESSP). Ceci est loin d'être atteinte à l'heure actuelle.

L'objectif de cette étude, réalisée pour la première fois au centre du Maroc, a été de décrire les facteurs qui ont influencé l'implantation et la pérennisation de la démarche qualité dans les ESSP de la ville de Fès située au centre du Maroc. Pour cela, nous avons réalisé une enquête auprès des responsables des ESSP de la ville de Fès. Nous avons également mené des entretiens avec les responsables du Service du Réseau des Etablissements de Santé qui gère les ESSP.

Sur les 36 ESSP touchés par la formation, le cycle qualité n'a pu être initié que dans 17 ESSP et n'a pu être achevé que dans 10 ESSP. Actuellement cette démarche a été abandonnée par toutes les équipes. L'analyse des résultats a révélé qu'il y a plusieurs facteurs qui ont entravé l'implantation et la pérennisation de la démarche qualité, dans le réseau ambulatoire de la préfecture de Fès.

Concernant les facteurs liés à l'environnement interne propice, nous avons enregistré l'insuffisance d'engagement des responsables du service central, l'insuffisance dans l'accompagnement, le suivi et la communication des responsables hiérarchiques de l'ensemble des ESSP impliqués dans notre étude. De même, l'insuffisance des ressources humaines et la surcharge du travail découragent les responsables des ESSP, à initier, à achever et à assurer la continuité du cycle d'amélioration de la qualité.

Concernant les fonctions de soutien, nous avons constaté que la supervision, la facilitation, la motivation et la récompense sont des facteurs déterminants qui ont fait défaut dans le contexte de cette étude.

Quant à l'organisation pour la qualité, cette étude a dévoilé aussi une insuffisance de la coordination des actions d'amélioration de qualité entre les acteurs opérationnels et de pilotage.

Mots clés : Démarche qualité, Facteurs de Pérennisation, Cycle d'amélioration de la qualité, Etablissements de soins de santé primaire, Préfecture médicale de Fès, Maroc.

1 Introduction

Historiquement, les démarches qualité se sont développées au début dans les entreprises industrielles. Par la suite, elles ont conquis les organisations non industrielles notamment le secteur de la santé [1].
Au Maroc, avec l'avènement des réformes politiques, institutionnelles, économiques et sociales engagées depuis les années 90 le contexte est devenu plus favorable pour l'introduction d'une approche qualité structurée dans les unités de soins [2]. Il s'agit notamment des audits cliniques, de l'approche d'équipe pour la résolution de problème, de l'élaboration des standards et des normes dans le cadre des différents programmes nationaux de santé publique... Ainsi en 1999, le Ministère de la Santé (MS) a développé un programme national d'assurance qualité (PNAQ), qui a constitué le cadre de référence du MS pour institutionnaliser l'assurance qualité à tous les niveaux du système de santé [2].
La région de Fès-Meknès est parmi les régions pionnières dans le domaine de la qualité. En effet, depuis la fin des années 90, un nombre important de personnes ont été formés en matière de démarches principes et outils qualité et des cercles de qualité (CQ) ont été constitués dans pratiquement tous les établissements de soins de santé primaire (ESSP). Cependant, sept ans après, cette démarche qualité (DQ) n'a pu être implantée que dans un nombre restreint d'ESSP.
Ces difficultés ont été même rencontrées dans des pays développés. En effet, la majorité des CQ, implantés aux établissements de santé au Canada ont rencontré des difficultés [3] et certains ont cessé leurs activités même avant de récolter des bénéfices. Le degré insuffisant d'implication des dirigeants, l'ambiguïté qui entoure leurs motivations et le contexte organisationnel à l'intérieur duquel ils exercent leurs fonctions sont autant de facteurs qui peuvent être incriminés [4].
L'implantation des CQ dans les établissements de santé exige le respect de plusieurs phases : allant d'une étude préalable, jusqu'à la mise en œuvre d'un plan d'action du CQ sans autant négliger les instruments de suivi et d'évaluation [5]. Elle demande également la convergence des efforts vers un but commun, des activités qui s'inspirent d'un processus décisionnel, l'implication de tous les niveaux hiérarchiques dans le maintien des points d'excellence et dans la correction des lacunes ainsi que l'identification des responsabilités des intervenants [6].
Plusieurs facteurs d'ordre organisationnels, culturels, économiques et environnementaux déterminent le succès ou l'échec des CQ [7]. Les dysfonctions et les obstacles qui influencent des CQ, n'apparaissent pas dans la majorité des cas, pendant la phase d'implantation, mais ils surviennent, au cours de la phase de la pérennisation [6]. Ces obstacles peuvent être classes en deux catégories : « barrière visible et invisibles ». Le première d'ordre technique et opérationnel et le deuxième est de nature stratégique et relationnel [8].
Les facteurs essentiels qui conditionnent le succès et la pérennisation des CQ peuvent aussi être regroupés en quatre catégories : stratégiques, techniques, structurelles et culturelles [9]. Une autre catégorie dite « réglementaire » a été ajoutée par Tabuteau [10] du fait que l'établissement de santé se gère autrement qu'une entreprise. De même, ils peuvent être classé en trois dimensions :1) celle liée à l'environnement interne propice, 2) celle liée à l'organisation pour la qualité et 3) celle liée aux fonctions de soutien [11].
C'est dans ce cadre qu'il nous a parut intéressant et nécessaire de s'interroger sur les éventuels facteurs qui ont influencé la pérennisation de la (DQ) dans les ESSP au niveau de la ville de Fès. Cette étude a été réalisée pour la première fois au centre du Maroc.

2 Matériel et Méthodes

Type d'étude

Il s'agit d'une étude descriptive rétrospective.

Milieu de l'étude

Cette étude s'est déroulée au niveau de la ville de Fès située au centre du Maroc et qui abrite 1079000 habitants. La ville comptait, durant la période d'étude, 36 ESSP. Chaque ESSP est géré par un médecin chef et un infirmier chef. Les ESSP sont gérés et encadrés par le Service des Réseaux d'Etablissements de Santé (SRES).

Population cible

Il est inclut dans cette étude une population rassemblant deux groupes d'acteurs, à savoirs: l'ensemble des gestionnaires (médecin et infirmiers chefs) des ESSP qui sont au nombre de 72 et les responsables du SRES.

Méthodes et instruments de collecte et analyses des données

Pour les médecins et infirmiers chefs des ESSP, nous avons réalisé une enquête via un questionnaire auto administré qui comportait des questions « fermées » et des questions « ouvertes ». Toutes les questions découlent du cadre de référence de l'étude.

Chez les responsables du SRES, nous avons mené des entrevus semi directives moyennant une grille d'entretien comportant les grands axes à discuter en relation avec la question de recherche.

Les données collectées ont été traitées et analysées à l'aide des logiciels Epi info (version 3.3.2 2005) et Microsoft office Excel 2007.

3 Résultats et discussion

L'ensemble des 36 ESSP ont été inclus dans notre étude. Sur les 72 questionnaires distribués, nous avons récupéré 71, soit environ 99% de répondant. 65% des répondants ont une ancienneté au poste supérieur à 3 ans.

Au niveau du SRES nous avons inclus 5 personnes impliquées directement dans la mise en place et la pérennisation du cycle qualités à savoir le médecin chef, le major et 3 facilitateurs qualité.

Implantation des CQ

Sur les 36 ESSP formé en DQ, 53% des ESSP n'ont pas pu initier le CQ. De plus, 20% des ESSP ont commencé un cycle mais n'ont pas put l'achevé. Pour le reste, 6 ESSP ont bouclé un seul CQ soit 16%, 2 ESSP ont complété deux CQ (6%), 1 ESSP a pu boucler 3 CQ (3%) et 1 ESSP a pu achever 4 CQ (3%) (Figure 1). Actuellement, tous les ESSP ont abandonné cette approche.

Plusieurs facteurs pourraient expliquer la difficulté d'initiation et de pérennisation de cette démarche au niveau des établissements de santé. Selon une étude initiée à l'Hôpital des Spécialités de la ville de Rabat au Maroc, les causes de non pérennisation du AQ qui ont été soulevées par les participants sont: le manque de la vision partagée de la qualité, l'insuffisance de l'implication de les responsables, l'échec de la coordination entre les structures et le non-contrôle de la méthode du projet de qualité [12].

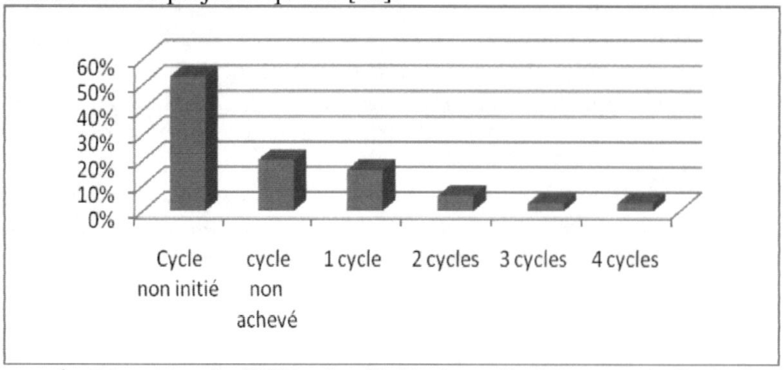

Figure 1 : Répartition des ESSP selon l'initiation et l'achèvement du Cycle Qualité

Formation des gestionnaires des ESSP en démarche qualité

Comme le montre la figure 2, 65% des participants à l'étude ont bénéficié d'une formation sur la qualité. Par contre les responsables du SRES, ont affirmé que la formation a été assurée à tout le personnel des ESSP relevant de la préfecture de Fès. Les 35% du personnel de santé non formés sont probablement nouvellement affectés au niveau de la ville de Fès.

La formation en DQ, constitue un facteur déterminant dans l'implantation et dans la pérennisation de la démarche qualité. Cependant, dans le contexte de notre étude, la formation ne se semble pas faire défaut, puisqu'un effort important en matière de formation a été déployé comme le prouve nos résultats. Ceci dit, nous pouvons nous interroger sur la qualité de cette formation. En effet, la mise en œuvre pérenne de la DQ, nécessite trois types de formation à savoir : (a) les compétences de bases en DQ, (b) l'encadrement du personnel lors de la réalisation des activités, et (c) la surveillance et la supervision des efforts du personnel en matière de DQ [11].

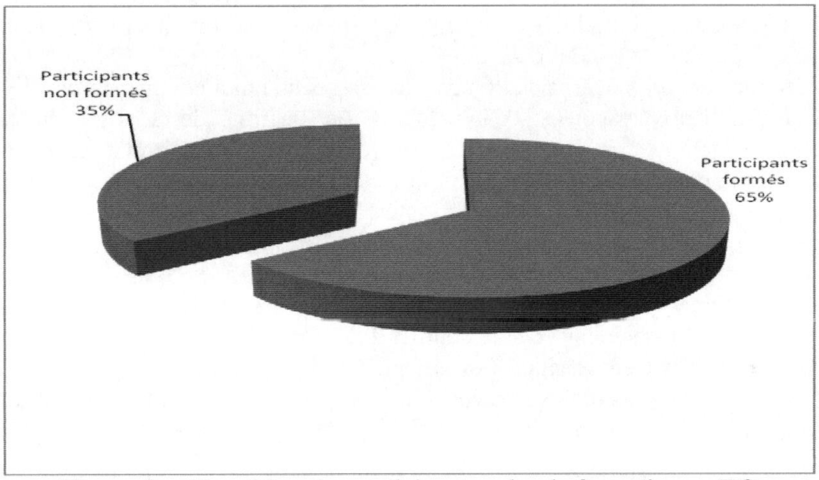

Figure 2 : Répartition des participants selon la formation en DQ

Supervision, suivi et évaluation des équipe qualité

Comme le montre la figure 3, 67% des ESSP qui ont initiés le CQ ont déclaré qu'ils n'ont pas fait l'objet d'une supervision, et qu'ils n'ont pas été convoqués par leurs supérieurs pour des réunions d'échange, du suivi et d'évaluation. Cela pourrait être une source de démotivation pour les équipes et ainsi constituer un facteur, dans le contexte de cette étude, pouvant entraver la pérennisation du CQ.

Ceci est compatible avec ce qui a été rapporté par certains auteurs [11, 13] qui ont affirmé que l'amélioration continue de qualité nécessite la surveillance, la supervision, le suivi du respect des normes et la mesure des réalisations en matière de la qualité à tous les niveaux. De même une enquête [14] réalisée par le centre national de la recherche scientifique français dans douze établissements de soins portant sur la perception de la qualité chez les professionnels des établissements de santé a conclu en la nécessité de favoriser une culture de l'évaluation qualité chez ces professionnels aussi bien au niveau des indicateurs mis en place qu'au niveau de la démarche qualité elle-même. Cela pour pouvoir maintenir les dynamiques parvenues des actions engagées au nom de la qualité.

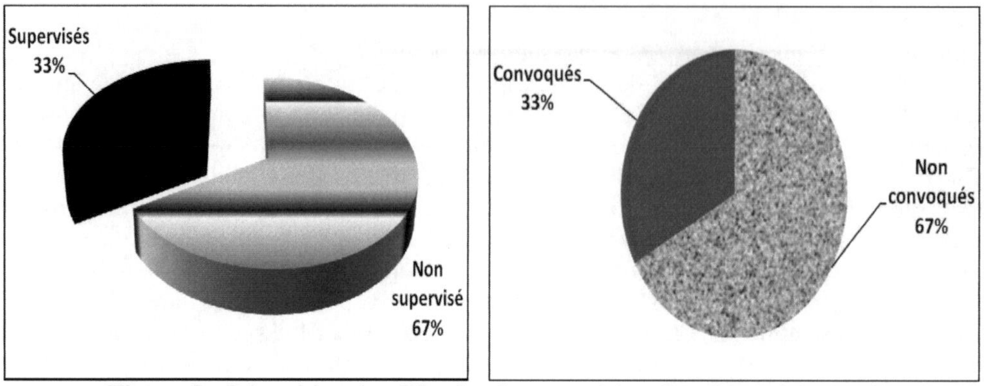

Figure 3 : Répartition des CS selon la supervision, le suivi et l'évaluation

Accompagnement (soutien et facilitation) par les responsables de SRES

56% des répondants ont déclaré qu'ils n'ont pas été accompagnés par leur responsable hiérarchique pendant la conduite du CQ (Figure 4).

Ce résultat ne concorde que partiellement avec tous ce qui a été avancé par les interviewés. En effet, les deux responsables de SRES ont affirmé le soutien, la facilitation et l'accompagnement systématique des équipes des CQ et la coordination avec les référents qualité pour les encadrer et les soutenir. Cependant, deux référents qualité sur trois ont signalé que leur soutien et facilitation n'est pas systématique, mais il est déclenché sous la demande de l'équipe de CQ.

Sachant que la pérennisation de DQ est difficile â obtenir, si les gestionnaires n'apportent pas un accompagnement et un encadrement solide à tous les niveaux. Cela pourrait être fait en démontrant leur attachement et leur soutien à une culture de qualité et aux personnes qui participent aux activités d'amélioration de qualité [15] et [12]. Nous pouvons considérer que l'insuffisance dans l'accompagnement est un facteur qui a influencé négativement la pérennisation de la DQ.

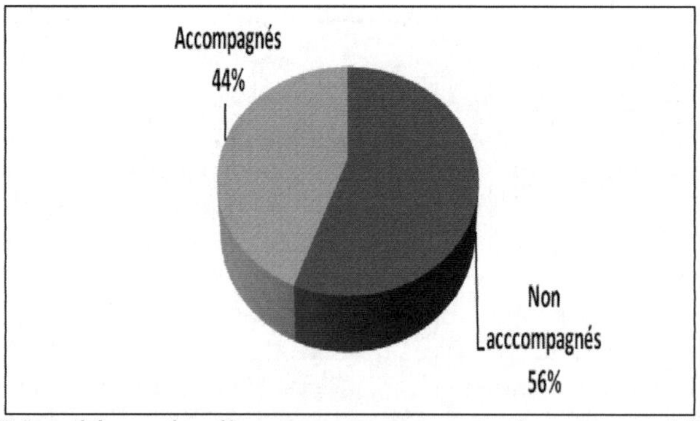

Figure 4 : Répartition selon l'accompagnement par les responsables de SRES

Disponibilité des ressources humaines

77% des responsables affirment ne pas disposer des ressources nécessaires pour effectuer les activités de la DQ (Figure 5). Ce constat a été confirmé par les responsables du SRES.

L'insuffisance des ressources humaines et la surcharge du travail sont deux facteurs qui peuvent freiner la pérennisation et le développement continu de CQ. En effet, l'insuffisance des ressources, surtout humains, retentit sur la motivation du professionnel pour exécuter les activités de la DQ [11] [6]. Ceci dit, l'insuffisance des ressources humaine est un problème national qui est parfois facilement avancé pour justifier certaines résistances au changement.

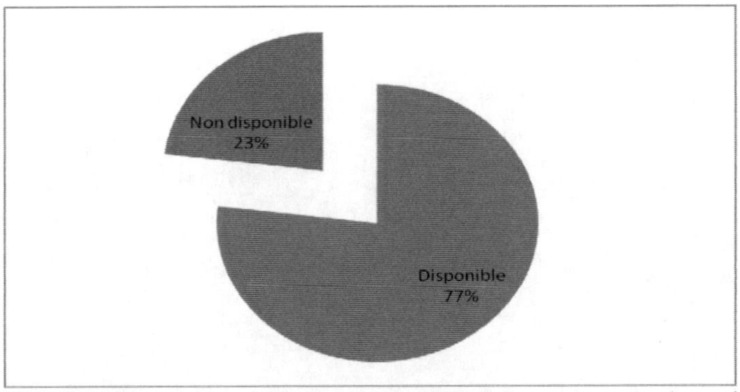

Figure 5 : Répartition selon la disponibilité des ressources humaine

Récompense des efforts qualité

81% des répondants appartenant aux ESSP où le CQ a été initié, déclarent qu'ils n'ont pas été récompensés pour leurs efforts en matière d'amélioration de qualité (Figure 6). De même, les responsables du SRES ont été tous accords que le manque de récompense est l'un des facteurs clés qui a entravé la pérennisation de la DQ dans les établissements de soins de santé primaire du Fès.

Le manque d'incitation démotive le personnel qui voit dans la démarche qualité une surcharge du travail [16]. Ainsi, la récompense symbolique ou matérielle, des équipes et des personnes qui réservent une partie de leurs temps et de leur effort à la DQ, pourrait jouer un rôle déterminant pour sa pérennisation au niveau des établissements sanitaire [11]. Dans le contexte de cette étude, cela montre que la non récompense des efforts qualité ont un impact non négligeable sur la non pérennisation de CQ.

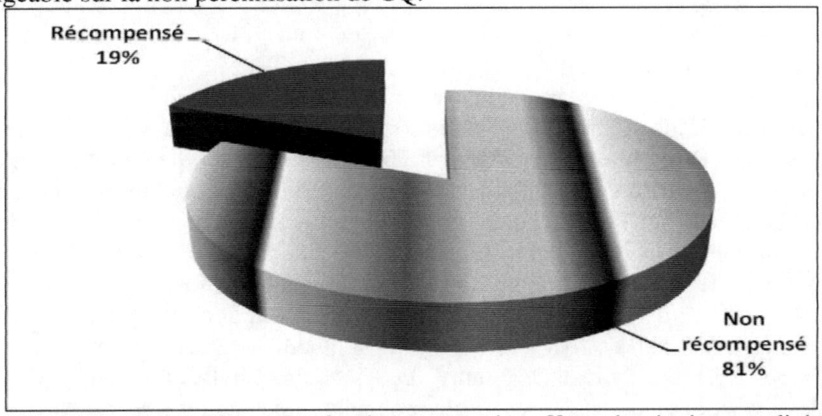

Figure 6 : Répartition selon la récompense des efforts des équipes qualité

Causes de non achèvement et pérennisation de DQ

Comme le montre la figure 7, les causes de non achèvement et de non pérennisation de la démarche qualité le plus fréquemment citées par les participants sont : la surcharge du travail (82%) et l'insuffisance des ressources humaines (73%). La démotivation, le manque d'esprit de volontariat et l'appui de chefs hiérarchiques ainsi que leur accompagnement sont citées par environ le un tiers des participants.

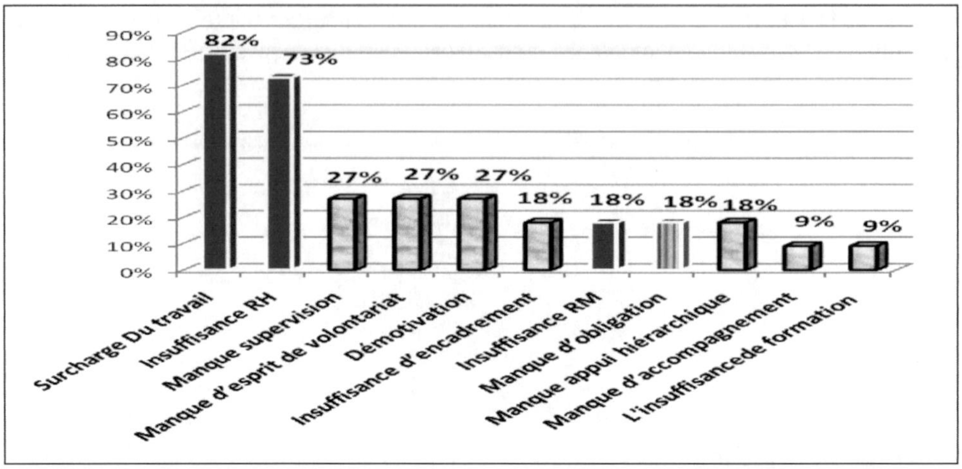

Figure 7 : Répartition selon les causes de non achèvement et pérennisation de DQ

Les résultats de l'entretien semi structuré avec les responsables de SRES confirment ce constat puisque ils ont précisé que les causes influençant négativement la pérennisation du CQ au niveau de réseau ambulatoire se présentent comme suit : l'insuffisance des ressources humaines et la surcharge du travail ainsi que le manque de la motivation à travers la récompense matérielle ou symbolique. La reconnaissance à travers la motivation pourrait rendre hommage aux équipes qualité et reconnaître leurs efforts en matière d'amélioration de qualité.

Les responsables de SRES ont noté également que la partialité et la subjectivité des auditeurs dans le premier prix du concours national qualité a démotivé complètement les équipes qui ont participé dans cette compétition nationale.

En outre, tous les interviewes ont souligné que l'insuffisance de la coordination entre les différents acteurs de cette démarche, la non implication et le non engagement des responsables au niveau du service central ont joué un rôle déterminant dans la non pérennisation de la DQ dans le milieu de cette étude.

Ce résultat est en accord avec une étude réalisée au Maroc au niveau de l'Hôpital des Spécialités de la ville de Rabat, qui a montré que le manque de la vision partagée de la qualité, l'insuffisance d'implication des responsables, la défaillance de coordination entre les structures et la non-maitrise de la méthode de la gestion de projet qualité, sont des causes de la non-pérennisation de la DQ [12].

De même, plusieurs auteurs [17, 11, 5, 18] ont affirmé que la réussite d'une politique d'amélioration continue de la qualité au sein des établissements de santé nécessite l'engagement explicite des responsables institutionnel et l'implication de tous les niveaux hiérarchiques. L'orientation des responsables pour la qualité est décisive pour dépasser deux types d'entraves : celui des résistances individuelles et structurelles au changement et celui d'éventuelles réactions de défense professionnelle quelquefois rencontrés dans les établissements de santé [19, 20].

Quant à leurs recommandations, les responsables de SRES ont tous suggéré la structuration de programme national d'assurance qualité, en lui affectant ses propres ressources humaines et financières, comme les autres programmes de santé.

4 Conclusion

Cette étude, a pu mettre en évidence certains facteurs affectant la capacité des ESSP de la préfecture de Fès à implanter et pérenniser la DQ, notamment: le manque d'engagement des responsables de service central, l'insuffisance dans l'accompagnement et l'appui de la hiérarchie, la surcharge du travail, le manque de récompense et l'insuffisance dans la coordination entre les acteurs opérationnels et de pilotage de la DQ.

La prise en considération des recommandations de cette étude sera d'un grand apport et d'un grand intérêt pour favoriser l'initiation et la durabilité de cycle d'amélioration de qualité. Cette étude s'est intéressée aux managers locaux, il serait intéressant de la généraliser auprès du tout le personnel impliqué dans les sites qualité.

Références

1. ANAES, (2002). Principes de mise en œuvre d'une démarche qualité en établissement de sante. Agence nationale d'accréditation et d'évaluation en santé, Paris.
2. Ministère de la santé, (2000). Plan nationale d'assurance qualité, Maroc.
3. Loseau. D, (2000). When the management of quality becomes a ritual. Inspiration and news bulletin for public managers, 15 (1).
4. Lozeau. D. « Les chemins tortueux de la gestion de la qualité dans les hôpitaux publics au Québec ». Gestion, Volume 27, N°3 Automne 2002. P 113-122.
5. Monteil, B, Périgord, M. et Raveleau, G (1985), les outils des cercles et l'amélioration de la qualité. Paris. Editions d'Organisation.
6. Grenier Raymond. « Le processus de gestion de la qualité des soins – services » ; Soins Cadres ; N° 43, Septembre 2002, pp : 29-34.
7. Bruno, F. (2008), Université du Québec à Trois-Rivières, Correspondance to Université du Québec à Trois-Rivières, C.P. 500, Trois-Rivières (Québec) G9A 5:7.
8. Jacqueyrie A. « Les obstacles à la qualité : barrières visibles et invisibles » ; actualité et dossier en santé publique ; N° 35 ; Juin 2001 ; pp : 42-43.
9. Shortell SM, Bennett CL, Byck GR. « Assessing the impact of continuous quality improvement on clinical practice : what it will take to accelerate progress » ; The Milbank Quarterly. Decembre 1998 ; Volume 76 ; Number 4 ; pp : 593–624.
10. Tabuteau B, Le management par la qualité dans les établissements de santé. Enjeux, freins et leviers d'action Thèse professionnelle pour l'obtention du Mastère spécialisé en Management par la Qualité, juillet 2008.
11. L.M. Frnco et al., Franco LM, Silimperi DR, Veldhuyzen van Zanten T *et al.*, Sustaining quality of health care: institutionalization of quality assurance. *QA Monograph Series*. Bethesda, MD: published for USAID by the Quality Assurance Project, 2002.
12. Salhi, N. (2014) Les facteurs qui entravent la pérennisation de la démarche qualité au niveau de l'hôpital des spécialités de Rabat. Mémoire de l'ENSP 2014. CONSULTBALE à l'URL : http://ensp.sante.gov.ma/CDS/Documents/Memoires/mem_2014/SALHI.pdf
13. Nicholas, D. (1999). Organisation de la qualité : option des programmes nationaux :
14. Claveranne J-P et col. « Les perceptions de la qualité chez les professionnels des établissements de santé » ; DHOS ; Ministère de la santé, de la famille et des personnes handicapées ; http://www.sante.gouv.fr/htm/dossiers/quali_profsante/qual_profes.pdf
15. Douguet F., Muñoz J. Les effets de l'accréditation et des mesures d'amélioration sur la qualité des soins et sur l'activité des personnels soignants. Paris : Direction de la recherche des études, de l'évaluation et des statistiques ; 2005, 172 p.
16. Boudin D., (2001). Accréditation et qualité des soins hospitaliers. .Les facteurs clés du succès d'une démarche qualité. Actual Doss Santé Publique, n° 35, p. 25-61.
17. Gautam KS. « A call for board leadership on quality in hospitals », Quality Management in Health Care. 2005 ; Volume 14 ; Number 1 ; pp : 18-30.

18. Weiner BJ, Shortell SM, Alexander J. « Promoting clinical involvement in hospital quality improvement efforts : the effects of top management, board, and physician leadership » ; Health Services Research 1997 ; Volume 32 ; Number 4 ; pp : 491-510.
19. Lucet B. "the place of the formation in the establishment of the culture quality"; Topicality and file in public health, N° 35, June 2001, p: 38-40.
20. Hassani E. 2010. Etude des facteurs influençant la reconduction du concours qualité: cas de la région du grand Casablanca. Mémoire INAS, 2010. Consultable à l'URL : http://www.sante.gov.ma/inas/mem/mem-2010/HASSANI%20MEHDI.pdf
21. D.R. Silimperi, L.M. Franco, T.V.V. Zanten and C. Macaulay, A framework for institutionalizing qualityAssurance. International Journal for Quality in Health Care. 14, 67–73 (2002)
22. J. Hermida, The road to institutionalizing quality assurance in Ecuador in an environment of health sector reform. Int J QualHealth Care; **11:** 447–450 (1999).
23. Project Report. Institutionalization of Quality Assurance. Bethesda, MD: published for USAID by the Quality Assurance Project, 2000.

Gestion du risque infectieux en en hémodialyse par la mise en place d'une démarche qualité : cas d'un centre hospitalier de la ville de Fès.

S. Berrada [1, 2, 3], T. G. Benjelloun [2, 4], L. Bennani [1, 4], B. Oumokhtar [4], L. A. El Ouali [1], H. F.Z. Squali [3], H.T. Sqalli[5]

(1) : Institut spécialisé des professions infirmières et techniques de santé de Fès. (2) : LRDEHM-Fès.
(3) : Laboratoire de neuroendocrinologie et environnement nutritionnel et climatique, faculté des sciences Dhar El Mahraz, Fès. (4) : Laboratoire de pathologie humaine, biomédecine et environnement, faculté de médecine, Fès.
(5) : Service de néphrologie, CHU Hassan II, Fès.

Résumé: Les infections nosocomiales constituent un problème de santé publique à l'échelle mondiale, avec des conséquences et des répercussions considérables, tant sur le plan individuel que sur le plan économique. Afin de réduire le risque infectieux au sein d'un centre d'hémodialyse hospitalier, nous avons mis en place une démarche qualité visant à apprécier et maitriser les éléments pouvant causer une contamination directe ou indirecte des patients tels que le respect des pratiques standards et spécifiques et la surveillance de la qualité de l'environnement des salles du traitement. Les objectifs ont consisté à évaluer les pratiques standards et spécifiques, et réaliser une surveillance microbiologique de l'environnement de ce centre.

Le 1èr volet réalisé pour évaluer le respect des précautions standards et spécifiques au centre, a reposé sur deux enquêtes descriptives observationnelles déroulées à un an d'intervalle, soit avant et après rénovation du centre. L'analyse globale a permis de montrer que le respect de ces pratiques est variable selon le type de mesures considérées, mais reste globalement insuffisant. Quant au second volet, nous avons effectué le contrôle de la qualité de l'air des salles d'hémodialyse et des surfaces des objets les plus communément manipulés par les patients. Ce contrôle a montré des taux de contaminations élevés, maximal dans le cas de l'air et très élevé dans le cas des surfaces (86,9%). Les points de surface les plus contaminés étaient les matelas, les télécommandes, les tensiomètres, les chariots et les balances. Les tables et les générateurs ont aussi révélé des taux de contamination élevés. L'identification des germes isolés a montré la présence de bactéries et de moisissures, avec une prédominance des bactéries. L'examen des moisissures retrouvés n'a révélé ni la présence d'Aspergillus, ni de Candida albicans. La répartition des bactéries retrouvées a montré une forte proportion des bactéries à Gram positif (85,81%) par rapport a celles à Gram négatif (14,19%). Ce taux élevé pourrait résulter du manque des mesures d'hygiènes et du respect des précautions standards par les patients et le personnel, que nous avons soulevés dans une étude antérieure.

Ce travail a permis de montrer une insuffisance de la pratique des précautions standards et spécifiques, une forte colonisation microbienne et une présence élevée de la flore bactérienne à caractère opportuniste et pathogène. Pour améliorer la qualité des soins et maîtriser le risque infectieux en hémodialyse, il serait indispensable de renforcer la formation du personnel en matière d'hygiène hospitalière, d'évaluer et d'optimiser le protocole de désinfection appliquée aux surfaces.

Mots clés : Démarche qualité, Infections nosocomiales, Environnement, Fès Hémodialyse, Précautions standards et spécifiques, Qualité des soins.

Keywords: Scienti•c grade CCD, MTF; modulation transfer function; laser speckle; spatial-frequency response

1 Introduction

Les infections nosocomiales constituent une situation préoccupante dans le monde entier du fait de leurs morbidité et mortalité élevées, mais également de leur retentissement humain et économique considérable [1–4]. En raison de l'exposition fréquente et prolongée à divers contaminants présents dans l'environnement de l'hémodialyse, de la multitude des portes d'entrée cutanées et des circonstances d'exposition, du déficit immunitaire des patients, les infections nosocomiales représentent en hémodialyse la seconde cause de mortalité après les maladies cardiovasculaires, le quart des hospitalisations en lien avec les infections d'accès vasculaire et les trois quarts des décès par infection en lien avec les bactériémies [5,6]. Si l'éradication de ces infections est impossible du fait que le risque de les contracter ne peut jamais être nul, la prévention quant à elle, reste le moyen pour freiner leur progression. Elle se base sur la maitrise et le contrôle de

l'environnement hospitalier, et le respect de précautions standards et spécifiques [5–8].
Dans le cadre de l'amélioration de la qualité des soins et la prévention du risque infectieux en hémodialyse, nous avons mis en place une démarche qualité visant à maitriser les éléments pouvant causer une contamination directe ou indirecte des patients. Réalisée au centre d'hémodialyse de l'hôpital Al Ghassani de Fès, notre étude a englobé deux volets et avait pour objectifs l'appréciation du respect des pratiques standards et spécifiques, et la surveillance de la qualité microbiologique de l'environnement des salles du traitement et l'évaluation des actions correctives mises en place.

2 Matériels et méthodes

Cadre et type d'étude

L'étude a comporté quatre enquêtes descriptives transversales, réalisées au centre d'hémodialyse de l'hôpital Al Ghassani de la ville de Fès (Maroc), soit avant et après rénovation du centre. Le 1èr volet était étalé sur une durée de 4 mois (février-mars 2012, mars-avril 2013), alors que le second volet, s'est déroulé sur une durée de six mois (avril, juin, septembre à novembre) de l'année 2012.

Population d'étude et procédure de collecte des données

Pour le 1èr volet, la population observée comprenait tout le personnel paramédical du centre ainsi que les patients communs traités pendant les deux périodes de l'étude. Les patients exclus de l'étude sont les nouveaux recrus au centre après rénovation et ceux ayant quitté le centre ou décédés après la 1ère enquête. Les informations étaient recueillies par observation et suivi de la population cible, sur des grilles anonymes élaborées à partir du guide des recommandations de la Société française d'hygiène hospitalière [7]. Ces grilles comportaient 58 questions et concernaient notamment l'hygiène des mains des patients et du personnel, le port de la tenue vestimentaire recommandée, le respect des précautions standards et spécifiques, ainsi que le nettoyage et la désinfection des surfaces des générateurs.
Pour le second volet, la population concernée était l'environnement des salles de traitement des malades. Les prélèvements de surface ont été réalisés entre les séances d'hémodialyse par la technique d'écouvillonnage, qui consiste à frotter un écouvillon stérile et humidifié sur une zone définie, d'une surface de 25 cm^2 [9]. Les points choisis étaient ceux les plus proches des patients tels que les générateurs, les tables et les matelas, ainsi que les objets les plus communément manipulés par les patients tels que les télécommandes. L'analyse des prélèvements a été pratiquée selon la méthode décrite par Meunier [10]. Chaque écouvillon a été immergé dans un bouillon nutritif liquide (Brain Heart Infusion [BHI]), puis incubé à 37 ± 1◦C pendant 18 à 24 heures. Par épuisement, ce bouillon a ensuite servi à ensemencer deux milieux de culture : la gélose au sang et le Sabouraud au chloramphénicol,incubés respectivement à 37 ± 1◦C pendant 48heures, et à 20 ± 2◦C pendant 5 jours. Quant aux prélèvements d'air, et en raison de l'absence de biocollecteurs, la technique de prélèvement utilisée a consisté à exposer pendantune durée de 16 minutes des boîtes de pétri ouvertes, contenant le milieu PCA, et à les incuber à 37±1°C pendant 48heures. L'identification des bactéries a été fondée sur les caractères culturaux, morphologiques et biochimiques classiques. Celle des moisissures est basée sur l'aspect, la taille et la forme. Les milieux de culture utilisés ont été préparés selon la norme NM 08.0.155 [11] et contrôlés avant utilisation (pH, stérilité). En outre, un contrôle qualité interne (Eau distillée, consommable, étuve, autoclave, conditions ambiantes de l'environnement des analyses,..), a été réalisé quotidiennement selon les lignes directrices canadiennes [12].

Éthique et confidentialité

Le protocole de l'étude a été soumis au comité d'éthique régional, qui nous a autorisé de débuter l'étude. La confidentialité des informations obtenues sur les sujets de l'étude a été respectée, car ni les noms des patients, ni ceux du personnel paramédical n'apparaissaient sur les documents de l'étude.

Analyse statistique

Toutes les variables sont résumées par l'utilisation des statistiques descriptives. Les variables qualitatives sont décrites en termes de proportions, et les variables quantitatives étaient décrites en termes de moyenne écart-type. L'analyse statistique des données a été réalisée avec le logiciel Epi Info 3.4 (version 2007). Une valeur de $p < 0,05$ était considérée comme significative. La saisie des données a été effectuée à l'aide du logiciel Excel.

3 Résultats et discussion

Le centre d'hémodialyse de l'hôpital Al Ghassani de Fès, a connu en 2012 une restructuration selon des normes nationales et internationales. Le centre rénové assure le traitement de plus de 132 malades atteints d'insuffisance rénale chronique terminale. En raison de nombreux facteurs tels que l'antibiothérapie fréquente et la multitude d'actes vasculaires invasifs, les patients traités par hémodialyse présentent un haut risque infectieux [13]. L'évolution du potentiel de transmission de ces infections a poussé les organisations nationales et internationales à émettre des recommandations relatives à leur prévention. Celles-ci concernent la conception des locaux, les règles d'entretien des équipements et des surfaces, les précautions standards et spécifiques destinées à minimiser le risque de transmission croisée des micro-organismes entre les soignants et les patients [7,8]. Afin d'améliorer la qualité des soins dans ce service et réduire le risque infectieux chez les patients hémodialysés, nous avons réalisé cette étude portant sur le respect des pratiques standards et spécifiques et la surveillance de l'environnement des salles de traitement des salles d'hémodialyse.

Fondée sur l'observation, nous avons mené deux enquêtes descriptives et rempli 344 grilles, soit 177 en 2012 et 177 en 2013, ce qui nous a permis d'évaluer le respect des précautions standards et spécifiques au centre avant et après aménagement, et de suivre leur évolution suite aux actions correctives que nous avons menées. Ces actions ont comporté la transmission au responsable du centre d'un rapport des points forts et des points faibles soulevés en 2012, et une sensibilisation de toute l'équipe soignante par exposition des résultats trouvés, tout en montrant sur leur rôle dans l'amélioration et en insistant sur les objectifs à atteindre [6].

Les précautions standards sont des mesures qui reposent essentiellement sur l'hygiène des mains et l'application des mesures de barrières lors de l'application de soins tels que les gants et la blouse [14–17]. Le respect de l'hygiène chez les patients a varié d'un type à l'autre, mais reste globalement insuffisant. Ainsi, lors du branchement, l'hygiène des bras des patients n'a pas été effectuée, mais elle a été constatée après le débranchement et s'est améliorée significativement en 2013. Les pourcentages de la pratique d'hygiène des mains avant le branchement et après le débranchement ont aussi changé. Cependant, l'amélioration significative de cette pratique n'est remarquée qu'avant le branchement. Ces résultats pourraient être liés à une méconnaissance de ces mesures, et devraient être améliorées par une campagne de sensibilisation portant sur le bon niveau d'hygiène quotidienne, le port d'une tenue propre et adaptée permettant de dégager la fistule, et le lavage systématique à l'aide d'une solution antiseptique moussante des mains et du bras où est localisée la fistule [5,7,8]. Chez le personnel soignant, l'observance de l'hygiène des mains était variable d'un type à l'autre. Ainsi, le lavage hygiénique n'a pas été pratiqué, le lavage simple des mains a diminué significativement (41,86% en 2012, 2,32% en 2013), alors que l'application de la friction hydro-alcoolique a connu une amélioration nettement significative entre les deux enquêtes (6,98% en 2012 contre 23,25% en 2013). Quoique le comité technique national des infections nosocomiales [CTIN], ait recommandé depuis 2001, la friction des mains par les solutions hydro-alcooliques en remplaçant le lavage des mains, son observance fait défaut malgré la disponibilité des solutions hydro-alcooliques dans le centre rénové [18]. Le manque d'hygiène des mains observé, montre que des efforts devraient être déployés pour rappeler et inciter le personnel soignant à respecter l'hygiène des mains puisqu'elle est la première mesure de prévention de la transmission croisée des germes entre patients et qu'elle doit être réalisée entre chaque patient et pour tout soin [7,19]. Il serait également intéressant de valoriser les avantages multiples des solutions hydro-alcooliques à savoir leur efficacité, leur disponibilité, leur tolérance et notamment lorsqu'elles contiennent des émollients, et leur rapidité d'action [20,21]. Tous ces avantages ont rendu la friction hydro-alcoolique la technique de référence de désinfection des mains et une alternative pour les pays à ressources limitées où l'approvisionnement en eau et les équipements mis à sa disposition constituent une véritable entrave à la pratique du lavage des mains [20] (Tableau 1).

Tableau 1 : Respect de la pratique d'hygiène par les patients et le personnel paramédical

Pratique d'hygiène	2012	2013	P
Patients			
Hygiène des bras avant branchement	0%	0%	-
Hygiène des bras après débranchement	2,90%	25%	<0,05
Hygiène des mains avant branchement	1,16%	10,46%	<0,05
Hygiène des mains après débranchement	16,25%	25%	>0,05
Personnel			
Lavage simple	41,86%	2,32%	<0,05
Friction hydro-alcoolique	6,98%	23,25	-
Lavage hygiénique	0%	0%	

Les gants représentent une barrière efficace contre la transmission croisée des germes puisqu'ils réduisent le niveau de contamination des mains par la flore acquise au cours des soins [21]. Ils doivent être portés systématiquement en cas de risque de contact avec du sang, ou tout autre produit d'origine humaine, lors de manipulations diverses de tubes de prélèvements biologiques, ou de matériels souillés, lors des soins [7,8 ,22]. Les résultats relatifs au respect de ces mesures sont représentés dans le tableau 2. En effet, nous avons constaté que cette barrière était utilisée systématiquement au cours des deux enquêtes, ceci a été objectivé par l'absence de notifications des cas d'hépatite virale. Le port de gants stériles était majoritaire aussi bien au cours du branchement qu'au cours du débranchement. Bien que les recommandations préconisent l'usage de gants propres, et leur changement entre deux patients et entre deux activités [5,7, 14], nous avons remarqué l'usage systématique de gants stériles et leur changement entre les activités et les malades. L'utilisation de gants stériles au lieu de gants propres pourrait représenter des dépenses inutiles puisque le coût des gants stériles est plus élevé que celui des gants propres. Quant à l'appréciation du port des précautions vestimentaires par le personnel, nous avons trouvé qu'elles étaient rarement respectées au cours de la 1ère enquête, soient des fréquences respectives de 4,07%, 10,46% et 5,23%. En revanche, une amélioration significative du port de masque et de la protection oculaire était notée en 2013. Cependant, la fréquence d'usage du masque reste relativement plus faible par rapport à celles mentionnées dans des travaux antérieurs [23-25]. Selon Girou et al (2002), le port des protections vestimentaires ne doit pas être systématiquement réalisé, la sur-blouse doit être portée lors de tout acte de soins exposant à une contamination de la tenue de travail par des liquides biologiques, le masque et les lunettes de protection doivent être mises lors de gestes exposants à des projections ou aérosolisations de liquides biologiques [14].

Tableau 2: Respect du port des gants et de la tenue recommandée.

Pratique	2012	2013	P
Port de gants stériles:			
Avant branchement	93,02%	97,67%	>0,05
Après débranchement	95,35%	98,83%	
Port de gants non stériles:			
Avant branchement	6,98%	2,33%	>0,05
Après débranchement	4,65%	1,17%	
Tenue vestimentaire			
Port de masque	5,23%	20,34%	<0,05
Port de la protection oculaire	4,07%	18,60%	>0,05
Port de la sur-blouse	10,46%	8,72%	

La compression des points de ponctions, présentée en tableau 3, a montré qu'elle était réalisée par les patients dans la quasi-totalité des cas observés (98,28% en 2012 et 99,42% en 2013). Quant à la mise en place du pansement sur les points de ponctions (tableau 3), elle a été effectuée fréquemment par le personnel soignant (67,44% en 2012 et 61,62% en 2013). Son exécution par les patients eux-mêmes, les autres patients et les aides-soignantes, a été aussi observée. La compression et la mise en place des pansements, effectuées par les mains des patients non lavées et colonisées par la flore commensale cutanée, pourraient générer des infections nosocomiales, résultant de la contamination par voie endogène [26].

Tableau 3 : Compression des points de ponction et mise en place des pansements.

Geste effectué	2012	2013	P
Compression des points de ponction effectuée par:			
Infirmier	1,72%	0,58%	>0,05
Patient lui-même	98,28%	99,42%	
Mise en place des pansements effectuée par/	67,44%	61,62%	>0,05
L'nfirmier	28,50%	33,14%	
Autre patient	2,32%	4,66%	
Patient lui-même	1,74%	0,58%	
Aide-soignante			

La pratique de la désinfection interne et externe des générateurs est présentée dans le tableau 4. Nous avons noté que la désinfection interne des générateurs entre les séances d'hémodialyses était systématique, alors que le nettoyage de leurs surfaces ne l'était pas. Cependant, nous avons constaté qu'il a augmenté significativement pour passer de 18,60% en 2012 à 40,12% en 2013, mais reste globalement insuffisant. Afin de prévenir la propagation d'agents pathogènes transmissibles de l'environnement, Karkar *et al* (2014) recommandent systématiquement le nettoyage et la désinfection des surfaces externes des générateurs, entre les sessions d'hémodialyse [5].

Tableau 4 : Nettoyage et désinfection des générateurs.

Désinfection	2012	2013	P
De la surface	18,60%	40,12%	<0,05
Interne	100%	100%	>0,05

Quoique la part des infections nosocomiales liées à une contamination d'origine environnementale soit difficile à apprécier, et l'importance du contrôle microbiologique soit controversé [27-29], les recommandations internationales indiquent actuellement les intérêts multiples de la surveillance microbiologique de l'environnement dans la prévention des infections nosocomiales, à savoir la prise en considération de la contamination des surfaces et la recherche des réservoirs microbiens à l'origine des cas groupés d'infections ou d'épidémies [18, 30]. Dans ce contexte et dans le cadre de la mise en place d'une démarche qualité dans ce centre, et avant toute intervention corrective, nous avons mené une surveillance de la qualité de l'air et des surfaces des salles de traitement des malades. Les résultats sont présentés dans le tableau 5.

Tableau 5 : Pourcentage de contamination des surfaces e de l'air.

Type de prélèvement	Point prélevé	Nombre de Point analysé	Pourcentage de contamination
Surface Nombre total:184	Générateur	84	79,8%
	Table	63	88,9%
	Matelas	21	100%
	Chariot	4	
	Télécommande	4	
	Tensiomètre	4	
	Balance	4	
Air Nombre total: 12	Salle 1	4	100%
	Salle 2	4	
	Salle 3	4	

La qualité de l'air intérieur dans les établissements de santé est devenue une préoccupation croissante, résultant de l'évolution des pratiques de soin et de la présence de personnes fragiles [31]. Son contrôle microbiologique a montré un taux de positivité maximal, causé dans la totalité des prélèvements analysés par une contamination bactérienne. Le niveau de contamination élevé a été rapporté par d'autres auteurs [32, 33]. Cependant, cette contamination ne présenterait pas un problème en soi si les contaminants resteraient en permanence dans l'air, et serait un risque réel si les contaminants se déposeraient sur les surfaces [34]. Ce risque s'aggraverait chez les patients à risque tels que les immuno-déprimés et les hémodialysés [35].

Quant à la surveillance microbiologique des surfaces, elle a montré un taux de contamination de l'ordre de 86,9%. Ce taux est comparable à celui retrouvé par d'autres auteurs. Meunier *et al* (2005), ont signalé à Strasbourg un taux de positivité de 87%. [10]. Saouide El Ayne *et al* (2014), ont rapporté à Kénitra, un taux de positivité de l'ordre de 92,85% [36]. Touijer (2014), a révélé un pourcentage de contamination de 97,92% lors d'une étude réalisée au sein de 4 services hospitaliers de la ville de Fès [33]. Cependant, Méité *et al* (2010), avaient noté à Abidjan un taux de positivité plus faible que celui que nous avons trouvé, soit 46,7% [39]. Barbut *et al*, (2006), notent que le niveau de contamination varie qualitativement et quantitativement au cours du temps et en fonction des services et des patients [37]. Les points de surface les plus contaminés étaient les matelas, les télécommandes, les tensiomètres, les chariots et les balances. Les tables et les générateurs ont aussi montré des taux de contamination très élevés. Ceci pourrait être lié au fait que ces objets sont communément manipulés par le personnel soignant et les malades, et d'autre part à un défaut des pratiques sanitaires, ce qui pourrait favoriser potentiellement la transmission des microorganismes [38]. Ces résultats rappellent ceux de Méité *et al* (2010), qui ont constaté que les sites les plus contaminés étaient ceux utilisés par le personnel ou les visiteurs [39]. Ces surfaces à contact fréquent situées dans les environs immédiats du patient, peuvent servir de réservoirs microbiens, et entrer en contact avec les patients soit directement, soit indirectement par l'intermédiaire de dispositifs médicaux ou les mains des patients et du personnel [10,38,40].

La fréquence des germes isolés des prélèvements d'air et ceux des surfaces est présentée dans le graphique 1. La répartition des germes retrouvés au niveau des prélèvements d'air, a montré l'absence de moisissures, et une prédominance des bactéries à Gram positif avec un pourcentage de 83,67%. Nous avons noté une prédominance des *Staphylococcus* et notamment de ceux à coagulase négative par rapport aux autres bactéries isolées (*Bacillus sp*, bacilles Gram négatifs oxydase positive non fermentaires (BGN Ox P NF). Ce résultat rappelle celui d'autres études [32,33], mais ne concorde pas avec celui retrouvé par Thilbaut (2011), qui avait noté la prédominance des *Staphylococcus aureus* par rapport aux autres bactéries isolées [41]. Les microorganismes saprophytes et pathogènes isolés, peuvent s'agglomérer et se fixer dans des milieux secs comme les poussières et les supports inertes, et sont en plus très résistants dans le milieu extérieur. En outre, une multiplication de ces germes pourrait se produire si les conditions nécessaires sont favorisées, d'autant plus si un entretien soigneux n'est pas assuré, ce qui pourrait aboutir à une concentration élevée ou critique de ces micro-organismes. D'autre part, la perturbation mécanique, continue ou discontinue des réservoirs microbiens, permet de libérer les microorganismes de leurs sources et d'être à l'origine d'une biocontamination, ce qui pourrait favoriser une contamination des malades par voie exogène [42].

L'identification des germes isolés des surfaces a montré la présence de bactéries et de moisissures, avec une prédominance bactérienne. L'examen des moisissures retrouvés n'a révélé ni la présence d'*Aspergillus*, ni de *Candida albicans*. Ce résultat ne concorde pas avec ceux d'autres auteurs qui avaient isolé le *Cladosporium sp*, l'*Aspergillus sp*, le *Penicillium sp* et le *Microsporum canis* au sein des surfaces contrôlées [43-45]. Cependant, les études de surveillance menées aussi bien Saouide El Ayne *et al* (2014) que par Méité *et al* (2010), n'ont signalé qu'une contamination bactérienne [36,39]. La répartition des bactéries retrouvées, a montré une forte proportion des bactéries à Gram positif (85,81%) par rapport à celles à Gram négatif (14,19%), ce qui est en accord avec des études antérieures [10,36], mais diffère du profil bactériologique signalé à par d'autres auteurs [39,45, 46,47]. Schmitt *et al*, (2009), notent que l'environnement constitue un réservoir aux bactéries Gram positives, très largement dispersées par l'activité humaine. Ces bactéries sont plus résistantes à la dessiccation que celles à Gram négatif et surtout si les surfaces ne subissent qu'un bionettoyage quotidien sans effet désinfectant du produit [48]. La flore bactérienne est représentée en grande partie par les *Staphylococcus* coagulase négative (61,70%), les *Bacillus sp* (12,78%), les *Streptococcus* (11,34%), les bacilles à Gram négatif non fermentaires (10,64%), et les bacilles à Gram négatif fermentaires (3,54%). La prédominance des *Staphylococcus* et notamment ceux à coagulase négative a été notée dans des études antérieures [36, 49]. La fréquence du genre *Staphylococcus* par rapport aux autres genres de bactéries ne concorde pas avec les résultats trouvés par d'autres auteurs. Touijer (2014), a signalé la prédominance de *Bacillus* sp par rapport aux *Staphylococcus* à coagulase négative et positive [33].

Si les *Staphylococcus* à coagulase négative et les *Bacillus* ont été omniprésents au niveau de toutes les surfaces contaminées, les *Staphylococcus aureus* n'ont été retrouvés qu'au niveau des générateurs et des matelas. Les *Streptococcus* ont été isolés à partir des générateurs, des matelas, des tables, des télécommandes et des balances. Les bacilles à Gram négatif (BGN) non fermentaires ont été présents sur tous les types de points sauf les balances, alors que ceux oxydase négative fermentaire n'ont été constatés qu'au niveau des matelas, des générateurs et des tables. La flore retrouvée sur les surfaces dépend en effet de plusieurs facteurs tels que l'activité humaine qui entraîne un apport de micro-organismes par les patients eux-mêmes et par le personnel soignant, l'inefficacité du bionettoyage, la qualité de l'air [37], ainsi qu'aux facteurs liés au microorganisme tels que la durée de vie sur les supports inertes, l'adhérence à la surface, la capacité à produire un biofilm et l'aptitude à résister aux conditions défavorables [36].

5 Conclusion

Ce travail s'inscrit dans le cadre de l'amélioration de la qualité des soins et de la réduction des infections nosocomiales au service d'hémodialyse de l'hôpital Al Ghassani. Il a montré que le respect des précautions standards et des pratiques d'hygiènes n'était pas perçue comme obligatoire aussi bien par le personnel soignant que par les patients. L'action corrective menée n'était pas efficace puisque l'application de ces mesures reste globalement non satisfaisante. Ceci pourrait être lié surtout à la réticence du personnel aux changements, au manque de motivation, à l'âge avancé, et à l'insuffisance de l'information, de la formation et de la sensibilisation.

Le contrôle de l'environnement des salles de traitement des hémodialysés, témoigne d'une forte colonisation microbienne aussi bien des surfaces que de l'air du centre. Le taux de contamination des surfaces est de 86,9%, celui de l'air est de 100%. Les points de surface les plus contaminés étaient les matelas, les télécommandes, les tensiomètres, les chariots et les balances. La flore bactérienne isolée était représentée en grande partie par les bactéries à Gram positif avec une nette prédominance pour les Staphylococcus coagulase négative.

Pour maîtriser le risque infectieux en hémodialyse, il serait indispensable de renforcer la formation du personnel en matière d'hygiène hospitalière, d'investir dans des programmes de formations efficaces et innovants à la fois pratique et théorique se basant sur des technologies éducatives et répondant au besoin du personnel et d'évaluer le protocole de désinfection appliquée à l'environnement du centre.

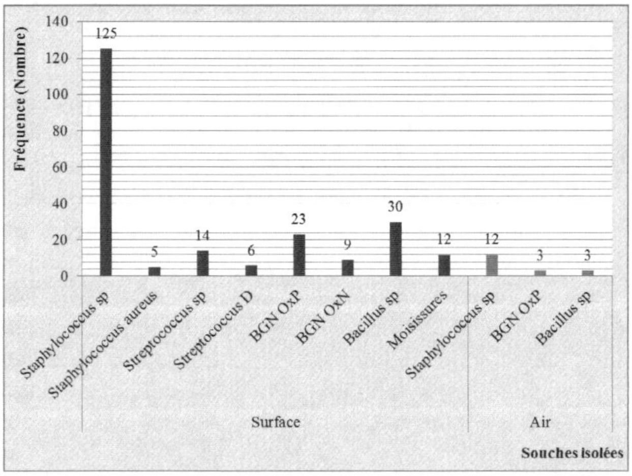

Graphique 1 : Fréquence des germes isolés des prélèvements d'air et de surfaces.

Références

1. R.W. Haley, D.H. Culver, J.W. White, W.M. Morgan, T.G. Emori, V.P. Munn, et *al*. The efficacy of infection surveillance and control programs in preventing nosocomial infections in US hospitals. Am J Epidemiol. **121**, 182-205(1985).

2. D. Pittet, S. Harbarth, C. Ruef, P. Francioli, P. Sudre, S. Pétignat. Prevalence and risk factors for nosocomial infections in four University hospitals in Switzerland. Infect Control Hosp Epidemiol.**20**,37-42 (1999).

3. K. El Rhazi, S. Elfakir, M. Berraho, N. Tachfouti, Z. Serhier, C. KAnjaa, et *al*. Prévalence et facteurs de risque des infections nosocomiales au CHU Hassan II de Fès (Maroc). Rev Sante Mediterr Orient.**13**, 56-63 (2007).

4. S. Berrada, T. G. Benjelloun, L. Bennani, A. S Diarra, B. Oumokhtar, L. A. El Ouali, H. F. Z Squali., H. T. Sqalli. Exploration microbiologique des surfaces d'un centre d'hémodialyse de la ville de Fès : étude descriptive transversale. Revue francophone internationale de recherche infirmière. **3**, 120-128 (2017).
5. A. Karkar, M.B. Bouhaha, M.L. Dammang. Infection control in hemodialysis units: a quick access to essential elements. Saudi J Kidney Dis Transplant. **25**, 496-519 (2014).
6. S. Berrada, H. T. Sqalli., B. Oumokhtar, L. Bennani, L.A. El Ouali, H. Hanin, S. El Fakirl, N. Benaich, H. F. Z. Squali. Évaluation de la conception et des pratiques standards d'un centre d'hémodialyse au Maroc. Revue francophone internationale de recherche infirmière. **1**,225-232(2015).
7. Jacques *et al.* Bonnes pratiques d'hygiène en hémodialyse. Recommandations de la SFHH. Hygiènes. **XIII** (2005).
8. Recommandations de bonnes pratiques médicales, affection longue durée, insuffisance rénale chronique terminale CIM 10 : N 18 Code ANAM: L008. Maroc: Ministère de la Santé (2013).
9. Norme ISO 14698-1. Salles propres et environnement maîtrisés apparentés. Maîtrise de la biocontamination. AFNOR; (2003).
10. O. Meunier, C. Hernandez, M. Piroird, R. Heilig, D. Steinbach, A. Freyd. Prélèvements bactériologiques des surfaces : importance de l'étape d'enrichissement et du choix des milieux de culture. Ann Biol Clin. **63**(5), 481-6 (2005).
11. Norme NM 08.0.155. Guide pour la préparation et la production des milieux de culture en laboratoire. 1-16 (2006)
12. Lignes directrices concernant l'application des contrôles de qualité en microbiologie. DR-12-SCA-02. Québec: Centre d'expertise en analyse environnementale du Québec. 1-36(2011).
13. B. Oumokhtar , M. El Azhari, M.Timinouni, K. Bendahhou, B. Bennani, M. Mahmoud, L.A. El Ouali, S. Berrada, M. Arrayhani, H.T. Squalli. *Staphylococcus aureus* nasal carriage in a Moroccan dialysis center and isolates characterization. Hemodialysis International. **17**, 542-547(2013).
14. E. Girou, R. Girard, C. Chémorin, A. Simon. Précautions standards. Reanimation. **11**, 257-9 (2002).
15. OMS. Manuel d'hygiène hospitalière et de prévention des infections nosocomiales. Royaume du Maroc: Ministère de la Santé(2009).
16. Centre de coordination de la lutte contre les infections nosocomiales inter-région sud-est. CCLIN. Rapport final du groupe d'experts concernant l'hémodialyse(2010).
17. M.L. Atif, A. Brenet, S. Hageaux, M.H. Fave, C. Cochet, E. Baticle, C. Pourrier, D. Wolny, P. Astagneau, Z. Kadi. Connaissances des précautions standards chez 4439 professionnels de santé dans 34 établissements de France. Médecine et maladies infectieuses. **43**,10-16(2013).
18. Comité technique national des infections nosocomiales (CTIN). Avis du CTIN du 5 décembre 2001 sur la place de la friction hydro-alcoolique dans l'hygiène des mains lors des soins. Bulletin officiel n° 2001-52.
19. Guide des bonnes pratiques pour la prévention des infections liées aux soins réalisés en dehors des établissements de santé Ministère de la Santé, de la Famille Et Des Personnes Handicapées (2002).
20. F. Dicko-Traore, C. Gire, V. Brevaut Malaty, M. Busutil,l A.S. Monnier, V. Brunel. Évaluation des connaissances et des pratiques d'hygiène des mains au niveau de l'unité de néonatologie et soins intensifs au service de médecine infantile et néonatologie de l'hôpital Nord, Marseille. J Pediatr Puericult **24**,172-7(2011).
21. E. Girou, R. Girard, C. Chemorin, A. Simon. Précautions standards. Réanimation. **11**, 257- 259(, 2002).
22. D. Thiveaud, A.M. Grimoud, N. Marty, C.Roques, J.P. Lodter, G.Chabanon. Hygiène : structures, matériels, méthodes. EMC- Ondontologie.**1**, 307-339(2005).
23. N. El Mikatti, P. Dillon, T.E. Healy. Hygienic practices of consultant anaesthetists: a survey in the north-west region of the UK. Anaesthesia. **54**, 13-18 (1999).
24. A. Carbonne, B. Veber, J. Hajjar , D. Zaro-Goni, S. Maugata, J.C. Seguier, A. Chalfine, K. Blanckaert, M. Aggoune, C. Auboyer. Évaluation des pratiques en anesthésie exposant au risque infectieux par transmission croisée. Annales Françaises d'Anesthésie et de Réanimation. **25**, 1158-1164 (2006).
25. A.J. Ryan, C.S. Webster, A.F. Merry, D.J. Grieve. A national survey of infection control practice by New Zealand anaesthetists. Anaesth Intensive Care. **34**, 68–74 (2006).
26. S. Anselme, S. Boileau, M. Vedel, C. Muller, M.F. Blech, H. Bouaziz . Evaluation des pratiques d'hygiène en anesthésie entre 1998 et 2007 en Lorraine. Annales Françaises d'Anesthésie et de Réanimation. **28**, 28-34 (2009).
27. T. Bauer, E. Ofner, H. Just, F.D. Daschner. An epidemiological study assigning the relative importance of airborne and direct contact transmission of microorganisms in a medical intensive care unit. J Hosp Infect. **15**, 301-309 (1990).
28. W.R. Jarwis, J.R. Edward, D.H. Culver. Nosocomial infection rated in adult and pediatric Intensive care units in the United States. AM J Med. **91**, 185-191(1991).
29. G.A. Ayliffe. Environmental Sampling in hospitals. Host, **6**, 3-5 (1992).
30. L. Sehulster, Y.W. Raymond, A. Matthew, Carpenter, P.E. Rodney-Donlan. Infection Control Practices Advisory Comitee. Recommandations of CDC and healthcare. Guidelines for environmental infection control in health care facilities. MMWR. **52**, RR10 (2003).
31. Guide. La qualité l'air intérieur dans les établissements du réseau de la santé et des services sociaux. Québec (2005).
32. M. El khadir. Surveillance microbiologique des surfaces de l'hôpital Ibn El Khateb de Fès. Mémoire de Master en Biologie, Université Sidi Mohamed Ben Abdellah, Faculté Des Sciences Et Techniques Fès, Maroc (2011).
33. H. Touijer. Prévention des infections nosocomiales : Ecologie bactérienne en milieu hospitalier et sensibilité aux antibiotiques et aux désinfectants. Mémoire de Master en Biologie. Université Sidi Mohamed Ben Abdellah, Faculté des Sciences Dhar Mehraz-Fès, Maroc (2014).

34. M. Combet. Salles propres à l'hôpital : un historique. Salles propres et maîtrise de la contamination. 05, 15-19 (2009).
35. F. Jacques *et al.* Surveiller et prévenir les infections associées aux soins. Hygiène. XVIII , **4**, (2010).
36. N. Saouide El Ayne, A. Echchelh, A. Chaouch., N. Auajjar, S. Hamama, A. Soulaymani. Rôle de l'environnement hospitalier dans la prévention des infections nosocomiales : Surveillance de la flore des surfaces à l'hôpital EL Idrissi de Kénitra- Maroc. European Scientific Journal. **10**, 238-247(2014).
37. F. Barbut, D. Neyme. Les difficultés d'interprétation des contrôles microbiologiques environnementaux. Revue Francophone des laboratoires. **382**, 27-32 (2006).
38. L.S. Munoz–Price, D.J. Birnbach, D.A. Lubarsky. Decreasing operating room environmental pathogen contamination through him proved cleaning practice. Infect Control Hosp Epidemiol. **33**, 897-904 (2012).
39. S., Méité, C. Boni-cissé, P. Monemo, A.P. Mlantanoa, H. Faye-ketté, H. Dosso. Surveillance microbiologique des surfaces au niveau d'un établissement hospitalier de niveau tertiaire : Exemple du CHU de Yopougon, abidjan, Cote d'ivoire. J sci pharm. biol. **11**, 73-81(2010).
40. Comité consultatif provincial des maladies infectieuses (CCPMI). Pratiques exemplaires en matière de nettoyage de l'environnement en vue de la prévention et du contrôle des infections dans tous les établissements de soins de santé. 2ème Edition (2012).
41. M. Thilbaut. Les infections nosocomiales : l'importance d'un suivi épidémiologique et de l'identification rapide des bactéries en cause (2011).
42. F. Squinazi. Analyses en microbiologie Environnement microbien (air, surfaces, eau). Techniques de l'ingénieur. **3**, 3551-3555 (2006).
43. J.T. Li, Y. Li. J. Wang. Surveillance on gram-positive bacteria isolated from patients with hospital acquired infections or community acquired infections. Zhonghua Yi Xue Za Zhi. **83**, 365-374 (2003).
44. P.E. Santos, S. Cordoba, A. Carrillo-Munoz, L. Rodero, E. Rubeglio, M. Soria. Epidemiology of fungaemia in a paediatric hospital of high complexity. Rev Iberoam Micol. **27**, 200-202 (2010).
45. C.P. Garcia-Cruz, M.J. Najera-Aguilar, O.E. Arroyo-Helguera. Fungal and Bacterial Contamination on Indoor Surfaces of a Hospital in Mexico. Jundishapur J Microbiol. **5**, 460-464 (2012).
46. R. Djerfaour, D.J. Benhaddouche, M. Bensenane, U. Bouk, C. Hacene, k Meguenni. Infections nosocomiales à bactéries multirésistantes en reanimation polyvalente 12 mois de surveillance sur 250 patients. J Magh' Réa Urg. **17**, 205-208 (2010).
47. C. Njall, D. Adiogo, A. Bita, N. Ateba, G. Sume, B. Kollo, F. Binam, R. Tchoua. Ecologie bactérienne de l'infection nosocomiale au service de réanimation de l'hôpital Laquintinie de Douala, Cameroun. Pan African Medical Journal. **14**, 140-148 (2013).
48. A. Schmitt, N.Glasser, D. Stainbach, O. Meunier. Études expérimentales de l'effet rémanent d'un détergent désinfectant pour surfaces sur une souche d'*Escherichia coli*. Pathologie Biologie. **57**, 463–469 (2009).
49. J. Nelson, A. Bivens, A. Shinn, L. Wanzer, C. Kasper. Microbial flora on operating room telephones. AORN J. **83**, 607-626 (2006).

Métrologie des balances dans un laboratoire multi domaines et activités

A. Chausse[1], C. Cecconi[1], C. Viarouge[1], et M. Gay[2]

1. *Université Paris-Est, Anses, Laboratoire de sécurité des aliments, F-94700 Maisons-Alfort, France*
2. *Anses, Laboratoire de sécurité des aliments, F-62200 Boulogne-sur-Mer, France*

1-2. *Anses, Mission Qualité des Laboratoires de sécurité des Aliments et de Santé Animale*

Résumé. Les laboratoires de sécurité des aliments (LSAl) et de santé animale (LSAn) de l'Anses (Agence nationale de sécurité sanitaire) sont répartis sur deux sites à Maisons-Alfort (neuf unités/missions scientifiques du LSAl et trois unités scientifiques du LSAn) et à Boulogne-sur-Mer (deux unités scientifiques du LSAl).
La refonte des procédures de métrologie des équipements de ces laboratoires a débuté en 2012 à l'occasion de la fusion des sites du LSAl. L'enjeu principal a été d'harmoniser les dispositions répondant aux spécificités des activités plurielles de ces laboratoires (recherche, prestations d'analyse accréditées*, référence interne) et concernant tous les champs d'expertise (bactériologie, virologie, parasitologie et physico-chimie des aliments - immuno-sérologie, bactériologie, virologie et parasitologie en santé animale - métrologie).
Dans ce contexte, la mission Qualité a développé spécifiquement des dispositions générales et un outil pour la métrologie des balances. L'objectif était d'apporter aux utilisateurs des consignes de vérification et des EMT (Erreur Maximale Tolérée) adaptées à leurs besoins. Seuls les essais de vérification ont été harmonisés.
Ce travail a été basé sur une analyse des pratiques déjà mises en œuvre dans ces laboratoires, une évaluation des données recueillies depuis de nombreuses années dans les unités, ainsi que sur une revue exhaustive de la littérature.

** Accréditations Essaie N°1-2246 et 1-5959, portées disponibles sur www.cofrac.fr*

Mots clés : Laboratoires; Métrologie; Balances; Pesées; Vérification; Qualité; Accréditation; Multi activités; Multi domaines

1 Introduction

La vérification métrologique d'une balance permet d'évaluer sa conformité par rapport à des besoins définis et vérifie la fiabilité de ses mesurandes.

La littérature scientifique apporte aux utilisateurs les outils pour mettre en œuvre des tests de vérification des balances appropriés à leurs activités. Néanmoins, les concepts sur la définition des spécifications (gamme de vérification, consignes et EMT [Erreur de Mesure Tolérée]) sont souvent imprécis.
Aux laboratoires LSA (acronyme désignant les laboratoires de Sécurité des Aliments [LSAl] et de Santé Animale [LSAn]) de l'Anses, nous avons observé que les paramètres de vérification mis en œuvre pour l'ensemble des balances étaient communs à toutes les activités (recherche, prestations analytiques, référence interne) et le plus souvent basés sur l'activité la plus exigeante (balances de précision utilisées pour les activités accréditées*). Ces procédures de vérification sont la conséquence des objectifs d'harmonisation des pratiques secondaires aux fusions successives des diverses activités scientifiques des laboratoires.
Or, les besoins sont bels et bien différents entre une balance de référence (en métrologie) et une balance d'analyse utilisée pour la pesée des échantillons à réception par exemple. Par ailleurs, les besoins peuvent être inconnus lorsqu'il s'agit d'une balance utilisée dans le cadre de projets de recherche.

Dans une structure où plusieurs activités coexistent, le risque de sur qualité est donc indéniable.

La mission Qualité des laboratoires LSA a donc élaboré et mis à disposition des utilisateurs de balances de laboratoire un outil permettant de réaliser une métrologie adaptée à leurs besoins spécifiques. Cet outil ainsi que la pertinence des tests à réaliser ont été évalués sur les balances de référence en métrologie.

2 Contexte

Les dispositions initiales élaborées pour toutes les unités du site de Maisons-Alfort préconisent la réalisation de trois tests (répétabilité, justesse et excentration) sur toute la gamme de pesée de chaque balance de laboratoire.
Les EMT sont définies selon une adaptation de la méthode décrite dans la norme Afnor NF EN 45501 [1] et les recommandations d'un fournisseur leader dans la distribution de balances de laboratoire.
Un échelon de vérification e a été calculé pour chaque marque et modèle de balance selon la formule $e = k \times d$, où d est l'échelon réel de la balance et k facteur compris entre 1 et 4.
L'EMT est ensuite calculé selon la norme [1] et la recommandation internationale OIML R 76-1 [4] décrite dans le tableau 1.

EMT	Classe I	Classe II	Classe III
± 1 x *e*	$0 \leq m \leq 50\,000\ x\ e$	$0 \leq m \leq 5\,000\ x\ e$	$0 \leq m \leq 500\ x\ e$
± 2 x *e*	$50\,000\ x\ e < m$ $m \leq 200\,000\ x\ e$	$5\,000\ x\ e < m$ $m \leq 20\,000\ x\ e$	$500\ x\ e < m$ $m \leq 2\,000\ x\ e$
± 3 x *e*	$200\,000\ x\ e < m$	$20\,000\ x\ e < m$ $m \leq 100\,000\ x\ e$	$2\,000\ x\ e < m$ $m \leq 10\,000\ x\ e$

Classe I : balance avec une cage de pesée solidaire de la carrosserie et un échelon d < 0,001 g. Balance dite de précision spéciale.

Classe II : balance sans cage de pesée solidaire de la carrosserie et un échelon 0,001 g < d < 1,000 g. Balance dite de précision fine.

Classe III : balance à bascule industrielle, dite de précision moyenne.

Tableau 1. EMT règlementaires des balances

Cette métrologie détournée des spécifications réglementaires utilisée pour classer les balances de précisions atteint rapidement ses limites dans des laboratoires d'analyses et d'essais multi-activités. En effet, le facteur *k* est évalué théoriquement sans analyse précise de chaque processus de mesure et sans utilisation des connaissances historiques associées à chaque balance. Aux laboratoires LSA, l'analyse des procédures montre que le facteur *k* a été défini en fonction de la résolution de la balance : plus celle-ci était faible et plus le facteur *k* était élevé. Pourtant, les balances d'analyse à faible résolution sont les plus critiques dans les processus d'analyse. Ainsi, $k = 1$ a été attribué pour une balance de résolution 10^{-1} utilisée pour la pesée des échantillons à réception et $k = 4$ a été attribué pour une balance de référence avec une résolution 10^{-6} utilisée comme référence en métrologie.

Le cas de la balance de référence présenté dans le tableau 2 est un exemple de dérive sur qualité non maîtrisée aux LSA.

EMT	Consignes	
± 0,000 004 g	$0 \leq m \leq 0{,}2$ g	Pesée maximale : 31 g
± 0,000 008 g	$0{,}2$ g $< m \leq 0{,}8$ g	$k = 4$ $d = 0{,}000\,001$ g
± 0,000 012 g	$0{,}8$ g $< m \leq 5$ g	Classe I

Tableau 2. Exemple de dispositions préexistantes aux LSA

Analyse des spécifications du tableau 2 :

- aucune masse étalon n'est capable de réaliser le processus défini (l'EMT règlementaire associée à une masse étalon de type E_1 de 0,200000 g est 0,000006 g, cf. recommandation internationale OIML R 111-1 [5]),
- les non-conformités sont le plus souvent constatées sur les masses de pesée proches de la limite maximale d'utilisation de la balance,
- elles aboutissent à des non-conformités systématiques lors des vérifications car bien qu'il s'agisse d'un instrument avec une précision élevée, ses performances ne répondent pas aux spécifications définies,
- les non-conformités donnent lieu à des études qui démontrent que l'impact des non-conformités est nul par rapport aux besoins.

3 Analyse des besoins

En raison des risques potentiellement élevés d'accepter un instrument non-conforme aux besoins ou au contraire de refuser un équipement conforme, il nous est apparu important de réaliser une étude précise de la valeur ajoutée de chaque spécification en mettant en perspective les recommandations de la littérature aux activités des laboratoires.

Pour définir une méthode adaptée, trois questions se sont posées :

- Quels essais réaliser ?
- Comment définir les consignes ?
- Quelles EMT appliquer et comment les définir ?

3-1 : choix des essais

La littérature propose la réalisation de plusieurs essais. Nous les avons confrontés aux pratiques de nos laboratoires. Le tableau 3 définit ces principaux tests.

Essais	Définition
Répétabilité	Vérification que la balance fournit des résultats concordants pour une même charge, mesurée dans les mêmes conditions.
Justesse	Vérification que la balance fournit un résultat de la mesure d'une charge concordant avec sa valeur vraie. Cet essai est réalisé pour plusieurs charges, souvent en deux temps : charge montante puis descendante.
Excentration	Vérification que la balance fournit des résultats concordants pour une même charge, quelques soit le point d'application de celle-ci sur le plateau de pesée de la balance.
Sensibilité	Vérification que la mesure d'une augmentation de charge réalisée par la balance est concordant avec sa valeur vraie.
Fluage	Vérification que, pour une même charge, la mesure relevée par la balance lors de la stabilisation et celle relevée après un temps défini sont concordantes.
Mobilité	Vérification que le dernier chiffre de résolution de la balance bascule bien d'un chiffre à un autre selon l'échelon réel de la balance.
Retour au zéro	Vérification du retour à zéro de la balance après une pesée.

Tableau 3. Définition des essais

La norme Afnor NF EN 45501 [1] et la recommandation internationale OIML R 76-1 [4] proposent d'autres essais complémentaires : vérification du temps de chauffage de la balance et de son endurance, influence des charges électrostatiques, influence des champs électromagnétiques de fréquence radio notamment.

L'ensemble des données de la littérature s'accorde sur la réalisation des trois essais majeurs suivant pour s'assurer de la fiabilité d'une balance d'analyse : la répétabilité, la justesse et l'excentration.

Selon le Guide Technique d'Accréditation du Cofrac LAB GTA 95 [6], l'essai de justesse doit correspondre au mode d'utilisation courant de la balance. Les masses qui sont pesées aux laboratoires, sur une même balance, sont constantes ou croissantes dans la plupart des cas. La revue de la littérature n'a pas permis cependant de définir la valeur ajoutée de la réalisation de ce test en charge croissante et décroissante. Par conséquent, cet essai est réalisé sur cinq masses (tel que défini dans la littérature) et seulement en charge croissante.

L'essai de sensibilité n'est pas systématiquement recommandé. Il correspond pourtant à une pratique courante dans les laboratoires : la pesée différentielle. Elle est utilisée lors des dilutions ou des vérifications des IVAP (Instrument Volumétrique à Piston) par exemple. Cet essai n'a pas été conservé en vérification complète d'un instrument car c'est une spécificité de quelques activités. Il sera indirectement vérifié en vérification hebdomadaire, en fonction de la criticité des pratiques (cf. § discussion).

Les mesures d'une même masse sur une durée prolongée ne sont pas faites dans nos laboratoires. Le test de fluage n'a donc pas été conservé.

Les performances des étalons de référence disponibles sur le marché ne permettent pas de réaliser le test de mobilité sur des balances dont l'échelon réel *d* est inférieur à 0,001 g. Par ailleurs, la criticité des processus de mesure réalisés sur les balances dont *d* est supérieur à 0,001 g ne nécessite pas un suivi métrologique précis.

La vérification de la bonne remise à zéro de la balance après une pesée a été intégrée aux essais de justesse et d'excentration : relevé de la valeur indiquée par la balance en fin de test.

3-2 : choix des consignes

Les consignes de vérification de chaque essai ont été définies selon les recommandations disponibles (cf. tableau 4), adaptées à la gamme d'utilisation réelle de chaque balance. En effet, nous nous sommes rendu compte que les balances des laboratoires LSA n'étaient pas toujours utilisées sur l'ensemble de leur gamme de pesée définie par leur constructeur. Ainsi, il a été défini le terme de "gamme d'utilisation" dans la documentation Qualité. Ladite gamme encadre la borne minimale m_{min} et la borne maximale m_{max} <u>d'utilisation</u> d'une balance.

Essai	Consigne
Répétabilité	1/2 de m_{max}
Justesse	m_{min} m_2, m_3, m_1 } *réparties sur la gamme de pesées ou réalisées quotidiennement* m_{max} m finale, à vide
Excentration	1/4 de m_{max} m finale à vide

Tableau 4. Essais retenus et consignes associées

3-3 : définition des EMT

L'expérience montre que la définition des EMT des balances dans nos laboratoires où coexistent plusieurs activités, ne peut pas découler d'une seule et unique méthode. Ainsi, plusieurs moyens ont été mis à disposition pour définir des EMT justes et en fonction des connaissances des processus analytiques associés à chaque balance.

La figure 1 présente le processus de définition des EMT des balances si les besoins sont connus pour chaque consigne de vérification. Ces besoins sont souvent indiqués dans les normes associées aux méthodes mises en œuvre ou bien définis lors du développement et de la validation de celles-ci.

La valeur minimale de *k* est fixée à 3 lorsque les pesées réalisées ne sont pas critiques. Dans le cas inverse, elle peut être fixée à 5. Lorsque le besoin n'est connu que pour une seule valeur de consigne, ce dernier est augmenté ou diminué proportionnellement pour les autres valeurs de consigne.

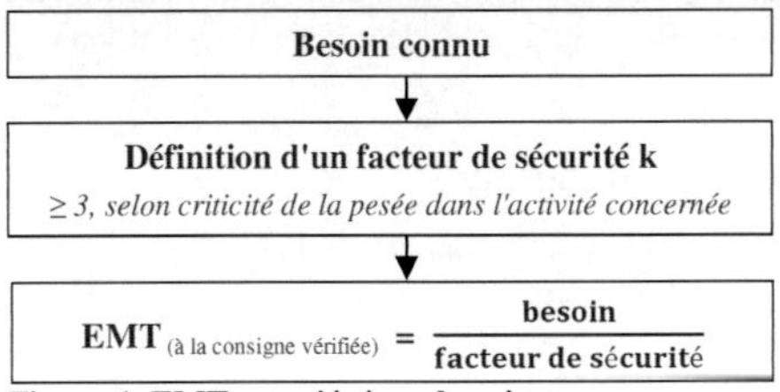

Figure 1. EMT associée à un besoin connu

Lorsqu'une balance est utilisée pour des activités de recherche (développement de méthode analytique par exemple), le besoin n'est pas toujours connu. Elle ne peut pas suivre le processus décrit précédemment. Dans ce cas, il est proposé de fixer des EMT en fonction de données issues de l'expérience.

Cette méthode est issue de la norme Afnor NF EN 45501 [1] et est proche de la méthode préexistante aux laboratoires. Pour chaque balance, l'échelon de vérification *e* est déterminé. Il est exprimé en unité de masse.

L'échelon de vérification est le produit d'un facteur *k* et de l'échelon réel de la balance : $e = k \times d$.

Le facteur *k* est défini en fonction des connaissances acquises sur la balance (Figure 2, "historique de la balance connu") et/ou de l'échelon réel *d*. Contrairement à la méthode précédente (Figure 1), plus la pesée est critique et plus *k* est petit. Les connaissances sur la balance nécessaires pour déterminer *k* sont des relevés journaliers d'une masse appartenant à la gamme d'utilisation, réalisés sur la balance et conformes aux EMT définies sans historique. Un minimum de cinquante relevés nécessaires a été fixé.

L'EMT est ensuite calculé selon la norme Afnor EN 45501 [1] et la recommandation OIML R76 [4] (cf. tableau 1).

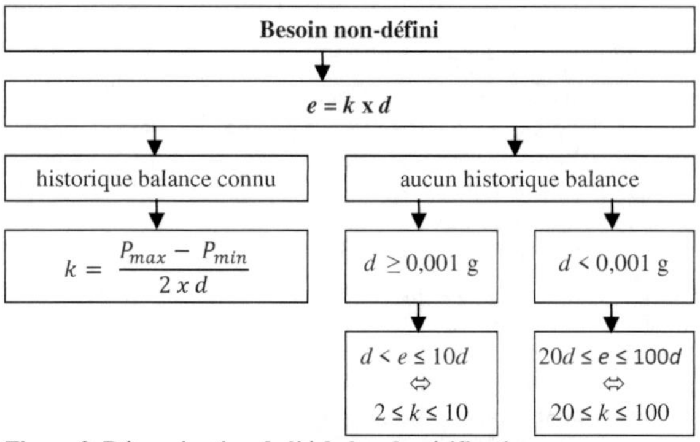

Figure 2. Détermination de l'échelon de vérification *e*

Dans le cas d'un besoin non-défini, il est important de porter à l'attention de l'utilisateur de la balance que l'EMT définie est théorique. Ainsi, il peut faire varier à tout moment les exigences de la balance notamment si l'EMT est une composante trop importante de l'incertitude globale de ses résultats d'analyse.

4 Etablissement des incertitudes

Deux types d'incertitudes sont développés dans la littérature : l'incertitude sur l'erreur d'indication de la balance et l'incertitude de la balance.

Seule l'incertitude sur l'erreur d'indication est utilisée pour établir la conformité de la balance pour chaque essai de justesse. Par ailleurs, elle est une composante de l'incertitude de la balance.
Cinq facteurs d'influence sont définis pour le calcul de l'incertitude de l'erreur d'indication.

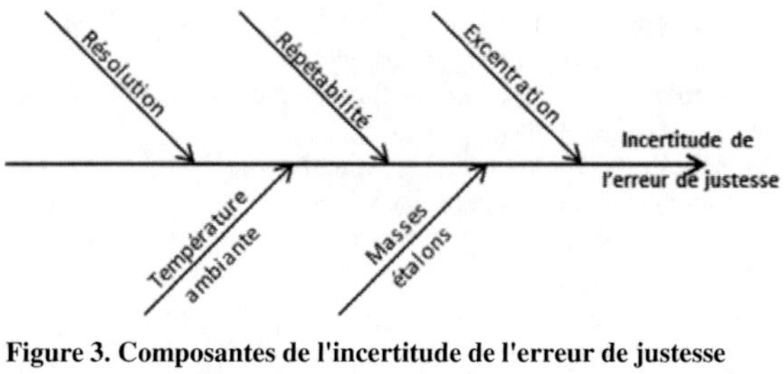

Figure 3. Composantes de l'incertitude de l'erreur de justesse

Type A - Répétabilité : il s'agit de l'incertitude due à la répétabilité du processus de pesée. Elle est estimée par le calcul de l'écart-type expérimental défini lors de l'essai de répétabilité.

Type B - Résolution : il s'agit d'une incertitude affectée à la lecture et fonction de l'échelon réel *d*. Celle-ci intervient deux fois pour la détermination d'un résultat de pesée : à l'équilibre à vide (d_0) et à l'équilibre en charge (d). Les valeurs d_0 et d peuvent être différente pour des balances à échelon multiples (plusieurs gammes avec des résolutions différentes).
La distribution de cette incertitude est de type triangulaire.

Type B - Excentration : il s'agit de l'incertitude due à la répartition de la masse sur le plateau de pesée. Les bonnes pratiques d'utilisation des balances préconisant de répartir les étalons de telle manière que leur centre de gravité se trouve à la verticale du centre du plateau de pesée, cette incertitude est considérée comme négligeable.

Type B - Température ambiante : l'estimation de cette incertitude est donnée par la littérature. Les paramètres qui interviennent sont le coefficient de variation de la pente de l'instrument *C* (nommé aussi coefficient de sensibilité de la balance) et la variation de la température durant l'étalonnage. *C* est une donnée fournie par le constructeur de la balance.

Type B - Masses étalons : les laboratoires travaillent avec des masses étalons de référence classées et étalonnées périodiquement. Ils prennent en compte la valeur conventionnelle établie après chaque étalonnage. Par conséquent, seule l'incertitude de l'étalonnage des masses est prise en compte. La conformité de l'évolution de la valeur conventionnelle des masses étalon est évaluée après chaque étalonnage selon les EMT du document règlementaire OIML R111 [5].
Lorsque plusieurs masses étalons sont utilisées pour une pesée, l'incertitude associée est la somme arithmétique des incertitudes-types de chacune.

Composante	Incertitude type
Répétabilité	$U_A = s$ s : écart type de répétabilité, défini pendant la vérification
Résolution	$U_{B1} = d/\sqrt{6}$ $U_{B2} = d_0/\sqrt{6}$ d : échelon réel en charge d_0 : échelon réel à vide
Température	$U_{B3} = C.[\Delta T/\sqrt{3}].m$ C : coefficient de sensibilité de la balance ΔT : variation de la température pendant la vérification m : masse vérifiée
Etalons	$U_{B4} = \Sigma u_{ét} = \Sigma U_{ét}/k_{ét}$ $U_{ét}$: incertitude d'étalonnage élargie de/des masse(s) $k_{ét}$: coeficient d'élargissement de l'étalonnage de/des masse(s)

Tableau 5.: Bilan des incertitudes

L'incertitude de la balance peut être calculée et mise à disposition des utilisateurs afin de déterminer l'erreur potentielle de la balance sur leurs résultats d'analyse finaux. Elle est sous la forme d'une équation du premier degré $ax + b$ où x est la masse mesurée dans le processus d'analyse.

5 Déploiement et exemple de spécifications

Afin de définir et de consigner aisément les spécifications pour chaque instrument de pesée, un outil Excel a été conçu, protégé contre les modifications intempestives et validé sur cinq instruments. Il guide l'utilisateur selon ses activités et ses besoins. Ce formulaire est conservé dans le dossier de vie de l'instrument et est révisé dès lors que les besoins et/ou les connaissances sur la balance évoluent.

L'exemple ci-après concerne la balance de référence du tableau 2, utilisée pour la vérification d'IVAP dont le volume nominal est compris entre 1 et 200 µL (soit en masse : entre 0,001000 et 0,200000 g d'eau).

Choix de la gamme de vérification : La portée minimale est définie par la plus petite pesée réalisée sur la balance, soit 0.001000 g (pour 1 µL).
Pour réaliser la vérification des IVAP, le plateau de la balance est équipé d'un récipient étanche appelé "réceptacle de pesée". La portée maximale est donc définie par la masse maximale d'eau pouvant être contenue dans ce réceptacle, soit 2,929073 g. Pour cette balance, la gamme d'utilisation et par conséquent de vérification est donc comprise entre 0,001000 et 3,000000 g.

Choix des consignes : les consignes sont définies en appliquant strictement les prescriptions du tableau 4.

Choix des EMT : dans le cas présent, les besoins sont clairement définis dans la norme NF EN ISO/CEI 8655 [8]. Les IVAP dont la métrologie est suivie sont des instruments critiques dans les processus d'analyse. Un facteur de sécurité $k = 5$ est choisi.

Masse de contrôle	Besoin [8]	EMT
Répétabilité		
1,500000 g	± 0,016000 g	± 0,003200 g
Justesse		
0,001000 g	± 0,000050 g	± 0,000010 g
0,010000 g	± 0,000120 g	± 0,000024 g
0,100000 g	± 0,000800 g	± 0,000160 g
2,000000 g	± 0,016000 g	± 0,003200 g
3,000000 g	± 0,040000 g	± 0,008000 g
Excentration		
1,000000 g	± 0,008000 g	± 0,001600 g

Tableau 6. Exemple de nouvelles spécifications

6 Discussion

Cette étude a permis de mettre à disposition un outil pour définir les spécifications métrologiques des balances adaptées à toutes les activités présentes dans les laboratoires. Ces spécifications sont consignées au travers d'un seul support qui peut être amendé aisément dès lors qu'une évolution des besoins est nécessaire.

L'exemple présenté permet de démontrer les limites de l'harmonisation des performances métrologiques des équipements d'une même grandeur.

Les dispositions du site de Maisons-Alfort étaient en vigueur depuis plus de dix années. Ainsi, la mission qualité s'est imposée des performances métrologiques bien trop importantes par rapport à ce qui était nécessaire sur sa balance de référence de résolution 10^{-6}. Par ailleurs, ce niveau de fiabilité était à la limite des performances de l'équipement. En conséquence de quoi il a fallu documenter au travers diverses non-conformités et dérogations l'absence d'impact des écarts constatés lors des vérifications périodiques.

Le tableau 7 présente l'évolution des EMT appliquées à cette balance de référence.

Masse de contrôle	EMT initiales	Nouvelles EMT	
Répétabilité			
1,500000 g	± 0,000012 g	± 0,003200 g	*x 260*
Justesse			
0,001000 g	± 0,000004 g	± 0,000010 g	*x 2,5*
0,010000 g	± 0,000004 g	± 0,000024 g	*x 6*
0,100000 g	± 0,000004 g	± 0,000160 g	*x 40*
2,000000 g	± 0,000008 g	± 0,003200 g	*x 400*
3,000000 g	± 0,000012 g	± 0,008000 g	*x 660*
Excentration			
1,000000 g	± 0,000008 g	± 0,001600 g	*x 200*

Tableau 7. Evolution des EMT

L'application de cette méthode montre une augmentation des EMT conséquentes et il est certain qu'elle induit un profond bouleversement des pratiques pouvant rebuter certains utilisateurs. Ils doivent donc être accompagnés pour qu'ils gardent confiance en la fiabilité de leurs instruments.

L'efficience de la vérification est d'autant plus renforcée qu'elle est faite sur la gamme réelle d'utilisation. Les erreurs de mesure étant d'autant plus fortes que la masse vérifiée est élevée, cette méthode permet d'exclure les erreurs de mesure pour des masses qui ne sont pas pesées en routine.

Bien qu'adaptée aux pratiques, cette procédure présente un certain nombre de contraintes :
- une communication efficace doit être faite pour que les utilisateurs soient informés de la gamme d'utilisation sur laquelle la fiabilité de la balance est assurée tout en spécifiant qu'elle peut évoluer aisément.
- une vérification hebdomadaire avant utilisation doit être effectuée en prenant en compte les spécificités des pesées le cas échéant. Par exemple, pour que la sensibilité de la balance présentée en exemple soit vérifiée, sa vérification hebdomadaire doit être réalisée avec l'accessoire additionnel nécessaire en routine. La fiabilité de cette balance pour la

réalisation de pesées différentielles (pesée par ajout de charge) est ainsi assurée.
- Pour les balances possédant plusieurs échelons réels *d* (balance à multi-résolutions), l'ensemble des spécifications est défini pour la gamme d'utilisation associée à chaque échelon réel.

L'incertitude de la balance dans les processus d'analyse n'est pas proposée. L'apport de la définition de cette dernière lors de chaque vérification est à déterminer selon les retours d'expérience. A noter que les utilisateurs peuvent utiliser l'EMT de vérification comme incertitude-type de la balance dans leur processus (limite : cette incertitude est surestimée).

7 Conclusion

La vérification métrologique des balances de laboratoire utilisées dans les laboratoires est indispensable pour déterminer leur performance et ainsi renforcer la fiabilité des résultats d'analyse produits quotidiennement.

Le risque principal des fusions d'activités et harmonisation des pratiques est d'imposer aux utilisateurs des équipements un niveau de performance trop élevé voir inadapté à leurs besoins réels. Lorsque ce risque n'est pas maîtrisé, l'utilisateur est contraint d'investir dans des équipements surqualifiés par rapport à ses besoins ou de justifier des non-conformités relevées à tort.

La présente méthode permet de réaliser la vérification métrologique des balances de laboratoire avec des critères adaptés aux travaux de l'utilisateur. En contrepartie elle implique un certain niveau de connaissance et donc de formation des agents en charge de la métrologie sur le terrain pour maintenir le niveau de maîtrise des équipements concernés.

Les objectifs d'harmonisation des pratiques restent accomplis car un socle commun a été défini. Il comprend les essais mis en œuvre et un outil mutualisé pour déterminer les spécifications métrologiques.

Références

1. Norme Afnor NF EN 45501 - Aspects métrologiques des instruments de pesage à fonctionnement non automatique - Juin 2015

2. Fascicule Afnor FD X07-017-1 - Procédure d'étalonnage et de vérification des Instruments de Pesage à Fonctionnement Non Automatique (IPFNA) - Décembre 1995 - Annulé le 13/09/2017.

3. Fascicule Afnor FD X07-017-2 - Procédure d'étalonnage et de vérification des Instruments de Pesage à Fonctionnement Non Automatique (IPFNA) - Décembre 1997

4. Recommandation Internationale OIML R 76-1 - Instruments de pesage à fonctionnement non automatique - Partie 1 : Exigences métrologiques et techniques - Edition 20016

5. Recommandation Internationale OIML R 111-1 - Poids des classes E_1, E_2, F_1, F_2, M_{1-2}, M_2, M_{2-3}, et M_3 - Partie 1 : Exigences métrologiques et techniques - Edition 2004

6. Guide Technique d'Accréditation Cofrac LAB GTA 95 - Etalonnage d'Instruments de Pesage à Fonctionnement Non-Automatique - Révision 00

7. Guide Technique d'Accréditation Cofrac LAB GTA 122 - Métrologie des masses - Révision 02

8. norme Afnor NF EN ISO 8655-2 - Appareil volumétriques à piston - Partie 2 : Pipette à piston - Avril 2003

Etalonnage des balances manométriques et modélisation des sections efficaces des ensembles piston-cylindre

P. Otal*, C. Yardin and N. Fischer

Laboratoire National de Métrologie et d'Essais, 1 rue Gaston Boissier, F-75015 Paris, France

Received:

Abstract. L'étalonnage des balances de pression au plus haut niveau métrologique consiste à déterminer les sections efficaces S_p de l'ensemble piston-cylindre en fonction de la pression. Les valeurs de ces sections efficaces sont ensuite analysées pour déterminer la section effective à pression nulle S_0 et, si celui-ci est significatif, le coefficient de déformation λ. Il existe plusieurs approches pour déterminer ces paramètres et les incertitudes associées qui peuvent donner des résultats significativement différents. Le LNE a une longue expérience dans l'étalonnage des balances de pression; il a par ailleurs développé un logiciel LNE- RegPoly qui estime la fonction d'étalonnage avec des méthodes de régression pondérée. Cet article décrit les différents modèles communément utilisés pour déterminer ces paramètres et présente, à partir de données numériques issues d'un projet Euramet, l'exploitation qui peut en être faite à l'aide du logiciel LNE-RegPoly diffusé par le LNE.

Keywords: balance de pression, balance manométrique, section efficace, coefficient de déformation, cross-float, moindres carrés pondérés, moindres carrés généralisés, incertitudes d'étalonnage.

1 Introduction

La balance manométrique est un instrument qui permet de matérialiser la pression à partir des grandeurs de base du système SI, et de la disséminer avec le meilleur niveau d'incertitude. Le principe de la balance de pression est d'équilibrer la force engendrée par la pression P appliquée à la base d'un piston de surface S bien définie par la force due au champ local de la pesanteur agissant sur la masse M placée sur la tête du piston [1]. A l'équilibre des deux forces, le piston flotte et la pression p_m reste pratiquement constante à une valeur calculable définie par l'équation (1):

$$p_m = \frac{\sum_i \left[m_i g(1-\rho_a/\rho_{mi})\right] + \Gamma C}{S_p\left[1+(\alpha_p+\alpha_c)(t-20)\right]} \quad , \qquad (1)$$

avec

m_i : masse réelle d'ordre i appliquée sur le piston,

g : accélération de la pesanteur au lieu d'utilisation de la balance,

ρ_a : masse volumique de l'air, considérée comme nulle en pression absolue ;

ρ_{mi} : masse volumique de la masse mi appliquée sur le piston;

S_p : section efficace de l'ensemble piston-cylindre à la pression p;

λ: coefficient de déformation de l'ensemble piston-cylindre.

α_p et α_C : coefficients de dilatation linéaire du matériau du piston et du cylindre;

t : température de l'ensemble piston-cylindre;

Γ est la tension superficielle de l'huile.

* Correspondance: pierre.otal@lne.fr

L'étalonnage d'une balance de pression est généralement réalisé par comparaison directe avec une balance de référence pour un nombre de points de pression fonction de l'incertitude recherchée. Des ajustages itératifs de masse sont nécessaires jusqu'à maintenir les balances dans leur position d'équilibre.

Les recommandations du BNAE (RM. Aero 802-21) [2] ou d'EURAMET (Cg3) [3], proposent deux méthodes d'étalonnage des balances de pression, identifiées A et B. La première consiste à fournir la pression mesurée par la balance dans des conditions spécifiées de température et d'accélération de la pesanteur. La seconde, présentée dans cet article, est plus complexe de mise en œuvre et applicable pour une incertitude relative d'étalonnage meilleure que 1.10^{-4}.

1 Etalonnage par détermination des paramètres de la balance (méthode B)

Cette méthode permet, à partir de l'équation (1), de remonter aux paramètres fondamentaux de la balance de pression. Elle consiste à déterminer les sections efficaces S_p de l'ensemble piston-cylindre en fonction de la pression p pour un nombre de points de pression. Les valeurs de ces sections efficaces sont ensuite analysées pour déterminer la section effective à pression nulle S_0 et, si celui-ci est significatif, le coefficient de déformation λ :

$$S_p = S_0\,(1+\lambda p)\,. \qquad (2)$$

Il existe différentes approches pour déterminer ces deux paramètres. Le projet Euramet 1125 [4] [5] avait pour objectif de vérifier numériquement les performances des différentes méthodes utilisées par quinze laboratoires nationaux de métrologie européens appliquées à des jeux de données simulés. Bien que cohérents avec les incertitudes, les résultats montraient des différences relativement importantes en termes de justesse et d'incertitude alors que tous les participants avaient les mêmes jeux de données.

Le LNE a une longue expérience dans l'étalonnage des balances de pression, il a par ailleurs développé un logiciel LNE-RegPoly [6] pour estimer la fonction d'étalonnage avec des méthodes de régression pondérée. L'exploitation des données numériques issues du projet Euramet 1125, en utilisant le logiciel LNE-RegPoly, est présentée dans les paragraphes suivants.

2. Données d'étalonnage

Parmi les quatre jeux de données d'étalonnage simulés, deux ont été sélectionnés dans le cadre de cette étude, un en gaz jusqu'à 10 MPa (section nominale 49 mm²) et un autre en huile jusqu'à 500 MPa (section nominale 2 mm²). Chaque étalonnage comprend 5 cycles et 10 points de pression. Tout d'abord, des valeurs théoriques arbitraires pour la section efficace à la pression nulle S_{0th} et le coefficient de déformation λ_{th} des ensembles piston-cylindre sous test ont été définies et considérées comme vraies, sans incertitude (tableau 1).

Tableau 1. Valeurs théoriques pour la section efficace à la pression nulle S_{0th} et le coefficient de déformation λ_{th} des ensembles piston-cylindre sous test.

	GAZ (10 MPa)	HUILE (500 MPa)
S_{0th} /mm²	49,019200	1,90292
λ_{th} / Pa^{-1}	-2,38E-12	7,80E-13

Une fois fixés les paramètres des sections efficaces des balances sous test, les autres paramètres sont définis de manière à satisfaire exactement l'équation de pression (1). Des erreurs de moyenne non nulle sont ensuite générées pour toutes ces données en utilisant un générateur de nombres pseudo-aléatoires. Les sections efficaces S_p des ensembles piston-cylindre sous test en fonction de la pression sont alors calculées, comme le métrologue a coutume de le faire en retournant l'expression (1). Le tableau 2 présente ces sections efficaces S_p avec leur incertitude type associée $u(S_p)$ ainsi obtenus. La figure 1 représente les sections efficaces S_p et les valeurs théoriques S_{thp} pour l'ensemble piston-cylindre gaz de section nominale 49 mm².

Par ailleurs, ces valeurs de section sont généralement fortement corrélées en raison de l'influence de facteurs communs. Toutefois, l'évaluation des covariances associées requiert une analyse longue et détaillée de chacune des sources d'incertitude. Dans cette étude, nous utilisons une méthode simplifiée qui consiste à distinguer deux groupes : les incertitudes dues à des effets systématiques et celles dues à des effets non systématiques. Elles sont présentées dans le tableau 3. Les covariances seront évaluées avec les incertitudes associées aux effets systématiques.

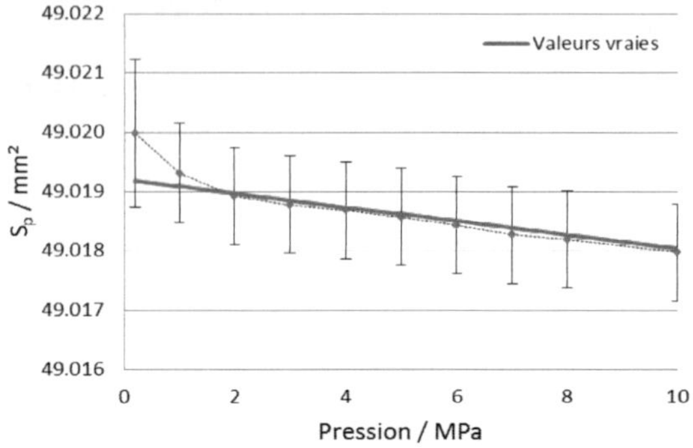

Fig. 1. Sections efficaces S_p et les valeurs théoriques S_{thp} pour l'ensemble piston-cylindre gaz de section nominale 49 mm². Les barres verticales représentent les incertitudes élargie associées.

Tableau 2. Sections efficaces S_p des ensembles piston-cylindre sous test en fonction de la pression ainsi que les incertitudes type associées $u(S_p)$.

GAZ (10 MPa)			HUILE (500 MPa)		
Pression nominale	Sp	*u(Sp)*	Pression nominale	Sp	*u(Sp)*
MPa	mm²	*mm²*	MPa	mm²	*mm²*
0,2	49,019 97	*0,000 62*	5	1,9028 26	*0,000 049*
1	49,019 31	*0,000 42*	52	1,9029 82	*0,000 026*
2	49,018 92	*0,000 41*	103	1,9030 70	*0,000 027*
3	49,018 77	*0,000 41*	155	1,9031 50	*0,000 027*
4	49,018 68	*0,000 41*	206	1,9032 16	*0,000 029*
5	49,018 57	*0,000 41*	258	1,9032 99	*0,000 031*
6	49,018 43	*0,000 41*	309	1,9033 77	*0,000 034*
7	49,018 26	*0,000 41*	361	1,9034 51	*0,000 036*
8	49,018 19	*0,000 41*	412	1,9035 31	*0,000 039*
10	49,017 97	*0,000 41*	515	1,9036 84	*0,000 047*

Tableau 3. Incertitudes sur les sections efficaces S_p dues à des effets systématiques et non systématiques.

GAZ (10 MPa)			HUILE (500 MPa)		
Pression nominale	$u(Sp_{sys})$	$u(Sp_{n/sys})$	Pression nominale	$u(Sp_{sys})$	$u(Sp_{n/sys})$
MPa	mm²	*mm²*	MPa	mm²	*mm²*
0,2	0,000 42	0,000 45	5	0,000 033	0,000 036
1	0,000 40	0,000 11	52	0,000 022	0,000 012
2	0,000 41	0,000 04	103	0,000 024	0,000 012
3	0,000 41	0,000 05	155	0,000 025	0,000 009
4	0,000 41	0,000 04	206	0,000 027	0,000 010
5	0,000 41	0,000 05	258	0,000 030	0,000 010
6	0,000 41	0,000 05	309	0,000 032	0,000 012
7	0,000 41	0,000 05	361	0,000 034	0,000 013
8	0,000 41	0,000 05	412	0,000 037	0,000 014
10	0,000 41	0,000 06	515	0,000 044	0,000 017

3. Méthodes d'estimation

A partir des données du tableau 2, le travail du métrologue est d'estimer la fonction d'étalonnage définie par l'équation (2). Puis il utilise la fonction estimée pour déduire la valeur de la pression mesurée par la balance sous test.
Pour déterminer les paramètres S_0 et λ de (2), trois méthodes type moindres carrés sont typiquement employées [7], les moindres carrées ordinaires (OLS), les moindres carrées pondérés (WLS) et enfin les moindres carrés généralisés (GLS).

3.1 Moindres carrés ordinaires (OLS)

Cette méthode est la plus couramment utilisée par les laboratoires de métrologie car elle est simple à mettre en œuvre. Elle suppose entre autre que l'incertitude sur les sections efficaces $u(S_p)$ soit constante (homoscédasticité) [4]. Toutefois, dans le cas des balances de pression, les incertitudes $u(S_p)$ varient généralement en fonction de la pression, en particulier lorsque le fluide utilisé est l'huile. Dans les exemples exposés ici, les incertitudes peuvent varier de plus de 50%.
L'application des OLS à ce type de données conduit souvent à des résultats éloignés des valeurs vraies et à des incertitudes systématiquement plus élevées que celles obtenues avec les autres méthodes (WLS et GLS). Comme indiqué à l'Annexe 1, la matrice de variances-covariances des paramètres estimés dépend de la structure d'incertitude des sections.

3.2 Moindres carrés pondérés (WLS)

La méthode des moindres carrés pondérés, dérivée des OLS, est adoptée par certains laboratoires, principalement des instituts nationaux de métrologie, afin de tenir compte de la variation de l'incertitude $u(S_p)$ en fonction de la pression. Dans ce cas, le poids associé à chaque point (S_p,P) correspond à l'inverse de l'incertitude $u(S_p)$.
En l'absence de covariances, cette méthode permet d'estimer correctement les valeurs des paramètres et également de propager les incertitudes $u(S_p)$ aux pressions estimées. Cependant, les valeurs des sections étant toujours fortement corrélées, les performances des WLS se dégradent si le poids associé au point (S_p,P) correspond à l'inverse de l'incertitude $u(S_p)$. Pour pallier à cette difficulté, nous proposons de pondérer les sections effectives par les incertitudes issues des facteurs non systématiques (voir § 2). Elles ne sont pas liées aux corrélations et elles expliquent la dispersion aléatoire des points autour du modèle vrai. Cette procédure permet d'estimer correctement les paramètres S_0 et λ, du modèle, les incertitudes associées aux paramètres doivent alors être augmentées de l'incertitude des effets systématiques (voir la formule donnée en Annexe 2).

3.3 Moindres carrés généralisés (GLS)

La méthode des moindres carrés généralisés, adoptée par quelques laboratoires en raison de sa complexité, considère l'ensemble des variances et des covariances associées aux sections S_p . Le poids attribué à chaque point (S_p,P) est issu d'une décomposition de la matrice de variances-covariances des sections S_p . La méthode des GLS, par son caractère complet, permet ainsi d'obtenir les incertitudes les plus faibles sur les paramètres S_0 et λ. Elle fournit aussi des estimations des paramètres, qui sont souvent les plus proches des valeurs vraies. Cette qualité est néanmoins relativement sensible à l'évaluation correcte des covariances.

4. Résultats

Le tableau 4 présente les valeurs des sections à pression nulle S_0 et des coefficients de déformation λ estimés par chaque méthode, pour les deux ensembles piston-cylindre. Les incertitudes associée $U(S_0)$ et $U(\lambda)$ correspondent aux incertitudes élargies exprimées en valeur relative dans le cas de la section à pression nulle S_0. Les écarts par rapport à la valeur vraie ont également été déterminés, pour le coefficient de déformation et pour la section à pression nulle.

Tableau 4. Résultats des estimations des sections effectives à pression nulle S_0 et des coefficients de déformation λ avec leur incertitude relative associée et écart respectif par rapport à leur valeur théorique S_{0th} et λ_{th}.

GAZ (10 MPa)	OLS	WLS	GLS
S_0 (mm²)	49.019 50	49.019 19	49.019 23
$U(S_0)/S_0 \cdot 10^6$	*18*	*17*	*17*
$(S_0-S_{th})/S_0 \cdot 10^6$	6.2	-0.3	0.7
$\lambda \cdot (10^6$ MPa)	-3.52	-2.57	-2.7
$U(\lambda) \cdot (10^6$ MPa)	*1.01*	*0.52*	*0.47*
$(\lambda - \lambda_{th}) \cdot (10^6$ MPa)	**-1.14**	-0.19	-0.32

HUILE (500 MPa)	OLS	WLS	GLS
S_0 (mm²)	1.902 881	1.902 908	1.902 923
$U(S_0)/S_0 \cdot 10^6$	*28*	*22*	*21*
$(S_0-S_{th})/S_0 \cdot 10^6$	-21	-6.4	1.8
$\lambda \cdot (10^6$ MPa)	0.836	0.796	0.813
$U(\lambda) \cdot (10^6$ MPa)	*0.056*	*0.054*	*0.051*
$(\lambda - \lambda_{th}) \cdot (10^6$ MPa)	**0.056**	0.016	0.033

Ces données sont représentées graphiquement dans les figures 2 et 3 ci-après.

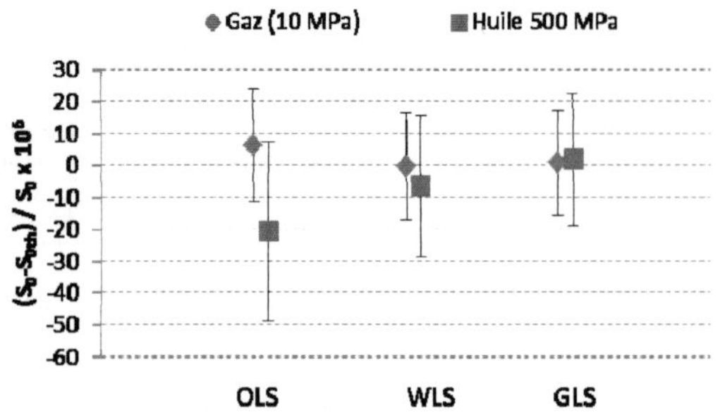

Fig. 2. Ecarts relatifs des sections effectives à pression nulle par rapport aux valeurs vraies en fonction de la méthodes d'estimation. Les barres représentent les incertitudes élargies associées.

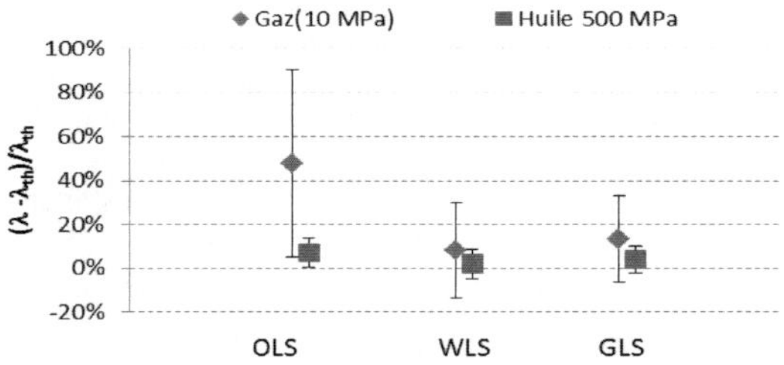

Fig. 3. Ecarts relatifs des coefficients de déformation par rapport aux valeurs vraies en fonction de la méthode d'estimation. Les barres représentent les incertitudes élargies associées.

5. Analyse

Les résultats montrent que les sections effectives à pression nulle S_0 estimées sont cohérentes avec les incertitudes associées $U(S_0)$ pour les méthodes employées. Toutefois, les OLS présentent un écart et une incertitude plus importants dans l'exemple d'étalonnage en huile. Les méthodes GLS et WLS montrent quant à elles des résultats satisfaisants avec des incertitudes sur ce paramètre relativement proches dans les deux cas de figure.

Concernant le coefficient de déformation λ, l'écart à la valeur vraie est supérieur à l'incertitude élargie dans l'exemple de l'étalonnage en gaz, pour les OLS et ce, malgré une incertitude environ deux fois plus importante que les autres méthodes. Dans le cas de l'huile, l'incertitude élargie correspond à cet écart.
Les deux autres méthodes, WLS et GLS présentent à nouveaux des résultats similaires sur la détermination de ce paramètre et l'estimation de son incertitude pour les deux ensembles piston-cylindre.

Par ailleurs, il est important de noter que les certificats d'étalonnage ne mentionnent jamais la covariance entre les deux paramètres S_0 et λ, alors que ceux-ci sont corrélés conduisant dès lors à une surestimation de l'incertitude sur la pression délivrée par la balance de pression.

6. Conclusion

La méthode des moindres carrés ordinaires (OLS), employée par la majorité des laboratoires lors de l'étalonnage des balances de pression pour la détermination des paramètres S_0 et λ conduit souvent à des résultats éloignés des valeurs vraies et à des incertitudes systématiquement plus élevées que celles obtenues avec les méthodes des moindres carrés pondérés (WLS) et des moindre carrés généralisés (GLS).
La méthode des OLS n'est donc pas adaptée à la modélisation des résultats d'étalonnage des balances de pression. La solution qui consiste à éliminer du modèle les points d'étalonnage présentant des incertitudes trop importantes est à éviter.

La méthode des GLS permet d'évaluer correctement les paramètres du modèle des sections efficaces, lorsque les incertitudes et notamment les covariances sont connues. En routine, l'effort demandé pour évaluer les covariances peut s'avérer trop important compte tenu des enjeux techniques et économiques. Une solution pour s'affranchir du calcul des covariances est d'utiliser la méthode des WLS modifiée. Les paramètres du modèle sont d'abord estimés en considérant seulement les incertitudes dues aux effets non systématiques. Puis, pour la prévision d'une section $\hat{S}_p$, l'incertitude issue de la modélisation est dégradée en lui ajoutant les incertitudes dues aux effets systématiques.

Par ailleurs, les méthodes WLS et GLS peuvent être mises en œuvre aisément avec le logiciel LNE-RegPoly disponible en accès libre sur le site internet du LNE.

Annexes

L'équation de la droite d'étalonnage (2) se réécrit dans une forme générale :

$$S_p = S_0\,(1+\lambda p) = b_0 + b_1\,p$$

En utilisant les notations matricielles, les données sont représentées par le vecteur colonne S qui regroupe les sections effectives, la matrice P = (1 p) à deux colonnes - composée du vecteur unitaire et du vecteur des pressions p - , le vecteur ligne $B = (b_0\ b_1)$. L'équation (2) devient :

$$S = P*B$$

La matrice V(S) comprend dans sa diagonale principale les variances et hors diagonale les covariances des valeurs des sections S_p.

A.1 - méthode des OLS

L'estimateur est donné par $B_{OLS} = (P'P)^{-1}P'S$ et sa matrice de variances-covariances par $Cov(B_{OLS}) = V[(P'P)^{-1}P'S]$
En développant, il vient :
$Cov(B_{OLS}) = (P'P)^{-1}P'V(S)P(P'P)^{-1}$

Cette expression se simplifie lorsque les valeurs de section ont la même incertitude σ et ne sont pas corrélées :
$Cov(B_{OLS}) = \sigma^2 (P'P)^{-1}$

A.2 - méthode des WLS
L'estimateur est donné par :
$B_{WLS} = (P'(M)^{-1}P)^{-1}P'(M)^{-1}S$
et sa matrice de variances-covariances par :
$Cov(B_{WLS}) = V[(P'(M)^{-1}P)^{-1}P'(M)^{-1}S]$
où M est une matrice diagonale représentant les poids.

En développant, il vient :
$Cov(B_{WLS}) =$
$(P'(M)^{-1}P)^{-1}P'(M)^{-1}V(S)(M)^{-1}P(P'(M)^{-1}P)^{-1}$

Lorsque la matrice M comprend les variances des valeurs de S sur la diagonale principale et ainsi, correspond à V(S), l'expression précédente se simplifie :
$Cov(B_{WLS}) = (P'V(S)^{-1}P)^{-1}$

References

1. P. OTAL, Métrologie des pressions, Afnor ; article III-20-30; 18p, 2010 ;
2. RMAéro 802-21, Étalonnage et utilisation des balances manométriques - Balance à application de masses
3. Calibration of Pressure Balances, EURAMET cg-3, Version 1.0 (03/2011)
4. P. OTAL et al., Evaluation of cross-float measurements with pressure balances - results of EURAMET project 1125, 2011 ; PTB mitteilungen ; heft 3 ; n°121 ; p294-297
5. I. Morgado et al, Evaluation of cross-float measurements with pressure balances – EURAMET project 1125
6. www.lne.fr/fr/logiciels/lne-regpoly
7. C. Yardin, Estimer la droite d'étalonnage avec les moindres carrés généralisés et évaluer le résultat de mesure, Revue Française de Métrologie, Volume 2012 – 3, n°31, pp. 21 – 39, 2013

Métrologie en Energie Solaire: un exemple de réétalonnage d'un pyranomètre réparé en remplaçant son hémisphère externe endommagé

S. Touré et M. Sidibé

Laboraatoire d'Energie Solaire, UFR SSMT, Université F. Houphoouët-Boigny Abidjan Cocody 22 BP 582 Abidjan 22. Email: siakaahtoure@yahoo.fr

Reçu:

Résumé. Notre Laboratoire est très souvent amené à effectuer des mesures d'éclairement solaire. Ces mesures se font dans le cadre de 'étude du gisement solaire. Elles se font aussi lors de l'étude expérimentale de systèmes de conversion thermique de l'énergie solaire tels que les cuisinières solaires, les chauffe-eaux solaire, les distillateurs solaires, les séchoirs solaires que nous construisons et testons. Elles se font aussi souvent lors de l'étude expérimentale de systèmes photovoltaïques que nous élaborons. Ce travail concerne la réparation et le réétalonnage d'un de nos pyranomètres Eppley PsP qui avait été accidentellement endommagé. L'hémisphère (coupelle) externe a été fissuré. Une autre coupelle a été fabriquée sur le modèle de celle qui a été endommagée. Un réétalonnage a dû être effectué. Le pyranomètre donne sous éclairement, une tension v en Volts. L'éclairement est donné par E = v/k. Avant l'incident, la valeur de la constante k était $k = 9{,}1.10^{-3}$. Nous disposons d'un second pyranomètre Eppley, en bon état, de constante $k = 10{,}41.10^{-3}$ qui a été considéré comme le pyranomètre normal servant d'étalon. Les mesures simultanées faites avec les deux pyranomètres ont donné des écarts importants entre les deux éclairements obtenus. Nous avons donc recherché une constante du pyranomètre réparé qui donne des valeurs correctes de l'éclairement. Le meilleur accord entre les deux mesures est obtenu pour $k = 8{,}2.10^{-3}$. Deux jours de test ont été considérés. Pour le premier jour, on a pour $k = 9{,}1.10^{-3}$, RMSE = 70,6 W/m² et pour $k = 8{,}2.10^{-3}$, RMSE = 22,14 W/m². Pour le second jour, on a pour $k = 9{,}1.10^{-3}$, RMSE = 62,75 W/m² et pour $k = 8{,}2.10^{-3}$, RMSE = 31,05 W/m².

Mots clés: Energie solaire, mesure d'éclairement; pyranomètre; constante solaire; estimation du rayonnement global

1 Introduction

On assiste aujourd'hui à un accroissement toujours grand de la population qui conduit à une demande croissante d'énergie dans tous les pays. La surexploitation des sources d'énergie dites fossiles telles que le pétrole et le charbon pose de sérieux problèmes d'environnement. Face à cette situation, les sources d'énergie renouvelables deviennent attrayantes. L'énergie solaire en particulier a de multiples applications. Les recherches qui se mènent dans ce domaine de même que l'évaluation des systèmes d'énergie solaire, requièrent une bonne connaissance du gisement solaire. Cette détermination du gisement solaire doit s'appuyer sur des instruments fiables de mesure du rayonnement solaire. L'un des instruments souvent utilisés dans ce domaine est le pyranomètre qui mesure le rayonnement global.

2 Evaluation et mesure du rayonnement solaire

2.1 Constante solaire et modèles d'estimation du rayonnement solaire

La constante solaire est définie comme étant l'énergie provenant du soleil par unité de temps qui atteint une surface unité perpendiculairement à la direction de propagation de la radiation solaire à la distance moyenne terre-soleil et en dehors de l'atmosphère. Cette constante solaire, qui est une valeur moyenne, vaut $G_{sc} = 1367\ W/m^2$. Il existe un certain nombre de modèles qui permettent d'estimer le rayonnement solaire. Ces calculs font intervenir la radiation extraterrestre E_{sc} qui varie en cours de l'année. D'après Spencer (1971), cette radiation extraterrestre s'écrit

$$E_{sc} = G_{sc}(1 + 0{,}033cos\frac{360n}{365D}) \quad (1)$$

Une autre relation est celle d'Iqbal(1983) [1] qui s'écrit

$$E_{sc} = G_{sc}(1{,}000110 + 0{,}034221cos\frac{(n-1)360}{365} + 0{,}001280sin\frac{(n-1)360}{365} + 0{,}000719cos2\frac{(n-1)360}{365} +$$

$0{,}000077 sin2 \frac{(n-1)360}{365})$ (2)

Plusieurs modèles sont utilisés pour estimer le rayonnement solaire reçu sur terre; Ainsi sont estimés:

- l'éclairement solaire I_h dû à la composante directe par ciel clair;

- l'éclairement solaire D_h dû à la composante diffuse;

- le rayonnement solaire global sur un plan horizontal

$$G_h = I_h + D_h \quad (3)$$

Ces modèles prennent généralement en compte la transmission due à la diffusion Rayleigh, la transmission due à l'absorption par les gaz (essentiellement O_2 et CO_2), la transmission due à l'absorption par l'ozone atmosphérique, la transmission due à l'absorption par la vapeur d'eau, la transmission due à l'extinction par les aérosols.

On peut citer le modèle de Bird & Hulstrom [1, 2, 3, 4,5]. On a aussi le modèle de Capderou [1, 6]

2.2 Mesure du rayonnement solaire et de la durée d'insolation

Le rayonnement direct est mesuré à l'aide d'un pyrhéliomètre. Quand au rayonnement solaire global sur un plan horizontal, il est mesuré à l'aide d'un pyranomètre. La durée d'insolation est généralement mesurée à l'aide de l'héliographe de Campbell - Stokes [7]

Notre étude porte sur le pyranomètre dont un schéma est donné sur la Figure 1

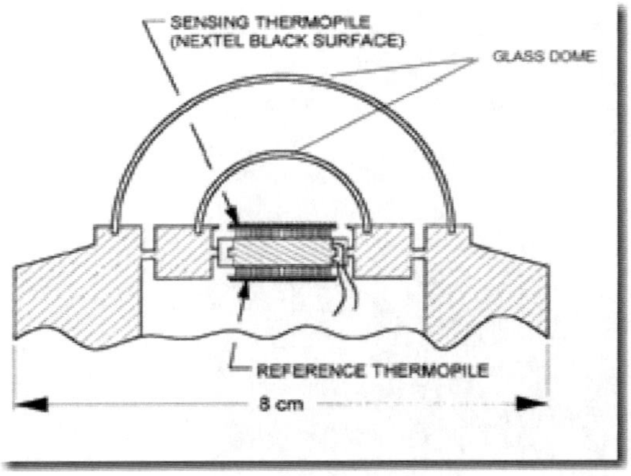

Fig. 1. Schéma de principe d'un pyranomètre montrant les deux coupelles

Les deux pyranomètres Eppley PsP intervenant dans la présente étude sont donnés ci-dessous. Le pyranomètre réparé est montré sur la Figure 2. Quand au pyranomètre étalon, celui qui n'a pas été endommagé, il est montré sur la Figure 3.

Fig. 2. Pyranomètre Eppley avec la coupelle extérieure renouvelée dont le coefficient était initialement, avant réparation, $k = 9{,}1.10^{-3}$.

. **Fig. 3.** Pyranomètre Eppley étalon en bon état, de coefficient $k = 10{,}41.10^{-3}$

Dans le principe, la plupart des pyranomètres utilisent la différence de température qui apparait entre une surface noire qui est un bon absorbant du rayonnement solaire visible et une surface blanche qui la réfléchit. [7]. La surface noire s'échauffe plus et la différence de température entre les deux surfaces est mesurée à l'aide d'un thermocouple qui délivre une tension v en mV. L'éclairement solaire E (W/m²) est donné par la relation

$$E == \frac{v}{k} \tag{4}$$

K (mV/W/m²) est une constante caractéristique du pyranomètre. Comme on le voit sur les Figures 2 et 3, l e récepteur (surface noire) est protégé des intempéries (vent, pluie, poussière…) par deux hémisphères ou coupelles transparents. Le pyranomètre mesure, sur un plan horizontal, le rayonnement solaire provenant d'un demi-espace [7]

3 Etude expérimentale

Lors d'une manipulation, la coupelle externe du pyranomètre de la Figure 2 a reçu un hoc et s'est fissuré. Une autre coupelle a été fabriquée sur le modèle de celle qui a été endommagée. Elle est montrée sur la Figure 4 ci-dessous

Fig. 4. Coupelle en verre fabriquée pour remplacer la coupelle externe du pyranomètre de la Figure 2 qui avait été fissurée

Après cette réparation, ce pyranomètre à réétalonner est représenté sur la figure 2. Le pyranomètre normal, celui qui servira à faire l'étalonnage st représenté sur la Figure 3. Deux journées d'expérimentation ont été choisies: le 04 avril 2008 et le 05 avril 2008. Pour chacune des deux journées, l'éclairement a été simultanément t mesuré à l'aide des eux pyranomètres. Chaque pyranomètre est branché aux bornes d'un multimètre et délivre ainsi une tension v qui est convertie en éclairement solaire en utilisant l relation (4). L'éclairement fourni par le pyranomètre normal est appelé Enor. Celui fourni par le pyranomètre à étalonner est appelé EEtalon1. Lee pyranomètre à talonner avait une constante $k = 9{,}1.10^{-3}$ mV/W/m². Quand au pyranomètre normal, sa constante est différente et vaut $k = 10{,}41.10^{-3}$ mV/W/m²

4 Résultats et discussions

Les valeurs de Enor et EEtalon1 obtenues avec ces deux constantes étaient importants. Nous avons donc recalculé EEtalon1 avec les valeurs suivantes de k: $k = 9{,}1.10^{-3}$; $k = 8{,}7.10^{-3}$; $k = 8{,}5.10^{-3}$; $k = 8{,}2.10^{-3}$ mV/W/m². La valeur de EEtalon1 obtenue est comparé à Enor. La Figure 5 donne la courbe de variation de l'clairement obtenu pour la journée du 04 avril 2008. Les courbes donnant Enor et EEtaalon1 pour les différentes valeurs de la constante k sont montrées. On constate que le minimum d'écart entre Enor et EEtalon1 et obtenu pour $k = 8{,}2.10^{-3}$ mV/W/m²

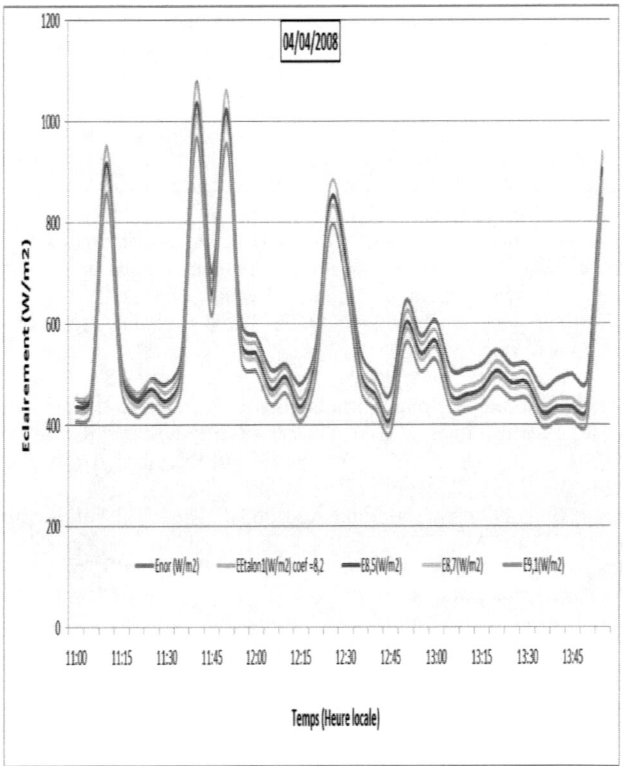

Fig. 5. Courbes de variation de Enor et de EEtalon1 le 04 avril 2008 pour $k = 9{,}1.10^{-3}$; $k = 8{,}7.10^{-3}$; $k = 8{,}5.10^{-3}$; $k = 8{,}2.10^{-3}$ mV/W/m².

Le minimum d'écart entre Enor et EEtalon1 entant obtenu pour $k = 8{,}2.10^{-3}$ mV/W/m², nous traçons sur la Figure 6 les évolutions comparées, avec le temps, de Enor et de EEtalon1 pour $k = 8{,}2.10^{-3}$ mV/W/m . On constate bien que sur plusieurs tranches horaires, les deux courbes sont pratiquement confondues.

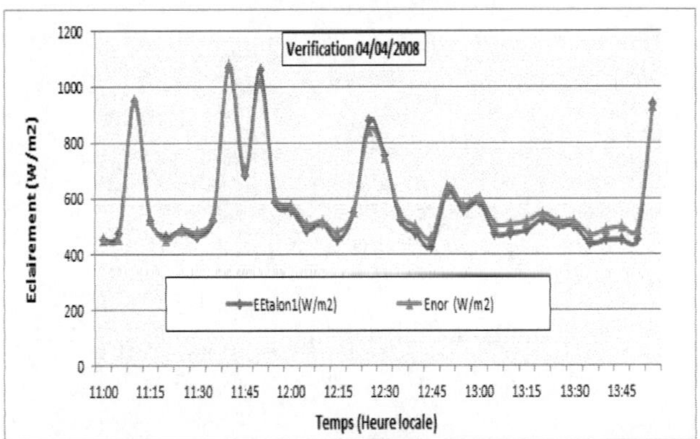

Fig. 5. Courbes de variation de Enor et de EEtalon1 le 04 avril 2008 pour $k = 8{,}2.10^{-3}$ mV/W/m².

Nous avons refait la même expérimentation le 05 avril 2008. La Figure 7 donne la courbe de variation de l'clairement obtenu pour la journée du 04 avril 2008. On y voit Les courbes donnant Enor et EEtaalon1 pour les différentes valeurs de la constante k . On constate encore que le minimum d'écart entre Enor et EEtalon1 et obtenu pour $k = 8{,}2.10^{-3}$ mV/W/m²

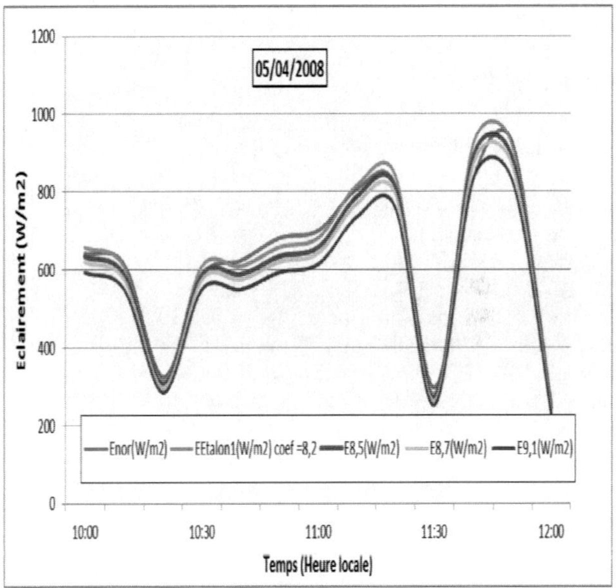

Fig. 7. Courbes de variation de Enor et de EEtalon1 le 05 avril 2008 pour $k = 9{,}1.10^{-3}$; $k = 8{,}7.10^{-3}$; $k = 8{,}5.10^{-3}$; $k = 8{,}2.10^{-3}$ mV/W/m².

Pur cette raison et comme dans le cas du 04 avril, nous traçons sur la Figure 8 les évolutions comparées, avec le temps, de Enor et de EEtalon1 pour $k = 8{,}2.10^{-3}$ mV/W/m . On constate encore que sur plusieurs tranches horaires, les deux courbes sont pratiquement confondues.

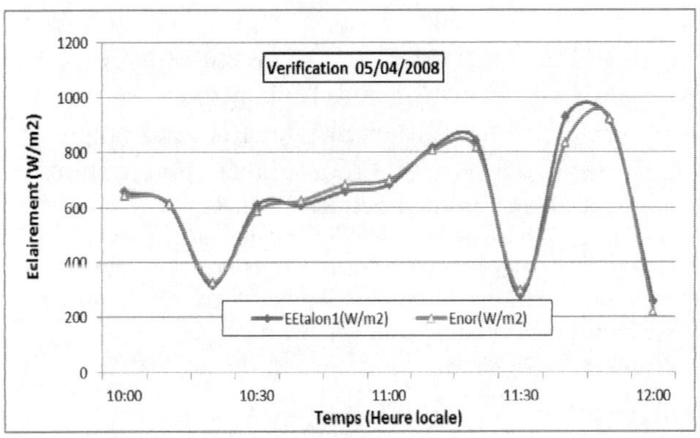

Fig. 5. Courbes de variation de Enor et de EEtalon1 le 05 avril 2008 pour $k = 8{,}2.10^{-3}$ mV/W/m².

Nous avons ensuite effectué une analyse statistique des résultats en utilisant un test d'ajustement qui est le "root mean square error (RMSE). Il s'agit d'évaluer la bonne concordance entre la valeur de l'éclairement obtenue avec le pyranomètre normal, et celle obtenue avec le pyranomètre réparé. Pour définir RMSE, , posons Fn = Enor (éclairement fourni par le pyranomètre normal) et Fe = EEtalon1 (éclairement fourni par le pyranomètre réparé). RMSE est alors défini de la manière suivante:

$$RMSE = (\frac{1}{N}\sum_{i=1}^{N}\left(f_{n_i} - f_{e_i}\right)^2)^{1/2} \quad (5)$$

N est la taille de l'échantillon

RMSE a été calculé pour les deux jours de test. Pour le premier jour, on a pour $k = 9{,}1.10^{-3}$ mV/W/m², RMSE = 70,6 W/m² et pour $k = 8{,}2.10^{-3}$ mV/W/m², RMSE = 22,14 W/m².
Pour le second jour, on a pour $k = 9{,}1.10^{-3}$ mV/W/m² , RMSE = 62,75 W/m² et pour $k = 8{,}2.10^{-3}$ mV/W/m², RMSE = 31,05 W/m². On constate, pour les deux jours de test, une forte baisse de RMSE lorsqu'on passe de $k = 9{,}1.10^{-3}$ mV/W/m², à $k = 8{,}2.10^{-3}$ mV/W/m²

5 Conclusion

L'expérience de réétalonnage que nous avons effectuée nous a montré que le récepteur du pyranomètre réparé n'a pas été endommagé lorsque sa coupelle externe a été fissurée. La courbe obtenue avec ce pyranomètre et celle obtenue avec le pyranomètre normal ont effectivement la même allure. Les écarts constatés entre les éclairements fournis par les deux pyranomètres nous ont indiqué que la constante k du pyranomètre réparé en changeant sa coupelle de verre externe, devait être corrigée. Plusieurs valeurs de k ont été essayées. Le minimum d'écart entre Enor (l'éclairement fourni par le pyranomètre normal) et EEtalon1 (l'éclairement fourni par le pyranomètre réparé) a été obtenu pour $k = 8{,}2.10^{-3}$ mV/W/m². Les calculs statistiques nous ont montré une forte baisse de RMSE lorsque nous passons de $k = 9{,}1.10^{-3}$ mV/W/m² à $k = 8{,}2.10^{-3}$ mV/W/m² pour le pyranomètre réparé. C'est cette dernière valeur de k qui est désormais retenue pour le pyranomètre réparé.

Références

1. M. Iqbal, An Introduction to Solar Radiation, Academic Press, Department of Mechanical Engineering, University of British Columbia, Canada (1983)

2. M. Mesri-Merad, L. Rougab, A. Cheknane, N.L. Bachari, Estimation du Rayonnement solaire au sol par des modèles semi-empiriques, Revue des Energies Renouvelables. **15**, 451–463(2012)

3. M. Koussa, A. Malek, M. Haddadi, Validation de quelques modèles de reconstitution des éclairements dus au rayonnement solaire direct, diffus et global par ciel clair, Revue des Energies Renouvelables. **9**, 307–332 (2006)

4. R. Hanane, F.S. Mohammed, C. Mohammed, Estimation de la composante directe normale du rayonnement solaire à partir des données satellites-cas de Rabat. ,16ème Journées Internationales de Thermique r(JITH 2013) Marrakech (Maroc) du 13 au 15 novembre 2013 (2013)

5. M. Sidibé., D. Soro, W.F.. Fassinou, S. Touré, Reconstitution of Solar Radiation on a site of the Littoral in Côte d'Ivoire, International Journal of Engineering Research and Technology ISSN 09774-3154 **10,** Number 1, 19–31 (2017)

6. A. Meffti, M.Y. Bouroubi, A. Khellaf, Analyse Critique du Modèle de l'Atlas Solaire e l'Algérie, Revue des Energies Renouvelables. **2**, 69–85. (1999)

7. J. M. Chassériaux, Conversion thermique du rayonnement Solaire, Dunod Paris France (1984)

Expérience du Centre de Recherche et Développement de l'Electricité et du Gaz-CREDEG Dans le domaine de l'accréditation de ses activités

I.KHELFANE - khelfane.ilhem@credeg.dz

Centre de Recherche et Devveloppement de l'Electricité et du Gaz , CREDEG ,filiale de SONELGAZ
Route de Ouled Fayet RN n°36, Colline des Grands Vents El Achour-Alger- Algérie

Received:

Abstract. L'accréditation est une reconnaissance formelle d'un organisme d'évaluation de la conformité de la compétence d'une entité à réaliser des activités spécifiques. L'évaluation de la conformité est au cœur de la vison managérial de la Direction Générale du Centre de Recherche et Développement de l'électricité et du gaz- CREDEG, depuis 2009, et il nous est apparu impératif d'aller vers une reconnaissance technique de nos compétences dans les activités clés du CREDEG à savoir l'étalonnage des compteurs d'énergie électrique selon le référentiel ISO/CEI17025-2005.
Le CREDEG a entamé le processus d'accréditation en 2009 par une pré-évaluation réalisée par les experts de l'Organisme Algérien d'Accréditation .

Keywords: Métrologie, étalonnage, accréditation; Management de la quaité

1.Introduction :

L'entreprise ne peut acquérir et donner l'assurance de ses moyens de contrôle de mesure et d'essai que si elle maîtrise la connaissance de leurs performances exactes ainsi que leurs limites d'emploi et leurs comportements dans le temps. La fonction métrologie dans l'entreprise est un investissement important qui concourt à la qualité des différents produits, de façon simple, efficace et économique.

A cet effet et afin de répondre au mieux aux attentes des filiales du groupe SONELGAZ, le Centre de Recherche et Developpement de l'Electricité et du Gaz-CREDEG a mis en place la fonction métrologie et a axé sa vision managérial sur l'évaluation de la conformité pour une reconnaissance technique de ses compétences dans son activité clé relative à l'étalonnage des compteurs d'énergie électrique.

2.Processus d'accréditation du laboratoire du CREDEG:

le CREDEG a entrpris un projet ambitieux scindé en deux phase:

la première consistait à l'implantation de la fonction métrologie au sein de l'entreprise suivant les étapes cités ci-dessous:

- Inventaire de tous les équipements qui interviennent dans le domaine de l'étalonnage;
- Élaboration d'une fiche de vie pour chaque équipements de mesure existant au laboratoire d'étalonnage;
- Identification des individus clés des laboratoires d'étalonnage du CREDEG avec la nomination d'un Responsable Technique et d'un Correspondant Qualité;
- Elaboration de fiche de poste pour le personnel du laboratoire d'étalonnage avec identification des taches et des responsabilités de chacun;
- Explication du rôle et de l'importance de la fonction métrologie au personnel des laboratoires en publiant des articles sur l'étalonnage dans la revue éditée par CREDEG ;
- Mise en place d'une veille technologique, normative et réglementaire au sein des laboratoires d'étalonnage ;
- Mise en place d'un système de management de la qualité selon le référentiel ISO/CEI 17025.

la seconde étape consistait à la mise en oeuvre du processus d'accréditation du laboratoire d'étalonnage des compteurs d'énergie électrique au laboratoire fixe et sur site client selon le référentiel ISO/CEI17025-2005, elle a débutée en 2009 avec une Pré-évaluation des capacités humaines et matériels du CREDEG réalisée par l'Organisme Algérien d'Accréditation (Algerac) en vu de la selection du CREDEG pour benéficier d'un accompagnement dans le cadre du programme (PME II) programme d'Appui aux PME/PMI dans les domaines de la qualité et du développement institutionnel.

Fig 1:Etalonnage laboratoire fixe

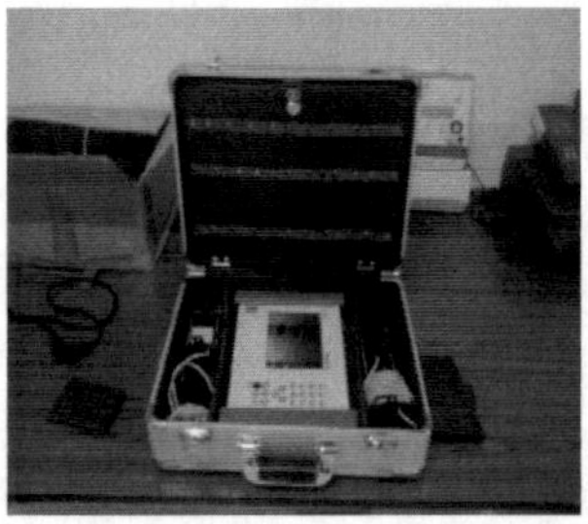

Fig 2:Etalonnage sur site

Au cours des deux années 2009 et 2010 le CREDEG a réalisé les actions listées ci-aprés afin de préparer son personnel au projet de l'accréditation:

- Sensibilisation du personnel du laboratoire à l'accréditation et son importance afin de susciter leur adhésion ;
- Formation du personnel aux exigences de la norme ISO/CEI 17025, formation réalisée par Institut Algérien de Normalisation IANOR;
- Mise en place d'une équipe chargée du suivi du projet d'accréditation;
- Identification du champs et de la portée d'accréditation.

Au cours de l'année 2011 un diagnostic des activités du CREDEG ,objet d'accréditation selon le référentiel ISO/CEI 17025, a été réalisé par les experts du Programme Moyenne Entreprise (PME II). A l'issu de ce diagnostic un certain nombre d'écarts a été constaté il a concerné notamment l'aspect formation du personnel et conformité des locaux de travail. Afin de lever toutes les non conformités et de se préparer à l'accréditation le CREDEG a bénéficié d'un accompagnement par le programme PME II d'une durée de 09 mois à raison d'une semaine par mois. L'accompagnement qui a débuté en 2012 a porté essentiellement sur la:

- Rédaction du Manuel qualité;
- Mise en place du système qualité;
- Rédaction des procédures techniques et création des enregistrements associés: (Formalisation du mode opératoire; identification et recensement des causes d'erreur et des facteurs influençant les opération d'étalonnage des compteurs d'énergie électrique, réalisation des cartes de contrôle statistique des équipements ayant une incidence sur la qualité des résultats d'étalonnage....ect);
- Mise en place des actions d'amélioration au niveau du laboratoire tel que le développement d'une application pour la gestion du planning d'étalonnage des équipements du laboratoire d'étalonnage.

En plus de ce qui a été cité , un plan d'action a été mis en oeuvre pour lever toutes les reserves constatées lors du diagnostic effectuée par le PMEII il a porté sur:

- La gestion rationnelle des équipements de mesure du laboratoire d'étalonnage des compteurs d'énergie électrique;
- Le raccordement métrologique des équipements de mesure du laboratoire d'étalonnage;
- L'étalonnages et la vérifications périodiques des équipements de mesure du laboratoire d'étalonnage;
- L'entretien et la maintenances préventives des équipements de mesure;
- l'utilisation des équipements de mesure par un personnel compétent habilité et autorisé;
- la mise en place d'un système d'identification et d'évaluation des formations ;
- L'orientation de l'organisation et du management vers l'amélioration des compétences;
- La surveillance et l'habilitation technique annuelles du personnel du laboratoire d'étalonnage;
- L'aménagement des locaux pour une adaptation aux activités d'étalonnage avec la mise en place d'un sas afin de maintenir la stabilité ambiante du laboratoire à (23±2) °C ;
- La surveillance des conditions d'environnement du laboratoire d'étalonnage (température et humidité) avec l'acquisition d'un enregistreur automatique en continu de température et d'humidité ainsi que la maitrise des conditions d'environnement du laboratoire avec l'élaboration de la cartographie du laboratoire pour l'obtention des conditions ambiantes (23±2)°C;
- L'accès limité et réglementé aux équipements de mesure, locaux, dossiers clients…etc.
- Réalisation d'une comparaison inter-laboratoire afin de valider et assurer la qualité des résultats du laboratoire ; le CREDEG a rencontré

certaines difficultés à réaliser cette action à cause des procédures douanières relatives à la mobilité des équipements et instruments de mesure vers l'étranger.

- Réalisation de formation sur l'estimation des incertitudes en énergie pour le personnel du laboratoire ;
- Réalisation de formation d'audit interne pour le personnel du laboratoire.

A la fin de la période d'accompagnement, le CREDEG a déposé une demande d'accréditation de l'activité étalonnage des compteurs d'énergie électrique au laboratoire fixe et sur site client auprès de ALGERAC qui après un audit lui octroyé une reconnaissance de la compétence de son personnel à réaliser les opérations d'étalonnage avec l'attribution d'une accréditation en 2014 pour une durée de 3ans. Cette dernière a été reconduite en 2017.

ORGANISME ALGERIEN D'ACCREDITATION

ALGERAC

Certificat d'Accréditation

N° du certificat : 1-1-004

ALGERAC, reconnu par le décret n° 05-466 du 06 décembre 2005, atteste que :

Le Laboratoire d'Etalonnage CREDEG

El Achour - Alger

Est accrédité selon la norme ISO/CEI 17025:2005 pour les activités suivantes :

Etalonnage des compteurs d'énergie électrique

décrites dans l'annexe technique qui fait partie intégrante du présent certificat.

L'accréditation est maintenue à condition que l'OEC continue à satisfaire les exigences d'accréditation d'ALGERAC.

Le Directeur Général

Date d'octroi : 19/01/2014
Date de fin de validité : 19/01/2017

Noureddine BOUDISSA

Fig3 : Certificat d'accréditation

3.Impact de l'accréditation sur le CREDEG:

L'accréditation a permis au CREDEG de s'imposer sur le marché des prestations d'étalonnage et de ganger la confiance et la périnnité de ses clients d'une part et d'autre pat d'obtenir la reconnaissance des pouvoirs publics.
Il est important de signaler que le chiffre d'affaire du CREDEG réalisé auprès des clients externes aux filiales du groupe SONELGAZ est passé de 20 à 30% du chiffre d'affaire globale du centre depuis l'obtention de l'accréditation. Cette reconnaissance de la compétence technique du personnel de CREDEG dans l'étalonnage des compteurs d'énergie électrique a garanti aux clients de CREDEG des rapports d'étalonnage fiable et reconnu par toutes les instances du marché au niveau international.
l'accréditation a permis l'amélioration de la satisfaction des clients ainsi que les parties prenantes du CREDEG.

Elle a permis de mobiliser le personnel autour d'un projet d'entreprise fédérateur et de maintenir les compétences technique du CREDEG.

par ailleurs, l'expérience ainsi que le savoir-faire acquis par le CREDEG dans le domaine de l'accréditation, lui a permis de developper une nouvelle activité qui est l'accompagnement. Actuellement le CREDEG accompagne les filiales du groupe SONELGAZ qui souhaitent être accréditées dans leur mise en place du système management de la qualité afin de se conformer aux exigences du référentiel de l'accréditation ISO/CEI 17025 version 2005 en vue d'obtention d'une accréditation.

4.Conclusion

Suite à l'expérience du CREDEG dans la mise en oeuvre du processus d'accréditation de son laboratoire d'étalonnage des compteurs d'énergie selon le référentiel CEI/ISO 17025 version 2005 un certain nombre de difficultés a été rencontré tel que la réalisation de l'opération de comparaison inter-laboratoire qui est une exigence du référentiel d'accréditation . A cet effet, il en résulte la néccessité de mise en place d'un réseau de laboratoires d'étalonnage en Algérie afin de permettre et faciliter les opérations de comparaison inter-laboratoires.

En tenant compte de l'impact positif de l'accréditation le CREDEG a décidé de faire l'extension de l'accréditation de ses laboratoires d'étalonnage en grandeurs électrique et la pression dans l'objectif d'améliorer les prestations d'étalonnage existantes et offrir ainsi des prestations conformes aux exigences de nos clients tout en respectant la réglementation nationale, les normes en vigueur et les règles déontologiques conformément au code d'éthique des sociétés du Groupe SONELGAZ.

En effet, le CREDEG, à travers les manifestations quelles organise contribue à la promotion de l'accréditation des laboratoires d'essai, analyse et étalonnage. Cette accréditation qui est à la base volontaire mais avec l'évolution du contexte règlementaire algérien elle tend à devenir dans le futur obligatoire dans de nombreux domaines. Actuellement, plusieurs entreprises du pays exigent l'accréditation comme préalable à un engagement contractuelle de prestation de service.

Estimation des Incertitudes de Mesures du Module de Rigidité : Cas d'essai de traction indirecte sur éprouvettes cylindriques

Hicham Mezouara [(1)], Latifa Dlimi [(1)], Abdelouahhab Salih [(2)], Mohamed Afechcar [(3)]

(1) Laboratoire Interdisciplinaire En Ressources Naturelles et en Environnement Département de Physique Faculté Des Sciences, Université Ibn Tofail de Kenitra, Maroc.
(2) PES Génie Mécanique LMD- E.N.S.E.T. B.P. 6207 Rabat – Maroc Responsable de l'Equipe de Recherche Instrumentation, Mesures et Essais, Auditeur Technique attaché au MCI, Consultant de l'ANPME.
(3) Directeur Technique du Laboratoire CNER. Rabat – Maroc.

hicham_dess@yahoo.fr

Résumé:

Cette étude traite des incertitudes de mesure que l'on peut rencontrer dans l'essai de module de rigidité d'enrobé bitumineux. On présente l'ensemble des capteurs installés sur des chaînes de mesure de module de rigidité ainsi que leurs plages d'incertitude, Plusieurs paramètres influencent sur la valeur du module de rigidité d'un enrobé telle que les paramètres liés aux conditions d'essai et d'autres sont plutôt liés à la spécification de l'appareillage sont la vitesse, le niveau de chargement, la température, la dimension de l'échantillon testé et l'acquisition des données…, tous ces facteurs ont une grande influence sur la valeur du module de rigidité. Pour qualifier les facteurs d'incertitude nous avons utilisé deux approches : approche1 est effectuée en suivant la démarche décrite par le GUM (Guide to the expression of uncertainty in measurement), l'approche 2 par la simulation numérique de Monte-Carlo. Les deux résultats sont alors comparés pour un intervalle de confiances de 95%.

Mots Clés : Module de Rigidité, Incertitude, Propagation des variances, GUM, Monte-Carlo.

Introduction

Dans les laboratoires des essais, la réalisation des essais implique l'utilisation des moyens de plus en plus performants aussi bien dans la production que dans le contrôle. L'utilisation des machines à mesurer s'est généralisée dans l'essai du module de rigidité d'enrobé bitumineux.

Toutefois, la connaissance des incertitudes de mesures dans les opérations de contrôle et de Métrologie demeure un problème majeur encore mal maîtrisé.

Les paramètres pouvant modifier les résultats de ces essais du module de rigidité sont multiples tels que les paramètres liés aux conditions d'essai et d'autres, plutôt, liés à la spécification de l'appareillage qui sont la vitesse et le niveau de chargement, la température, la dimension de l'échantillon testé et l'acquisition des données… . Tous ces facteurs ont une grande influence sur la valeur du module de rigidité en vue de qualifier les facteurs d'incertitude, nous avons utilisé deux approches : L'approche 1 est effectuée en suivant la démarche décrite par le GUM, l'approche 2 par la simulation numérique de Monte-Carlo [3] [2]. Les deux résultats sont alors comparés pour un intervalle de confiances de 95%.

L'essai de traction indirecte sur éprouvettes cylindriques du module de rigidité se base sur la normalisation EN 12697-26 « Mélanges bitumineux – Méthodes d'essai pour mélange hydrocarboné à chaud – Partie 26 : Module de rigidité », apparue en 2004 [1]. Des cinq annexes correspondant à autant de méthodes d'essais, nous nous intéressons ici à l'Annexe C (Essai de traction indirecte sur éprouvette cylindrique IT-CY).

Machine d'essai et capteurs :

Pour la réalisation des essais, une presse hydraulique de capacité 50 kN est utilisée. Les Caractéristiques principales sont les suivantes :

- Définir les différents paramètres d'essai se fait à l'aide d'un logiciel spécifique.
- Créer les signaux de sollicitation voulus. La commande de la presse et de l'enceinte thermique ainsi que tous les éléments nécessaires à la programmation d'un essai.

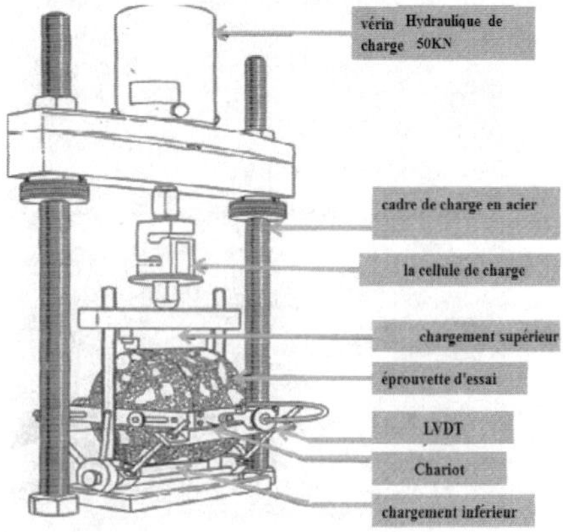

Fig 1 : Appareillage d'essai de module de rigidité (EN 12697-26)

La commande de la presse se fait à l'aide du logiciel. Ce programme permet de définir les différents paramètres et de créer les signaux de sollicitation voulus : la commande de la presse et de l'enceinte thermique ainsi que tous les éléments nécessaires à la programmation d'un essai.

Instrumentation :

Les mesures se dérouleront dans une salle, interne du laboratoire d'essai, identifiée sous « Salle » et maintenue aux conditions climatiques ambiantes.

La machine d'essai de module logée dans une enceinte thermo-régulée étalonnée/vérifiée en externe, dans laquelle une température constante d'essai, entre 0 et 40°C peut être maintenue, à proximité des éprouvettes, avec une exactitude de ±0,5°C.

- La machine est suivie métrologiquement par des cartes de contrôle obtenues à partir des essais sur un étalon de travail (Anneau étalon).

- Le système de mesure de déformation constitué de deux capteurs linéaire (LVDT : Linear Variable Differential Transformers), capable de mesurer la déformation diamétrale transitoire de l'éprouvette pendant l'application d'une impulsion de charge avec une exactitude meilleure que 1µm.
- Un peson (ou capteur de force) pour la mesure de la charge appliquée avec une exactitude de 2%. Les deux capteurs de force et de déplacement sont étalonnés séparément par un organisme externe.

- Les thermocouples adaptés, étalonnés en externe, capables de mesurer à ±0,1°C la température de l'éprouvette et des conditions de stockage et d'essai.

- Le pied à coulisse étalonné en externe, permet de mesurer les épaisseurs et les diamètres des éprouvettes avec une exactitude de ± 0,1mm.

Mesure de module de rigidité [5-6-8-9-10]

Selon la norme NF EN 12697-26 : 2004 [1], sur des éprouvettes compactées, de diamètre Φ100mm, d'épaisseur 53mm et de masse volumique 2451kg/m^3, des essais de traction indirecte ont été effectués.

La détermination du module de rigidité a été réalisée à l'aide d'une presse pneumatique (fig 1), située dans une enceinte thermostatique pour contrôler la température.

L'essai consiste à appliquer une charge cyclique de compression diamétrale sur l'éprouvette. On mesure la variation du diamètre horizontal.

La durée de l'impulsion de la charge appliquée doit être de 124 millisecondes, suivi d'une période de repos de 3 secondes. L'amplitude de la charge est nécessaire pour produire une augmentation transitoire de 4 microns du diamètre horizontal de l'éprouvette.

Pendant l'essai, sont appliquées d'abord 10 impulsions de charge de conditionnement pour permettre à la presse de caler la magnitude de la charge et la durée. Puis 5 autres impulsions de charge sont appliquées pour chaque direction, on mesure la variation de la déformation diamétrale horizontale et la charge appliquée. Le module de rigidité est calculé à l'aide des mesures des 5 impulsions de charge selon la formule suivante :

$$E = \frac{F*(\upsilon+0.27)}{(Z*H)}$$

Où :

E est le module de rigidité mesuré, exprimé en MPa ;
F est la valeur de la charge verticale appliquée, exprimée en N ;
Z est l'amplitude de la déformation horizontale obtenue pendant le cycle de charge, exprimée en mm ;
H est l'épaisseur de l'éprouvette, exprimée en mm ;
υ est le coefficient de poisson une valeur de 0,35 a été prise ;

Le tableau 1 résume les conditions des essais :

Déformation horizontale visée	5 ± 2 µm
Fréquence en Hz	10
Nombre d'impulsions	10
La période de répétition des impulsions	3 ± 0,1 s
Temps de montée en charge	124 ± 4ms
Coefficient de poisson	0,35
Température d'essai	15 C

Tableau 1

Les résultats des essais :

Module de Rigidité moyenne mesuré (E en Mpa)	6503,125
Module de Rigidité moyenne corrigé (E' en Mpa)	6696

Avec ,
Module de rigidité corrigé donné par la formule suivante

$$E' = E \times [1 - 0,322 \times (\log(E) - 1,82) \times (0,6 - K)]$$

Calcul des incertitudes selon la méthode GUM [4-14] **:**

Nous allons structurer le calcul d'incertitude en quatre étapes:

- Spécifier le mesurande :

La définition du mesurande avec l'écriture du modèle mathématique le représentant de chaque grandeur d'entrée du modèle est estimée et la valeur du résultat (mesurande) est déterminée.

Avant de commencer les mesures, il est important de bien définir ce que l'on va mesurer, nous nous sommes basées sur la norme NF EN 12697-26 :2004 et le dossier technique d'essai de module de rigidité :

La force F
Le déplacement Z longitudinal
L'épaisseur de l'éprouvette h
Le coefficient de poisson
Le facteur de charge k

- Identifier les sources d'incertitudes :

Les sources d'incertitude ont été recensées par la méthode des 5M et sont présentées dans le schéma suivant.

Les facteurs qui peuvent influencer la valeur du module de rigidité de l'enrobé, sont principalement : la température, la vitesse de chargement et le niveau de contrainte, la fréquence ou le temps de chargement, La dimension de l'échantillon testé et répétabilité du processus d'essai. Tous ces facteurs ont une importance de premier ordre sur la valeur du module.

La méthode des 5M

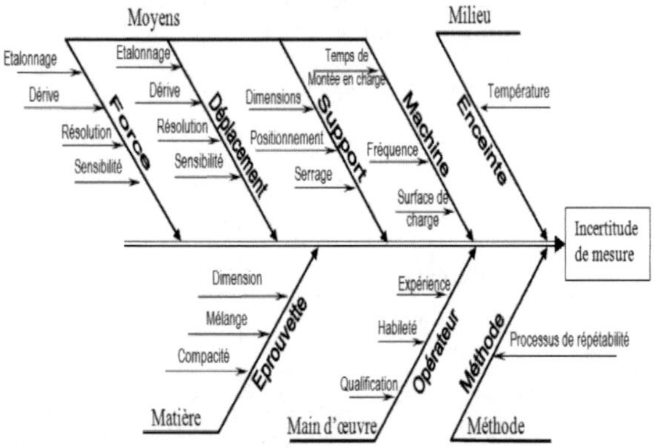

- Quantifier les sources :

Incertitude-type du type A : Répétabilité du processus d'essai (U_A):

Le processus complet de détermination du module (E) du matériau est effectué n fois d'une façon indépendante, Le résultat est obtenu automatiquement par le logiciel de pilotage de la machine.

Le processus de mesure est caractérisé par l'estimation S_X (écart-type expérimental) de la répétabilité de E :

$$u_A = S_X$$

Où $S_X = \sqrt{\frac{\sum_i^n (E_i - \overline{E})^2}{n-1}}$ avec $\overline{E} = \frac{\sum E_i}{n}$

Incertitude-type du type B : (u_{B1})

$$u_{B1} = \sqrt{\left(\frac{0,62 \times u_F}{Z \times h}\right)^2 + \left(\frac{0,62 \times F \times u_Z}{Z^2 \times h}\right)^2 + \left(\frac{0,62 \times F \times u_h}{Z \times h^2}\right)^2}$$

Incertitude obtenue à partir de la loi de propagation des incertitudes sur le mesurande équation du module de rigidité on obtient de l'équation suivante en (MPa) :

Avec

$$u_{B1}^2(y) = \sum_{i=1}^{n} \left[\frac{\partial f}{\partial x_i}\right]^2 .u^2(x_i)$$

La corrélation entre les variables est négligeable.

Pour chaque capteur, l'incertitude de mesure u est donnée par: $u = \sqrt{u_{ET}^2 + u_{der}^2 + u_{res}^2 + u_s^2}$

L'incertitude-type u provient de :

u_{ET} : L'incertitude liée à d'étalonnage de peson (capteur de force)

u_{der} : L'incertitude liée à la dérive dans le temps,(pour la 1er étalonnage on prendra ($u_{der} = u_{ET}$)

u_{res} : L'incertitude liée à la résolution d'indication de la valeur mesurée,

u_s : L'incertitude liée à la sensibilité de température, Les essais n'ont été réalisés qu'entre 0 et 40°C, à température constante. A température fixée, il n'y a pas de dérive des mesures des capteurs avec la température.

Pour déterminer ces incertitudes on se réfère à l'ensemble des informations (données observées, constats de vérification, certification d'étalonnage, avis d'expert, fiches techniques, données constructeur…) et notamment les guides suivantes [JCGM -100-2008 et GUM 1995].

- Bilan des incertitudes-types : voir Tableau 2

- Détermination de l'incertitude élargie :

L'incertitude élargie correspond à une grandeur définissant un intervalle, autour du résultat d'un mesurage, dont on puisse s'attendre à ce qu'il comprenne une fraction élevée de la distribution des valeurs qui pourraient être attribuées raisonnablement au mesurande .

$U(E') = k.u(E')$ où K est le facteur d'élargissement, on pourra prendre comme facteur d'élargissement K=2 pour avoir un niveau de confiance de 95% le résultat final exprimé avec deux chiffres significatifs, en utilisant la règle d'arrondissage de Gauss .

L'incertitude élargie sur le module corrigé :

$$U(E') = 2u(E')$$

$$\underline{U(E') = \pm 39,06 Mpa}$$

Si on prend en considération toutes les sources d'incertitude, donc on aura une incertitude élargie [7] :

$$U_{GUM} = 2u_{GUM}$$

Avec $u_{GUM} = \sqrt{u_A^2 + u_F^2 + u_Z^2 + u_h^2 + u_k^2 + u_{B_2}^2 + u_{B_3}^2}$

= 382 ,0085 Mpa

L'analyse de contribution consiste à identifier parmi l'ensemble des paramètres du modèle ceux qui ont une influence sur les essais du module de rigidité.
Pour déterminer les paramètres les plus influents, L'analyse de contribution sert à identifier les paramètres entrants contribuant le plus à l'incertitude des résultats finaux. Ils sont caractérisés par une incertitude et une sensibilité élevée.
Cependant, un paramètre possédant une sensibilité démesurée et une incertitude petite, ou l'inverse, peut constituer un contributeur non négligeable.

Code u_i	**Sources d'incertitude**		**Loi**	**Incertitude-type** u_i **(Demi étendue)**	**Coefficient de sensibilité** $Si = \frac{\partial E}{\partial x_i}$	**Incertitude** (Si*ui)	**Contribution (les indices de sensibilité)** Si en (%)
	Composantes						
u_F	Capteur de force (en N)	Peson : u_{ET} (Etalonnage)	Loi normale	1	/	/	/
		Peson : u_{Der} (Dérive)		1	/	/	
		Peson : u_{Res} (Résolution)	Loi uniforme	2.88675135	/	/	
		Peson : u_s (Sensibilité)	Loi arcsinus	0	/	/	
		u_F	Loi normale	**1.914854216**	**2.924528302**	**5.600045347**	**0.03**
u_z	Capteur de déplacement LVDT : déformation (en μm)	LVDT : u_{ET} (Etalonnage)	Loi normale	0.00890956	/	/	
		LVDT : u_{Der} (Dérive)		8.9096E-06	/	/	
		LVDT : u_{Res} (Résolution)	Loi uniforme	4.0825E-05	/	/	
		LVDT : u_s (Sensibilité)	Loi arc-sinus	0	/	/	
		u_z	Loi normale	**0.00840008**	**1674.292453**	**14.064191**	**2.15**
u_h	Epaisseur de l'éprouvette (en mm)	Pied à coulisse : u_{ET} (Etalonnage)	Loi normale	0.001266144	/	/	
		Pied à coulisse : u_{Der} (Dérive)		0.001266144	/	/	
		Pied à coulisse : u_{Res} (Résolution)	Loi uniforme	0.002106028	/	/	
		Pied à coulisse : u_s (Sensibilité)	Loi arc-sinus	0.000163379	/	/	
		u_h	Loi normale	**0.180165144**	**0.126361695**	**0.022765973**	**0.00254**
u_k	Facteur de surface de charge	u_k	Loi uniforme	**0.01**	/	**0.003**	**0.00143**
Calcul d'incertitude – Type composée sur l'équation $u_{B1} = u_E$ (en Mpa)							**15.13811397**
Calcul d'incertitude – Type composée sur l'équation $u_{E'}$ (en Mpa)							**19.53299021**
u_{B_2}	Temps de montée en charge (en ms)		Uniforme	155.4919745	1	155.4919745	23.72
u_{B_3}	Température (en C°)		Loi arc-sinus	183.9361515	1	183.9361515	28.06
u_A	Répétabilité		Type A	296.507257	1	296.507257	45.23

Tableau 2

Analyse de contribution des paramètres :

Alors nous avons une incertitude élargie :

$U_{GUM} = \pm 764{,}0170$ Mpa

Les contributions des paramètres sont représentées sous forme d'histogramme.

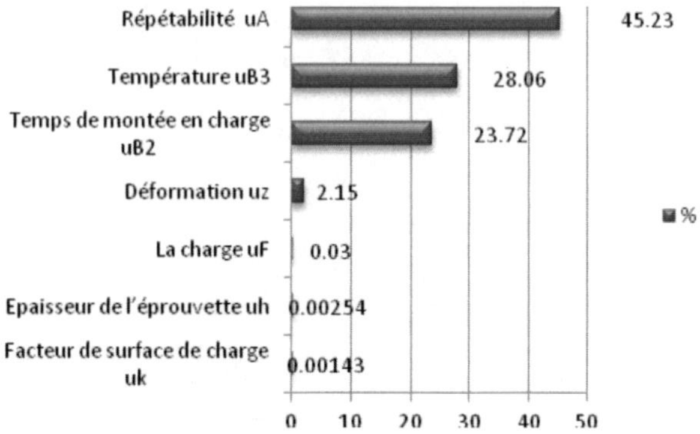

Nous avons sélectionné 3 facteurs (temps de montée en charge 23 %, températures 28% et Répétabilité 47 %), ceux ayant les pourcentages des indices les plus élevés sont les factures ayant le plus d'influence dans leur plage de variation sur les essais du module de rigidité.

On peut remarquer que les trois facteurs ayant des indices de pourcentage du premier ordre supérieures aux facteurs (capteur de force, capteurs de déplacement LVDT et l'épaisseur de l'éprouvette), cela s'explique par les valeurs des incertitudes de ceux-ci qui sont négligeables devant les incertitudes dues aux facteurs suivants temps de montée en charge, à la températures et à la Répétabilité .

Calcul des incertitudes selon la méthode Monte-Carlo :

La méthode de Monte Carlo numérique [11-13] est alors une alternative nécessaire. Pour la mettre en œuvre, il faut tout d'abord définir les facteurs d'influence de la grandeur de sortie et les associer via un modèle analytique ou numérique. On peut remarquer que cette étape était déjà nécessaire pour la méthode linéaire. A chaque facteur d'influence, on associe une distribution statistique.

On utilise ensuite un générateur aléatoire pour générer des tirages de chaque facteur d'influence [12].

Choix des distributions pour les grandeurs d'entrée.

Les densités de probabilité de chaque grandeur d'entrée sont définies dans le tableau 3 de la méthode GUM, Les écarts-types de chaque variable sont obtenus en prenant les incertitudes-types calculées par l'approche GUM.

Source d'incertitude	Type de distribution	incertitude-type
La charge u_F en N	Loi normale	2,5648
Déformation u_z en μm	Loi normale	0,034567
Epaisseur de l'éprouvette u_h en mm	Loi normale	0,04359
Facteur de surface de charge u_K	Loi uniforme	0,25
Temps de montée en charge u_{B2} (en ms)	Loi uniforme	149,65767
Température u_{B3} (en C°)	Loi arc-sinus	184,6527
Répétabilité u_A	Type A	297,56

Tableau 3 : densité de probabilité des gradeurs d'entrée

Lorsque toutes les distributions des grandeurs d'entrée ont été définies, on peut alors générer 10^6 réalisations de chaque grandeur d'entrée par tirage dans leur fonction de densité de probabilité, il est nécessaire de disposer d'un générateur de nombres aléatoire suffisamment performant, le calcul est réalisé dans un logiciel spécifique (MC-Ed) [2] Il permet de définir un module pour chaque grandeur du module (La charge, Déformation, Epaisseur de l'éprouvette, Facteur de surface de charge, etc.) puis de les assembler en un métamodule . Enfin, il choisit la valeur numérique de chaque terme du modèle, son incertitude associée et la fonction de probabilité.

Les simulations de Monte Carlo de 10^6 valeurs obtenues de la grandeur de sortie, ce qui permet de construire la distribution empirique du mesurande Fig 2

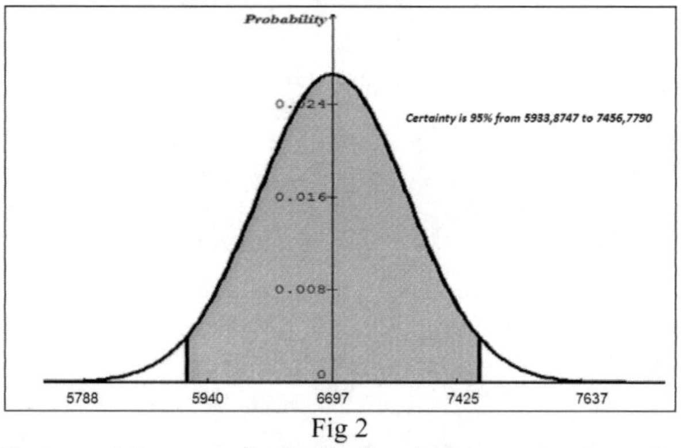

Fig 2

Nous constatons que la distribution de forme gaussienne, Le maximum de la valeur de module de rigidité (7456,7790Mpa) et le minimum (5933,8747 Mpa) définissent un intervalle qui contient 95 % des valeurs attribuables au mesurande. La valeur moyenne est de 6697,02 Mpa et l'écart-type 380,8446 Mpa.

Avec,

$$u_{Monte\ carlo} = \sqrt{u_A^2 + u_F^2 + u_Z^2 + u_h^2 + u_K^2 + u_{B_2}^2 + u_{B_3}^2}$$

Finalement, le résultat est donné avec un intervalle de confiance I_p (E') = [E'_{low} , E'_{high}] correspondant à une probabilité p de 95 % (Fig 2) :
- Ecart-type = 380,8446 Mpa
- Intervalle élargie, $I_1(95\%)$ (E') = [5933,8747 ; 7456,7790]Mpa

Etude comparative entres les deux méthodes (GUM et Monte Carlo)

Les résultats obtenus par la méthode de GUM et par la méthode Monte-Carlo pour l'évaluation des incertitudes de mesures du module de rigidité.

Grandeur	Méthode GUM	Méthode Monte-Carlo
E'	6696 Mpa	6697,02 Mpa
u	382,0085 Mpa	380,8446 Mpa
Intervalle élargie en Mpa	[5931,9830 ; 7460,0170] (K=2)	[5933,8747 ; 7456,7790] (à 95%)

Nous constatons que la différence entre les deux intervalles de confiance obtenus est très faible et que l'intervalle calculé par simulation numérique de Monte-Carlo est inclus dans celui de la propagation des incertitudes. De plus, Ces résultats sont donc tout à fait en accord l'un par rapport à l'autre et l'on peut considérer que les résultats donnés par la simulation numérique de Monte Carlo valident la loi de propagation des incertitudes.

Nous avons également appliqué le critère de comparaison décrit dans le document (BIPM . JCGM 10)[3]. En effet, il y est conseillé d'appliquer la loi de propagation des variances (GUM) en y ajoutant des termes de plus haut degré si nécessaire, et de donner un intervalle de confiance de 95 % pour la variable de sortie. Ensuite, pour valider la loi de propagation des variances, il faut appliquer la simulation numérique de Monte Carlo afin de fournir une incertitude-type et un intervalle de confiance de 95 %. Il faut alors déterminer si les intervalles de confiance obtenus par la Méthode de Monte Carlo et la loi de propagation des incertitudes sont en accord avec un degré d'approximation calculé de la manière suivante :

Nous exprimons l'écart- type sous la forme $a \times 10^r$ où a est un entier de 2 chiffres (correspondant au nombre de chiffres significatifs, ici 2) et r un entier. La précision de la comparaison est alors : $\delta = 0,5.10^r$.

On compare les incertitudes élargies obtenues par chacune des méthodes. On forme les différences :

$d_{low} = \left| E' - \text{EMBED Equation.3} - E'_{low\,(MONTE-CARLO)} \right|$

$d_{high} = \left| E' + \text{EMBED Equation.3} - E'_{high\,(MONTE-CARLO)} \right|$

Si ces différences sont toutes les deux inferieures à la tolérance préalablement déterminée, alors les résultats obtenus par la méthode GUM sont validés.

Si nous prenons 2 chiffres significatifs pour, $u_{Monte-Carlo}$ nous avons : E'=6696 Mpa

$$u_{Monte-Carlo} = 380\ Mpa = 38.10^1 Mpa$$

Donc $\delta = 0,5.10^1 = 5$

$$d_{low} = 1,89173$$
$$d_{high} = 3,23795$$

Les résultats obtenus montrent que les deux quantités d_{low} et d_{high} ne sont pas plus grandes que δ , alors l'approche analytique GUM est validée par l'approche Monte-Carlo.

Comparaison de deux variances $u^2_{(Monte\_Carlo)}$ et $u^2_{(GUM)}$ (Test de Ficher):

Le test de comparaison de Fisher compare les variances de deux approches de calcul d'incertitude, la loi de propagation des incertitudes(GUM) et la simulation numérique de Monte-Carlo sous populations, il confronte les hypothèses suivantes:

$$H_0 : u^2_{(Monte\_Carlo)} \approx u^2_{(GUM)}$$
$$H_1 : u^2_{(Monte\_Carlo)} \neq u^2_{(GUM)}$$

La statistique du test F est donc définie par :
Un risque de α=0,05 (5%)

Dans notre cas $F = \dfrac{u^2_{(GUM)}}{u^2_{(Monte\_Carlo)}}$;

Les degrés de liberté :

- $n_{GUM} - 1 = 6$
- $n_{Monte\,Carlo} - 1 = 6$

On calcule :

$$F = \frac{u^2_{(GUM)}}{u^2_{(Monte\_Carlo)}} = \frac{(382,0085)^2}{(380,8446)^2} = 1,00612 \quad ;$$

On compare cette valeur à la valeur tabulaire du F dans la table de la loi F :

$$F^{n_{GUM}-1}_{n_{Monte\,Carlo}-1} = F^6_6 = 4,284$$

Extrait de la table F

$F_{.05}(\nu_1, \nu_2)$

ν_2 \ ν_1	1	2	3	4	5	6	7	8
1	161.448	199.500	215.707	224.583	230.162	233.986	236.768	238.882
2	18.513	19.000	19.164	19.247	19.296	19.330	19.353	19.371
3	10.128	9.552	9.277	9.117	9.013	8.941	8.887	8.845
4	7.709	6.944	6.591	6.388	6.256	6.163	6.094	6.041
5	6.608	5.786	5.409	5.192	5.050	4.950	4.876	4.818
6	5.987	5.143	4.757	4.534	4.387	4.284	4.207	4.147
7	5.591	4.737	4.347	4.120	3.972	3.866	3.787	3.726

On conclut que le rapport observé est plus petit que le rapport de référence : F < $\mathbf{F_6^6}$ et donc on ne rejette pas l'hypothèse $\mathbf{H_0}$.

Conclusion et recommandation

La méthode analytique (GUM) permet d'effectuer facilement une analyse complète de l'incertitude : elle permet de calculer l'incertitude des scores d'impact, leur sensibilité à la variation des paramètres entrants et la contribution de l'incertitude d'essai du module de rigidité d'après GUM la plus grande part d'incertitude provient des trois facteurs (temps de montée en charge 23 %, températures 28% et Répétabilité 47 %).
La comparaison entre l'incertitude calculée à l'aide de la méthode analytique et les résultats de la méthode Monte Carlo n'ont montré aucune différence significative, c'est à cause de la linéarité des modèles de mesure utilisée pour chacun des tests et l'indépendance des effets des contributions à l'incertitude considérés.
Les simulations de Monte Carlo réalisées ont permis de montrer que le module de rigidité est gaussien donc il est facile de donner un intervalle de confiance, avec Le maximum de la valeur de module de rigidité (7456,7790 Mpa) et le minimum (5933,8747 Mpa) définissent un intervalle qui contient 95 % des valeurs attribuables au mesurande. La valeur moyenne est de 6697,02 Mpa et l'écart-type 380,8446 Mpa .
Certaines fonctionnalités de Monte Carlo sont réduction de l'effort d'analyse requis pour les modèles complexes ou non - linéaires, en particulier depuis les dérivées partielles de première ou d'ordre supérieur utilisé pour fournir des coefficients de sensibilité pour la loi de propagation de l'incertitude (GUM) ne sont pas nécessaires.

La méthode analytique reste très pertinente dans la mesure où les cas de non linéarité sont rares dans les ordres de grandeur pratiques des sources d'incertitudes et dans les processus complexes.
Les deux méthodes sont donc faisables et il est intéressant d'effectuer ces deux calculs en parallèle pour vérifier son résultat.

Principalement, pour l'évaluation des incertitudes de mesures d'essai du module de rigidité. Il est recommandé de procéder l'approche GUM. La facilité de son utilisation, sa rapidité et la quantité d'informations essentielles à l'analyse de l'incertitude qu'elle fournit. Rendre disponible cette méthode permettrait à l'analyse de l'incertitude de gagner en popularité, améliorant l'interprétation des résultats d'essai du module de rigidité.
L'emploi de la méthode analytique (GUM) permettrait, de surcroît, d'améliorer la qualité des analyses de l'incertitude, puisque la sensibilité fait ressortir rapidement les paramètres entrants susceptibles de contribuer beaucoup à l'incertitude des scores d'impact.

Références

[1] NF EN 12697-26- Annexe C, Méthodes d'essai pour mélange hydrocarboné à chaud : module de rigidité .

[2] PLATEL F., « Mise en pratique de la méthode de Monte-Carlo Projet Monte-Carlo Editor (MC-Ed) », MetGen, Dossier métrologie 25

[3] JCGM , Evaluation of measurement data-supplement 1 to the Guide to the expression of the measurement _propagation of distributions using a Monte-Carlo method , BIPM . JCGM 10.

[4] NF ENV 13005 Guide pour l'expression de l'incertitude de mesure. Afnor 1999.

[5] Huet C. représentation de module et complaisances complexes arithmétique et logarithmique. Crope fr Rgéole tome 1-5. Nov 1947 page 237.

[6] Cornil P. détermination du module de rigidité et Essais de fatigue en flexion sur éprouvettes de matériaux hydrocarbonés encastrées à une extrémité Rapp rech. CRR Bruxelles, 1968.

[7] JCGM, « Vocabulaire international de métrologie - Concepts fondamentaux et généraux et termes associés (VIM) », BIPM, JCGM 200:2008 (E/F)

[8] Di Benedetto, H., M. N. Partl, et al. (2001). " Stiffness testing for bituminous mixtures." Materials and Structures 34: 66-70.

[9] Kim, Y. R., Y. Seo, et al. (2004). "Dynamic modulus testing of asphalt concrete in indirect tension mode." Transportation Research Record 1891: 163-173.

[10] Nunn, M. E. et T. M. Smith (1997). Improvements to the indirect tensile stiffness modulus test. 2nd European Symposium - Performance and durability of bituminous materials, Leeds.

[11] ISO/CEI Guide 25 :1990 Prescriptions générales concernant la compétence des laboratoires d'étalonnage et d'essais.

[12] James E. GENTLE, (2003). "Random Number Generation and Monte Carlo methods" – Springer, Statistics and Computing, second Edition.

[13] H. SCHWENKE, B.R. L. SIEBERT, F. WÄLDELE, H. KUNZMANN, (2000). "Assessment of Uncertainties in Dimensional Metrology by Monte Carlo Simulation: Proposal of a Modular and Visual Software" – Annals of the CIRP Vol. 49/1/2000.
[14] ISO/IEC Guide 98-3/Suppl.1:2008(E) Uncertainty of measurement - Part 3: Guide to the expression of uncertainty in measurement (GUM:1995) Supplement 1: Propagation of distributions using a Monte Carlo method. Geneva (Switzerland): ISO, December 2008, 98 p.

Bavures d'usinage et ébavurage : Méthode de sélection des procédés et allocation optimale des machines

A. Bouzid, V. Songmene*, J.P. Kenné
École de Technologie Supérieure (ÉTS), 1100 Notre-Dame Street West, Montréal (QC) H3C 1K3, Canada

Résumé. Les industriels dans la plupart des domaines de fabrication mécanique par usinage font encore face à d'importants obstacles lorsqu'il s'agit de fabriquer des pièces de précision ou d'excellente finition, parmi lesquels la formation des bavures. La formation des bavures est un phénomène néfaste qui diminue la qualité de la pièce et augmente le coût de production. Pour éliminer ces bavures, on doit impérativement passer par des opérations d'ébavurage. Il existe une grande variété de procédés d'ébavurage et de finition de surface. Cette variété est à l'origine de la complexification du problème de détermination du procédé d'ébavurage le plus approprié en présence des exigences de qualité, de santé et sécurité du travail, et d'économie. Le but de cette étude est de proposer une stratégie de sélection des meilleures méthodes d'ébavurage. Une étude approfondie de la littérature a été menée, notamment sur le mécanisme de formation et la caractérisation des bavures, l'influence des facteurs technologiques sur la formation des bavures, les aspects économiques et de santé/sécurité des différents procédés d'ébavurage. Une base de données dynamique a été construite, ensuite un algorithme itératif de sélection des meilleurs procédés d'ébavurage a été conçu. Cet algorithme permet de rechercher dans la base de données les procédés en fonction des critères préétablis associés aux matériaux, à la bavure et aux spécificités des procédés d'ébavurage. La faisabilité de l'approche a été illustrée à travers un premier exemple numérique. Un modèle de minimisation des coûts a permis de faire une allocation de la production aux machines d'ébavurage sélectionnées. Un deuxième exemple numérique et une analyse sensibilité ont permis de déterminer les quantités allouées à chaque machine et de valider les résultats de l'étude.

Mot clés : Usinage, qualité de pièces, bavure, caractérisation et mesure, ébavurage, optimisation

1 Introduction

Aujourd'hui, en raison de la concurrence mondiale, les industries manufacturières doivent fournir des produits de haute qualité et à prix abordable en respectant les délais pour rester compétitifs. Les pièces mécaniques de bonne qualité incluent celles ayant une meilleure finition et texture de surface, des précisions de dimension et de forme, une contrainte résiduelle réduite et des pièces sans bavure. La formation de bavures est l'un des phénomènes indésirables les plus fréquents qui se produisent dans les opérations d'usinage, ce qui réduit la qualité des pièces usinées et celle des assemblages. Par conséquent, il est souhaitable d'éliminer les bavures ou de réduire l'effort nécessaire pour les enlever.

Généralement, pour obtenir une pièce sans bavure, le passage d'une opération de finition par ébavurage après l'usinage est nécessaire. Toutefois, selon [1], les opérations d'ébavurage sont longues et coûteuses, elles sont considérées comme des opérations non productives, sans aucune valeur ajoutée. Selon [2], les opérations d'ébavurage peuvent atteindre 30% du coût total de l'usinage d'une pièce, spécialement quand les pièces sont petites ou les bavures sont épaisses, et que l'accès aux bavures est difficile. Pour remédier à ces problèmes, il convient de bien connaître le domaine technico-économique des différents procédés d'ébavurage pour choisir la solution adaptée à la configuration des pièces, à la forme des bavures et à leur accessibilité tout en respectant l'intégrité des surfaces et les caractéristiques dimensionnelles des pièces.

Il existe plusieurs informations et données relatives à l'ébavurage dans le milieu industriel. Ces informations sont très utiles dans l'amélioration de qualité de surface de la pièce, ainsi que l'optimisation des méthodes d'ébavurage. Malgré leurs importances, il n'existe pas d'outils qui permettent le stockage et la protection de ces données précieuses. Dans cette recherche, nous avons commencé par la collecte des données afin d'établir une base de données solide et fiable. Nous avons également réuni les informations nécessaires à la bavure et aux méthodes d'ébavurage. En deuxième étape, nous avons étudié le mécanisme de formation de bavure et de caractéristique de différentes méthodes d'ébavurage dans le but de proposer des critères de choix des méthodes d'ébavurage. Par la suite et en nous basant sur la base de données préalablement établie, nous avons développé un outil de décision permettant la sélection des meilleures méthodes d'ébavurage pour une application donnée. Ensuite nous avons établi un modèle d'optimisation afin d'assurer la bonne répartition des pièces sur les machines et minimiser le coût d'ébavurage. Enfin nous avons conçu une interface graphique pour faciliter la communication entre le programme et l'utilisateur.

*Corresponding author: Victor.songmene@etsmtl.ca

2 Établissement d'une base de données

Une bavure est définie comme une projection indésirable du matériau formé à la suite de déformation plastique au cours d'une opération d'usinage, formage, découpage ou cisaillement.

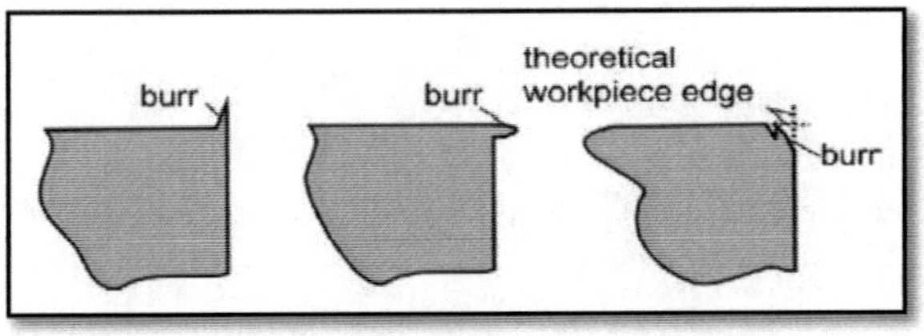

Fig. 1. Différents types de bavure [3]

Ces bavures sont inévitables et indésirables. Elles causent plusieurs problèmes dans l'assemblage, l'inspection, l'interaction des composants en opération et sont une cause fréquente de blessures chez les opérateurs. Afin de remédier à ces problèmes on doit impérativement passer par des opérations d'ébavurage, telles que l'ébavurage manuel, mécanique, électrochimique, par vibration ou par jet abrasive. Dans le but de développer une stratégie de sélection des méthodes d'ébavurage, l'établissement d'une base de données qui réunit le maximum d'informations relatives aux bavures, à l'ébavurage et aux méthodes d'ébavurage est nécessaire.

2.1 Classification et mesure de bavure

Il existe plusieurs différentes classifications de bavures selon l'application, le processus de fabrication, la forme, le mécanisme de formation et les propriétés des matériaux (voir tableau 1).

La bonne sélection des méthodes de mesure de la taille de bavure dépend essentiellement du niveau de qualité souhaité et de la précision de mesure demandée. La figure 2 résume les différentes méthodes de mesure de bavure :

Tableau 1. Différents types de bavure selon l'opération

Opération	REF	Type de bavure
Perçage	[4]	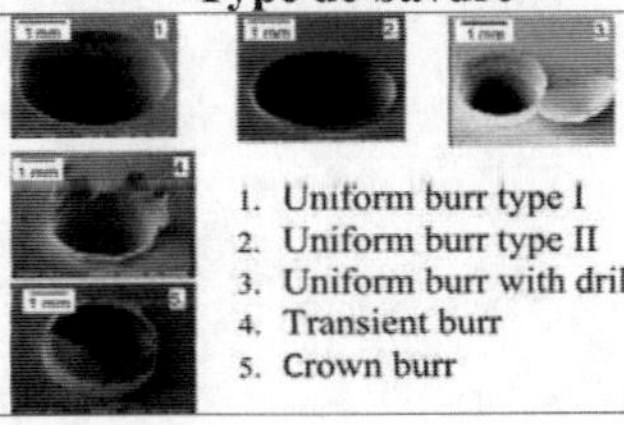 1. Uniform burr type I 2. Uniform burr type II 3. Uniform burr with drill cap 4. Transient burr 5. Crown burr
Meulage	[5]	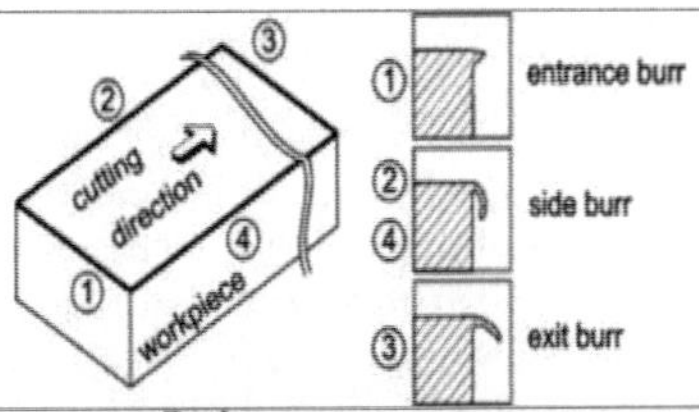
Fraisage	[6]	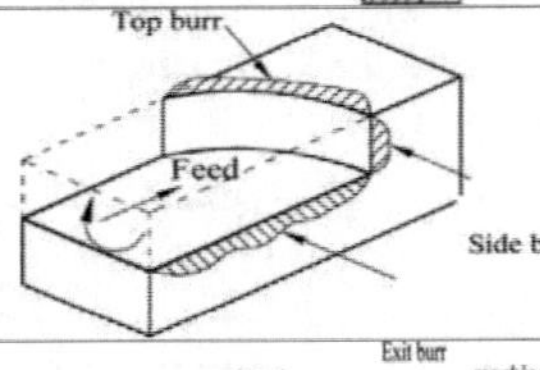
Surfaçage	[7]	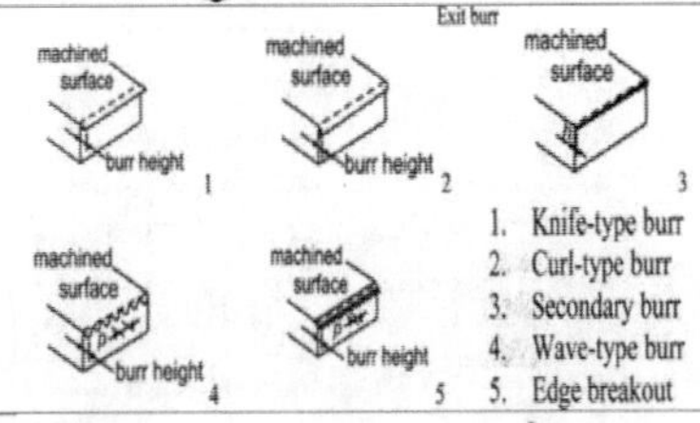
Divers	[8]	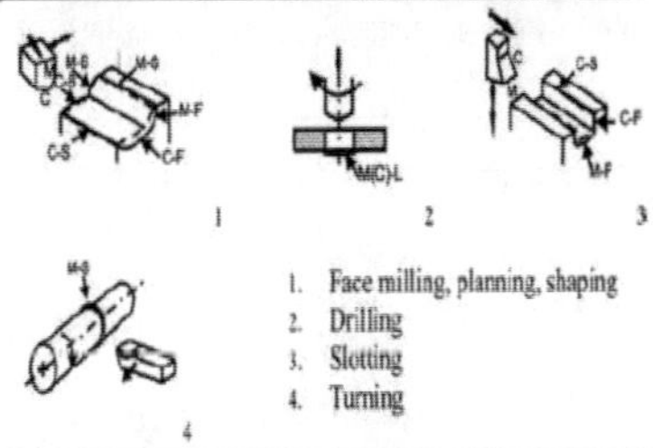

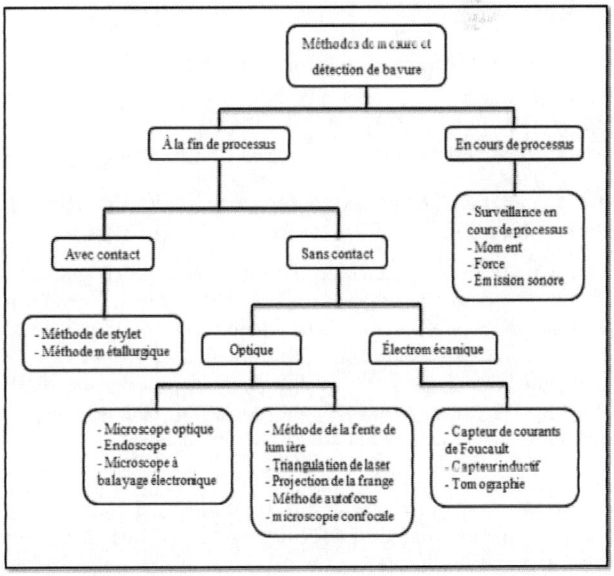

Fig. 2. Méthode de mesure et détection de bavure [3]

2.2 Critères de choix de méthodes d'ébavurage

Pour pouvoir sélectionner une méthode d'ébavurage adéquate, nous devons nous baser sur des critères solides et pertinents. En considérant l'étude de différents procédés d'ébavurages, la formation et la caractérisation de bavure nous avons conclu que le choix d'un procédé d'ébavurage doit tenir compte des critères déterminants liés à la bavure, à la pièce et au procédé d'ébavurage récapitulés à la figure 3, avec la géométrie de la bavure illustrée à la figure 4.

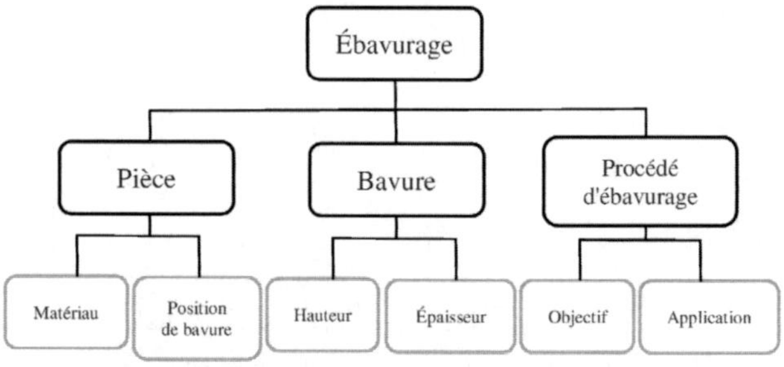

Fig. 3. Critère de choix de méthode d'ébavurage

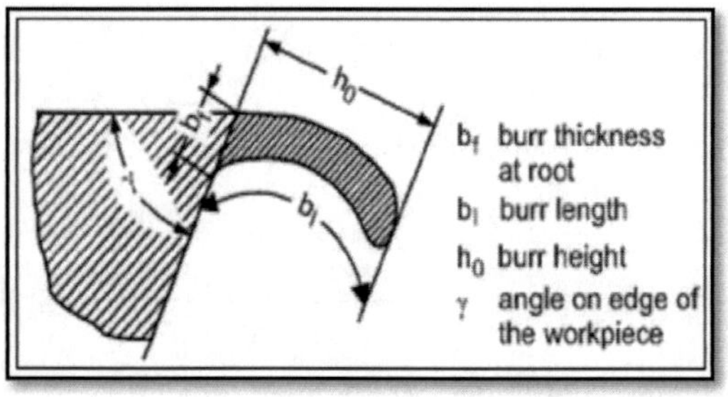

Fig. 4 Caractérisation dimensionnelle de la bavure d'usinage, Tirée de (J. Aurich et al., 2009)

Nous avons travaillé sur les quinze procédés d'ébavurage les plus utilisés, recensés par [2] et présentés dans le tableau 2.

On se basant sur les critères de choix présentés précédemment et les informations relatives aux différentes méthodes d'ébavurage recensés durant cette étude, nous avons réussi à établir une base de données qui présente les performances des méthodes d'ébavurage avec les différents critères de sélection. Le tableau 3 présente un exemple de la capacité de chaque méthode d'ébavurage avec le critère "Matériau".

Six tableaux similaires au tableau 3 ont ainsi été établis. Ces tableaux contiennent les performances de chaque méthode d'ébavurage avec chaque critère de choix. L'ensemble de ces tableaux représente la base de données qui sera adoptée dans le reste de travail pour développer une stratégie de sélection des meilleures méthodes d'ébavurage.

Table 2. Les quinze procédés d'ébavurage les plus utilisés

N°	Procédés d'ébavurage	Quantité dans le monde (1997)
1	Ébavurage manuel	800 000
2	Ébavurage par brosse	100 000
3	Sablage	50 000
4	Ébavurage par jet d'abrasif	40 000
5	Finition par vibration	30 000
6	Ébavurage par coupe mécanisé	20 000
7	Tonneau d'ébavurage	16 000
8	Tonneau de finition centrifuge	2000
9	Ébavurage par broche de finition	1200
10	Ébavurage électrochimique	1200
11	Ébavurage robotique	1200
12	Ébavurage par jet d'eau	800
13	Ébavurage thermique	700
14	Grenaillage	?
15	Ébavurage thermique	30

? : Manque de donnée publié

Table 3. Méthodes d'ébavurages appropriées par matériau de la pièce.

	Matériaux										
Méthode D'ébavurage	Fer	Fer doux	Ac. dure	Ac. inoxy	Lait.	Zinc	Alum	Plas	Cér.	Cui.	Fon.
Ébavurage Manuel											
Brossage											
Sablage											
Jet abrasive											
Finition par vibration											
Coupe mécanisée											
Tonneau d'ébavurage											
Tonneau de vibration centrifuge											
Ébavurage robotique											
Broche de finition											
Ébavurage électrochimique											
Jet d'eau											
Ébavurage thermique											
Grenaillage											
Ébavurage ultrasonique	?	?	?	?	?	?	?	?	?	?	?

? : Manque de données publiées

: Certains plastiques   : Réalisable   : Non réalisable

3 Optimisation et stratégie de sélection

L'un des principaux objectifs de cette recherche sur l'ébavurage consiste à élaborer un outil de décision permettant de sélectionner des méthodes d'ébavurage fiables et efficaces. Une stratégie efficace contribuera à réduire le coût d'ébavurage en ayant une meilleure qualité de surface. Après avoir déterminé les critères de choix nécessaires pour sélectionner une méthode d'ébavurage, nous avons mis en place une stratégie permettant de sélectionner la meilleure méthode d'ébavurage pour une application donnée, en nous basant sur la base de données préalablement établie.

Cette stratégie fonctionne comme suit : au début le programme demande à l'usager de saisir les critères de choix selon ses exigences d'ébavurage. Dans la deuxième étape, le programme commence à balayer les tableaux de base de données pour vérifier la validité des critères de choix saisis par l'usager avec chaque méthode d'ébavurage. S'il trouve des méthodes d'ébavurage qui sont compatibles aux exigences de l'usager, il va les retenir, classifier puis les afficher. Si au moins un seul critère n'est pas compatible avec les performances des méthodes d'ébavurage, le programme va le rejeter et affichera le résultat « Méthode non disponible »; ensuite il demandera à l'usager de changer les critères de choix. Le diagramme suivant représente l'algorithme de fonctionnement de la stratégie de sélection.

Après l'implémentation du programme de sélection des méthodes d'ébavurage sur Matlab, nous avons conçu une interface graphique en utilisant l'outil « GUI » sur Matlab afin de faciliter l'interaction entre le programme et l'usager. Cette interface se compose de trois sections. La section 1 permettant la sélection de différents critères de choix, la section 2 réservée à l'exécution de programme, et la section 3 constituée d'un champ vide consacré à l'affichage des résultats.

4 Modèle d'optimisation des coûts d'ébavurage

4.1 Fonction objectif

La notion de coût de l'ébavurage devrait impérativement être estimés et incluse dans le modèle d'optimisation pour garantir un meilleur choix technologique. Dans cet objectif, nous avons établi un modèle permettant la minimisation du coût d'ébavurage en déterminant une solution d'ébavurage optimale.

En utilisant la programmation linéaire, nous allons résoudre un problème d'allocation des ressources. L'application de sélection des méthodes d'ébavurage établi préalablement nous a fourni plus qu'une méthode d'ébavurage pour le même produit. Le modèle d'optimisation permet de répartir les pièces sur les différentes machines d'ébavurage d'une façon optimale afin de sauver le temps et l'argent. En effet ce modèle permet de comparer le coût et le temps d'ébavurage de différentes machines d'ébavurage fournis par l'application de sélection, ensuite et en respectant les contraintes de travail, le modèle alloue une quantité des pièces à la machine la moins chère et qui nécessite moins de temps pour effectuer l'ébavurage des pièces, une fois la capacité maximale de la machine épuisée (elle ne peut plus prendre d'avantage des pièces en charge). Le modèle allouera le reste des pièces à ébavurer sur la machine la moins chère suivante et ainsi de suite jusqu'à la fin des pièces à ébavurer.

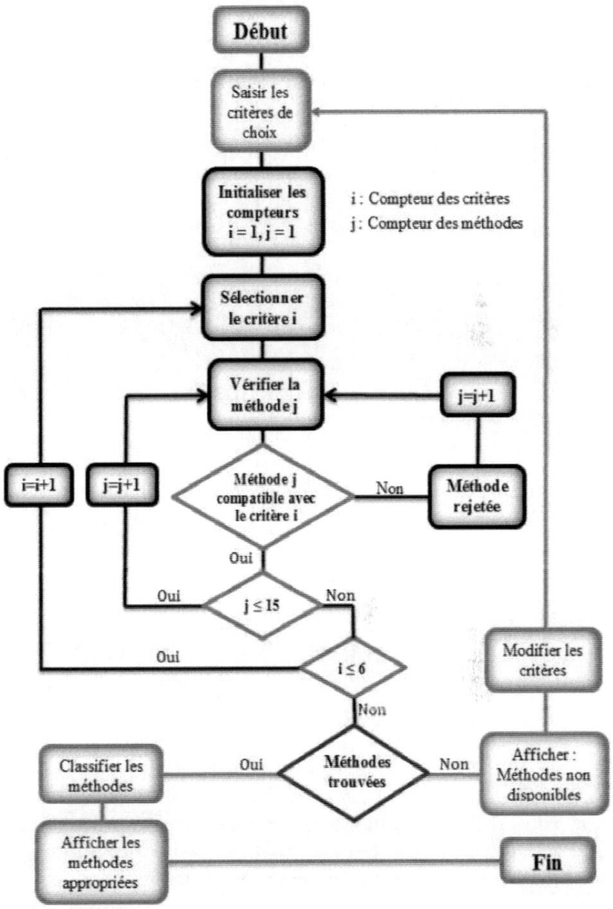

Fig. 4. Stratégie de sélection de méthode d'ébavurage

Le modèle d'optimisation est représenté par la fonction objectif de minimisation de coût suivante :

$$Min\ Z = \sum_{i=1}^{n} \sum_{j=1}^{3} C_{ij} T_{ij} P_{ij} M_{ij} \quad (1)$$

Ce modèle est établi à l'aide de la commande «Solveur» d'Excel, en utilisant la programmation linéaire. Les variables du modèle sont définies comme suit :

Cij : Le coût associé à la machine d'ébavurage.

Tij : Le temps d'ébavurage d'une pièce.

Pij : La quantité des pièces i associée à la machine j.

Mij : La machine j associée à la pièce i.

La variable de décision dans cette fonction est Pij, désignant la quantité des pièces allouée à chaque machine.

4.2 Identification des contraintes

Les contraintes associées à cette fonction objectif sont les suivantes :

- Le temps d'ébavurage doit être inférieur à la disponibilité de la machine.

$$\sum_{i=1}^{n}\sum_{j=1}^{3} P_{ij}T_{ij} \leq D_{ij} \quad (2)$$

avec D_{ij} désignant la disponibilité de la machine.

- La quantité des pièces à ébavurer doit être inférieure à la capacité maximale de machine.

$$\sum_{i=1}^{n}\sum_{j=1}^{3} P_{ij} \leq V_{ij} \quad (3)$$

avec V_{ij} désignant la capacité maximale de la machine

- Le nombre des machines fonctionnelles est fixé à trois.

$$\sum_{i=1}^{n}\sum_{j=1}^{3} M_{ij} = 3 \quad (4)$$

Dans cette recherche, nous avons fixé le nombre de machines juste à titre d'exemple, mais en réalité le nombre de machines est variable de décision. Donc le modèle complet peut s'écrire sous la forme suivante :

$$Min\ Z = \sum_{i=1}^{n}\sum_{j=1}^{3} C_{ij}T_{ij}P_{ij}M_{ij} \quad (5)$$

Sujet à

$$\sum_{i=1}^{n}\sum_{j=1}^{3} P_{ij}T_{ij} \leq D_{ij}$$

$$\sum_{i=1}^{n}\sum_{j=1}^{3} P_{ij} \leq V_{ij}$$

$$\sum_{i=1}^{n}\sum_{j=1}^{3} M_{ij} = 3$$

i : Numéro de pièce

j : Numéro de machine

5 Résultats et analyse de sensibilité

5.1 Interface graphique

Pour résoudre le problème d'allocation des pièces sur les machines d'ébavurage, nous avons pris comme exemple trois produits différents (P1, P2 et P3) qui seront répartis sur neuf machines, chaque produit sur trois machines. Afin de réaliser cette tâche, nous avons conçu une interface graphique qui permet l'interaction avec le modèle d'optimisation. En effet, cette interface permet d'introduire les données d'entrée du modèle telles que les machines opérationnelles, la disponibilité de chaque machine et la quantité des pièces à ébavurer (voir partie supérieur d'interface graphique). Elle permet également d'afficher les résultats tels que les répartitions de chaque produit sur leurs machines appropriées et le coût d'ébavurage de chaque produit (voir partie inférieur de l'interface graphique présentée à la figure 5).

		Machine 1	Machine 2	Machine 3	Quantité pièces	Quantité Max
P1	Machine(s) opérationnelle (s)	M1	M2	M4	5300	5400
	Disponibilité des machines (h)	600	600	600		
P2	Machine(s) opérationnelle (s)	M5	M7	M8	9500	9600
	Disponibilité des machines (h)	600	600	600		
P3	Machine(s) opérationnelle (s)	M3	M6	M9	9100	9200
	Disponibilité des machines (h)	600	600	600		

Répartition des pièces sur les machines

	Machine(s) sélectionnée (s)	M1	M2	M4	Temps/ Produit (h)	Coût/ Produit ($)
P1	Répartition des pièces	500	2400	2400	1700	1229
	Temps d'ébavurage/Machine (h)	500	600	600		
	Coût d'ébavurage / unité ($)	0.6	0.25	0.15		
P2	Machine(s) sélectionnée (s)	M5	M7	M8	1750	1520
	Répartition des pièces	2400	6000	1100		
	Temps d'ébavurage/Machine (h)	600	600	550		
	Coût d'ébavurage / unité ($)	0.7	0.5	1		
P3	Machine(s) sélectionnée (s)	M3	M6	M9	1725	590
	Répartition des pièces	6000	700	2400		
	Temps d'ébavurage/Machine (h)	525	600	600		
	Coût d'ébavurage / unité ($)	0.35	1,5	0,5		
	P1 P2 P3				Coût Optimisé	3339 $

Fig. 5. Interface graphique de modèle d'optimisation

5.2 Analyse de sensibilité

L'objective de cette analyse est de quantifier l'influence de variables d'entrée de notre modèle sur la variable de sortie. Elle consiste à changer la valeur d'un paramètre du modèle en fixant les autres paramètres, et d'analyser l'impact de ce changement sur la solution optimale. Dans l'exemple suivant, nous allons étudier l'effet de variation du coût et du temps de production de P1 sur la répartition des pièces sur les machines (M1, M2, et M3). Tous d'abord on commence par fixer les valeurs de coût et de temps sur toutes les machines (table 3), puis on relève le résultat de répartition des pièces (figure 7).

Table 3. Fixation des paramètres d'entrée

Machine	M1	M2	M3
Coût ($)/pièce	1	1	1
Temps (h)/pièce	0.25	0.25	0.25

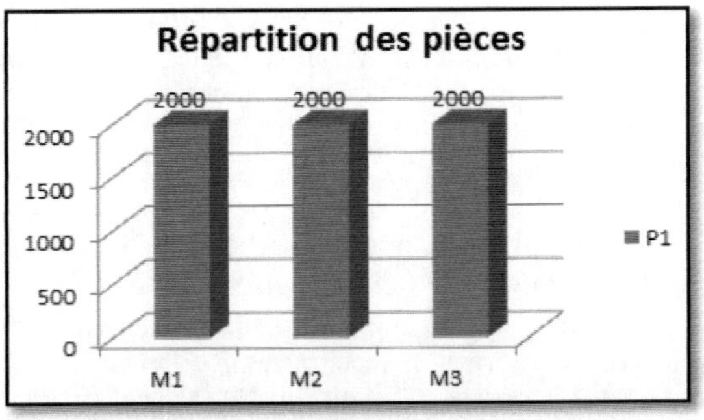

Fig. 6. Répartition de produit P1 sur les machines M1, M2 et M3, (Temps et coût fixe)

Ensuite on augmente la valeur de coût en laissant les valeurs des autres paramètres fixes (table 4), puis on relève le résultat (figure 8).

Table 4. Variation de coût

Machine	M1	M2	M3
Coût ($)/pièce	**2**	1	1
Temps (h)/pièce	0.25	0.25	0.25

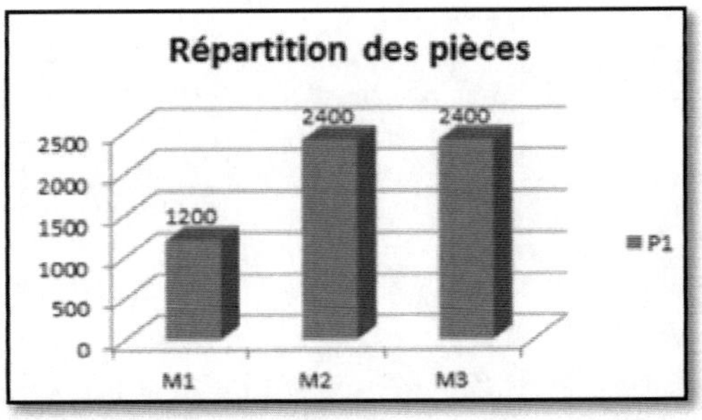

Fig. 7. Répartition de produit P1 sur les machines M1, M2 et M3 (temps fixe, coût variable)

On remarque dans la figure précédente que la quantité des pièces allouées à la machine M1 a diminuée par rapport aux autres machines. Cette diminution s'explique par l'augmentation du coût d'ébavurage sur cette machine.

Dans l'exemple suivant, nous avons augmenté la variable de temps de la machine M2 pour voir son influence sur la répartition des pièces.

Table 5. Variation de temps

Machine	M1	M2	M3
Coût ($)/pièce	1	1	1
Temps (h)/pièce	0.25	**1**	0.25

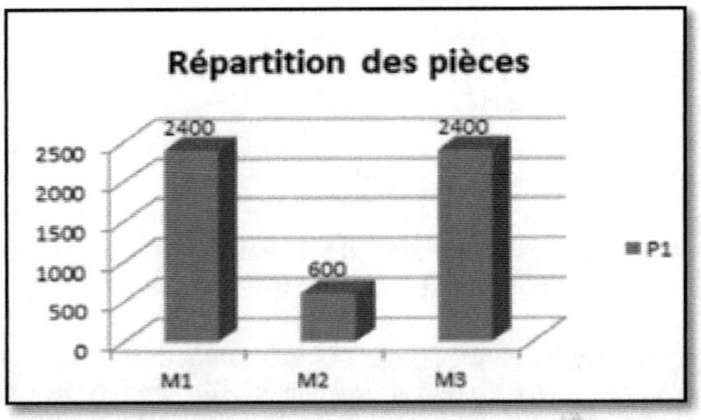

Fig. 8. Répartition de produit P1 sur les machines M1, M2 et M3 (temps variable, coût fixe)

On remarque dans la figure 9 que la quantité des pièces allouées à la machine M2 a chuté à cause de l'augmentation de temps d'ébavurage sur cette machine.

Ces exemples démontrent que la variation des paramètres du modèle d'optimisation a une influence directe sur la solution optimale. En effet, chaque augmentation de coût ou de temps d'ébavurage sur une machine particulière, engendre la diminution de la quantité des pièces allouées à cette machine. Par conséquent, on obtient une répartition optimale de pièces sur l'ensemble des machines et par la suite un coût minimal.

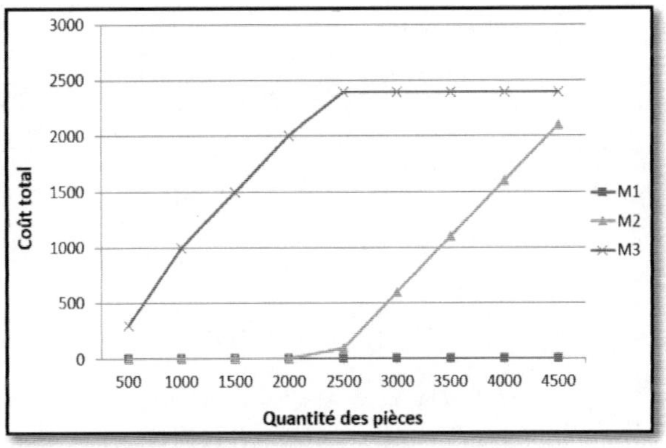

Fig. 9. Comportement de cout total en fonction de variation de quantité de pièces pour chacune des machines M1 à M3.

La figure 9 démontre le principe de fonctionnement du modèle d'optimisation. Comme illustré dans la figure 9, le modèle commence à allouer des pièces à la machine M3, puisqu'elle est la moins chère, jusqu'à la saturation de cette machine. Ensuite il alloue le reste des pièces à la machine M2 puisqu'elle est moins chère que la machine M1, jusqu'à la fin de stock.

6 Conclusion

Cette étude nous a permis de conclure que l'établissement d'une base de données relative à l'ébavurage est indispensable afin de minimiser, uniformiser et prédire la génération des bavures, et par la suite faciliter leur enlèvement et améliorer la qualité de surface de la pièce. Après l'étude de l'influence des facteurs technologiques sur la formation des bavures, nous avons déterminé les critères de choix des méthodes d'ébavurage. En utilisant la base de données, nous avons établi les critères de choix développé une stratégie permettant la sélection des meilleures méthodes d'ébavurage pour une application donnée. Ensuite, et dans le but d'optimiser les opérations d'ébavurage, un modèle de minimisation de coût d'ébavurage a été établi. Le rôle de ce modèle est de résoudre les problèmes d'allocation des ressources. Ce modèle assure la répartition des pièces à ébavurer sur les différentes machines d'ébavurage d'une façon optimale afin de minimiser le coût et le temps d'ébavurage. Enfin, une analyse de sensibilité a été réalisée pour confirmer la validité du modèle d'optimisation.

Références

1. Gillespie, L. K. (1981). Deburring technology for improved manufacturing: Society of Manufacturing Engineers, Dearborn, MI.

2. Gillespie, L. K. (1999). Deburring and edge finishing handbook: Society of Manufacturing Engineers.

3. Aurich, J. C., Dornfeld, D., Arrazola, P., Franke, V., Leitz, L., & Min, S. (2009). Burrs—Analysis, control and removal. CIRP Annals-Manufacturing Technology, 58(2), 519-542.

4. Kim, J., Min, S., & Dornfeld, D. A. (2001). Optimization and control of drilling burr formation of AISI 304L and AISI 4118 based on drilling burr control charts. International Journal of Machine Tools and Manufacture, 41(7), 923-936.

5. Barth, C., Dollmeier, R., & Warnecke, G. (2001). Burr formation in grinding of hardened steel with conventional and superabrasive wheels. Transactions-North American Manufacturing Research Institution of Sme, 273-278.

6. Hashimura, M., Chang, Y., & Dornfeld, D. (1999). Analysis of burr formation mechanism in orthogonal cutting. Transactions-American Society of Mechanical Engineers Journal of Manufacturing Science & Engineering, 121, 1-7.

7. Chern, G.-L. (2006). Experimental observation and analysis of burr formation mechanisms in face milling of aluminum alloys. International Journal of Machine Tools and Manufacture, 46(12), 1517-1525.

8. Nakayama, K., & Arai, M. (1987). Burr formation in metal cutting. CIRP Annals-Manufacturing Technology, 36(1), 33-36.

Mutualisation des pratiques métrologiques dans les laboratoires de recherche : IRD Sénégal

M. Gueye[1,2], H. Bassene[3], M. Cissoko[4], E-J. Diatta[5,2]

[1]LEMSAT, Laboratoire d'Ecologie Microbienne des Sols et Agroécosystèmes Tropicaux, IRD-Bel air route des hydrocarbures, Dakar, Senegal; [2]LMI IESOL, Intensification Ecologique des Sols Cultivés en Afrique de l'Ouest, IRD-Bel air route des hydrocarbures, Dakar, Senegal; [3]URMITE, Unité de recherche sur les maladies infectieuses et tropicales émergentes, IRD-Hann route des pères maristes, Dakar, Senegal; [4]LCM, Laboratoire Commun de Microbiologie IRD-Bel air route des hydrocarbures, Dakar, Senegal; [5]LAMA, Laboratoire des Moyens Analytiques, IRD-Bel air route des hydrocarbures, Dakar, Senegal.

Résumé. La démarche qualité est un outil indispensable dans les structures de recherche où la mesure est omniprésente. La métrologie en fait partie et constitue l'un des facteurs permettant d'assurer la pertinence des résultats scientifiques obtenus. Les prestataires en métrologie sont rares et la baisse des budgets alloués aux laboratoires de recherche oblige à optimiser la gestion des instruments de mesure. Les responsables métrologie des différents laboratoires certifiés ISO 9001:2015 à l'IRD Dakar (URMITE, LEMSAT, LAMA, LCM) se sont engagés dans la mise en place de mécanismes de mutualisation des instruments et d'harmonisation des pratiques métrologiques pour une meilleure prise en charge de cette activité. Pour ce faire nous nous sommes organisés en groupe de travail et avons recensé les appareils que nous avons en commun sous surveillance métrologique ou qui doivent l'être. Des procédures et instructions communes sont rédigées selon les normes en vigueur. Les étalons et certains appareils de contrôle sont mis en commun sous accès contrôlé et utilisés par des personnes habilitées. Pour certaines vérifications réglementaires, un contrat est établi entre notre institut et l'organisme d'inspection en spécifiant nos exigences afin que le même inspecteur fasse les contrôles en suivant la même procédure pour l'ensemble des laboratoires. Nous avons également mis en place des outils qui nous permettent de vérifier la conformité des résultats de certains appareils pour lesquels nous ne possédons pas d'étalons de vérification ni de prestataire au niveau national. Cela nous a permis d'optimiser les périodicités d'étalonnage et de réduire les coûts des prestations. Certains instruments sont maintenant étalonnés en interne par des étalons raccordés au SI en utilisant les compétences en interne. Cette démarche a permis l'amélioration de la qualité du travail, ce qui s'est traduit par un gain de temps pour la réalisation de certaines activités et une motivation des acteurs. De plus, elle a permis de nouer de nouvelles collaborations scientifiques et techniques du fait de la fiabilité et de la pertinence reconnues des mesures.

Mots clés: Recherche, démarche qualité, Mutualisation, harmonisation ,ISO 9001

1 Introduction

Le Laboratoire d'Ecologie Microbienne des Sols et Agroécosystèmes Tropicaux (LEMSAT), l'Unité de recherche sur les maladies infectieuses et tropicales émergentes (URMITE), le laboratoire commun de microbiologie (LCM), le laboratoire des moyens analytiques (LAMA), implantés à Dakar, se sont engagés dans une démarche qualité depuis une dizaine d'années. Cette démarche se propose de contribuer à la qualité de nos recherches grâce à une bonne organisation, une documentation adaptée, de la traçabilité et de la fiabilité. Nous faisons partie de ceux qui ont osé franchir le pas de la certification ISO 9001 [1] en recherche en Afrique et introduit un management de la qualité dans la pratique de la recherche. La certification atteste que la structure possède un management de la qualité, c'est-à-dire qu'elle a organisé son travail selon les exigences de la norme ISO 9001 [2].

Dans la recherche une telle démarche vise à satisfaire une demande que ce soit du porteur de projet ou du financeur de recherche, ou à répondre à un objectif de recherche. Le processus de production de résultat passe par un ensemble d'étapes permettant de vérifier la validité des résultats et d'en assurer la reproductibilité [3].

L'ensemble des activités qui assurent la maîtrise de la qualité des résultats de mesures est la métrologie. Il convient d'une part d'étalonner les instruments, d'autre part de vérifier la stabilité de leurs performances. Le laboratoire doit définir et appliquer une procédure d'étalonnage et de vérification dont l'objet est de s'assurer que tout équipement impliqué et utilisé au cours d'un processus d'analyse possède des qualités de justesse telles que le résultat ait une valeur aussi proche que possible de la valeur vraie, avec une incertitude maîtrisée. Il importe donc que les opérations d'étalonnage et de vérification soient effectuées, que leurs résultats aient été validés et enregistrés et que les utilisateurs aient accès à ces informations au moment de l'utilisation des équipements [4].

Cependant au Sénégal les prestataires de la métrologie sont rares. Par exemple il n'y a qu'un seul prestataire intervenant dans les domaines des masses et températures. La demande étant forte il est souvent difficile qu'il puisse assurer toutes les prestations en temps voulu. Ces prestations ont également un coût et avec la baisse des budgets alloués aux laboratoires de recherche c'est une forte contrainte pour les directeurs de laboratoire et acteurs de la métrologie. Pour une meilleure prise en charge de cette activité les responsables métrologies des différents laboratoires certifiés ISO 9001:2008 à l'IRD Dakar (URMITE, LEMSAT, LAMA, LCM) se sont donc engagés dans la mutualisation des instruments et l'homogénéisation des pratiques métrologiques.

2 Organisation

Nous nous sommes organisés en groupe de travail piloté par un des responsables métrologiques (celui du LEMSAT) sous la responsabilité de l'Ingénieur Qualité sécurité environnement (QSE) de l'IRD au Sénégal. Cependant les autres responsables métrologie participent également en s'assurant de l'état de leurs équipements de mesure et d'analyse. Les directeurs d'unités fixent la politique et les objectifs de leurs laboratoires respectifs et allouent les moyens d'action nécessaires pour son bon déroulement. L'ingénieur QSE assure le relais entre les responsables métrologie et la représentation (Figure1). La coordinatrice prépare et anime des réunions périodiques. Les besoins y sont discutés afin de partager, sensibiliser et agir ensemble. Une analyse objective des besoins est effectuée. Après chaque réunion du groupe de travail, un compte rendu est envoyé aux directeurs des laboratoires afin qu'ils prennent connaissance de l'état d'avancement des objectifs et puissent les ajuster si besoin, soient alertés des problèmes rencontrés et soient informés des actions à prendre pour y remédier, et plus largement pour améliorer le système de management.

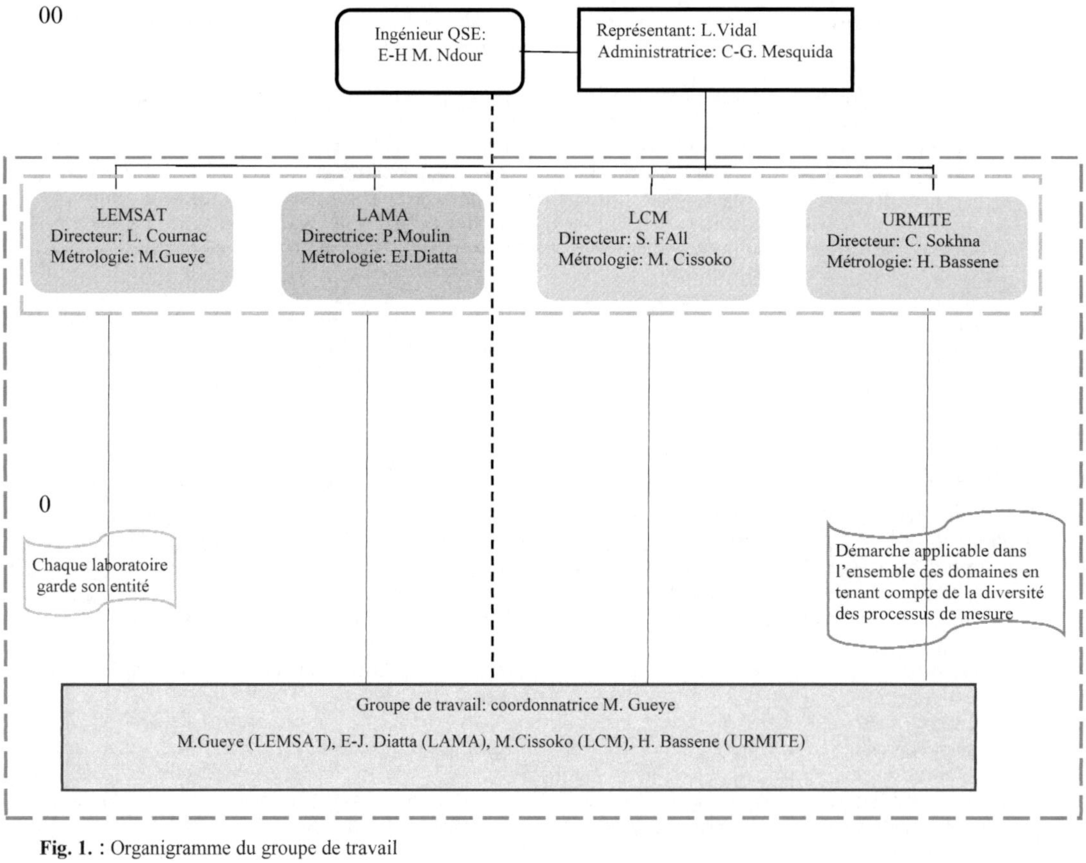

Fig. 1. : Organigramme du groupe de travail

3 Choix des équipements de travail

A partir de la connaissance des besoins de chacun d'avoir des résultats scientifiques pertinents, de nous départir autant que possible des prestataires et d'amoindrir les coûts, l'état des lieux au niveau de chaque structure a été fait. Pour ce faire l'inventaire des équipements a été réalisé par le responsable métrologie correspondant. Chaque unité en fonction de ses activités a recensé les instruments qui ont des incidences sur ses résultats d'analyse. Puis pour chaque équipement a été décidé s'il était nécessaire d'assurer un suivi métrologie ou pas et si oui le type de suivi à effectuer (interne ou externe). Puis nous avons sélectionné les appareils que nous avons en commun sous surveillance métrologique. A la suite de cela nous avons défini notre mission et analysé nos forces et faiblesses pour sa réalisation. Pour finir nous avons identifié nos objectifs.

4 Gestion des équipements

Chaque unité continue la prise en charge de la gestion de ses équipements sous la responsabilité du responsable métrologie correspondant. Cependant elle devient accessible si besoin est aux autres équipes en fonction de sa disponibilité et en respectant les règles mises en place au niveau de chaque structure.
Une étude comparative des procédures ou instructions utilisées au niveau de chaque laboratoire pour chaque appareil sous suivi métrologie est effectuée. Afin de mieux structurer notre action nous avons procédé à l'homogénéisation des procédures par appareil. Pour cela après recensement et étude des procédures mises en place dans les différents laboratoires nous avons pris la procédure qui nous semblait la meilleure et l'avons améliorée en nous basant sur les normes en vigueur [5]. Chaque laboratoire l'adopte en mettant son logo et son entête et l'intègre dans son système. Les périodicités de vérification ou d'étalonnage sont gérées par chaque laboratoire en fonction de ses besoins pour certains appareils et sont communes pour d'autres. Cependant les procédures ne sont pas figées car les membres du groupe réalisent des retours d'expériences afin d'identifier les améliorations nécessaires à apporter après validation par tous.

Les étalons et les appareils de contrôles de chaque laboratoire sont rassemblés et stockés auprès de la coordonnatrice afin de coordonner leur archivage et leur mise à jour. Elle veille également à leur raccordement au Système International d'unités (SI) par des organismes habilités. Cela est fait avec la participation financière de chaque laboratoire. Les documents externes, la fiche de vie de l'équipement, qui sert à l'enregistrement de toutes les utilisations ou interventions, les procédures d'étalonnage, de vérification, de maintenance et d'utilisation [6] de même que les certificats d'étalonnage relatifs à ces instruments sont mis à la disposition des membres du groupe de travail. Les flux d'entrée et de sortie des étalons sont tracés et leur bon fonctionnement est vérifié à chaque fois avant chaque sortie et à leur retour devant l'emprunteur qui doit être une personne habilitée. Une procédure écrite qui explique tout le procédé est mise en place.

5 Vérifications réglementaires

Un contrat de prestation de service est établi entre notre institut et l'organisme d'inspection, sous la direction de l'Ingénieur QSE et de l'administratrice, après validation par les responsables métrologies. Nos exigences sont spécifiées dans le contrat afin que le même inspecteur fasse les contrôles en suivant la même procédure pour l'ensemble des laboratoires. Chaque laboratoire prend en charge les coûts relatifs à ses prestations et gère ses documents et reçoit son ou ses rapports d'inspection. Une copie de chaque rapport est remise à l'Ingénieur QSE pour un meilleure suivi.

6 Vérification d'appareils en absence d'étalons et de prestataire

Dans certains cas il n'existe pas de prestataire local pour la prise en charge de certaines prestations et nous n'avons pas accès à des étalons afin de les réaliser nous-même. Nous avons alors mis en place des outils ad hoc qui nous permettent de vérifier autant que faire se peut la conformité des résultats générés. Par exemple pour les hottes aspirantes nous faisons des tests périodique avec le test de fumée (contrôle visuel) pour vérifier l'absence de sortie d'air de l'intérieur du volume de travail vers l'extérieur de celui-ci, au niveau du plan de travail.

En ce qui concerne les hottes à flux laminaires notre objectif principal c'est que la hotte soit stérile, qu' il n'y ait pas de contamination des échantillons. Nous faisons un contrôle bactériologique de l'air du volume de travail Pour ce faire nous avons mis des boites de milieu nutritif sous la hotte à différents temps d'exposition. Ces boites sont scellées et misent en incubation à l'étuve. Il s'ensuit des phases d'observation pendant 72h. Si rien ne pousse sur ces boites on se dit que la hotte est stérile parcontre s'il y'a une ou plusieurs colonies qui poussent sur les boites alors la hotte n'est pas stérile. Dans ce cas il faut proceder à la décontamination de la hotte et le processus de vérification est refait. Cette étape est d'habitude suffisante pour supprimer toute contamination. Cependant au cas où la contamination persiste il est pévu de faire intervenir le service technique et nous essayerons de nettoyer le filtre. Le processus de vérification doit être repris.

Par rapport aux thermocycleurs nous introduisons 1 ou 2 témoins positifs lors des PCR que nous positionnons à des endroits différents au niveau des puits du thermocycleur, tout est fonction du nombre d'échantillon. Si l'un des témoins positifs ne marche pas on peut se dire qu'il y'a un "soucis" par rapport au puit car il pourrait s'agir d'un effet manipulateur. Ensuite une pcr est reprise avec remise du témoin positif au même endroit pour vérification Ceci aprés avoir pris toutes les précautions lors de la préparation PCR pour éliminer tout effet manipulateur. A la suite de cela s'il y'a encore probléme avec le témoin positif alors on pourra dire qu'il y'a un probléme avec ce puit. Ce dernier sera identifié et ne sera plus utilisé et les puits adjacents seront aussi vérifiés.

7 Utilisation d'un outil d'auto-évaluation

L'étude du processus de mutualisation et de ses facteurs de maîtrise induit l'utilisation d'un outil d'auto-évaluation permettant la surveillance et la progression des pratiques. L'outil est basé sur un tableur automatisé qui permet une évaluation rapide du processus mis en place par les principaux acteurs. La grille d'évaluation comprend 7 bonnes pratiques [1- Pilotage du groupe par les Directeurs d'unités 2- Pilotage du groupe par la coordinatrice 3- Gestion prévisionnelle des ressources humaines dans le laboratoire 4- Gestion documentaire des équipements 5- Disponibilité des équipements de mesure 6- Confirmation métrologique des équipements 7- Conditions environnementales d'utilisation et de stockage de l'équipement] qui sont détaillées chacune par 5 à 7 critères de réalisation. L'utilisateur répond aux propositions selon une échelle de véracité à six niveaux : Faux unanime (0%), Faux (20%), Plutôt faux (40%), Plutôt vrai (60%), Vrai (80%), Vrai prouvé (100%). L'ensemble des résultats est ensuite présenté en temps réel, dans un diagramme 'radar' de synthèse à 7 branches (Figure 2). Ces résultats peuvent dès lors être imprimés, et capitalisés dans le processus de mise en place de la mutualisation des pratiques [7].

8 Résultats et discussion

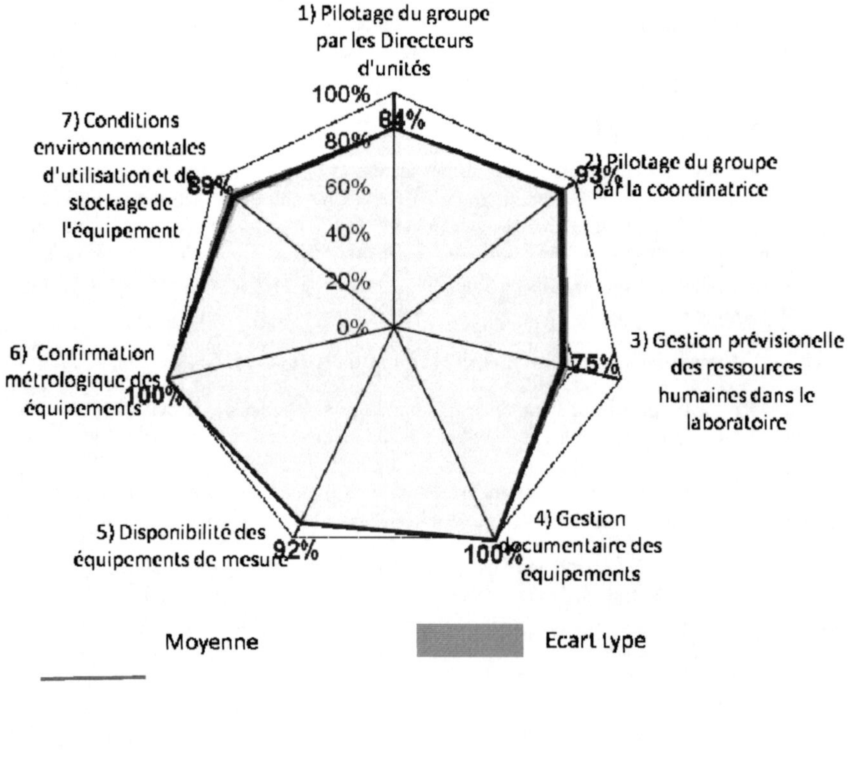

Fig . 2. Résultat de l'auto-évaluation de la mutualisation des pratiques métrologiques

Les membres du groupe de travail ont procédé à l'application de l'outil d'autoévaluation, soit 4 personnes. Selon leur évaluation, le processus de mutualisation est assuré à 91%. Les écart-types varient de 0 à 3%. La Figure 2, récapitule le pourcentage de maîtrise moyenne obtenu pour chaque bonne pratique. Trois des facteurs obtiennent moins de 90% de maîtrise à savoir : le pilotage du groupe par les directeurs d'unité (84% ± 0%), la gestion prévisionnelle des ressources humaines du groupe (75% ± 2%) et les conditions environnementales d'utilisation et de stockage de l'équipement (86% ± 3%).
Le système mis en place est assez robuste. Cependant afin de cerner les points d'améliorations des processus ayant des taux de maîtrise inférieurs à 90%, nous nous sommes intéressés aux réponses apportées à chaque critère.
Il ressort que malgré la prise en charge des moyens pour la confirmation métrologique des équipements par les directeurs d'unités et leurs bonnes volontés nous n'avons pas encore les moyens d'acheter certains étalons de vérification pour être plus autonomes. Nous avons prévu de faire une étude comparative des coûts de prestation externe par rapport à l' achat d'étalons pour le raccordement en interne de certaines prestations comme c'est déjà le cas pour les balances, pipettes, pH mètre, et spectrophotomètre.

Des points d'amélioration sont à apporter également au niveau du processus de la gestion des ressources humaines prévisionnelles. En effet malgré l'octroi de formations par le pôle RH, il s'avère que le personnel n'est pas suffisamment formé surtout pour la prise en charge de certaines prestations en interne. Il ressort aussi le fait que le personnel n'est pas suffisant pour le travail demandé car tous les membres du groupe ne sont pas seulement des responsables métrologie. Ils ont d'autres activités au sein de leurs laboratoires respectifs. Ceci ralentit notre dynamique de mutualisation et d'homogénéisation des pratiques et cela se traduit également par la tenue de réunions très espacées. L'identification du personnel d'entretien des équipements manque au niveau du processus utilisation et stockage des équipements. Cependant il faut noter que chaque personne utilisant un équipement a la responsabilité de le rendre propre et en bon état; ceci est vérifié après chaque retour d'équipement.

L'utilisation d'un outil d'auto-évaluation a permis de quantifier le niveau de la mutualisation et de l'homogénéisation des pratiques dans nos laboratoires de recherche, et de cibler les points critiques. Des propositions d'amélioration ont été faites. Leur réalisation sera une première démarche dans la résolution de ces problèmes.

9 Conclusion

La mise en place du processus de mutualisation nous a permis d'optimiser les périodicités d'étalonnage et de réduire les coûts des prestations. Certains instruments sont maintenant étalonnés en interne par des étalons raccordés au SI en utilisant les compétences internes. Cette démarche a permis l'amélioration de la qualité du travail, ce qui s'est traduit par un gain de temps pour la réalisation de certaines activités et une motivation des acteurs. De plus, elle a permis de nouer de nouvelles collaborations scientifiques et techniques du fait de la fiabilité et de la pertinence reconnues des mesures. L'utilisation de l'outil d'auto-évaluation, développé dans le cadre de la démarche qualité dans les laboratoires de recherche et d'analyse, nous a permis de quantifier le niveau de maîtrise des processus mises en place, d'identifier les points critiques et les axes d'amélioration prioritaires.

References

1 . NF EN ISO 9001, Système de management de la qualité – Exigences, Ed. Afnor® 2008,

2 . E. Giesen, Démarche qualité et norme ISO 9001, Une culture managériale appliquée à la recherche IRD éditions (2013)

3 . J-P. CHIPPAUX, La Paz, juillet (2008)

4 . NF EN ISO 10012 : 2003, Système de management de la qualité – Principes essentiels et vocabulaire

5 . Gérer et maîtriser les processus et les équipements de mesure, volume 1, Ed. Afnor® (2005)

6 . E. Fargier, M. Priel, Organisation d'un laboratoire d'étalonnage, Techniques de l'ingenieur (2007)

7 . S. Bousbiat, démarche qualité en recherche, UTC, (2010)

Le développement d'outils intégrés : un travail collaboratif pour améliorer l'organisation d'un laboratoire de recherche

V. Molinéro-Demilly[1], S. Pelletier[1], S. Gaillard[1], C. Landes[1], E. Vergne[1], A. Charki[2], B. Lyonnet[3] et C. Jeoffrion[4]

1 Institut de Recherche en Horticulture et Semences (IRHS) - UMR 1345 INRA/Agrocampus Ouest/Université d'Angers - 42, rue Georges Morel - BP 60057 - 49071 BEAUCOUZE Cedex - FRANCE
2 Laboratoire Angevin de Recherche en Ingénierie des Systèmes (LARIS - EA7315), Université d'Angers, 62 avenue Notre Dame du Lac 49000 Angers, France
3 Institut d'Economie et Management de Nantes - réseau des IAE Université de Nantes, Chemin de la Censive du Tertre BP 52231, 44312 Nantes Cedex 3, France
4 Laboratoire de Psychologie des Pays de la Loire (LPPL - UPRES EA 4638), Département de Psychologie, Université de Nantes, BP 81 227, 44312 Nantes cedex 3, France

Received:

Résumé. L'IRHS (Institut de recherche en Horticulture et Semences) est un laboratoire de biologie végétale créé en janvier 2012 suite à la fusion de quatre unités mixtes de recherche. Ce laboratoire est composé de 230 personnes provenant de trois tutelles : l'Institut National de la Recherche Agronomique (INRA), l'école d'ingénieurs dans le domaine de l'agronomie et de l'horticulture (AGROCAMPUS-OUEST) et l'Université d'Angers. La démarche qualité a débuté dans les années 2000 à l'INRA et, depuis 2013, une ingénieure qualité est en charge de déployer et d'harmoniser un Système de Management de la Qualité (SMQ) au sein de l'IRHS. L'objectif de cette communication est de montrer comment, avec l'appui de l'équipe Bioinformatique, des outils intégrés peuvent structurer l'organisation d'un laboratoire de recherche et faciliter l'intégration d'un SMQ dans le quotidien du travail des scientifiques.

Mots-clefs : Management de la qualité, système d'informations, outils intégrés

1 Introduction

Depuis quelques années, plusieurs organismes de recherche publics se sont engagés dans une démarche qualité pour améliorer notamment leur organisation (1). En France, l'Association française de normalisation (Afnor) préconise l'utilisation de la démarche qualité par les acteurs scientifiques (2). Cependant, une démarche qualité appliquée à un organisme public peut rencontrer des difficultés différentes d'un organisme privé (3). De plus, l'activité de recherche nécessite une organisation rigoureuse et transparente dans la production des connaissances et présente des spécificités en termes d'objectifs, de moyens et d'organisation pouvant être bien différentes du secteur de l'industrie où la démarche qualité a été traditionnellement élaborée. Nous allons voir comment des outils intégrés peuvent structurer l'organisation d'un laboratoire de recherche et faciliter l'intégration d'un Système de Management de la Qualité (SMQ) dans le quotidien du travail des scientifiques.

2 Contexte du changement

L'IRHS (Institut de Recherche en Horticulture et Semences) a été créé en janvier 2012, sous les tutelles de l'Institut National de la Recherche Agronomique (INRA), d'une école d'ingénieurs dans le domaine de l'agronomie et de l'horticulture (AGROCAMPUS-OUEST) et de l'Université d'Angers. Ce laboratoire est composé de 230 personnes réparties en 14 équipes. Le laboratoire conduit des projets de recherche visant à répondre aux questions de qualité et de santé des produits du « végétal spécialisé (semences horticulture) » Il développe des approches intégrées en coordonnant les efforts et expertises en génétique, épigénétique, génomique, en pathologie, physiologie, écophysiologie, biochimie, en modélisation, statistiques et en bio-informatique.

Avant 2012, les équipes étaient réparties dans quatre Unités Mixtes de Recherche (UMR) et la maturité de la démarche qualité dépendait de la proportion d'agents de chaque tutelle. Notamment les équipes sous tutelle INRA ont initié une démarche qualité depuis les années 2000 selon le référentiel 1 de l'INRA (4). La mise en place d'un Système Management Qualité global à l'unité selon le référentiel INRA version 2 (5) a débuté en septembre 2013 avec le recrutement d'un ingénieur qualité-prévention. Ce recrutement est en cohérence avec la démarche qualité définie par l'INRA dont la finalité est de contribuer à l'excellence scientifique, à l'attractivité et à la créativité dans ses unités de recherche et d'expérimentation.

En parallèle, deux des trois Centre de Ressources Biologiques (CRB) hébergés au sein du laboratoire (CRB Fruits à pépins et rosiers et CRB Apiacées) ont initié une démarche de certification selon le référentiel ISO 9001(6). Le troisième, la collection française de bactéries associées aux plantes (CFBP), est certifié ISO 9001 depuis 2008.

Pour accompagner ce changement, alors qu'en 2012 les équipes étaient alors réparties sur 8 sites de la technopole d'Angers, en 2015 toutes les équipes ont été regroupées sur le site de l'INRA grâce à la construction d'un bâtiment supplémentaire.

3 Les acteurs de la qualité

Le SMQ constitue un outil de maîtrise et de pilotage des activités de l'unité (5). Le laboratoire a choisi de développer une approche intégrée de la qualité, en prenant en compte des aspects liés à la prévention et au développement durable. Un mode de management de type participatif a été choisi par la direction pour la mise en place du SMQ (7) de manière à stimuler les échanges inter-équipes et inter-tutelles. Nommé en septembre 2013, l'ingénieur qualité a pour missions de déployer et piloter un système qualité commun à l'ensemble des équipes de recherche du laboratoire. Il dispose d'une grande autonomie pour mener à bien ses missions et d'un budget de fonctionnement. Il participe aux réunions mensuelles du comité de pilotage du laboratoire, et les points relatifs à la qualité et à la prévention y sont abordés si nécessaire.

Le risque aurait été que l'ingénieur qualité reste seul face à l'ampleur du travail. Avec le soutien du directeur, une organisation a alors été mise en place faisant intervenir plus de 70 acteurs dans le laboratoire : directeur, chefs d'équipe, un correspondant qualité pour chaque équipe et chaque CRB (soit un total de 17 personnes) et des correspondants matériel réparti dans chaque bâtiment (soit un total de 45 personnes). Les correspondants qualité se réunissent tous les deux mois et les correspondants matériels une fois par an pour planifier les vérifications internes et externes du matériel. Une lettre de mission a été rédigée pour chacun des acteurs.

Afin d'aider la cellule qualité du laboratoire (ingénieur et correspondants qualité) à déployer la démarche qualité au sein des équipes de recherche, l'ingénieur qualité s'est appuyé sur l'implication d'étudiants en stage au laboratoire. Les conseils de leur enseignant tuteur, spécialiste en management de la qualité et en métrologie, ont été très importants pour stimuler la mise en œuvre du SMQ en coopération avec les personnes concernées. Cette collaboration étroite a débouché sur de nombreuses réalisations (certaines visibles sur le site Web du laboratoire: https://www6.angers-nantes.inra.fr/irhs) telles qu'une cartographie des processus, un manuel qualité, des procédures de gestion documentaire et des équipements, une aide à la formalisation de processus et de modes opératoires (8).

La démarche d'amélioration continue initiée par la cellule qualité a été mise en pratique dans les équipes de recherche. Cette démarche rejoint les objectifs de développement de l'équipe Bioinformatique. Elle a formalisé les besoins des autres équipes en termes de gestion de données et intégré les productions des stages en qualité quant à la traçabilité, la gestion du matériel et des documents. L'équipe Bioinformatique, en développant et en déployant des outils intégratifs, vient ainsi appuyer l'action de la cellule qualité.

4 Les actions collectives et élaboration des cahiers des charges

Une réflexion a été menée pour développer une démarche par projet au niveau du laboratoire en s'appuyant sur le diagramme d'Hishikawa nommé les 7M (9). En effet, la communauté de la recherche est d'accord sur le principe que les publications scientifiques doivent être fondées sur des données scientifiques fiables et obtenues grâce à la maîtrise de tous les facteurs (Fig. 1) pouvant influencer la qualité d'un résultat. Ces facteurs peuvent être ventilés selon la méthode évoluée du diagramme d'Ishikawa en 7 grandes catégories : les équipements (matériel), les méthodes, les produits (matière), l'environnement (milieu), le personnel (main-d'œuvre), le management et la mesure.

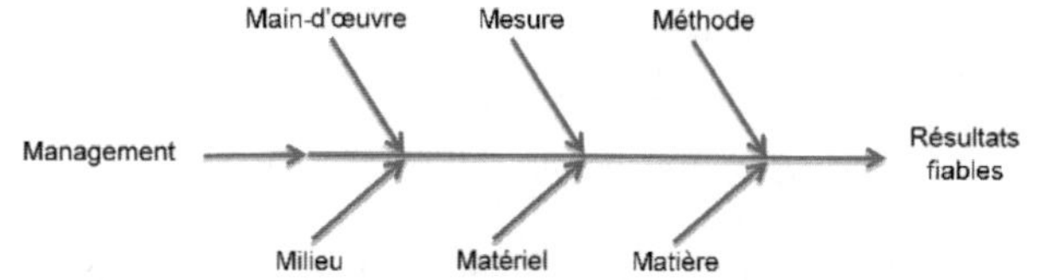

Figure 1 – Diagramme d'Ishikawa évolué (principe des « 7 M »).

L'intérêt de cette démarche est de formaliser les interactions entre les différents acteurs et d'identifier les éléments nécessaires au suivi de projet. Pour cela, le projet est découpé en fonctionnalités : la problématique, la ou les questions de recherche et hypothèses, les objectifs et les activités.

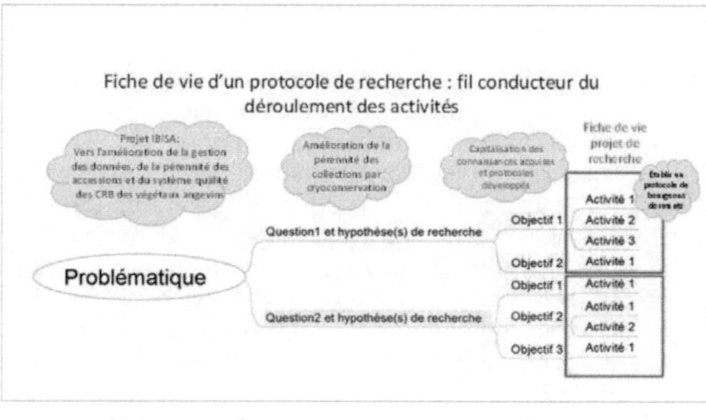

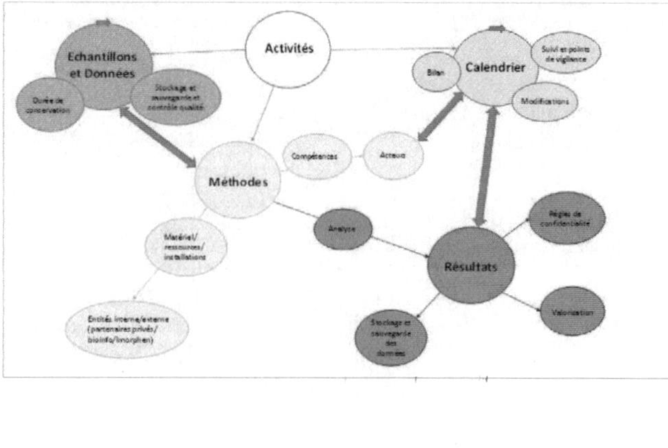

Figure 2 – Formalisation des interactions entre les acteurs et les éléments nécessaires au suivi de projet.

Cette réflexion a conduit à imaginer un projet global de base de données pour gérer tous les éléments nécessaires au suivi de projet. Avec l'appui de l'équipe Bioinformatique, les correspondants qualité des équipes et des correspondants matériels aidés par des stagiaires d'école d'ingénieurs ont travaillé en partenariat afin de développer des outils informatiques. Les étudiants 'Qualité' ont réalisé un travail d'enquête auprès des correspondants qualité et matériel de manière à élaborer des cahiers des charges répondant aux besoins des utilisateurs. Ces cahiers des charges sont des documents très utiles à l'équipe Bioinformatique pour réaliser les développements. Les cahiers des charges réalisés à ce jour concernent la gestion documentaire, la gestion du matériel et la gestion des échantillons.

5 Les outils intégrés développés par l'équipe Bioinformatique

L'équipe Bioinformatique a mis en place un système d'informations intégré construit en plusieurs modules. Il est dédié à la gestion des données produites par les équipes ainsi que du matériel support de leurs études, et intègre la gestion du matériel biologique et des résultats issus des recherches, des projets de recherche (élaboration de fiche de vie permettant de suivre le projet de sa conception à la valorisation), des équipements scientifiques, des consommables et de la documentation. Il prend en compte la gestion des projets et utilise une gestion des utilisateurs par rôles (gestion des droits de lecture, modification et suppression).

A ce jour, le module permettant la traçabilité des données d'analyses transcriptomiques (résultats des expériences de microarray et RNA-seq et métadonnées associées) est en test auprès des utilisateurs. La gestion des échantillons biologiques, intégrée dans les outils de gestion des CRB, est opérationnelle. Le module complémentaire de gestion des échantillons extraits à partir du matériel biologique (ADN, ARN, protéines) est en cours de développement. Il va permettre d'optimiser l'identification des échantillons, leur localisation et la traçabilité des données associées.

Ces développements impliquent la programmation d'interfaces utilisateurs conviviales pour l'interrogation et la saisie des données, garants de l'utilisation future. Les outils développés sont testés au fur et à mesure de leur conception (développement en cycle court) par les correspondants qualité et un panel d'utilisateurs au sein de l'IRHS, afin d'être au plus près des habitudes de travail des utilisateurs finaux.

L'ensemble des développements de l'équipe Bioinformatique est publié sous licence libre (CeCILL) sur la forge publique SourceSup de Renater afin de faciliter sa diffusion dans d'autres laboratoires.

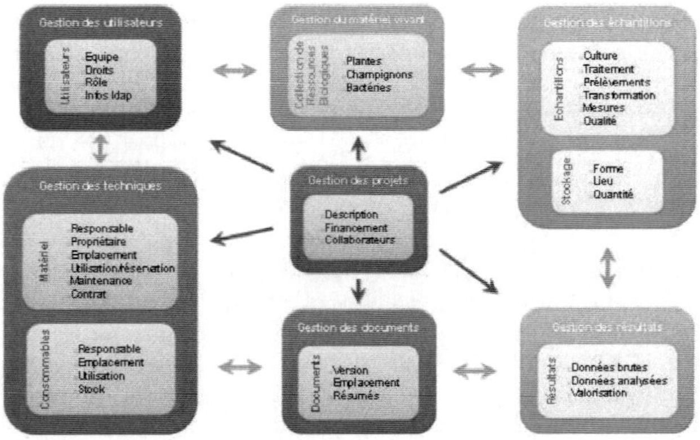

Figure 3 – Cartographie des outils développés dans la base de données.

6 Difficultés rencontrées

Les difficultés rencontrées par la cellule qualité et l'équipe Bioinformatique se rejoignent sur plusieurs points car ces deux activités sont transversales et touchent l'ensemble des personnels des laboratoires. Nous avons identifié des difficultés de quatre ordres :

- Le premier concerne les ressources humaines. Les forces de développement informatiques et les forces nécessaires à la mise en place de la démarche qualité ne sont pas aussi conséquentes qu'il le faudrait pour une unité de 230 personnes. Une réflexion a donc été menée pour prioriser la réalisation de certains modules et choisir des outils temporaires pour d'autres en attendant que l'équipe Bioinformatique soit disponible pour leur programmation. Actuellement la priorisation a été mise sur le module de gestion des échantillons, notamment ceux qui concernent les CRB, car c'est un outil indispensable pour leur certification. En ce qui concerne la gestion documentaire et la gestion du matériel, des solutions intermédiaires ont été trouvées : par exemple l'utilisation du logiciel ALFRESCO pour gérer la documentation et l'utilisation d'Excel pour la gestion du matériel. Nous avons prévu deux réunions annuelles entre l'équipe Bioinformatique et la cellule qualité pour mettre à jour l'avancement de la cartographie des outils intégrés développés, puis diffuser l'information à l'ensemble du personnel.

- Le second concerne la difficulté des experts informatiques et qualité à aider les personnels des laboratoires à définir leurs besoins. La méthodologie utilisée depuis 2018 à l'INRA en matière de qualité se rapproche de celle proposée par la norme ISO 9001 (6) version 2015. La méthodologie INRA met l'accent sur l'évaluation des risques et des opportunités des projets du laboratoire en s'appuyant sur les '7M' du diagramme d'Ishikawa (9). Dans le domaine de la qualité, les solutions pour répondre aux besoins sont multiples et peuvent souvent venir directement des personnes des laboratoires, tandis que pour l'informatisation d'une solution (par exemple, la gestion des échantillons), seuls les experts informatiques connaissent le langage et doivent faire une traduction des besoins, ce qui peut parfois conduire à des erreurs. Par exemple, le terme 'une année de notation' employé par le personnel scientifique pour une variété de poirier a été compris par les informaticiens par le traitement des données relevées sur un arbre durant une année civile. C'est par hasard qu'après 4 ans d'utilisation du programme informatisé des données, que les deux parties (scientifiques et informaticiens) se sont rendu compte de la mauvaise interprétation de ce terme : pour le scientifique, une année de notations correspondait en fait à ce que les informaticiens ont traduit ensuite par 'une campagne de notation' qui débute à la période de floraison de l'année n et se termine à la période de floraison de l'année n+1. Les deux parties sont en train d'analyser les conséquences de cette incompréhension sur les cultures et les résultats des recherches. Ceci confirme l'intérêt des échanges entre les différents acteurs d'un projet (10).

- Le troisième concerne les langages et les concepts spécifiques utilisés en informatique et dans le domaine de la qualité (11) pour lesquels l'ensemble des personnes des laboratoires ne sont pas formées, ce qui demande un temps d'appropriation et bouscule le quotidien. Par exemple, dans le domaine de la 'qualité', le mot 'protocole' est régulièrement utilisé par le personnel des laboratoires pour désigner un mode opératoire, c'est-à-dire que ce document opérationnel décrit de manière détaillée comment réaliser une opération ou une tâche réalisée en laboratoire ou sur le terrain. Le protocole de recherche désigne dans le référentiel INRA version 2 (6) un document synthétisant les objectifs par rapport à la question de recherche et des activités, responsables et ressources mis à contribution. Au sein du laboratoire pour ne pas perturber les utilisateurs, nous avons renommé le 'protocole de recherche' par 'fiche de vie d'un projet de recherche'.

- Le quatrième concerne la communication à l'ensemble du personnel sur l'état d'avancement de la démarche qualité au laboratoire et du développement des outils informatisés. En ce qui concerne la démarche qualité, des panneaux d'affichage présentant la politique qualité du laboratoire, les objectifs et des diagrammes de progression selon les objectifs définis ont été installés à l'entrée de chaque de bâtiment de manière à informer les personnels du laboratoire, mais aussi les visiteurs. Une page sur l'internet du laboratoire est consacrée à la qualité et la métrologie du laboratoire. En qui concerne le développement des projets informatiques, l'équipe bioinformatique teste utilisation d'un outil informatique nommé 'WIKI' qui sert de 'cahier de laboratoire' à l'équipe, et qui permet aux équipes scientifiques de suivre en direct les avancées concernant leurs projets.

7 Conclusion

Les outils intégrés facilitent la mise en place et le maintien d'un SMQ dans un laboratoire de recherche car ces outils permettent d'assurer la traçabilité des connaissances et des résultats (12). Cependant la limitation des ressources humaines dans le domaine de l'informatique en freine le développement. Il est important d'être vigilant sur l'expression des besoins des utilisateurs et leur traduction en langage informatique. La démarche qualité et le développement d'outils intégrés nécessitent du temps et il est important de savoir communiquer avec l'ensemble des personnels du laboratoire pour les tenir informés des avancements des objectifs et ne pas susciter de frustrations.

Remerciements

Correspondants qualité : Sophie Aligon, Marie-Noëlle Bellanger, Béatrice Bonnet, Nathalie Brouard, Annie Chastellier, Cécile Dubois-Laurent, Remi Gardet, Arnaud Guyader, Bruno Hamon, Julien Jeauffre, David Lalanne, Sylvain Gaillard, Perrine Portier, Aurélia Rolland, Pascale Satour, Magali Tabuteau, Émilie Vergne.
Correspondants matériels : Sophie Aligon, Matthieu Barret, Abdelilah Benamar, Marie-Noëlle Bellanger, Juliette Benejan, Daniel Beucher, Sophie Bonneau, Marie-Hélène Bouvet, Chrystelle Brin, Nathalie Brouard, Maryline Bruneau, Sophie Cesbron, Aurélie Charrier, Elisabeth Chevreau, Caroline Denancé, Cécile Dubois-Laurent, Cécile Dutrieux, Pascale Expert, Rémi Gardet, Matthieu Gaucher, Arnaud Guyader, Latifa Hamama, Bruno Hamon, Sébastien Huet, Christelle Heintz, Laurence Hibrand-Saint-Oyant, Julien Jeauffre, David Lalanne, Marion Le seaux, Joseph Ly-Vu, Muriel Marchi, Martine Neveu, Laurent Ogé, Maria-Dolores Perez Garcia, Aurélien Petiteau, Sandrine Pierre, Anne Prévaux, Roland Robic, Aurélia Rolland, Pascale Satour, Vanessa Soufflet-Freslon, Anita Suel, Géraldine Taghouti, Christophe Vilfroy, Linda Voisine.
Stagiaires : Alexiane Goujon, Maha Cheneau, Abraham Padi, Victor Brunet, Thomas Vallée et Hervé Andres.

References

(1) G. Granier, L.-Y. Mas, L. Finot, B. Arnoux, N. Pasqualini, V. Dollé. La démarche qualité dans la recherche publique et l'enseignement supérieur. Versailles : Editions Quæ (2009)

(2) A. Jaime, M. Gardoni, J. Mosca, D. Vinck. La démarche qualité, cadre de la capitalisation des connaissances dans les organismes de recherche. In: Proceedings of the CITE'2003 Conference – Cooperation, Innovation et Technologies. Troyes, France, p ; 193-204 (2003)

(3) A. Matei, C. Antoni C. The New Public Management within the complexity model. Procedia-Social and Behavioral Sciences, 109 : 1125-1129 (2014)

(4) Inra. Mission Qualité. Référentiel Qualité Inra, version 1, 2003-2005. Paris, Inra, 6p. (2009)

(5) Inra Mission Qualité. Référentiel Qualité Inra pour les unités de recherche et expérimentales, version 2. Paris. Inra Sciences et impact, 19p. (2013)

(6) NF EN ISO 9001. Systèmes de management de la qualité. Exigences. AFNOR, 31 p. (2015)

(7) F. M. Beyer. Langages et stratégies au travail saisis par les normes d'assurance qualité. Sociologie du travail, Juillet, 41 (3) : 235-254 (1999)

(8) NF X50-553, Management des activités de recherche. Paris, Afnor, 34 p. (2014)
(9) V. Molinero-Demilly, A. Charki, C. Jeoffrion, B. Lyonnet, S. O'Brien, L. Martin. An overview of Quality Management System implementation in a research laboratory. Int. J. Metrol. Qual, 9. Eng. (2018) https:/articles/ijmqe/abs/2018/01/ijmqe170027/ijmqe170027.html
(10) M. Detchessahar. Quand discuter, c'est produire… Pour une théorie de l'espace de discussion en situation de gestion. Revue française de gestion, 132 :32-43 (2001)
(11) NF EN ISO 9000. Systèmes de management de la qualité. Principes essentiels de vocabulaire. Paris, Afnor, 51p. (2000)
(12) C. G. Begley, A. M. Buchan, U. Dirnagl. Robust research: Institutions must do their part for reproducibility. Nature, 525 : 25-27 (2015)

Comite African de Metrologie (CAFMET)
62 av. Notre Dame du Lac
49000 Angers
France

CURRAN ASSOCIATES INC.
proceedings.com

ISBN 978-1-5108-7471-8
9 781510 874718